RADIATION AND HUMAN HEALTH

Updated and Abridged

John W. Gofman, M.D., Ph.D.

Pantheon Books, New York

Library of Congress Cataloging in Publication Data

Gofman, John William.
  Radiation and human health.

  Bibliography: p.
  Includes index.
  1. Ionizing radiation—Toxicology. 2. Tumors,
Radiation-induced. 3. Radiation—Dosage. I. Title.
RA1231.R2G56 1983   616.9'897   83-2135
ISBN 0-394-71360-5 (pbk.)

Manufactured in the United States of America

First Edition

To the Quest for Scientific Truth in the Issues of Human Health

Acknowledgments

The reader of this book will learn that we have a very large fund of accumulated knowledge concerning the effects of low doses of radiation on human health. Yet, the information available is not very useful in its crude, unintegrated form. A major goal of the author of this book is to present and analyze the evidence concerning effects of low doses of radiation upon humans, and to demonstrate that a systematic and consistent evaluation of the evidence is now possible, with very useful practical results for the scientist, the physician, the public health profession, the public, and the attorney.

The endeavor to present scientific material in an appropriate sequence is always difficult for one who has been deeply immersed in a subject for decades. Therefore, the author is especially indebted to colleagues who have volunteered to study the manuscript, to question all the concepts and calculations critically, and to suggest numerous improvements in organization, with the view to clarity and logical consistency. The assistance of Egan O'Connor in meticulous "testing" of the entire manuscript in these respects has been invaluable, as have been the excellent suggestions made by André Bruwer, M.D., and William Marks, M.D..

Daniel Moses, Editor-in-Chief of Sierra Club Books, and his associate, JoAnn Pluemer, were totally cooperative and made many improvements in the presentation in the course of editing of the unabridged edition of the book. It has been a privilege to have their contribution to this effort.

Diana Landau did the excellent and difficult task of abridging and revising the original edition. Any residual errors are, however, to be attributed to the author.

CONTENTS

FOREWORD

I AM GLAD for this chance to tell the reader about a few things that have happened since the publication of the unabridged hardcover edition of *Radiation and Human Health* in October 1981. One of these was the public response to the book and its subject, and I will start by relating the most common question asked me when I appeared on a series of television and radio call-in programs related to the book. By the way, unfamiliar terms used in the Foreword are explained in the book, and most can be located with the Index.

What About Unmeasured Medical and Dental Doses?

"Why can't the doctor and dentist tell me what radiation doses they are giving me?"

That was the most common question and complaint I heard. The simple answer is this: Many cannot tell you because they do not know. Almost none of them is skilled in dose measurement or dose calculation. There are wholly separate professions, called health physics and radiation physics, whose expertise is in measuring and calculating radiation doses. While it is simple indeed to measure a radiation dose at the surface of the skin in open air, it is more difficult to ascertain the dose to internal organs such as the brain or the stomach (see the Index to this book, under "Dosimetry").

If you ask, "Why don't my doctor and dentist hire an independent health physics service to measure the customary doses they are giving on their standard examinations?" the answer again is simple. They don't do it because their patients have not yet insisted on receiving this information. When doctors and dentists realize that an ability to provide their patients with such information gives them a competitive edge over their less informed colleagues, they will certainly offer it. Most large hospitals and clinics do employ the services of a health physicist or radiation safety officer. First-class medical facilities, the Mayo Clinic for example, now invite their patients to ask for the dose from every radiological procedure performed there.

A general rule to keep in mind is this: If an office giving you a medical or dental examination has been *measuring* the dose it customarily gives for a particular kind of exam, that office is probably making a real effort to *minimize* the dose. However, when an office claims to know its own doses, the claim may mean nothing at all unless that office is using an independent health-physics service to determine them. A true story may help to illustrate the problem. When I was a guest on a radio health program a caller identified himself as a radiologist and told the audience, "I assure my patients that a gastrointestinal series gives about the same dose as flying across the country." It pained me to have to correct him so publicly, but he was dispensing cockamamie assurances. The reality is that flying across this country gives a whole-body dose of about 2 millirads (see Index, "Air travel"), whereas an average GI exam gives an abdominal dose of about 3,000 to 26,000 millirads (see Index, "Medical irradiation").

How serious is the risk of suffering later cancer or leukemia from medical irradiation? There is no single answer for an individual, because your risk depends not only on the size of the dose but also on your age (young children are far more easily injured than adults) and on the particular part of the body receiving the radiation (for example, a dose of 15 rads to the knee carries a trivial risk compared with 15 rads to the abdomen or chest). Readers of this book will be able to determine the risk from various examinations (see Index, "Cancer-risk determination").

Determining the risk, which starts with *knowing* the dose, can always be helpful in one of two ways. Either the knowledge will remove unnecessary and exaggerated worries, or it will help patient and physician to weigh more intelligently the possible benefits versus the quantified risks of a contemplated procedure.

I would urge people not to focus on *past* medical and dental exposures. Reconstruction of the dose received is impossible, in general. And life is too short and sweet for even a moment of one's own life, or anyone else's, to be poisoned by what cannot be remedied. In my opinion, readers who use this book to avoid overdosing in the *future* are on the right track.

A Grand Opportunity: Preventing a Million Cancers

One of the most encouraging trends since the original publication of this book is a growing awareness of the opportunity to do something big and yet simple against the scourge of cancer, an opportunity made clear by the book's findings. A truly simple set of actions, described below, could prevent about one million cancer fatalities which would otherwise be induced in the United States during the next thirty years. Aside from cessation of cigarette smoking, there is no greater single opportunity on the horizon to prevent so much cancer.

What is involved? We just need to cut the average radiation doses from medical and dental examinations to a third of what they are now. We do *not* need to eliminate a single desirable diagnostic X-ray; we need only eliminate the unnecessarily high doses. Measurements have shown that medical and dental doses vary by as much as 50-fold from place to place for the same exam, and even in different rooms of the same facility (see chapter 13). The average dose can fall by two-thirds when the places delivering doses in the high ranges "clean up their act." And this is a task which is easy for them to do, even without new equipment. K. W. Taylor's work demonstrates that, without any loss of diagnostic information, dose reduction can be achieved on existing equipment (see chapter 13).

The opportunity to save a million lives in this simple way creates no conflict whatsoever between the professions of radiology and dentistry and the concerns of patients. The contrary is true. Independent radiologists and dentists enhance their practices by understanding the truth about radiation side effects (such as cancer), reducing the doses, and building loyal clienteles of customers who tell others, "That office measures its doses and really knows what it is doing." Moreover, such offices may avoid malpractice suits over excessive radiation exposures.

Independent radiologists seem eager to study the evidence in this book for themselves; they have been avid buyers of the original edition, from which they learn, for instance, that the effects of low doses (below 50 rads) are *not* extrapolated from evidence at high doses. Many are greatly surprised to find that the average dose of the exposed Japanese atom-bomb survivors was approximately 30 rads—a dose comparable to some common diagnostic exams in American medicine. (Indeed, current dose revisions for Japan may show that the average dose to bomb survivors was even appreciably lower.) It is heartening, also, to see the interest of radiologists in the newest "digital radiography" equipment, now coming on the market, which can reduce X-ray doses drastically, as well as their interest in imaging techniques (such as nuclear magnetic resonance or NMR, sonar, and infra-red) which do not use ionizing radiation at all. It remains to be seen whether or not the non-ionizing techniques create harmful side effects of their own; the evidence is not yet in.

I am confident that most independent radiologists are giving their wholehearted cooperation to reducing radiation doses as they begin better to understand the severe side effects of current average diagnostic dose levels, and as they begin to understand the magnificent benefits they will contribute by reducing that average dose by two-thirds.

Today, the average American receives the equivalent of at least 0.050 rads (50 millirads) of whole-body radiation from medical and dental diagnostic examinations each year. During the next 30 years, about 250 million people will live in the United States. Therefore, the aggregate dose from diagnostic medical-dental radiation *each year* will be the product of (250 million persons) times (0.050 rads), which gives us 12,500,000 person-rads of dose. In chapter 6 we find that for a population of mixed ages, 268 person-rads will produce *one* fatal cancer. When we divide 12,500,000 person-rads by 268 person-rads per fatal cancer, we discover that 46,600 fatal cancers will be induced annually by these exams. In thirty years (essentially one generation), this represents some 1,400,000 radiation-induced cancer fatalities. When the average dose is cut to one-third, then two-thirds of these radiation-induced cancers will not occur. Close to *one million people* in a single generation will be spared the unnecessary occurrence of this tragic disease.

In my medical career, I have known of few opportunities for people to do so much good for public health in such a straightforward and simple manner. A million lives—sixteen times more than all the American fatalities in Vietnam—how many such opportunities exist? Individually, we all have been helpless witnesses to massive suffering in other countries caused by the antihuman activities of a few. At least we are *not* helpless when it comes to saving one million Americans from the terrible suffering of radiation-induced cancer from unnecessary overdosing.

There will be some who believe that radiation can't be as harmful as the best estimates in this book. If they believe it is only half as harmful, such people are still looking at the exciting possibility of saving 500,000 Americans per generation from radiation-induced cancer! The saving of lives starts on the very day that a facility somewhere measures its doses and takes the steps required to reduce them.

Dental X-rays: Some Surprises

Apparently I threw some physicians into a tizzy when I stated on the *Phil Donahue Show* (November 1981) that one out of every 2,000 children who receive 1 rad of radiation to their brains will get brain cancer sometime during their remaining life-span. To be more exact, one out of every 2,600 three-year-old boys who receive 1 rad to their brains (not to be confused with their skulls) will later develop fatal brain cancer. This number, and figures for other ages and for females, are fully explained and supported in this book (see Index, "Specific-organ cancer dose").

Because I am concerned about the exposure of children's brains to dental X-rays, I agreed to do some additional analysis for the American Dental Assistants Association (Chicago); the three-part analysis was published in the *ADAA Journal* of July, September, and November 1982. The surprise, to me, was to find out that this analysis revealed radiation-induced cancer in the buccal cavity (including pharynx, lips, tongue, salivary glands, and floor of mouth) to be an even greater concern than brain cancer.

Another surprise was to find such widespread misinformation about the "average" dose from a dental film. For instance, a very commonly used table states that one X-ray to the front teeth usually gives a "mean active bone-marrow dose" of 2.9 millirads. That is true, but only because such a small fraction of the body's entire active bone marrow is located in the jaw. According to a government study (HEW, 1976), the *skin dose* from dental X-rays is most commonly 1,000 millirads (1 rad) per film. This skin dose may mean, roughly, a dose of about 250 millirads per film to the buccal cavity —quite a difference from 2.9 millirads!

The same report revealed that doses range from 100 millirads to more than 5,000 millirads per dental film, depending on the office. I admit feeling shocked to think someone's child can have a 50-fold higher risk of cancer induced from dental care if that child is taken to one office rather than to another. According to the report, the *highest* skin dose required to produce high-quality dental films is about 550 millirads per film, and 100 millirads

are sufficient with some machines and films. Yet doses are commonly between 900 and 1,100 millirads per film. Beware of the office that glibly says
"Only 2.9 millirads" and offers no additional information.

What Does the Newest Evidence Show?

Additional scientific data about low-level radiation effects have, of course,
been published since the original edition of *Radiation and Human Health* went
to press in mid-1981. Readers of this edition may wonder, quite reasonably, "Does it need revising, in view of the newest evidence?" The answer
is no. Definitely not. The new papers appearing in the scientific literature
strongly confirm and support the findings and methods of this book, and
do so on three issues of *central* importance to making correct risk estimates.

This book set forth the evidence existing in 1981 that the following
statements are correct:

1. The relative risk method for estimating cancer risk from radiation is
far superior to the so-called absolute risk method.

2. The cancer risk from radiation is much greater for those irradiated
at 0–9 years of age than for those irradiated at 10–19 years of age, and the
risk declines even further for those irradiated at higher ages.

3. When people of the same age are exposed to radiation, the excess
cancer induced by radiation is directly proportional to the dose received
(the linear dose-response "curve").

All three of these statements are anathema to those whose mission in life
appears to be to downplay the serious hazards of ionizing radiation. But all
three statements have been strongly fortified, and their correctness
confirmed, by the latest data from studies of the Japanese atom-bomb survivors.

In a recent paper by H. Kato and W. J. Schull, "Studies of the Mortality
of A-Bomb Survivors: 7. Mortality, 1950–1978: Part 1. Cancer Mortality" (in
Radiation Research **90**:395–432, 1982), both statements (1) and (2) are
strongly confirmed. On page 408 of the Kato-Schull paper, we have the
following statement:

*Thus, though in the recent BEIR report (9), two different models, i.e., the relative risk
model and the absolute risk model, have been used for projection of risk beyond the period
of observation, the present data support the relative risk model projection more strongly.*

So much for the claim of radiation downplayers about the absolute risk
method.

Also on page 408, we have the following statement:

*For age-at-death specific groups the relative risk for all cancer except leukemia (Table
1V) is higher the younger the age ATB (ATB stands for At Time of Bombing).*

Thus, this report lends powerful additional support to statement 2, above,
from *Radiation and Human Health*. Furthermore, Figure 4 of the Kato-Schull

paper shows a declining relative risk with increasing age at irradiation, with very high relative risk for those 0–9 years of age at the time of bombing. Kato and Schull's Figure 4 is virtually identical with figure 4 of this edition of *Radiation and Human Health*. The new, additional evidence could hardly be *more* supportive of the earlier conclusions in the original edition.

Finally, we come to statement 3, one of the most crucial of all. Those who would try to downplay the serious cancer hazard of radiation are fond of repeating *ad nauseam* that "the linear hypothesis undoubtedly overestimates the cancer risk of radiation." But all the evidence presented in *Radiation and Human Health* indicated that the linear hypothesis (that cancer risk is proportional to radiation dose) *underestimates* the risk, if indeed it does not predict it precisely.

It has been fashionable among the apologists for radiation to say that the linear hypothesis derives much of its support from the evidence at Hiroshima, and that the results at Hiroshima supported linearity because there was a sizable dose from *neutrons* in the Hiroshima dose. If the "neutron story" collapsed, their entire house of cards would collapse with it. In the original edition of *Radiation and Human Health*, I had deduced the absurdity of this fashionable "neutron explanation" by showing that it was quite inconsistent with the evidence itself. The final dagger in the heart of this absurd neutron explanation came while the original edition was going to press. Mendelsohn and Loewe published a series of papers showing that neutrons simply were not present in anything approaching the quantity that had been previously claimed to exist at Hiroshima! So the "neutron story" has indeed now collapsed. Another new paper also is important in this regard, this one by Wakabayashi, Kato, Ikeda, and W. J. Schull entitled "Studies of the Mortality of A-Bomb Survivors: Report 7: Part III. Incidence of Cancer in 1959–1978, Based on the Tumor Registry, Nagasaki" (in *Radiation Research* **93**:112–146, 1983). This paper presents evidence based on a large series of cases studied at *Nagasaki only*, where there never has been a claim for a "neutron explanation." A previous report on Nagasaki, based on the Leukemia Registry, had shown that linearity is supported. Now Wakabayashi and co-workers make the following statement for all cancers other than leukemia: "Thus the linear model appears to be the better for all cancers except leukemia."

A scientific group known as the BEIR Committee tried as a last straw to cling to a quadratic model for the dose-response relationship (which would make the cancer risk at low doses smaller than does the linear model). In reply to a rump group of the BEIR Committee, Wakabayashi and co-workers offer the following, *based upon the evidence:*

In the dissenting section in the BEIR III report, Rossi (19) stated that the dose-response for mortality from all cancers in Nagasaki (1950–1974) fits a quadratic model best. The present analysis does not support this. Rather, the data suggest a linear model or at least a linear-quadratic model. . . .

And they add, concerning the linear-quadratic model:

The linear term is significant in the L-Q model, whereas the quadratic term is not.

So, it is clear that the new evidence is completely in support of the analyses in *Radiation and Human Health,* both the original and present editions.

Does Anyone Wish to Obscure the Truth?

The stakes for personal and family health are very high, as I have indicated, in the low-dose-radiation issue. One might *hope* that no one would be willing to injure a million people, for instance, by blocking or trying to obscure the truth on any health issue. But reality doesn't always match hopes. Reality in this case includes the failure of employers to warn millions of asbestos workers about the known dangers of their work. Reality includes the continuing resistance of some manufacturers that use toxic chemicals to revealing even the names of the substances to their employees and to the surrounding communities. Reality includes similar behavior by managers of some government operations. It seems there are plenty of people who are willing, if rewarded, to help kill people by concealing and manipulating *information.*

So it would be naive not to ask, "Who might have an interest in distorting or covering up the effects of ionizing radiation?" Certain commercial interests are obvious. More interesting is a noncommercial interest—the U.S. Department of Defense—whose strategy of nuclear deterrence is said to be injured by findings like mine about low-dose radiation. Sad to say, the government began to issue false assurances about radiation effects back in the early 1950s, as radioactive fallout from American and Soviet bomb-testing was polluting the world.

In the fall of 1982, a suit came to trial against the U.S. government concerning fallout from the bomb tests done in Nevada. The suit was brought by injured Utah civilians. Because I testified at that trial against the government and on behalf of some of the civilians, because I have also helped some of the "atomic veterans," and because I speak out loud and clear about nuclear pollution from military as well as civilian programs, some readers will be surprised by my statement that I emphatically support the U.S. policy of nuclear deterrence and nuclear-weapons research. While I understand the true consequences of nuclear pollution and nuclear war very well indeed, I understand also the unspeakable physical and moral costs of surrendering freedom and losing human rights. I think it is a moral imperative of the highest order for the United States to build a fearsome and respected nuclear retaliatory force of unquestionable diversity, survivability, and readiness, because in my opinion such a force, and the clear will to use it if necessary, can *prevent* both nuclear holocaust and nuclear blackmail.

The defense of freedom and human rights has never in all history been costless; one of the modern costs is nuclear pollution, which can and should be reduced to a minimum, rather than denied or belittled with half-truths about its consequences. It is not right to pretend the cost of freedom is lower than it really is. Americans will pay the cost only if they have a government whose information they can trust. It pains me to see such trust undermined seriously by the utter rubbish about radiation put into wide circulation by some defense apologists. Among the worst enemies of the nuclear-weapons program are those whose chronic use of deception on the radiation issue helps undermine the credibility of the Pentagon in general. I find it particularly nauseating when such low behavior is used in the "service" of a goal so noble as liberty.

Long Live the Difference!

It came as no surprise to me that several attempts were made to discredit this book after its original publication, in letters published in *Nuclear News*, for instance. The most remarkable attack, having special implications for the health of children, was one published in the *Canadian Medical Association Journal*, May 1, 1982. This review was written by David Myers of the Chalk River Nuclear Laboratory, who claims that "the available epidemiologic data" do not support my conclusion that radiation induces more excess cancer when young people are exposed than when older people are. Indeed, the reviewer asserts that this conclusion is merely an "assumption" by me, even though this book shows all the data that made it, by 1981, an inescapable *conclusion.* I have referred previously in this Foreword to the additional and overwhelming support for my conclusion from the recent studies of Nagasaki A-bomb survivors.

Even when critics pretend to be discussing a book's real substance, they may (to put it kindly) be just bluffing. There is no reason for some critics to let facts interfere with what they write, if their mission is actually to retard understanding of the evidence a little while longer. Most often, such critics avoid discussing evidence and substance at all. They give themselves away by resorting to "arguments from authority"; they can do no better than name and count the alleged authorities whose opinions they prefer! But truth is not revealed by majority vote; it is revealed by logic applied correctly to real-world evidence. Criticism that truly addresses such substance (logic and evidence) contributes to the advance of knowledge in a most welcome way.

No one, so far, has validly refuted any of this book's substance, or found a hole in its reasoning. Critics have mostly resorted to pointing out the obvious, which I state myself in chapter 1: that my conclusions differ from those of the quasi-official radiation committees like BEIR, UNSCEAR, NCRP, and ICRP. Indeed they do differ! The virtue of my conclusions is their difference. I would be ashamed to put my name on any of the principal documents issued so far by the quasi-official committees.

Readers who are resolved to protect their own health, and the health and genetic integrity of their loved ones, may be most interested in a review of this book (unabridged edition) written by Dr. Victor Archer, who has made truly solid and major contributions of his own in radiation health research. His review, published in the *Journal of the American Medical Association* March 19, 1982, said in part:

This remarkable and important book enables any intelligent person with a high school education to understand the complexities involved in assessing the risks to man from low levels of ionizing radiation. Gofman not only demonstrates his mastery of this complex subject, but . . . uses a rational and innovative model to calculate the risk of induced cancer for each year after exposure to ionizing radiation. . . . He contrasts his risk estimates with those of official committees, carefully pointing out the reason for different results. One does not have to agree with all of Gofman's assumptions and estimates to appreciate the quality of this book. It will not soon be out of date, as new data can easily be inserted into the formulations to obtain current risk estimates.

Pantheon Books earns high marks for making this abridged version available to a much wider readership than would otherwise be possible. The 900-page original edition remains in print for those who decide to explore all the details.

JOHN W. GOFMAN
San Francisco, 1983

[Chapter 1]

Introduction to Radiation and Human Health

N<small>O ONE SERIOUSLY</small> doubts the overwhelming evidence that ionizing radiation causes a wide variety of injuries to the health of human beings. Many of these injuries either are fatal or guarantee a life of misery. The injuries evaluated in this book are cancer, leukemia, and chromosome damage (whose consequences can be a whole variety of diseases, caused to a newly conceived child in the uterus, or even earlier to the sex cells from which the child takes life).

Whose Concerns Does This Book Address?

The issues surrounding radiation injury to health are of broad interest to diverse individuals and groups, including:

☐ Physicians, nurses, radiological technicians, and medical students
☐ Patients contemplating medical irradiation procedures for themselves, and parents making such decisions for their children
☐ Radiographers, pilots, flight attendants, soldiers, nuclear-power workers, truck drivers and loaders of radioactive cargoes, and numerous other workers exposed to radiation
☐ Public-health officials, politicians, and their staffs
☐ Citizens active in the environmental movement
☐ Attorneys
☐ Journalists and television reporters
☐ Nuclear engineers and health physicists
☐ Epidemiologists, students of the various public-health sciences, radiobiologists, cancer researchers, and geneticists

An Assurance About Numbers

The first thing a flip through this book will show is that it contains many *numbers*. Numbers terrify some people (including many, many physicians). So the author offers the following assurance: Anyone who can understand *miles per gallon, dollars per pound,* or *18% interest on your unpaid balance* can understand every bit of math in this book. Numbers are necessary the moment we pass beyond the generalization that ionizing radiation is harmful and ask, *how* harmful is it? If a reader does not now appreciate the beauty of numbers for expressing certain kinds of useful information, by the time he (she) finishes chapter 6, section 4 ("Who Really Bears the Brunt of Population Exposures?"), he may have acquired a real fondness for them. For a single number can sometimes convey information so succinctly that its use with other numbers makes it easy to ponder many concepts at the same time without getting confused.

Moreover, numbers make it possible to understand why experts disagree about how harmful radiation is. In order to evaluate this author's conclusion that radiation is more dangerous than is claimed by quasi-official bodies, one needs to consider the *numbers*.

Some readers may have difficulty at first in grasping the meaning of two-part numbers like 3.6×10^6 (which is 3,600,000) and 3.6×10^{-6} (which is 3.6 millionths). The use of *10 to some power* to express either very large or very small numbers is essential in the quantitative sciences. Readers encountering the 10-power notation for the first time will find that mastering it will eliminate a real barrier between them and the "professional literature" on many, many topics (besides radiation) that may interest them.

An Intention to Demystify

This book is not bedtime reading. It is a reference book with which one can answer numerous practical questions, and it is also a book that demystifies a whole field of science, a field now dominated around the world by a small circle of prominent experts.

It is the author's certainty that this book will make the field comprehensible to anyone with a real interest in comprehending it. It is the author's desire to make it as easy as possible, not as difficult as possible, for the reader to join the club of those who understand the field.

Furthermore, the author believes that many readers will become able on their own to appraise all *future* announcements, reports, and papers in this field. During 1980, two rather sensational reports, one on employment at Lawrence Livermore National Laboratory "causing" an excess of deadly skin cancer, and the other on medical X-rays causing no detected harm, received considerable attention on television and in the press. Since one report would tend to scare people about radiation exposure, and the other would tend to tell them that all fears are groundless, the public surely became more confused than ever. Both reports are examined in this book (in chapters 5 and 14), not because they are important studies, but because their analysis here will help some readers to detect poor science and poor reporting for themselves in the future.

The author has made every effort to produce a self-contained book, with which the reader can find out the meanings of all terms and concepts used by the author without having to seek out reference books in a library. For some readers, prior studies will have made many of the terms and definitions familiar. Others will not have such a background. Therefore, background information is provided in various parts of the book for those who need it. For instance, explanations are provided for terms like *rad, curie, biological half-life, internal* versus *external exposure, cancer dose, doubling dose, linearity,* and *risk* (not so obvious as it seems; see chapter 8, section 5). In particular, chapter 2 presents many basic concepts and definitions, some of which "expert" readers may pass up. Many others will find all of chapter 2 essential for their understanding of the remainder of the book.

The Kinds of Practical Questions Answered in This Book

The author expects that some readers will use the book mainly to answer practical questions concerning personal and public-health protection, such as:

□ I am a radiographer who received 78 rads of whole-body radiation exposure when I was 24 years old in an accident caused by faulty equipment. My attorney wants to know, what is the medical probability that I will get a radiation-induced cancer? My attorney also wants to answer a separate question: What is the medical probability, if I develop a cancer, that it was caused by the radiation and not by some "natural" cause? (See chapter 6.)

□ I am the physician for a 15-year-old patient with hyperthyroidism. I am considering treating her with 14 millicuries of radioactive iodine. If I do, what would be her risk of dying from a radiation-induced cancer somewhere else in her body? (chapter 13)

□ My son injured his knee-joint in sports when he was 17 years old, and the X-rays he then received gave him a dose of about 17 rads to the left knee. What is the chance that he will get cancer as a result? (chapter 7)

□ I am an airline stewardess who is planning to have children. How big a risk of cancer and leukemia do I give my child if I am working during my early pregnancy? (chapters 12 and 15)

□ I am age 20 and thinking about going into nuclear work. If I work 10 years and receive the "permissible" occupational dose of 5 rads per year, what is my risk of dying from radiation-induced cancer? (chapter 12)

□ To what extent am I increasing my radiation exposure if I insulate my house? (chapter 9)

□ I am a 23-year-old woman who received 25 rads of exposure to my breasts during some medical diagnostic procedures. What is the chance that I will get a breast cancer as a result? If I do develop breast cancer, what is the probability that it was caused by the radiation rather than by some other cause? (chapter 7)

□ A nuclear-power plant exposed 5 million people to an average estimated whole-body radiation dose of 20 millirads each. Will anyone die because of the low-dose exposure? (chapter 8) If so, how many, and what share will be children? (chapter 7)

□ Is it true that I receive a real dose of radiation from my spouse when we cuddle in bed? (chapter 12)

□ How big a dose of radiation do we get from our color television? (chapter 12)

□ They claim nuclear power is "clean," but I hear that the radioactive residue just from mining the fuel is killing lots of people. Is that true, and if so, how many people are we talking about? (chapter 9)

□ How many Americans are killed by "natural" radiation exposure? Is it a big risk to live in Denver where the dose is higher? (chapter 12)

This book answers these questions and others, and more important, enables the reader to answer independently countless additional questions.

Full Disclosure of How Answers Were Found

There will be many readers who want more than both the answers to specific questions and the ability to answer further specific questions as they arise. They will want to understand what is known about *how* ionizing radiation causes biological harm. And they will want to know why it is scientifically reasonable to treat the evidence as we do, precisely how the quantitative answers are obtained, and where the evidence is meager or lacking. For these readers, we will devote considerable attention to the nature of the cell, of cell division, of chromosomes and chromosome injuries, and to the relationship of all these to the development of cancer and genetic injury (chapters 3 and 15). Also, we shall note a clue (chapter 8) that the evidence from human radiation may be providing about the as yet unknown, but common, mechanism that is presumed to initiate cancers of all varieties.

As noted in the Foreword to this edition, the author's methods and calculations are presented in full in the 1981 edition of *Radiation and Human Health,* and in less complete form here. The material in the unabridged edition is arranged so that the reader can delve as deeply as he (she) wishes into any of the methods developed here for handling the human evidence. Those who are active in research in this field will assuredly go over some of the methods and calculations meticulously and critically. This edition, aiming at simplification, bypasses some of the more detailed methodology to make use of the final estimates to answer practical questions.

In chapters 4, 5, and 6, all the human epidemiological evidence is analyzed in some detail. Some readers will not yet understand the difference between *epidemiological* evidence and what we call *anecdotal* evidence in medicine. Epidemiological evidence is quantitative evidence in which groups of persons who experienced a measured exposure to radiation are compared with a *control* group that was not irradiated. If the irradiated group develops much more cancer (for instance) than the unirradiated group, we consider that finding to be good reason for believing that the radiation caused the excess cancer. The issue of "much more" (statistical significance, or a *significant* effect) is discussed in chapters 5, 7, and 14.

By contrast, anecdotal evidence consists of reports about single, unrelated cases without controls. Although such evidence by itself provides little if any justification for claiming a cause-and-effect relationship, it is often the inspiration for conducting important epidemiological research. A good illustration of such inspiration is related in chapter 5.

In chapters 4 through 7, the reader will "participate" in the development of a new method to analyze existing epidemiological evidence, a method that permits scientifically valid, comprehensible generalizations to be made. Previously, there existed no way to compare or combine evidence from different studies, for the reasons explained in chapter 4. The absence of such a method has been both a source of great confusion within the field and a severe obstacle to making practical use of the existing studies to assess the personal and public-health impacts of exposure to ionizing radiation. With the method set forth in this book, however, both past and future studies can be readily analyzed in a useful manner, and radiation risks in the United States and other countries can be assessed.

When Experts Disagree, Whom Shall We Believe?

While it is widely agreed that ionizing radiation produces serious effects like cancer and leukemia, one is constantly bombarded with variants of the two following statements, in spite of an enormous body of scientific information proving them false.

1. "Oh yes, ionizing radiation does indeed produce harmful effects, but only if the dose is very high. We do not know the effects of low-level radiation."

2. "There was a release of radiation today, but the amount was small, and no harm will be done to the public health."

Scientists, public-health officials, engineers, physicians, journalists, and just about everyone else are thoroughly confused by such statements, particularly when they read or hear statements by this author and other scientists asserting that we *do* know the effects of low-dose radiation, and that both evidence and logic tell us there is *no harmless amount of radiation exposure* (chapter 8). Whom shall we believe?

The author of this book has a straightforward answer to this question. It is not necessary to believe any expert on faith, when the evidence is now available for all to examine. Since the author thinks that evidence, not faith in certain authorities, should be the foundation of opinion, he has endeavored in this book to present all the existing human evidence. In this effort, it is absolutely essential to meet the highest scientific standards, which means presenting not only evidence and conclusions but also the basis for relating them to each other, so that the reader can independently check the conclusions reached. And for those who wish to go back to the original scientific papers from which the raw evidence was taken, a list of references is provided in the back of the book.

Assumptions and Approximations

Throughout history, at any time before a particular problem was fully solved, it was inevitable that certain pieces of information important to the solution of the problem were simply not available. Either no one had chosen to seek the information, or the opportunity to do so had not presented itself. Under such circumstances, there were and are two possible approaches. One alternative is to walk away from the problem by saying, we simply don't know *everything*, and therefore we can do *nothing*. The other approach is to make reasonable approximations where they are needed, and to identify them clearly and unequivocally. Sometimes it is possible to say just what degree of uncertainty is introduced by a particular approximation.

The author would like to share with the reader a lesson of enormous importance he learned from the great chemist Kenneth S. Pitzer, when he took a course in quantum mechanics from Dr. Pitzer. On one examination, a problem was presented without all the data necessary to solve it. One piece was missing. Later, we learned that the omission was no accident. We were meant to try out a wide range of imaginary values in order to discover whether the exact value of the one missing piece would really make much of a difference in the final answer. If it did not, an approximation would clearly provide a "ballpark" answer valid for many purposes, and would certainly be preferable to no answer at all! Said Pitzer, "Any scientist who walks away from a problem just because he can't have a certain datum is not much of a scientist."

In still other instances, one must make certain assumptions about the *relationships* between hard data. One must not be apologetic about assumptions; they are part and parcel of scientific procedure. It is simply of the highest importance that assumptions be labeled as such. In this book they are always clearly identified.

Significant Figures

In science, there is a general rule that one can never get answers that are more precise than the numbers put into a calculation. We can indicate the precision of a number through appropriate use of *significant* figures. Suppose a certain measurement is made and the result is 127 by our measurement technique. We could write our number as 000127, but the extra zeros to the left of the 1 do not add to the precision at all. We say that those zeros are *not* significant figures when they are to the left of the 127. However, we may wish to indicate that the measurement is so good that we can count on the answer for much more precision than is indicated by writing 127 as the answer. We might write 127.00 for our number. Now we mean that this value is "good" out to the second decimal place. That is, we mean that the real value lies between 126.99 and 127.01. If we were to write the answer as 127.0, we would mean that the real answer lies between 126.9 and 127.1. When we write just 127, we mean that the real value lies between 126 and

128. So, the use of zeros to the right of the decimal point tells us a great deal about the precision of a number.

In this book, answers are often listed with more significant figures than the precision of the input information would justify. The author has done this so the reader will be able to follow the various calculations more readily than he would if the numbers were always rounded off. But the author does not, of course, mean to imply that the precision of a final answer is ever better than the precision of the input numbers. Thus, in a certain problem, our most uncertain measurement might be written as 14, by which we would mean we consider the real value to lie between 13 and 15. So our uncertainty is about 7% for this input number. Out of a calculation involving this input number, we can never hope to get a final answer with a precision of better than approximately 7%. Thus, if a final answer were obtained, and written in this book, as 12.462, the reader must realize that the real value lies between 12 and 13, and that this is the most precision we can hope for in the final answer. In every calculation and estimate in this book, the reader must keep in mind that the final answer cannot ever be more precise than the least precise of the input numbers.

The author has avoided the term *accuracy* here. *Precision* refers to the exactitude of a measurement. *Accuracy* refers to the closeness of the measured value to the *true* value. A very precise measurement can be far from the *true* value, if the measuring system is biased or inappropriate.

"Selection" of Data from the Literature

Obviously, it would be poor science indeed to select from the existing literature those papers that provide evidence favoring one conclusion, and to neglect those papers that favor a different conclusion. To the best of his knowledge, the author has included every study of radiation and cancer development which meets the criteria of providing some reasonable estimate of radiation dose and of reporting a meaningful follow-up period for the exposed persons. Negative studies (those that find *no* effect from radiation) as well as positive studies have been included. Studies excluded are cited, so the reader can determine if the exclusion was appropriate.

Wishful thinking and science don't mix. As a physician, the author has seen and cared for many miserably ill patients. He would be more comfortable in every way to discover that radiation below a certain dose does not add to human misery. But as a scientist, his inner driving force has always been to learn the truth.

Whether or not we can assess the effects of ionizing radiation, those effects inexorably go on being whatever they are! The desire of this author is to come as close as possible to figuring out the truth about those effects. How he and others decide to respond to the information provided here depends, first, on the information itself, and only then on their views concerning health, voluntary versus involuntary risks, and so forth.

The author would like to say that, whenever he contemplates the mystery of cell division—the intricate production, mobilization, and proper attachment of "threads" (of some sort) to each of the 46 human chromosomes, and the "pulling" (somehow) of each in the proper direction—and when he considers the other steps in the healthy growth and maintenance of a human being, all of which are directed and controlled by the chromosomes and genes within the cell, he feels profound awe and humility. So, he also feels deeply concerned about activities that pollute and destroy this exquisite information machinery, from which all future humans must originate.

The author knows that it is just by chance, in the random shuffling of mankind's genes, that he did not receive the damaged genes and chromosomes that produce very low intelligence, severe emotional disorders, or major physical disorders or early death. Luck, not merit. Those of us who were lucky may express our gratitude not only by helping those who were unlucky but also by working to protect the integrity of the species' genetic materials from unnecessary injury.

What Will Be Found, and Not Found, in This Book

This book does not cover acute radiation sickness (and death) from very high-dose radiation delivered to the whole body in a brief time—the sort of exposure one would receive during a nuclear war or during a catastrophic nuclear-power accident. Nor does this book cover noncancerous, nongenetic effects (usually from high, localized doses) such as damage to the brain, induction of cataracts, or weakening of the jaw and teeth. These very serious effects are omitted simply because their analysis would require another book, and because there exists for them no quantitative human evidence comparable to the evidence for cancerous and genetic effects. Injury to the central nervous system from in utero radiation is treated in chapter 15.

The reader will also encounter many tables. Every parent, worker, physician, and nurse, every public-health official, every attorney, every health physicist, nuclear engineer, and environmentalist who deals with matters of radiation exposure will find constant use for the tables in this book, some of which condense a world literature into a few pages.

Included in the array are tables that provide, for both sexes, the number of rads of whole-body radiation required to guarantee one cancer death, whether that radiation is given to one person or is distributed among a group of people. These values are given for radiation at every age, from early infancy on through advanced age (chapter 6). The tables in chapter 6 give the number of rads of whole-body radiation required to guarantee one cancer death when a population of mixed ages is irradiated. Similar information for leukemia is provided in the tables of chapter 14.

In many situations radiation is delivered to specific organs rather than to the whole body. The tables in chapter 7 permit estimation of the number of rads required to guarantee one cancer death from cancer in a specific organ if only that organ is irradiated.

Plutonium has become almost a household word. A table in chapter 10 gives the number of lung-cancer deaths that would be produced annually for various degrees of containment of plutonium in a nuclear-energy economy. The assumptions underlying this estimate are clearly presented in chapter 9.

Nuclear energy has by-product radioactive wastes that must be contained just as plutonium must be contained. In chapter 11 are tables giving the number of cancer fatalities per year to be expected with various degrees of perfection of containment of these by-products.

The reader will learn the shocking uncertainty about both the dose delivered by common diagnostic medical irradiation (chapter 13) and the dose delivered even today by nuclear power (chapter 11).

The reader is also offered an introduction to what is known today about chromosome injury and disease (chapters 3 and 15). Genetic injury from low-dose radiation has been evaluated too, to the extent permitted by existing evidence (chapter 15).

Some readers of this book will find food for thought about the nature of personal versus public-health protection, about the very nature of that tricky concept "risk," about the nature of cancer, the nature of genetic injury, and the nature of scientific inquiry. It would be correct for the author to state that this book is not *exclusively* about radiation.

CHAPTER 2

ENERGY INTERCHANGES AND HEALTH

O UR ENVIRONMENT can have an injurious impact upon our health in two major ways. First, material (chemical) poisons, such as dioxin, asbestos, and lead, and second, energy transfers from the environment to our body, can affect us. The subject of this book is the latter, and indeed, we shall restrict ourselves to one very large field of energy transfers, those involving ionizing radiation.

SECTION 1: THE RELATIONSHIP OF IONIZING RADIATION TO OTHER FORMS OF ENERGY

FORMS OF ENERGY

Energy, while a household word, can mean many different things.

To be sure, energy forms are interconvertible. Energy can neither be created nor destroyed, with the one exception that matter can be converted to energy, and energy can be converted to matter. So more accurately, we say that "matter-energy" can neither be created nor destroyed, but only interconverted.

Energy exists in various forms. A bullet or other projectile traveling at high velocity is said to possess *kinetic* energy (also called mechanical energy), the energy of motion. When that projectile is stopped by a solid object, the kinetic energy is converted into *heat* energy. When an object is lifted away from the earth, it acquires a still different form of energy, known as *potential* energy. That such a body has been endowed with energy is readily apparent from the fact that *kinetic* energy is acquired as the body falls back to earth. Still another form of energy is *electrical* energy.

The interconvertibility of energy can be readily understood from the process of generating electrical energy from water. We convert water into steam by the application of heat energy, convert this energy into kinetic energy when the steam turns a turbine, and then convert the kinetic energy into electrical energy in the generator by the motion of an electrical conductor through a magnetic field. Finally, in our homes, we reconvert the electrical energy into motion (kinetic energy) as in a motor, or into heat energy, as in a toaster.

Lastly, and most relevant for the discussions in this book, is that form of energy known as *radiation* energy, or *radiant* energy. Some forms of radiation energy are very familiar: light energy, which we perceive directly through our eyes; infra-red energy, which we perceive as heat; and radio-wave energy, which carries signals through the world and from outer space and finally reaches us, after amplification, on radio and television.

There are other radiation energies that are beyond visual perception, but quite similar to light energy, including ultra-violet radiation, X-rays, and gamma rays (these to be described later). In principle, all the forms of radiation energy are similar in physical nature. Until recently, radiant forms of energy were physically described as *wave motion,* capable of transmission even in a vacuum. Although the wave-motion description is adequate for many of their properties, it does not explain certain discoveries of the twentieth century. Instead, these phenomena are much better explained by considering radiant energy to be concentrated in the form of extremely minute *packets* of energy, a single packet of which is designated by the term *photon.*

This leads us to an exceedingly important and simplifying way of describing different types of radiant energy for practical purposes, namely, by the *quantity* of energy possessed by a single photon. An enormous range exists of differing energies *per packet* or *per photon,* from the extremely small quantity of energy per photon of radio-wave energy to the extremely large quantity of energy per photon of gamma rays emitted from the nuclei of unstable atoms. The range of such energies is measured in *electron-volts:* that of radio waves is from approximately 1.24×10^{-5} to 1.24×10^{-10}, whereas that of gamma rays is from 155 to millions of electron-volts. (Readers unaccustomed to working with powers of ten should keep in mind that 10^{-5} equals one hundred-thousandth, 10^{-10} equals one ten billionth.) The simple rule is: The shorter the wavelength of a form of radiation, the greater will be its energy per photon.

In addition to energy per photon, there is another property of photons that concerns us here, namely, their interaction with matter. This interaction depends on both the kind of photon and the kind of matter involved. For example, visible light will not penetrate a thin sheet of black paper, but will penetrate an inch of glass. We refer to the glass as *transparent* to photons of visible light, a phenomenon specific to the energy of the photons and to the composition (including the arrangement of atoms) of the glass.

In 1895, Roentgen discovered the important form of radiant energy, now commonly understood and familiar, known as X-rays. The special property of X-rays was their ease of penetration through all sorts of solid objects, objects that would *not* permit the transmission of radiant energy in the form of visible light. Although the X-rays of Roentgen and the light rays of sunlight are both photons of energy, the X-ray photons each possess an enormous quantity of energy compared to the light photons. The term *X-ray* is used to cover a whole group of photons, differing from each other in the quantity of energy per photon. It is important to remember this variation in energy per photon, for many differences in biological effectiveness depend upon the\differences in X-ray energies within the group of radiations all known as X-rays.

How did Roentgen produce his X-rays? The understanding of this requires that attention be turned to some of the basic properties of all matter, living and inanimate.

ATOMS AND IONS

Matter, as we think of it (outside the realm of subatomic physics) is reducible to 92 naturally occurring forms, known as chemical *elements.* Hydrogen, carbon, oxygen, nitrogen, iron, lead, and uranium are all chemical elements. All of these elements can be described as having a central dense core, the *nucleus,* surrounded by a very large region (relatively) that occupies most of the space of the atom, in which outer region are particles known as *electrons* in motion about the central core. These electrons are precisely the same particles that are in motion in an electrical wire carrying electric current.

The simplest element known to man is the familiar substance hydrogen. Its central core (nucleus) has one unit of positive charge in the form of a particle known as a *proton.* Also in the hydrogen atom is one electron in motion about the nucleus; this electron carries one unit of negative charge. The proton of the nucleus, while of the same electrical charge as the electron (although its charge is positive instead of negative), has a mass some 1,840 times as large as the mass of the electron. We say that the simplest element, hydrogen, has an *atomic number* of 1, the atomic number designating the number of protons in the nucleus.

In a *neutral* atom, the number of orbiting electrons is equal to the number of protons in the nucleus. We shall return later to discussion of another nuclear particle, the neutron.

With the application of sufficient energy, it is possible to separate the electron from the hydrogen atom. In so doing, we produce a separated electron, of one unit of negative charge, and the core of a hydrogen atom, of one unit of positive charge, now called a *positive* hydrogen *ion.* A positive ion is produced by the physical subtraction of a negative charge, an electron, from a neutral atom, leaving a positively charged remainder. A *negative ion* is produced by adding an electron to a neutral atom. Thus an electron, extracted from a neutral hydrogen atom, can attach itself to another neutral atom, converting that atom into a negative ion. Since the hydrogen atom has only one electron, it is obviously possible to remove only one electron from it, leaving a hydrogen ion with a charge of $+1$. From other neutral atoms, with many electrons orbiting their nuclei, it is possible to produce ions of charge $+2$, $+3$, or more by removing two, three, or more electrons, respectively.

Ions are very familiar in the world of chemistry and biology. Common table salt (also called *sodium chloride*) is made up of one atom of the element sodium combined with one atom of the element chlorine. But in table salt there are no sodium or chlorine *atoms*. Instead, every unit of table salt is made up of +1 sodium ions and −1 chloride ions. In solid crystals of salt there is a precise lattice work of sodium and chloride ions, and while each positive ion is exactly balanced by a negative ion, it is impossible to say that any particular sodium ion "belongs" to any particular chloride ion. If the salt is dissolved in water, however, the crystal lattice is broken down into single ions of sodium (written as Na^+) and single ions of chlorine (written as Cl^-). Our body fluids are filled with ions, as are our body cells, not only of sodium and chlorine but also of potassium (K^+), magnesium (Mg^{++}), calcium (Ca^{++}), iodine (I^-), and many other chemical elements. A great part of our physiology and biochemistry is based upon the behavior of ions and upon the movement of ions into and out of cells.

The process of creating ions from atoms is known as *ionization*. The creation of positive ions from neutral atoms requires the expenditure of energy, in an amount known as the *ionization potential*, to wrest electrons out of their orbits. The attachment of a free electron to certain neutral atoms can yield energy. More complex forms of ions are created when groups of atoms are attached to each other.

DISCOVERY AND DEFINITION OF IONIZING RADIATION

With a variety of techniques, it is possible to separate electrons from atoms to create positive ions, indeed to create a whole region of positive charge (a lack of electrons), and similarly to create whole regions of negative charge (an excess of electrons). Between such positive and negative regions, an *electrical field* is said to exist, and it can be described quantitatively in units known as *volts per centimeter*. Since the separated regions differ in voltage (in volts per centimeter), electrons will leave the negative region (or what is called the *negative electrode*), will migrate through a gas or vacuum toward and finally to the positive region (or what is called the *positive electrode*).

In a vacuum tube with a high-voltage difference between the positive and negative electrodes, electrons leave the negative electrode and acquire an enormous velocity in traveling toward the positive electrode. An electron moving at high speed has kinetic energy, the energy of motion. When the electron strikes the positive electrode, all its kinetic energy is dissipated in the positive electrode, most of which is converted into ordinary heat.

But Roentgen discovered that, in this process of electrons giving up their energy in the positive electrode, something else was occurring: a new form of radiant energy was simultaneously produced, which would pass through glass and through a variety of materials that would stop ordinary light rays. Only a small fraction of the electron energy went into the production of this new form of radiant energy. Additionally, it was determined that the larger the voltage drop from positive to negative electrode, the greater was the kinetic energy acquired by the electrons, and the more penetrating was the radiation. This new form of radiation was given the name *X-rays*, since its nature was unknown.

Somewhat later it was discovered that X-rays, now known to be photons of radiant energy, could, on passage through gas, liquid, or solid matter (living or nonliving), *produce ions from neutral atoms or molecules*, and so were described as *ionizing radiation*. We will encounter other forms of ionizing radiation later. The biological importance of the ionizing capacity of X-rays is profound. Ordinary light of any color can induce many chemical reactions —for example, conversion of carbon dioxide and water into sugars in green plants. No photon of light, however, has enough energy to rip an electron away from a neutral atom or molecule. Photons of ultra-violet light have more energy per photon than do those of visible light, but neither do they have sufficient energy to eject electrons from neutral atoms. Photons of energy from Roentgen's evacuated high-voltage tubes did indeed have enough energy to strip an electron from neutral matter. Ionizing capacity became an important (though arbitrary) dividing line between forms of radiant energy. In the remainder of this book we will concern ourselves with those radiations that are sufficiently energetic to produce ionization.

It should be noted that both ionizing radiation and non-ionizing radiation share the same velocity of travel—the speed of light, if the radiation is in the form of photons. We shall later encounter some *particles* that can also produce ionization which do not travel at the speed of light.

THE ENERGY PER ELECTRON

An electron acquires energy in a high-vacuum tube in proportion to the voltage through which it falls, finally acquiring, at the moment of impact with the positive pole, a total (kinetic) energy that can be described by the multiplication of its charge by the voltage. Thus, if a single electron (carrying one unit of charge) falls through a difference in electrical potential of 10 volts, we say it has acquired a kinetic energy of 10 *electron-volts*. The electron-volt is abbreviated *ev*. Since an ev is a unit of energy, it can be converted to any other form of energy unit, such as the calorie, the BTU, the erg, or the joule, if we wish to do so.

If an electron migrates between two electrodes separated by a potential difference of 1 million volts, the energy of motion acquired at the moment of impact with the positive pole will be 1,000,000 ev. For certain purposes it is convenient to use a simpler set of units. Thus, if two poles have a potential difference of 1,000 volts, we say that the difference is 1 *kilovolt*, which we abbreviate to *kv*. (*Kilo-* is a prefix meaning "one thousand.") If they are separated by a potential difference of 1,000,000 volts, we call that difference 1 *megavolt*, which we abbreviate to *mv*. (*Mega-* means "one million.") We use a corresponding system to describe energy. Thus, an electron that has acquired 1,000 electron-volts of energy is said to have an energy of 1 *kev,* and an electron that has acquired an energy of 1,000,000 electron-volts is said to have an energy of 1 *mev.*

In Roentgen's X-ray tube, now commonly seen in doctors' and dentists' offices, voltages across the tube (between positive and negative electrode) range from 50,000 to 250,000 volts, or, expressed in other units, between 50 and 250 kv. Correspondingly, the electrons hurtling through the vacuum inside such tubes acquire energies, respectively, of 50 to 250 kev.

The Law Connecting X-ray Energy with Electron Energy

We stated previously that most of the energy of electrons striking a positive electrode is converted into heat. A small, but highly important, part of their energy is converted into the photons of X-rays. A fundamental law was discovered relating the energy of the electrons with the energy per photon of the X-rays emitted from the tube. If the voltage across the tube is 50 kv, the energy acquired by each electron in moving from negative to positive pole is 50 kev, and the *maximum* energy of the emitted X-rays will be 50 kev per X-ray photon. There is an additional feature of importance, however. Some of the electrons are slowed down before their energy is converted into X-rays, so that not only are X-rays of the maximum energy emitted by the tube, but X-rays of all the lower energies as well. But it is impossible for a tube with 50 kv of potential difference between electrodes to produce any X-rays of energy higher than 50 kev per photon. So, we see a continuum of X-ray energies being produced, up to a maximum value that corresponds to the voltage across the tube. In a 50-kv tube, most of the X-rays produced will be of energies below 50 kev, and the maximum energy of X-rays produced will be 50 kev. Similarly, in a 250-kv tube, a continuum of X-ray energies will be emitted, from a very low level of energy per photon to a maximum energy of 250 kev per photon.

All X-ray tubes emit additional X-rays known as *characteristic X-rays.* These depend upon the nature of the chemical element of which the positive pole, or *target,* is made. A tungsten target produces different characteristic X-rays than does a chromium target. Provided the tube voltage is high enough to "excite" the characteristic X-rays, their actual energy depends on the target element and not on the tube voltage. They originate by a process different from that which produces the continuum of X-ray energies described above. Some of the electrons hurtling into the target eject an electron from what is called the *inner shell* of a target atom, leaving a vacancy. When an electron falls into that inner shell, energy is given off in the form of characteristic X-rays, the energy of an X-ray depending on the difference in energy of the electron in the inner shell and its energy in the outer shell from which it falls. These characteristic X-rays have specified, discrete energies, in contrast to the continuum of X-ray energies previously described. Generally, the characteristic X-rays make up about 10% of all the X-rays emitted from the tube. If an X-ray tube is operated at a voltage too low to eject those inner electrons from the target, then that set of characteristic X-rays will not be produced.

THE PENETRATION OF MATTER BY X-RAYS

Everyone who has seen a chest X-ray film knows that at least some of the X-rays must be able to penetrate through the entire chest; otherwise there would be no X-rays left to blacken the film itself. Moreover, it can be shown, by interposing varying thicknesses of material between an X-ray source and an X-ray detector (film or other), that the quantity of X-rays penetrating the material depends on:

a. The upper energy limit of the X-rays themselves
b. The thickness of the material interposed
c. The nature of the atomic composition of the material interposed,
whether it is tissue, iron, aluminum, lead, or copper

X-rays of *one specific energy* (recall that an ordinary X-ray tube emits a whole spectrum of energies) will be reduced in number by a certain fraction for each unit of thickness of the material through which they pass. For a certain X-ray energy and for a certain material—lead, for example—that number of X-rays by which the incident X-ray beam is reduced is a *universal* number. It will be the same for any X-ray source at any place on earth. It does not depend on the kind of detector we use to measure the X-rays. For a different material, say, copper instead of lead, and for the same X-ray energy, there will be a different number to characterize what we call the *absorption* of the X-rays, or the *attenuation* (meaning reduction) of the beam by the interposed material.

    If we have X-rays of, say, 50 kev of energy, and we measure how much copper must be interposed to cut the number of 50-kev X-ray photons getting through it in half, that specific thickness of copper is known as its *half-thickness* for 50-kev X-rays. If one impinges a half-thickness of copper with 1,000 50-kev photons, it will be found that 500 of the 50-kev photons get through it. The interesting point about the fact that a certain fraction of the 50-kev X-rays is stopped by a certain thickness of absorber is that *the fraction does not change* as the rays go through an additional equal thickness of absorber. Let us illustrate this by starting with 1,000 X-ray photons of 50 kev in energy. With one half-thickness of copper interposed, 500 of the 50-kev photons will get through. If we now interpose an additional half-thickness of copper in the beam, 250 of the 50-kev photons will get through. If we interpose a third half-thickness of copper in the beam, 125 of the 50-kev photons will get through, and so on. The rule is that there is no specific distance of passage through a material which can be regarded as a "range of travel" for X-rays of a specific energy. Instead there is a fractional reduction with each thickness of absorbing material. We shall need this rule later in estimating dose to tissues from X-ray beams incident upon the skin of humans. (We shall later discuss other ionizing radiation in the form of particles, whose behavior is quite different, and where a certain amount of material stops the radiation entirely.)

In a practical sense, if we interpose enough half-thicknesses of material, very, very few X-rays will emerge through that material, and we can say that the X-rays have been virtually stopped. But if we start with a sufficiently large number of X-ray photons, some must come through even a large number of half-thicknesses of absorber.

An important point must be realized concerning the biological effects of X-rays. Any X-ray that passes through a thickness of tissue and still emerges with its original energy, say 50 kev, will have done no biological harm whatever to the tissue.

Of course, the key question is about the X-rays that do *not* pass through the absorber, whether the absorber is copper or human tissue. These X-rays produce major chemical and biological effects, and we must now turn to the mechanisms by which they produce their effects.

SECTION 2: HOW IONIZING RADIATION INTERACTS WITH LIVING TISSUE

X-RAY INTERACTION WITH MATTER

Let us consider the fate of X-ray photons of any energy passing through matter. For purposes that will become apparent shortly, we shall restrict our attention at first to X-rays of energies less than 1.02 mev. There are two ways X-ray photons can interact with matter and give up their energy; these ways are described by the terms *photoelectric effect* and *Compton effect*.

Let us recall that all matter, whatever elements it is made of, from element 1 (hydrogen) to element 92 (uranium), is composed of atoms which themselves have central cores (nuclei) and orbiting electrons.

When the photoelectric effect occurs in any material interacting with X-rays, *all the energy* of an X-ray photon is transferred to one of the orbiting electrons of an atom in the material. Some energy is consumed in pulling the electron out of its orbit, but all the rest of the X-ray energy is imparted to the electron, which is thereby placed in motion at a very high velocity. The precise velocity of the electron thus set in motion depends on how many kev there were in the X-ray photon that set it in motion. In the photoelectric process, the original X-ray *disappears* as an entity. All subsequent effects are due to the newly activated high-velocity electron. At this point we shall not ask what this electron does, but simply insure that it is realized that the *only* effect of this particular photon is to set an electron in linear motion—no more, no less.

The second type of interaction is the Compton effect. When this occurs, instead of *all* the energy of the X-ray photon being given up to the electron it sets in motion, only *part* of the X-ray energy is expended. The remainder of the energy of the X-ray appears in a new X-ray photon, of reduced energy compared with the energy of the original photon. The Compton effect is the process by which most of the X-rays of biological interest affect matter.

The X-ray photon of reduced energy newly created by the Compton effect can itself do exactly what the original photon could do. It can interact with another atom causing the photoelectric effect and giving up all its energy to set an electron in motion, or it can itself undergo the Compton effect, setting an electron in motion and creating a new X-ray photon of an energy still further reduced. Through these two processes, those X-rays that do interact with matter finally give up all their energy to *set electrons in motion.* So the *real* effects of X-rays are the secondary effects of all the electrons they set in motion.

We must now return to those X-ray photons of energy greater than 1.02 mev. While these photons can and do cause the photoelectric effect and the Compton effect, they also have an additional capability. In the vicinity of an atom, they can actually *disappear,* and in the process create new matter in the form of one negative electron and one positive electron, or *positron.* A positron is a particle of the same size and mass as a (negative) electron, but a positron has one unit of *positive* charge. In order to create this "pair" (a positron plus an electron), exactly 1.02 mev of energy is used up in the conversion of energy into matter. But the X-ray (or gamma ray) that creates the "pair" may have had much more energy than 1.02 mev. Any residual energy is distributed equally to the electron and positron in the form of kinetic energy. Thus, if we start with an X-ray of 2 mev, 1.02 mev is used up in creating the electron and positron, leaving 0.98 mev. The created electron gets 0.49 mev of kinetic energy, and the created positron gets 0.49 mev of kinetic energy.

The fate of the electron, set in high-speed motion, is the same as the fate of any electron set in motion by the photoelectric or the Compton effect. This we shall discuss shortly. The fate of the positron is different. It will expend some of its energy by interacting with atoms of the material in which it has been set in motion; finally it will meet a negative electron, and the two will annihilate each other. The electron and the positron will both disappear in this annihilation, and two new gamma rays will appear, each having 0.51 mev of energy. So in the annihilation we get back the total of 1.02 mev of energy it took to create the electron and positron. These newly created gamma rays will simply do what any other 0.51-mev gamma rays do, namely, interact by the photoelectric effect and the Compton effect.

Again, aside from the interactions of positrons with matter, *all* of the energy of X-rays or gamma rays that *is* expended in matter finally ends up as the energy of electrons in motion. It will be *the interactions of those electrons with matter* that will determine all the biological effects of radiation, be those effects cancer production, leukemia production, or genetic injury. Before considering these interactions, we must turn our attention to the crucial comparison of the magnitude of the energies of the high-speed electrons with the magnitude of the energies involved in ordinary chemical reactions, inside or outside the body.

HIGH-SPEED ELECTRON ENERGIES VERSUS CHEMICAL AND BIOLOGICAL ENERGIES

Essentially all chemical processes, whether they occur in inanimate matter or in living, biological tissue, are accompanied by energy changes. It may be necessary to put energy in either to create a new substance or to break apart an existing chemical substance. In other reactions, energy may be released during the formation or destruction of a chemical substance. How do these energy changes compare, quantitatively, with the energies of the high-speed electrons set in motion when X-ray energy is absorbed by matter in the processes we have just described?

In living tissue we have such atoms as carbon, hydrogen, nitrogen, oxygen, sulfur, and phosphorus combined in a variety of ways into thousands of different chemical compounds, or molecules. Some of these compounds are the familiar proteins, amino acids, sugars, fats, hemoglobin, urea, enzymes (thousands of them), hormones, water, carbon dioxide, and ammonia. The atoms in all such chemical compounds are said to be "bound" to each other, in chemical terms, by what we call *chemical bonds*. Thus we have many carbon-to-carbon bonds, carbon-to-hydrogen bonds, carbon-to-nitrogen bonds, carbon-to-phosphorus bonds, phosphorus-to-oxygen bonds, and so on. If our bodies are to break such chemical bonds in the course of biochemical processes, energy must be put in to break the bonds. Often we do not need to put in all the energy needed to break a particular bond, because energy is released in the simultaneous *formation* of some other chemical bond. Broadly, we can say that the energy involved in the breaking of chemical bonds is of the order of 5–7 electron-volts. The energy involved in many chemical reactions is less, simply because some bonds are made while others are broken. So we speak of chemical bonds as being characterized by *binding energies* of 5–7 electron-volts.

If an X-ray of 100 kev transfers its energy during the photoelectric effect to an electron and sets it in motion in biological tissue, that electron will have 100 kev of energy minus the very small amount (comparatively) of energy required to tear it out of its atom. This is an *enormous* amount of energy compared to the energies of chemical bonds. Indeed, 100 kev is enough energy to break 14,000–20,000 ordinary types of chemical bonds, on the average. *There is no chemical bond in biological tissue which is strong enough to resist breakage by such energy,* since even the most powerful chemical bonds are of energies of about 1/14,000 the energy of the high-speed electron. In actual fact, however, the electron with 100 kev of energy, set in motion by the X-ray, does not simply break 14,000 or 20,000 separate bonds; its interactions are far more complex than this. Some of the 100 kev of energy goes into knocking additional electrons out of atoms or compounds of atoms (this process being the familiar *ionization*). Some of the energy is expended in what is called *excitation* of electrons to a higher energy state, without actually knocking the electrons out of their atoms. A compound containing excited electrons is said to be in an *unstable,* higher energy state, in which a variety of chemical reactions, otherwise not possible, become possible. Compounds that have lost an electron by ionization and are in a very unstable state can rearrange themselves into new compounds, or can react vigorously with other compounds. Compared to the orderly, precise ways by which low quantities of energy are ordinarily transferred from atom to atom, molecule to molecule, in the exquisitely functioning biological tissue, the introduction of an electron with 100 kev (100,000 ev) can only be described as chemical and biological mayhem—a veritable bull in a china shop.

What about the electrons that have been ripped out of atoms or molecules by the first very-high-speed electron? They can themselves rip electrons out of atoms of additional compounds, although these secondary electrons do not have nearly as much energy as the original 100-kev electron. So there is a cascading effect: an X-ray sets an electron into high-speed motion; that electron rips other electrons out of atoms and molecules, excites other electrons; the secondary electrons, ripped out, go on to rip still further electrons out of atoms or molecules, until finally all the 100 kev has been expended. All kinds of chemical reactions and rearrangements of atoms in molecules have occurred as a result of the excitation and ionization.

If we measure the number of actual ionizations that have occurred, it turns out that 33.7 ev will have been expended for each ionization, *on the average.* This does not mean that it takes 33.7 ev to produce an ionization, since we know that some of the energy went into exciting electrons in atoms, without ionizing the atoms. It is just an accounting process in which we divide the number of ions produced into the total energy expended, and arrive at 33.7 ev per ion-pair produced. We use the term *ion-pair* to mean a positive ion plus the electron or negative ion produced when the electron attaches itself to a neutral atom or compound.

To be sure, after all the reactions have occurred, including all the secondary reactions, caused by a single 100-kev electron set in motion by an X-ray, finally some of the original order may be restored. A particular carbon atom, broken away from a particular nitrogen atom to which it was attached, may reunite with its partner nitrogen atom. For *this* pair of atoms it can be said that no damage was sustained. But unfortunately, this is not the general expectation. Rather, the general expectation is that chaos has been created out of order, chemically. If it were not for the fact that multiple copies of many important biological compounds are available and the fact that new copies *can* be synthesized, X-rays would cause far more serious effects on living systems than they do. As we shall see, their effects are serious enough.

WHAT IS SO SPECIAL ABOUT THE CREATION OF IONS WITH RADIATION?

We know that ions are created all the time in chemical reactions. For example, when sodium (metal) reacts with chlorine gas to produce sodium chloride, an electron is transferred from a sodium atom to a chlorine atom, thus creating a sodium ion (Na^+) and a chloride ion (Cl^-). But in this reaction, no electron is set free to roam around in space for distances that are thousands of times atomic distances. When sodium reacts with chlorine, an electron is transferred over distances measured in *angstroms* (1 angstrom represents 10^{-8} centimeters), and at no time is that electron endowed with a kinetic energy of thousands or more of electron-volts, as is commonly the case with ionizing radiation. It does take 5.1 ev to wrest the electron out of the sodium atom, but 3.6 ev is regained when the electron attaches to the chlorine atom, and then further energy is released from the binding of the positive sodium ion to the negative chloride ion, again of the order of a few electron-volts.

When any of a host of chemical reactions occur, we visualize that electron transfers occur. For example, when a Fe^{++} ion (ferrous ion) is oxidized chemically to Fe^{+++} (ferric ion), an electron is transferred to the oxidizing agent, whatever that oxidizer may be. Here again, the movement of the electron is over distances measured in angstroms, not millimeters or centimeters. And the energy change accompanying the reaction is commonly 0.5 to 2 electron-volts, *not* 20, 200, 2,000, 20,000, or 200,000 electron-volts, which are the energies with which electrons can be endowed by ionizing radiation processes.

To summarize, with ionizing radiation, electrons are removed from their atoms and endowed with energies huge compared to those in ordinary chemical reactions. Such electrons maraud for great distances (compared with atomic dimensions in angstroms) and have the chemical capability to break any kind of bond one might care to visualize. In biochemical systems, reactions are carefully controlled, often by special geometric juxtaposition of the reactants. A marauding high-speed electron simply does not notice all this elegant juxtaposition—it can break anything, anywhere. And once it has ripped an electron out of an atom in a molecule, that molecule is itself at such a high-energy level that it can produce all kinds of chemical reactions that would never have been possible without the ionizing radiation.

THE OTHER IONIZING RADIATIONS: ALPHA, BETA, AND GAMMA RAYS

In the discussion above, we stated that X-rays and gamma rays have identical properties, both being high-energy photons. But we did not explain that their *origins* differ.

Not long after Roentgen's discovery of X-rays, Becquerel made a related and in many ways far more fateful discovery, namely, that salts of the element uranium (atomic number 92) emitted radiations that were able to penetrate matter in a manner similar to X-rays and totally different from ordinary light radiation. We must understand that these rays were emitted from uranium without benefit of any high-vacuum tubes or high voltages. Becquerel thought for a short time that the uranium was activated by sunlight to emit these special radiations, but he soon realized that its emissions were spontaneous, not caused by sunlight or other outside influences. This was the discovery of *radioactivity*, the emission of radiation by supposedly inert substances without help from any energy source outside. Of course, subsequent work revealed that uranium is not the only natural substance that emits radiation. Several other chemical elements do so as well, some of them created from uranium by radioactive decay. The discoveries of Becquerel are among the truly astounding ones of science.

While it is simple to relate now, it took very astute experimentation and observation finally to prove not only that the radiation was a property of uranium itself, rather than of any of its chemical compounds, but also that the radiations from uranium were far more complex than Roentgen's X-rays.

First of all, there were uranium radiations that were photon in nature —the gamma rays—and were essentially identical to Roentgen's X-rays except that some had far higher energies per photon than any X-rays Roentgen had produced in his machines. Our current understanding is that we can regard X-rays and gamma rays as identical in nature, except that in general X-rays are made in high-voltage machines, while gamma rays originate from the nuclei of atoms. (Not all X-rays are produced in machines, since some nuclear reactions are accompanied by X-ray emission.) For our purposes here, we shall make no error by considering the interaction of X-rays and gamma rays with biological tissue as identical, once we have accounted for the actual energy of the ray. We shall return later to the question of how the energy of the ray influences its biological effect.

The other radiations coming from the uranium or its decay products turned out not to be photons at all, but rather two types of *particulate* radiation.

The first type are the so-called *beta rays*, which are not rays at all, but rather the familiar particles, electrons, emitted from the nuclei of decay products of uranium and traveling at high speed. Once emitted, the properties of the beta rays are no different from those of any other source of high-energy, high-speed electrons.

The second type, originally called *alpha rays*, were also not rays at all, but particles quite different from beta particles. The alpha particles, emitted from the nuclei of uranium, turned out to be "stripped" nuclei of the element *helium*. Helium is of atomic number 2, which tells us that each of its nuclei must have two protons, giving the nucleus a charge of $+2$, and that in the neutral atom of helium, there must be two orbiting electrons. The alpha particle bursting out of a uranium nucleus (or a nucleus of radium, or radon) is nothing other than the nucleus of a helium atom, with the two orbiting electrons missing. Ultimately, all alpha particles emitted from such substances as uranium find two electrons in the environment and become atoms of helium gas.

The radiations emitted from such naturally unstable (radioactive) atoms as uranium are commonly much more energetic per unit than the X-ray photons from Roentgen's machine, though not all are more energetic. Some of the gamma rays from uranium and other naturally radioactive substances have energies in the range of millions of electron-volts per photon—compare these with 50–100-kev photons of ordinary X-ray machines. Gamma rays from unstable nuclei do all the things that X-rays do, such as cause the photoelectric effect, the Compton effect, and the production of electron-positron pairs.

The most energetic beta particles (electrons) from unstable nuclei also have energies in the million-electron-volt range, although we shall see later that these highly energetic beta rays are always accompanied by beta rays of lesser energies ranging down to nearly zero energy. The alpha particles (helium nuclei) commonly have energies in the 5-million-electron-volt range, when emitted from naturally occurring unstable nuclei.

In the discussion of X-rays it was pointed out that those X-rays which do *not* produce such effects as the photoelectric or Compton effect, but go right through the body, will have no biological effect at all. Precisely the same is true for gamma rays. The facts are quite otherwise for alpha and beta particles. These particles interact at every millimeter along their path through human tissue, so if they gain access to tissue, biological harm is guaranteed.

Besides the difference in the magnitude of energy in nuclear-emitted gamma rays and the X-rays of a Roentgen machine, another important difference exists. In an X-ray machine, X-rays are produced with energies ranging from a high energy, which corresponds to the voltage of the machine, down to very low energies—a continuum of energies. Gamma rays emitted from unstable nuclei are either all of the same energy or are of discrete sets of energies. Thus, an unstable nucleus may emit one set of gamma rays, all of 1.5 mev, or it may emit two sets of gamma rays, some of 1.5 mev and some of 0.8 mev. Still other unstable nuclei may emit four, five, or six sets of gamma rays, differing from each other in energy, but will emit no rays with energies in between those of the discrete sets and no very low energies such as we find for X-rays.

BETA- AND ALPHA-PARTICLE ENERGIES AND THEIR INTERACTION WITH TISSUE AND OTHER MATTER

The beta particles emitted from a radioactive element are not all of the same energy. What is found is that there is some *maximum* energy of beta particles emitted from a particular radioactive substance. Beta particles of the maximum energy are emitted along with others of every energy down to zero energy. The reason for this is that some energy is carried off in a particle known as the *neutrino,* with which we will not concern ourselves here because of the virtual absence of neutrino interaction with tissue. The average energy of the beta particles emitted from a radioactive substance can be taken, as a very good practical approximation, to be *one-third* of the maximum energy. We shall need this approximation later in calculating the radiation received from beta particles.

Alpha particles emitted from a radioactive element are either all of one discrete energy, or of a few sets of discrete energies, as in the case of gamma rays. Radioactivity tables provide information as to whether there is one alpha-particle energy or two energies, and what they are numerically. Thus, in the case of a radioactive decay with only one set of alpha-particle energies, the maximum alpha-particle energy is identical with the average alpha-particle energy.

The beta particle, originating from the nucleus of an unstable atom, is a high-speed electron in motion. Once it has come out of the nucleus, it behaves in every way exactly as does any other high-speed electron of the same energy. Thus a beta particle (electron) of 100 kev in energy will do exactly the same amount and the same kind of damage in tissue as will be done by a 100-kev electron set in motion by an X-ray or gamma ray.

The alpha particle produces its effects in tissue by ionization, too. The alpha particle interacts with atoms to rip out electrons; then those electrons do all the things in tissue that electrons from any other source would do, if they were of the same energy.

LINEAR ENERGY TRANSFER, OR "LET"

We have noted thus far that X-rays, gamma rays, beta particles, and alpha particles all interact in tissue by ejecting electrons from atoms (ionization). If this is true, then all the biological effects of all these radiations should be the same, corrected for their differing energies. To a first approximation this *is* true, but some important second approximations exist.

First, the efficiency with which a charged particle ejects an electron depends upon how much charge is on the particle—precisely, upon the *square* of the charge. Since an alpha particle has twice the charge of a beta particle (2 versus 1), an alpha particle should be four times (2^2) as efficient in ionizing, per collision, as is a beta particle, all other features being equal.

Second, another important effect depends on the speed at which a charged particle is traveling, and this effect is the opposite of what one might intuitively think. It turns out that the more slowly a particle is traveling, the greater is the chance of ionization. This means that as a high-speed electron slows down, as it imparts energy by ionization, it becomes progressively *more* effective in causing new ionizations per collision with atoms. The same is true for alpha particles. Of course, both kinds of particles finally reach such low energies that they are no longer able to ionize at all.

In order to express the combined effects of charge and speed in determining ionization effectiveness, the term *linear energy transfer* has been introduced. It describes the amount of energy (ionization plus electron excitation) transferred *per unit of path traveled* by the ionizing particle (electron, alpha particle, or other). There is good reason to believe that biological injuries of some sorts are more severe when the ionizations are closely spaced than when they are farther apart. For this reason, linear energy transfer (known as LET) is important in the assessment of biological effects.

Distances in biological tissues are measured in *micrometers* (also called *microns*). One "micro-meter" is one-millionth of a meter. The reason for the use of this unit is that cells in tissue are on the order of 10–30 micrometers in diameter. The convenient unit for describing linear energy transfer is *kev per micrometer.* The average LET for a 1-kev electron is 12.3; the average LET for a 100-kev alpha particle is 260 (kev per micrometer). Of course, since electrons and alpha particles slow down as they do their ionizing damage in tissue, the LET for a particular particle is a constantly changing value. One can describe the average LET for the particle throughout its travel path, but we must remember that this obscures the fact of a steadily changing LET as energy is lost by the particle. Some writers speak of certain radiation as being of low LET (what they call "sparsely ionizing") and of other radiation as being of high LET ("densely ionizing"), but that tends to be deceptive in an important respect. An electron can start out with 1 mev of energy, at which energy it is "sparsely ionizing," or of low LET, but later on, as it slows down, it becomes progressively more densely ionizing, or of higher LET. In this sense, all originally low LET radiation becomes high LET radiation during the later part of its travel path in tissue.

What is the LET of an X-ray or gamma ray? The answer is that there is none so long as the ray remains a photon, since from all our discussions above, there is no interaction with tissue until the photon sets an electron in motion. Now, since the *maximum* energy of an electron set in motion by an X-ray is equal to the X-ray energy, it follows that high-energy photons can produce electrons of lower LET than can low-energy photons.

Lest the reader be confused by the statement above that the LET of an X-ray or gamma ray is zero, we will clarify. In the literature, X-rays and gamma rays are discussed as low LET radiation. This designation really means that the *electrons* set in motion *by* such radiation are low in LET compared to such radiations as alpha particles. Strictly speaking, the correct designation is zero—so long as a 100-kev photon remains a 100-kev photon, it has transferred no energy and has produced no biological or chemical effect. While some generalizations can be made that high LET radiation may be more harmful, for the same total energy delivered to tissue, than is low LET radiation, this is by no means a law of nature. It is not necessarily true that all biological effects depend on the closeness of the spacing of ionizations in tissue. Some undoubtedly do, and in those instances, high LET radiation will necessarily be more effective per unit of energy delivered. Some very probably do not, and in those instances, high LET radiation may hardly be any more effective than low LET radiation, for the same total energy delivered. Note in all instances that the qualifier is *for the same energy delivered.* No one doubts that the more energy delivered in toto, the greater will be the effect.

THE TRAVERSAL OF TISSUES BY BETA AND ALPHA PARTICLES

In the case of X-rays and gamma rays, we have already shown that there is a *statistical* chance that any particular X-ray will interact in traveling a certain distance. It either does interact or does not. That is why some X-rays can travel through quite a distance in tissue and come through unaltered, and why we can describe *half-thicknesses* for X-rays and gamma rays.

But beta and alpha particles start interacting and producing ionizations in tissue from the very beginning of their travel paths, and they slow down as such ionizations reduce their energy (energy transfer). This means that there is a *finite* distance, known as the *range,* over which an alpha or beta particle will travel in tissue. Beyond that distance, no alpha particles or beta particles will penetrate. They have no half-thickness. To be rigorous, we can say that there is a small variation in range, even for alpha particles of the same energy, simply because the loss of energy in every micrometer of path is not exactly the same. This is also true of beta particles. In general, the range of alpha particles in tissue is on the order of 30–40 micrometers, or about 3 or 4 cell diameters, and no alpha particle of interest to us will travel more than 100 micrometers in tissue. (Of course, alpha particles of differing initial energies will travel a different distance before coming to rest.) Beta particles travel much farther because they lose less energy per micrometer. In general, we are dealing with beta particles that travel distances on the order of millimeters, rather than micrometers, unless the initial energy of a beta particle is very low, in which case its range will be very low too.

There is a curious misconception in some quarters about alpha particles. Those who are endeavoring to assure the public about the safety of nuclear power are fond of a little demonstration they make. They place an alpha-emitting source near a machine that counts the emissions, and show the counter whirring. Then a piece of paper is placed between the source and the counter, and the whirring ceases, showing that no alpha particles are getting through the paper. What the public is supposed to construe from this demonstration is the "weakness" of alpha particles for causing biological damage. "After all, they can't even make it through a sheet of paper." The reader by now knows how ludicrous this demonstration is. The reason the alpha particles do not get through the paper is that they are so effective in damaging chemical bonds in the paper that they transfer all their energy in just the thickness of the sheet of paper. The appropriate conclusion is that alpha particles should be expected to be very damaging in going through tissue. If an alpha-emitter is lodged, for example, in the lining epithelium of the bronchi (where lung cancer originates), three or four sensitive cells there will get an enormous blast of energy as one alpha particle expends its energy in passing through them. To be sure, however, an alpha-emitter on the surface of the body cannot produce radiation injury to *internal* tissues.

SECTION 3: THE NATURE OF RADIOACTIVE DECAY AND ITS MEASUREMENT

NUCLIDES: STABLE AND RADIOACTIVE

In our prior discussion of the chemical elements, we noted that the number of protons (each carrying a single positive charge) determines the identity of a chemical element. It would be perfectly correct to say that six protons in a nucleus *defines* the element carbon, which has the atomic number 6. The neutral carbon atom always has six protons in its nucleus and six orbiting electrons.

Life was simple in science until it was discovered that there still existed a way for there to be more than one kind of nucleus for a certain element, that is, a way for a nucleus to be different even though the number of protons, and hence the atomic number, remained the same. This possibility is a reality because of a nuclear particle known as the *neutron.* A neutron is of very nearly the same mass as a proton but carries no electrical charge. Since neutrons do not affect the charge of a nucleus, their presence does not alter the atomic number of the atom to which they belong, and hence does not change the elemental identity of the atom. However, the mass of the nucleus, which is very close to the sum of the masses of neutrons and protons, depends on how many neutrons there are in addition to the fixed number of protons for a particular element. The sum of the number of neutrons and protons in the nucleus is called the *mass number.*

Let us illustrate the variation in neutron content by considering hydrogen, the simplest element. In a neutral atom of hydrogen, there is one proton in the nucleus and one orbiting electron. It turns out, however, that ordinary hydrogen in the hydro-geosphere and biosphere is really a mixture of two major, stable forms called hydrogen and *deuterium.* Both show virtually the same chemical behavior (but not exactly the same), and they do so because neutral atoms of both hydrogen and deuterium have only one proton in the nucleus and one orbiting electron. But deuterium, also called *heavy hydrogen,* has a neutron in each nucleus in addition to a proton, whereas "light" hydrogen has no neutron. The mass number of deuterium is 2, whereas that of the "light" hydrogen is 1, simply because neutron mass is very close to proton mass, which is 1 on an arbitrary scale.

Although a neutron in the nucleus has very little influence on the *chemical* properties of an atom, there are some chemical reactions in which the neutron's mass can make a difference. For example, in a reaction where the rate of movement of the atom can make a difference, the behavior of hydrogen and deuterium does differ; but for most reactions in which hydrogen is incorporated in a larger molecule, the mass difference is largely ineffectual in determining chemical properties.

What is possible for hydrogen, namely, having two stable forms, also occurs for elements throughout the periodic table of elements. We find several stable varieties of some elements, differing from each other in the number of neutrons in the nucleus. For example, the element tin, of atomic number 50, has ten different stable forms. Different forms of the same element are known as *nuclides* (or *isotopes*) of the element. We differentiate between *stable nuclides*, or stable forms of an element, and *radionuclides*, or unstable forms which undergo radioactive decay. Hydrogen, as it occurs in nature, has two major stable nuclides, hydrogen and deuterium. There does exist a third form of hydrogen, a radionuclide present at very low levels in nature, known as *tritium* (also called *hydrogen-3*), which decays by emitting beta particles and becoming helium. The reason that tritium exists in nature (wholly aside from man's production of it), is that cosmic rays keep producing it as the tritium already present decays. We shall discuss tritium in more detail later. (Radiations originating extraterrestrially are known as cosmic rays.)

There is a rather widely agreed-upon convention for describing nuclides, stable or radioactive. The two features needed to describe the nuclide are the atomic number and the mass number. The atomic number tells us which element we are dealing with. The mass number tells us the total number of particles in the nucleus, that is, the sum of protons plus neutrons. The convention is illustrated as follows:

For hydrogen the stable nuclides are:
"Light" hydrogen, designated as ^1_1H (one proton, no neutrons)
Deuterium, designated as ^2_1H (one proton, one neutron)
For hydrogen, the radionuclide is:
Tritium, designated as ^3_1H (one proton, two neutrons)
For the next element in the periodic table, helium, the stable nuclides are:
Helium-3, designated as ^3_2He (two protons, one neutron)
Helium-4, designated as ^4_2He (two protons, two neutrons)
There is also one very unstable radionuclide of helium:
Helium-6, designated as ^6_2He (two protons, four neutrons).

The general procedure is to use the chemical symbol of the element, to place a subscript on the left indicating the atomic number (the number of protons in the nucleus), and to place a superscript on the left to indicate the mass number (the sum of the number of neutrons and protons). It is immediately apparent that the number of neutrons in the nucleus is obtained by subtracting the subscripted number from the superscripted number, or

number of neutrons = mass number − atomic number

The element uranium has *no* stable nuclides in nature. Three radionuclides exist in nature: $^{238}_{92}U$, $^{235}_{92}U$, and $^{234}_{92}U$. Man has produced a number of additional radionuclides of uranium.

None of our nomenclature tells us directly whether a nuclide is stable or radioactive, or if radioactive, how rapidly it decays. This information must be obtained by measurement.

In the literature, the subscript for atomic number is often left out. So the reader will commonly encounter ^{235}U instead of $^{235}_{92}U$. It is assumed the reader knows that uranium has the atomic number 92.

RADIOACTIVE DECAY RATES

All kinds of questions concerning the health effects of radiation depend on knowing how fast particular radionuclides decay, and what types of radiation they emit when they decay. The fact that a radionuclide decays at all tells us that it is seeking a more stable state (a state of lower energy). Depending on the element and the ratio of neutrons to protons in the nucleus of an unstable radionuclide of that element, a more stable state can be achieved by emission of a negative electron, by emission of an alpha particle, or by emission of a positron. Many of these emissions are accompanied by the additional emission of one or more gamma rays. Some radionuclides have been produced (and some occur naturally) which decay solely by gamma-ray emission, with no accompanying particle emission. These radionuclides are referred to as *meta-stable* forms. Lastly, one encounters a special form of electron emission accompanying some gamma-ray emissions, known as *internal-conversion electrons*. In such cases, instead of a gamma ray being emitted, the gamma ray gives up all its energy to an orbiting electron, and the electron is emitted. It is the conversion of the gamma-ray energy to electron energy which leads to the name. In sharp contrast to beta particles originating in a nucleus, which have a continuum of energies, these conversion electrons have a single energy.

Radionuclides each have a characteristic decay rate, which we must now consider. These rates differ enormously among the many hundreds of radionuclides known to exist, and they are very important, since there is some confusion about the effects of radionuclides in the body during the period *before* they decay.

The fundamental law of radioactive decay is that each pure, radioactive species is characterized by what *fraction* of its atoms are decaying during a given unit of time (say, per second). Another way of stating this is that for each pure, radioactive species, there is a specific, fixed (constant) probability that any particular atom in a sample will decay during a second; this probability is constant regardless of the size of the pure sample or its age.

Intuitively, it may seem that the longer a particular atom of a radioactive nuclide has been around, the greater the chance it will decay. That intuition is simply wrong. The *chance* that any atom of a radionuclide will decay is always the same, no matter how "old" the atom is.

Since a certain fraction of atoms decay per unit time, there exists a predictable length of time during which half of the atoms one starts with will have decayed. The length of time during which one-half of a sample of species A will have disintegrated (decayed) is called the radioactive *half-life* for species A. *The larger the fraction decaying per second, the shorter the half-life.*

The relationship between a species' fixed fraction of decay and its half-life can be expressed by a very simple equation:

$$X = \frac{0.693}{T\frac{1}{2}}$$

X = the fraction of atoms decaying per unit time (X has a different value for different radioactive species)

$T\frac{1}{2}$ = the half-life, or the time required for one-half of the atoms in a pure sample to decay

With this equation, anyone who knows the decay fraction (X) for a radioactive species can easily calculate its half-life. And anyone who knows its half-life can easily calculate the fraction of atoms decaying per unit time.

Let us consider tritium, ^3_1H. It is a radionuclide of the element hydrogen, and it decays by emitting a beta particle (a negative electron). Its half-life is 12.3 years.

As each atom of ^3_1H decays, it becomes an atom of helium-3, or ^3_2He. In essence, the tritium has achieved stability by converting one of its two neutrons into a proton. When a neutron is converted into a proton, an electron is emitted too, and that accounts for the beta-particle emission from tritium. The *maximum* energy of the tritium beta particle is very, very low—0.018 mev (this could also be written as 18 kev).

How do we interpret the half-life? For tritium, if we have 1,000,000 atoms at this moment, a half-life of 12.3 years tells us that in 12.3 years we will have about 500,000 atoms left, and 500,000 will have been converted to ^3_2He. Because of the statistical nature of the half-life concept, i.e., the *chance* that any one tritium atom will decay in a certain time interval, we can expect certain fluctuations in how many atoms actually decay in that interval. In the sample above, we can expect that in 12.3 years the number of tritium atoms which will have decayed by beta-particle emission will be very close to 500,000, but it will not be exactly that in every trial with 1,000,000 tritium atoms. If we start with a much smaller number of tritium atoms, the spread will be much greater between the expected number of decays and the observed number. Thus, if we start with 10 atoms of tritium, in 12.3 years the *expected* number of decays is 5.000. But if we do the experiment several times, we shall sometimes find that 4 have decayed, or 6, or 7, or 3, in the 12.3-year interval. This is precisely what is expected for such a statistical process using small samples. But if we do the experiment 10,000 times, each time with 10 atoms at the start, we shall have tested 100,000 atoms; and if we average the number of decays per experiment, we shall find the average to be very close to 5.000. The larger the number of trials, with 10 atoms per trial, the closer the average number of decays will be to 5.000.

There is a source of potential confusion concerning radionuclides, which decay by emitting particulate or photon radiation or both. Up to the very instant in which a particular atom of tritium decays (that is, transforms itself into $^3_2$He) it behaves chemically in every way the same as does hydrogen (except for the small effect of its greater weight). *Until the instant of decay, there is no radiation at all coming from that particular tritium atom.* None at all. A particular tritium atom can exist for 25, 50, or 100 years, and if it is not one which has emitted a beta particle in transforming itself to helium-3, that tritium atom has not emitted *any* radiation during that time. And during that time, the tritium atom can participate in all kinds of chemical transformations: it can combine with oxygen to produce water (we would call it *tritiated water*); the water containing the tritium can be absorbed by humans, be re-excreted in urine, can go into the biosphere and form sugar molecules, be eaten, and the tritium reconverted into water, and so on. But someday, possibly one day from now, possibly one hundred years from now, that tritium atom will, in a fraction of a second, emit a beta particle, and become an atom of helium (helium-3). It is only during that fraction of a second that this particular tritium atom is *ever* emitting any radiation. Before that instant, the tritium atom has always done chemically what hydrogen does; forever after that instant, it will always do what helium does chemically.

Thus it is absolutely crucial to differentiate between *radiation* and *radioactivity.* The radiations we deal with are X-rays, gamma rays, electrons (positive or negative), and alpha particles. The radioactive nuclides of an element are not themselves radiation, but instead are chemical substances showing all the chemical properties of the element of which they are nuclides, and they have one more property: in a certain time period, some number of them, determined by their half-life, will undergo spontaneous transformation. It is only those undergoing transformation which provide any radiation; the rest produce no radiation at all.

Units of Radioactive Decay: Curies

Ultimately our objective here is to ascertain the energy delivery from radioactive substances to biological tissue. Since the energy delivered must come from the radioactive transformations (decays) themselves, it follows that the energy transfer to biological tissues depends upon two factors:

a. The number of radioactive decay-events per unit of time from the radioactive material present (this rate is referred to as the *source strength*)

b. The amount of energy released by each of the transformations that does occur

For a variety of health-study purposes, we need a method of describing the "strength" of a radioactive source, and we need to know how that strength changes over time. It is evident that the strength of a source (whether concentrated all at one point or distributed among tissues) is a measure of the number of radioactive events occurring per unit time, for example, in one second.

Historically, the unit used as the standard rate of disintegration was related to the number of disintegrations occurring per second from 1 gram of pure radium, $^{226}_{88}$Ra. This number was named the *curie*, in honor of Madame Marie Curie. But since that number could change with time as more purified samples of radium became available for measurement of the disintegration rate, and since measurement accuracy could change with time, it was felt that a more stable standard rate was needed. So it was decided to reset the standard rather close to, but not tied to, the decay rate for pure radium. The curie is now defined, for any radionuclide as a source, as that quantity of radionuclide which is disintegrating at a rate of 37 billion disintegrations per second (3.7×10^{10} disintegrations per second). It is common in physics, chemistry, and medicine to use subunits or multiples of units to describe either very small quantities or very large quantities. For radioactively decaying substances, some of the common units encountered are:

☐ The *megacurie*—a source showing 3.7×10^{16} disintegrations per second

☐ The *kilocurie*—a source showing 3.7×10^{13} disintegrations per second

☐ The *millicurie*—a source showing 3.7×10^{7} disintegrations per second (37 million disintegrations per second)

☐ The *microcurie*—a source showing 3.7×10^{4} disintegrations per second (37,000 disintegrations per second)

☐ The *nanocurie*—a source showing 3.7×10^{1} disintegrations per second (37 disintegrations per second)

☐ The *picocurie*—a source showing 3.7×10^{-2} disintegrations per second (0.037 disintegrations per second, or just over 2 per minute)

☐ The *femtocurie*—a source showing 3.7×10^{-5} disintegrations per second (0.000037 disintegrations per second)

The astute reader will immediately ask how it is possible to get 0.000037 disintegrations in one second, the definition for the femtocurie. Disintegrations either occur or they do not; they cannot be fractional. The answer is that if the source strength is one femtocurie, there will be one disintegration every 27,027 (1/0.000037) seconds, on the average.

The curie, its multiples, and its subunits are now totally independent of radium, which was involved only in the original definition. The curie units can be used to describe any radionuclide of any element and any half-life.

Let us compare two vastly different radionuclides, $^{135}_{54}$Xe (xenon-135, familiar because it was prominently described as one of the radioactive gases emitted in the Three Mile Island accident), with a half-life of 9.1 hours, and $^{239}_{94}$Pu (the major form of plutonium, formed in reactors, and used in atom bombs), with a half-life of 24,400 years. As different as these are, it is still true that 1 curie of $^{135}_{54}$Xe undergoes 37 billion disintegrations per second and 1 curie of $^{239}_{94}$Pu also undergoes 37 billion disintegrations per second. *A curie is a curie no matter what radionuclide is decaying.*

Of course, there are major differences between the xenon and the plutonium. First of all, a huge number of plutonium atoms are required to make a curie (i.e., to achieve a disintegration rate of 37 billion atoms per second) compared to the number of xenon atoms required. Expressed in a common unit of weight, it takes 16.3 grams of $^{239}_{94}$Pu to give 1 curie, while only .392 micrograms of $^{135}_{54}$Xe are needed (a microgram is a millionth of a gram). Second, there is a very important difference in how the strength of the source changes with time. In 9.1 hours, the original $^{135}_{54}$Xe curie has decayed in half, so our source strength is now only 0.5 curies. But in 9.1 hours, which is very short compared with 24,400 years, the $^{239}_{94}$Pu source is still essentially 1 curie (actually 0.999999 + curies). It would take 24,400 years for the plutonium source to decay to 0.5 curies.

For certain purposes it may be useful for the reader to be able to compare the mass required to represent a curie of a substance with a short half-life, with the mass required to represent a curie of a substance with some very different half-life.

HALF-LIFE VERSUS BIOLOGICAL HAZARD

While it is logical to ask, "Is a long half-life more dangerous biologically than a short half-life?" this question does not permit of a single biological answer. We must ask the question in more specific forms.

For illustration we shall consider two nuclides about which the public is inevitably going to hear a great deal, both nuclides of plutonium: $^{238}_{94}$Pu and $^{239}_{94}$Pu. Most of the plutonium on earth today is man-made; tons of ^{239}Pu have been made. For ^{238}Pu, the half-life is 86 years, and the alpha particles emitted in its decay have an energy of 5.5 mev. For ^{239}Pu, the half-life is 24,400 years, and the alpha particles emitted in its decay have an energy of 5.1 mev.

Since the energy of the alpha particles is very similar, it is only the half-lives that differ markedly. (At this point, the author wishes to point out that the reader will encounter slightly differing values for half-lives—and for the energies of emitted alpha particles—in various reference books. The reason is that new measurements are continually being made to improve the accuracy of some of these values.) Would 1,000 atoms of $^{238}_{94}$Pu absorbed into the bloodstream produce more biological hazard than 1,000 atoms of $^{239}_{94}$Pu?

Since they are radionuclides of the same element, both $^{238}_{94}$Pu and $^{239}_{94}$Pu will behave essentially the same as to biological properties, such as where in the body they will concentrate and to what extent. The bulk of plutonium going into the bloodstream will concentrate in the liver and bones. Let us consider the problem of the bones, from which plutonium is excreted so slowly that it takes about 100 years for even half of it to be eliminated, via the urine. So for practical purposes, we can say that during an individual's lifetime, very little of any plutonium lodged in his bones will be excreted.

Let us consider a period of 30 years. During that time, 220 of the 1,000 atoms of $^{238}_{94}$Pu will have emitted a damaging alpha particle, the energy of which is available to do biological harm. During that same 30-year period, less than 1 atom out of the 1,000 atoms of $^{239}_{94}$Pu will have emitted an alpha particle. Thus, in a 30-year period, the $^{238}_{94}$Pu (with the shorter half-life) has produced over 220 times as much biological damage as has the $^{239}_{94}$Pu.

However, the question can now be asked in a different way. Let us ask about the difference between one microcurie of $^{238}_{94}$Pu and one microcurie of $^{239}_{94}$Pu getting into the bloodstream, both concentrating in the liver and skeleton of man. Which will produce more damage, the $^{238}_{94}$Pu, with its shorter half-life, or the $^{239}_{94}$Pu, with its longer half-life? At the outset, since we have 1 microcurie of each radionuclide, there must be, according to the definition of microcurie, 37,000 disintegrations per second for each of the radionuclides. Since the alpha particles have nearly similar energies, the rate of delivery of ionizing radiation to tissues will be virtually identical (within 10% of each other, correcting for alpha-particle energies), and hence the biological damage will be identical in the early period after administration of the nuclides.

But what about 10 years, 20 years, or 30 years after the deposition of 1 microcurie of each in the body? During that period there will be a much greater loss of the shorter-lived $^{238}_{94}$Pu. Shown below are the strengths of the two sources at any time after such time periods.

Time	$^{238}_{94}Pu$	$^{239}_{94}Pu$
0 years	1.00 microcurie	1.00 microcurie
10	0.92	0.9997
20	0.85	0.9995
30	0.78	0.9992

It is evident that, while the sources were of equal strength at the outset, the $^{238}_{94}$Pu source is declining in strength much more rapidly than is the $^{239}_{94}$Pu. And this means that the ^{238}Pu is emitting fewer alpha particles *per second* than is the ^{239}Pu at all times beyond the beginning of the study. Therefore, the longer-lived ^{239}Pu is doing more damage per unit time, at any time after deposition.

The reader will note that this is the *opposite* conclusion from that reached when we asked about injecting equal numbers of atoms rather than equal numbers of microcuries. The key is how the question is framed. Putting in sources with the same number of *atoms* will mean that the nuclide of the shorter half-life will do more damage. Putting in sources with the same number of *disintegrations per second* will mean that the nuclide of the longer half-life will do more damage.

There is a special case we should consider, relating to long and short half-lives of nuclides of the same chemical element. That has to do with the question of *access* to the human body. Let us consider the production of two radionuclides of the element krypton in a nuclear reactor: $^{85}_{36}$Kr, with a half-life of 10.3 years, and $^{90}_{36}$Kr, with a half-life of 33 seconds.

For the purpose of illustration, let us imagine that initially there are equal numbers of atoms of each of these produced in the fissioning of uranium in a nuclear reactor. In nuclear reactors, if they are built and functioning correctly, there are "hold-up" systems for potential gaseous radionuclide emissions. Let us assume that the hold-up system prevents any krypton produced from getting out before one hour. In one hour, we have gone through 109 half-lives of the $^{90}_{36}$Kr, so we can say there is essentially *none* of that radionuclide left (every 20 half-lives cuts the amount down by a factor of 1,000,000). But, in one hour, the $^{85}_{36}$Kr has hardly decayed at all, so virtually all of it is still present, can go out of the stack into the air, and is capable of irradiating people.

In this comparison, it is obvious that the nuclide of longer half-life can do harm, whereas under the conditions postulated, the nuclide of shorter half-life can do virtually no harm at all, simply because its radioactivity is dissipated before any of it gets out to irradiate people.

SECTION 4: DOSES: AN ENERGY TRANSFER IS AN ENERGY TRANSFER

INTERNAL VERSUS EXTERNAL RADIATION

The question whether internal radiation or external radiation is more dangerous to health has been a long-term source of confusion. The central reason for the confusion has been the failure to appreciate that biological damage depends on the quantity of energy from ionizing radiation that is *deposited in a particular tissue.* For the moment, we will defer the question of the rate of delivery of the radiation and simply assume that the rate of delivery is the same from external and internal sources.

One often hears statements such as "Radionuclides are more dangerous than external sources of radiation such as X-rays and gamma rays *because* the radionuclides *inside* the body can do more damage." Note carefully that this statement misses the entire point, for it says nothing about the actual energy delivered to the tissue in question. The statement just talks about external versus internal radiation. A variant of this statement is: "Beta-emitting radionuclides taken into the body are more dangerous than external X-rays or gamma rays because beta particles are more damaging than are X-rays and gamma rays."

Both of these statements are grossly misleading and deserve no credence whatever. First, let us recall all we have developed above showing that X-rays and gamma rays produce harmful effects only to the extent that they set high-speed electrons in motion. Such high-speed electrons are identical

with beta particles emitted from internally deposited radionuclides. Therefore, it is evident that if the same number of high-speed electrons produced
by gamma rays or X-rays come into the tissue from outside as there are beta
particles emitted inside, the biological effects must necessarily be the same.
Furthermore, it should be evident that there are not "favorite" radionuclides (another common fallacy) in terms of damage done to tissue, *if* we
are talking about the same amount of energy delivered to tissue. For the
same energy delivered, we must expect the same damage. If we look at
another facet of the problem, we can identify one major source of the confusion.

Let us consider external radiation in the form of X-rays coming from
an X-ray machine. Let us suppose the kilovoltage of the machine is 100 kev.
Recalling our earlier discussion, we realize that the X-rays from this machine
will have a distribution of energies from 100 kev down to very low amounts.
In fact, most of the X-ray output will be of energies well below the maximum
energy. For each range of X-ray energies in the X-ray beam there will be a
characteristic half-thickness of penetration into the body. If a specific tissue
lies deep within the body, many of the initial X-rays in the beam (particularly
those of low energy) will be filtered out by intervening tissues before the
beam penetrates to the specific tissue. On the other hand, an internally
deposited radionuclide, right in the specific tissue, does not have this problem of penetration to the specific tissue. It is emitting its beta particles right
in the tissue of interest.

The author predicts that in any instance where it is alleged that beta
particles, as a source of internal radiation, are worse than external radiation,
someone has failed to do the proper homework in calculating how much of
the external X-radiation actually got through to the tissue studied. We must
carefully avoid comparing apples and oranges! Figuring out how much
energy *reaches* a tissue, and figuring out the *effect per unit dose,* are two separate
matters.

The actual calculation of how much of the X-ray beam reaches a particular tissue is a difficult and important problem that engages the efforts of
careful physicists, skilled in such measurements. Therefore, when one ex-
amines a report on cancers produced by X-rays and wishes to compare the
results of that report with results for internal radiation or with results from
someone else's report on X-radiation, the first question to ask is, how was
the energy delivery measured or calculated? Often the reports give the X-ray
source strength as measured at the skin surface, which is called the *skin-
entrance dose* in the literature. Translation of that skin-entrance dose into the
true dose received in deep tissue requires knowing the kilovoltage of the
machine, whether the electrical supply produced one-phase or three-phase
electricity, and what kinds of absorbers were in the X-ray beam before it
reached the body.

Another method for estimating an internal dose from external sources
is to set up "phantoms" of material closely approximating the composition
of living tissue, to place dosimeters in various positions within the phantom,

and then expose the phantom to X-rays delivered at various kilovoltages, with various absorbers in the beam.

One should view with caution any report of the health effects of external radiation where care has not been taken to estimate the true energy delivered. It is regrettable that many reports in the literature are quite deficient in providing several of the items of information that would be required to get a valid estimate of the actual ionizing radiation energy deposited in tissues. As a result, the subject of cancer induction by ionizing radiation has been muddied unnecessarily.

The only caveat in all this is that we must consider the possibility of differing LET values. Beta particles emitted by tritium that have a maximum energy of 18 kev have an average LET much higher than the average LET of beta particles of some other radionuclide, which have a maximum energy of 500 kev. To the extent that LET is important, there can be a difference in carcinogenic effect even when the same total amount of energy is delivered. The question of the importance of LET in radiation carcinogenesis will be considered later (chapters 8 and 9).

Just as there are serious technical problems in estimating the true dose delivered to a specific tissue from external X-rays, so there are different but equally serious problems in estimating the dose to a tissue from internally deposited radionuclides. For each radionuclide there are several crucial factors that will determine how much energy is actually deposited in the tissue, including:

a. The route of entry of the radionuclide into the body.

b. The fraction of the administered dose that actually reaches the tissue of interest.

c. The biological rate of removal of the radionuclide from that tissue.

d. The amount of radiation the tissue of interest receives from the portion of the radionuclide deposited in tissues other than the one of interest (so-called *cross-fire radiation*). In most instances, but not all, this will not be a serious problem for beta-particle radiation.

e. The number of microcuries of the radionuclide taken in (crucially dependent on the correct measurement of the strength of the radionuclide source).

f. Careful calculation of the average energy of the beta particles emitted, of any ancillary gamma rays emitted, and of any loss of radiation out of the specified tissue.

g. Metabolic or other factors that might alter the distribution of the radionuclide in the various tissues of the people studied.

Clearly there is no easy way to translate all this into the energy deposited in a particular tissue by several hundred different radionuclides of some sixty different chemical elements. So it should not be surprising that the literature continues to report erroneous conclusions concerning specific radionuclides—claims that one is more or less harmful than another.

The problem of assessing energy delivery to a particular tissue is difficult, but not unmanageable. The Society of Nuclear Medicine has taken a leadership role in the effort to determine true energy delivery from internally administered radionuclides and has published a series of available reports, known as the MIRD reports (short for *medical internal radiation dose*). These reports have provided tables for numerous radionuclides, utilizing the best available information for the parameters (listed above) which can make a difference in dose. Inevitably, some of the data available at this time will prove to be erroneous, and will have to be revised later.

"NATURAL" VERSUS "MAN-MADE" IONIZING RADIATION

It is certainly true that human beings have been exposed to natural sources of ionizing radiation for millions of years. And, with the exception of a small part of the cosmic radiations, the natural sources are very similar to the many sources that man has added. A curious notion is commonly expressed, that such natural sources of radiation (which we shall consider in much detail later) are less damaging than man-made ionizing radiation. A variant of this myth is that natural radiation can be held up as some sort of evidence for the lack of harm from ionizing radiation. The subtle, and sometimes less than subtle, suggestion is made that "since man has lived with natural radiation for millions of years, it follows that doses of radiation comparable in size to those received from natural sources must therefore not be harmful." As this suggestion stands, it is sheer nonsense.

However, it is a valid question whether cancer is produced less effectively at low doses of radiation (either man-made or natural) than at high doses (always man-made) *per unit of energy delivered to tissue*. Much of the discussion in later chapters of this book will address that question. But that is a very different matter from suggesting that natural radiation is *harmless* simply because it has been with us for a long time! Exonerating natural radiation as a cancer producer by resorting to a "grandfather clause" is a scientific hoax.

THE MEANING OF "RAD"

A key feature of all ionizing radiations in producing carcinogenic damage and genetic damage in human beings is the energy delivered to sensitive tissue, expressed as energy per unit weight of tissue. A second feature, the importance of which is less certain for some health effects of radiation, is the LET of the radiation, with which we shall deal later. The author will point out now that no scientific law exists that tells us that the spacing of ionization events along the path of a high-speed electron is crucial for a specific health effect. This must be determined empirically for each type of effect. Thus, it is entirely possible that the induction of cataracts of the eye may be sensitive to the linear spacing of ions along the track of the electron, whereas cancer induction may not be.

There are two ways of expressing energy delivered per unit weight of tissue. One way is by simply dividing the total ionization energy delivered to a macro-sample of tissue (*macro-* in this context meaning amounts measured in grams or kilograms) by the mass in grams or kilograms of the tissue. This is what we do ordinarily, but while doing so, we realize that the important issue is the dose delivered to some very tiny region within a single cell. The critical events that lead to such diseases as cancer, as we shall see, are highly likely to occur in a small structure within a small cell. So we are really interested in the field called *micro-dosimetry,* which describes the actual dose received in the sensitive region, or volume, of the cell. Practically, however, we must measure the macro-dose.

In describing the energy delivered per unit mass of tissue by ionizing radiation, *any* unit of energy could be used: calories, BTUs, ergs, joules, watt-seconds, electron-volts, or any other.

Historically, the *erg* has been used to describe energy delivered by ionizing radiation. If 100 ergs of energy are deposited in 1 gram of tissue, that tissue is said to have received 1 *rad* of radiation. More recently, there is a move to use a unit in the international system of units, the *gray,* defined as the absorption of 1 *joule* of energy per kilogram of tissue. One gray = 100 rads. We shall use the rad throughout this book, rather than the gray, since most of the current literature gives doses in rads. The reader should be familiar with the gray, however, since future literature will most likely express dose in grays.

The definition of the rad says nothing about the *time* it takes to deliver 100 ergs per gram of tissue. In some cases good reason exists to be concerned about the *rate* of delivery of radiation, and in these cases we would express radiation doses in terms of rads per minute, rads per hour, or rads per year. For many purposes, we shall be concerned with total rads delivered, and not with their rate of delivery.

As with the curies, sometimes a larger or smaller unit is useful in dealing with radiation dose. Therefore, the following units are also defined:

- ☐ 1 *megarad* = 1,000,000 rads
- ☐ 1 *kilorad* = 1,000 rads
- ☐ 1 *millirad* = 0.001 rads (or 10^{-3} rads)
- ☐ 1 *microrad* = 0.000001 rads (or 10^{-6} rads)

The reader will commonly encounter the unit *microrads per hour* in descriptions of low-intensity radiation exposures.

THE MEANING OF "REM" AND "RBE"

Note also that the definition of the rad says nothing about the kind of radiation that delivers the 100 ergs per gram of tissue. The radiation could be delivered by alpha particles, beta particles, X-rays, or some other source. We know that the linear energy transfer (LET) is much higher for some radiations than for others. For those biological effects where LET matters, the rad unit must be modified to a unit that shows the greater effectiveness of one kind of radiation over another. A term has been introduced, the *relative biological effectiveness*, or RBE, to express this difference in effectiveness.

Let us consider a hypothetical case in which alpha-particle radiation produces ten times as much health effect per rad as does beta-particle radiation. The RBE *for that particular health effect* would be 10. A combined unit, the *rem*, is commonly encountered, defined by

$$\text{rems} = (\text{rads}) \times (\text{RBE})$$

In the illustration given, we would say that 1 rad of the alpha-particle radiation represents 10 rems. No mystique or magic determines the RBE for one type of radiation versus another, and there is *no* adequate theory that tells us what the RBE should be, or must be, for a particular kind of radiation. Furthermore, the RBE for alpha particles may be 10 for one biological effect, whereas it may be 1 or 2 for some other biological effect. This must always be determined for the particular biological effect *empirically*, which means that we must find out how many rads of alpha-particle radiation are required to produce the same health effect as a particular number of rads of X-radiation, for example, produces. And for some other health effect the RBE for alpha-particle versus X-radiation may be quite different. It is important to realize that the RBE for one radiation compared to another is *not* a fixed quantity. The literature suggests all too often that one can use a single RBE value to describe alpha-particle radiation, for example, in comparison with X-rays or beta-particle radiation.

HANDLING CUMULATIVE DOSES OF RADIATION

It was stated above that the *rate* of delivery of radiation may or may not be of any importance in determining its health effects. That must be determined empirically by observation of effects produced by differing rates of radiation delivery. But, for any particular rate of delivery, it is clear that health effects are *cumulative*, that is, health effects increase with an increase in the total amount of radiation delivered to a particular tissue, whatever the rate of delivery may be.

A major caveat must be introduced concerning the handling of cumulative radiation doses; it centers on the issue of *the age at which the radiation dose is received*. As we shall learn later, age at irradiation is all-important in determining cancer induction by radiation: the young are far more sensitive to radiation than the old. This will be documented in extenso from the human evidence.

Because of this caveat, it would not be appropriate, for example, to add the rads of radiation received at 1 year of age to the rads received at 25 years of age, if we wished to determine the cancer-induction effect. What we should do is determine the cancer-production risk from the rads received at 1 year of age, and the cancer-production risk from the rads received at

25 years of age, and then add the risks instead of the rads. On the other hand, if we are dealing with ages at irradiation which are very close to each other, it is appropriate to add directly the rads received.

While the effect of age at irradiation has been known and emphasized by some workers for over a decade (Gofman and Tamplin 1969–70), the scientific literature is rife with a lack of appreciation of the importance of age at irradiation. The reader is therefore warned to be on the lookout for inappropriate handling of this issue in new reports on cancer induction by radiation.

The reader will recall discussions on television during the Three Mile Island accident in which doses were commonly described in millirads (or millirems) per hour, and in which no comment at all was made about the cumulative effect of such doses. It is the cumulative dose that matters. One millirad per hour sounds like a small number, but if the irradiation continues for a week, or a period of 168 hours, then the cumulative dose is 168 millirads, not 1 millirad. It is the 168 millirads that will determine the increase in cancer risk, not the 1 millirad per hour.

WHOLE-BODY RADIATION VERSUS PARTIAL-BODY RADIATION

Most of the important health effects of radiation are *direct* in nature. By this we mean that the effect in a particular organ is due to the radiation received by that organ. Thus, if we are concerned with lung-cancer induction by radiation, then we are concerned with the radiation dose received by those cells of the *lung* which are vulnerable to cancer induction. We are not, for that particular purpose, concerned about radiation received by the arms or legs. Some possible *indirect* effects require consideration. For example, there is evidence that some of the hormones produced by the ovary can influence the development of breast cancer. Thus, if sufficient radiation were delivered to the ovary to shut down its hormone production, there could be an indirect effect on the breast with respect to cancer induction even if the breast itself received none of the radiation. It would be fair to state that such indirect effects are rare, and that the major effects of radiation, and those with which we shall concern ourselves, will be the direct effects.

If the genetic effects of radiation are being considered, it is the dose in rads received by the *gonads,* that is, the testes in the male and the ovaries in the female, which will determine the effect. The reader will commonly encounter the term *gonadal dose,* which expresses this important point. The term *gonadally significant dose* will also be encountered; it generally has an additional, subtle meaning, referring not only to the direct dose received by the gonads but also taking into account the prospect that the recipient of the radiation will subsequently procreate.

For cancer or leukemia induction, a wide variety of organs can be susceptible to radiation effects. Certain leukemias are considered to arise in the bone marrow. Bone marrow is spread over the entire body since the bones themselves spread throughout the body. Therefore, it is important to know how large a fraction of the bone marrow received a radiation dose if one is to assess the risk of leukemia induction by radiation. Irradiation of the total body is more leukemogenic than irradiation of a single region of bone marrow.

Solid cancers can arise in a large number of different organs in the body. Irradiation of one region of the body subjects only the organs in that region to cancer induction. However, whole-body radiation subjects numerous organs of the body to cancer induction. Since it only takes *one* cancer to kill a person, it is evident that whole-body radiation is a much more serious matter for increasing cancer death risk than is partial-body radiation.

The rad unit addresses the problem of the dose to a specific tissue, in terms of ergs per gram of that tissue. In describing a radiation exposure we cannot simply say there was an exposure of 50 rads. We need to specify the fraction of the body that received 50 rads. Thus we can speak of 50 rads of whole-body radiation, 50 rads to the head, 50 rads to the neck, or 50 rads to the chest, but we *must* specify how much of the body received the radiation if a meaningful assessment of cancer induction risk is to be made.

Many, many people are still confused about this point. One will hear someone speak of having received 1 rad of radiation, for example, in a dental examination, but that person may not realize that this is very different in implication from having received 1 rad of whole-body radiation.

From external radiation it is generally hard to get *uniform* whole-body irradiation. The absorption of some of the radiation by intervening tissues will, in such circumstances, reduce the amount of radiation received by deeper tissues. This is further complicated by the fact that a particular organ will get some of its radiation by the "back-scattering" of radiation from deeper tissues. So, while we commonly see statements that a particular dose of whole-body radiation has been received, we must realize that an accurate assessment of its effects requires a determination of precisely how much radiation was actually received by various organs separately, since they will not all have received the whole-body dose of radiation. This task can be quite complicated and require the persistent efforts of physicists and health physicists.

A case in point is the exposure of the populations of Hiroshima and Nagasaki. The radiation received there is commonly spoken of as whole-body radiation by gamma rays or by a combination of gamma rays and neutrons, and the unwary may assume that all organs received the stated dose of radiation. Indeed, many papers in the literature carelessly assume this in assessing the effects of radiation received at Hiroshima and Nagasaki. Recently, much more care has been taken in discussions of the dose, with correction factors introduced, so that one can estimate the true dose received by breast or bone marrow or thyroid gland, or by several deep-lying tissues. Errors of a factor of 2 can be introduced in estimates of cancer or leukemia induction if these correction factors are not taken into account.

True whole-body radiation, with all organs receiving precisely the same number of rads, is an unusual situation. It can occur, however, with internal administration of tritium, which will distribute itself in the body everywhere that water is present, if the tritium is administered as HTO (tritiated water), in time reaching all body compounds that have hydrogen in them (and these include all the organic compounds of the body). So, if a person were constantly exposed to tritium, he would receive almost uniform whole-body radiation, although even this case would be characterized by a different dose to the bones. Introduction of the radionuclide $^{137}_{55}$Cs (cesium-137), which will also distribute itself into all the cells of the body, would likewise approximate the case of true whole-body radiation.

The situation is most complex for external radiation from X-ray machines, commonly operated with a maximum kilovoltage of 50–250 kv. We recall from our discussion of the X-ray emissions of such machines that a continuum of X-ray energies is produced from a maximum energy (50–250 kev for voltages of 50–250 kv, respectively) down to very low energies, and that most of the X-ray emission is not of the maximum energy. If a person's entire body were exposed to the X-rays from such a machine, there would be considerable variation in the actual dose received by different organs. A dosimeter placed on the skin can tell us what the skin-entrance exposure is in rads, but it is a complicated matter to determine the dose received by lungs, by stomach, by colon, or by pancreas. The problem is complicated by the fact that the various X-rays making up the continuum each have differing penetrations to the deep tissues, depending on their actual energies.

THE MEANING OF "ROENTGEN"

A common older unit, the *roentgen*, is often used to describe radiation exposure from X-ray machines. This unit is formally defined as

that amount of X- or gamma radiation such that the associated corpuscular emission per 0.001293 grams of air, at 0°C, and 760 mm mercury of pressure produces, in air, ions carrying one electrostatic unit of quantity of electricity of either sign (+ or −).

Quite formidable! It turns out that 1 roentgen corresponds to an absorption of 83 ergs per gram of air, or 93 ergs per gram of tissue at the body surface. It is for this reason that one will encounter statements in the literature that 1 roentgen is approximately 1 rad (which itself refers to absorption of 100 ergs per gram of tissue). The roentgen unit, like the rad, tells us nothing of the penetrating qualities of the radiation, about how much will get to tissues deep in the body. In the early period of the study of radiation effects on humans, studies were so crude that the errors introduced by failure to convert roentgen exposure to true dose in rads to the tissues of interest were small compared with the many other errors made. But in the current era and in the future, when critical efforts are being made to understand cancer-induction mechanisms, and in particular whether radiation effects are similar or different from tissue to tissue, accurate assessment of true dose in rads to the tissues studied becomes of very great importance.

THE ENORMOUS EFFECTIVENESS OF IONIZING RADIATION

Thus far we have not concerned ourselves with the special properties of ionizing radiation except to note that the energy of a beta particle, for example, can be 100,000 or even 1,000,000 or more times greater than the energy required to break even a strong chemical bond in biological tissue. But that does not tell us the whole story about the enormous effectiveness of ionizing-radiation energy in producing devastating biological effects such as cancer and even virtually immediate death.

Just how much energy is represented by 1 rad? And how effective is that energy in producing biological injury compared with other modalities that might deliver energy to tissues? As an interesting comparison, we may compare the biological effectiveness of energy from ionizing radiation with energy from heat (Gofman 1960).

The *calorie* is the familiar unit in chemistry that describes energy transfers involving heat. One calorie is that amount of energy which will raise the temperature of 1 gram of water by 1 degree centigrade. (This definition does change some at different temperatures of water, but for our purposes here we can neglect those small changes.)

The best estimates are that approximately 400 rads of whole-body radiation, if delivered rapidly, are sufficient to cause 50% of the exposed humans to die within a period of days to weeks. This is the so-called acute radiation sickness. Is this a great deal of energy in heat terms? In fact, it is not; a simple calculation shows that 400 rads produce only 10^{-3} calories per gram.

Biological tissue is quite comparable to water in the amount of heat required to raise its temperature by 1 degree centigrade. So we shall say that the required amount is 1 calorie per gram for biological tissue too. Therefore, our 10^{-3} calories/gram from the absorption of 400 rads of ionizing radiation energy would be enough to raise the temperature of biological tissue by 0.001° centigrade. Not much of a fever! We tolerate fevers of several degrees centigrade (not thousandths of a degree) in a variety of infectious diseases. Yet the amount of ionizing radiation that can kill half of the humans exposed to it, would—if converted first into heat—raise temperatures only by 0.001° centigrade.

This points up the biologically deadly difference between energy in the form of heat versus the same amount of energy in the form of ionizing radiation. Why is the effect of ionizing radiation so much larger?

The difference resides in the fact that the energy of ionizing radiation is not distributed the way the thermal energy of a fever is, the latter being about evenly distributed among all the molecules of a gram of tissue. Instead, the energy of ionizing radiation is transferred from photons to single electrons, which in turn transfer all their energy to *relatively* few electrons in *relatively* few molecules. The transfer occurs in extremely concentrated fashion compared with the even diffusion of heat energy. Therefore, the energy delivered by ionizing radiation is energetic enough to break *any* chemical bond, even the strongest ones in living tissue. We shall learn later that certain chemical bonds in cells are crucial, and breaking just a few of these bonds may set a cell on the path to cancer.

CHAPTER 3

THE ORIGINS OF HUMAN CANCER AND THE ROLE OF RADIATION

NOT RARELY, one will read that the cause of human cancer is unknown. On the contrary, we know a number of *proved* causes of human cancer and leukemia, and ionizing radiation is certainly one of them. In medicine, we refer to the cause of a disease as its *etiology*. If multiple agents cause the disease, we say there are multiple etiological factors. While we can say, with assurance, that we know several etiological factors in the genesis of human cancer, we do not know the precise sequence of events in the development of the cancer, from the period of its inception to the point of clinical detection. Such a sequence of events is known as the *pathogenesis* of a disease. The pathogenesis of human cancer does indeed remain unknown, although we have many pieces of information that are highly suggestive of some of the steps in the process. We do not know the key intracellular event that sets a certain organ or tissue on the path to cancer development.

WHAT IS MEANT BY "RADIATION CAUSES CANCER"?

We must comment a bit further on the subject of "cause." The word *cause* seems to mean different things to different people. In an effort to clarify, some have spoken about remote causes and proximal causes. For example, if radiation increases the number of cancers observed in a population, it may be referred to as a remote cause of cancer. The specific cellular change or changes which are set in motion by the radiation and which lead the cell to become the progenitor of a cancer are referred to as the *proximal cause* or *causes*.

When we refer to radiation as a cause, we do not mean that it causes every case of cancer or leukemia. Indeed, the evidence we have indicting radiation in the causation of cancer and leukemia shows that not all cases of cancer are caused by radiation. Second, when we refer to radiation as a cause of cancer, we do not mean that every individual exposed to a certain amount of radiation will develop cancer. We simply mean that a population exposed to a certain dose of radiation will show a greater incidence of cancer than that same population would have shown in the absence of the added radiation.

It is not at all necessary that we know the initial cellular event on the road to cancer or the steps in the pathogenesis in order to prove that ionizing radiation causes human cancer. We can make this proof by statistical observations of persons who have been exposed to ionizing radiation and of persons who have not been so exposed. We can make our case even more powerful if we study people exposed to different doses of radiation and are able to demonstrate an association of increasing risk of cancer development with increasing dose. This is known as a study of the *dose-response relationship.* We shall consider a large number of studies of human beings, which provide information on the dose-response relationship between ionizing radiation and the development of many different types of human cancer and leukemia, and we shall consider this evidence in a highly quantitative fashion.

The Issue of Very Low Radiation Doses

There will be some stumbling blocks in our way. We are very concerned about the number of cancers that occur as a result of exposure to very low doses of ionizing radiation. But this is precisely the dose region in which it is most difficult to get valid human evidence. The problem is almost wholly the numbers of cases available at low-dose exposure. Ascertainment of the shape of the dose-response curve at very low doses requires huge numbers of persons under study, numbers which are not available and are not likely ever to be available. That is why it would be enormously helpful if we understood the pathogenetic sequence of events set in motion by ionizing radiation when such radiation increases the risk that a person will develop a fatal cancer or leukemia. If we knew that sequence of events at the cellular, or the molecular, level, we could probably *predict* the shape of the dose-response curve down to the very lowest doses.

Understanding the events that go on at the cellular level in the development of any human cancer would be worthwhile for its own sake. If that understanding could enable us to predict the effect of low doses of radiation, it would also be an enormous practical assist. For these reasons, we shall devote much of the remainder of this chapter to describing the nature of the events we think *may* be crucial in the evolution of a full-blown clinical cancer or leukemia, and separately, to describing the events occurring at the cellular level when persons are exposed to ionizing radiation. Consideration of the events going on at the cellular level can teach us which mechanisms of cancer production are reasonable and which are unreasonable, on a quantitative basis.

Some readers may wish to defer such considerations, in which case they can go right on to chapter 4 and to subsequent chapters that deal with the quantitative human evidence. Then they can return later to this chapter, when they wish to understand how we apply our knowledge of cellular and subcellular mechanisms of radiation injury, and our knowledge of the cellular and subcellular events in cancer pathogenesis, to the problem of trying to predict radiation effects at dose levels for which direct human evidence may be lacking.

There is no controversy about the issue of whether ionizing radiation causes cancer and leukemia. We have good human data proving the induction of cancers and leukemia by fairly low doses, by moderate doses, and by high doses of ionizing radiation. From those data, we can tell whether the number of cancers induced is proportional to the radiation dose received. But then we must ask, if proportionality holds in the region of doses for which we do have evidence, will it hold at lower doses too?

The Proportionality Question Simply Stated

To the extent that there is any controversy over the induction of cancer by ionizing radiation, it is over this question of the proportionality of dose and effect. Let us state the question simply. If 10 rads cause 1,000 cancers in a large population sample, will 1 rad cause 100 cancers, and will 0.1 rad cause 10 cancers, and will 0.01 rad cause 1 cancer? If we knew the details of the pathogenetic steps, we might be able to answer this question unequivocally, based upon physical principles, without requiring the study of millions of exposed persons.

There is a mammoth field of endeavor known as radiobiology. Many of the studies in this field have dealt with the effects of various ionizing radiations on cells cultured in laboratories, as well as with the effects on cells in whole animals and in man. Some of these studies could be brought to bear on our question of dose versus response in cancer induction, *if* we knew the steps in the pathogenesis of cancer. But some of these radiobiological studies have been grossly misapplied to the cancer problem, the misapplication resulting from the rather arrogant assumption that certain key steps in cancer pathogenesis are known, when they truly are not known (BEIR-III 1979, Draft Report, Minority Report).

SECTION 1: WHAT IS CANCER?

THE SINGLE-CELL ORIGIN OF CANCER

The author considers the overall body of scientific evidence to be in favor of the concept that human cancers ultimately result from events that take place in a *single* cell of the body. This of course would not rule out "multicentric" cancers, if we mean by that the occurrence of more than one cancer in a single organ of a human being. Further, the origin of cancer from a single cell does not rule out influences on the *rate of development* of the cancer, influences that may be the result of tissue changes in an area surrounding the cell that is the site of origin of the cancer. Nor does it rule out hormonal influences on the development of the cancer, such hormones coming from some distant organ. Surely we do have evidence that some hormones can accelerate or retard the growth rate of certain cancers in the human being. Lastly, origin from a single cell does not rule out the possible influence of an immune reaction that may either destroy an incipient cancer or retard its development.

There exists cogent evidence to indicate that the key carcinogenic events within the cell where cancer originates almost certainly occur in the *nucleus* of the cell. This is not beyond all doubt, but a very strong case can be made for the nuclear origin of human cancers. The aspect of the nucleus that most prominently suggests its central role in carcinogenesis (whether by ionizing radiation or other cause) is the presence in it of the great bulk of cellular DNA. The DNA represents the information base for the enormous biochemical capabilities of the cell, including instructions for carrying out the remarkable process of *mitosis.* Mitosis is the process in all human cells except the gonadal cells that leads to the formation of new cells. (Mitosis does go on in the spermatogonial cells of the testes, but the final process that leads to sperm formation requires *meiosis,* a process we shall consider later.)

Few phenomena of life are more remarkable than the ones which insure that human cells divide—increasing their numbers when an increase is required, or re-creating themselves in just sufficient numbers to replace dead or dying cells, as they do every few days, for example, in the lining of the entire intestinal tract. Even more remarkable is the fact that cells do not divide and increase in numbers in adults when such division is not required to preserve integrity of structure and function in specialized tissues. The cells throughout the body of the human being are "team players." Whatever may be its nature, the regulatory function that maintains this system in health is commonly referred to as a manifestation of cellular *control,* or cellular *regulation.*

DEFINING CANCER

Cancer is widely regarded as some type of disturbance of this control function, resulting in proliferation of cells that are not only not needed but ultimately cost the life of the host individual.

Some may debate that the "death-of-the-host" requirement should be part of the description of cancer itself, but others (the author included) adhere strongly to the idea that "cancer is what cancer does." And cancer does kill. This is not academic. And it is important to realize that decades of study have failed to demonstrate a single reliable histological (microscopic) or pathological (gross) criterion of cell structure or behavior that clearly identifies a *neoplasm* (new growth) as truly a cancer (a malignancy). Descriptions of the minutial features of neoplastic cells under the microscope abound, yet no single such feature reliably announces that a new growth is cancerous, rather than just a benign tumor. Unless the new growth has been removed or successfully destroyed, the final criterion is that it is a cancer if it is killing its host. Even this criterion can be clouded by the fact that certain benign tumors can kill by exerting pressure on vital organs.

A variety of features of proliferating accumulations of cells, if considered together, lead with pretty high reliability to the labeling of a true cancer:

a. Certain microscopic features of the cells themselves

b. Invasion of the capsule of an organ (a covering layer) by some of the proliferating cells, for those organs with capsules

c. Invasion of the lymphatic vessels by proliferating cells, with resultant spread beyond the initial focus of growth

d. Invasion of the blood vessels, with resultant spread of proliferating cells to distant organs (known as *metastasis*)

e. Death of the host, generally following debilitation of health

At any point in the evolution of a particular cancer, some of the features listed above may be absent, and only the cellular features may suggest that the growth is a cancer. At some (variable) later time, capsule invasion, lymphatic invasion, or bloodstream spread may occur. In still other cancers, bloodstream invasion and spread can occur very early, long before any clinical examination can reveal the presence of a cancer. Some have erroneously claimed that radiation-induced cancers may differ in certain of the properties just mentioned, but such claims have fallen by the wayside on more careful examination. *There is no reason to regard radiation-induced cancers as different from cancers in general* (Tamplin and Gofman 1970b; Beebe 1980).

Some cancer cells show both structural and functional features extremely similar to those of the normal cells of the organ in which the cancer has arisen. Others show virtually none of the features of the normal cells, and are then described as being in an undifferentiated state. In such a state, they are regarded as primitive kinds of cells, and the cancers to which they belong are called *anaplastic* cancers.

In the "universe" of cancers, not only do cancer cells display a myriad different features under the microscope, but masses of cancer cells also exhibit numerous gross features. For example, some are richly supplied by the ingrowth of new blood vessels, whereas others are poorly supplied with blood. Some cancers invade and even destroy adjacent organs, whereas others remain well contained within a fibrous capsule. Some spread very widely to distant organs; others rarely do so.

So bewildering is the *apparent* array of differences in this "universe" of cancers that some scientific observers have even suggested that it is a mistake to speak of cancer as a single disease. To these observers, the displays of diversity mean that there are more than 100 separate diseases, falsely lumped together under the name *cancer*. For very cogent reasons that we shall consider here, the author does not share this point of view and considers it a step backward in the quest to understand the cancer process. Indeed, it is remarkable that ionizing radiation has been shown to be capable of causing almost every type of human cancer known. That would be quite a coincidence if cancer were truly 100 different diseases. Let us now consider a number of other features that suggest a considerable unity in the midst of this seemingly bizarre and bewildering diversity.

UNIFYING FEATURES OF CANCER

First, it must be emphasized and re-emphasized that when a cancer is induced by ionizing radiation, the structural and functional features of the cancer cells, and the gross cancer itself, show *nothing specific to ionizing radiation*. Once established, a radiation-induced cancer cannot be distinguished from a cancer of the same organ arising from the unknown causes we so commonly lump together as "spontaneous." (*Spontaneous* is an elegant term for describing our ignorance of the cause.) The fact that radiation-induced cancers cannot be distinguished from other cancers itself indicates that there are profound common features among cancers, likely far more important than the differences.

The fact that radiation and other known carcinogens seem to add to the number of cancers already occurring in people, rather than to produce new varieties of cancer, suggests, along with other evidence, that the process of carcinogenesis is one form of biological reaction by organized living systems to certain classes of biological insults. Just as certain microbes and irritants call forth what we call an inflammatory reaction in tissues, another class of agents, which we label carcinogens, calls forth a reaction in human (and other) cells which we call cancer.

One feature does indeed tie together the diverse cancers, and that is the unregulated, uncontrolled proliferation of the descendants of a single changed cell. It is not that cancer cells necessarily divide more rapidly than normal cells; rather it is that they keep on dividing when there is no need for them.

SECTION 2: CHROMOSOMES: AN INTRODUCTION

EVENTS IN THE CELL NUCLEUS

It behooves us to look into the cell nucleus for a possible explanation for deregulation of certain cells, for the absence of "team playing," and for an explanation of both the similarities and the differences in various malignant cells. There are at least two major sites in the nucleus to consider in seeking an explanation for malignant behavior.

First, the DNA molecule, as we know from the elegant work of Watson and Crick, is the gene. In a human cell it is estimated that there are in the neighborhood of 25,000 to 100,000 genes (DNA molecules), which are involved in coding for the production of proteins and enzymes. There exists, in addition, an even greater amount of DNA in the cell nucleus, which is not involved in coding for protein production; and it is not at all clear what the function of this additional DNA is.

Some scientists think there may exist a single specific gene that is *the* crucial seat of the regulated behavior of the cell. And they believe further that a *mutation* (a broad term meaning change, without specifying the nature of the change) of the DNA molecule constituting that "regulatory" gene may alter its function as a regulator or destroy its function entirely. According to this view, with the regulatory gene missing or nonfunctional, the cell proliferates without control, wholly irrespective of any need for that type of cell, and the result is a clinical cancer. Whether or not this proposed mechanism is correct for any type of cancer is hard to say. There is no really good evidence in favor of this concept, but it cannot be ruled out as a possibility for some cancers. In any event, there are many reasons to doubt seriously the general applicability of this explanation for cancer.

The Chromosomes

We must also consider another level of organization of the DNA genetic material in the nucleus of the human cell. The DNA molecules do not exist as isolated entities floating around in the nucleus of the cell—far from it. Instead, in the human being, the nuclear DNA is contained in 46 separate objects known as *chromosomes.* Other species also have chromosomes, but of different appearance and in different numbers per cell. There are strong reasons to suggest that the comparison of chromosomes can tell us a lot about the evolutionary history of various species.

Human (and other) cells are commonly described as having a *cell cycle,* broadly comprising the actions of the cell other than cell division as well as the actions involved in cell division. Through most of the period of the cell cycle, the individual chromosomes are not discernible under the microscope as discrete entities. However, as the cell enters the early stages of cell division (called the *prophase*), the individual chromosomes become visible as such under the modest magnification of the light microscope (500- to 1,000-fold magnification). There is a wealth of information that convinces scientists that the 46 chromosomes are still there as discrete objects even during the period when they are not visible as such. It is considered that the chromosomes are grossly elongated and "thin" before prophase, which makes them hard to discern, and that they undergo a considerable condensation and "thickening" when the cell enters prophase. The chromosomes are known to contain DNA, some RNA, and proteins. The precise nature of the condensation process—what type of coiling and rearrangement occurs in preparation of the cell for division—currently represents an exciting area of investigation, but only the dimmest outlines of these processes are now available.

Cell Division

Cell division in all human cells (aside from certain divisions in the gonads) leads to the production of two daughter cells, each of which will have, when cell division is complete, its own complement of 46 chromosomes, which will be replicas of the 46 chromosomes present in the parent cell. And each of the 46 chromosomes will have all of the DNA molecules of the parent cell. Therefore, it is clear that all the DNA in the parent cell must have undergone replication to provide the DNA material for a new, additional set of chromosomes. This DNA replication takes place during the period of the cell cycle known as the *S phase* (*S* for synthesis), which is completed well before prophase. There is excellent evidence to support the idea that reproduction of the DNA occurs in the chromosome structures themselves, even though those structures are not visible while DNA replication is occurring.

The process of DNA replication is well described elsewhere (Watson 1970). For our purposes in the consideration of cancer and deregulation, we shall simply accept that a full new complement of 46 chromosomes is produced in the steps preparatory to cell division. One feature is important for our considerations: the two sets of 46 chromosomes are not randomly separated in the parent cell before division is complete. Rather, for each chromosome, there are now two chromosomes (at this stage called *chromatids*), and they are tied together in a region called the *centromere*.

At a time slightly later than prophase (measured in minutes), the chromosomes are still tied together at the centromere, but they are shortened and thickened still further than in prophase. Again, what is going on mechano-chemically in this further shortening and thickening remains obscure. This new phase, which follows prophase, is called the *metaphase* of cell division, and it is during metaphase that the chromosomes are most amenable to study.

CHROMOSOMES UNDER THE MICROSCOPE

Examination under the microscope shows that the 46 double-chromosomes are arrayed on a plate (called the *equatorial plate* because of its central position in the cell).

For decades it was hard to study the double-chromosomes at metaphase because of much overlapping. Through a fortunate, but carefully observed, laboratory error, Hsu and co-workers (1953) opened a new and important chapter in the study of human chromosomes. Cells were immersed in a solution containing less than the usual amount of salt, and this caused them to swell. When the cells were deposited on a microscope slide (a very clean slide), it was found that the 46 double-chromosomes were well separated from each other and were readily studied in detail under the microscope. This method of preparing cells for study is now called the *hypotonic* method (denoting the lower-than-normal salt content of the solution). It has revolutionized the study of chromosomes and the genetic information they carry, a field now known as *cytogenetics.*

In the early studies in cytogenetics, two criteria were available to describe chromosomal properties. First, there is the *length* of the chromosomes in metaphase. This length is very different from one class of chromosome to another. Second, there is the *position* of the centromere along that length. Simple examination of figure 1 shows the differences in length and position of the centromere among the chromosomes.

One additional crucial feature of human chromosomes must be described. Since human beings originate through the fertilization of the female ovum by the male sperm, and since normal human cells (in the embryo, the fetus, the child, and the adult) all contain 46 chromosomes, it is clear that the sperm and ovum must each provide fewer than 46 chromosomes to the fertilized ovum. In fact, we know that each provides 23 chromosomes, so that the new human being receives 23 chromosomes from the male parent and 23 from the female parent.

The 46 chromosomes of the normal human cell (except for certain stages of the sperm and ova cells) are truly made up of 23 pairs of chromosomes, but the partners are separate. For example, chromosomes A-1 from the father is not attached to chromosome A-1 from the mother. With one exception, the two members of each pair appear quite similar to each other. The exception is the pair that determines sex. So in both the male and the female of the human species, there are 22 of what we can call *grossly* identical pairs of chromosomes. We call these paired chromosomes the *autosomal chromosomes,* or simply *autosomes.* In the human female, there is one additional pair of relatively long chromosomes called the *X-chromosomes.* The presence of two X-chromosomes means the individual is a female. In the male, the twenty-third pair is not matched; instead there is one X-chromosome and one very short Y-chromosome. When an X and Y pair is present, the individual is a male. (See figure 1.)

In the last decade, an enormous amount of progress has been made in determining which genes are located on particular autosomes, and which are located on the X-chromosome. It is considered that very little genetic information is located on the Y-chromosome. Zellweger and Simpson (1977) stated that only two genes have been discovered on the Y-chromosome. One of these genes is a testis-developing gene. From recent work, it is not only becoming known which autosome carries a particular gene, but in some cases where along the length of the autosome the gene is located. Migeon and Miller (1968) did some of the earliest work in this area.

We have thus far treated the chromosomes as though they were always intact. We know, however, that there is variation beyond that caused by the mutation of genes. Small, and sometimes fairly large, pieces of a particular chromosome may actually be missing, and this means that tens or hundreds or even thousands of genes may be missing. There are also cases in which one of the chromosomes may have an extra piece attached, either to an autosome or to an X-chromosome. Nature is not very tolerant of such

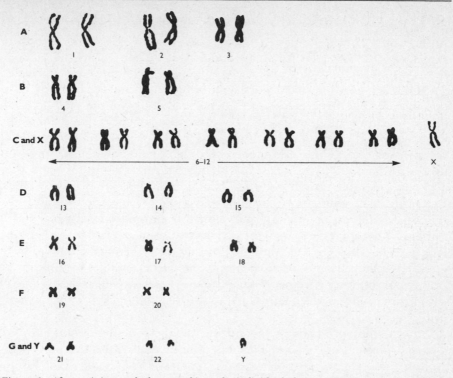

Figure 1: After staining and photographing, the individual chromosomes are cut out, and the various autosomes are paired based upon length of arms and position of the centromere. The classification shown is an arbitrary one, known as the Denver *classification. This is the type of picture seen without benefit of any of the special banding stains (see text).*

Detail is limited in this procedure. While some authors attempt to differentiate the chromosomes in the C 6 to C 12 group, most do not, since the detail is simply not good enough. This group is commonly referred to as the C6-C12 *chromosomes. Similarly, it is difficult to distinguish among the D-13 to D-15 chromosomes, or between F-19 and F-20, or between G-21 and G-22. Most of these resolutions can be made in favorable samples prepared with banding stains.*

The Y-chromosome is often hard to distinguish from G-21 and G-22 in routinely stained preparations. Similarly, the X-chromosome is often hard to distinguish from some members of the C-6 to C-12 group of chromosomes.

This karyotype (the chromosomal characteristics of this particular cell) would be found in almost any other somatic cell of this man if a metaphase of mitosis were studied. The "almost" proviso covers the rare cells that are tetraploid in normal persons, which cells would show a karyotype with twice as many chromosomes in all classes as are shown here.

defective chromosomes, and probably the reason most of us have 46 normal-looking chromosomes, at least so far as we can see them under the microscope, is that either fertilization will not occur if a defect is present, or we lose the defective embryo by spontaneous abortion. Infants who are born alive with defective chromosomes in all or many of their cells almost always suffer from defective development or severe disease.

Detecting Damaged Chromosomes

In the post-1970 period, a variety of techniques have been introduced for preparing chromosomes for study, and for the staining of the microscope slides with chromosomes present. These new techniques have revealed considerably more internal detail than just the length and the position of the centromere. The detail becomes evident, depending on the method used, in the form of regions of greater or lesser intensity of staining along the length of the chromosome *arms* (the arms are the regions on either side of the centromere). These techniques of differential staining are quite reproducible—though not yet of the quality we might hope for—and they allow considerable further detection of abnormalities in the chromosomes. But more than that, these "banding techniques" (so called because the differential staining appears as bands along the chromosome arms) allow for rather positive identification of the various autosomes. When we had just the length of the chromosomes and the position of the centromere to go by in identifying the various chromosomes, errors were possible, because in the process of shortening in the passage from prophase to metaphase, some of the chromosomes occasionally failed to shorten and thicken within a single cell.

The earlier, pre-banding literature is full of erroneous identifications of a chromosome as one type of autosome when it really was some other type. Not only does the banding considerably increase the certainty of the assignment of chromosomes to classes, but it allows detection of moderate-sized pieces of chromosomes missing or added, a fact that, as we shall see, is of great importance for cancer.

HOW DO THE CHROMOSOMES OF DIFFERENT ORGANS DIFFER?

Since all cells in the fully developed individual originated from one cell, the fertilized ovum, we expect that all cells of the individual will have 46 chromosomes, and that the genes of each chromosome will have all the expected loci. This would be the case if no errors were made. If all the chromosomes and genes in an individual are the same from cell to cell, why do the various specialized tissues and organs differ from each other? Why is a liver not a lung?

An older idea, now thoroughly discredited, held that the chromosomal constitution changed as tissues differentiated. Today we see that, in some way, the genes in each chromosome can be influenced to function or not function, and that it is whether certain genes are in the functional or nonfunctional mode which accounts for the differentiation into specialized tissues and organs. By no means do scientists think that liver cells have different sets of chromosomes from kidney cells or from bone-marrow cells. Precisely how the genes are "turned on or off" is a major area of current study in biology. The answers are far from available at this time.

Section 3: Chromosome Abnormalities in Human Cancer Cells

We have just stated that liver cells and kidney cells and bone-marrow cells all have the normal complement of 46 chromosomes. What about cancer cells in the human being—do they always have the normal chromosome complement too? The answer is a resounding no. Indeed, it may be true that *not one* cancer cell has 46 normal chromosomes, each chromosome having the normal, internal, structural composition. Unfortunately, our techniques are far from good enough to detect minor structural alterations in a specific chromosome, so it is difficult to test the question rigorously. However, we shall now consider the evidence that points overwhelmingly to the abnormal chromosomal constitution of the cancer cell in the great majority of human cancers.

The Birth of an Idea

Well before 1900, even without the modern improvements in methodology for the study of human chromosomes, semiquantitative observations were made. Makino (1975) points out that as far back as 1890, there was general agreement among pathologists that the one common, predominating feature of cancer is the occurrence of chromosomal and mitotic irregularities in the cancer cells. It became evident very early, even with crude techniques, that cells from a variety of human cancers could have 50, 60, 70, 80, and even more chromosomes per cell, in contrast to the closely controlled number of 46 chromosomes in normal, nonmalignant cells. (An error was propagated through the literature for decades that the normal human cell had 48 rather than 46 chromosomes.)

Additionally, and particularly as the techniques for studying chromosomes improved, it became evident that there were often extensive structural alterations in some of the chromosomes of cancer cells, over and above the abnormality in numbers of chromosomes per cell. Many of the alterations found in such cells were similar to the alterations produced by the irradiation of human cells. So here was an important link in the relationship of ionizing radiation and cancer.

The idea began to be considered that the cellular cause of cancer might be some error in cell division causing an abnormal distribution of numbers of chromosomes to daughter cells, or it might be an injury to certain of the chromosomes directly.

In spite of a mountain of evidence that it is rare to find a cancer cell with the normal number of chromosomes or the normal structure of the chromosomes present (the literature containing this evidence is well referenced in Makino's book *Human Chromosomes* [1975]), many scientists are far from convinced that a change either in the composition of chromosomes or in their numbers per cell could be the *cause* of human cancer. The reason for their skepticism is that there is a bewildering array of differences from cancer to cancer in both areas of chromosomal alterations.

These scientists have taken the position that such observations would argue much more strongly that the cancer comes first, and that as a *result* of the cancer, somehow all these bewildering chromosomal alterations occur. Thus, their thesis is that cancer causes chromosomal alterations, rather than that chromosomal alterations cause cancer. It is interesting that such scientists overlook the fact that radiation damages chromosomes promptly when the irradiation is applied, and that cancer is a later result.

THE WORK OF THEODOR BOVERI ON THE CHROMOSOMAL ORIGIN OF CANCER

In 1914, the first edition of an important book appeared, authored by Theodor Boveri, a great German embryologist. In this book, Boveri put forth a seminal concept of the origin of human cancers from chromosomal alterations both in structure and in number per cell. His ideas were remarkably advanced in that he appreciated intuitively and foresaw many of the remarkable developments of genetics and cytogenetics in the modern era, and that he did this some fifty to seventy years before these advances occurred.

Boveri suggested that there is a closely controlled balance of genetic information (which we now recognize to be in the DNA molecules) in the normal cell, which it achieves by having the same number of and types of chromosomes from cell to cell. So long as this *balance* of genetic information is maintained, Boveri reasoned, the cell will exhibit regulated behavior. As we have described above, the regulated behavior of cells is represented by cell division taking place only when needed. Boveri did not think the specific mechanism of injury to the cell was important. Rather, he was concerned about *any* injury that could upset the closely controlled balance of the various types of chromosomes, either by changing the total number of chromosomes per cell or by causing a *structural change,* that is, by adding or removing a piece of some chromosome.

As an illustrative mechanism of injury, Boveri suggested that an injury to the *cell-division mechanism* could result in an abnormal cell division, followed by an abnormal number of chromosomes in each of the daughter cells. Boveri stressed that the injury to the cell-division mechanism was not his primary concern. Instead, he was concerned about the final, abnormal balance of chromosomes in one of the daughter cells, no matter what injury mechanism may have operated to cause it.

Once a cell had achieved an abnormal number of chromosomes (or a structural abnormality, by the gain or loss of a piece of chromosome), causing an imbalance in the number of genes of various sorts, the entire regulatory mechanism for control of cellular proliferation would be upset, and the cell would be on the path to development of cancer. For once a cell had acquired an imbalance in chromosomal information, that cell would pass the imbalance on to each of its daughter cells in division, setting in motion the unchecked proliferation of such cells, none of them responding to regulatory influences.

The Boveri concept suggested an explanation for the diverse properties of human cancers, and for the differences in behavior of the cancers of a single organ from person to person. Boveri stated that one particular chromosome imbalance might be crucial for upsetting the regulatory mechanism, but that obviously, in a faulty mitosis, there might be all sorts of abnormal distributions of chromosomes (and their genes), which would account for the diversity of behavior of cancer cells in different individuals. Thus, in one person, the event that set off the cancer might cause the initial cancer cell to have a very different total distribution of chromosomes than the initial cancer cell in another person would have. For Boveri, the crucial issue was that a particular imbalance had to be present to insure loss of regulation, but beyond that, much variation in chromosome content could be expected. We know from extensive human evidence that the presence or absence of a single gene, and certainly the presence or absence of a whole chromosome, can have profound biochemical effects on the cell.

Boveri did not claim that a single, specific chromosome imbalance was the *only* imbalance that could lead to a loss of regulation and hence to cancer. Rather, he was saying that certain imbalances could be essential to cause loss of regulation, and that the many other incidental imbalances which could accompany a crucial imbalance would account for the great diversity in properties of cancers—such as rate of growth, metastasis or nonmetastasis, and output of hormones. Boveri himself did not have the opportunity to follow up his suggestions experimentally.

THE LATER HUMAN EVIDENCE PERTAINING TO BOVERI'S IDEA

Studies made since Boveri's time of the chromosomal constitution of human cancers leave no doubt that the vast majority of human cancer cells studied do indeed show an abnormal number of chromosomes, often deviating very widely from the normal number. Moreover, it is very common to find structurally altered chromosomes in the cancer cells.

Cancers have been reported with most of the cells showing 133 chromosomes per cell (Ishihara and Sandberg 1963), one has been reported with most of the cells showing 35 chromosomes per cell (Sandberg and co-workers 1967), and essentially every number in between has been found for at least one cancer in humans. Numbers in the range between 46 and 69 are most frequent, although numbers above 69 chromosomes per cell are also frequent.

The reader will encounter a specific terminology in the literature for the range of chromosome numbers in cancer cells, with which it is important to be familiar. In the sperm and ova cells there are 23 chromosomes each. This number, which is half the number found in all the cells of the somatic tissues of the body, is known as the *haploid* number for the human being. In the somatic cells, which comprise all the cells of the body except the ones that give rise to sperm and ova, and which all derive from the fertilized ovum, we have what is called the *diploid* (meaning double) number, which for the human being is 46 chromosomes. If a cell is found with three times the haploid number, it is said to be *triploid;* with four times the haploid number, to be *tetraploid.* In cancers where the number of chromosomes found is near but below the diploid number of 46, the cancer is said to be *hypodiploid.* In cancers where the number is near but above the diploid number, the cancer is said to be *hyperdiploid.* Correspondingly, there are cancers which are hypo- and hypertriploid, and hypo- and hypertetraploid.

In a single cancer, one also finds a certain number of cells with twice or four times the number of chromosomes, called the *modal* number, shown in most of the cells of that cancer. Thus in a cancer with most of the cells showing 73 chromosomes per cell, one also may find some with 146 chromosomes and some with 292 chromosomes per cell!

In a cancer with 73 chromosomes per cell as the modal number, one also finds some cells with chromosome numbers above and below that modal number. Thus, cancer cells in such a case will be found with 74, 75, 76, and 77 chromosomes and with 72, 71, 70, and 69 chromosomes. Since the technique for the preparation of slides for chromosome study is not perfect, it is possible to lose one or even a few chromosomes from a cell during preparation. One tries, in scoring the number of chromosomes, to search out cells showing no evidence of such disruption and loss, but it is never possible to be sure no chromosomes have been lost. However, it is much more difficult to explain the existence of cells with a few *more* chromosomes than the modal number on the basis of the technique of preparation.

Therefore, it seems far more likely that in each cell division, particularly for cells with large numbers of chromosomes and with injured chromosomes (a subject to which we shall shortly return), *errors in division* account for one daughter cell getting 72 chromosomes and the other daughter cell 74. This would provide a mechanism of deviation from the modal number. It would also provide a mechanism for "evolution" of the cancer to a more slowly or more rapidly growing variety, since its genetic balance has become altered. Clinically we know that cancers which have been dawdling along will, at a certain point, take off and grow rapidly.

The First Cancer Cell Versus the Cancer Cells in a Clinical Cancer

A fundamental difficulty stands in the way of testing the Boveri concept concerning the nature of the critical imbalance that sets a cell on the path to cancer. (It is not necessary that there be only *one* way of achieving a critical imbalance that permits escape from regulation.) The difficulty arises from the fact that the initial event occurs in a single cell. *We have no way of studying this initial event.* Instead, some 10, 20, or 30 years later, when that one cell has multiplied to 1 billion or 100 billion cells, we become aware that a cancer process has been going on. So when we initiate a chromosome study of the cancer at this later time, we must necessarily expect that we are studying very distant descendants of that initial cancer cell. Such initial cells do indeed undergo "evolution" (as discussed above) by losing or gaining a chromosome in cell divisions and by other mechanisms.

We do know that the chromosomal constitutions we see at this later stage of the cancer *successfully proliferate,* and certainly they show no regulated behavior, for they are at this point killing their host.

So the study of clinical cancers can never be expected to test the Boveri concept that certain specific imbalances are the initiating event. Instead we can examine the findings in studies of cells of proliferating cancers, and ask ourselves whether radiation can produce changes such as those noted in these "successful" human cancer cells. And we can ask ourselves, further, whether the production of such cells by radiation is proportional to the dose of radiation or shows some other relationship between dose and response.

The fact that we cannot see that initial change in a cell which sets it on the path to cancer should have one salient effect, namely, the introduction of a bit of humility into the cancer investigator.

The author is appalled, on reading the Minority Report of the BEIR-III Draft Report (1979), to find scientists talking about the use of radiobiological theory in the prediction of the relationship of radiation dose to frequency of induction of human cancer. It is quite amazing to find scientists invoking radiobiological theory about a process that none of us, they included, have the ability even vaguely to describe, since that first cancer cell cannot be seen. The BEIR Minority Report invokes the unknown mechanism initiating cancer in order to proclaim a law about how the evidence must "behave," whereas the author will do the reverse: in chapter 8, section 2, he will suggest possibilities for the unknown mechanism based on a clue from the *evidence.*

SECTION 4: IONIZING-RADIATION INJURY TO CELLS AND THE DEVELOPMENT OF CANCER

Ionizing radiation produces cancer and leukemia in humans. We shall consider the direct evidence in much of the remainder of this book. Such radiation also provokes a variety of chromosomal and cellular injuries that lead to an imbalance of the chromosomal information content of the cell. Since we do have a well-described set of mechanisms by which ionizing radiation injures the chromosomal system of cells, it is reasonable to suspect that one of those mechanisms may very well be *the* mechanism which sets the cell on the path to cancer. We cannot test this directly in the human being. But there is something we *can* do with regard to each of the mechanisms by which radiation injures chromosomes or alters the number of chromosomes per cell. We can study radiation effects upon cells outside the body. If the quantitative aspects of the production of a given injury by radiation disagree with the quantitative findings in epidemiologic studies of human cancer induction by radiation, then it follows that this particular mechanism of radiation injury studied *in vitro* (outside the body) cannot, by itself, represent the key initiating event in cancer. The mechanism by which radiation induces cancer must have quantitative dynamics that agree with what we observe epidemiologically. The epidemiologic data are, for certain types of cancers, far from ideal, but some of the data are very good indeed, and would permit ruling in or out certain mechanisms of radiation induction of cancer.

We must now consider some of the specific ways in which those high-speed electrons set in motion in tissue by ionizing radiation produce cellular and chromosomal injuries. In order to do so, we must first look a little more closely at that remarkable process, mitosis, in the somatic cells.

THE MITOTIC PROCESS (CELL DIVISION) AND POSSIBLE ERRORS

We have already discussed the replication of the chromosome preparatory to the process of cell division, leading to the presence of two daughter chromatids (at metaphase), tied together at the centromere. During the latter phases of mitosis, known as metaphase and anaphase, some other important events occur, leading to the division of the centromere into two centromeres, one for each daughter chromatid. Following this, the two chromatids "migrate" away from each other to widely separate points in the cell, all 46 chromosomes (or 92 chromatids) undergoing this process.

In the final phase (telophase), a new nuclear membrane forms around each new group of 46 chromosomes. (Once it has its own centromere, each daughter chromatid is called a chromosome.) Finally, the cell's cytoplasm undergoes cleavage, creating at last two cells where formerly there was one.

In a cancer cell, or other abnormal cell, mitosis also occurs. If the cancer cell has 79 chromosomes, all 79 will undergo duplication.

One can imagine a number of errors that could occur in the mitotic process, and a number of defects that could be produced in the chromosomes themselves, the centromeres themselves, and the centrioles themselves. As is so often the case in medicine and biology, if one can dream up a possible defect, it is likely that the defect will occur. It is "Murphy's law" in biology: if anything *can* go wrong, it *will,* sometime. Whether the defective cell will survive is another matter. Unfortunately, some *do* survive, and reproduce. Certain of these aberrant cells may well be the progenitors of human cancer.

Polyploidization and Radiation

This formidable word, *polyploidization,* describes a very straightforward process, namely, the production of a cell with multiples of 46 chromosomes, e.g., 92 or 184 chromosomes per cell. The author and every other researcher who has looked at many thousands of cells in mitosis have seen some cells in normal human material that show 92 and more chromosomes. There is a tendency in the literature to write this phenomenon off as unimportant for cancer, simply because it is seen in normal tissues. That may be a very erroneous tendency, since it has been found that ionizing radiation can increase the frequency of development of polyploid cells.

Polyploid cells arise from failure to complete a normal cell division. In some cases, all kinds of final distributions of chromosomes to daughter cells are possible, so the second and later generations of such cells can exhibit many different chromosome numbers.

Polyploidy can originate from a variety of causes, including radiation injury. The specific chromosome injuries that can lead to polyploidy are thought to be translocations and the formation of dicentric chromosomes, both discussed below. It is possible that polyploidy is the most important of all mechanisms in the induction of cancer by ionizing radiation; we simply do not know.

THE VARIETY OF RADIATION-INDUCED CHROMOSOMAL INJURIES TO HUMAN CELLS

The Simple, Single Break

For most of the cell cycle, we are dealing with a single-chromosome structure, although it is double-stranded with respect to its DNA molecules. It is only after replication of all the DNA, preparatory to cell division, that we have a double-chromosome of two individual, but joined, chromatids. As a result it is presumed that most of the injuries to cells will occur while the chromosome is single, rather than while it is composed of two chromatids. However, we do know that single-chromatid injury can and does occur.

We shall discuss here the kinds and consequences of injuries that occur while the chromosome is a single structure.

Ionizing radiation, in the form of high-speed electrons, primary or secondary (e.g., set in motion by X-rays), can shear off part of a chromosome at any place along the length of the chromosome. Some scientists suggest that, possibly, certain sites along the length of a chromosome are more readily sheared, but this is not well documented for human chromosomes. Since there are 46 chromosomes in a somatic cell, and with the entire length of the chromosomes subject to such shearing, an enormous variety of final results is possible.

One result which undoubtedly occurs is that the sheared piece of chromosome rejoins the remainder of the chromosome from which it was removed. The process of rejoining is known as *restitution*. The term *restitution* implies that no harm has been done to the chromosome. However, there is evidence which indicates that damage can be done in the region of the break, and that the functions of all the genes may not be restored.

Another result of radiation injury is the failure of the sheared piece of chromosome to rejoin the main body of the chromosome from which it was removed. In this case that piece which was lost is said to represent a *deletion*. Sometimes the term *deleted chromosome* is used for the residual chromosome. During duplication of the chromosomes preparatory to cell division, the residual chromosome (after deletion) will duplicate itself without the sheared piece. And, separately, the deleted piece will duplicate itself, except that the deleted piece has no centromere. When we come to the metaphase of cell division, we actually see the shortened chromatids of the chromosome that has suffered the deletion (provided the piece was large enough). We also see two so-called *acentric fragments* (meaning fragments without centromeres). It is rare for these acentric fragments to become incorporated into the nuclei of the daughter cells, so they are generally lost to the cells. This is one mechanism for radiation production of a loss of chromosomal information. A very large body of information exists to show that the number of deletions produced is directly proportional to the dose of radiation delivered, in the low-dose range (Brewen and Preston 1973; Sasaki 1975). Since plotting of dose versus number of deletions on a graph produces a straight line (direct proportionality always graphs as a straight line), the deletion effect is said to be *linearly* related to dose.

If the cell is able to complete its cell division, the part of the chromosome that still has the centromere will go through the remainder of mitosis normally. Whether the daughter cells with the missing piece of chromosome are viable and able to divide again depends upon how serious to cellular metabolism was the loss of the genes on the deleted piece. No doubt many of the cells suffering a deletion do die, but we are also certain that some of them can live and go on to divide further.

We must ask why it turns out that deletions are linearly related to dose, for both low and high LET radiations. There is every reason to believe that deletion of a piece at the end of a chromosome, called a *terminal* deletion, is what is known as a *one-track event*. In a one-track event a high-speed electron (or a high-speed proton, or a high-speed alpha particle) can produce a deletion without any help from another ionizing particle. Therefore, it is reasonable to expect that the number of deletions should be directly proportional to the dose of radiation, since the number of ionizing particles (electron or other) is directly proportional to dose received.

Radiation-Induced Terminal Deletions and Cancer Induction: Are terminal deletions induced by radiation involved in cancer production? We simply do not know how large a part of the total cancer and leukemia production by radiation is the result of terminal deletions. First of all, as mentioned earlier, we do not get to see that "first cell" in the development of a human cancer, so we cannot say that deletion of a chromosome is or is not a primary event. Second, small terminal deletions would be hard to detect in the chromosomes of cancer cells even if they were present in the first cancer cell and persisted throughout the entire history of a cancer in a particular person. In general, it is true that we are missing *most* of the small terminal deletions by current research techniques, even including the recent banding techniques. The one point to be made is that to the extent to which deletions should turn out to be a causal event in cancer production by radiation, it would be expected that the cancer incidence would be proportional to the dose of radiation, down to the lowest doses that could be considered.

The Philadelphia Chromosome and Chronic Myelogenous Leukemia: An outstanding discovery, made by Nowell and Hungerford (1960), is that chronic myelogenous leukemia is characterized, in the large majority of cases, by cells showing an apparent deletion of a part of the long arm of the chromosome G-22. Most scientists today would regard this as the discovery that the leukemia was *caused* by this chromosome alteration, though not all would agree to causality. This was the first clean illustration of a single, specific chromosome change related to a specific malignancy.

Later observations by Rowley (1973) and others indicate that the missing piece of chromosome G-22, rather than simply being deleted, was transferred to another chromosome. This association between a *translocation* and a fatal disease is one of many reasons why the author rejects the common claim that simple translocation of a chromosome piece produces no, or very little, biological effect.

Interstitial Deletions, Translocations, and Inversions Produced by Ionizing Radiation in Human Cells

The terminal deletion involves one break in a chromosome. But more than one break can occur in a single chromosome, and breaks occurring in two different chromosomes can interact.

The Interstitial Deletion: If there are two breaks in a single chromosome, caused either by one ionizing track or by more than one ionizing track, there can be left a terminal piece of chromosome, an intermediate piece, and the large bulk of the chromosome still containing the centromere. Both pieces without the centromere can get lost, in which case we have produced two deletions. What happens in some cases is that the intermediate piece does indeed get lost, but the terminal piece is rejoined with the bulk of the chromosome containing the centromere. The deleted piece, in this case, is referred to as an *interstitial* deletion. Whether we detect an interstitial deletion depends upon its size. We shall discuss one interstitial deletion involved in the hereditary transmission of risk of a particular cancer, so we know they can be detected by banding techniques if of adequate size. But small interstitial deletions, which may still involve large numbers of lost genes, are probably missed quite often. Both for this reason and because of our inability to study early cancer cells, we are in no position to state anything about interstitial deletions as a possible cause of cancer. Such deletions are produced both by one-track and two-track radiation events. The linear, one-track dose-response curve predominates in the region at least up to between 50 and 100 rads in human cells (Brown 1976, 1977; Evans et al. 1979).

Translocations Produced by Ionizing Radiation: Ionizing radiation can produce complex and important changes which involve two, three, or even more chromosomes. Consider two separate chromosomes, with a break occurring in one arm of each chromosome. If nothing further happened, we would have two separate chromosomes, each having suffered a terminal deletion. But rejoining in various special ways can occur, which gives rise to new chromosomes. The terminal pieces of two broken chromosomes can become transposed, or translocated; this is referred to as a *reciprocal* translocation, for obvious reasons. In a reciprocal translocation, there are no acentric fragments left over. So, aside from injury to genetic material in the break region itself, there is no major loss of pieces with genetic information. Reciprocal translocations are a common effect of ionizing radiation in human cells.

Alternatively, the bulk of one chromosome, containing a centromere, can join with the bulk of another chromosome, also retaining its centromere. The terminal pieces are left over from both chromosomes, as acentric fragments. The composite chromosome formed from the two large pieces will now have two centromeres, having acquired one from each chromosome involved in the translocation.

Such dicentric chromosomes cause trouble at mitosis, during anaphase, whenever the two centromeres "want" to migrate in opposite directions. The entire cell division may be inhibited; instead of division into two cells, a tetraploid cell may result. Or the division may be completed, with the dicentric chromosome left out of both daughter nuclei. Obviously, an *enormous* number of possible combinations of chromosomes can enter into the formation of such dicentrics. It would be arrogant indeed to make statements about the fate of all the possible end products of dicentric formation.

A rarer, but definitely occurring, translocation is known as the *tricentric chromosome.* As the name suggests, it involves three chromosomes in the formation of a new chromosome with three centromeres. The difficulties in mitosis just described for dicentrics also apply here.

Yet another form of translocation can be regarded as peculiar in the sense that all the events take place in a single chromosome. If a piece is broken off of the short arm of a chromosome, and separately, a piece is broken off of the long arm of that same chromosome, we would, if nothing else happened, have a residual chromosome with two terminal deletions. There would, of course, be the acentric fragments, representing each deleted piece of chromosome. But something else can and does happen. The two ends of the doubly deleted chromosome can get together and join, forming what is known as a *ring chromosome.* Ring chromosomes, having only a single centromere, can go through the mitotic process, providing ring chromosomes to each daughter cell. The acentric fragments are lost during one of the very earliest divisions after deletion. Ring chromosomes are not rare in cancer cells. But on the other hand, there is no evidence to suggest that the type of translocation within one chromosome that leads to ring structures is specially related to carcinogenesis. The quantitative relationships to radiation dose, for ring-chromosome formation, would be expected to be similar to those for translocations in general, with some one-track events and some two-track events.

Lastly, there is the form of translocation known as *inversion.* In the description above of the interstitial deletion, we spoke of two separate breaks in one arm of a chromosome, which can either give rise to a double deletion or, if the end piece joins the main part of the chromosome arm, to an interstitial deletion. But there is still another possible combination. The intermediate piece of chromosome need not get lost as an interstitial deletion. It can, instead, turn around end for end, and all pieces can thereafter be rejoined. Finally, no block of chromosomal material has been lost in this event, although there may well be some injured genic material in the neighborhood of the breaks. The process of reassembly, after the end-for-end turn, is known as *paracentric inversion.* As a variant of the inversion phenomenon, we can consider a break in one arm of the chromosome and a break in the other arm of the chromosome. Then the entire body of the chromosome turns around, end for end, and the various pieces rejoin to form a chromosome that has lost no pieces. The piece broken off the short arm is now rejoined to the long arm, and the piece broken off the long arm is rejoined to the short arm. The resultant chromosome is said to have undergone a *pericentric inversion.* Any biological effects that result from paracentric or pericentric inversions must be due either (a) to injury in the break regions, or (b) to the effect of position of the genes within the chromosome arm.

There is no information concerning whether such inversions are of special importance in cancer formation, simply none.

Translocations: Dose-Response Relationships

All translocations require two separate chromosome breaks. Sometimes both breaks are produced by a single ionizing track, a single electron, for example, creating both of the breaks. In events such as this, we expect that the number of translocations produced is proportional to the radiation dose —the linear relationship. On the other hand, the two breaks may be caused by two separate electron tracks, in which case we expect that the number of translocations will be proportional to the square of the radiation dose. Since both are possible mechanisms and since both occur, it is not surprising that the final result is some combination of one-track and two-track events. The

quantitative relationship between dose of radiation and number of translocations will reflect the combined mechanisms. At the low end of the dosage
scale, the one-track mechanism will predominate; somewhere along the
dosage scale, the two mechanisms will provide equal contributions; and
finally, at still higher doses, the two-track mechanism will predominate. As
Brown (1967, 1977) and others have shown, for human cells, the one-track
linear mechanism appears to predominate below 100 rads of radiation (see
chapter 8).

We shall discuss shortly an interesting and important illustration of an
inherited translocation that predisposes offspring to a very high risk of kidney
cancer (Cohen, Li, et al. 1979a). But that does not address the question
whether a translocation can be a crucial event in setting a cell itself on the
path to cancer. To that question we simply do not know the answer.

Aside from the general problem we have of not being able to see that
"first cell," we have a very serious problem in identifying the existence of
many, if not most, translocations. If a dicentric chromosome is formed, it
stands out clearly. Two centromeres in a chromosome are readily identified.
But if the translocation is of the symmetrical type, with terminal ends exchanged between two chromosomes, then we have serious difficulty. If the
exchanges are fairly large pieces, the banding techniques may be able to
reveal that a translocation has occurred. However, if the pieces exchanged
are small, the banding techniques will not be good enough to identify the
existence of a translocation. So even if translocations were crucial, we might
very well miss them with current technology.

RADIATION-INDUCED CENTROMERE DEFECTS: ISOCHROMOSOMES AND CANCER

One potentially important mechanism for producing a chromosomal imbalance has not yet been discussed: direct injuries to the *centromere* of the
chromosome itself, either by ionizing radiation or by other chromosome-
injuring agents.

A form of important injury produced by ionizing radiation and other
chromosome-injuring agents is the *misdivision* of the centromere so that
instead of dividing to separate the two chromatids, it divides at right angles
to the way it normally would. What then happens is that the two long arms
of the chromatid pair get a centromere and become a new type of chromosome. At the same time the two short arms of the chromatid pair get a
centromere and become a new type of chromosome. The two new chromosomes produced by this misdivision of the centromere have arms that are
mirror images of each other, and hence are called *isochromosomes* (*iso-* meaning "equal"). The original chromosome may have had one very long arm
and one short arm. The first isochromosome has two very long arms. The
second has two short arms. Thus the daughter cells are strongly unbalanced
in chromosome gene information.

As we shall see in our later discussions of congenital and genetic disorders, far smaller informational imbalances than these provoke serious errors in development. It would not be surprising if the kind of imbalance in information produced with isochromosome formation were important with respect to cancer formation. But again, we simply do not know if isochromosome formation initiates cancer. We do have information that indicates isochromosome formation may have important effects in the progression of certain malignant diseases, notably chronic myelogenous leukemia.

NONDISJUNCTION AT MITOSIS

Nondisjunction is a process whereby both chromatids of one type go to one daughter cell, instead of one chromatid to each daughter cell. The result of nondisjunction is the production of one daughter cell lacking one chromosome, and one daughter cell having one chromosome in excess. This creates a chromosome imbalance within each of the daughter cells. There is no doubt whatever that a certain number of human cancers are characterized by 47 chromosomes per cell as the modal number of chromosomes, although no single chromosome has been identified as consistently in excess in such cases. Whether a nondisjunction was the *initial* event that led to the cancer which later manifests a chromosome complement of 47 per cell cannot be stated with the evidence at hand.

The evidence concerning radiation induction of the nondisjunction phenomenon is not at all consistent. This evidence will be examined in detail in chapter 15, which concerns itself with congenital and genetic disorders.

CHROMOSOMES IN THE HEREDITARY TRANSMISSION OF CANCER RISK

While in clinical cancers we have found a great variety of chromosome changes—most of them inducible by ionizing radiation—it is not possible to identify a specific change as the initial event in a human cancer. We have been discussing changes in chromosome numbers per cell, and chromosome structural alterations, either of which might set a particular cell on the path to becoming a full-blown clinical cancer 5, 15, 25, 35, or 50 years later. When chromosome injury occurs to some of a person's somatic cells, the vast majority of his body cells still have a normal chromosome complement.

By contrast, when we consider *inherited* chromosome aberrations, we are looking at an entirely different phenomenon. Here we see chromosome abnormalities that are common to *all the cells* of a person, and we ask if those abnormalities increase the risk that their owner will develop some type of cancer. The results already obtained are of very great importance, particularly with respect to ionizing radiation.

Inherited diseases that have been associated with various types of chromosome injuries include Wilms' tumor (a cancer of the kidney, or of tissues around it), retinoblastoma (a serious cancer of the eye), and renal-cell carcinoma.

A PREDICTION AND ITS RADIATION IMPLICATIONS

The author predicts that the discoveries to date of increased risk of specific cancers associated with deletions and translocation—all hereditarily transmitted—are only the tip of the iceberg. It is the fact that the deletions and translocation were *large* enough to be readily discerned in the laboratory which brought the syndromes discussed to discovery. With improved technique and diligent search, there can be no doubt that many more relationships will be found.

It would not surprise this author if it turned out that transmitted chromosomal lesions may be a major part of the increase in cancer risk which certain individuals carry and of which, in most instances, we are not aware.

The implications of the existing findings are profound for the role of ionizing radiation. Even at low doses of radiation, deletions and translocations are produced by ionizing radiation, and the production of such aberrations is directly proportional to the dose of radiation received down to the lowest doses studied. It has not been proved that all the chromosome injuries in the cases studied were radiation-induced, but it is certain that radiation can produce these types of lesions. Deletions and translocations are the "classical" chromosomal injuries from ionizing radiation. There are, no doubt, chemical agents, and possibly viruses, that can also produce deletions or translocations. But since exactly these types of chromosome lesions are produced by ionizing radiation, we can predict with confidence that the diseases here mentioned will, in some cases, have been caused by radiation.

Various committees speculate on the genetic effects of ionizing radiation. It may well turn out that the inherited risk of cancer due to a chromosomal aberration is one of the major areas they should be studying. Much will be learned in this area in the next ten years.

CHAPTER 4

THE INDUCTION OF CANCER BY IONIZING RADIATION: FROM "IDEAL" STUDY TO A METHOD FOR HANDLING REAL DATA

I T IS UNIVERSALLY AGREED that leukemia and virtually all forms of solid cancers in humans *can* be induced by ionizing radiation. That statement is, of course, very different from the statement that all cancers and leukemias in humans *are* induced by ionizing radiation. There does exist a minority opinion which suggests that *all* cancers and leukemias are caused by ionizing radiation, but the author considers the evidence overwhelming that radiation is only one of a number of causal agents.

Our objective in this book is to develop a quantitative estimate, for all kinds of ionizing radiations, of the numbers of cases of cancer and leukemia that will be caused by exposure to specified quantities of ionizing radiation energy. We may not know for decades or centuries the intimate cellular details of precisely *how* ionizing radiation causes cancer, but this in no way precludes our making close estimates of how *many* cancers will be caused in a population receiving some specified number of units of ionizing radiation. Surely, if we did know the precise mechanism of causation, we might be able to calculate the numbers of cancers without recourse to human observation, but for now such knowledge eludes us, and we must determine the results empirically.

There does exist a considerable body of information concerning the effects of radiation upon human (and other) cells. In the effort to resolve certain thorny problems concerning the induction of cancer by ionizing radiation, we shall refer to such information, but only as a supplement to the direct evidence. It can be stated flatly, however, that at this time we simply do not know which, of the many kinds of interactions that occur between radiation and cells, is (or are) crucial for the causation of cancer.

SECTION 1: CARCINOGENESIS: THE EFFORT TO QUANTIFY

Faced with the difficult enough problem of having to rely on actual observations, we will encounter some special features that make the task of quantifying the carcinogenic effects of radiation even more difficult. When human cancer is produced by ionizing radiation or other agents, there is generally a very long period, measured in years or decades, between the time of the causal event and the time the cancer becomes detectable in a physician's office or hospital. The only exception is the case of in utero radiation, in which there may be less than a year between exposure to the carcinogen and the observation of the cancer clinically.

THE LATENT PERIOD: QUANTITATIVE ASPECTS

A special term has been given to that long time-interval between causal event and clinical appearance of the cancer: the *latent period.* Unfortunately, the literature is quite equivocal with respect to the precise definition of the latent period.

The latent period is sometimes taken to mean the time it takes to be able to *prove* that a population of exposed persons is experiencing a higher rate of development of a particular form of cancer than would be expected for that same population without it, in the cases of interest to us, the added ionizing radiation. Or, if we had two truly matched population samples, one sample exposed, the other not exposed to radiation, the latent period would be the minimum time required to be able to prove, statistically, that there was a real difference in the rate of development of cancer between the two population samples.

While this definition has in the past been commonly used, there are some real difficulties with it. If one is studying 100 persons in the two population samples, and if the particular cancer under study is infrequent in occurrence rate, it may take 25 years before one can prove, statistically, that the cancer occurrence rate differs between the exposed and unexposed groups. On the other hand, if one is studying 1,000,000 persons in the two population samples, a provable difference may become evident in 10 years. Obviously, a definition is not very useful if it depends on the number of subjects studied.

For this very reason, the reader should view with skepticism any statement that a particular form of cancer due to radiation, e.g., breast cancer, cannot occur before, say, 12 years after exposure. Whoever determined that 12-year figure did so from a finite sample of persons. Had the investigator studied 100 times as many people, he might have reached the conclusion that radiation-induced breast cancers can appear 5 years or even 3 years after exposure.

It is because of difficulties such as these that the older definition of the latent period would best be eliminated. Most of the recent literature does not use it. One commonly finds now that when investigators refer to the latent period for cancer development, they refer to the time, *for a specific individual,* between exposure to the ionizing radiation and the clinical observation of the cancer. Even this is inexact because of the term *clinical observation.* Whether a cancer is found at a particular time depends on how hard one looks.

There is one definition of the latent period that is free of ambiguity, namely, the time from the exposure of a particular person to that person's death from cancer. While unambiguous, this way of stating the latent period can miss the development of cancers induced by radiation for decades, since some cancers may become clinically evident at, say, 10 years, but not cause death for another 10 or 20 years.

Perhaps the best approach is to recognize the difficulty and deal with it by *specifying* the manner in which any particular study was done. Provided the exposed and unexposed persons are examined in the same way, then one can base the latent period, for each study, upon the time between exposure and discovery of cancer by that type of examination. A study may use death from cancer as its end-point. Provided exposed and unexposed subjects are both studied this way, there should be no problem with the results. Clinical discovery of cancer must be matched with clinical discovery. Deaths must be matched with deaths.

Whatever method of cancer detection is used, clinical incidence or death, two other terms are commonly used, the *median* and *mean latent period.* If all the cancers that are ever going to occur from a particular exposure have already occurred, then one can add up all the latent periods for the cancers, divide by the total number of cancers, and thus arrive at the mean latent period. The median latent period can also be obtained with such data, by simply finding the period of time before and after which the same number of cancers have occurred.

Unfortunately, on this issue of using either mean or median latent period, the existing literature is exceedingly messy. Investigators of radiation effects have reported a mean latent period for a particular cancer as, let us say, 11.3 years, when their total period of follow-up of the exposed persons is only 15 years. Such a reported mean latent period means absolutely nothing. In such a limited follow-up period, all the radiation-induced cancers have not yet occurred, so the reported mean latent period excludes a large part of the evidence. A mean latent period determined by the convenience of the investigator in setting the follow-up period does nothing but confuse the scientific evidence. One of the chief tasks of this book will be to correct the erroneous conclusions reached from such studies. The true mean or median latent period can be determined only when all the cancer cases which will ever occur have been discovered.

THE NATURE OF THE LATENT PERIOD

Why should it take years or decades for a cancer produced by radiation to become clinically evident or to cause death? We do not have any rigorous answer to this question, but we do have some ideas about how to answer it.

The general view shared by most investigators, though not by all, is that cancer has its origins in changes *in a single cell* of an organ susceptible to the development of cancer. The author considers that the evidence taken as a whole supports this view. For example, in experimental animal studies, it has been demonstrated repeatedly that cancer can be transmitted from one animal to another by the transfer of *one* cancer cell from one animal to the other. This is not of itself conclusive, since one might be transferring a cancer-causing virus at the same time. Other, perhaps more cogent, evidence is the fact that in certain cancers, there are features common to all the cancer cells—for example, a particular abnormal chromosome (see chapter 3). Let us regard the theory that cancer arises from a single cell as one based on opinion, not one thoroughly proved.

A single cell in a human is a very, very small object, with a diameter in the neighborhood of 10–20 micrometers. Some human cells are smaller than this, and some are a little larger, but this is the general order of size. In a gram of tissue, if all the tissue were made of cells, without any fibers, there would be roughly 100 million to one billion cells. Clinically, it would be very difficult to diagnose an internal cancer before there are some 10 to 1,000 grams of cancer cells present in the patient. One might diagnose a skin cancer or even a breast cancer with as little as a fraction of a gram of cancer cells, but these are special cases.

Thus, *if* a single cell is set on the path of cancer development by ionizing radiation, that cell must divide many times by the process known as mitosis in order to produce one billion or ten billion cells, which is in the neighborhood of what it takes for clinical observation of the cancer. While we regard uncontrolled cell division as a prime feature of cancer, we do not know the factors which determine, for a particular cancer, what the time interval will be between successive cell divisions. Of one thing we can be certain: the older idea that cancer cells divide extremely rapidly is not correct in general. Experimental data indicate a wide variation in the time between divisions for different cancers, and the factors involved remain obscure. And particularly, since we are never able to observe the cancer until it has become clinically manifest, we certainly do not know the rate of cell divisions of the cancer in its early stages, nor do we know how that rate compares with the rate in the clinically manifest cancer. It would make a large difference in the latent period if the time between cell divisions were months or years rather than days or weeks.

Furthermore, as a cancer develops, for example, in the breast or lung or intestine, it must acquire its own blood supply for nourishment and removal of the waste products of its cellular metabolism. This is accomplished by the ingrowth of new small blood vessels in the cancer itself. This process of vascularization is of grossly variable efficiency for different cancers. This one feature probably has a great deal to do with the time it takes for the cancer to grow to a size that is clinically detectable. The microscopic study of cancers has shown that there are often large regions in a cancer with dead and dying cells, probably the result of the cancer cells outgrowing their blood supply, while in other regions of the cancer the cells are growing well and show no signs of cell damage or death. Thus, the precarious balance of blood need and blood supply can keep the cancer from growing, as some cells die and others proliferate. To what extent this balance of growth and necrosis (death) of cells may prolong the latent period we cannot say.

The blood-supply problem can have another effect too. Cancer cells are able to synthesize some of the biochemicals they need for further cell division, but it is certain that some of the chemicals needed for cell division must be brought to the cell from body sources. If the blood supply is not adequate, the growth of the cancer may be limited by the availability of needed biochemicals, and this too may be a factor prolonging the latent period. It is somewhat ironic that cancers have any ability at all to call forth a network of new blood vessels, to be provided by the host, who is going to be killed by the cancer. That is a facet of biology we have yet to understand.

Another factor that has been invoked in the explanation of the very long latent periods for certain cancers is some sort of immune surveillance system. It is postulated that under ordinary circumstances cancer cells may incite a cellular immune reaction, which results in the destruction of at least some of the cancer cells. To the extent that any such immune reaction operates, it might result in a balancing, for long periods, between new cell proliferation and cancer-cell destruction. It is unclear, at present, whether such an immune system operates at all, or operates for some cancers only, and if it does how it affects the rate at which cancers grow to clinically observable size.

Also, we must realize that the radiation insult which ultimately produces a cancer is only the first step in what may well be a long, tortuous process. As we have seen in our earlier discussions, cancers can be regarded, at the cellular level, as a kind of microcosm of the evolutionary process. The information system of the cancer cell, as of any other cell, resides in the genes of the cell, and these, in turn, are present in the structures known as chromosomes. At every cell division, there is a chance of misdistribution of chromosomes, and hence of the genes. Out of such changes in the informational system may come cells that compete more favorably in the body environment, and these may accelerate the rate of development of the cancer. Others may find the environment unfavorable and die out, thus impeding the total growth rate of the cancer.

And we must remember that each latent period goes with only one human host. Humans are not biochemically identical. The milieu for a radiation-injured cell in one person may be favorable for the rapid growth and development of descendant cancer cells, which makes for a relatively short latent period, while the milieu in another person may be quite unfavorable to a burgeoning cancer, resulting in a very long latent period.

Lastly, there are possibly important mechanical effects. A growing cancer can impinge on normal tissues in its immediate vicinity, with disturbance to the nerve and blood supply, which disturbances can themselves alter the nutrition supply to the cancer, and change the time it takes to grow to a clinically observable size.

For the many reasons given, and probably for many others that could apply, we should *expect* what is actually observed: that cancers induced by radiation in one specific organ demonstrate a wide range of growth rates. This, in turn, means that there will be a wide range of observed latent periods, from person to person. It is a *fact* that some radiation-induced cancers become clinically evident in fewer than 5 years, and it is also a fact that some take 40 to 50 years to become clinically evident.

The astute reader will, no doubt, ask how we know that cancers occurring 40–50 years after irradiation have anything at all to do with the radiation. The answer is that there are *some studies* in which radiation is localized to an organ that has a very low spontaneous rate of cancer development. Hence, when a number of cancers occur in an exposed population 50 years after radiation, and when that number far exceeds the expected spontaneous number, we can be confident of the radiation basis of the cancers, even after such a long period. For all we know at present, it is entirely possible that some radiation-induced cancers may develop 60 or 80 years after irradiation.

SOCIO-POLITICAL ASPECTS OF THE LATENT PERIOD

As a society, we are accustomed to being able to "see" the relationship between the purported cause of a disease and the disease itself. And to "see" such a relationship has generally meant to us that a *short* time interval must elapse between the institution of the cause and the observation of the effect. Radiation-induced cancer was the first disease to add a new dimension to this problem of cause and effect. This new dimension has been fiercely resisted in many quarters, even ridiculed, in the face of a mountain of evidence that the time period between insult and disease can be measured in decades, not days, weeks, or months. Indeed, as we develop here the quantitative evidence concerning radiation-induced cancer, we shall see that events which occur in a population before its members are 20 years of age are probably going to be the major determining factor in the number of cancers to occur in that population for the remainder of its life-span!

An industrial worker can be very unfairly treated as a result of a long latent period between radiation insult and development of a clinical cancer if he is asking for worker's compensation. Lawyers, judges, juries, and physicians have all tended to disbelieve that present cancers can result from radiation exposures twenty years ago. Even today, when we know beyond a shadow of a doubt that this occurs, the worker making a claim of occupationally induced cancer has a tough time winning his case. We can hope for some enlightenment on this issue, but it will be slow in coming.

An interesting illustration of the lack of appreciation of the long latent period between radiation and cancer development occurred in the post–World War II period. The United States initiated a follow-up study of the persons who were exposed to and survived the atomic bombings of Hiroshima and Nagasaki. Within the first five years, no excess of cancers developed in the exposed individuals, although an excess of leukemia did become manifest. The author, then working in an Atomic Energy Commission–supported laboratory, recalls the self-congratulatory attitude then prevalent —even with the large doses of radiation received, no cancers were occurring. But that early jubilation, based on a total lack of appreciation of the length of the latent period for cancer, soon turned to disappointment. As the years have passed, cancers have indeed begun to occur in the survivors of the bombings, and by now, the cancers have exceeded the leukemias. It is inevitable that the numbers of cancers from the bomb radiation will increase appreciably in the next decade and beyond, particularly as those who received their radiation in early youth approach the ages at which most of the cancers are much more common. We shall see that radiation appears to increase the frequency of cancers at whatever ages the cancers tend to occur spontaneously in unexposed persons.

Medicine has also failed to appreciate the long latent period for cancer development. One can still find some recent papers on the long-term consequences of administering radionuclides to patients for diagnostic and therapeutic purposes, which report, with self-satisfaction, that few if any cancers have resulted from the use of the radionuclide. When one looks at the follow-up period, it is sometimes as short as 9 years. A post-irradiation period like 9 years is just the beginning of the radiation-cancer story, not the story itself.

If the reader discovers such a short follow-up in a report suggesting that no cancers have been induced from a particular use of radionuclides, there is only one thing to do—simply disregard it. Some studies are hardly more competent, but superficially they look better. For example, it may be reported that the follow-up of exposed persons lasted anywhere from 6 to 23 years. That sounds good, what with 23 years of follow-up for some of the people. But the key question is, what is the *average* period of follow-up? Is it closer to 6 years, in which case the study provides no meaningful information on radiation-induced cancer, or is it closer to 23 years, in which case the results may be quite important?

SECTION 2: THE "IDEAL" STUDY TO ASSESS THE RISK OF RADIATION-INDUCED CANCER

Fortunately, the human species is not barbaric enough to *do* the "ideal" study that would be required to assess the real cancer impact of a specified amount of radiation delivered to persons of a particular age. But if we are to know how well or how poorly we *are* measuring the cancer price from the planned or unplanned exposures that have happened to human beings (including bombing victims, radiation workers, medically irradiated persons), it is essential to discuss what an "ideal" study would be.

We have already mentioned the central importance of age at the time of irradiation. There are additional variables. For instance, at present it is not certain whether there is or is not a measurable difference in sensitivity to cancer induction by radiation for one sex versus the other. Claims of differential sensitivity are poorly supported. It is possible that a sex effect exists, and this further complicates our "ideal" study. Another possibility is that the radiation effect per unit dose (measured in rads) is not the same for all total doses delivered, so we would have to consider setting up separate studies for doses of 1 rad, 10 rads, etc. Further, there is the possibility that the *rate* of delivery of the radiation is important in determining the effect, so we would have to consider setting up studies in which the dose is delivered instantaneously, say, in a second or less, others where the dose is delivered in hours, and still others where the dose is spread over weeks or months. And we would of course study both sexes with each variation. We have already outlined a very large study indeed, but that is only the beginning of the study. Since the really hard part of this study comes after the beginning, we shall discuss just one small segment of the "ideal" experiment to show how we would go about gathering the critical information required.

Suppose we consider a single group, males at 0+ years of age (very early infancy). Suppose further that we limit ourselves to one single dose level and rate, 10 rads delivered acutely, within 1 second. And for further simplification, suppose we restrict the radiation to one source, low LET radiation (X-rays, for example) uniformly spread over the entire body.

If we wish to know just how many excess cancers are produced by this amount of radiation exposure and just how many years of life expectancy are lost by the radiation-cancer victims, we would have to start with a very large population sample of males 0+ years old, say, 200,000.

The first step would be *randomization,* meaning that we would divide the entire group into two groups, each having 100,000 of our subjects, and divided so that the two groups are as nearly alike as possible in all respects, except for their radiation exposure. This can never be done perfectly, but the more careful we are to randomize *without any bias,* the closer we will come to matched groups of 100,000 each. Note that we are not trying to get 100,000 persons of 0+ years of age who are all alike in all details; rather, we are trying to insure that *within* both groups of 100,000, any peculiarities, genetic or other, are equally represented. Thus, if 5% of one group of 100,000 is characterized by some genetic predisposition to the development of cancer, we would try to insure that 5% of the other group of 100,000 is also so characterized.

Unless such randomization is done, we face the possibility of doing a useless and false experiment. We could confound the effect of radiation in causing cancer with some other cancer cause, if such an alternative cause existed only in the irradiated group. In an "ideal" experiment, we would not allow such a possibility to arise.

It is important to note here that natural sources of radiation do indeed exist, but the point is that the cancer effect of natural radiation will be the same in both groups. In such a large experiment, it is also fair to assume that both groups will receive the same *average* dose in a lifetime from medical and occupational irradiation. And, of course, we expect fully that both groups will be exposed to a variety of other carcinogens; but again, this creates no problem because with true randomization, both groups will be equally affected.

Having once succeeded in choosing our two groups of 100,000 male infants, we are prepared to start the experiment. Let us suppose that Group Y receives 10 rads of whole-body radiation, and that Group Z receives no such supplemental radiation.

The next task would be to observe these two groups (of 100,000 each) to determine how many cancers develop each year after the irradiation of Group Y. How long would one have to go on observing the two groups? Since we do not know *in advance* how long the radiation, delivered in infancy, will continue to produce cancers, obviously the only way to assess the price in radiation-induced cancers would be to follow both groups for the remainder of the life-span of all the 100,000 individuals in each group. That means about 90 years of follow-up observation! Had we started this "ideal" experiment (barbaric as it is to contemplate) at the turn of the century (A.D. 1900), the experiment would not be complete until the year 1990. And 1900 was just five years after Roentgen's discovery of X-rays.

The results of this ideal experiment are summarized with an illustrative example.

Column 1	Column 2	Column 3	Column 4	Column 5
94,119	26	24.5	45	20.5

Column 1 shows for the Group Z (unirradiated) subjects what is known as a *life table,* which describes how many people are left alive at each successive age, starting with 100,000 in infancy. To illustrate, if we look at the entry for 35 years of age in column 1, we find that there are still 94,119 alive out of the initial 100,000 infants. (These are real data for the United States for the year 1976.) Obviously these are the only persons left from Group Z to be subject to the development of cancer. But of those 94,119 who are survivors (of all prior causes of death), some will die of cancer during their thirty-fifth year of age.

To figure out how many members of Group Z will die of cancer during that year, we must use a second column of data, which gives the *age-specific cancer mortality.* Column 2 tells us how many people out of 100,000 alive at their thirty-fifth birthdays will die of cancer in the next year—that is, before their thirty-sixth birthdays. We find this age-specific cancer mortality to be 26 persons out of 100,000. But from column 1 we know that there are only 94,119 persons left alive, not 100,000. Therefore, we calculate the number of cancer deaths in that year as follows:

$$\frac{(94,119)}{(100,000)} \times 26 = 24.5 \text{ deaths from cancer during the thirty-fifth year}$$

This number, 24.5, is our entry for age 35 in a third column, which gives *actual spontaneous cancer deaths*. With precisely the same procedure, we derive all the entries for column 3, for every age up through 90. Column 3 gives us a quantitative description of how many die of cancer and at what age, throughout the entire life-span, *without any added radiation*. When finally all the initial 100,000 persons in Group Z have died (at 90+ years beyond the start of the study), we can also know what fraction of the entire group died of cancer, by simply adding all the entries in column 3, and dividing by 100,000. We find that this fraction is 0.182. Or, if we prefer, this figure can be multiplied by 100% to give us the percentage, 18.2%, who have died of cancer, at some time between infancy and old age. The importance of the life-table method is that it takes care of other causes of death, and hence does not overestimate the number of cancer deaths.

Now we must turn to the question of the actual number of cancer deaths at each age for Group Y, all members of which received 10 rads of whole-body radiation at infancy. Since our experiment as a whole is hypothetical, (although columns 1–3 contain real data), we shall use hypothetical entries in a fourth column of data. Let us suppose that the entries in column 4 are truly observed numbers of cancer deaths for Group Y. Now, since the two groups, Y and Z, were perfectly matched at infancy, it follows that subtracting the entries in column 3 from those in column 4 will give us the *extra*, or excess, cancer fatalities *at each age* caused by the 10 rads of radiation delivered at infancy. For the thirty-fifth year of age, the entry in column 4 is 45 cancer deaths; the entry in column 3, we noted, is 24.5 cancer deaths. The difference, 20.5 deaths, entered in column 5, is the number of excess cancer deaths caused by the irradiation in infancy. This is true because the numbers in columns 3 and 4 would have been identical *in the absence of radiation*, since the two groups were perfectly matched. (Of course, in the real world, statistical fluctuations would have made the numbers slightly different. We would have ironed out these statistical fluctuations by plotting smoothed curves. But we are in a hypothetical world here.) We enter all the differences (column 4 entry minus column 3 entry) in column 5, and call them *extra cancer deaths due to radiation*.

If now we add all the entries in column 5, out to 90+ years, we obtain the total number of premature cancer deaths that were caused in our 100,000 members of Group Y by the radiation delivered in infancy. That total number is 15,182.

The author is sure that by now the astute reader is worrying about an error in the tabulations. In Group Y there are, at each year, those extra cancer deaths caused by the irradiation. Therefore, the entries in column 1 would be decreasing slightly faster than shown, for the Group Y people. In a rigorous treatment of the problem, this small correction should indeed be made, but it is not important to the general points being made here.

Observed Versus Expected Values

Two terms, used in the professional journals and in this book, can now be understood. The entries in column 4 for the irradiated group are by custom called the *observed* values, while the entries in column 3 for the control group are by custom often called the *expected* values, even though the cancers in the control group were also observed, and real. This could be a source of confusion to some readers, and it might help them to think of it this way: the expected values always correspond to the values you would *expect* to see if you had *not* introduced any radiation exposure (which is the variable being tested)—in short, if you had not done any experiment at all.

The Person-Rad

We shall also introduce here another term which will be used widely in the remainder of this book. It has great importance beyond its illustrative use in this chapter. That term is the *person-rad* (had we been measuring dose in rems, we would be using the term *person-rem*). The number of person-rads is obtained by multiplying the number of persons irradiated by the number of rads each person received. In our present example we irradiated 100,000 infants each with 10 rads. Therefore, the number of person-rads is

$$(100,000 \text{ persons}) \times (10 \text{ rads}) = 1,000,000 \text{ person-rads}$$

By adding all the entries in column 5, we found a total of 15,182 extra cancer deaths caused by this radiation. So with 1,000,000 person-rads, we produced 15,182 extra cancer deaths.

The Whole-Body Cancer Dose and Specific-Organ Cancer Doses

We are now in a position to ask another question. What is the number of person-rads required to guarantee *one* extra cancer death if infants are irradiated? This we obtain by simply dividing two numbers:

$$\frac{1,000,000 \text{ person-rads}}{15,182 \text{ extra cancer deaths}} = 65.87 \text{ person-rads per extra cancer death}$$

We shall define the *whole-body cancer dose* as the number of person-rads per extra cancer death. With this definition, our experiment has led to a whole-body cancer dose of 65.87 person-rads. We could have done this whole set of tabulations using the data for specific cancers instead of dealing with all cancers together. For example, we could have made the entries for leukemia, colon cancer, or pancreas cancer. Then, instead of arriving at the whole-body cancer dose, we would have arrived at the *leukemia dose,* the colon-cancer dose, the pancreas-cancer dose, etc. We stated earlier that a

preponderance of the evidence indicates that the effect of radiation in inducing cancer is *direct*, meaning that cancer in any specified organ arises as the
result of radiation of that organ. So we need not have used whole-body
irradiation in this example if we were interested just in the lung-cancer dose.
We could have derived that dose from an idealized experiment with just the
lung fields irradiated.

Proportionality

Why is the "cancer dose" so important? As we shall see in subsequent
discussion, the evidence is strong, from direct human observations, that at
least within the usual dose ranges of concern (between 0 and 200 rads), the
number of excess cancer deaths produced is either very close to proportional, or exactly proportional, to the dose received. We shall consider all
the arguments about such proportionality in great detail later (in chapter 8),
but let us accept for the purposes of this illustration that the author is correct
in the statement that proportionality holds.

Proportionality means that if we expose a population to 10 rads and find
100 extra cancer deaths, then exposure to 20 rads will produce 200 extra
cancer deaths, and exposure to 1 rad will produce 10 extra cancer deaths.
So long as proportionality holds, it turns out that all we need to know, for
an exposed age group, is the total number of person-rads if we wish to
calculate the total number of extra cancer deaths produced. Thus, it is not
necessary that all subjects get the same dose of radiation. We simply calculate, for each person, the person-rads of dose (which, of course, is his dose
in rads multiplied by 1), and then sum all these numbers of person-rads for
the whole population sample. When we then divide this sum of person-rads
by the whole-body cancer dose, we have the number of extra cancer deaths
produced in the remainder of the life-span of the population.

One crucial point! So far we have calculated the whole-body cancer
dose only for irradiation at infancy. We would have to go through the entire
procedure separately, by the same general methods outlined, to calculate
the whole-body cancer dose for radiation at any other age. Indeed, we shall
do just that later in this book, using real human evidence rather than a
hypothetical example.

Note that we can calculate the extra cancer deaths to be expected in a
group of irradiated individuals in two ways: (a) by direct proportionality,
and (b) by the use of person-rads and the whole-body cancer dose. If we
know the actual number of extra cancer deaths caused by a certain amount
of radiation in one group (as in our hypothetical experiment above), we can
apply proportionality to estimate the excess deaths in another group, as
long as we correct for any differences in the size of the sample and dose.
Using the second method, we do not need a "known" result for comparison;
we can calculate the extra cancer deaths in any group as long as we know
the total person-rads received by the group and the whole-body cancer
dose. Both methods of calculation will give very close to identical results.

This is valid if proportionality holds between radiation dose and cancer induction, as we propose to prove later on in this book.

APPLICATION OF THE WHOLE-BODY CANCER DOSE TO AN INDIVIDUAL

We are, for certain purposes, interested in the consequences of radiation delivered to large population samples. But we are equally interested in providing, *for the individual,* an estimate of the risk of premature cancer death for a specified radiation dose at a specified age. We have just shown the public-health consequences in extra cancer deaths (hypothetical here, actual later on in the book) for irradiation of 100,000 infants with 10 rads of radiation. Suppose we now ask, what is the risk to one infant of premature cancer death as a result of receiving those 10 rads in infancy?

We have one infant receiving 10 rads. The number of person-rads for that infant is (1 person) × (10 rads) = 10 person-rads. But the whole-body cancer dose is 65.87 person-rads. Thus, the extra cancers for that infant are

$$\frac{10 \text{ person-rads}}{65.87 \text{ person-rads per cancer}} = 0.152 \text{ extra cancers}$$

We must think through the meaning of this fractional expectation of extra cancers. It is this child's personal probability of dying prematurely of cancer somewhere in his body as the result of that radiation. In percentage terms, there are 15.2 chances out of 100 that he will die prematurely of cancer from the radiation. This means that if there were 100 such individuals, 15.2 of them would die prematurely of the radiation-induced cancer. We shall shortly consider *how* premature the cancer death will be, on the average.

In the case of irradiation accepted voluntarily by an *adult,* he must know the risk of his action is to be genuinely voluntary. Knowledge is also the key when he has to make such a choice for his children. An individual may be told he needs a certain diagnostic X-ray procedure that will give him 10 rads. Surely he should be told what the increased chance of cancer death is from such a procedure done at his age, so he can carefully weigh this against the reasons for accepting the extra 10 rads. He should also be told what the chances are that his disease will kill him if it is not thoroughly diagnosed and treated (assuming treatment *is* available). If the chance is 50 out of 100— or any risk substantially greater than that posed by the radiation—he may very well choose to have the X-ray procedure and accept the extra risk of cancer death at some later time in life.

If estimates of the cancer risk from radiation can be made—and they can—then the person and his physician can mutually arrive at a reasonable decision. If irradiation of a *child* is contemplated, such considerations are even more important because of the extra sensitivity of children to radiation injury.

No doubt *most* physicians will be deeply relieved and pleased to have at last a comprehensible basis for making responsible recommendations. Patients and lawyers are surely going to come to understand these issues, and physicians will want to be able to justify the X-ray, nuclide scanning, fluoroscopic, angiographic, CAT-scanning, and other radiological procedures they order, and to be sure they have made clear to their patients what risks are involved from these procedures.

The days are rapidly passing when a physician orders an extensive set of X-ray procedures, for instance, without considering their consequences. Every medical student should be learning the principles outlined in this book, for they apply not only to radiation hazards, but also to some non-radiation medical procedures and medications.

THE LOSS OF LIFE EXPECTANCY IN THE RADIATION CANCER VICTIMS

Tabulations such as those in our hypothetical experiment can provide additional valuable information beyond the *number* of extra premature cancer deaths induced by radiation. What is at least as important is an estimate of the actual average loss of life-span for those who do develop radiation-induced fatal cancers. Obviously, if this average loss were a few hours or days, one would take a very different view of the matter than if it were 15 years.

Which is it, years or hours? Let us see how our experiment can be expanded to provide this information. Data from the National Center for Health Statistics have been computed by the Metropolitan Life Insurance Company into what is known as the *expectation of life* at each age. This represents the average number of years a person can expect to live under current health circumstances. If, therefore, someone at age 25 has an expectation of 46.5 years, and if that person becomes a fatality of radiation-induced cancer at 25, he has lost 46.5 years of life. This provides us with a methodology for estimating the life-span lost by radiation.

For each year of age from 1 to 90, we multiply the number of radiation-induced cancers by the life expectation for that year. This gives us the total number of years of life lost by radiation-cancer victims for that age. If we sum those numbers for all ages, we get the total number of years of life lost by all the radiation-cancer cases: 198,232 years. But from column 5, we found that we had produced a total of 15,182.4 radiation-induced cancer fatalities. Therefore, the *average* number of years of life lost for the irradiated infants is obtained by division: $198,232/15,182.4 = 13.06$ years. Far from days or hours! Although this entire calculation is a hypothetical one, when we examine the real human evidence, this turns out to be an appropriate estimate of loss of life. The reader must bear in mind that this is the *average* number of years of life lost. *Some* radiation cancer victims will lose 40 or 50 years of life; others, only a few years.

SECTION 3: FROM "IDEAL" EXPERIMENT TO THE REAL-LIFE PROBLEM

We have outlined here what it would take to find out the radiation-cancer price for one dose of radiation, of one type, administered to infants only, and to infants of one sex. Obviously, to expand this study to include different doses, both sexes, different ages at irradiation, and to study all the groups for some 90 years of follow-up (somewhat shorter periods for those older at irradiation) is a mammoth experiment that (a) is never going to be done, and (b) even if it were done, would not help us to know the cancer effects of radiation while the experiment was under way—for the next 50 to 100 years. We need these answers now; indeed, it is already rather late, with the widespread use and abuse of radiation extant.

The situation is not at all discouraging. We can get answers that should be quite close to what an ideal experiment would show, and we can get those answers now. A large number of observations have been made of human beings of all ages, even in utero, exposed to radiation under a variety of conditions. The follow-up periods are variable, but quite a number of studies have follow-up periods long enough to be useful. A few approximations are going to be needed in carrying through the necessary calculations, and they will be carefully identified as such. This will all be explained in the following sections and in later chapters, where all the existing human evidence is analyzed and put into a systematic framework which permits us to have working answers today instead of waiting 50 to 100 years. We shall identify approximations carefully as the evidence is presented and analyzed, and shall show why those approximations are reasonable. No doubt the purist will say, "But you haven't confirmed this with a 90-year study." The author doubts whether society is going to allow such purists either to conduct barbaric experiments or to go on babbling that "we don't know the effects of low-level radiation."

THE HUMAN EVIDENCE

We do indeed have a large body of information on human cancer induced by ionizing radiation. Unfortunately, Hiroshima and Nagasaki *were* bombed, and the follow-up of the survivors has produced much information concerning cancer and leukemia induction in humans. We have a large body of information on human cancers induced by ionizing radiation used for diagnosis and therapy, the use of much of which was ill-advised. In fact, some of our information comes from medical uses of radiation for diseases we now think never existed in the first place. We have important information on the induction of human cancers from occupational exposure to ionizing radiation.

None of this information was accumulated under "ideal" experimental conditions. There are, to be sure, many, many defects in the combined base of information available to us. The task before us is to develop a method that circumvents as many of the defects as possible.

Dosimetry Problems

The doses received by irradiated subjects are often poorly measured. In many of the studies, dose received has been reconstructed many years after the radiation, and this certainly introduces uncertainties into the dose estimates.

For example, an elaborate set of studies has been carried out on the survivors of the atom bombing of Hiroshima and Nagasaki. This required an estimate of the gamma-ray and neutron dose of the survivors based on their recollection of where they were at the time of the bombing, coupled with an estimate of the shielding that would have been present between them and the source of radiation. Noble and difficult as this effort has been, it is not unreasonable to believe that there may be a sizable error in the dosimetry for the survivors. Certainly there must be appreciable errors for individuals. Nevertheless, the data are very valuable, for they allow reasonable segregation of the survivors into major classes of dose.

A second valuable source of information has been derived from the exceedingly careful study (Court-Brown and Doll 1965) of some 14,000 persons in Great Britain who received spinal irradiation with X-rays as therapy for the disease known as ankylosing spondylitis (a form of rheumatoid arthritis of the spine). The British have conducted a remarkable follow-up effort to ascertain the number of leukemias and cancers produced as a side effect of the spinal irradiation. It is impossible in such therapy to restrict the X-rays to the spine itself, and as a result, a number of other body organs and tissues received radiation. Cancer or leukemia has developed in a significant number of the spondylitis patients during a long-term follow-up. The problem of estimating accurately what the radiation dose was to the various organs inadvertently irradiated, in the course of delivering radiation to the spine, has been formidable. Over a 20-year period, various individuals and groups have wrestled with efforts to assess, in retrospect, what the true dose was to such organs as the lung, lymph nodes, stomach, intestine, and pancreas. The dose estimates have varied by factors of 4 or 5 for some of these organs. Obviously, the cancer effects *per unit dose* will also vary by those factors. The tenuous state of affairs in this important study is best illustrated by the fact that in 1979, some two decades into the study, a new, determined effort is under way to try again better to estimate the dose to various organs (UNSCEAR 1977, p. 408).

Another very valuable source of information has arisen from the occurrence of radiation-induced breast cancer as a result of fluoroscopic X-rays taken in the course of so-called pneumothorax and pneumoperitoneum treatment of tuberculosis in women. These treatments consisted of injection of air into the thorax (pneumothorax) or into the peritoneal space (pneumoperitoneum) for the purpose of collapsing the lung, to rest it.

Fluoroscopic examinations were made either before and after, or just after, the injection of air to ascertain whether the desired collapse had been achieved. These treatments for tuberculosis have been superseded by chemical therapy, but they were undergone by thousands of women in several countries. The radiation dose was not accurately estimated at the time of examination by fluoroscopy, so, in retrospect, estimates have been made for each woman's breast dose based upon the type of X-ray machine used, the positioning of the patient with respect to the machine's beam (beam to anterior or posterior part of the chest), the number of seconds the fluoroscopic beam was on (a rough measure at best), and the number of fluoroscopic procedures carried out. It would not be surprising if the true dose is known to only within a factor of 2 or even worse.

There is also a series of women who received therapy with X-rays in the treatment of benign diseases of the breast, and who later developed breast cancer as a result.

Children, in large numbers, were irradiated a few decades ago during the first few months of infancy with X-rays to the neck for the supposed treatment of enlargement of the thymus gland (an enlargement which few physicians today believe ever existed in those children). An appreciable excess of thyroid cancers has developed in such children over what would have been expected without radiation, such cancers developing *decades* after the irradiation in infancy. This has been a valuable source of information, but reconstruction of the dose to the thyroid gland itself has been difficult, to say the least.

Additionally there are available a host of separate studies of a variety of medical conditions treated with ionizing radiation where radiation-induced cancers have been looked for during follow-up periods of varying duration. Some of these studies provide sufficient information to make a reasonable approximation of the dose received, and these will be included in our analysis. In some of these studies, the dose is simply impossible to reconstruct, and after careful explanation these will be excluded.

There have been two separate, major analyses of the occurrence of cancer in radiation-exposed workers at the Hanford Atomic Facility in Hanford, Washington. The dose of external radiation to these workers was carefully measured by film badges. Although there is less certainty about possible internal doses, these studies are a valuable adjunct to our data base.

Lastly, there are the elegant studies of Dr. Alice Stewart and her colleagues in Great Britain on the effects of ionizing radiation on infants in utero, including subsequent leukemia and cancer in childhood, together with the confirmatory studies of this phenomenon by MacMahon in the United States. Even for these studies estimation of dose is difficult because of changing practices in diagnostic radiology.

So there are formidable problems with accurate dose estimation for virtually all the available studies of human cancer induced by ionizing radiation. But there are some important mitigating factors that operate in our favor, provided we make use of a great variety of separate studies around the world, which we shall indeed do. There is no reason to expect all the estimates of dose to be "off" in the same direction in all these unrelated studies. Rather, there is good reason to believe that dosimetry errors will tend to cancel each other out. Therefore, as a result of dosimetry problems, the uncertainty in the final estimated "effectiveness" of radiation in producing cancer may be well below two-fold in either direction.

Another Problem: Inadequate Follow-up Periods

Even more troublesome than dosimetry, in making use of most of the human radiation experience, is the fact that so many of the studies are made over exceedingly *limited follow-up periods*. Compared with the 80–90 year follow-up of the "ideal" experiment described in the preceding section, the actual follow-up periods of 10–30 years are short indeed. And unfortunately, most of the available studies are well below 30 years in follow-up.

As a general rule, the reported studies will lead to an *under*estimate of radiation-induced cancers if no effort is made to correct the findings for the short follow-up period. Section 4 of this chapter will present a method which allows us to deal with follow-up deficiencies.

Some Estimate Versus No Estimate At All

Strangely enough, many authors seem to take pride in saying that no one should attempt to extrapolate their data beyond the exact follow-up period of their study, that we should not use their data for any rate of radiation delivery other than the one reported in their study, and that we should not try to use data from one country to tell us anything about radiation induction of cancer elsewhere.

We might as well claim that a chemical reaction achieved in Peoria cannot be trusted to be possible in Paducah. To deny the validity of making generalizations about radiation from specific studies is to deny the validity of the inductive reasoning on which all science is based, and is to say further that none of the data on human irradiation can be put to any really useful purpose. Just as physicists were able to generalize to the laws of gravity and of radioactive decay long before they could measure accelerations or half-lives to a gnat's eyebrow, so can scientists in other fields use imperfect measurements to arrive at valid generalizations.

This author considers cautions against inductive reasoning in radiobiology to be hogwash, calculated to make another century or two go by before we have any "permissible" estimates of the personal and public-health risks from ionizing radiation. In this book, we *are* going to use all the available data, imperfect as they are; we are going to make some reasonable approximations; and we are going to make some necessary assumptions where data are unavailable. We shall spell out explicitly what is assumption, approximation, and hard evidence.

A word about statistical tests and statistical significance is in order. Essentially all the data to be used have already been tested for statistical significance, which means it has been determined whether the association between radiation and cancer induction could have occurred simply by chance. And as we merge the evidence from all sources, the data base becomes much larger than for the individual studies, making chance alone a totally remote explanation of the findings.

We shall end up, in this book, with the ability to estimate the personal and public-health consequences of cancer induction by ionizing radiation based upon the evidence currently available. The true risk (if we could know it) may be twice or half as high as the best estimate we can make now. But our choice is some imperfect estimate or *no* estimate, and it will always be so. We will never have a "perfect" estimate because we will never perform perfectly controlled experiments on human beings.

Should any scientist be able to *prove* that the estimates presented here are in error, or that a better way of making the estimates is now available, such proof would be most welcome. Otherwise, our approach should be to make use of the estimates presented here, while we continue to evaluate new information on dosimetry, future data as irradiated people already under study are followed up for longer periods, and new information from epidemiologic studies not yet accomplished. Five years from now, and every five years thereafter, new evidence will undoubtedly allow for the replacement of some approximations by hard evidence, and of certain assumptions by data. The *methods* of this book will, however, remain valid.

DOSE RATE, FRACTIONATION, AND DOSE-RESPONSE RELATIONSHIPS

It is theoretically possible that delivering ionizing radiation rapidly may produce a greater (or lesser) incidence of cancer than delivering it slowly. It is theoretically possible that fractionation of the dose of radiation (giving it in split doses at intervals of time) may increase or decrease the incidence of cancer. The human evidence comes from various schedules of radiation administration. We shall, in all treatments in this discussion, assume that for a particular age, all that counts is the total quantity of radiation in rads that is delivered. This assumption is based on evidence that will be discussed in the next chapter and later chapters. But let it be clear how the data will be handled.

With respect to the dose-response relationship, it is theoretically possible that the number of cancers produced, for a particular age at irradiation, is directly proportional to the dose of radiation received, over a large range of doses, but it is also possible that some other relationship may operate over some part of the range of doses. We shall, in the treatment here, use direct proportionality, and defer to a later chapter (chapter 8) the large body of evidence that supports direct proportionality in the range of doses of interest to us. The question of the shape of the dose-response curve is best addressed once the reader is familiar with the various epidemiological sources of evidence.

In chapter 8, the author intends to prove that the old saw, "the linear hypothesis gives just an upper limit for the effects of radiation—the true effects are much smaller or zero," is simply in error. In general, it is a self-serving statement in support of industries involved in releasing radioactivity into the environment, and has no scientific basis in human evidence.

SOME KEY TERMS

The human evidence is treated with a jargon that needs to be understood. It is exceedingly simple to understand, once the various terms are explained and illustrations given of their use.

"Observed and Expected" Ratios and Percent Increases

The studies of human beings exposed to radiation are of several major types. With the first type, we are dealing with a sample of people exposed to radiation of an estimated dose plus a separate sample of people, otherwise *equivalent* (in the best studies), who have not received that supplemental radiation. So we have an *irradiated group* and a *control group* corresponding to Groups Y and Z in the "ideal" experiment of section 2 of this chapter. In such a study, we count the number of cancers in both groups during some specified follow-up period after irradiation, and learn the differences between groups. This situation is rather straightforward. A variation of this situation may be that we have the ability to divide the exposed group into subgroups, each subgroup characterized by having received a different average amount of radiation. This situation is also readily understood.

But there are some instances in which we do not have a well-matched, unexposed group for comparison with the irradiated group. A variety of techniques have been employed to compensate for this lack of a control group. Sometimes the siblings of the exposed individuals are used as a control group directly. Sometimes a group with the same disease as the irradiated group is available with similar ethnic and demographic features; such individuals, unirradiated, may be used by investigators as a control group. Matching is never perfect, but investigators do the best they can, and we must always be on guard to see that they have not introduced any confounding information by an inappropriate choice of control group.

Lastly we come to the situation in which a control group is not available for direct follow-up, and in this case the investigators may use the vital statistics of the region, or of a region as closely comparable as possible, to estimate how many cancers would be *expected* for a group of the same age and sex, without irradiation. This expected cancer rate is then compared with the cancer rate *observed* directly in the sample population that has received some specified radiation dose.

In most of the papers in the literature, the reporting scientist has already calculated such expected rates for us, and if we think he is a reliable investigator, we may accept his calculation. If we are skeptical, we can go to the original Vital Statistics source ourselves (see Bibliography) and check whether he did his homework correctly. How? Illustrating how we would do this will clarify what is done later in this chapter.

Let us imagine, for illustrative purposes, that 568 people, all age 26, were irradiated with 50 rads, and then observed for 15 years, post-irradiation (from age 26 through 41). Suppose, during the 15-year follow-up, that we *observe* a total of 25 cancer deaths in those irradiated persons. Are 25 cancer deaths more, less, or the same number we would *expect* to see in a comparable, unirradiated control group (for which we will use U.S. population between ages 26 and 41)?

The first step to answer this question, since the vital statistics are given in cancer deaths per 100,000 people per year, is to convert our 25 cases per 568 persons into the rate we would have observed had we irradiated 100,-000 persons of the same age with the same dose. We ask, 25 cancer deaths relates to 568 persons as how many caancer deaths (x) relates to 100,000 persons?

$$\frac{25 \text{ cancer deaths}}{568 \text{ persons}} = \frac{x \text{ cancer deaths}}{100,000 \text{ persons}}$$

So it is correct to say that the cancer *rate* we observed in the irradiated group is 4,401.4 cancer deaths/100,000 persons. Now the observed number and the expected number (which we will get from the vital statistics) will be in the same terms: cancer deaths per 100,000 persons. There is nothing magical about using 100,000 as the base number at risk. For other purposes, the reader will note that rates are expressed as number of cancers per 1,000 or per 1,000,000 people. All one has to do is be *consistent* in comparing the irradiated group with the control group, or with the expected value from vital statistics when no direct control group has been observed.

The next step in finding out how many cancers we would have expected in our sample even without irradiation would be to look up in vital statistics cancer deaths per 100,000 for persons of age 26, age 27, and so on through age 41. The *sum* of these rates for the 15 years would give the expected rate per 100,000 people for the follow-up period. Say the sum comes to 2,000 cancers per 100,000 people.

Now that we know both the observed and expected numbers of cancer deaths per 100,000 persons, we can express this relationship as a ratio:

$$\frac{\text{number of cancers observed}}{\text{number of cancers expected}} = \frac{4,401.4/100,000}{2,000/100,000} = 2.20$$

(The 100,000 values cancel each other out, so we are really dividing 4,401.4 by 2,000.)

Our "finding" in this illustration is that the irradiated group has a cancer *rate* which is 2.20 times the rate of the unirradiated group.

From this point on, we will abbreviate the ratio of observed to expected as *O/E*, for simplicity of notation. In our illustration, O/E is 2.20/1, or "2.20 to one." It is customary not to express a 1 in the denominator of a ratio, and that is why what may look like a simple number (2.20) can be a ratio.

It is often convenient in science, if magnitudes must be compared, arbitrarily to set a value of 1.0 (or 100%, or *unity*) on whatever will be used as the standard for comparison. Furthermore it is customary and useful to regard the rate in the control group (the expected value) as 100%, and to refer all values for the irradiated group to this 100% value, since the expected rate of cancer mortality is our standard for measuring the effect of radiation.

Therefore, since the cancer rate in the irradiated group is 2.20 times the rate in the control group, the latter *expressed in percent* is 220%. The *excess percent* due to irradiation is 120%.

Since this kind of presentation will be used again and again in this book, it is worth noting that the terms *% excess* and *% increase* are interchangeable.

In this book, we are going to treat most of the evidence in terms of *% increase* (or *excess*) in *cancer rate per rad.* That constitutes straightforward treatment of the data, and it implies no hypothesis, no theory. Whatever is the value observed for the number of excess cancers (O − E), it is *some* percentage of the spontaneous or control value. A little later, we will see the great simplifications and new insights made possible by treating the data in this manner.

Meanwhile, let us illustrate what is meant by *% excess per rad.* In the illustration we have just been considering, in which the dose was 50 rads, the *% excess per rad* would be:

$$\frac{120\%}{50 \text{ rads}} = \frac{2.4\%}{\text{rad}}$$

Now let us reflect upon this number, 2.4% per rad. It is valid as the overall *% excess cancer mortality rate per rad* only for the period between 26 and 41 years of age, since those are the only years covered by the follow-up in this limited experiment. But our *requirement,* if we are to evaluate the true impact of these 50 rads of radiation, is to know the % excess cancer mortality for every year of life for the remainder of the life-span of the sample.

After describing a few more terms used in the literature, we shall turn our attention, in section 4 of this chapter, to converting limited follow-up data into lifetime estimates.

Person-Years

In the hypothetical situation just described above, all persons who had been irradiated were followed up for 15 years, and they were all of the same age at irradiation. In many of the studies reported in the scientific literature, some individuals in a group are followed up for 5 years, others for 12 years, others for 17 years, etc. We need a technique for handling variable follow-up periods; we find one in the use of the term *person-years.*

This term means what it says: multiplication of the number of persons by the number of years of follow-up. If we have 12 persons, each followed up for 15 years, we have $12 \times 15 = 180$ person-years. (If the group consists only of women, we can write 180 woman-years, etc.) This term permits us to use the evidence for a group of individuals followed up for a varying number of years. Twelve persons followed up for 15 years (180 person-years) can be combined with 10 persons followed up for 20 years (200 person-years) to get a total number of person-years for the combined group: 380 person-years. If we want the average follow-up period, we simply divide the total person-years by the total persons: in this case, 380 person-years/22 persons = 17.27 years.

We will have numerous occasions to deal with person-years in the analysis of the literature.

Age-Specific Cancer Rates

The number of people who die of cancer out of every 100,000 depends on the age of those 100,000 people. These rates vary with age; they also vary from country to country even at the same age. And the change in cancer rate among specific cancers is not exactly the same with changing age.

Many fallacious statements are based on failure to take into account the *age-specific* rates of cancer death, which means the number of cancer deaths per 100,000 persons (of one sex) at a specified age. As an example, one might hear someone say that the death rate from cancer of some organ is going up in the United States each year. Yet when one looks at the age-specific cancer death rate, one finds that the statement is not true for that cancer, that is, the rate is not going up each year. The answer is that the population is changing in *average age* with time, and more people are reaching the age of high cancer rates. So while we may get a higher number of total cancer deaths per year, the age-specific cancer death rate may be the same.

In analyzing radiation induction of cancer, we shall use age-specific rates, since that is the correct way to handle the data. Furthermore, when appropriate, we shall distinguish between mortality rates and incidence rates. A mortality rate is a death rate, whereas an incidence (or morbidity) rate is the rate at which an illness is diagnosed.

SECTION 4: THE USE OF PEAK PERCENTS AND CONVERSION FACTORS

Earlier, we mentioned that incorrect analysis of the available studies has led to underestimates of the effect of radiation in the production of cancer. Failure to appreciate the importance of age at irradiation, which importance will be demonstrated in future chapters, is one factor in the underestimates.

The rest of this chapter deals with an additional, large source of error and confusion, namely, the failure to deal properly with the *shortness* of the follow-up periods of irradiated people and with the *variation* of the follow-up periods both in their duration and in the particular post-irradiation years studied. The shortness of most follow-up periods (fortunately, a few exceptions exist) has led directly to underestimates of radiation effect. The variation in follow-up periods has led to findings that cannot be compared with each other, or combined with each other for greater statistical significance and stability, or interpreted in any meaningful way.

The entire body of human epidemiological evidence is next to useless and even quite deceptive unless one converts the evidence to *a common base.* The method devised and proposed in this chapter, of converting all values to *peak percent excess cancer mortality rate per rad,* provides a common base. Before explaining peak percent increase (or excess) per rad, and the conversion factors required to obtain such peak percents, we will simply illustrate their use; the reader is assured that explanations will follow.

Illustration

Suppose two studies (called Studies A and B) were reported of 10,000 male children who had been equally irradiated, say, with 17 rads each, at age 10 years. It does not matter whether these studies were of two different sets of irradiated children, or of the same set of irradiated children.

Suppose Study A included a follow-up from the time of irradiation out through the fourteenth year post-irradiation. Suppose Study B included a follow-up from the beginning of the sixth post-irradiation year through the twentieth post-irradiation year. Studies A and B both represent 15 years of follow-up. Can the value for the observed percent excess cancer rate per rad reported in Study A be directly compared with the observed percent excess cancer rate per rad from Study B?

The answer is that a very serious error would be made by assuming that one can compare the observed values directly. Suppose Study A reported a value of 1% excess cancer rate per rad, and Study B reported a value of 4% excess cancer rate per rad. In many papers in the professional literature, the authors blithely treat the findings as if Study B were showing four times the cancer effect from radiation as was Study A. This is grossly erroneous. These two studies would give precisely the *same* cancer effect per rad if they were converted to a common base (peak percent excess cancer rate per rad) by the use of appropriate conversion factors.

Let us turn to table 2 for our conversion factors. Table 2, which will be used repeatedly in subsequent chapters, provides separate sets of conversion factors for various ages at irradiation. We go to the one, in this case, for irradiation at 10 years of age.

For Study A, we look up the conversion factor for follow-up from the time of irradiation out through the fourteenth year post-irradiation, and find the factor to be 30.8. What do we do with this factor? We take the *observed* percent excess cancer rate per rad of Study A (which may be precisely 0.98%) and multiply it by the conversion factor (which is 30.8) to get the *peak percent increase* (or *excess*) *cancer rate per rad,* which turns out to be 30.2%.

For Study B, we look up the conversion factor for follow-up time from the sixth year post-irradiation through the twentieth year, and we find the factor to be 7.5. Then we take the observed percent excess per rad of Study B (which may be precisely 4.04%) and multiply it by the conversion factor (which is 7.5), to get the peak percent excess cancer rate per rad, which turns out to be 30.3%.

Let us tabulate findings from these two hypothetical studies, plus a third one which will be discussed later. These findings are in table 1.

Throughout the remainder of this book, as we analyze the *real* human epidemiological evidence on radiation effects, we shall use the tables of conversion factors to obtain a common base, which is the peak percent increase (or excess) in the cancer *death* rate per rad. If we are dealing with cancer *incidence* rates, in both the irradiated and the control groups, we will obtain the peak percent increase (or excess) in the cancer incidence rate per rad.

In the following sections, it will be shown why failure to convert findings from limited follow-up periods to a common base leads to nonsensical errors in assessing and predicting the effects of radiation exposure.

DIVERGING CURVES: OBSERVED VERSUS EXPECTED

In the illustration just provided, why was the observed percent excess per rad so much higher in the 15-year follow-up between the sixth year and the end of the twentieth year post-irradiation, than it was in the 15-year follow-up starting immediately after irradiation and finishing at the end of the fourteenth year post-irradiation?

The main reason is that radiation-induced cancers neither appear nor kill people immediately after irradiation—the latent period was discussed early in this chapter. It takes about 10 years, after the irradiation of a group of people, before excess mortality from solid cancers can be detected—and it may take longer to detect if the irradiated group is small in numbers.

We shall, for almost every purpose in the remaining sections of this book, separate the consideration of leukemias from the consideration of solid cancers and solid tumors. The evidence itself indicates that many of the time parameters for leukemias are quite different from those for solid cancers as a class. In the present discussion, we will deal with solid cancers, leaving the leukemias for later analysis.

Excess cancer mortality, which is barely detectable 10 years post-irradiation, increases gradually in the eleventh, twelfth, and subsequent post-irradiation years, as illustrated in figures 2a and 2b. Let the curve in figure 2a describe the age-specific cancer mortality rate for a control group of children who grow up without irradiation (except for natural background irradiation). In figure 2b we repeat the curve and add another curve, describing the gradually rising age-specific cancer mortality rate which is observed in our hypothetical group (Studies A and B), which received 17 rads at 10 years of age. This second curve (the *observed curve*) does not even start

TABLE 1: ILLUSTRATIVE USE OF CONVERSION FACTORS IN RADIATION STUDIES

	STUDY A	STUDY B	STUDY C
	Follow-up from irradiation through 14th post-irradiation year	*Follow-up from the 6th through the 20th post-irradiation years*	*Follow-up from the 23rd through the 33rd post-irradiation years*
	(15 follow-up years)	*(15 follow-up years)*	*(11 follow-up years)*
E = total number of cancer cases expected (counted in control group)	12	16	46
O = total number of cancer cases observed in the irradiated group	14	27	212
Observed % excess $\left(\dfrac{O-E}{E}\right) \times 100\%$	$\dfrac{2}{12} \times 100\% = 16.67\%$	$\dfrac{11}{16} \times 100\% = 68.75\%$	$\dfrac{166}{46} \times 100\% = 360.8\%$
Observed % excess per rad	$\dfrac{16.67\%}{17 \text{ rads}} = 0.98\%/\text{rad}$	$\dfrac{68.75\%}{17 \text{ rads}} = 4.04\%/\text{rad}$	$\dfrac{360.8\%}{17 \text{ rads}} = 21.2\%/\text{rad}$
Conversion factor	30.8	7.5	1.43
Peak percent excess cancer rate per rad	30.2% per rad	30.3% per rad	30.3% per rad

*For explanation of Study C, see the later section titled "When Does the O/E Value Reach Its Peak in Human Beings?"

to diverge from the curve of unirradiated children (the *expected curve*) until the irradiated group reaches the age of 20 years.

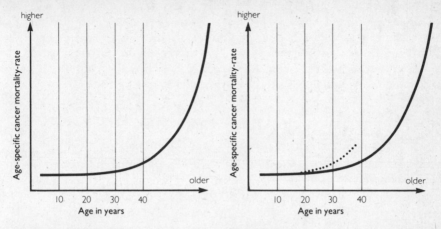

Figure 2a   Figure 2b

Since the number of cancers observed in the irradiated group includes those which would have occurred without irradiation *plus* the excess cases caused by the radiation, it is evident that the age-specific rate of cancer deaths in the irradiated group will be higher, age for age, than the comparison value for the unirradiated control population, after the minimal latent period is past.

Now, Study A presented the total number of cancers seen in the unirradiated control group as it was followed for 15 years, from the beginning of the tenth year of age through the end of the twenty-fourth year of age, and also the total number of cancers observed in the irradiated group for that same time-span. We get the excess number of cancers by subtracting the total expected (by counting the cancers in the control group) from the total observed in the irradiated group: O − E. If we then divide the excess by the expected, (O − E)/E, we have the ratio of excess to expected, which, multiplied by 100%, gives the observed percent excess (see table 1).

But, from the curves in figure 2b, we know that for 10 of the 15 years of follow-up, there was *no* excess. So, in effect, in Study A only 5 years of excess are being divided by 15 years of expected, to get the % excess. However, in Study B—which covered the period from the sixth year through the twentieth year post-irradiation—10 years of 15 show an excess. Therefore, *the excess percent per rad* is "found" to be higher in Study B than in Study A. The disparity is the result of the total excess in Study A being more seriously "diluted" by the latency period than is the total excess in Study B.

There is an additional and important reason for the disparity. In Study A, by the last year of the follow-up (by the end of the fourteenth year post-irradiation), the observed curve in figure 2b had just *begun* diverging from the expected curve. In Study B, by the last year of the follow-up (at the end of 20 years post-irradiation), there is good evidence that the distance between the two curves (and therefore, the excess cancers) has been continuously growing every year since the curves first diverged. Therefore, the value for the excess (which is O minus E) is greater in the twentieth year post-irradiation, and consequently, *it should not surprise us* that the effect of radiation per rad seems greater in Study B than in Study A! In fact, (O − E) can be shown, in this period, to have increased *faster* than E itself.

What is the evidence that the distance between the two curves keeps increasing more and more after the minimal latent period?

POST-IRRADIATION BEHAVIOR OF THE O/E RATIO

In every report that is capable of addressing the issue (namely, how long the % excess cancer continues to increase after irradiation), it has been found that the curve for the irradiated group is still diverging from that for the control group even out to periods of 20 to 35 years (to an average of 27.5 years) post-irradiation, for different kinds of cancers, and for groups in different parts of the world. The O/E ratio is still increasing out to at least 27.5 years post-irradiation. This is for solid cancers, not for leukemia.

All the major studies of the human evidence on radiation-induction of cancer in which the follow-up periods are long enough to be significant indicate that the O/E ratio may peak anywhere from 20 to more than 40 years post-irradiation, with most of the evidence concentrating at the high end of that range.

When Does the O/E Value Reach Its Peak in Human Beings?

From the evidence available, it seems reasonable to conclude that 30 years is certainly too short a post-irradiation period for the O/E ratio to have reached its highest, or peak value. Some of the data suggest it may be leveling off somewhere in the neighborhood of 40 years after irradiation, although the leveling off might be at 35 years, 45 years, or never.

With respect to our illustrative studies A and B, where 15-year follow-ups of irradiated people produced different "findings," the important point to grasp is this:

The fact that the O/E ratio is *increasing* for so many years post-irradiation *accounts* for the fact that two studies produced different results, when the follow-up period of one is mostly for years when the irradiated curve is far above the control curve, and the follow-up period of the other is mostly for years when the curve for those irradiated has barely diverged from the control curve.

The reader can see the importance of the follow-up effect most strikingly now by considering a third hypothetical study, which we will call Study C, in which the same group of 10,000 irradiated boys as were followed in Studies A and B, are followed from the start of the twenty-third through the end of the thirty-third year post-irradiation. *Because, in those post-irradiation years, the O/E ratios are higher than they were in Studies A and B*, the % excess cancer rate per rad revealed in Study C appears to be 21 times higher than revealed in Study A, and 5 times higher than revealed in Study B (see table 1). However, the reader can see that all three studies are really revealing the *same* story when the findings are converted to a common base, namely, to the peak percent increase in cancer rate per rad.

How Does the O/E Ratio Behave Beyond 40 Years Post-irradiation?

As we pointed out early in the chapter, when we described an *ideal* experiment, we need to assess the full cancer consequences of irradiation. We have shown above that some existing studies tell us about the crucial O/E ratio out to about 30–40 years post-irradiation, which is far from the full lifetimes of people irradiated as infants, children, adolescents, and young adults. So in the absence of data beyond 40 years post-irradiation, we need a reasonable estimate of what is going to happen to the O/E ratio.

In the early, extensive development of this method, generally known as the *relative risk* method, Gofman and Tamplin (1971) simply assumed a single value for O/E beyond 15 years post-irradiation. The BEIR Committee (1972) followed with a similar assumption. In this book we can now do much better.

It is possible from the human evidence now available to see (as we did earlier in this chapter) that the O/E ratio increases gradually, by degrees, every year after the minimal latent period, and that the *rate* at which it increases appears to slow down after 30 years post-irradiation, O/E probably reaching its highest or peak value at 40 years post-irradiation.

Then what? Does the O/E ratio stay the same? Since there are no adequate follow-up studies for solid tumors for longer than 40 years post-irradiation (we cannot use the radium-dial painters for reasons to be explained in chapter 9), the author has considered the evidence from radiation-induced leukemias, which start to appear much earlier than solid tumors after irradiation. The O/E ratio for leukemia seems to reach a peak at 10–15 years post-irradiation, and then it declines. The author feels it is reasonable to expect that the solid cancers will behave as leukemia does, but over a markedly extended time-frame.

The author will handle the solid-tumor data from various human series (studies) by using 40 years after irradiation as the time the peak O/E ratio is reached, and by assuming that the O/E value will start to decline thereafter in a manner symmetrical with its rise during the period 0 to 40 years post-irradiation. Bone sarcoma (see chapter 9) appears to be an exception among solid tumors; it has time-frames more like leukemia than like the other solid cancers.

To assume a declining O/E ratio after 40 years post-irradiation will be to *underestimate* the cancer risk of radiation if the true value does not decline, particularly for those who are young at the time of irradiation. However, a decline instead of a plateau does seem the most reasonable assumption in the absence of data, if one takes the shape of the O/E curve of leukemia into account.

It is useful for the reader to realize that, when the ratio of observed to expected cancers is still increasing in the 30–40-year period after irradiation, it means that the radiation effect is growing even more rapidly than the spontaneous cancer rate—which is itself growing with advancing age until about 70 years of age. The only way for O/E to keep rising is for the radiation-induced cancers to increase at a rate faster than the increase in the spontaneous rate.

And it follows that if O/E reaches a peak at 40 years post-irradiation, so does the % excess cancer mortality rate per rad reach a peak at 40 years.

Now, if the reader thinks back to table 1, he will realize what the peak percent excess cancer rate per rad means. It is the highest percent increase in cancer mortality per rad, and it is assumed to occur in about the fortieth year post-irradiation.

It is important to realize that *peaking* of the O/E ratio and of the % excess cancer rate per rad at 40 years after irradiation, does *not* mean that after 40 years, no excess cancers will occur. It means the O/E ratio will be declining, but that observed cancers will still exceed expected cancers; the irradiated people will still have a higher cancer rate than the unirradiated people. As pointed out before, this is an assumption based on real observations of radiation-induced leukemias; it is possible that the O/E ratio for solid tumors will *never* decline from its peak value. It is also possible that it will plunge from its peak in an asymmetrical fashion.

THE BASIS FOR THE CONVERSION FACTORS

Plotted in figure 3 is a curve that describes all the features just discussed of the post-irradiation behavior of the O/E ratio, and therefore, of the % excess cancer rate per rad values:

No excess mortality during the first 9 years after irradiation

The peak percent excess cancer rate per rad in the fortieth year post-irradiation

A decline in the % excess per rad after the 40th post-irradiation year

The upward side represents an approximation based on existing tumor data, and the downward side represents an assumption based upon the existing leukemia data, with an extended time-frame for solid cancers.

Since this curve provides the basis for deriving the *conversion factors*, which will enable us to convert findings from follow-up studies of varying durations and years to a common base, it is worthwhile to discuss the curve more fully.

Someone may well say, "How do you know that this is the exact curve for every type of human cancer?" The answer is that we do not know this to be the exact curve for every type of human cancer. In 30 to 40 years, we will know a lot more about minor variations from this curve as a result of follow-up studies of longer duration for many different cancers. For now, this curve is an exceedingly reasonable approximation derived from valid human evidence that we have in hand right now, and that is why it makes good sense to use it.

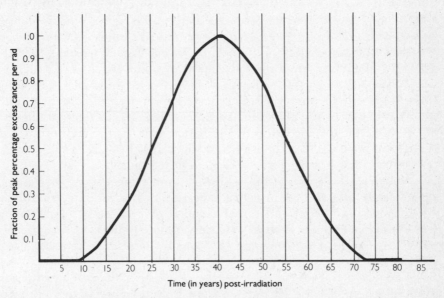

Figure 3: **The Follow-up Conversion Curve.** *This curve provides the fraction of the peak percentage excess per rad for successive years following irradiation.*

Is the Curve of Figure 3 Applicable to All Ages?

The cautious reader will certainly be asking himself whether the follow-up conversion curve of figure 3 can be applied no matter at what age the irradiation occurred. It certainly can. It was developed from human data extending from irradiations at infancy to irradiations at 25–30 years of age, and with some follow-ups out to age 60 and beyond. There is every reason to use the same curve for all ages at irradiation, until someone can prove it should be modified for certain ages.

If anything, the curve will *underestimate* the risk, since it says that O/E will be falling by the time irradiated infants and children reach the older ages at which their spontaneous cancer rates will be increasing.

The reader must realize that, because infants and children are much more sensitive than adults to radiation injury (chapter 6), age at irradiation has an enormous effect on the % excess cancer rate per rad, and therefore also on the *peak* percent excess per rad. Nevertheless, the follow-up conversion curve is independent of age at irradiation because it is depicting something else, namely, *when* the excess cancer mortality occurs in the post-irradiation years, *not how big* the excess mortality rate will be.

The author doubts that application of figure 3 to all ages will mislead us in our estimate of the personal and public-health risks of radiation.

Reading off the Follow-up Conversion Curve

In figure 3, the peak percent excess per rad occurs at 40 years post-irradiation, and it is given no specific value. Instead, in this curve, it is set at 100%, or 1.0, because the peak percent excess per rad is serving as the *standard* against which values for % excess per rad from all studies will be evaluated.

Since 1.0 stands for the highest % excess cancer mortality per rad, occurring in the fortieth post-irradiation year, values for the excess at other post-irradiation years will be fractions of that peak value of 1.0. From the curve, we see that, whatever value the % excess per rad may carry in the twenty-fifth year post-irradiation, that value will always be 0.50 (or one-half) of the value for the fortieth post-irradiation year. In the eighteenth post-irradiation year, the % excess per rad will always be 0.22 (or the fraction 22/100) of what it will be in the fortieth post-irradiation year.

Thus, when we accept the follow-up conversion curve as a *reasonable approximation* of what all post-irradiation follow-up studies would show about the changing O/E ratios, if the studies were carried on long enough and were large enough, then we can use the curve to find out what the peak percent excess is, if we know the % excess for any single post-irradiation year.

For example, if we are told that the % excess in the seventeenth post-irradiation year is 15% per rad, we know from the curve that 15% excess in the seventeenth post-irradiation year is 0.20 (or one-fifth) of the peak percent excess. So what will the peak percent excess be? Let p = the peak percent excess per rad.

$$15\% \text{ excess per rad} = 0.20 \text{ p, or p} = \frac{15\%}{0.20} = 75\% \text{ excess per rad}$$

This is the peak percent excess per rad. It is the common base we need to compare and make sense of the existing studies.

The curve also enables us to find out what the peak percent excess (the common base) is if we know the % excess reported for a particular group of follow-up years. For if the % excess reported in *single* post-irradiation years bears a fixed relationship to the peak percent excess, then the % excess for a particular *group* of post-irradiation years must also bear a fixed relationship to the peak percent excess. That relationship cannot be read directly off the curve; it must be calculated, and it is expressed by a *conversion factor*.

The conversion factor can be defined by the following equation:

$$conversion\ factor = \frac{\text{peak percent excess cancer mortality per rad}}{\text{\% excess per rad in the limited follow-up period}}$$

With a little reflection, the reader will realize that each different combination of post-irradiation follow-up years will have to have its own special conversion factor, since it has its own special, fixed relationship with the peak of the follow-up conversion curve. It is a laborious process indeed to obtain all the conversion factors needed to handle the variety of follow-up studies in the literature. The author has done that job for the reader: huge numbers of conversion factors are provided in table 2.

The reader may well ask why we must consider the way *groups* of post-irradiation years relate to the fortieth year, instead of reading the fractions for *single* post-irradiation years directly off the curve. The reason is this: the follow-up studies in the literature do not provide information in terms of single years, and even if they did, the information would be statistically unstable because of the small numbers involved. The fluctuations of pure chance cancel each other out when large numbers are dealt with, but these fluctuations can remain when only small numbers are involved. This is commonly referred to in science as "the small numbers problem."

Therefore, with only a few exceptions, the follow-up studies of irradiated human beings lump together the total excess cancers observed in the irradiated group during *all* the years of follow-up combined, and they lump together the total cancers observed in the control group during all the years of the follow-up combined. That way, the investigators can get larger and more statistically significant results. Typical studies report the same sorts of findings that we illustrated earlier in this chapter with Studies A, B, and C: *total* number of cancers expected during the entire follow-up. As Study A illustrates, even in a very large study (10,000 boys irradiated), only 14 cancers might have been observed during a follow-up extending for 15 years, starting immediately after irradiation. It is only in Study C that the numbers are appreciable, and there are mighty few instances in which 10,000 irradiated people were tracked down and studied 23–33 years after irradiation.

So that is why we have to deal with groups of post-irradiation years instead of single years, as we convert values for % excess per rad from various follow-up years and durations of years into a common base: the peak percent excess per rad.

Employing conversion factors involves accepting one additional approximation: that the age-specific cancer mortality rate trend of the whole population is not very different from the age-specific cancer mortality rate trend of control groups. This is a completely reasonable assumption. In any specific study where it can be shown that the control group has a very special set of age-specific cancer mortality rates, the conversion factor can be adjusted accordingly.

Trends in the Conversion Factor Tables

The reader who looks at any part of table 2 (the conversion factors) will see a trend he should have expected. Since the conversion factor = peak percent excess per rad/% excess per rad in limited follow-up, and since he knows from earlier discussion that the *% excess per rad* in follow-up studies is far smaller near the time of irradiation than near the fortieth

TABLE 2: CONVERSION FACTORS FROM LIMITED FOLLOW-UP PERIOD TO PEAK PERCENT PER RAD

Age = 0 Years at Irradiation

Beginning of Year Follow-up Starts (post-irradiation)	Year-End of End of Follow-up Period																			
	14th	15th	16th	17th	18th	19th	20th	21st	22nd	23rd	24th	25th	26th	27th	28th	29th	30th	31st	32nd	33rd
1	43.7	35.0	26.5	19.0	15.7	12.8	11.4	10.0	8.6	7.3	6.05	5.4	4.8	4.2	3.8	3.54	3.23	2.95	2.69	2.48
2	40.0	32.0	24.8	18.2	14.9	12.1	10.6	9.2	8.0	6.9	5.81	5.2	4.6	4.1	3.7	3.45	3.17	2.92	2.67	2.44
3	37.0	29.7	23.6	17.5	14.2	11.4	9.9	8.6	7.4	6.5	5.6	5.0	4.5	4.0	3.65	3.35	3.08	2.85	2.62	2.41
4	33.8	27.2	22.1	16.6	13.4	10.7	9.3	8.0	6.9	6.1	5.36	4.8	4.3	3.9	3.59	3.26	3.02	2.80	2.58	2.37
5	30.6	24.7	20.2	16.0	12.8	10.1	8.7	7.4	6.4	5.8	5.12	4.6	4.1	3.8	3.47	3.15	2.92	2.71	2.50	2.32
6	27.6	22.3	18.7	14.5	11.3	9.5	8.2	7.0	6.1	5.5	4.92	4.5	4.0	3.7	3.40	3.05	2.85	2.65	2.45	2.28
7	24.8	20.3	17.3	13.7	10.2	8.8	7.7	6.7	5.9	5.2	4.71	4.33	3.91	3.59	3.30	2.97	2.78	2.59	2.41	2.22
8	22.0	18.2	15.6	12.5	9.4	8.3	7.2	6.3	5.5	5.0	4.53	4.17	3.77	3.47	3.19	2.89	2.70	2.51	2.33	2.19
9	19.2	16.1	13.8	11.2	8.5	7.7	6.7	5.9	5.2	4.8	4.34	3.99	3.65	3.37	3.10	2.82	2.64	2.46	2.29	2.14
10	16.5	14.0	12.2	10.1	7.8	7.2	6.3	5.7	5.0	4.5	4.14	3.81	3.52	3.25	2.99	2.73	2.55	2.37	2.20	2.08
11	14.1	12.1	10.5	8.8	7.2	6.7	5.9	5.4	4.8	4.3	3.98	3.68	3.40	3.15	2.90	2.65	2.48	2.30	2.15	2.03
12	12.2	10.2	9.0	7.7	6.5	6.3	5.6	5.2	4.7	4.11	3.82	3.55	3.27	3.03	2.80	2.58	2.42	2.26	2.11	1.99
13						5.9	5.3	4.9	4.45	3.94	3.68	3.45	3.16	2.93	2.71	2.52	2.36	2.21	2.07	1.95
14						5.5	5.0	4.6	4.16	3.79	3.54	3.33	3.05	2.83	2.62	2.45	2.30	2.16	2.02	1.91
15						5.2	4.8	4.4	4.00	3.65	3.41	3.23	2.94	2.73	2.52	2.37	2.22	2.09	1.98	1.87
16						4.8	4.5	4.14	3.80	3.50	3.28	3.13	2.83	2.63	2.44	2.30	2.17	2.05	1.93	1.82
17											3.13	2.97	2.72	2.53	2.35	2.23	2.11	2.00	1.89	1.78
18											2.99	2.83	2.61	2.44	2.28	2.16	2.05	1.95	1.85	1.75
19											2.83	2.68	2.48	2.33	2.19	2.08	1.98	1.88	1.79	1.71
20											2.70	2.55	2.40	2.26	2.13	2.02	1.92	1.82	1.73	1.66
21											2.58	2.43	2.29	2.17	2.05	1.95	1.86	1.77	1.69	1.62
22																1.88	1.79	1.71	1.63	1.57
23																1.83	1.75	1.67	1.59	1.53
24																1.77	1.69	1.62	1.55	1.50
25																1.71	1.63	1.56	1.49	1.44
26																1.64	1.57	1.51	1.44	1.40

AGE = 10 YEARS AT IRRADIATION

Year-End of End of Follow-up Period

Beginning of Year Follow-up Starts (post-irradiation)	14th	15th	16th	17th	18th	19th	20th	21st	22nd	23rd	24th	25th	26th	27th	28th	29th	30th	31st	32nd	33rd
1	30.8	25.5	20.0	15.2	12.3	10.4	9.0	8.0	6.9	5.9	5.02	4.5	4.0	3.5	3.2	2.76	2.6	2.4	2.2	2.0
2	29.3	24.3	19.1	14.4	11.8	10.1	8.8	7.8	6.75	5.81	4.92	4.40	3.94	3.45	3.14	2.72	2.53	2.31	2.08	1.93
3	27.8	23.1	18.2	13.7	11.4	9.8	8.5	7.57	6.55	5.63	4.80	4.29	3.84	3.36	3.04	2.68	2.47	2.24	2.05	1.91
4	26.2	21.7	17.1	12.9	10.9	9.4	8.2	7.30	6.31	5.43	4.70	4.20	3.76	3.29	2.93	2.64	2.40	2.16	2.02	1.89
5	24.4	20.3	16.0	12.0	10.3	9.0	7.9	7.00	6.10	5.30	4.59	4.10	3.70	3.25	2.87	2.62	2.35	2.10	2.00	1.87
6	22.5	18.9	15.1	11.6	10.0	8.6	7.5	6.65	5.85	5.08	4.44	3.98	3.61	3.21	2.86	2.57	2.34	2.09	1.96	1.84
7	20.3	17.3	14.1	11.3	9.7	8.2	7.2	6.38	5.68	5.00	4.32	3.88	3.52	3.17	2.85	2.53	2.33	2.08	1.95	1.82
8	18.1	15.6	12.9	10.7	9.2	7.7	6.8	6.02	5.36	4.74	4.18	3.75	3.40	3.06	2.83	2.47	2.30	2.07	1.93	1.80
9	15.9	13.8	11.7	10.1	8.7	7.3	6.4	5.67	5.16	4.57	4.03	3.61	3.27	2.98	2.80	2.43	2.28	2.06	1.92	1.79
10	13.8	12.2	10.5	9.1	7.8	6.7	6.0	5.30	4.85	4.30	3.88	3.50	3.20	2.95	2.75	2.38	2.25	2.05	1.90	1.77
11	11.8	10.8	9.3	8.3	6.8	6.4	5.7	5.07	4.62	4.11	3.73	3.39	3.12	2.87	2.65	2.33	2.18	1.98	1.84	1.73
12	9.7	9.4	8.2	7.3	6.3	6.0	5.4	4.77	4.35	3.87	3.59	3.30	3.04	2.80	2.59	2.27	2.12	1.95	1.81	1.71
13						5.6	5.1	4.62	4.21	3.81	3.43	3.16	2.91	2.68	2.48	2.22	2.08	1.92	1.79	1.69
14						5.2	4.8	4.35	3.97	3.61	3.29	3.04	2.80	2.58	2.39	2.16	2.02	1.88	1.75	1.66
15						4.8	4.4	4.06	3.70	3.40	3.15	2.93	2.72	2.50	2.30	2.11	1.96	1.83	1.70	1.62
16											3.04	2.84	2.65	2.45	2.27	2.06	1.93	1.81	1.68	1.60
17											2.91	2.72	2.54	2.36	2.19	2.01	1.88	1.77	1.66	1.58
18											2.78	2.60	2.42	2.25	2.08	1.96	1.84	1.73	1.63	1.56
19											2.65	2.48	2.31	2.16	2.00	1.91	1.79	1.70	1.61	1.54
20											2.54	2.38	2.23	2.09	1.95	1.86	1.76	1.68	1.60	1.52
21																1.81	1.72	1.65	1.58	1.50
22																1.76	1.68	1.61	1.53	1.46
23																1.71	1.63	1.56	1.48	1.43
24																1.66	1.58	1.51	1.45	1.40
25																1.62	1.55	1.49	1.43	1.38

Note: Most follow-ups have started by the tenth year post-irradiation. If any values are desired that are not in this table, they can be obtained by extrapolation to a very good approximation.

TABLE 2: CONTINUED

AGE = 20 YEARS AT IRRADIATION

Year-End of End of Follow-up Period

Beginning of Year Follow-up Year Starts (post-irradiation)	14th	15th	16th	17th	18th	19th	20th	21st	22nd	23rd	24th	25th	26th	27th	28th	29th	30th	31st	32nd	33rd
1	28.3	22.4	17.9	14.3	10.7	8.5	7.3	6.3	5.5	4.7	4.0	3.50	3.10	2.85	2.55	2.36	2.16	2.00	1.88	1.75
2	26.8	21.4	17.3	13.8	10.5	8.25	7.10	6.07	5.31	4.54	3.95	3.48	3.10	2.84	2.55	2.34	2.14	1.99	1.87	1.75
3	25.3	20.5	16.5	13.2	10.2	8.00	6.88	5.88	5.14	4.43	3.89	3.46	3.10	2.83	2.55	2.32	2.12	1.98	1.86	1.74
4	23.9	19.6	15.8	12.6	9.8	7.75	6.67	5.70	4.94	4.33	3.83	3.43	3.10	2.82	2.55	2.30	2.11	1.97	1.85	1.74
5	22.4	18.7	15.1	12.0	9.5	7.56	6.50	5.50	4.75	4.20	3.78	3.41	3.10	2.82	2.55	2.29	2.09	1.96	1.84	1.73
6	20.7	17.3	14.4	11.5	9.2	7.30	6.28	5.30	4.61	4.12	3.71	3.35	3.04	2.76	2.52	2.26	2.07	1.94	1.83	1.72
7	19.1	16.0	13.4	11.0	8.9	7.05	6.06	5.11	4.48	4.04	3.64	3.29	2.98	2.71	2.49	2.24	2.06	1.93	1.82	1.71
8	17.4	14.6	12.4	10.4	8.6	6.75	5.81	4.92	4.35	3.95	3.56	3.23	2.92	2.65	2.45	2.22	2.04	1.91	1.81	1.70
9	15.3	12.8	11.0	9.5	8.0	6.40	5.50	4.74	4.21	3.86	3.48	3.16	2.86	2.60	2.41	2.20	2.02	1.89	1.80	1.68
10	13.2	11.1	9.7	8.5	7.2	6.09	5.25	4.60	4.10	3.80	3.41	3.10	2.80	2.55	2.38	2.17	2.00	1.88	1.79	1.67
11						5.85	5.09	4.48	4.00	3.70	3.33	3.03	2.74	2.51	2.34	2.15	1.98	1.86	1.78	1.66
12						5.60	4.93	4.32	3.89	3.60	3.25	2.96	2.68	2.47	2.30	2.12	1.97	1.85	1.76	1.65
13						5.35	4.76	4.16	3.78	3.50	3.17	2.89	2.62	2.43	2.26	2.09	1.96	1.84	1.75	1.64
14						5.00	4.50	4.00	3.67	3.40	3.08	2.83	2.57	2.38	2.22	2.06	1.95	1.82	1.73	1.63
15						4.72	4.34	3.90	3.57	3.30	3.00	2.76	2.51	2.34	2.18	2.04	1.93	1.81	1.72	1.62
16											2.91	2.68	2.45	2.29	2.13	2.00	1.89	1.78	1.69	1.60
17											2.82	2.60	2.39	2.24	2.09	1.96	1.85	1.75	1.66	1.58
18											2.72	2.52	2.33	2.18	2.04	1.92	1.81	1.72	1.63	1.55
19											2.62	2.44	2.27	2.13	1.99	1.88	1.77	1.69	1.60	1.53
20											2.52	2.35	2.21	2.08	1.95	1.85	1.74	1.66	1.57	1.49
21																1.81	1.70	1.62	1.54	1.48
22																1.77	1.68	1.60	1.52	1.46
23																1.72	1.65	1.58	1.51	1.44
24																1.67	1.62	1.55	1.49	1.42
25																1.63	1.58	1.52	1.47	1.40

AGE = 30 YEARS AT IRRADIATION

Year-End of End of Follow-up Period

Beginning of Year Follow-up Starts (post-irradiation)	14th	15th	16th	17th	18th	19th	20th	21st	22nd	23rd	24th	25th	26th	27th	28th	29th	30th	31st	32nd	33rd
1	22.6	18.0	15.1	12.2	9.7	7.58	6.60	5.55	4.80	4.35	3.88	3.55	3.20	2.87	2.59	2.38	2.20	2.03	1.91	1.80
2	21.9	17.5	14.7	11.9	9.5	7.48	6.47	5.49	4.75	4.31	3.83	3.53	3.18	2.86	2.58	2.37	2.20	2.03	1.91	1.80
3	21.2	17.0	14.3	11.6	9.3	7.35	6.36	5.41	4.72	4.28	3.80	3.50	3.16	2.85	2.57	2.36	2.19	2.04	1.91	1.80
4	20.4	16.3	13.7	11.3	9.2	7.23	6.25	5.34	4.71	4.26	3.78	3.47	3.14	2.83	2.56	2.35	2.19	2.04	1.91	1.79
5	19.6	15.7	13.2	11.0	8.9	7.10	6.10	5.27	4.70	4.25	3.76	3.44	3.12	2.82	2.55	2.34	2.18	2.04	1.91	1.79
6	18.7	14.9	12.5	10.4	8.5	6.90	6.00	5.14	4.49	4.10	3.69	3.35	3.07	2.79	2.53	2.32	2.16	2.03	1.89	1.77
7	17.5	14.2	12.1	10.1	8.4	6.70	5.83	5.07	4.37	3.99	3.63	3.29	3.02	2.76	2.51	2.30	2.14	2.02	1.87	1.76
8	16.2	13.2	11.4	9.6	8.0	6.48	5.64	5.00	4.27	3.90	3.58	3.25	2.97	2.73	2.48	2.29	2.12	2.01	1.86	1.75
9	14.4	12.0	10.4	8.8	7.5	6.26	5.51	4.96	4.16	3.80	3.52	3.19	2.92	2.68	2.45	2.27	2.10	1.99	1.85	1.73
10	12.9	10.8	9.4	8.0	7.0	6.04	5.35	4.93	4.10	3.75	3.47	3.13	2.88	2.65	2.43	2.25	2.09	1.96	1.84	1.72
11						5.80	5.16	4.76	4.03	3.66	3.40	3.09	2.82	2.59	2.38	2.22	2.07	1.94	1.82	1.70
12						5.53	4.98	4.57	3.94	3.58	3.33	3.03	2.76	2.54	2.33	2.19	2.04	1.91	1.80	1.68
13						5.28	4.78	4.37	3.83	3.48	3.24	2.95	2.70	2.48	2.28	2.15	2.02	1.89	1.78	1.67
14						5.03	4.58	4.18	3.73	3.39	3.15	2.87	2.64	2.42	2.24	2.12	1.98	1.86	1.75	1.66
15						4.74	4.33	3.98	3.60	3.28	3.06	2.81	2.58	2.37	2.20	2.09	1.96	1.84	1.73	1.65
16											2.97	2.76	2.51	2.31	2.16	2.05	1.93	1.81	1.71	1.63
17											2.88	2.68	2.44	2.26	2.12	2.01	1.90	1.79	1.69	1.61
18											2.76	2.57	2.37	2.21	2.08	1.97	1.87	1.76	1.66	1.59
19											2.66	2.47	2.31	2.15	2.04	1.93	1.83	1.73	1.64	1.57
20											2.54	2.38	2.24	2.10	2.00	1.88	1.80	1.70	1.63	1.55
21																1.83	1.75	1.66	1.60	1.52
22																1.78	1.70	1.62	1.57	1.49
23																1.73	1.65	1.58	1.53	1.46
24																1.68	1.61	1.54	1.49	1.43
25																1.63	1.57	1.51	1.46	1.40

TABLE 2: CONTINUED

AGE = 40 YEARS AT IRRADIATION

Beginning of Year Follow-up Starts (post-irradiation)	Year-End of End of Follow-up Period																			
	14th	15th	16th	17th	18th	19th	20th	21st	22nd	23rd	24th	25th	26th	27th	28th	29th	30th	31st	32nd	33rd
1	24.0	20.2	16.5	13.3	10.3	8.1	7.00	6.30	5.50	4.80	4.15	3.70	3.30	2.90	2.75	2.61	2.35	2.25	2.10	2.00
2	23.3	19.6	16.1	12.9	10.0	7.9	6.90	6.25	5.45	4.73	4.11	3.65	3.26	2.89	2.74	2.60	2.35	2.25	2.10	2.00
3	22.4	18.8	15.2	12.1	9.6	7.8	6.84	6.20	5.40	4.67	4.07	3.60	3.22	2.88	2.73	2.59	2.35	2.25	2.10	2.00
4	21.7	18.2	14.6	11.5	9.2	7.7	6.80	6.15	5.35	4.61	4.02	3.55	3.19	2.86	2.71	2.57	2.35	2.25	2.10	2.00
5	20.8	17.4	14.0	10.9	8.8	7.5	6.75	6.10	5.30	4.55	3.99	3.50	3.15	2.85	2.70	2.55	2.35	2.25	2.10	2.00
6	19.5	16.4	13.3	10.5	8.6	7.3	6.53	5.86	5.14	4.51	3.92	3.47	3.14	2.85	2.68	2.53	2.32	2.21	2.07	1.98
7	18.0	15.3	12.6	10.2	8.4	7.1	6.31	5.60	4.96	4.43	3.85	3.44	3.13	2.85	2.66	2.50	2.29	2.17	2.04	1.95
8	16.5	14.0	11.9	9.9	8.3	6.8	6.09	5.41	4.83	4.35	3.78	3.41	3.12	2.85	2.64	2.47	2.26	2.13	2.01	1.93
9	14.9	12.8	11.0	9.3	7.8	6.6	5.86	5.17	4.62	4.24	3.69	3.38	3.11	2.85	2.62	2.43	2.23	2.09	1.98	1.90
10	13.2	11.4	9.9	8.5	7.2	6.2	5.50	5.00	4.50	4.20	3.61	3.35	3.10	2.85	2.60	2.40	2.20	2.05	1.95	1.88
11						5.9	5.31	4.86	4.38	4.01	3.52	3.27	3.03	2.78	2.55	2.36	2.18	2.03	1.93	1.83
12						5.7	5.19	4.75	4.28	3.86	3.42	3.18	2.94	2.71	2.50	2.31	2.16	2.02	1.92	1.82
13						5.4	4.91	4.49	4.05	3.65	3.32	3.09	2.86	2.65	2.45	2.27	2.14	2.01	1.90	1.81
14						5.2	4.74	4.34	3.91	3.51	3.22	2.99	2.77	2.59	2.40	2.23	2.11	2.00	1.89	1.78
15						4.8	4.37	4.03	3.65	3.34	3.11	2.90	2.69	2.52	2.35	2.19	2.09	1.99	1.88	1.77
16											3.00	2.81	2.63	2.46	2.31	2.13	2.03	1.93	1.76	1.66
17											2.89	2.71	2.53	2.37	2.23	2.09	1.99	1.89	1.74	1.64
18											2.78	2.60	2.43	2.28	2.14	2.03	1.93	1.83	1.72	1.62
19											2.66	2.49	2.33	2.18	2.08	1.97	1.88	1.79	1.69	1.60
20											2.56	2.42	2.28	2.15	2.04	1.92	1.82	1.73	1.66	1.58
21																1.86	1.78	1.69	1.62	1.54
22																1.80	1.72	1.65	1.58	1.50
23																1.73	1.65	1.61	1.54	1.48
24																1.69	1.61	1.57	1.50	1.45
25																1.64	1.58	1.53	1.47	1.43

AGE = 50 YEARS AT IRRADIATION

Year-End of End of Follow-up Period

Beginning of Year Follow-up Starts (post-irradiation)	14th	15th	16th	17th	18th	19th	20th	21st	22nd	23rd	24th	25th	26th	27th	28th	29th	30th	31st	32nd	33rd
1	26.1	22.0	18.0	14.3	11.0	9.1	7.9	7.00	6.20	5.40	4.70	4.30	3.75	3.50	3.25	2.96	2.65	2.50	2.35	2.25
2	25.3	21.5	17.7	14.4	11.2	8.9	7.7	6.89	6.04	5.30	4.65	4.25	3.75	3.49	3.22	2.93	2.65	2.49	2.32	2.22
3	24.3	20.7	17.0	13.8	10.8	8.7	7.6	6.76	5.88	5.20	4.57	4.20	3.75	3.48	3.19	2.89	2.65	2.48	2.30	2.20
4	23.2	19.7	16.3	13.2	10.3	8.5	7.4	6.57	5.71	5.10	4.50	4.15	3.75	3.46	3.17	2.86	2.65	2.46	2.27	2.17
5	22.0	18.7	15.5	12.8	10.1	8.2	7.2	6.40	5.50	5.00	4.44	4.10	3.75	3.45	3.15	2.84	2.65	2.45	2.25	2.15
6	20.5	17.6	14.8	12.3	10.0	7.8	6.87	6.12	5.32	4.84	4.32	3.93	3.59	3.28	3.04	2.79	2.62	2.42	2.23	2.13
7	18.8	16.1	13.7	11.7	9.7	7.6	6.61	5.89	5.17	4.70	4.23	3.74	3.42	3.12	2.92	2.73	2.59	2.39	2.21	2.11
8	17.3	14.9	12.7	10.9	9.3	7.3	6.35	5.56	4.96	4.51	4.10	3.62	3.31	3.02	2.85	2.69	2.56	2.36	2.19	2.09
9	15.6	13.4	11.5	10.0	8.6	7.0	6.09	5.38	4.80	4.36	4.00	3.49	3.19	2.91	2.77	2.64	2.52	2.33	2.17	2.07
10	13.5	11.7	10.1	8.9	7.7	5.5	5.70	5.10	4.60	4.20	3.88	3.40	3.10	2.80	2.70	2.60	2.48	2.30	2.15	2.05
11						5.3	5.50	4.88	4.44	4.07	3.77	3.31	3.04	2.76	2.65	2.55	2.42	2.25	2.12	2.01
12						5.9	5.21	4.72	4.29	3.94	3.65	3.26	2.99	2.72	2.60	2.49	2.36	2.20	2.08	1.97
13						5.5	4.95	4.53	4.12	3.78	3.50	3.15	2.92	2.68	2.55	2.42	2.30	2.15	2.05	1.93
14						5.2	4.73	4.37	3.97	3.64	3.37	3.11	2.88	2.64	2.50	2.35	2.24	2.10	2.01	1.89
15						4.8	4.43	4.08	3.75	3.44	3.20	3.02	2.82	2.61	2.45	2.29	2.19	2.06	1.97	1.86
16											3.08	2.87	2.69	2.51	2.37	2.23	2.13	2.01	1.92	1.82
17											2.95	2.77	2.60	2.45	2.31	2.17	2.07	1.96	1.87	1.78
18											2.85	2.66	2.49	2.37	2.24	2.10	2.01	1.91	1.82	1.74
19											2.70	2.56	2.40	2.29	2.16	2.03	1.95	1.85	1.76	1.69
20											2.57	2.45	2.32	2.21	2.09	1.96	1.89	1.80	1.71	1.64
21																1.91	1.83	1.75	1.67	1.62
22																1.84	1.77	1.70	1.63	1.57
23																1.77	1.71	1.65	1.58	1.53
24																1.69	1.65	1.59	1.53	1.47
25																1.65	1.58	1.53	1.49	1.46

post-irradiation year, he should expect larger conversion factors for a fol-low-up from the third through the fourteenth years post-irradiation, than for a follow-up from the twenty-third through the thirty-third year post-irradiation. And this is what table 2 always shows.

The conversion factors are not quite the same for different ages at irradiation, as one will note in perusing table 2 carefully. Table 2 provides conversion factors separately for irradiation at 0 years, 10 years, 20 years, 30 years, 40 years, and 50 years of age. Many studies in the literature are for people irradiated at some interim age, for example, at age 16. Let us illustrate the use of table 2 in such cases. We will assume that our group, irradiated at age 16, is followed up from the beginning of the fifth year after irradiation out to the end of the sixteenth year after irradiation. How do we obtain the appropriate conversion factor from limited follow-up to peak percent value?

From table 2, we look up the values for age 10 at irradiation and for age 20 at irradiation, since our desired value, for age 16 at irradiation, must lie between those two values. For 10 years of age at irradiation, and a follow-up from the fifth through the sixteenth years, table 2 gives us a conversion factor of 16.0. For 20 years of age at irradiation, and for a follow-up from the fifth through the sixteenth years, table 2 gives us a conversion factor of 15.1. Our desired value, for irradiation at 16 years of age, lies between 16.0 and 15.1. Indeed, since 16 years is 6/10 of the way between 10 and 20 years, we know our factor must lie 6/10 of the way between 16.0 and 15.1. So we obtain our factor as follows: $16.0 - [(6/10) \times (0.9)] = 16.0 - 0.54 = 15.46$. (This process is called *interpolation* between two values, and is standard in such matters.) Whatever excess percent per rad is obtained for the limited follow-up period between the fifth and sixteenth years must be multiplied by 15.46 to obtain the peak percent increase per rad for that particular study.

The Power of the Curve and the Conversion Factors

The "magic" of the tabulation (table 1) for Studies A, B, and C is no mystery now. Rather, it is an illustration of how the follow-up conversion curve (figure 3) and the table of conversion factors (table 2) enormously enhance our power to handle various human studies of limited follow-up duration. Thus, with figure 3 and table 2, we can convert a study of limited duration into a set of numbers that permits comparison of different studies, and permits estimation of the cancers to be induced for the remainder of the life-span of the exposed populations. With these tools, we can make some worthwhile use of studies of limited follow-up duration instead of just be-moaning their limitations, as so many scientists are wont to do.

The author would like to give credit where credit is due. One of the first radiobiologists to realize that it would be nonsensical to accept the evidence from limited follow-up studies as if it were the full story was Dolphin (1968). His early suggestion was that the number of excess cancers found in a limited follow-up of irradiated people ought to be multiplied by a factor that took into account the excess cancers yet to come in later follow-up years.

Is the Peak Percent Value a "Universal" Value?

There is no scientific law which rules that the peak percent value obtained for irradiation at a specified age in *Japan* must be the same as that obtained for the same age in Sweden or the United States or elsewhere. But we will observe, in the study of the human evidence, that there appears to be little, if any, difference in such values from country to country. We intend to derive composite values from data around the world. We shall, in this book, make the approximation, which is consistent with the evidence at hand, that the peak percent value, for a specified age at irradiation, is a "universal" value that applies to radiation in any country. If some scientist can show that a different set of numbers for peak percent increase in cancer rate per rad applies for a particular country, that will be just fine, and we shall all use his numbers for that particular country.

This does not mean that the *spontaneous* cancer rates, expressed as age-specific rates, are the same from country to country. They are assuredly *not* the same. We are saying that, whatever the spontaneous rates may be, no evidence exists to show that the % increase per rad over that spontaneous rate, corrected to the common base of peak percent values, is any different from one country to another. Hence, the peak percent values, finally ascertained by combination of the worldwide data, will be applicable to calculations for any specific country.

THE HUMAN EPIDEMIOLOGICAL EVIDENCE

We now have the tools at our disposal to make use of the human epidemiological evidence. Our goal is the prediction of personal and public-health consequences from exposure to ionizing radiation. The first step on the route to that goal is necessarily the conversion of all the human evidence to a common base, the peak percent increase in cancer rate per rad, *for each age at irradiation.*

We shall use all the epidemiological evidence with adequate dosimetry and with a meaningful follow-up period. Some studies will disagree with others, giving a higher or lower radiation risk per rad. We shall use *all* the studies, and shall weight them in the final results only in proportion to the number of cancer cases included in each study, since this is the largest determinant of their reliability, provided all the investigators have applied equal diligence and honesty. As we will see, on completion of our analyses, the evidence will lead us to a very consistent set of answers.

The various human studies were conducted in different manners, depending on the circumstances faced by the investigator. We shall reference the sources in the literature for each study, as some scholars undoubtedly will want to go to the sources to assure themselves that nothing was overlooked or mishandled by the author of this book.

"Absolute" Risk Versus "Relative" Risk Methods

In chapter 7, the author shows why the evidence indicates that the *relative* risk method, which describes the number of radiation-induced cancers in relation to the number of spontaneously occurring cancers, is a better method of analysis than the *absolute* risk method. Many groups present both methods of calculating expected radiation-induced cancers. The absolute risk method has no theory at all; it simply counts and tabulates cancer deaths after irradiation. In a 90-year experiment, the absolute and relative risk methods *must* give the same answer, since there is always only *one correct* answer. In a limited follow-up study, the absolute risk method always gives a lower expected number of cancer deaths per unit of radiation than does the relative risk method. If, say, 5 cancers per year were noted in the early years of follow-up in an irradiated population sample, the absolute method would suggest that 5 cancers per year would be observed in future years, even if the spontaneous cancer incidence per year were rising, and rising steeply.

Since we know that the O/E value is rising over the period when E itself is rising, it is clear that the absolute risk method is providing the wrong answers when it suggests that the number of radiation-induced cancers will stay the same over a large number of years. The author considers this sufficient reason to discard the absolute risk method entirely, and none of the analyses in this book will use it.

Only time and more evidence can tell us whether the relative risk method is or is not a perfect method for describing what is happening with radiation and cancer. As of now, the evidence strongly favors it (see chapter 7).

[CHAPTER 5]

THE HUMAN EVIDENCE: STUDIES INVOLVING EXTERNAL EXPOSURE

IN THIS CHAPTER, we shall treat carcinogenesis from external exposures to any kind of radiation source. Later in the book (chapter 9), we shall also consider the matter of *internal* exposures to alpha particles; such exposures present quite different problems of analysis, best addressed separately. Our objective in this chapter is to ascertain a best estimate for peak percent cancer increase per rad. These data represent the first *essential* step in estimating personal and public-health radiation risk.

In this chapter, we will include quantitatively adequate studies involving *neoplasms* (tumors), including "benign" ones. In doing this, the author does not differ from the BEIR and UNSCEAR radiation committees. As the reader will see, the evidence shows that radiation increases the incidence of *both* malignant and "benign" tumors, and it is generally presumed that a comparable mechanism is at work. The reader will recall (from chapter 3) that there is no clear distinction between the two kinds of tumors until their behavior differs at quite advanced stages of their growth: cancer *is* what cancer *does*.

When the reader sees in chapters 6 and 7 how the data from this chapter are used, he will see for himself that the use of data for *nonlethal* tumors will *not* cause an overestimate of the risk from radiation, because the data are used only to ascertain an appropriate factor by which to multiply the spontaneous occurrence of *lethal* tumors. The only way an overestimate of risk could be introduced would be if "benign" tumors were to have a consistently higher *% excess per rad* than malignant ones, and there is no evidence at this time that they do.

Also, we will include (as do the BEIR and UNSCEAR radiation committees) quantitatively adequate studies that report on the *incidence* (diagnosis) of tumors rather than on mortality. One can use either incidence or mortality studies provided the control (or expected) values are appropriately matched. One must always compare cancer *deaths* in irradiated groups with cancer *deaths* in control groups, and cancer *incidence* in irradiated groups with cancer *incidence* in control groups.

We must make one qualification here. The development of the follow-up conversion curve (figure 3) is based on O/E (Observed/Expected) values derived partially from studies of incidence of cancer, and partially from studies of cancer deaths (see chapter 4). So when we say that the peak percent increase per rad is reached at approximately 40 years after irradiation, we are using a "hybrid" value. For some cancers, for example, lung cancer, where the interval between diagnosis and death is short, it hardly matters whether we are using cancer *death* or cancer *incidence* data. But for those cancers for which the interval between diagnosis and death is several years, on the average, we would necessarily expect that everything would be shifted on the follow-up conversion curve by approximately this average interval between clinical diagnosis and death.

For a highly refined study, the author feels that one would wish to have separate follow-up conversion curves for cancer-incidence data and for cancer-death data. We are far from having sufficient data at this time to justify separate curves and the separate handling of the data implied by the use of separate curves. Possibly ten years from now, this might be justified by the accrual of new evidence. The author wants the reader to know that there is an approximation involved in using a single follow-up conversion curve based on both kinds of data.

It is important to reiterate that, in spite of the "hybrid" nature of the conversion curve, within any single study cancer deaths must be matched with cancer-death expectations, and cancer incidence must be matched with cancer-incidence expectations.

It should be noted that the use of death data instead of incidence data for definitely deadly tumors in the Japanese and spondylitic series will tend to cause an *underestimate* of the effect of radiation, since some radiation-induced cancers are not counted simply because, at the end of a follow-up period, they had not yet killed their hosts.

SECTION 1: THE JAPANESE BOMB SURVIVORS

In a very detailed paper, Beebe, Kato, and Land (1978) present mortality from cancer (and other diseases) in 82,000 A-bomb survivors who registered as such in a census taken on October 1, 1950.

This group of 82,000 survivors constitutes what is known as the *Life Span Study*. It does not represent all survivors of the bombing. But it is a group for which a careful effort has been made to assess individual radiation dose and for which the follow-up is given special attention, compared with that for other survivors. The additional 27,000 persons who were not in the city at the time of the bombing, but who are also followed up carefully, make up an addition to the 82,000 survivors described above and together these 109,000 persons are referred to as members of the *extended Life Span Study*.

While Beebe and co-workers present data on the additional 27,000 persons who were not in the city at the time of the bombing, we have no need to use those data, since we wish to deal only with the bomb survivors. We shall not deal with leukemia in this section, but we shall deal with all deaths due to solid cancers. We shall for purposes of this analysis combine the data for Hiroshima and Nagasaki. The data in the Beebe et al. paper are such that one can analyze them separately by age groups *at the time of the bombing (ATB) in 1945:*

Age at time of bombing	
0–9 years of age	(mean age = 4.5 years)
10–19 years of age	(mean age = 14.5 years)
20–34 years of age	(mean age = 27.0 years)
35–49 years of age	(mean age = 42.0 years)
50+ years of age	

For the purposes of this analysis, we shall combine the data for males and females. There are a number of studies of Hiroshima-Nagasaki survivors other than these death-record studies of Beebe and co-workers, and they will be analyzed in a subsequent section.

DOSIMETRY

The doses are given in what is known as *T-65* rad units, developed by Auxier and colleagues (1975) at Oak Ridge National Laboratory. For each subject both the distance from the hypocenter of the bomb and an estimate of shielding were obtained from the individual, and from these data the T-65 dose was developed. The T-65 dose is what is known as the *kerma* value in rads. It does not give us the direct dose to various organs. The kerma value is the tissue dose in rads if the tissue were in air at the location of the survivor. In order to obtain the actual organ doses received in rads, correction factors are needed for the effect of intervening tissues of the body. Such factors are now available, and we shall correct all of the T-65 air doses presented by Beebe et al. to obtain the appropriate deep-tissue doses in rads to the organs developing reported cancers.

From the work of Jones and co-workers (1965), the following factors are suggested to correct from the T-65 kerma dose in air to the absorbed dose in bone marrow:

☐ For gamma rays, a factor of 0.55

☐ For neutrons, a factor of 0.26 + 0.07 = 0.33 (this includes the contribution from protons set in motion by the neutrons, plus gamma rays produced by neutron capture in tissue nuclides)

For breast tissue, the corresponding factors are:

☐ For gamma rays, a factor of 0.80
☐ For neutrons, a factor of 0.60

In a study of cancers overall, we take into account that some tissues are very deep, others more superficial, such as the breast. As a reasonable approximation for the dose to all the tissues susceptible to cancer, we shall use factors between those for bone marrow and for breast. Therefore, for cancers overall:

    □ For gamma rays, a factor of 0.62
    □ For neutrons, a factor of 0.47

(When we come to specific analyses of thyroid and breast cancers, and of leukemia, we shall use correction factors specifically appropriate to those tissues to convert T-65 doses into actual absorbed doses.)

DERIVING THE AVERAGE DOSE BY AGE GROUP

The author considers it essential to use *all* the data from Japan, not just the high-dose data, as some reports do. This addresses the criticism, "You get your information from high doses; but it does not apply to low-dose radiation." We shall use every bit of data, including data involving doses as low as 1 rad. For various age groups, Beebe, Kato, and Land give the doses in several categories:

    □ Less than 1 rad—the *zero-dose group*
    □ Between 1 and 9 rads
    □ Between 10 and 49 rads
    □ Between 50 and 99 rads
    □ Between 100 and 199 rads
    □ Between 200 and 299 rads
    □ Between 300 and 399 rads
    □ Over 400 rads

We will show that there is an even larger effect per unit dose at *low total doses* than at *high total doses*. (See chapter 8.)

Beebe, Kato, and Land also provide separate tables of gamma-ray and neutron doses for each dose category, so that the correction from T-65 kerma dose to absorbed dose in tissue can be calculated. For each age group, we shall combine all the cases from 1 rad to 400+ rads, so that all radiation doses are utilized.

In order to get a weighted average dose for *all* persons in each age category who received one rad or more, we must know how many people are in each dose category, or preferably (since some of the exposed persons did not survive for long), how many *person-years* are represented in each dose category (chapter 4, section 4).

The data of Beebe et al., when so treated, give us the *mean absorbed dose* for all age groups; these results are presented in table 3.

TABLE 3: MEAN ABSORBED DOSE, IN RADS, FOR ALL AGE GROUPS IN 1950–1974 FOLLOW-UP

Age Group (in years)	Mean Absorbed Dose in Rads
0–9	23.0
10–19	31.4
20–34	31.0
35–49	28.1
50+	23.6

CONVERSION FROM LIMITED FOLLOW-UP TO PEAK PERCENT VALUES

We have already described the necessity of converting all limited follow-up data to peak values at 40 years post-irradiation. The Japanese data are for a follow-up period from 1950 to 1974. Since the bombing occurred in 1945, this is a follow-up from the fifth through the twenty-ninth year. We obtain all the conversion factors from table 2, chapter 4, making appropriate interpolation corrections for age group. The values obtained are as follows:

Age Group	Conversion Factor to Peak Percent Per Rad
0–9 years	2.91
10–19 years	2.47
20–34 years	2.33
35–49 years	2.49
50+ years	2.84

Overall Cancers, Leukemia Excluded, for the Group 0–9 Years of Age ATB

In Table VI of the Beebe, Kato, and Land paper the raw data are presented for all cancers, excluding leukemia, which is treated separately both there and in this book.

The results are as follows:

Group	Number of Cancers	Person-Years	Cancers per Million Person-Years
Unexposed	8	158,400	50.5
All doses above 1 rad	18	203,700	88.3

The reader deserves an explanation of how one calculates the values in the column, "Cancers per Million Person-Years"; this *kind* of calculation is behind a great many of the values to be found in tables in this book.

The tabulation states that in the unexposed group, 8 cancers occurred per 158,400 person-years. Our first step is to find out how many cancers would have occurred for 1 person-year. This is obtained by dividing 8 by 158,400, which gives a quotient of 0.0000505. Since it is inconvenient to work with numbers such as 0.0000505, we commonly ask a question such as, "How many cancers would have occurred per *million* person-years?" To find out how many cancers would have occurred per million person-years, of course we must multiply 0.0000505 by 1,000,000, and such multiplication provides the value of 50.5 cancers per million person-years found in the tabulation.

Since we are expressing all values in cancers per million person-years, the O/E value is 88.3/50.5, which is 1.75. Therefore, we have an excess of 75% in cancers for a mean dose (table 3) of 23.0 rads.

$$\text{Percent excess cancer rate} = \frac{75\%}{23.0 \text{ rads}} = 3.26\% \text{ per rad}$$

But this is for the limited follow-up. Conversion to the peak percent increase per rad requires multiplication by 2.91.

$$\textit{Peak percent increase in cancer rate} = (2.91) \times (3.26)$$

$$= \textit{9.5\% per rad,}$$
for ages 0–9 at irradiation

The procedure just described is used in the same way to obtain values for the peak percent increase in cancer rate per rad for each of the remaining age groups. The results are summarized in table 4. The findings in table 4 will be discussed further in section 10 of this chapter.

TABLE 4: PEAK PERCENT INCREASE IN CANCER RATE PER RAD, ALL AGES, JAPAN (CANCERS, OVERALL, LEUKEMIA EXCLUDED)

Age group ATB	Mean dose in rads	Peak percent increase in cancer rate per rad
0–9 years	23.0	9.5
10–19 years	31.4	3.5
20–34 years	31.0	1.47
35–49 years	28.1	0.82
50+ years	23.6	No Increase Provable

The findings in table 4 will be discussed further in section 10 of this chapter.

THE ISSUE OF AGE SENSITIVITY

It would be difficult to imagine a clearer confirmation, from these Hiroshima-Nagasaki death data (not cancer-incidence data, not "benign" tumor data), of the original Gofman-Tamplin demonstration in 1969–1970 that the % increase per rad is highest when irradiation occurs at an early age, and declines steadily with increasing age at the time of irradiation. The author suspects that there is likely to have been *some* increase in the 50+ age group too, and that it is a sampling problem which leads to no increase at all, for cancers overall, in that group. But the cancer effect must be quite small, since the Hiroshima-Nagasaki data for that oldest age group are hardly based on small numbers, in a statistical sense. We shall see, in the analysis of the leukemia data, that an effect from radiation *was* observed in the 50+ age group.

SECTION 2: PATIENTS IRRADIATED FOR ANKYLOSING SPONDYLITIS

The group of patients irradiated for treatment of ankylosing spondylitis, already alluded to, has provided considerable information concerning the late occurrence of both cancer and leukemia in irradiated human beings. The difficulties in dosimetry, for many of the organs in which cancer developed, were described in chapter 4. Another difficulty that led to some early skepticism centered on the question whether or not the disease *itself* might *predispose* to the development of cancer, in which case it would not have been appropriate to use expected values from the population at large for control estimates. This problem has been resolved by Smith, Doll, and Radford (1977), with the demonstration that ankylosing spondylitis patients *not* treated by radiation show no excessive development of the cancers at issue. Hence, the expected values for cancer rates can be obtained from population statistics.

DOSIMETRY

While the effort is still going on to improve the dosimetry for the "spray" radiation that incidentally reached a variety of body organs during X-ray treatment of the spine, some recent estimates have been provided. We will use those estimates since they are the best available at this time. They certainly are better than those suggested in the BEIR-I report (1972). The recent estimates are listed in table 5.

In the early reports on the spondylitis cases, it was not pointed out that some of the patients received *multiple* courses of therapy with X-rays, and that as a result the precise follow-up period was uncertain. In the data to be presented here, from Smith and Doll, unpublished data communicated to the BEIR-III Committee, we shall be considering the results only for those patients who had a single course of therapy, since these are not equivocal with respect to follow-up time. The data are for 6,838 patients, each of whom received a single course of X-ray therapy and was followed up for a mean period of 11.3 years. The follow-up period began with the sixth year post-irradiation, and ended 17.3 years (mean value) post-irradiation. By excluding the first 5 years post-irradiation, the investigators were confident that, at the time of diagnosis, no one diagnosed as spondylitic was suffering instead from such diseases as metastatic cancer of the spine or pancreatic cancer.

Conversion Factor from Limited Follow-up to Peak Percent per Rad

Through the use of table 2, chapter 4, and an estimate of age at irradiation of 30 years, we obtain a conversion factor to peak percent increase per rad of 9.8 for the follow-up period described above, including the appropriate interpolation correction for the 0.3 years beyond the seventeenth year. This factor, of course, will apply for all the kinds of cancers studied in the ankylosing spondylitis cases.

TABLE 5: ESTIMATED DOSES (IN RADS) TO THE VARIOUS ORGANS IN THE SPONDYLITIS CASES

Site of Cancer	Dose in Rads[a]
Leukemia (all bone marrow)	214
Lymphoma (assuming origin in mediastinal nodes, excluding Hodgkins disease)	306
Esophagus	306
Stomach	67-89[b]
Colon	57
Pancreas	90
Bronchus (of lung)	197[c]
Spinal Cord and Nerves	698
Kidney	46[d]
Bladder	31[e]

[a]All these calculations are based on an average spinal marrow dose of 505 rads.

[b]This range is given because it is recognized that different configurations of the stomach can result in different doses.

[c]This dose estimate is based on the assumption that 80% of the bronchial epithelium is irradiated.

[d]This is one of the areas usually referred to in the spondylitis studies as *lightly irradiated*. The estimate given is based upon the assumption that 10% of the organ is irradiated.

[e]Also one of the lightly irradiated sites. The estimate given assumes that 33% of the organ is irradiated.

All these estimates should be regarded as provisional; they are the best available at the present time. The author doubts that the dosimetry problem is either better or worse, a priori, for these spondylitis cases than for any other of the human epidemiologic studies.

These data are presented in BEIR-III (1979, Draft Report), Table 1, p. 277.

SUMMARY OF THE FINDINGS FOR THE ANKYLOSING SPONDYLITIS SERIES

Again following the same procedure described in section 1 (but without, in this case, the need to convert from kerma doses), we obtain the peak percent increase in cancer rate per rad for each type of cancer studied. These are summarized in table 6.

Since our ultimate purpose in considering all the human epidemiological data is the ascertainment of the *best* value of the peak percent increase in cancer rate per rad, with a separate value for each age group at time of irradiation, it is now essential to combine the spondylitis series results into a single value that we can later use toward that goal. The spondylitis series gives us one age at irradiation, approximately 30. The summary findings in table 6 are then combined to provide a composite value.

The Composite Peak Percent Increase per Rad

For two reasons, the composite value should be obtained by weighting the various peak percent values by the *number* of observed cancers. The first reason is that, for overall cancer calculations, we want the various cancers weighted according to their numerical importance in the total of observed cancers of all types (chapter 6). The second reason is that the statistical weighting of each value is related to the number of cancers actually observed.

TABLE 6: PEAK PERCENT INCREASE IN CANCER RATE PER RAD, SPONDYLITIS DATA

Type of Cancer	Number of Cancers Observed	Peak Percent per Rad
Bronchogenic Cancer, Lung	101	2.25%
Cancer of the Large Intestine	18	6.5%
Cancer of the Pancreas	12	6.6%
Cancer of the Stomach	36	5.8%
Cancer of the Esophagus	9	3.5%
Lymphoma	13	3.1%
Cancer of the Kidney	7	26.5%
Cancer of the Urinary Bladder	8	10.8%
Hodgkins Disease	0 (2 cases expected)*	0.0%

*In combining the findings for various cancers to achieve a composite peak percent increase in cancer rate per rad, the best weighting to give a cancer with 0 cases observed is the expected value for that cancer. Using the observed value would give no weighting at all.

Obtaining a composite value for the ankylosing spondylitis experience requires that each peak percent value be multiplied by the number of cancers corresponding to that value, and that all these products be summed.

Then that sum is divided by the total number of cancers in the series. This will give a weighted average value for the peak percent increase in cancer rate per rad.

(Number of Cancers) × (Peak Percent)		Number of Cancers Observed	
101 × 2.25 = 227.3		101	Lung
18 × 6.5 = 117.0		18	Large Intestine
12 × 6.6 = 79.2		12	Pancreas
36 × 5.8 = 208.8		36	Stomach
9 × 3.5 = 31.5		9	Esophagus
13 × 3.1 = 40.3		13	Lymphoma
7 × 26.5 = 185.5		7	Kidney
8 × 10.8 = 86.4		8	U. bladder
2 × 0.0 = 0.0	(expected)	2	Hodgkins
Totals = 976.0		206	

Therefore, weighted average peak percent increase is

$$\frac{976.0}{206} = 4.74\% \text{ per rad,}$$ for age approximately 30 at irradiation

SECTION 3: MALIGNANT LYMPHOMA AND MULTIPLE MYELOMA IN JAPAN

Many of the studies of Hiroshima and Nagasaki survivors are reported separately from the main studies, and may be based on either cancer incidence or cancer deaths. Nishiyama and colleagues (1973) provide one such study for malignant lymphoma and multiple myeloma. There is some controversy as to whether these two cancers should be grouped together. A large segment of the medical-research community holds the view that they should be grouped together. In any case, we can treat these two malignancies here without debating that issue.

We shall combine the data for Hiroshima and Nagasaki. These studies are based on the population comprising the Life Span Study group, so that the population composition and doses in the Beebe, Kato, and Land report can be used to estimate average age and doses. We shall estimate the mean age for those receiving zero rads separately from that for those in all irradiated groups combined. As we shall see, the mean ages are very close for the two groups, and we shall be able to use the average of the two.

The Unirradiated Groups		The Irradiated Groups	
Mean Age ATB	Person-Years Follow-up	Mean Age ATB	Person-Years Follow-up
4.5 years	158,400	4.5 years	203,700
14.5 years	165,000	14.5 years	233,500
27.0 years	156,800	27.0 years	206,300
42.0 years	170,800	42.0 years	215,500
50+ years	80,200	50+ years	97,500

The mean ages are obtained by multiplying, for each age group, the mean age by the person-years, then summing these values, and then dividing by the sum of the person-years. When this is done with the data just listed, the mean ages are:

Unirradiated group: Mean age = 25.9 years
Irradiated group: Mean age = 25.3 years

The average of the values is 25.6 years, which shall be taken as the mean age for the overall group.

For the mean doses, we shall use the corrected absorbed doses presented in table 3 for overall cancers in deep tissues in the body. To obtain the mean dose for the overall irradiated population, all ages combined, we multiply each value of person-years for the irradiated group by its mean dose, sum all these products, and divide that sum by the total person-years. The result is a mean dose in rads of 28.0 rads. This is the dose we shall use for the malignant-lymphoma case analysis.

The population at risk, unexposed, is 29,973 persons at Hiroshima plus 4,702 persons at Nagasaki, for a total of 34,675 persons. The population at risk, all groups exposed to more than 1 rad, is 30,325 persons at Hiroshima plus 14,184 persons at Nagasaki, for a total of 44,509 persons.
Occurrence of cases among the unexposed:

Malignant lymphoma = 14 cases
Multiple myeloma   = 2 cases

Occurrence of cases among the exposed groups (all doses above 1 rad):

Malignant lymphoma = 23 cases
Multiple myeloma   = 6 cases

For the purposes of this analysis, in which we are interested in the overall group, we shall combine malignant lymphoma and multiple myeloma cases. Therefore, the total number of cases for the unexposed is 16; the total number of cases for the exposed is 29. The analysis proceeds in the same way as demonstrated in section 1. The resulting peak percent increase in cancer rate = 10.1% per rad. This value applies to the combined group, malignant lymphoma plus multiple myeloma.

SECTION 4: CANCER AND ADENOMA OF THE THYROID

There are, by now, numerous studies in the scientific literature supporting the induction both of thyroid cancer and benign tumors (known as *adenomas*) of the thyroid gland by ionizing radiation. However, either because of inadequate information on dosimetry or potentially biased methods of obtaining the follow-up data, many of these studies are not suitable for ascertaining values of the peak percent increase in cancer or benign neoplasms as the result of radiation.

The studies to be analyzed quantitatively here are those for which the dosimetry and follow-up do meet the criteria of adequacy. Whether the risk per rad is high or low is totally irrelevant in the decision to use or not use a particular study. The author notes that the UNSCEAR and BEIR Committees utilize the same studies as are included here. We shall consider the data and analysis for thyroid carcinoma and thyroid adenoma from childhood irradiation first; then the data for combined ages from the Japanese bomb survivors; and last, the data from the Adult Health Study in Japan.

THE STUDIES BY HEMPELMANN AND CO-WORKERS OF THYROID-CANCER INCIDENCE

A long-term study of the development of thyroid tumors in 2,872 persons who received irradiation to the neck region in the first few months of infancy has been in progress for over two decades. Hempelmann and colleagues (1975) recently published the fourth in a series of reports on the follow-up of these children. The follow-up includes 5,055 siblings of the irradiated children as controls, in an effort to eliminate any variables that might be confounded with the radiation itself. Many of these persons, originally from upstate New York, have now been followed up into the fourth decade of life. The final response rate in the survey was 85.4%, which is considered quite good for a study of this duration.

Two separate subpopulations are identifiable in the overall sample, based on the fact that one subgroup (designated by Hempelmann as *Subgroup C*) was treated by one particular radiologist with much larger doses than the remainder of the sample received. Subgroup C also differs in that 48% of it is designated as Jewish, based on surnames, whereas 4% of the remainder of the population sample is so designated. There is some evidence of a higher spontaneous rate of thyroid cancer in Jewish persons (UNSCEAR 1977, p. 380). We shall treat the Subgroup C sample separately from the sample designated as *All Others*.

Dosimetry for the Thyroid Gland

Hempelmann and co-workers report the following dose estimates, in actual rad dose to the thyroid gland:

2,872 Subjects, All Groups   *261 Subjects, Subgroup C*

Average thyroid dose, 119 rads   Average thyroid dose, 399 rads

The average thyroid dose for All Others, calculated from these data, is 91 rads.

Thyroid Cancer in the *All Others* Group

Ideally one would prefer to use the *measured* thyroid-cancer incidence rate in the sibling group as the control value. However, no thyroid cancers occurred in the unirradiated sibling group, owing to the rarity of this cancer. Hempelmann appropriately elects to use the incidence rate for comparable groups, matched by age and period of follow-up, from the annual cancer rates for upstate New York. The observed number of thyroid cancers was 11 cases, in All Others. The expected number of thyroid cancers was 0.25 cases, based on vital statistics. The O/E value was $11/0.25 = 44$. Therefore, there is a 4,300% excess cancer rate in All Others for a mean thyroid dose of 91 rads. The value seems shocking but it *is* correctly stated.

The excess cancer per rad = 4,300%/91 rads = 47.3% per rad for the limited follow-up period.

The average age of the overall group when responding to the follow-up survey was 24.9 years. Since the irradiation was in the first few months of life, the initiation of follow-up was effectively at 0 years of age. The average age at follow-up of Subgroup C was 33 years. The average age at follow-up of All Others is calculated to be 24.1 years. So, for the All Others, the follow-up period was effectively 24.1 years, since irradiation took place in early infancy. For irradiation at 0 years of age, and a follow-up through 24.1 years, table 5 provides a conversion factor of 5.98.

$$\text{Peak percent increase in cancer rate} = (5.98) \times \frac{47.3\%}{\text{rad}}$$

$$= 282.9\% \text{ per rad}$$

Lest the reader be shocked, he should be reminded that this group received its radiation in early infancy, and all the data we shall examine show the extreme sensitivity of the very young infant to the induction of cancer by ionizing radiation.

Thyroid Cancer in Subgroup C

As has been stated, Subgroup C received a higher radiation dose to the thyroid, and contained a high proportion of subjects with Jewish surnames, according to Hempelmann. We shall make a correction for the difference in incidence of thyroid cancer in Jewish subjects, on the assumption that Hempelmann's surname approach has some meaning. As we shall see, when properly analyzed, the risk of thyroid cancer *from radiation* is less for Subgroup C than for All Others, contrary to the conclusions of Hempelmann and co-workers.

The observed number of cancers in Subgroup C was 13. For the expected number, we will make a correction for the proportion of Jewish-surnamed subjects. From data presented in UNSCEAR (p. 380), it appears that Jewish subjects show a spontaneous incidence of thyroid cancer that is 3.56 times higher than that for non-Jewish subjects, among males, and 5.5 times higher than that for non-Jewish subjects among females. We will use an average factor of 4.5.

Since 48% of Subgroup C have Jewish surnames, the following approach is taken to calculate the expected rate of thyroid cancer. The general expected risk is 0.04, from Hempelmann. For the 48% Jewish group, we multiply the general risk by 4.5, to obtain 0.18. The expected risk for Subgroup C is then calculated to be 0.107. Using our standard procedure, the result obtained for the peak percent increase in cancer rate is 74.9% per rad.

Thus, even with the increased spontaneous risk of thyroid cancer in Jewish subjects, and with corrections to account for this, the peak percent increase per rad for Subgroup C is about 1/3 what it was for All Others. Since we should feel approximately equal concern about the goodness of the estimates of thyroid dose in both groups, and since the numbers of observed thyroid cancers are about equal—11 versus 13 cancers—the most reasonable procedure is to average the two values for peak percent increase per rad. The final value, from the Hempelmann studies, thus obtained, is *178.9% per rad*, for irradiation in early infancy. The age at irradiation is a crucial point.

When one is endeavoring to assess the true dose to the thyroid, one realizes the serious difficulty of knowing beam factors for the gland itself. The author would not be surprised if the dosimetry for these studies might be in error by a factor of two. That would still not alter the *extreme* seriousness indicated for irradiation in early infancy.

THE STUDIES BY SHORE AND CO-WORKERS OF THYROID-CANCER INCIDENCE

Shore and co-workers (1976) carried out a follow-up study of 2,215 children who received irradiation of the scalp in the treatment of tinea capitis (ringworm of the scalp). The treatment was delivered at 7.9 years of age, on the average. It is estimated that the dose to the thyroid gland was between 6 and 9 rads, but we shall use the BEIR value of 8 rads average dose to the thyroid gland. The average age of the individuals at follow-up was 28.4 years, so the average duration of follow-up was 20.5 years, from the time of irradiation. No cancers of the thyroid gland were observed in this group (there were thyroid adenomas, which will be analyzed separately).

Therefore, for this series, the *peak percent increase in thyroid-cancer rate* is *0% per rad*. Ordinarily, in a case like this, we would use the number of thyroid cancers expected without radiation to weight this result, as we suggested was our general policy. However, Shore and co-workers do not present expected values, except to state that two cases would have been expected based on Modan's results (1977). Since Shore uses Modan's results, we shall do the same, except that we will make a formal calculation.

Modan reports a very high thyroid-cancer rate for a similarly treated group. We shall use the comparative size of the populations at risk and the duration of follow-up in the two studies in our calculation.

For Shore and co-workers, (2,215 persons) $\times$ (20.5 follow-up years) gives us 45,408 person-years. For Modan and co-workers, (10,900 persons) $\times$ (17.5 follow-up years) gives us 190,750 person-years. Since Modan observed 10 thyroid cancers, we shall say that Shore's cancer value, if the results were in agreement, would have been (45,408/190,750) $\times$ (10) = 2.4 thyroid cancers, to be our observed value.

Since we must, of course, use all negative findings as well as all positive findings, we shall, in the final estimates of a "best" peak percent per rad, use Shore's value of 0.0%/rad for thyroid cancers and weight his value as for a series of 2.4 cancer cases. This would appear to be a reasonable way to handle these data.

THE STUDIES BY JANOWER AND MIETTENEN OF THYROID-CANCER INCIDENCE

Janower and Miettenen (1971) report on a follow-up study of 466 persons irradiated in Massachusetts for ostensible enlargement of the thymus gland, and of 506 unirradiated subjects with similar illnesses, as one control group. The reader of this book may find the circumstances under which these children were irradiated interesting. Quoting from the Janower and Miettenen paper:

From 1924 to 1946, it was the policy of the Massachusetts Eye and Ear Infirmary in Boston to apply prophylactic irradiation in every case in which an "enlarged" thymus gland was diagnosed in infancy. The assessment of the size of the thymus gland was based on an anteroposterior roentgenogram of the chest taken in expiration with the patient in the supine position. Whenever the width of the superior mediastinum was at least half the width of the heart the gland was characterized as "enlarged" or "suspicious," and the child was given radiation treatment; if the gland was less than half the width of the heart the child was not given radiation. On the basis of these criteria, 1,131 children received thymus gland radiation in the 22-year period. (p. 753)

The author would only add one point, for perspective. There never has existed any scientific evidence that irradiation produces *any* "prophylactic" benefit in children with "enlarged" thymus glands.

In this study, the irradiated children were an average of 4.7 years at exposure (Janower and Miettenen refer to this age as "infancy"). The average age at the termination of the follow-up period was 34.8 years, so the average follow-up period was 30.1 years. Complete follow-up was achieved in 466 out of 511 subjects (91.1%), which is quite good.

Dosimetry and Observations

Janower and Miettenen report that the irradiation was generally delivered
in 4 treatments of 100 roentgens (air dose) each, at 10-day intervals over
a total elapsed time of 30 days. In 78% of the irradiated patients, the
cumulative air dosage was 400 roentgens. In 11% of the cases, the total dose
was listed as "less than 400 R." Only 1% received more than 400 R (air
dose). The other 10% of patients are not accounted for by Janower and
Miettenen. Given the uncertainties involved concerning what radiation actually reached the thyroid gland, it would be unproductive to say much more
than that these children received about 400 rads to the thyroid. This is an
illustration of a study that is borderline where inclusion here is concerned,
on the basis of uncertain dosimetry. But since other studies are also uncertain on this issue, in different ways, this one will be included.

The result, obtained via our standard procedure, is *23.9% per rad*, for
children irradiated at a mean age of 4.7 years.

The Studies by Modan and Co-workers of Thyroid-Cancer Incidence

Modan and co-workers (1977) report on the development of thyroid cancer
in a series of 10,902 Israeli children who received scalp irradiation for the
treatment of tinea capitis, with X-rays. Their exact age at irradiation is not
given, just "before 15 years of age." We shall use 7.5 years of age as average
age at irradiation. This series is similar to the Shore and co-workers series.
Modan matched these children with 16,400 unirradiated children. The follow-up period for these children was between the twelfth and the twenty-
third year post-irradiation, for those children followed longest, but the *mean*
follow-up period was between 12 and 17.5 years after irradiation. The data
for thyroid cancer are as follows. The observed number of thyroid cancers
in 10,902 irradiated children was 10. The original report of Modan lists 12
cancers, but this must be corrected to 10, because 2 of the cancers were
found to have occurred in children who had more than one course of
therapy with X-rays. The expected number of cancers for the controls,
corrected to the same number of subjects as for the irradiated group,
was 2.

Dosimetry and Observations

The Modan series suffers from the same problem as does the Shore et al.
study, namely, the difficulty of obtaining an accurate assessment of the dose
to the thyroid gland when the scalp is irradiated. The best estimate for the
Modan series is between 6 and 9 rads. We shall use the middle of this range:
7.5 rads to the thyroid. Modan points out that if there had been some
movement of the child or some misalignment during therapy, the thyroid
dose could have been appreciably higher. The BEIR Committee finally did
its calculations on the basis of 6–9 rads, and we shall too, keeping in mind

that a possible dose underestimate may exist. The O/E value is $10/2 = 5.0$, for the limited follow-up. The peak percent increase in thyroid cancer rate is calculated to be *366.7% per rad*, for an estimated age of 7.5 years at irradiation.

The scientific community was somewhat surprised by the extremely high value for the excess thyroid cancers in the Israeli series. On the other hand, one may also be surprised by the extremely low value (zero) for the Shore study. But because we are dealing with small numbers of cancers, large variations in results should not surprise us. It would be *totally* inappropriate to manipulate the data to exclude either very large or very small increases in cancer incidence. Instead, we realize that as we combine a sufficient number of series, our number of cases builds up, and the reliability of the *peak percent increase in cancer rate per rad* increases markedly compared with the estimate from a single series of reported cases. Here we shall, of course, utilize both the Shore and the Modan data. There is no reason to exclude either. The Modan data are not *surprising* when compared with the Hempelmann findings for irradiation of a much younger group, although they are still high compared to those of Hempelmann.

All these series will undoubtedly be studied further, to lengthen their follow-up periods. New reports should be carefully studied to determine whether revisions in peak percent excess values are needed.

THE STUDIES BY HEMPELMANN OF THYROID ADENOMA

While thyroid adenoma is not considered a malignant disease (that is, a cancer), it is considered to be neoplastic, and its incidence has been shown in many studies to be increased by ionizing radiation. The author will consider, as do others, the quantitative aspects of induction of thyroid adenoma.

The thyroid-adenoma data from Hempelmann (1975) are for the same series of subjects already described in connection with thyroid cancer. The reader will recall that these subjects are divided into two subgroups, Subgroup C and All Others. The dosimetry has also already been presented.

The data used for the determination of expected rates of occurrence of thyroid adenomas were obtained from the sibling control groups, rather than from Tumor Registry data for New York. Hempelmann and co-workers give a value of 3.42 adenomas for the combined subgroups; they give a zero value for Subgroup C, since the matched siblings for Subgroup C developed no adenomas. The author disagrees on principle with the use of zero expected values. Unless there is reason to think that a particular group is blessed with immunity from adenoma, *some* adenoma must be expected, even if it is a fraction of a case for a small sample. To get an expected value for the control group of Subgroup C, we will divide the *total* expected into appropriate parts for Subgroup C and for All Others.

Hempelmann is not sure that Jewish people have as strong a tendency for adenoma as for thyroid cancer, but he indicates that they have some increased tendency to develop adenoma. In the absence of more definitive data, we shall assume that the Jewish factor is the same for adenoma as for thyroid cancer, and that the ratio of expected *cancer* in Subgroup C to expected cancers in All Others equals the ratio of expected *adenomas* in Subgroup C to expected adenomas in All Others.

The peak percent increases obtained from calculations were as follows:

Thyroid adenoma rate in the All Others group = *81.3% per rad*
Thyroid adenoma rate in Subgroup C = *11.4% per rad*

Combined Results for Thyroid Adenoma

Whether the lower value for Subgroup C compared to All Others is any reflection of an overcorrection for the Jewish factor cannot be known for certain. It may be. However, where uncertainty exists we would prefer not to overestimate cancer induction by radiation, so we shall use the calculated value for Subgroup C presented above.

To obtain a weighted final value for thyroid adenoma, we can weight the two values obtained in proportion to the corresponding numbers of thyroid adenomas. This gives a weighted peak percent value of 54.4% per rad for age 0 at irradiation. However, we shall use the separate values (81.3% and 11.4%) in the final tabulations for all groups (table 7).

THE STUDIES BY SHORE AND CO-WORKERS OF THYROID ADENOMA

Shore and co-workers (1976) present data for thyroid adenomas in those same children with scalp irradiation whom they studied for the development of thyroid cancer. There were 6 thyroid adenomas observed in the original 2,215 children irradiated. None were observed in the 1,395 control children. However, a zero expected value is inherently unreasonable, and also would make any observed value infinitely larger per rad, which would be absurd. Since Shore does not provide an expected value, an estimate can be obtained by comparing his series with that of Hempelmann. While Shore's subjects were older at irradiation, the age difference is just about balanced by Hempelmann's longer follow-up.

With the appropriate calculations performed, a resulting peak percent increase in the thyroid adenoma rate is obtained, of *189.0% per rad,* for age 7.9 years at irradiation.

The problem of sampling variation with small numbers is seen here. Whereas the Shore series shows a *lower* peak percent for thyroid *cancer* than does the Hempelmann series, the Shore series shows a *higher* value than does the Hempelmann series for thyroid *adenoma.* In order to cancel out errors inherent in "small numbers," we are building up a big series of values by combining as many valid literature reports as possible. And the appropriate way to build up the total base of observations is with the peak percent values rather than with the raw data, because of the varying doses and follow-up periods in the individual series.

The Studies by Janower and Miettenen of Thyroid Adenoma

The dosimetry for the Janower-Miettenen (1971) series was already presented in our review of their study of thyroid cancer. Janower and Miettenen use three separate control groups. We shall combine all the control groups into a single group. The data for thyroid adenoma in this series are as follows:

Group	Number of Thyroid Adenomas	Person-Years	Adenomas per Million Person-Years
Exposed	9	14,037	641.1/million
Controls	10	71,110	140.6/million

The peak percent increase in this study is calculated to be *2.6% per rad,* for irradiation at age 4.7 years.

It will be noted that this value is much smaller than those from any of the other series. This, the author believes, is the result of the very difficult problem of thyroid dosimetry for irradiation performed to treat the thymus gland. It is certainly possible in the Janower-Miettenen series that the thyroid gland was missed in some of the irradiations, and hence that the mean dose is far lower than the 400 rads used here. But we cannot know this, so we shall use this value, weighted by the number of observed adenoma cases. Dosimetry is assuredly not without its problems in all the other series too.

Thyroid Cancer in the Hiroshima-Nagasaki Groups

Thyroid cancer in the Japanese studies will be handled here, separately from the overall cancers already treated above. The thyroid cancer data are not for deaths but for incidence of cancer, from two separate studies of the Hiroshima-Nagasaki survivors. We shall consider both of those studies.

The Data from the Japanese Thyroid Tumor Registry

Beebe, Kato, and Land (1978) present, in their Table XVII, the incidence of thyroid cancers for Hiroshima and Nagasaki combined, for all ages *at exposure* combined, by dose group. The observed numbers of thyroid cancers and the person-years of exposure from 1959 to 1970 (the years for which the cancer incidence is available from the Registry) are as follows:

Group	Thyroid Cancers	Person-Years	Cancers per Million Person-Years
Exposed to 1 rad or more	87	466,400	186.5
Unexposed	48	356,400	134.6

There are two additional items of information needed: (a) the mean age at exposure, and (b) the mean dose to the thyroid gland for the exposed individuals.

The Mean Age at Exposure: Since this is essentially the same population at risk as was considered in the lymphoma calculations previously, we shall use the same mean age, 25.6 years, as the mean age at exposure.

Dosimetry: In the calculations for lymphoma, a mean dose of 28.0 rads was estimated for the exposure of the lymph glands. That estimate was based on the conversion of the kerma air dose to deep-tissue dose using factors of 0.62 for gamma rays and 0.47 for neutrons. The thyroid gland is not as deeply situated as the other tissues considered in the sections on the development of cancers overall. So the dose to the thyroid must be considered to have been somewhere between the deep-tissue dose and the kerma dose. As a reasonable approximation for the thyroid dose, we shall raise the deep-tissue dose estimate by 20%, which means estimating the thyroid dose to be halfway between the deep-tissue and kerma doses. This gives a value of 33.6 rads as the estimated dose for the thyroid gland. Further calculations result in a peak percent increase in thyroid cancer incidence of *3.3% per rad,* and this value is for exposure at age 25.6.

The Data from the Clinical Cases in the Adult Health Study

UNSCEAR (1977, p. 378) presents data for 40 thyroid cancers diagnosed clinically in the Adult Health Study for Hiroshima and Nagasaki. There is some overlap in cases between this study and the Tumor Registry data. Nevertheless, this study was conducted differently on a well-followed group, so it deserves independent analysis and crediting in our overall evaluation of peak percent values. The data are presented separately for the 1–49-rad exposure group and the over-50-rad (kerma) exposure group. Unfortunately the person-years data needed to combine these groups are simply not provided, so we shall have to approximate the final result.

For the 1–49-rad dose group, the observed number of cancers is 6, and

UNSCEAR estimates an expected number of 3.9. For all other exposure groups the data are as follows:

Group	Number of Thyroid Cancers	Person-Years	Cancers per Million Person-Years
Unexposed	9	101,000	89.1
Exposed, at 50 rads or more (kerma dose)	25	52,000	480.7

From our subsequent calculations, the peak percent increase in thyroid cancer rate = (4.2% per rad) × (2.85) = *12.0% per rad,* for exposure at a mean age of 25.6 years (using the mean age for the overall series from Beebe, Kato, and Land, since no specific value is provided for this group).

THE STUDIES BY CONTI AND CO-WORKERS: A NEGATIVE RESULT FOR THYROID-CANCER AND ADENOMA INCIDENCE

In a study of infants receiving X-radiation to the anterior mediastinum, the region where the thymus gland is located, Conti and co-workers (1960) report on a follow-up of 1,564 persons. These include 1,340 infants who received between 75 and 200 roentgens to a small area of the anterior chest for the following reason (we quote a passage from Conti and co-workers which follows a discussion of the treatment of 224 children with presumed thymus enlargement with 200–450 roentgens to the chest):

Since upper respiratory infections also seemed to be less prevalent in the treated children, it was decided to give all children born between June, 1944 and May, 1946 small doses of X-rays to the manubrial region. Ninety-five of the 1,340 children so treated were given 150 r and the remainder received 75 to 100 r. [All treatments were within 7 days of birth.] (p. 386)

The reader can glean from this passage that all it took to get an unnecessary dose of radiation at the Pittsburgh Hospital in those days was simply *to be born.* The reader should also glean from this how primitive medicine was as recently as the 1940s, when the notion was expressed that 75 to 150 R of radiation to the chest was a "small dose."

The Follow-up Findings

The majority of the children in the group of 1,564 (actually, 1,340 of them) were treated between June 1944 and May 1946. We can take 1945 as the mid-point for the treatment. Follow-up was conducted between 1956 and 1958. We can take 1957 as the average time at which follow-up was conducted. Thus we have a follow-up from irradiation out to a point 12 years later.

Some 10% of the total group could not be followed up. The results for the treated group and for untreated siblings are as follows for thyroid cancer:

Treated Children (1,564)		Untreated Siblings (2,923)	
Expected	Observed	Expected	Observed
0.03	0	0.07	0

For a 12-year follow-up, which is an inordinately short one, it is clear that the observed thyroid cancers did not exceed the expected, but it could hardly have been otherwise. With 3/100 of a case expected, it would have taken only 0.3 of a case to exceed the expected by ten-fold. And if indeed 0.3 of a case were occurring, we would expect to observe *zero* cases about two times out of three. Of further interest is that table 2 would indicate that *any %* excess per rad obtained in a 12-year follow-up would have to be multiplied by about 40 to get the peak percent per rad.

With such small numbers, stemming from such a short follow-up, this study is surely marginal with respect to inclusion here. Nevertheless, we shall include this study as one which is negative with respect to the production of thyroid cancer from thymus irradiation. Since thyroid adenoma is not mentioned, nothing can be said about that tumor. In weighting this series along with all other series, we shall credit it with a weight of 0.5 of a case, which takes into account a possible expected value for thyroid adenoma. This is likely a very generous weighting.

The authors of the study do point out two reasons why the thyroid-cancer production was so low compared with other reported series of thymus irradiation in infancy. One possibility is the bias introduced by the missing 10% of cases where follow-up was unsuccessful. It is possible that among the missing cases might be a subject who had died of radiation-induced cancer. Second, they point out that the port through which the radiation was delivered was considerably smaller than those used in studies where a thyroid-cancer effect was shown. So the possibility does exist that the thyroid gland was simply missed by the beam.

A much longer follow-up period would, of course, have been highly desirable, but the author of this book has found none, and none is mentioned by even the most recent BEIR and UNSCEAR reports. It is hoped that some investigator is still conducting a follow-up on this group of irradiated newborns. If someone were able to evaluate the dose to any irradiated organs near the thymus, this group could potentially yield additional information about radiation carcinogenesis from exposure near the beginning of life. As the Conti study now stands, however, it provides no dose estimate to other organs, no values for expected (spontaneous) cancer rates for the other organs which may have been irradiated, and no adequate follow-up time.

We shall simply use this as a series with 0% per rad for thyroid cancer or thyroid adenoma, with a weighting of 0.5 cases expected.

SECTION 5: SALIVARY-GLAND TUMORS

Several studies have reported on the occurrence rate of salivary-gland tumors following ionizing-radiation exposure. Most of these are in the parotid gland (which is the salivary gland best known for its involvement in mumps).

THE STUDIES BY SHORE AND CO-WORKERS

The difficulty with several observations on salivary-gland tumors following radiation is that no dose estimates are provided for the salivary glands. However, in the tinea capitis scalp-irradiation studies of Shore, Albert, and co-workers (1976), an estimate from Harley (1976) of 39 rads is provided for the dose to the parotid gland.

Shore, Albert, and co-workers report finding 4 total salivary-gland tumors (3 benign and 1 malignant) in the 2,215 exposed children, with follow-up through 1973. They report a total of 44,300 person-years in the exposed group. Since there are 1,413 control children (BEIR-III report), the person-years for controls should be $(1.413)/(2.215) \times (44,300)$, which is 28,260 person-years of follow-up. There are *no* salivary-gland cancers reported for the control group. No expected value is provided for the control group, but we shall use 1 salivary-gland tumor as the expected value, realizing that this may be too high, and may hence underestimate the effect of radiation. If we use these data and approximations, we have:

Group	Person-Years	Observed Number of Salivary-Gland Tumors	Tumors per Million Person-Years
Exposed	44,300	4	90.2
Controls	28,260	1 (approximated)	35.3

The peak percent increase in salivary-gland tumor rate is calculated to be *36.0% per rad.* This value is for a group at a mean age of 7.9 years at irradiation.

THE MODAN STUDY OF CHILDREN IRRADIATED FOR TINEA CAPITIS

The BEIR-III report (1979) presents an update on the occurrence of salivary-gland tumors in the Modan study of Israeli children irradiated for tinea capitis. The data presented are as follows:

☐ 7 tumors (4 malignant, 3 benign) in 10,902 exposed children
☐ 1 tumor (benign) in 16,400 control children, unexposed
☐ Duration of follow-up = 15 years beyond the eleventh post-irradiation year

From these data, and with the use of Harley's estimate of 39 rads as the dose to the parotid gland in similar irradiation of the New York children, we obtain the following:

Group	Persons Followed Up	Number of Tumors	Tumors per Million Persons
Exposed to 39 rads	10,902	7	642
Unexposed	16,400	1	60.9

The peak percent increase in salivary-gland tumor rate in this study is calculated to be *69.8% per rad*, for children irradiated at a mean age of 7.5 years.

Comparison of this value with the 36% per rad from the Shore series shows that agreement is quite good, particularly since the expected value in the Shore series is based on an approximate occurrence of 1 case in the controls, which, as we mentioned, may be too high. We shall use both the Shore and Modan values as they stand, even though the Shore value may underestimate the risk of radiation.

THE TAKEICHI STUDIES OF SALIVARY-GLAND TUMORS IN HIROSHIMA

Takeichi and co-workers (1976) report on the occurrence of salivary-gland tumors in exposed and unexposed subjects in Hiroshima City, occurring in the 19 years between 1953 and 1971. From Table 3 of their paper we ascertain the following data:

(1953–1971) Group	Person-Years	Number of Salivary Tumors	Tumors per Million Person-Years
Exposed	1,490,146	31*	20.8
Unexposed	4,333,814	30†	6.9

*Of the 31 tumors in the exposed group, 17 are listed as malignant and 14 as benign.
†Of the 30 tumors in the unexposed group, 5 are listed as malignant and 25 as benign.

We shall, for consistency with the other studies, combine the listed malignant with the listed benign tumors. The appropriate mean age at exposure for the overall study is approximately 25.6 years of age, as noted for the lymphoma series.

Dosimetry and Observations

Since this study is restricted to Hiroshima alone, we shall ascertain the mean dose for Hiroshima, rather than the mean dose for the combined cities, as was done for other studies of the bomb survivors. We obtain the data for estimation of doses from Table II of Beebe, Kato, and Land.

The salivary glands can appropriately be regarded as lying about as deep in the body as the vulnerable tissues of the breast. Using the appropriate correction factors to convert from kerma to absorbed tissue dose, we obtain a mean absorbed dose of 31.4 rads.

Finally, after the usual calculations, we find that the peak percent increase in salivary-gland tumor rate is *16.1% per rad.* This value applies for persons exposed at a mean age of 25.6 years.

From Ohkita and co-workers (1978), who also consider this series, we ascertain that the incidence rate of *benign* salivary-gland tumors among the exposed individuals was 1.8 times higher than among the unexposed individuals, and that (for the same average radiation dose) the incidence rate of *malignant* salivary tumors among the exposed was 10 times higher than among the unexposed. We shall not attempt to handle the benign and malignant salivary neoplasms separately, because of the small numbers of cases available at this time.

SECTION 6: BRAIN TUMORS INDUCED BY IONIZING RADIATION

Data have been reported for two studies of brain tumors where both an estimate of radiation dose and a reasonable follow-up period are available. Both will be analyzed here.

THE STUDIES BY SHORE, ALBERT, AND CO-WORKERS OF BRAIN TUMORS

For the 2,215 children who were irradiated for tinea capitis, Shore and co-workers report (in the BEIR-III report, 1979) the following results.

In the irradiated group 8 brain tumors were observed. There were no brain tumors in the 1,395 control children. Instead of using zero for the control group, data from the Connecticut Tumor Registry are used to estimate what would have been expected in a group of the same size as the irradiated group. That value is 1.1 brain tumors (BEIR-III, p. 658).

The average age at irradiation was 7.9 years. It is estimated that the dose of radiation penetrating to the brain from the scalp was approximately 140 rads. The mean follow-up period for the overall group was 25 years (from irradiation to 25 years later). The peak percent increase in brain-tumor incidence = *21.1% per rad,* for irradiation at a mean age of 7.9 years.

THE STUDIES BY MODAN OF BRAIN TUMORS IN CHILDREN WITH TINEA CAPITIS

The data from Modan et al. (1977) are for the same children, irradiated for tinea capitis, for whom the occurrence of thyroid cancer and salivary-gland tumors was reported. The follow-up period is the extended one between the eleventh and twenty-sixth year post-irradiation, a 15-year period. The mean dose to the brain from the scalp irradiation is estimated at 150 rads. The data on observations in the irradiated and control groups are as follows (Modan, 1974):

Group	Number of Persons	Number of Brain Tumors	Brain Tumors per Million Persons
Exposed	10,902	16	1467.6
Controls	16,400	3	182.9

The peak percent increase in brain-tumor incidence = *13.4% per rad*, for children irradiated at a mean age of 7.5 years.

SECTION 7: SKIN CANCER

Some investigators seem to have already made the decision that *they* think skin cancer is not readily induced by radiation, so they do not include it in evaluations. There is no logical reason to exclude skin cancer from our tabulations, so we shall analyze the two series for which dosimetry appears adequate and a reasonable follow-up period is available.

THE STUDIES BY SHORE AND CO-WORKERS OF SKIN CANCER

Shore and co-workers also provide skin-cancer data for the tinea capitis patients treated with X-rays to the scalp. BEIR-III (1979, p. 666) provides an update of these data. The data can be treated separately for heavily irradiated sites and for lightly irradiated sites on the skin. The mean dose estimated for the heavily irradiated sites is 700 rads; the estimated dose for the lightly irradiated sites is 40 rads. (Because no tumors appeared in non-Caucasians, the study was limited to Caucasians.)

For the heavily irradiated sites, the data are:

Group	Person-Years	Number of Cancers	Number of Cancers per Million Person-Years
1685 irradiated persons	28,820	24	832.7
1046 controls	17,124	2	116.7

The peak percent increase in skin-cancer rate = *3.7% per rad*, for children irradiated at 8.0 years of age.

For the lightly irradited sites, the data are:

Group	Person-Years	Number of Cancers	Number of Cancers per Million Person-Years
1685 irradiated persons	28,820	5	173.4
1046 controls	17,124	2	116.7

The peak percent increase in skin-cancer rate = 5.2% per rad, for irradiation at 8.0 years of age. It is interesting that the peak percent values for the widely differing total doses are quite close to each other. However, one cannot make too much of this since the number of control cases for both the heavily and the lightly irradiated groups is small (2 in each group), making appreciable room for sampling variation.

THE STUDIES BY HEMPELMANN OF SKIN CANCER

Hempelmann and co-workers provide data concerning skin-cancer induction in the series of children followed up subsequent to thymus irradiation in infancy (see our review of their thyroid-cancer results). There were 2,878 irradiated subjects and 5,055 sibling controls in this study of skin-cancer occurrence. The mean dose to the area of skin studied was 330 rads. The observations (from BEIR-III, 1979, p. 670) follow:

Group	Person-Years	Number of Skin Cancers	Cancers per Million Person-Years
Exposed	50,226	9[*]	179.1
Sibling Controls	89,625	3	33.4

*Of the 9 skin cancers, 6 were basal-cell cancers and 3 were malignant melanomas.

The peak percent increase in skin-cancer rate = 5.0% per rad. It must be emphasized that this value is for infants irradiated at essentially zero years of age.

SKIN CANCER STUDIES WITH NEGATIVE RESULTS

This author has emphasized that one must be just as interested in reports which show no radiation effect, as in those which do. The proper approach is to weight all the studies by the number of observed cancers in each series, so that appropriate credit is given based on the statistical goodness of the observations. It should never surprise the reader to find a study reporting a negative effect of radiation when that study is based on small numbers of observed cases.

The Hiroshima-Nagasaki Experience

The BEIR-III report (1979, p. 673) presents the details of the observations made in the Adult Health Study, a subset of the overall Hiroshima-Nagasaki survivor sample. An extensive dermatological evaluation was made on 9,646 persons, including 1,830 who received doses of 90 or more rads (kerma dose) and 2,081 persons who received 10–89 rads. These persons were compared with 2,696 others who were in the city at the time of the bombing but received doses of 1 rad or less. BEIR-III reports that the sample was "carefully drawn" and the examinations were conducted 19–21 years after irradiation. BEIR-III also reports that the Japanese have spontaneous skin-cancer rates of only 1/40 to 1/30 those of Caucasians in similar environments.

Out of the entire irradiated group *plus* the control group, only *one* person developed a skin cancer, and that one was in the control group. This is obviously a very small sample of cancers from which to draw any conclusions. Nonetheless, we must include this as a sample of subjects with a *zero* peak percent increase in skin cancer per rad, and it shall be weighted as based on 1 cancer in toto, for a mean dose of 50 rads skin dose, at an approximate age of 25.6 years (like the overall Japanese series).

The Studies by Shore and Co-workers

We shall consider the postpartum mastitis cases in detail in connection with the subject of breast-cancer induction by radiation. Here we shall be concerned only with the skin-cancer problem in these subjects. Shore and co-workers (1977) (BEIR-III 1979, p. 679) present the following data:

Group	Number of Subjects	Number of Skin Cancers	Cancers per Million Persons
Irradiated	571	6	10,507.8
Controls	993	13	13,091.6

It is evident that in this study, no skin-cancer induction can be demonstrated for an estimated 280 rads to the skin and an average follow-up period of 25 years in a group of women averaging 27.5 years of age at irradiation. This *negative* result will be entered in our final tabulations, with a weighting based on the number of cancers in the irradiated group, which was 6.

SKIN CANCER STUDIES EXCLUDED FROM QUANTITATIVE CONSIDERATION

There are a number of studies in which evidence of skin-cancer induction by radiation has been either a primary or a secondary result, as well as some in which skin cancers might have been expected as a consequence of radiation but were not observed. However, for various reasons, all of the following studies lack sufficient data to be included in our quantitative analysis:

skin-cancer occurrence in the ankylosing spondylitis series; studies by Delarue and co-workers of patients who had received multiple fluoroscopies
(1975); the Myrden fluoroscopy studies; studies by Sevcova and co-workers
of uranium miners (1978); studies by Matanowski and co-workers of physicians (1975); studies by Takahashi of skin cancer in the Japanese (1964); and
studies by Conard and co-workers of Marshall Islanders exposed to fallout
from weapons testing (1975). In some of these cases, the data on the "expected," or control, group is not available; in others the dosimetry is too
uncertain, or the study is incorrectly based on death data rather than incidence data (as it should be, in view of the very low mortality rate for skin
cancer). It should be emphasized that these studies do not affect our analysis
one way or the other; they are neither positive nor negative.

The Study by Austin of Malignant Melanoma in Lawrence Livermore Laboratory Employees

Austin released a report in 1980 entitled "A Study of Cancer Incidence in
Lawrence Livermore Laboratory (LLL) Employees." The report demonstrates that there was a significantly higher incidence rate of malignant
melanoma in LLL employees than in the population of the same area *not*
employed at LLL. There were 19 cases of melanoma in the years 1972–
1977, inclusive, among the laboratory employees, 17 in males and 2 in
females. For the males the expected number of melanomas would have been
5.13 cases. The excess is highly significant statistically, according to the
Austin report.

Nevertheless, there are multiple reasons why the Austin study cannot
be used to ascertain peak percents.

In the first place, it is not even a *radiation* study at this time. Although
the press and indeed some physicians have jumped to the conclusion that
exposure to ionizing radiation is the cause of the reported excess of malignant skin cancers, neither Austin nor the author of this book does so. In fact,
the latter is not *yet* convinced that an excess of malignant melanoma in the
laboratory employees even exists. Every physician knows that when one
starts looking for something more carefully, one starts finding more of it.
After the first few cases of melanoma were diagnosed in LLL employees, it
could easily have been that LLL employees were then examined far more
carefully than was the general population of that area. Indeed, LLL employees have a periodic medical examination at the lab itself, wholly in
addition to medical care they receive on the outside. There is also room for
suspicion that not all 19 cases diagnosed as *malignant* melanoma are really
malignant at all. If this were a mortality rather than an incidence study, that
suspicion would not exist, of course.

Austin addresses these problems in his report as follows:

*The greater than expected number of cases of malignant melanoma among the employees
of the LLL during that period is not the result of an unusual pattern of disease reporting,
diagnosis or medical care. (p. 13)*

However, nothing in the report itself substantiates this claim.

Austin intends to explore the rate of other malignancies at LLL in the future. The findings will be interesting. Certainly, if ionizing radiation is under consideration as a basis for the melanomas observed (if we assume there is a *real* excess), it would be extremely important to know whether squamous-cell and basal-cell carcinomas of the skin are also in excess in the LLL employees. Both of these cancers are known to be caused by ionizing radiation, so it could be expected that if ionizing radiation were responsible for the melanomas in LLL employees, it would also have caused an increased frequency of squamous- and basal-cell cancers.

Whenever radiation exposure is considered as a cause of cancer excess, dose estimates must be provided. In the case of occupational exposure, we must also have some way of knowing, in either an incidence or a mortality study, how soon after hire the cancer appeared or killed, since during the latency period it would not be possible to see any difference between the workers and the general population. Because the Austin study is not at this time a radiation study, it includes none of these data.

WHY ARE THE PEAK PERCENTS FOR SKIN CANCER SO LOW?

As the reader will find throughout this book, this author considers it highly likely that the *true* peak percent will not vary much, if at all, for any one type of cancer from that for any other type. Yet, it is evident from the studies reported here that the *observed* peak percents are definitely lower for skin cancer than for any other type of cancer studied. (See Table 7.)

It is this author's opinion that there is a valid explanation for this low peak percent for skin-cancer induction by ionizing radiation. The skin is the one organ of the body which is exposed to ultra-violet light (from the sun). Ultra-violet light is a known carcinogen. Therefore we are, in all probability, never observing a true control group, since the controls for our ionizing radiation groups are exposed to ultra-violet light. The "ideal" study would be of populations with and without ionizing radiation, with both groups *not* exposed to sunlight. Such a study is essentially impossible.

If ultra-violet radiation acts similarly to ionizing radiation in *cancer production,* then the "spontaneous" skin-cancer rate includes the effect of what can be regarded as "equivalent rads" from the ultra-violet radiation (see Section 14, this chapter).

In this book we are using the results as they stand for skin cancer, even though we suspect they provide falsely low peak percents, simply because the author cannot prove that his surmise is correct. By inclusion of the skin-cancer findings we may underestimate the true peak percent values for cancers, overall, because of the low contribution from skin cancers. But we prefer to underestimate, where uncertainty exists, rather than to overestimate radiation effects.

SECTION 8: PELVIC CANCERS

THE STUDIES BY BRINKLEY AND HAYBITTLE OF PELVIC CANCERS

Brinkley and Haybittle (1969) have been following a group of 277 women in whom an artificial menopause was induced by X-rays directed toward the ovaries. They state that the central pelvic dose was generally 700 R delivered in two treatments in an overall time of five days, except that some patients of differing body-build got as much as 1,000 R. We can cite their statement, following:

Unless these cases are already predisposed towards cancer of pelvic sites, even before treatment, there would seem to be a definite suggestion that X-ray induction of the menopause increases the risk of subsequently dying from pelvic cancer. The increases are most marked in the intestines and rectum, and although it is not possible to give precise values for the doses received by these organs, it is unlikely that they could have received more than 20 percent above the prescribed central dose to the ovaries. (p. 519)

It would seem reasonable to include these studies, since the dosimetry problems do not seem appreciably different from those of most of the studies we are utilizing. In order to take care of the fact that some subjects received a dose of 1,000 R, the exact number of subjects not being specified, we shall use a value of 800 rads as the dose to the pelvic organs. We will consider the follow-up period to have been between the fifth post-irradiation year and the mean follow-up duration of 16.1 years reported by Brinkley and Haybittle. The mean age of the women at irradiation was 46.4 years.

Observed pelvic cancers (the heavily irradiated sites) were 14. The expected number of cancers was obtained from registrations at the Cambridge Cancer Registration Bureau. This number was 4.29, for the same organs as considered for the irradiated cases. The peak percent increase in pelvic cancers = *4.1% per rad.* This value applies to women irradiated at 46.4 years of age. Since we know of no reason to consider that the indication for X-ray-induced menopause, namely, excessive menstrual bleeding, predisposes to the cancers observed, we shall use these data in our tabulations. The UNSCEAR Committee also includes this series in its studies. We would prefer, however, not to include too many data based on doses as high as 800 rads, because there is evidence that cancer induction per rad decreases at very high doses, and there is also some speculation that cells which sustain cancer-inducing injuries from high doses *also* sustain other radiation-induced injuries which have a high probability of killing the cells.

THE STUDIES BY SMITH AND DOLL OF INTESTINAL AND OTHER PELVIC CANCERS

Smith and Doll (1976) also report on the development of cancers in the pelvic organs following irradiation of the ovaries for metropathia hemorrhagica (excessive menstrual bleeding) in three Scottish centers. The UNSCEAR report suggests that the following doses are reasonable to apply to the Smith-Doll studies:

For small and large intestines, dose = 133 rads
For all other pelvic organs, dose   = 400 rads

We shall use these doses and analyze the cancers of the small and large intestines separately from all others, because of the dose difference. The mean follow-up period was the same for all cancer observations, that is, between 5 and 19 years post-irradiation.

From the data for all cancers taken from Table IV of the Smith-Doll paper, the peak percent increases are calculated: for cancer of the small and large intestine = *4.3% per rad;* for all other pelvic cancers = 0.65% per rad. Both apply to women irradiated at a mean age of 45.2 years.

SECTION 9: RADIATION-INDUCED CANCERS FROM JOB-RELATED EXPOSURES

Two major groups of occupational workers have developed cancer as a result of radiation from alpha-particle exposure internally: radium-dial painters and uranium miners. We shall handle these groups when we consider alpha-particle emitters; they are not suitable for inclusion in this analysis of external radiation exposure.

Mancuso, Stewart, and Kneale (1977) recently gave us a group suitable for inclusion here: gamma-ray-exposed workers at the Hanford Atomic Works in Washington State. Studies of this type are likely to yield important additional data in the early future, so we will explain their nature and principles below.

Gofman (1979) performed an independent analysis of the raw data provided to him by Dr. Mancuso. Neither the Mancuso nor the Gofman paper deals with *peak* percent per rad evaluation. However, the % increase per rad is presented. From Mancuso and co-workers, the best estimate for the follow-up period used is 2.97% per rad, for all forms of cancer combined, for males. From Gofman, the estimate is 2.30% per rad for all forms of cancer combined, for males. These two values, for an average age circa 41 at hire, are derived by considerably different handling of the data, but are quite consistent with and confirmatory of each other.

THE HANFORD DEATH STUDY

In the Hanford death study a comparison is made of a high-dose group and a low-dose group, with respect to the ratio of cancer deaths to noncancer deaths. It will be shown here that the difference in the two ratios is directly related to the % increase in cancer risk per rad. In truth, the Hanford study, based on film-badge measurements of occupational exposure to external radiation, really shows no truly high-dose exposures. The "high-dose" group consists of those who accumulated 10 or more rads of external exposure during the course of employment; the average dose in this group is 23.0 rads. The average dose for the low-dose group is 0.73 rads. The follow-up study includes all those who survived at least 15 years beyond the dates they were hired at Hanford.

Findings and Implications

The actual observations at Hanford were as follows:

2,547 males in the lower-dose group died noncancer deaths.
  646 males in the lower-dose group died of some sort of cancer.
   81 males in the higher-dose group died noncancer deaths.
   34 males in the higher-dose group died of some sort of cancer.

After the appropriate calculations and corrections have been made, we obtain a value for the % increase in cancer death per rad, compared with the spontaneous risk. This value = 2.3% per rad, for the limited follow-up period. The problem of converting this value into peak percent per rad is not at all straightforward. The difficulty is that in the case of the Hanford workers, the radiation dose was accumulated over a very long period of time. Indeed, for those who got over 10 rads of total accumulated external dose, and a mean total dose of 23 rads, the dose was accumulated over a period of 20.5 years. In no other study we have analyzed has the dose been accumulated over a period so long compared to the follow-up period.

This raises several questions, the answers to which are not immediately clear. First, is the total dose the effective dose in producing the cancer deaths observed in these workers, or should any dose received less than 10 years before death be neglected, in order to take the latency period for cancer into account? If some of the later part of the dose were neglected, the increase in cancer rate per rad would be even larger than reported here. Second, and related, is the question of the choice of the mean time of irradiation to be used in correcting to the peak percent increase in cancer rate per rad.

No elegant answer to these questions is currently available. Rather than making questionable assumptions about the appropriate manner of handling such very long-term irradiation, it is preferable not to use the Hanford data in any compositing procedure with other data, all derived from short-term irradiation. We shall, therefore, omit the Hanford evidence from the composite picture.

We should explore the implications of certain reasonable treatments, however. Let us suppose that the entire dose of the higher-dose group (23 rads, average) was received during the seventh year of work (the entire employment period was 20.5 years, average). This supposition would minimize the peak percent per rad in two ways: it would subtract none of the dose received during the last years of employment, and it would lower the conversion factor somewhat, by crediting all the dose received during the eighth through the twentieth years with a longer-than-actual follow-up period. The latter effect is largely offset by simultaneously crediting the dose received before the seventh year with a shorter-than-actual follow-up period.

Supposing that the time of irradiation was 7 years beyond the date of hire means that the follow-up period would have its "zero" year in the seventh year and would extend for 16 years, since 23 years was the average interval from hire to death for those in the study. For a follow-up period from 0 to 16 years, the approximate conversion factor is 17.7 for approximately 48 years of age at irradiation. Therefore, the *peak percent increase per rad* = $(17.7) \times (2.3\%$ per rad$) = 40.7\%$ *per rad*, for overall cancer induction in the Hanford workers.

Comments

This value is far, far higher than for other people irradiated at about the same age. In particular, it is in gross disagreement with the observations of the Hiroshima and Nagasaki survivors. The dosimetry in the Hanford workers is about as good as one could hope for, since it is based on periodic film-badge measurements. This should certainly give data far superior to data obtained from a reconstruction of the radiation dose at Hiroshima and Nagasaki years after the bombing.

One possible factor to consider is that there may have been some unmeasured internal radiation dose at Hanford as a result of slow ingestion or inhalation of radionuclides, with such intake having increased, on the average, with an increase in external dose. In that case, the true dose has been underestimated, and the true cancer induction per rad has been overestimated. There did exist measurements of internal dose at Hanford, and cases with appreciable known internal doses are excluded from the analysis. However, it is doubtful that measurements of internal dose would have been good enough to rule out unappreciated internal doses.

Another factor to note is that the Hanford results rest largely on one measurement: the number of cases of cancer from cumulative doses over 10 rads. That number is 34, and is subject to considerable sampling variation error. Additional studies of occupationally exposed workers are under way, and it is hoped that some of the questions surrounding the Hanford sample will be resolved in time.

Lastly, when data may be telling us something surprising, it is well to keep one's mind open and receptive. One cannot rule out some unexpectedly large increase in carcinogenic effect from irradiation at a very slow dose rate. In chapter 8, we will explore why such a large increase may occur.

A STUDY OF ARMY TECHNOLOGISTS: A POSSIBLE NEGATIVE STUDY WITH RESPECT TO INDUCTION OF CANCER BY OCCUPATIONAL EXPOSURE TO RADIATION

Jablon and Miller (1978) conducted a 29-year follow-up of 6,560 Army radiological technicians and of 6,826 medical, laboratory, or pharmacy technologists. No excess death-rate from cancer was observed among those who had been radiological technicians compared with all other technologists. Unfortunately, there are no studies of the radiation dose which was received by either group of technologists. One might suspect that the radiological technicians did receive a higher radiation dose than did the other technologists, but there is simply no way to estimate the dose. For this reason, the study is not included here for consideration. However, the author feels it is important that the reader know about the existence of this potentially negative study with respect to radiation carcinogenesis.

SECTION 10: INTEGRATION OF ALL THE MISCELLANEOUS CANCER DATA

Table 7 on the following pages represents a synthesis of the peak percent values, appropriately weighted, for all the admissible studies combined. A composite peak percent value for each age group at irradiation is provided; it is calculated as shown for the youngest age group.

A POTENTIAL INCREASE IN THE CARCINOGENIC EFFECT PER RAD IN THE HIROSHIMA-NAGASAKI EXPERIENCE

When an analysis of the type presented in this chapter is performed, the expected value used for O/E is assumed to be the value without added radiation. The Beebe, Kato, and Land presentation (1978) indicates that the control group received a dose below 1 rad (T-65 units). The control group is the population sample which was located 2.50 kilometers and farther from the hypocenter of the bomb.

However, in the analyses of linearity (chapter 8) and leukemia (chapter 14), we will present evidence from the Hiroshima-Nagasaki observations which strongly suggests that this "zero-dose" group received over 5 rads, T-65 dose, probably from fission-product fallout. This is a startling finding. Nevertheless, because the statistical test of this phenomenon gives a result of $p = 0.07$ (7 chances out of 100 that the phenomenon occurred by chance), and most scientists would not accept a result good at that level, we did *not* incorporate this finding into the peak percent per rad analyses in this or any other chapter.

Instead of incorporating this finding into our composite results, we present it in this section for those who wish to know how much it would alter

TABLE 7: SYNTHESIS OF ALL HUMAN EPIDEMIOLOGICAL DATA FOR PEAK PERCENT INCREASE IN CANCER RATE PER RAD FOR DIVERSE CANCERS AND TUMORS (LEUKEMIA EXCEPTED)*

Age Group: Infancy, Near 0 Years of Age at Irradiation

Age (years)	Peak Percent Increase per Rad	Observed Number of Cancers	Expected Cancers**	Mean Dose in Rads	Type of Study	Kind of Cancer or Tumor
0	282.9	11	(0.25)	91	thymus irradiation	thyroid cancer
0	74.9	13	(0.107)	399	"	thyroid cancer
0	81.3	32	(2.39)	91	"	thyroid adenoma
0	11.4	20	(1.03)	399	"	thyroid adenoma
0	5.0	9	3	330	"	skin cancer
0	0.0	0	(0.5)	50–450	"	thyroid adenoma or thyroid cancer

*Deaths due to breast cancer are included in table 14 for the Japanese data only; a much larger number of breast cancers are separately studied.

**Numbers in parentheses are *calculated* expectations (see text).

- -

BEST ESTIMATE OF COMPOSITE PEAK PERCENT VALUE

(Peak Percent Value) × (Number of Cancers)		Number of Cancers†
(282.9) × (11)	= 3,111.9	11
(74.9) × (13)	= 973.7	13
(81.3) × (32)	= 2,601.6	32
(11.4) × (20)	= 228.0	20
(5.0) × (9)	= 45.0	9
(0.0) × (0.5) =	0.0	0.5
Totals	6,960.2	85.5

Best estimate of peak percent per rad, for 0 years of age at irradiation = 6,960.2/85.5 = *81.4% per rad.*

†Observed number used except when it was zero. In that event, expected value used.

Age Group 0–9 at Irradiation

Age (years)	Peak Percent Increase per Rad	Observed Number of Cancers	Expected Cancers	Mean Dose in Rads	Type of Study	Kind of Cancer or Tumor
4.5	9.5	18	8	23	bomb survivors	cancer deaths, overall
7.8	0.0	0	(2.4)	8	scalp radiation	thyroid cancer, incidence
4.7	23.9	2	(0.059)	400	thymus radiation	thyroid cancer, incidence
7.5	366.7	10	(2)	7.5	scalp radiation	thyroid cancer, incidence
7.8	189.0	6	(2.24)	7.5	scalp radiation	thyroid adenoma, incidence
4.7	2.6	9	10	400	thymus radiation	thyroid adenoma, incidence
7.9	36.0	4	(1)	39	scalp radiation	salivary gland neoplasms
7.5	69.8	7	1	39	scalp radiation	salivary gland neoplasms
7.9	21.1	8	(1.1)	140	scalp radiation	brain tumors, incidence
7.5	13.4	16	3	150	scalp radiation	brain tumors, incidence
8.0	3.7	24	2	700	scalp radiation	skin cancers, incidence
8.0	5.2	5	2	40	scalp radiation	skin cancers, incidence

Best estimate of composite peak percent per rad = *55.4% per rad.*

Mean age for this age group = 772.5/111.4 = 6.9.

TABLE 7 (CONTINUED)

Age Group: 10–19 at Irradiation

Age (years)	Peak Percent Increase per Rad	Observed Number of Cancers	Expected Cancers	Mean Dose in Rads	Type of Study	Kind of Cancer or Tumor
14.5	3.5%	86	42	31.4	bomb survivors	cancer deaths, overall

Since there is only one value available, the best estimate of composite peak percent per rad = *3.5% per rad.*
Mean age for this age group = 14.5.

In a later compositing with the breast-cancer data, we shall need two products:

(Peak Percent Value) × (Number of Cancers) = (3.5) × (86) = 301.0

(Mean Age) × (Number of Cancers) = (14.5) × (86) = 1,247.0

Age Group: 20–29 at Irradiation

Age (years)	Peak Percent Increase per Rad	Observed Number of Cancers	Expected Cancers	Mean Dose in Rads	Type of Study	Kind of Cancer or Tumor
27.0	1.47	266	169	31.0	bomb survivors	cancer deaths, overall
25.6	10.1	29	16	28.0	bomb survivors	lymphoma + myeloma
25.6	3.3	87	48	33.6	bomb survivors	thyroid cancer, incidence
25.6	12.0	31	9 + (3.9)	33.6	bomb survivors	thyroid cancer, incidence
25.6	16.1	31	30	31.4	bomb survivors	salivary gland neoplasms
25.6	0.0	0	1	50.0	bomb survivors	skin cancer, incidence
27.5	0.0	6	13	280.0	mastitis X-rays	skin cancer, incidence

Best estimate of composite peak percent per rad = *4.08% per rad.*
Mean age for this age group = 11,925.4/451 = 26.5.

Age Group: 30–39 at Irradiation

Age (years)	Peak Percent Increase per Rad	Observed Number of Cancers	Expected Cancers	Mean Dose in Rads	Type of Study	Kind of Cancer or Tumor
30	2.25	101	(69.5)	197	ankylosing spondylitis	bronchogenic cancer (lung), deaths
30	6.5	18	(13.1)	57	"	large intestine cancer, deaths
30	6.6	12	(7.5)	90	"	pancreas cancer, deaths
30	5.8	36	(24.6)	78	"	stomach cancer, deaths
30	3.5	9	(4.3)	306	"	esophagus cancer, deaths
30	3.1	13	(6.59)	306	"	lymphoma, deaths
30	26.5	7	(3.16)	46	"	kidney cancer, deaths
30	10.8	8	(5.98)	31	"	urinary bladder cancer, deaths
30	0.0	0	(2)	306	"	Hodgkins disease, deaths

Best estimate of composite peak percent per rad = *4.74% per rad.*
Mean age for this age group = 6,180/206 = 30.0.

TABLE 7 (CONTINUED)

Age Group: 40–49 at Irradiation

Age (years)	Peak Percent Increase per Rad	Observed Number of Cancers	Expected Cancers	Mean Dose in Rads	Type of Study	Kind of Cancer or Tumor
42.0	0.82	931	675	28.1	bomb survivors	cancer deaths, overall
46.4	4.1	14	(4.29)	800	X-ray-induced menopause	pelvic cancers
45.2	4.3	24	(13.86)	133	X-ray therapy of excess menstrual bleeding	intestinal cancers
45.2	0.65	35	(26.23)	400	"	pelvic cancers

Best estimate of composite peak percent per rad = *0.94% per rad.*

Mean age for this age group = 42,418.4/1,004 = 42.2.

Age Group: 50+ at Irradiation

Age (years)	Peak Percent Increase per Rad	Observed Number of Cancers	Expected Cancers	Mean Dose in Rads	Type of Study	Kind of Cancer or Tumor
50+	0.0	811	692	23.6	bomb survivors	cancer deaths, overall

Best estimate of peak percent per rad = *0.0% per rad. (See text for explanation of this zero value.)*

For later compositing with breast-cancer data we shall need two values:

(Peak Percent Value) × *(Number of Cancers)* = *(0.0)* × *(811)* = *0.0*

Number of cancers = 811

the carcinogenic effect per rad. As the author points out in chapter 14, there is nothing magical about the p = 0.05 level of statistical significance, which some scientists regard as the maximum acceptable possibility that a thing occurred by chance. And as the author also points out in chapter 14, when p = 0.07, then the odds are 13 out of 14 that we should take the finding seriously.

The estimate presented in chapter 14 is that the extra dose beyond 2.5 kilometers from the hypocenter was 5.7 rads at Hiroshima and 5.2 rads at Nagasaki, with an average of 5.5 rads *in T-65 dose units* for the two cities combined. In this chapter, we showed that 0.62 for gamma rays is a reasonable conversion factor from T-65 dose to absorbed dose for most of the organs involved in cancer development from whole-body radiation. Therefore, 3.4 rads [(0.62) × (5.5 rads)] is a reasonable estimate of the *increment* of radiation in *absorbed dose* received by the control group at a distance beyond 2.5 kilometers from the hypocenter. Remember that the lowest range of dose in the observed group was 0–9 rads. Beebe, Kato, and Land treat the group beyond 2.5 kilometers as having effectively received zero dose, which this author regards as incorrect. This group may, indeed, have received a virtually zero gamma and neutron dose as *direct* bomb radiation, but our analysis (chapters 8 and 14) shows that they nevertheless received about 3.4 rads *more* absorbed dose than the 0–9-rad group closer to the bomb.

The mean absorbed dose for the so-called 0–9-rad group = 2.2 rads. Since our control group is now estimated to have received 3.4 rads *more* than the 0–9-rad dose group, we must finally estimate that the unexposed, or control, group really received 3.4 + 2.2 = 5.6 rads in total absorbed dose (*not* T-65 dose). The *corrected* peak percent increases for each age group, based on this increase in absorbed dose, are summarized in tabular form (table 8).

TABLE 8: CARCINOGENIC EFFECT PER RAD IN THE HIROSHIMA-NAGASAKI EXPERIENCE, UNCORRECTED AND CORRECTED VALUES

Age Group (years ATB)	Peak Percent Increase per Rad, Uncorrected	Peak Percent Increase per Rad, Corrected
0–9	9.5	16.6
10–19	3.5	4.74
20–34	1.47	1.89
35–49	0.82	1.05

However, the values in the composite tabulations will not be raised, for the reason already stated. The reader has the corrected values here, should he (she) choose to use them instead.

Since we were unable to demonstrate any effect of radiation in the 50+ age group, we can apply no correction.

The Problem of "Built-In," Fraudulent Thresholds

The underestimation in the Japanese series of from 22% to 43% in excess cancer rate per rad is appreciable. However, there is an even more serious implication of the finding that there is an *increment* in dose of 3.4 rads to the population at 2.5 kilometers from the hypocenter and beyond, both in Hiroshima and Nagasaki. As the data become more refined, with further follow-up at Hiroshima and Nagasaki, we shall wish to compare the control group with the lowest-dosage groups, to test for carcinogenesis at very low doses. The *wrong* answers will be obtained from the Hiroshima-Nagasaki data unless the correction for the dose *increment* at a distance is taken into account.

As matters stand now, no study appreciates this source of error. If the increment is real, and is not taken into account, we will find in the future that there is a lower cancer rate in the 0–9-rad dose group than in the zero-rad dose group. And it is likely that this finding will be explained as the identification of a "safe radiation threshold." The reader of this book, after reading chapters 8 and 14, will understand why this "built-in" threshold will be fraudulent, the result of failure to correct for the *increment* in dose beyond 2.5 kilometers from the hypocenter.

SECTION 11: THE INDUCTION OF HUMAN BREAST CANCER BY IONIZING RADIATION

Breast cancer currently accounts for 19.9% of all cancer deaths in women in the United States. The history of radical, disfiguring surgery to treat this disease helps account for the special fear of breast cancer. Not only because of its quantitative importance and its psycho-social implications, but also for other salient reasons, breast cancer deserves prominent attention in considerations of the role of ionizing radiation in the genesis of human cancer in general.

One reason for giving breast cancer special consideration is that we now have more quantitative data for assessing how many breast cancers will occur for a specified dose of radiation than for any other solid cancer. Moreover, the spontaneous incidence of breast cancer, compared with that of many other cancers, occurs relatively early in life, which means that we start to see the breast-cancer consequences of childhood irradiation when it is still too early to see other adult cancers induced by childhood irradiation.

There are two additional, critical reasons why breast cancer deserves and receives special attention here. First, a large number of young women are engaged in occupations associated with radiation, such as hospital work, and for them, the evidence that radiation can induce cancer, specifically of the breast, is important. Second, in recent years, the technique of *mammogra-*

phy (a radiological examination of the breast) for seeking out early, and hence allegedly treatable, diseases of the breast has been widely promoted.

Major criticisms of mammography, particularly for young women, have recently been voiced, based on the estimate that there will be more breast cancers induced by the procedure than there will be women saved from breast-cancer death by early discovery of lesions. As a result of the criticisms by Bailar (1976 and 1978) and by the Ad Hoc Working Group on Mammography of the National Cancer Institute, the dose given in mammography has recently been grossly reduced, and new work in progress attempts to reduce it even further.

Bailar (1978) recently discussed the question of mammography further and continued to express his many reservations concerning the use of mammography, particularly for women under 50 years of age, to whom no benefit from the procedure has been demonstrated. There are conflicting claims in the literature as to whether the benefits of screening to women over 50 years of age are the result of the *mammographic* examination itself. Since there were many parts to the examination of the women over 50 years of age, beyond the mammography, it is not at all certain that early breast cancers would have been less efficiently detected even without the mammography. There is considerable controversy concerning the usefulness of mammography, and it is not likely that a clear picture will very soon emerge.

Whatever does emerge concerning potential benefits from the mammographic procedure, it is still *essential* that we have good, quantitative estimates of the induction of breast cancer by ionizing radiation at various ages, as an input for intelligent decision making by both the patient and the physician.

The analysis in this chapter will be incorporated into the calculation of the *cancer dose* (chapter 6) and thus into the *breast-cancer dose* (chapter 7). The *breast-cancer dose* is that dose of ionizing radiation which provides essentially 100% risk (or certainty) of development of breast cancer.

The Modern Era of Investigation

The work of a Nova Scotia physician, Dr. Ian MacKenzie, was central in initiating serious quantitative study of radiation-induced breast cancer. MacKenzie's studies of women who had undergone multiple fluoroscopies during treatment of tuberculosis showed a strong association between the X-radiation used in the treatment and subsequent development of breast cancer. MacKenzie's work, in turn, provided the stimulus for Wanebo, working with the Atomic Bomb Casualty Committee, to investigate the epidemiology of breast cancer among the atomic-bomb survivors. This study too showed positive results.

In 1970, Tamplin and Gofman (1970c) published the first formal analysis of both the MacKenzie and the Wanebo data in modern terms, namely, as the % increase in cancer incidence (over spontaneous incidence) per rad of exposure to X-rays (MacKenzie) and to A-bomb radiation (Wanebo et al.).

They reported:

a. For the Wanebo data, for women at a mean age of 28.1 years at irradiation (ATB), the best estimate of the increase in breast-cancer incidence per rad is 5.21% per rad. At the time of the Wanebo analysis, the number of cases in the unexposed (expected) group were so few that there was room for a large sampling error in the O/E value and thus in Tamplin and Gofman's 5.21% per rad excess. Newer data, based on many more cancer cases, suggests a lower % increase per rad.

b. For the MacKenzie data, for women at approximately 25 years of age at irradiation (from fluoroscopic X-rays), the best estimate of the increase in incidence per rad is between 5.08% and 2.18%, with the uncertainty resulting from the uncertainty in dose *per* fluoroscopic examination.

c. In both cases, the data are highly consistent with linearity, meaning that the induction of breast cancer is essentially proportional to radiation dose. The Wanebo data support this conclusion all the way down to a dose of 10 rads to the breast.

The similarity in these results is remarkable, and the fact that the two groups received their irradiation in different ways is crucial. The women in Japan received their radiation in one acute dose; the women in Nova Scotia received their total dose of radiation in small fractions, spread over months and years. The similarity of effects, by now abundantly confirmed (as we shall see below), went a long way toward demolishing the myth that fractionation of radiation dose can mitigate the development of cancer.

In the years since 1970, a wealth of new data has become available. The broad conclusions of 1970 remain unchanged, but we are now in a position to address many additional questions, particularly concerning the critical importance of age at exposure, and to formulate a general picture of the quantitative aspects of breast-cancer induction by ionizing radiation.

SECTION 12: QUANTITATIVE ANALYSIS OF RADIATION-INDUCED BREAST CANCER

Several very different types of studies are now available for quantitative analysis by modern methods. As these studies exist in the literature, they are generally not analyzed in a way that makes them integrable, but sufficient data are usually provided so that they *can* be so analyzed. Unless such analysis is made, including the determination and use of the peak percent increase per rad for breast cancer, grossly erroneous estimates of the risk of breast cancer can be obtained.

Let us recall our general discussion of the objective of such analyses. We desire to ascertain the % increase in breast-cancer risk (over spontaneous risk) per rad of radiation for various ages at irradiation. In particular, we seek the *peak percent increase in breast-cancer risk per rad,* taken to occur at 40 years post-irradiation (from chapter 4). With these values of peak percent per rad and life tables, we will be able to calculate the overall price in breast cancer for the remainder of the life-span of a population irradiated at a particular age (see chapter 7).

Even though 589 cases of breast cancer, in toto, are available in the combined studies analyzed here, it is still true that for the individual studies, once the cases are broken down by age group or by dose group, small numbers of cases are often encountered. The statistical reliability of estimates for certain individual categories of age or dose will be poor in such instances. But, when all the results are combined appropriately, most of the statistical uncertainties will balance each other, affording results of quite acceptable reliability for the purposes we intend.

It is self-evident that over time many, many more breast cancers will unfortunately occur in the various series under study; in time, therefore, estimates can be refined. It is worth reminding the reader that the assurance that better estimates will be available 30 years from now is no help at all in making decisions which must be made *now.*

The analyses of currently available breast-cancer data are provided here in an abbreviated form, and the conclusions are presented in section 13.

As will become evident from the summary of our analyses, the picture we can draw of breast-cancer induction by ionizing radiation is a remarkably consistent one, despite grossly differing circumstances of irradiation, and data from throughout the world. There is every reason to believe that our results are applicable throughout the world.

FURTHER STUDIES OF THE NOVA SCOTIA WOMEN WITH TUBERCULOSIS

Myrden and Hiltz (1969) extended the follow-up period for the Nova Scotia Sanatorium patients whom MacKenzie had studied in his original, now classic work. Myrden later provided additional data from his studies to the BEIR Committee. These studies provide data for many more breast cancers than were available at the time of MacKenzie's work. Additionally, the crucial datum, *woman-years at risk,* is available in the Myrden studies. Lastly, the most refined of Myrden's studies are based on a follow-up period beginning 10 years after fluoroscopic radiation, thus eliminating many cases of early death and providing a series better restricted to the crucial period for radiation carcinogenesis, that is, beyond 10 years after irradiation. Myrden's is an incidence report.

For this analysis, all the breast-cancer cases will be considered in one group, with mean age at irradiation 25.4 years. Over the entire period of follow-up (ranging from 10 years for some patients to as long as 25 years for others), 5 breast cancers developed in 306 non-fluoroscoped women (no artificial pneumothorax therapy), and 27 breast cancers developed in 243 women who were fluoroscoped. The data, together with the woman-years of follow-up, are as follows:

Group	Women	Woman-Years*	Number of Cancers of the Breast*	Breast Cancers per Million Woman-Years
With Pneumothorax	243	2,607.5	27	10,354.7
Without Pneumothorax	306	3,250	5	1,538.4

*The woman-years of follow-up include the period through 1966, while the actual number of breast cancers includes some cases through 1971. The author agrees with the BEIR Committee that for O/E values, the 1966 data for woman-years can be utilized together with the 1971 data for breast cancers.

O/E = 10,354.7/1,538.4 = 6.73, so there was a 573% excess in breast cancers. We must now turn to the question of dosimetry for these patients.

Dosimetry: Some of the treated patients received bilateral pneumothorax therapy; others received unilateral pneumothorax therapy. We estimate that of the 243 women who received pneumothorax treatment, 188 cases received unilateral and 55 cases received bilateral treatment. From Myrden's data on the number of fluoroscopies received by each patient (0–300 + treatments), we obtain an average number of fluoroscopies per patient of 162.8. (This is obtained by multiplying the number of patients by the average number of fluoroscopies, summing all the products, and dividing by 243 [the irradiated patients]).

The most uncertain datum for the Nova Scotia series is the *true average dose per fluoroscopic examination,* because this depended on how long the individual physician kept the machine in operation. At best, the dose estimate is a reasonable approximation. After correcting for several factors, we calculate a dose of 7.5 rads per fluoroscopic examination. Then we calculate the total average breast dose received by each age group: for the 188 unilaterally irradiated women, this is 741 rads; for the 55 bilaterally irradiated women, it is 1,221 rads. For all 243 patients, therefore, the average dose to the breasts was 850 rads. From this we obtain a % excess per rad of 0.67% per rad, for the follow-up period of this study.

The reader may raise his eyebrows about the "very high" doses in this study (see sections 7 and 8). However, 850 rads were not received all at once; each dose was approximately 7.5 rads, and doses were separated by days or weeks. The fractionation of the dose in this series will be considered further in chapter 8.

Finally, we calculate that the peak percent increase in breast-cancer rate per rad = *3.4% per rad,* for women irradiated at a mean age of 25.4 years. It is desirable in any study to segregate the cases by age group, and to develop a peak percent value for each age group. For the Nova Scotia series, however, the number of breast-cancer cases is simply too small to warrant subdivision by age.

An extremely interesting event in this series is this: one *child* was irradiated before age 9, and this one child (the entire "population sample" of children) *did* develop breast cancer during the follow-up period. This could have happened by chance, or it could be telling us something about the increased sensitivity of the young to cancer induction from irradiation. We will see additional indications of increased sensitivity at early ages when we come to the breast-cancer series from Hiroshima-Nagasaki.

THE MASSACHUSETTS FLUOROSCOPY STUDIES

Boice and Monson (1977) conducted a study of women exposed to fluoroscopic X-radiation in the course of tuberculosis therapy in sanatoria in Massachusetts. This study of breast-cancer incidence provides a totally independent check of the findings obtained in Nova Scotia.

It is estimated that the average dose per fluoroscopy was much lower in the Massachusetts series. In the Massachusetts series, over 75% of the examinations were conducted with the woman's back to the X-ray tube, giving a lower dose to the breast than would be the case if the women were facing the tube, as was usually the case in the Nova Scotia series. Thus, Boice and Monson estimate that the average dose received by the breast was 1.5 rads per fluoroscopic examination, versus 7.5 rads for the Nova Scotia series.

Peak Percents Categorized by Age at Irradiation: It is possible to break the Massachusetts patients into two age groups without causing the number of cases per age group to be dangerously small:

□ Group I : All women 29 years of age and younger at exposure
□ Group II: All women 30 years of age and older at exposure

From Table 10 of the Boice and Monson paper, we obtain the following data for Group I:

Group I (avg. age: 20.3 yrs.)	Woman-Years	Number of Breast Cancers	Breast Cancers per Million Woman-Years
Pneumotherapy	21,522	33	1,533.3
No Pneumotherapy	14,642	10	682.9

From these data we calculate a peak percent increase in breast-cancer rate for Group I of *2.3% per rad.* From the data of Boice and Monson (Table 5 of their paper), it is estimated that the mean age at irradiation for the group under 30 years of age was 20.3 years, so it is to this mean age that the estimate of 2.3% per rad applies.

For Group II Boice and Monson present the following data:

Group II (avg. age: 37.6 yrs.)	Woman-Years	Number of Breast Cancers	Breast Cancers per Million Woman-Years
Pneumotherapy	5,902	8	1,355.4
No Pneumotherapy	4,383	5	1,140.7

For Group II, the peak percent increase = *0.49% per rad.* The mean age at irradiation for the women in Group II, from the Boice data, was 37.6 years.

Comparison of the two values just derived shows a marked *decline* in peak percent increase in breast-cancer rate per rad (from 2.3% per rad to 0.49% per rad) with increase in age at exposure. The total number of cases in the Massachusetts series precludes a further breakdown into more age groups at irradiation.

THE HIROSHIMA-NAGASAKI SERIES

The Hiroshima-Nagasaki data of Beebe, Kato, and Land, already analyzed in section 1, include *deaths* from breast cancer. However, a much larger number of breast-cancer cases is available for analysis if *incidence* of breast cancer is examined instead. New data on breast-cancer incidence for Hiroshima-Nagasaki were presented, for the 1950–1969 follow-up, by McGregor and co-workers in 1977, and were analyzed by Land and McGregor in 1979. Data for the 1950–1974 follow-up were presented by Boice and co-workers in 1979. By 1969, 231 breast cancers had been observed in the exposed and unexposed groups combined; five years later, 360 cancers had been observed.

These numbers provide a much larger data base than was available to Wanebo in his initial studies. Although no one reported on breast cancer until the late 1960s, follow-up can be said to have begun in 1950, since records were kept long before their analysis.

The paper by McGregor and co-workers showed that there is no significant difference between the findings from Hiroshima and those from Nagasaki, and that there is no evidence to suggest that an RBE value for neutrons other than 1.0 (indicating no difference in effectiveness) is needed. In other words, we shall treat rads absorbed from neutrons just like rads absorbed from gamma rays, in terms of their cancer-producing effects. However, in correcting kerma doses in air to absorbed tissue doses, we shall use appropriate factors for gamma rays and neutrons.

From the 1979 Boice paper, a dose estimate (including, of course, zero dose for the controls) is available for 351 of the 360 breast-cancer cases. This large series will also permit age-grouping.

Dose Groups Considered

In the analysis of the Beebe, Kato, and Land data for cancer deaths, it was emphasized that *all* groups from 1 rad and up were utilized. This practice prevents the criticism that an analysis is based only on high-dose exposures.

The mean doses received by the irradiated age groups in this breast-cancer analysis will likewise include all radiation doses at or above 1 rad. After correcting for kerma doses, the data for the Life Span Study groups give the following mean doses, in breast-absorbed dose:

Age Group years ATB	Mean Breast-Absorbed Dose (gammas plus neutrons)
0–9	29.7 rads
10–19	43.3 rads
20–34	40.0 rads
35–49	36.2 rads
50+	30.5 rads

The procedure for deriving these mean doses is explained in our analysis of the overall cancer death rate of Beebe, Kato, and Land (section 1). There would appear to be one correction that should be considered in the dosimetry of the 0–9-year-old group. The undeveloped breast tissue in this age group is very thin, so the usual correction factor for kerma to absorbed dose should probably not be used. For this reason, the value 29.7 rads will be adjusted upward by a factor of 10/8 or 1.25, giving an absorbed tissue dose of 37.1 rads for the 0–9-year age group. This group, Group 1, will be analyzed last, because some special considerations are required.

Group II: Women Ages 10–19 ATB:

Group	Woman-Years	Number of Breast Cancers	Breast Cancers per Million Woman-Years
Unexposed	180,742	31	171.5
Exposed to 1 rad or more	115,590	43	372.0

The peak percent increase in breast-cancer rate = *6.2% per rad*, for a group exposed at a mean age of 14.5 years.

Group III: Women Ages 20–29 ATB:

Group	Woman-Years	Number of Breast Cancers	Breast Cancers per Million Woman-Years
Unexposed	154,764	44	284.3
Exposed to 1 rad or more	94,739	38	401.1

The peak percent increase in breast-cancer rate = *2.3% per rad*, for a group of women exposed at a mean age of 24.5 years.

Group IV: Women Ages 30–39 ATB:

Group	Woman-Years	Number of Breast Cancers	Breast Cancers per Million Woman-Years
Unexposed	144,282	49	339.6
Exposed to 1 rad or more	84,925	34	400.3

The peak percent increase in breast-cancer rate = *1.1% per rad,* for women exposed at a mean age of 34.5 years.

Group V: Women Ages 40–49 ATB:

Group	Woman-Years	Number of Breast Cancers	Breast Cancers per Million Woman-Years
Unexposed	116,794	38	325.3
Exposed to 1 rad or more	73,395	24	326.9

$O/E = 326.9/325.3 = 1.005$. This excess is insignificant, so we can say that *no* excess of breast cancer can be demonstrated for women 40–49 years of age when exposed to 38 rads of radiation.

Two explanations are possible. First, this may simply represent the effect of sampling variation, a small-numbers problem. Second, it is *possible* that the absence of radiation effect on the breast in this group is real. Boice and co-workers suggested, as Smith and Doll did previously, that irradiation of the ovaries (as part of whole-body radiation, such as the Japanese experienced) may itself have suppressed the risk of breast cancer. This would be a quite different situation from irradiation of the breasts alone. Since no such effect was found in the younger women, this explanation requires a different sensitivity of ovaries to irradiation, by age.

The ultimate solution of this question can only come with the acquisition of more data on the Japanese. For now, there is no choice but to find *zero* breast-cancer induction per rad for the 40–49-year age group.

Group VI: Women Over 50 ATB:

Group	Woman-Years	Number of Breast Cancers	Breast Cancers per Million Woman-Years
Unexposed	82,190	26	316.3
Exposed to 1 rad or more	50,071	19	379.4

The peak percent increase in breast-cancer rate = *1.7% per rad,* for women irradiated at age 50 or older.

Group 1: Children Ages 0–9 ATB: Since a vast accumulation of evidence (most of it detailed in this book) indicates that the risk of cancer induction per rad is greatest at very young ages at irradiation, one would presume that among investigators of Hiroshima and Nagasaki the greatest interest would center around the group 0–9 years old ATB. In the unabridged version of this book the BEIR-III report (1979) was used as the information source concerning 5 cases of breast cancer occurring in those 0–9 years old ATB. That source refers (p. 382) to "only one (nonexposed) breast cancer . . . found in the 1950–1969 LSS series." A little further on the BEIR report states, "Five cancers in the same age group were found in the 1950–1974 series, including one with a breast tissue dose of 57 rads and four with doses of less than 20 rads," The reasonable interpretation of this, given that 1 case was "unexposed," was that all the other 4 had some dose different from zero. But a later paper by Tokunaga states that 2 of the 4 had zero doses, so the BEIR report was misleading on this small series.

A little earlier, when the UNSCEAR report (1977) was written, only 1 breast cancer, in the unexposed group, had occurred. Based on this, the UNSCEAR committee stated:

For example, it is not yet known whether those exposed at age 0–9 will show a large excess when they reach the age at which hormonal or other influences determine a full expression of "latent" cancers, or will show only a minimal excess because only a few breast cells had developed, and were exposed to radiation, at the time of the bomb explosion. (p. 389)

We find it difficult to fathom the UNSCEAR logic concerning "few breast cells" exposed, since these cells must necessarily be the progenitors of all future breast-tissue cells. So the UNSCEAR logic is simply faulty in suggesting that the possibly sensitive cells are not yet there.

The author of this book stated in the original edition that he would willingly go out on a limb to predict that there were going to be a goodly munber of breast cancers in those exposed in this 0–9-year age group (ATB).

Recently, at an informal workshop on low-dose radiation, Jablon of the Hiroshima-Nagasaki study group reported that the "theory" about the very young not having the required hormonal influence to get the radiation effect is "now totally exploded." He stated that the excess of breast cancers being found in this group simply wipes that "theory" out. That is very gratifying to this author, who found the idea absurd, as stated above.

We do not yet have the format report of Jablon, so we cannot use his informal statements to do any quantitative analysis for breast cancer in the 0–9-year age group of Hiroshima-Nagasaki.

A Comment on Statistical Significance

The author hopes that the reader will appreciate the unreliability of small numbers, and will always ask, is this *five* really different from this *one*? Or would a different random sample give a *three* and a *two* under the same circumstances?

If the reader also remembers that the error band on numbers grows smaller, relatively, as the numbers grow larger, he (she) will understand why the *combined* studies in this book provide the most *reliable* findings in existence.

The reader, it is hoped, will also be alert to the "phenomenon of banished evidence." Readers unfamiliar with the scientific literature may be surprised to learn that evidence is routinely banished if there is 1 chance in 10 (p = 0.10) that it is "not real." Thus, findings which have 9 chances out of 10 of being "real" are sometimes never revealed at all to the outside world, or even to other investigators in the same field of interest! When p = 0.10, findings are said to be "not statistically significant," or (in a far more misleading way) it is said that "evidence was lacking" or "no evidence was found."

It is indeed dangerous that scientists can disallow findings that they do not *like* because the findings have "only" 9 chances in 10 of being real! In this author's opinion, if the numbers are so small that their statistical significance is in doubt, it is far better science to say so than simply to discard the data.

It is not commonly recognized that investigators can often control statistical significance by the way they *group* their data. The reader can see that the radiation induction of breast cancer in Japanese females irradiated at young ages would be "found" sooner at a statistically significant level if the age grouping were 0–14 years ATB instead of 0–9 years, simply because *more* observed cases would fall into the broader age category and would reflect statistical significance sooner. Using a 15-year instead of a 10-year age grouping is not a far-fetched idea: several reports on the Hiroshima-Nagasaki data routinely use categories like 20–34 years of age. On the other hand, the reader can also see that the radiation induction of breast cancer would be "found" much later if age groupings such as 0–4.5 years ATB and 4.5–9 years ATB were used.

To consider an extreme example, let us realize that investigators could almost make the whole of human evidence on radiation carcinogenesis *disappear* by the simple device of grouping data by *single* years of age at irradiation. Then each age group would contain only a very few cases, with large error bands. Since there would be *no* group providing statistically significant observations, we could declare that no substantial evidence in controlled studies was found for radiation carcinogenesis, and all go home.

THE ROCHESTER ACUTE MASTITIS THERAPY SERIES OF SHORE AND CO-WORKERS

In 1969, Mettler and co-workers published the first paper on the development of breast cancer in 606 women who had been treated with X-rays for acute postpartum mastitis (an inflammatory disease of the breast occurring in the early nursing period). In that study it was shown that the breast-cancer incidence was double the expected rate, which was drawn from age-specific breast-cancer rates for upstate New York. Recently, this incidence study has been significantly extended, and the results published by Shore and co-workers (1977).

There existed certain questions about possible confounding variables in the Mettler et al. study. Could acute postpartum mastitis itself increase breast-cancer incidence? Was there a familial factor in the women with postpartum mastitis which accounted for excess breast cancer? In the new, enlarged study, three control groups were added, in addition to the control group provided within the series itself by the unirradiated breasts (two-thirds of the women received treatment to only one breast). While some very useful information is provided by the additional control groups, it is this author's view that the best control group by far is represented by the unirradiated breasts.

As a control for familial predisposition to breast cancer, 554 sisters of the irradiated group were followed up. As a control for an effect of postpartum mastitis itself in increasing breast cancer, 539 women with postpartum mastitis treated *without* X-ray therapy (in another New York hospital) were followed. Lastly, as a control for this group of 539, their sisters, also not receiving X-ray therapy, were followed up.

It became clear that the X-irradiated women with postpartum mastitis showed a breast-cancer incidence rate in excess of the rate for any of the control groups, and in excess of the breast-cancer rate for the untreated breasts of the women irradiated unilaterally. It was of interest that all three additional control groups showed higher breast-cancer incidence rates than would be expected based on the New York State Cancer Registry data. A possible explanation is that Shore and co-workers sought out cases more diligently than is usual for data reported to the New York Registry.

One question necessarily remains open. Is it possible that a breast inflamed because of mastitis is more sensitive to radiation injury than an uninflamed breast? If this were true, the findings could not claim the general applicability we seek here. While this question cannot be answered definitively, there are two points to be made. First, the possibility of a special sensitivity is only speculated. Second, if it were true that inflamed breasts were especially sensitive to radiation induction of breast cancer, the data for this series would show much higher values for % excess incidence per rad than do all the other series, which involve uninflamed breasts. This is *not* the case. Therefore, we shall use the data from this series as one component in the composite picture of radiation induction of breast cancer.

The Findings

The patient's ages at therapy ranged from 14 to 44, except for one case. Of the 606 women in the series, 571 responded to the follow-up questionnaire. The follow-up started at 10 years post-irradiation, for analytic purposes.

While the longest follow-up was to 34 years post-irradiation, the mean follow-up for the entire group was to 24.8 years post-irradiation.

While one would like to break this series into categories of age at irradiation, this will not be done because the data for the unirradiated breasts of the mastitis patients are provided only for the overall series. Since we do not wish to omit this important control data, we shall treat the entire series as one group, with a mean age of 27.5 years at time of treatment.

Shore and co-workers studied 1,142 breasts (in 571 patients), of which 392 were not irradiated (in the 392 patients who received unilateral treatment). Thus, 750 breasts (1,142 − 392) received radiation, with a mean dose of 377 rads.

The data are as follows:

Group	Breast-Years at Risk	Number of Breast Cancers	Breast Cancers per Million Breast-Years
1. Breasts exposed to 377 rads	12,055	33	2,737.4
2. Unirradiated breasts in treated women	6,323	3	not calculated separately
3. Combined additional control groups	31,857	28	not calculated separately
Total of 2 and 3	37,857	31	818.8

The peak percent increase in breast-cancer rate = *2.0% per rad,* for women irradiated at a mean age of 27.5 years.

Breast-Years Versus Woman-Years

Some readers may say, "Well, that is the peak percent increase for *one* breast, and so I must double it if both breasts get irradiated." Not so! The peak percent increase per rad is the increase over a spontaneous rate, and it applies to both the spontaneous rate of cancer *per breast* and the spontaneous rate of breast cancer *per woman*. The % excess per rad and the peak percent increase per rad will be the *same* whether incidence per breast-year or incidence per woman-year is studied. And consequently, a *composite* value can be obtained from the five series examined in this chapter.

THE SWEDISH EXPERIENCE: STUDIES BY BARAL AND CO-WORKERS

Baral and co-workers (1977) were able to follow up 1,037 of 1,115 women who had been treated at the Radiumhemmet, a treatment center in Sweden, with X-rays for several different nonmalignant conditions of the breast between 1927 and 1957. The follow-up period started at 5 years post-irradiation and extended to an average of 31.5 years post-irradiation. The distribution of cases by the disease for which X-ray therapy was utilized follows: 855 patients were treated for fibroadenomatosis, 120 for acute mastitis, 49 for chronic mastitis, 13 for unilateral hypertrophy of the breast.

In this incidence series, 115 cancers developed in the irradiated breasts. Radiation treatment was given over a period of 12 months in 85% of the cases, over 12–60 months in 11% of the cases, and over a period in excess of 60 months in 4% of the cases.

Baral calculated control values from the Swedish national rates for the year 1970 because he had no other control series. Baral points out that lower breast-cancer rates must have prevailed before 1970 (since Swedish rates rose 2% per year after 1958). This means, if anything, that the 1970 expected rates he used may be somewhat too high, and hence the O/E values somewhat too low. Thus, radiation effects may be underestimated. However, it is unlikely that an underestimation of any consequence would result, since any overestimation of expected rates would be partly balanced by under-reporting in the national incidence rates (physicians failing to report). We noted in the mastitis series, for instance, that official incidence statistics in New York reported a lower rate than the rate actually found in the control groups.

The Baral data do lend themselves to categorization by age at exposure. The peak percent values are given here in table 9; see "X-ray therapy of benign lesions."

Comments on Age Sensitivity and on High Doses

The series of patients studied by Baral and co-workers show an age trend in peak percent increase in breast-cancer rate per rad that is strikingly similar to the trend shown by the combined Hiroshima-Nagasaki group. Taking these two studies together, the evidence is overwhelmingly in favor of a marked *decrease in sensitivity* of the breast to induction of cancer by ionizing radiation *with increase in age*. This is also in accord with the trend for overall cancers, and is also in accord with the trend demonstrated by Gofman and Tamplin over a decade ago.

The reader's initial impression in examining the doses delivered in the Baral series (given in table 9) may be that the entire study is based on very-high-dose radiation. And since we have noted that the risk per rad has been observed to *decrease* at very high doses, the reader may worry that we will underestimate the effect at low doses by incorporating this study with others. As we shall see in chapter 8, that is a possibility.

On the other hand, the *opposite* effect of high doses has been proposed (but not observed) by some investigators, on the presumption that the effect per rad will *increase* with dose if simultaneous injuries at two cell sites are involved in carcinogenesis (see chapters 3 and 8). The probability of simultaneous two-site injuries depends on dose *rate*. If the total dose is fractionated, with adequate time between treatments, it is the dose given each time that would be operative for causing any such two-track events. All the total doses in the series of Baral and co-workers were given over a period of 12 months or more (over even 60 months in some cases). The individual doses per treatment, likely to be no more than 50–100 rads, are quite comparable to the Hiroshima-Nagasaki dosage, where the mean dose, delivered acutely, was in the neighborhood of 40 rads. The reader will find the issues of high versus low doses and dose rates examined further in chapter 8.

Section 13: Integration of All the Breast-Cancer Data

Our objective, in examining these independent studies of the induction of breast cancer by ionizing radiation, is to obtain the best values, *for each age group at irradiation,* for *peak percent increase in breast-cancer rate per rad.* These best values will be used to help determine the personal and public-health risks of breast cancer from radiation. Table 9 presents the assembled values from all the various series, arranged in ascending order of age at the time of irradiation. Since all the values are presented in the form of peak percents per rad, we have effectively converted disparate follow-up studies into a body of results resting on a common base.

As in table 7, we weight the peak percent value for each study according to the number of observed breast cancers in that study.

In table 9, we calculate the best value for each decade of age at irradiation and the mean age at irradiation within each decade from the ages in the individual series, again weighting by the number of observed cancers per series.

Section 14: What Is the Effect of Natural and Medical Radiation on Cancer Calculations?

The reader will note that in all the calculations where O/E values are used, the E value (unless explicitly stated otherwise) represents the value for the spontaneous occurrence of cancer. This is not precisely correct, since there are two sources of radiation, natural-background and medical radiation, which will have affected both the "irradiated" and the "control" groups. Let us explore what magnitude of error these might introduce.

We can use as an example one of the calculations from this chapter. In considering the data for persons 20–34 years old at irradiation in Hiroshima and Nagasaki, we used the following data:

□ Cancers per million person-years (unexposed) = 1,077.8
□ Cancers per million person-years (1 rad or more) = 1,289.3
□ Mean dose for the irradiated group = 31.0 rads

TABLE 9: SYNTHESIS OF ALL HUMAN EPIDEMIOLOGICAL DATA ON BREAST CANCER FOR PEAK PERCENT INCREASE IN CANCER RATE PER RAD

Age Group: 0–9 at Irradiation

Age (years)	Peak Percent Increase per Rad	Observed Number of Cancers	Expected Cancers	Mean Dose in Rads	Type of Study	Kind of Cancer
4.5	38.8	4	1	37.1	bomb survivors	breast cancer

Best estimate of peak percent per rad = 38.8% per rad
(Obviously so because there is only one value available)

We shall later need three additional items:
(Peak Percent Value) × (Number of Cancers) = (38.8) × (4) = 155.2
(Mean Age) × (Number of Cancers) = (4.5) × (4) = 18.0
(Number of Cancers) = 4

Age Group: 10–19 at Irradiation

Age (years)	Peak Percent Increase per Rad	Observed Number of Cancers	Expected Cancers	Mean Dose in Rads	Type of Study	Kind of Cancer
14.5	6.2	43	31	43.3	bomb survivors	breast cancer
15.0	5.0	2	(0.25)	285	X-ray therapy of benign lesions	breast cancer

TABLE 9: (CONTINUED)

Best estimate of composite peak percent per rad = 6.15% per rad.
Mean Age for this group = 653.5/45 = 14.5.

Age Group: 20–29 at Irradiation

Age (years)	Peak Percent Increase per Rad	Observed Number of Cancers	Expected Cancers	Mean Dose in Rads	Type of Study	Kind of Cancer
25.4	3.4	27	5	850	Nova Scotia TB	breast cancer
20.3	2.1	33	10	150	Massachusetts TB	breast cancer
24.5	2.3	38	44	40	bomb survivors	breast cancer
27.5	2.0	33	31	377	X-ray for mastitis	breast cancer
22.0	4.6	13	(1.1)	450	X-ray therapy of benign lesions	breast cancer
27.0	3.1	18	(2.3)	430	"	breast cancer

Best estimate of composite peak percent per rad = 2.65% per rad.
Mean age for this group = 3,966.2/162 = 24.5.

Age Group: 30–39 at Irradiation

Age (years)	Peak Percent Increase per Rad	Observed Number of Cancers	Expected Cancers	Mean Dose in Rads	Type of Study	Kind of Cancer
37.6	0.49	8	5	150	Massachusetts TB	breast cancer
34.5	1.1	34	49	38	bomb survivors	breast cancer
32.0	1.35	17	(3.4)	600	X-ray therapy of benign lesions	breast cancer
37.0	0.36	11	(4.9)	720	"	breast cancer

Best estimate of composite peak percent per rad = 0.98% per rad.
Mean age for this group = 2,424.8/70 = 34.6.

AGE GROUP: 40–49 AT IRRADIATION

Age (years)	Peak Percent Increase per Rad	Observed Number of Cancers	Expected Cancers	Mean Dose in Rads	Type of Study	Kind of Cancer
44.5	0.0	24	38	38	bomb survivors	breast cancer
42.0	0.44	13	(4.8)	840	X-ray therapy of benign lesions	breast cancer
47.0	0.17	7	(4.1)	940	"	breast cancer

Best estimate of composite peak percent per rad = 0.16% per rad.
Mean age for this group = 1,943.0/44 = 44.2.

Age Group: 50+ at Irradiation

Age (years)	Peak Percent Increase per Rad	Observed Number of Cancers	Expected Cancers	Mean Dose in Rads	Type of Study	Kind of Cancer
50+	1.7	19	26	30.5	bomb survivors	breast cancer
53.3	0.26	5	(2.47)	932	X-ray therapy of benign lesions	breast cancer

Best estimate of composite peak percent per rad = 1.4% per rad.
Mean age for this group will be given as 50+

Let us now "correct" the unexposed group for the natural plus medical radiation. Of course, we will also correct the exposed group by the same amount. We will use a cumulated natural exposure of approximately 2.7 rads (27 years at 0.1 rad/year) and a cumulated dose of approximately 2.5 rads for medical exposure (a less certain value). Then the true dose for the exposed group would be $31.0 + 2.7 + 2.5 = 36.2$ rads. The true dose for the "unexposed" group would be $2.7 + 2.5 = 5.2$ rads.

Now we calculate the % excess cancer per rad, which equals 0.654% per rad. In section 1 of this chapter, we found a value of 0.632% per rad, without taking the natural and medical radiation into account. So there is a small correction upward when we do take these into account. However, even this small correction upward will not operate fully. The reason is that we use the % excess per rad value as a multiplier with the spontaneous rate of cancer deaths in order to arrive at the *number* of cancer deaths produced per rad. And since the "spontaneous" cancer deaths have natural plus medical radiation built in, we must now correct the "spontaneous" values for the group 20–34 years old ATB for natural and medical radiation.

Comparison of the uncorrected values for cancer deaths per rad with values corrected for natural and medical radiation shows that these values are identical, within rounding errors. The correction of % excess cancer per rad is exactly offset by the decline in "spontaneous" cancer rate to which the % excess of cancers per rad is applied.

However, there are enormously important implications from this *type* of correction of the observed % excess cancers per rad. In section 7, it was proposed that ultra-violet light might provide "equivalent rads" with respect to production of skin cancer. Although ultra-violet light is not ionizing, it represents energy-per-packet just below what is required for ionization (see chapter 2). In Shore's series of "lightly irradiated" cases (section 7), we found 1.23% excess cancer per rad for 40 rads of *ionizing* radiation. Suppose, for illustration, that ultra-violet light (from the sun) contributed 70 "equivalent rads" to both the irradiated and control groups.

The calculation of k would be as follows:

$$O/E = 1.49 = \frac{1 + 110\,k}{1 + 70\,k}$$

So, $k = 0.086$, or an increase of 8.6% per rad. Applying the conversion factor of 4.2 yields a *peak percent increase* of 36.1% per rad, which is far more in line with the results for other cancers than the result obtained without ultra-violet correction. Since we do not *know* the true "equivalent rads" for the ultra-violet, this calculation must remain *illustrative,* but illustrative concerning a very important issue in radiation induction of cancer.

[Chapter 6]

Whole-Body Cancer Doses and Their Practical Application

WE HAVE NOW REVIEWED and analyzed all the human epidemiological evidence which is suitable for determining the peak percent increases in cancer rate per rad. Our first objective in this chapter is a set of peak percent values that can be used for dealing with the problem of overall cancer development. From these values we will then derive whole-body cancer doses for irradiation at any age. Finally, we will see, through concrete examples, how this information can be used to answer a great variety of practical questions about the risk of cancer from irradiation.

In chapter 5, all the evidence for miscellaneous cancers and breast cancer was assembled, and the best estimates of peak percent were obtained by weighting the individual studies according to the number of cancers observed in the irradiated groups. Examination of those data shows that the Hiroshima-Nagasaki data for deaths from overall cancer (leukemia excluded) weigh heavily in those analyses, particularly for ages over 10 years at irradiation.

Section 1: Composite Values for Peak Percents, by Age

We shall now combine the miscellaneous cancer data with the breast-cancer data to obtain an overall peak percent value which takes *all* the cancer data into account, for each age group. As before, we shall weight according to the number of cancers observed in the irradiated groups of the individual studies. Ideally, we would like also to weight each study according to the importance of its particular cancer in the overall spontaneous incidence of cancer—e.g., if breast cancer accounted for 10% of all cancer deaths, then the evidence from the breast-cancer studies would be weighted as 10% of the evidence overall. The radiation data base for some major types of cancer is just too sparse for that ideal treatment, however. The best attainable approximation is represented by the combination of the data the literature does provide, for as many different cancers as possible. We shall show later (chapter 7) that there is good reason to believe that the peak percent values, *for a specific age at irradiation,* do not differ appreciably from each other (if at all) for at least the major forms of solid cancer. For this reason, the author considers it appropriate to use *all* the literature data on radiation cancer induction, even though the various cancers are not necessarily represented in such data according to the ratio of their spontaneous occurrence.

The results of this synthesis of miscellaneous cancer analyses with breast-cancer analyses is summarized here.

SUMMARY OF COMPOSITE VALUES OF PEAK PERCENT BY AGE GROUP

The final values of peak percent per rad for all cancers combined are as follows:

Age at Irradiation (years)	Peak Percent Increase in Cancer Rate per Rad
0	81.4%
6.85	54.8%
14.5	4.41%
25.9	3.71%
31.2	3.78%
42.3	0.91%
50+	0.04%

HIGH, MEDIUM, AND LOW ESTIMATES FOR AGES BELOW 20 YEARS

A best fit for the composite values above is plotted in figure 4, curve 4a. The reader will note the sharp rise in peak percent values as we go to ages below 15 years at irradiation. The truth may very well be just what the plot indicates. However, the author has certain reservations about using curve 4a to interpolate the peak percent values for each of the youngest ages at irradiation.

Use of curve 4a would mean that below 10 years of age, we would be generalizing largely from the high peak percents for thyroid cancer and adenoma, and from the *incidence* of several sorts of tumors, "benign" as well as malignant ones (see table 7, chapter 5). We do not *know* that the % excess per rad is the same for benign as for malignant tumors; in an older group (20–29 years of age), the % excess per rad was far greater for malignant salivary-gland tumors than for benign ones, but there is evidence pointing in the other direction, too. We do know there is a difference in behavior

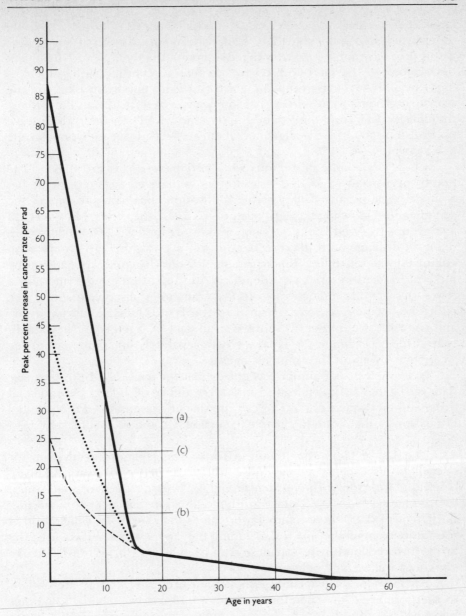

Figure 4: **The Peak Percentage Excess in Cancer Rate per Rad Versus Age at Irradiation.** *Curve (a) represents the values obtained from the overall data (see text). Curve (b) represents the values obtained from the* Japanese *data (those derived from the Hiroshima and Nagasaki observations).*

Curve (c) represents the weighted *average (see text), where the Japanese data are given a weighting of one.*

between leukemia and solid cancers, and we cannot rule out a possible difference between "benign" and malignant tumors. So the author prefers *not* to give very much weight to the assumption that benign and malignant tumors behave the same with respect to peak percent increase per rad.

The only two age groups in which this is an important issue are the newborn group and the 0–9-year group. As a scientist, the author prefers the *stronger* data, from the Japanese series and based on *deaths,* which leave no question about the malignancy of the "effect" from radiation on the 0–9-year-olds.

There are additional reasons why the Japanese data are strong. The bomb survivors are a unique series in that we have *all* ages represented in a single, well-organized, large-scale follow-up. Thus, comparisons of the age effect can be made between age groups *within* the series. Moreover, all age groups received about the same mean dose, and whatever errors were made in dosimetry will tend to be uniform over all the age groups, also enhancing the reliability of internal comparisons. By contrast, many of the medical-irradiation series provide no cases in some age groups, and only a few series provide enough cases to make any internal comparison of age effect. For all these reasons, the author regards the Japanese data as strong, and since they count heavily in the overall data for age groups beyond 10 years, we will examine the Japanese data separately for a moment to see what they say about the youngest ages.

Nevertheless, the author recognizes that the *weakness* of the Japanese data is that they may well lead to an underestimate of the risk per rad at all ages, and he therefore wants to call the reader's attention to the detailed discussion of that issue in chapter 5, section 10, and in chapter 14.

The Curve from the Japanese Data: The Japanese death data for miscellaneous cancers among those who were below 20 years ATB are combined with (only) the incidence data for breast cancer for that group, to produce curve 4b. We are faced with the situation that curve 4b, reflecting the Japanese data, shows much lower values than curve 4a, which reflects the values from all the sources, including the Japanese. Even if we used the upward correction for the Japanese data from chapter 5, section 10, curve 4b would still be well below curve 4a.

For the reasons given above, the author prefers to give greater weight to the Japanese data. Therefore, in addition to curves 4a and 4b, another curve will be plotted, 4c, which will weight the Japanese data (4b) two times and the overall data (4a) one time. Curve 4c will be known as the *weighted average curve,* and the author will use it as the primary basis for all assessments of risk of cancer from irradiation at young ages. All three curves have virtually merged by age 16, so what is at issue is which curve most closely approximates the truth at ages below 15 at irradiation. Because we cannot prove that the weighted average curve is the best choice, in some subsequent calculations we shall also provide the values that would obtain if curve 4a or 4b were used.

When additional evidence becomes available in the future, readers will be able to apply whichever of the alternatives that evidence supports most strongly. In using the weighted average curve, the author realizes he may be underestimating both the true risk of radiation-induced cancer for persons young at the time of irradiation and the consequences of irradiating whole populations of mixed ages.

FINAL PEAK PERCENT VALUES FOR EVERY AGE AT IRRADIATION

The weighted average curve (4c), the Japanese curve (4b), and the overall cancer curve (4a) give rise to values for every age at irradiation. These are presented in tabular form in the unabridged edition of this work, and are one of the essential ingredients in calculating whole-body cancer doses, individual-organ cancer doses, and all types of personal and public-health risk estimates per unit of radiation. We discussed these objectives in chapter 4, but pointed out there that data out to 90 years of age simply are not available. Now, with peak percent values for all ages, we are in a position to use the existing epidemiological evidence to *calculate* values which would otherwise be unobtainable for an additional 40 to 50 years.

SECTION 2: DERIVATION OF THE WHOLE-BODY CANCER DOSES, BY AGE

The reader will recall from chapter 4 that we defined the term *whole-body cancer dose* as the number of person-rads required to guarantee 1 extra cancer death. In addition to the peak percent values for every age at irradiation (read directly from figure 4), several other factors are taken into account in calculations of the whole-body cancer dose.

One of these is a set of values read from figure 3, the follow-up conversion curve (chapter 4); these represent the fraction of the peak percent value that applies to any specific year *after* irradiation.

Another factor is the life table. As we saw in chapter 4, this is a table providing the number of survivors at each year of age from an initial 100,000 live-born infants. To obtain the best results, the life-table data used in any calculation should be as up-to-date and specific as possible, e.g., separate tables for male and female infants.

The final factor, also encountered in chapter 4, is the age-specific cancer death rate, expressed in numbers of "spontaneous" cancer deaths per 100,000 persons alive at the beginning of each age interval. Like the life table, these data ideally should be recent, sex-specific, and place-specific (as noted previously, the age-specific rate varies among countries and even within countries).

These, in sum, are the elements used in calculating the whole-body cancer dose. Some readers may be interested to see just how this dose, for irradiation at any age, is calculated.

However, the task of making these calculations for all possible ages at irradiation is laborious, so the author has made them for the reader. All the whole-body cancer dose estimates are presented here, both for males (table 10) and females (table 11). A third column in each table estimates the average loss of life expectancy in years for any age at irradiation.

SECTION 3: PRACTICAL APPLICATIONS OF THE WHOLE-BODY CANCER DOSE: EXPOSURE OF INDIVIDUALS

There is no better way to demonstrate the practical application of the whole-body cancer dose values, which we now have available in tables 10 and 11, than to ask a number of concrete questions, the kinds of questions which come up again and again, legally, medico-legally, and from the general public's interest in radiation hazards.

QUESTION 1: *I am an industrial radiographer, working with a gamma-ray source. Through a malfunction in the equipment, the source was still present when I moved to an unshielded area. It was estimated that I received 78 rads of equivalent whole-body radiation. This happened to me about a month after my twenty-fourth birthday. I am of the male sex.*

a. Is my risk of developing cancer increased by this exposure? If it is, by just how much?

b. If I do develop cancer from this radiation, by how much will my life be shortened, on the average?

ANSWER: The risk of cancer somewhere in the body is certainly increased by the exposure. We can analyze just how much in the following manner:

Exposure occurred in the beginning of the twenty-fourth year of age. The whole-body dose was 78 rads. From table 10, whole-body cancer dose = 200.9 person-rads per cancer.

Since in this case one person received 78 rads, the person-rads delivered were $(1) \times (78) = 78$ person-rads. If 200.9 person-rads guarantee one fatal cancer, it follows that 78 person-rads will produce $(78)/(200.9) = 0.388$ fatal cancers.

Of course, fatal cancers either occur or they do not occur, so the 0.388 value means that there are 38.8 chances out of 100 that the industrial radiographer will die prematurely of cancer caused by this industrial accident. Let us round off to 39 chances in 100. Some people have difficulty understanding the meaning of 39 chances in 100. So we will put it a little differently: If 100 industrial radiographers had this accident, 39 of them would die prematurely of radiation-induced cancer.

TABLE 10: WHOLE-BODY CANCER DOSES FOR MALES, ALL AGES AT IRRADIATION

In the second column the value based on the weighted average curve is surrounded by a lower value, corresponding to the overall cancer curve, and a higher value, corresponding to the "Japanese" curve.

Age at Irradiation (years)	Whole-Body Cancer Dose (person-rads per cancer)			Average Loss of Life Expectancy (in years)
0	(33.5)	63.7	(116.5)	22.3
1	(33.0)	64.5	(123.4)	21.9
2	(32.9)	65.5	(129.6)	21.4
3	(33.6)	67.5	(136.2)	20.9
4	(34.1)	69.0	(141.1)	20.5
5	(34.7)	70.8	(147.7)	20.1
6	(35.4)	73	(156.1)	19.6
7	(36.9)	76	(161.5)	19.2
8	(38.9)	80	(168.8)	18.7
9	(41.1)	83	(169.6)	18.2
10	(44.3)	87.8	(172.4)	17.9
11	(48.1)	92	(174.6)	17.4
12	(60.1)	107	(176.8)	17.0
13	(76.0)	123	(178.1)	16.6
14	(120)	160	(182.8)	16.2
15	(164.4)	178.1	(187.5)	15.9
16	(178.3)	185	(188.5)	15.6
17	(186.2)	190	(190)	15.1
18	(194)	194	(194)	14.9
19	(197)	197	(197)	14.6
20		200.1		14.2
21		200.2		13.9
22		200.4		13.6
23		200.6		13.4
24		200.9		13.1
25		201.4		12.8
26		203		12.6
27		208		12.3
28		214		12.1
29		222		11.8
30		234.2		11.6
31		250		11.4
32		268		11.2
33		288		11.0
34		308		10.8
35		327.6		10.6
36		370		10.4

TABLE 10 (CONTINUED)

Age at Irradiation (years)	Whole-Body Cancer Dose (person-rads/cancer)	Average Loss of Life Expectancy (in years)
37	410	10.2
38	450	10.0
39	490	9.8
40	537.5	9.6
41	625	9.4
42	730	9.2
43	860	9.0
44	1020	8.9
45	1232.5	8.7
46	2000	8.6
47	3000	8.4
48	5000	8.3
49	9000	8.1
50	13434	8.0
51	15300	7.8
52	16700	7.7
53	17800	7.5
54	18700	7.4
55	19590	7.1

1. All values at five-year intervals were calculated in step-by-step fashion. All other values were obtained by interpolation.

2. With the very low radiation sensitivity above 55 years of age, in terms of cancer production, there is little reason for carrying the calculations beyond this age at irradiation.

3. Readers who know that an acute radiation dose of 400 rads to the *whole body* will kill about 50% of people from acute radiation sickness may be puzzled at first to see whole-body cancer doses well over 400 rads in this table. They must remember two things: (a) the whole-body cancer dose says nothing about the *rate* of the exposure, which means that fractionation of the dose to a single individual would spare him from acute radiation death but would not spare him from a radiation-induced cancer later, and (b) the whole-body cancer dose is expressed in *person-rads* per cancer, which means the exposure may be distributed among *numerous* individuals, and still one cancer would be guaranteed.

4. Average loss of life expectancy applies to those who *do* develop radiation-induced cancer, not to the overall group receiving the radiation.

5. The *lower* whole-body cancer doses for males than for females mean that it takes *less* radiation exposure to guarantee a male death, but this does *not* mean male tissues are more sensitive to radiation. At any given age, we use the same peak % excess per rad for males as for females. What the lower whole-body cancer dose means is that men worldwide have a higher *spontaneous* cancer death rate than women, in general (see table 12, in section 4). The lower the spontaneous cancer rate is, the higher will be the whole-body cancer dose.

TABLE 11: WHOLE-BODY CANCER DOSES FOR FEMALES, ALL AGES AT IRRADIATION

(See table 10 for explanation of column headings.)

Age at Irradiation (years)	Whole-Body Cancer Dose (person-rads per cancer)			Average Loss of Life Expectancy (in years)
0	(35.9)	68.3	(124.9)	28.9
1	(35.8)	70.0	(133.9)	28.4
2	(36.4)	72.5	(143.5)	27.9
3	(37.3)	75.0	(151.3)	27.3
4	(38.3)	77.5	(158.5)	26.8
5	(39.0)	79.6	(166.0)	26.3
6	(40.2)	83	(177.5)	25.7
7	(42.7)	88	(187.0)	25.2
8	(45.2)	93	(196.2)	24.7
9	(48.5)	98	(200.3)	24.2
10	(52.3)	103.6	(203.5)	23.6
11	(60.1)	115	(211.8)	23.1
12	(72.4)	129	(213.2)	22.5
13	(91.6)	148.3	(214.7)	22.1
14	(138.0)	184	(222.6)	21.5
15	(200.5)	217.2	(228.6)	21.0
16	(221.8)	230	(234.3)	20.5
17	(231.3)	236	(236.0)	20.1
18		241		19.6
19		245		19.1
20		248.5		18.6
21		250		18.2
22		250		17.8
23		250.5		17.3
24		251		17.0
25		251.6		16.6
26		254		16.2
27		260		15.9
28		267		15.5
29		274		15.2
30		284.6		14.8
31		298		14.4
32		315		14.1
33		340		13.8
34		368		13.4
35		398.7		13.0
36		420		12.7

TABLE 11 (CONTINUED)

Age at Irradiation (years)	Whole-Body Cancer Dose (person-rads per cancer)	Average Loss of Life Expectancy (in years)
37	465	12.4
38	510	12.1
39	570	11.8
40	636.1	11.5
41	750	11.2
42	875	11.0
43	1030	10.8
44	1200	10.5
45	1412	10.2
46	2100	10.0
47	4100	9.8
48	7800	9.6
49	11700	9.5
50	14615	9.3
51	16700	9.2
52	18600	9.0
53	19800	8.8
54	20500	8.6
55	20960	8.5

Notes at the foot of table 10 also apply to table 11.

The second part of the question has to do with the loss of life expectancy from any cancer resulting from the accident. For those extra radiation-induced cancers which do occur, each one will shorten life, on the average, by 13.1 years (table 10). But since this man cannot be sure that he will be one of those who does get a radiation-induced cancer, he must figure that his life expectancy has been shortened, on the average, by $(0.388) \times (13.1$ years$) = 5.08$ years.

It is not immediately obvious why this is correct, so let us look at this problem in a different manner. Suppose, again, that 100 radiographers experienced this accident. We have shown above that 38.8 of them will die prematurely of radiation-induced cancer, and 61.2 of them will not die of radiation-induced cancer from the accident. For those who will not die of radiation-induced cancer, there is no shortening of life expectancy. For those who will die of radiation-induced cancer, the total loss of years of life $= (38.8) \times (13.1) = 508.3$ years of life. Since this is the total number of years of life lost per 100 persons, the average loss of life expectancy is $(508.3)/(100) = 5.08$ years, which is the same answer as given above.

QUESTION 2: *(from the radiographer): Suppose I do develop a cancer at 55 years of age, which will ultimately prove fatal to me. In a compensation case, what will my lawyer be able to say about the chance that the cancer was due to radiation rather than just to "natural" causes?*

ANSWER: This is an important question, and it will recur often. Let us provide a quantitative answer. Note that this question calls for a different approach than for the first question. Now, instead of being asked for the risk of dying prematurely of a radiation-induced cancer, which we showed above was 0.388, we are being asked to compare the radiation-induced risk with the spontaneous risk.

To answer this question we need the following information: (1) the number of spontaneous cancer deaths during a one-year period at age 55, deriving from a population sample of 95,943 males. This population sample represents the number of survivors at age 25 (the age at irradiation). The spontaneous cancer deaths are obtained by multiplying the number of survivors from the original population sample by the age-specific cancer rate (see section 2). (2) We also need the number of radiation-induced cancer deaths per rad of radiation delivered in the twenty-fourth year. This is obtained by multiplying the number of spontaneous cancer deaths at age 55 (item 1) by the percent increase per rad that applies to the total number of years post-irradiation.

All the necessary calculations to obtain this information have been made for the reader and are tabulated in table A, in the Appendix. There we provide radiation-induced cancers per rad and spontaneous cancers for every age beyond irradiation, with irradiation at 5-year intervals. We could use both the tabulations for age 20 at irradiation and those for age 25 and interpolate for age 24, but we will come close enough to the answer we want if we just use the table for irradiation at 25 years of age.

Our radiographer, irradiated at 24, develops cancer at 55, that is, 31 years later. So, as a close approximation, we can say that if he had been 25 at irradiation, we would look up cancer rates for $25 + 31 = 56$ years of age. From table A we find that at age 56, during a one-year period: spontaneous cancer deaths are 293 (for a population sample of 95,943 persons at 25 years of age); and radiation-induced cancer deaths are 8.88 per rad delivered at age 25 to the same population. Our radiographer received 78 rads. (78 rads) $\times$ (8.88 cancer deaths per rad) $= 692.6$ cancer deaths in a population of 95,943 persons who received 78 rads at 25 years of age:

$$\begin{aligned} \text{Total cancer expectancy} &= \text{spontaneous} + \text{radiation-induced} \\ &= 293 \qquad\qquad + 692.6 \\ &= 985.6 \end{aligned}$$

The radiation-induced share is:

$$\frac{692.6 \text{ per } 95,943 \text{ persons}}{985.6 \text{ per } 95,943 \text{ persons}} = 0.703$$

And this is *precisely* the answer the lawyer would need. Of any cancers that occur in these individuals of age 56, who were irradiated at age 25, we can say 0.703 or 70.3% of them are radiation-induced. Or, in the legal parlance for such matters, we can say that the medical probability is 70.3% that the radiation was the cause of this man's cancer.

Table A, dealing with such matters of occupational exposure, can be used for radiation occurring at any age and cancers occurring at any later age.

QUESTION 3: *I worked in a nuclear power plant for 5 years, between age 21 and age 26. My whole-body radiation doses, measured on a film badge, were as follows:*
21st year: 4.6 rads
22nd year: 3.9 rads
23rd year: 3.7 rads
24th year: 4.4 rads
25th year: 4.0 rads
My employer told me that since I never exceeded the permissible dose of 5.0 rads per year, there is no chance that any harm could accrue to me. Is it true that my risk of cancer development was not increased by this exposure? If I do have an increased risk of cancer from this work, just how large a risk is it?

ANSWER: It is certainly *not* true that there is any harmless dose of radiation; any exposure increases a person's risk of cancer (see chapter 8, section 5). The designation of a so-called permissible dose of radiation was made for the convenience of the nuclear industry and should never be misinterpreted to mean a *safe* dose with respect to cancer induction. But we can say much more than that: we can provide a quantitative estimate of just how large this person's risk of cancer is, as a result of those 5 years of work in a nuclear facility.

From table 10, we obtain the whole-body cancer doses that go with each year of work:

Year of Work	Person-Rads Received	Whole-Body Cancer Dose
21st year	$(1) \times (4.6) = 4.6$	200.2 person-rads
22nd year	$(1) \times (3.9) = 3.9$	200.4 person-rads
23rd year	$(1) \times (3.7) = 3.7$	200.6 person-rads
24th year	$(1) \times (4.4) = 4.4$	200.9 person-rads
25th year	$(1) \times (4.0) = 4.0$	201.4 person-rads

Therefore:

$$\text{in 21st year, risk of cancer added} = \frac{4.6}{200.2} = 0.0230$$

$$\text{in 22nd year, risk of cancer added} = \frac{3.9}{200.4} = 0.0195$$

$$\text{in 23rd year, risk of cancer added} = \frac{3.7}{200.6} = 0.0184$$

$$\text{in 24th year, risk of cancer added} = \frac{4.4}{200.9} = 0.0219$$

$$\text{in 25th year, risk of cancer added} = \frac{4.0}{201.4} = 0.0199$$

Total risk of cancer added in the
five years of work: $= 0.1027$

Another way of stating the risk caused by this worker's occupational radiation is that there are 10.27 chances out of 100 that he will die of a *radiation*-induced cancer. Or, expressed still another way, if we had 100 such workers, 10.27 of them would die of a radiation-induced cancer. We cannot of course say *which* 10.27 out of 100 would fall victim to radiation-induced cancer. So the "permissible" dose of radiation is *anything but safe*, especially for the younger workers. We have just shown how even less than the annual permissible dose, for only five years of work, could kill one out of ten of the younger workers.

In later chapters, we shall have occasion to take up a number of additional practical questions concerning individual exposure, as some of the sources of ionizing radiation are considered.

SECTION 4: PRACTICAL APPLICATIONS OF THE WHOLE-BODY CANCER DOSE: EXPOSURE OF POPULATIONS

A separate, important set of questions arises when we consider the exposure of populations comprising individuals of all ages. In this section, the reader will be introduced to an additional concept, and calculations will be made of its value. That concept is the whole-body cancer dose *for a population of mixed ages,* and it is essential for the estimation of public-health consequences from radiation exposure.

DERIVATION OF THE WHOLE-BODY CANCER DOSE FOR A POPULATION OF MIXED AGES

Tables provided in the unabridged edition of this work, 1980, demonstrate how the whole-body cancer dose for a population of mixed ages is derived, by calculating the effect of delivering one rad per person to separate populations of 118,947,000 males and 131,100,000 females—a so-called equilibrium population of 250,000,000 for the United States. In an equilibrium population the death rate per year from all causes combined is exactly balanced by the birth rate. While the United States is not in equilibrium now, it seems to be moving in that direction, and it seems more rational to estimate public-health consequences on the basis of an equilibrium population than on the population as it currently stands, with a changing birth rate.

The following whole-body cancer doses, in person-rads per cancer death, were derived for populations of mixed ages. To consider the whole population, it is really close enough for most purposes to use the average for males and females combined. The results, *in person-rads per cancer death,* are as follows:

	From "Overall" Curve	From "Wgt. Av." Curve	From "Japanese" Curve
Males, mixed ages	147.3	235.0	334.7
Females, mixed ages	186.6	300.2	431.7
Population	167.0	267.6	383.2

We will use these figures to answer a number of practical questions.

QUESTION 4: *If we were to "give" 1.0 rad of whole-body radiation to every person in the population, what would be the ultimate consequences in extra radiation-induced cancer deaths?*

ANSWER: This is precisely the situation treated in the tables found in the unabridged edition, in which the whole-body cancer dose for a mixed-age population is derived. We find that each time we introduce 1.0 rad of whole-body radiation into the population, we add:

For males, 506,130 cancer deaths (limits 355,348 to 807,788)
For females, 436,663 cancer deaths (limits 303,650 to 702,646)
Total extra cancer deaths = *942,793 radiation-induced cancer deaths.*

It should be self-evident that giving 1 rad of whole-body radiation to everyone in this population would be a major public-health disaster. It must be noted that the deaths would not occur immediately; this number, 942,793, represents the extra, premature cancer deaths that would occur as all the members of the population live out their lives.

QUESTION 5: *What if 1.0 rad of whole-body radiation is delivered to the population every year, instead of only once?*

ANSWER: From Question 4, it is clear that 942,793 radiation-induced cancer deaths are the price of delivering 1.0 rad to the population. Suppose 1.0 rad whole-body dose per person were delivered in 1980 to an equilibrium population of 250 million. If in the next year, we again were to deliver a 1-rad dose to everyone, we would add an *additional* 942,793 cancer deaths to those already caused by the radiation exposure of the previous year. Of course, the radiation-induced cancers would show up gradually, not as a block in a single year.

It can readily be shown that if we continued that rate of population exposure indefinitely (1 rad whole-body dose per person per year), we would arrive at a time when we would see 942,793 radiation-induced cancer deaths *each* year. Just for simplification, suppose that all radiation-induced cancers showed up exactly 20 years post-irradiation, none earlier and none later. Then:

Year of Population Exposure to 1.0 Rad Whole-Body Dose per Person	Corresponding Radiation-Induced Cancer Deaths Observed Annually
1980	0
1981	0
1982	0
1983	0
2000	942,793 from exposure in 1980
2001	another 942,793 from exposure in 1981
2002	another 942,793 from exposure in 1982
2003	another 942,793 from exposure in 1983

. . . and so forth

QUESTION 6: *Suppose a nuclear-power-plant accident releases some "puffs" of radiation. Let us assume that a populated area containing 5 million people is exposed, so that each person averages 20 millirads of whole-body radiation from the releases. How do we calculate the number of extra cancer deaths produced?*

ANSWER: First we must calculate how many males and females are in the population of 5,000,000 persons. In doing so we find that there are

2,380,000 males and 2,620,000 females. As to dosage, 20 millirads is the same as 0.02 rads.

So the males received (2,380,000) × (0.02) = *47,600 person-rads*, and the females received (2,620,000) × (0.02) = *52,400 person-rads*. For males, the whole-body cancer dose for a mixed-age population is 235.0 person-rads per cancer death. We can calculate the number of extra deaths caused by this radiation to be 203 extra cancer deaths. For females, from table 24, the whole-body cancer dose for a mixed-age population is 300.2 person-rads per cancer death. Therefore, the 0.02 rads of radiation will cause 175 extra cancer deaths. The total cost of the nuclear "incident" is 378 extra cancer deaths.

QUESTION 7: *It is said that the United States population receives about 100 millirads of whole-body radiation from natural sources per year. If this value is correct, how many extra cancer deaths are caused each year by natural radiation, if we have an equilibrium population of 250,000,000 people?*

ANSWER: The natural radiation is a mixture of internal and external radiation. For this illustration, we shall assume that the 100 millirads apply to gamma-ray plus beta-particle irradiation, so that the relative biological effectiveness (RBE) is the same as for the whole-body irradiation we have been considering.

Of 250,000,000 people, approximately 131 million are females and 119 million are males. A dose of 100 millirads is the same as 0.1 rad. Female dose = (131,000,000) × (0.1) = 13,100,000 person-rads. Male dose = (119,-000,000) × (0.1) = 11,900,000 person-rads. For females the result is 43,-638 extra cancer deaths; for males it is 50,638 extra cancer deaths. Total extra cancer deaths = 94,276 per year.

The reader will certainly wish to know if we are actually experiencing 94,276 extra cancer deaths per year from natural radiation *right now*, since natural radiation has been unchanged for many millennia. The answer is that the actual number of extra cancer deaths right now in the United States must be in the neighborhood of about one-half of 94,276, but that answer has *nothing* to do with changes in natural radiation. Rather, the reason for the lower number is that the radiation-induced cancer deaths occurring now are primarily in the older segment of the population, that older segment having arisen from a smaller original population of roughly 125,000,000 persons. But if we have a population of 250,000,000, and keep it steady at that level, we can anticipate that the number of cancer deaths induced each year by natural radiation will finally approach 94,276. This subject is treated in detail in chapters 9 and 12.

WHO REALLY BEARS THE BRUNT OF POPULATION EXPOSURES?

If we examine table A, in the Appendix, we find that the *spontaneous* cancer death rate is quite low in children and very young adults, compared to the cancer rates steadily rising with increasing age. One must be on guard against a serious error of thinking, namely that children suffer the consequences of radiation-induced cancer less than do adults. *Exactly the opposite is true.* We can see this in several different ways.

First, we can use the data from table 10, which provides values of the whole-body cancer dose for males at various ages. Let us compare the values for male infants with those for males 35 years of age, both ages, of course, being the *age at irradiation.*

Age at Irradiation	Whole-Body Cancer Dose
0 years (infancy	63.7 person-rads/cancer
35 years	327.6 person-rads/cancer

Now, suppose 100,000 infants and 100,000 35-year-olds each receive a dose of 1 rad of whole-body radiation. One hundred thousand person-rads are delivered to each group.

For the infants, the additional cancer deaths (radiation-induced) are:

$$\frac{100{,}000 \text{ person-rads}}{63.7 \text{ person-rads per cancer}} = 1{,}570 \text{ cancer deaths}$$

For the 35-year-old males, the additional cancer deaths (radiation-induced) are:

$$\frac{100{,}000 \text{ person-rads}}{327.6 \text{ person-rads per cancer}} = 305 \text{ cancer deaths}$$

Clearly the infants are suffering far greater injury than the 35-year-old adults, with the same dose of radiation. Many scientists have been confused about this relationship, because they make inappropriate comparisons. If one looks at these two groups, say, at 20 years post-irradiation, there will be more radiation-induced cancers in the older group than in the younger group. This comparison is inappropriate because it compares 20-year-old males with 55-year-old males (the groups' ages 20 years post-irradiation). A more appropriate comparison is to measure the excess cancers induced by radiation when both groups have reached one particular age, which means comparing the excess cancer rate in the infants when they have reached 50 years of age with the excess cancer rate in the 35-year-olds when *they* have reached 50 years of age. That comparison would be *less* faulty.

The *most* appropriate material for comparison, however, is the two numbers, 1,570 and 305 radiation-induced cancer deaths. Only these numbers tell the *whole story,* because they incorporate the lifetime effects for each of those two irradiated groups.

A second approach to demonstrating how large a part of the burden of radiation is borne by the young is to consider whole populations. If we look at the radiation-induced cancer deaths for those irradiated at successively greater ages, in a mixed, equilibrium population, we find that 506,130 radiation-induced cancer deaths result from 1 rad delivered to every male member of the population. Now let us see how many of these cancers develop in those who were young at irradiation. These values are tabulated here.

Age at Irradiation	Total Number of Cancers Produced
0–5 years of age	152,169
6–10 years of age	105,652
11–15 years of age	67,539
16–20 years of age	43,276
0–20 years of age	368,636

Thus, we find that $368,636/506,130 \times 100\% = 72.8\%$ of all the cancers develop in people at or below 20 years of age at irradiation. Those 0–10 years of age at irradiation develop $257,821/506,130 \times 100\% = 50.9\%$ of all the cancers.

These illustrations present a simple and clear message. The young pay a very high price in the form of premature deaths, though delayed in manifestation, from radiation-induced cancer.

How Do Changes in Spontaneous Cancer Rates Affect the Whole-Body Cancer Dose?

In chapter 4, the difference between total cancer mortality in a country and age-specific cancer mortality rates in the same country was discussed. In the United States, there are currently (1981) about 400,000 cancer deaths per year. The author feels certain that this number is going to increase, over time, to a value close to 600,000 per year. The reasoning behind his expectation of increase is simple. When the population reaches an equilibrium of about 250 million people, there will be as many deaths per year as there are births. In such a population the number of births (or deaths) will be 3,438,000 per year. Averaging male and female cancer death rates, approximately 17% of all deaths are due to cancer. Therefore, there will occur $(0.17) \times (3,438,000) = 584,460$ cancer deaths per year.

Even while this large increase in the total number of cancer deaths occurs, the whole-body cancer dose for the United States will *not* change, *provided* the age-specific cancer mortality rates do not change, since it is the age-specific cancer mortality rates that enter into the calculation of the whole-body cancer doses.

But age-specific cancer mortality rates can, in principle, change over a period of years and decades. There is much controversy over whether the changes in age-specific cancer mortality rates in some countries are really as great as the data may suggest. Some scientists believe that the improving quality of diagnoses, better standards of reporting, and other factors, including even the desire of families not to have cancer reported as the cause of death on a death certificate, can all change the apparent age-specific cancer mortality rates for a particular country. We need not debate this issue. We can simply state it is possible for *real* changes in age-specific cancer mortality rates to occur. How would they change the whole-body cancer dose?

If the age-specific cancer mortality rates go up, for example, two effects are possible. Either (a) the peak percents increase in cancer rate will stay the same, in which case the total number of radiation-induced cancers will also go up, and the whole-body cancer doses (including the ones for mixed ages) will go down, or (b) the peak percents increase in cancer rate will go down, in which case the total number of radiation-induced cancers could stay the same, and the whole-body cancer doses could also stay the same. The author doubts that a third possibility need be considered, namely, that the peak percent values go up along with the age-specific cancer mortality rates, in which case the whole-body cancer doses would necessarily go down.

Of course, if the age-specific cancer mortality rates were to go down, then either (a) the peak percents increase would stay the same, in which case the total number of radiation-induced cancers would also go down, and the whole-body cancer doses would go up, or (b) the peak percent values would go down too, in which case the total number of radiation-induced cancers would go down more appreciably and the whole-body cancer doses would go up.

At present, there simply are not any data that permit us to know how peak percent values would change with a change in age-specific cancer mortality rates, so it is impossible, based on hard evidence, to predict whether whole-body cancer doses would change one way or another. This question will probably be answered definitively in the next fifty years or so, if continuing follow-up studies are reported.

On the basis of a variety of indications that radiation seems to act as a multiplier of other carcinogenic influences (a point not agreed to by all investigators), the author predicts that peak percent values will not change even if age-specific cancer mortality rates do change. But time and facts alone will tell. Of course, if age-specific rates do not change in any appreciable manner, time will *not* tell.

APPLICABILITY OF THE WHOLE-BODY CANCER DOSE IN DIFFERENT COUNTRIES

In the development of the peak percents increase in cancer rate per rad, data from all around the world were used. There is good reason to believe, since there was no consistent deviation by geography, that the peak percent values are "universal" in applicability, at least so far as the evidence at this time goes. More extensive follow-up data may change that opinion, and we must keep an open mind on this issue.

But the whole-body cancer dose is quite another matter! Even if peak percent values *are* universal, whole-body cancer doses are not.

Why is this so? Because the total number of radiation-induced cancers enters into the final determination of the whole-body cancer dose. That total number of radiation-induced cancers is obtained by multiplying appropriate percent increases, year by year in the post-irradiation period, *by the spontaneous cancer rates* in the particular country being studied.

The treatment in this chapter is based on United States spontaneous cancer mortalities in the years 1973–1974. If every spontaneous cancer rate in the United States had been half of the 1973–1974 value, for example, then every calculated radiation-induced cancer rate would have been half as high, and as a result the final whole-body cancer dose would have been twice as high. So, while the peak percent value is taken to be "universal," the whole-body cancer dose definitely is not. The whole-body cancer dose will be identical for any two countries for which the spontaneous age-specific cancer rates are identical.

A simple procedure will permit calculation of the whole-body cancer dose for any country, starting with the whole-body cancer dose for the United States. Let us see how this procedure is applied.

For all countries, one can obtain what is known as the *standardized age-specific cancer mortality rate* (see table 12). What this value provides is a comparison of age-specific cancer mortality rates adjusted to a common age base, for example, 50 years of age. Let us suppose that in "Country X" the standardized age-specific cancer mortality rate is twice that of the United States. The final total number of radiation-induced cancers would also be twice that for the United States. Since that number appears in the denominator of the calculation of whole-body cancer dose, the final whole-body cancer dose for Country X will be *one-half* that of the United States. Therefore, the general relationship is as follows:

Whole-body cancer dose in Country X =

$$(\text{whole-body cancer dose in U.S.}) \times \frac{(\text{standardized cancer rate, U.S.})}{\substack{(\text{standardized cancer rate,} \\ \text{Country X})}}$$

For most practical purposes, this relationship will serve very well in estimating whole-body cancer doses for various countries. The peak percent values, it must be reemphasized, can be taken to be universally applicable.

COMPARISON OF THE ESTIMATES OF RADIATION-INDUCED CANCER IN THIS BOOK WITH THOSE OF OTHER SCIENTIFIC GROUPS

There are two sources of estimates of radiation-induced cancer similar to those presented in this chapter. One source is the Advisory Committee on the Biological Effects of Ionizing Radiation (the BEIR Committee); the

TABLE 12: AGE-ADJUSTED CANCER DEATH RATES PER 100,000 POPULATION AROUND THE WORLD (1974–1975)

Country	Cancers Overall, Leukemia Excepted		Leukemia	
	Males	Females	Males	Females
*United States	152.5	101.8	6.9	4.3
Australia	156.8	97.5	6.4	4.5
Austria	183.1	119.0	6.3	4.4
Belgium	194.2	111.3	6.2	3.9
Bulgaria	118.4	75.0	6.3	4.7
Canada	150.6	105.1	7.0	4.2
Chile	143.1	118.1	3.9	3.3
Costa Rica	119.8	101.3	7.8	4.7
Czechoslovakia	205.9	113.3	7.3	4.7
Denmark	158.9	122.8	6.6	4.4
Dominican Rep.	35.0	35.9	1.7	1.2
England & Wales	183.9	119.3	5.8	3.9
Finland	176.3	93.4	5.7	4.9
France	187.5	94.2	7.0	4.5
Germany, Fed. Rep.	176.1	117.0	6.3	4.3
Greece	127.9	72.9	7.1	4.4
Honduras	27.3	40.7	1.9	1.3
Hong Kong	165.6	93.9	3.8	2.9
Hungary	188.7	124.3	6.5	4.7
Iceland	130.6	111.8	5.2	3.6
Ireland	158.8	129.5	6.3	2.8
Israel	123.0	112.9	6.6	5.6
Italy	162.7	96.3	6.5	4.4
Japan	137.1	84.9	4.2	3.1
Luxembourg	190.6	103.1	2.8	3.0
Mexico	55.4	71.3	2.6	2.2
Netherlands	186.8	109.7	6.6	4.1
New Zealand	167.1	117.0	7.4	4.8
N. Ireland	164.0	115.0	6.3	3.1
Norway	130.1	97.6	6.7	4.2
Panama	75.0	61.4	3.4	1.5
Philippines	53.6	44.1	3.0	2.7
Poland	154.9	97.5	5.5	3.7
Portugal	121.9	81.2	5.6	4.1
Puerto Rico	116.8	75.8	4.7	3.9
Romania	120.5	82.9	4.6	3.2
Scotland	200.2	125.1	4.8	3.6
Singapore	158.2	87.2	3.9	3.0

TABLE 12 (CONTINUED)

Country	Cancers Overall, Leukemia Excepted		Leukemia	
	Males	Females	Males	Females
Spain	138.2	85.8	4.7	3.2
Sweden	139.9	107.4	6.7	4.9
Switzerland	169.4	99.5	5.8	4.0
Thailand	33.4	24.2	0.9	0.7
Trinidad & Tobago	103.6	97.8	1.1	5.1
*Uruguay	187.8	118.3	5.1	4.6
Venezuela	97.3	97.2	3.7	3.2
Yugoslavia	122.8	79.6	4.4	3.3

Data taken from "Cancer Around the World," part of "Cancer Statistics, 1980," prepared by Edwin Silverberg, Project Statistician, Department of Epidemiology and Statistics, American Cancer Society, New York, New York, and appearing in *Ca-A Cancer Journal for Clinicians*, Vol 30, No. 1., January/February, 1980. Silverberg's original source cited as *World Statistics Annual, 1977-1978*.

These are precisely the type of data referred to in the text (this chapter) as *standardized for age*, and are precisely the data needed to obtain the whole-body cancer dose for any particular country from the whole-body cancer dose for the United States, by the "Country X" relationship shown in the text.

Since leukemia is handled separately for all radiation calculations, the data are presented here for all cancers, leukemia excepted, and for leukemia as a separate entry. In the original references, these two entries are added together.

*United States is out of alphabetical order, and appears first in the table.

other is the United Nations Scientific Committee on the Effects of Atomic Radiation (UNSCEAR). Let us compare the estimates presented by those committees with those presented here. We will see that there are sharp differences in the estimates of radiation-induced cancers per rad of whole-body radiation. Since all scientists have access to the same literature describing human epidemiological studies, some are either making different assumptions or grossly misusing the evidence in their analyses.

In their 1979 draft report (BEIR-III), the BEIR Committee presents a Table 5 (p. 342), labeled "Comparative Lifetime Cancer Risk Estimates for the General Population from Exposures to Low-Dose, Low LET Radiation, Single Exposure and Continuous Exposure, Both Sexes Combined." We shall restrict our attention to the cancer mortality data for a single exposure of a population of 1 million to 1 rad of radiation. Elsewhere in this chapter, we estimated that 942,793 radiation-induced cancer deaths would occur if 1 rad were delivered to everyone in a population of 250,000,000. For a population of 1,000,000, the estimate would be 942,793/250 = 3,771 radiation-induced cancer deaths. Now we can compare the values presented here with those of BEIR and UNSCEAR (1977). The UNSCEAR value is 37.7 times lower than this author's. The highest BEIR value is 10.7 times lower than this author's, and the lowest BEIR value is 53.9 times lower than this author's. These are very serious discrepancies indeed and deserve an explanation.

Source of Estimate	Radiation-Induced Cancer Deaths per Million Person-Rads, Delivered to a Population of Mixed Ages
BEIR, relative risk method (p. 342)*	177–353
BEIR, absolute risk method (p. 342)*	70–124
UNSCEAR (p. 414)	100
This author (see above)	3,771

*BEIR (1979)

Flaws in the BEIR-III Analysis

Let us dispense first with the estimates made by BEIR-III by the absolute risk method. This method, for reasons discussed in chapters 4 and 7, gives falsely low estimates of the cancer hazard of radiation, and the author feels it is not worthwhile even to discuss the estimates made in this case by that method. The BEIR-III estimates made by the relative risk method, which is the method used throughout this book, are also seriously lower than our estimates and deserve our serious attention.

There is no mystery at all about how this author arrived at his estimate; all the evidence, every assumption, and each step of every calculation are presented in this book. Unfortunately, the reader of the BEIR-III report will have extreme difficulty ascertaining how BEIR members did their analysis, because the presentation of that analysis is simply inadequate. In the sections that follow, we will do what we can to figure out how the BEIR-III Committee made its estimate.

Shuffling of the Data: The BEIR calculation of the extra cancer deaths produced if 1 rad of radiation is delivered to one million persons of mixed ages is based exclusively on the Hiroshima-Nagasaki mortality data, which we analyzed in chapter 5. Sufficient attention has been given in this chapter to the signal importance of the great sensitivity of the young to irradiation, and to the relatively large development of cancer in the young when a population is irradiated. So it comes as quite a surprise to find the following statement in the BEIR-III draft report:

For ages under 10 years at exposure, the relative risk ratios obtained appear unreliable, and the ratios for ages 20–29 years at exposure are substituted for them. (p. 324)

In a lifetime of scientific research, this author has never seen a more shocking mishandling of scientific evidence than is manifested in this statement. In effect, the BEIR Committee is saying, we are unhappy with the large % excess cancer rate per rad in the 0–9-year age group since it does not have the statistical base we would like, so we will find a group, *grossly less sensitive according to every item of evidence available,* and substitute the value from that group for the high value that makes us uncomfortable. Please overlook the fact that, while we claim our interest is in reliability, we have simply substituted one unreliable (because totally inapplicable) value for the unreliable value which we did not like.

Handling data that way, one can "prove" just about anything one would like to prove. The BEIR procedure above can be rejected out of hand, since the nature of the error is all too obvious. It would be interesting to know what the BEIR Committee would have done with the "unreliable" data for the 0–9-year age group if the risk had turned out to be unusually low rather than high.

Use of the Wrong Percent Excess per Rad: Another error in the BEIR presentation is the use of percents increase in cancer rate per rad that are in conflict with the existing evidence, resulting in the much lower estimates of extra cancer deaths produced by 1 rad in a mixed-age population, and suggests the possible means by which the error was introduced.

One way, for example, would be to calculate the % excess in cancer rate per rad by considering all age groups combined, which would obliterate the large effect of radiation on the relatively young. This is why, in the correct method, we calculated the percentages separately for the various age groups, and then weighted them by their corresponding numbers of persons, or person-years.

In the 1980 BEIR-III Final Report, the estimate of cancer mortality from 1 rad introduced into a population of 1 million persons of mixed ages was lowered to 266 deaths (for the relative risk model), compared to 177–353 deaths in the Draft Report. This was justified by the use of a combined linear-quadratic model for radiation dose-response, a model that is not upheld by the epidemiological evidence. Later in this book the author will present evidence that supports a linear or even a supralinear model.

Effective Percent Increase Versus Peak Percent Increase: A further source of error lies in the BEIR report's failure to take account of the limited follow-up of the Hiroshima-Nagasaki study, and to correct for a common base. However, there does exist a way to avoid these flaws and to obtain an "effective" percent increase that describes the *average* increase in cancer risk over the lifetime of an exposed population. This effective percent increase is obtained in a different manner than is our familiar peak percent increase, by calculating backward from the whole-body cancer dose. The value so obtained, 2.19% per rad, is the value that should be set alongside the values of 0.103–0.272% presented by BEIR-III.

Does the Author Ever Combine Data in the "Incorrect" Way? The author has emphasized here that it is absolutely *forbidden* to combine the observed cancers for all irradiated age groups and the observed cancers for all unexposed age groups when, clearly, one must obtain instead the *correctly weighted percent* excess per rad in order to estimate the risk from irradiation of a mixed-age population. Is it *ever* permissible to combine age groups in the manner we labeled "incorrect" in our discussion of the BEIR-III results?

Yes, and as a matter of fact, the reader will find that the author himself has done so in chapters 7 and 8, *for wholly different purposes.*

The author's purpose in chapter 10 is to render some death data comparable with some corresponding incidence data. His purpose in chapter 8 is to test the linear relationship through various *dose* groups. The percents excess per rad from both those analyses cannot be used for calculating the health effects of radiation precisely because the age effect was obliterated.

Flaws in the UNSCEAR Analysis

The UNSCEAR analysis produces a value that corresponds to a whole-body cancer dose of 10,000 person-rads per cancer death, for exposure of a mixed-age population. The values in this book are in the neighborhood of 235–300 person-rads per cancer death. Examination of the UNSCEAR report shows that the analysis is inadequate in many ways:

1. In the analysis of the Hiroshima-Nagasaki data, UNSCEAR simply neglects the age effect altogether, lumping the data for all ages together to arrive at a value corresponding to a whole-body cancer dose in the neighborhood of 10,000 person-rads per cancer death. Such an analysis is both unacceptable and useless.

2. UNSCEAR bases its analysis of the Japanese data on kerma dose in rads, failing to correct to true absorbed dose. This introduces an error on the order of a factor of about 2.

3. There is no meaningful treatment in the UNSCEAR report of the problem of correcting for limited duration of follow-up, again leading to a possibly large underestimate of the cancer risk per rad.

For all these reasons, the author considers that the UNSCEAR analysis can hardly be taken as a serious effort to assess the true risk of cancer from population exposure. In most respects, the UNSCEAR analysis is even less satisfactory than the BEIR-III analysis, which is itself seriously flawed.

Possibly a Larger Disparity

In his treatment of the evidence for determining composite peak percent per rad values, this author went into detail about the problems with the group under 15 years of age at irradiation (chapter 6, section 1). The fact is that the Japanese data suggest not a *higher* radiation risk for this group compared with all other studies combined, but rather a *lower* radiation risk (see chapter 5).

Nevertheless, the author has weighted the Japanese data twice as heavily as the overall data, which may mean that his weighted average value for those young at irradiation *underestimates* the true risk for such persons. That is why, in the tabulations of whole-body cancer doses, both for mixed ages and for single ages, the author provides the reader with alternate estimates.

If this author has indeed underestimated the risk for those young at irradiation, then the BEIR and UNSCEAR estimates are even further from reality than they already appear to be.

[CHAPTER 7]

PARTIAL-BODY IRRADIATION AND CANCER DOSES FOR SPECIFIC KINDS OF CANCER

U P TO THIS POINT, we have been concerned with developing and using peak percents increase in cancer rate to determine the cancer consequences of whole-body radiation. That is important and essential. However, a separate and large problem remains, namely, evaluation of the cancer consequences of irradiation of a single organ or a single region of the body. Many of the practical problems we face concern such *partial-body* irradiation. It is evident, upon reflection, that fewer cancers will be produced by radiation if only part of the body is irradiated with a particular dose of radiation, than if the whole body is irradiated with that dose.

The procedures for estimating the *breast-cancer dose,* the *stomach-cancer dose,* the *lung-cancer dose,* or the cancer dose for any other organ are identical with the procedures we have applied to estimate the whole-body cancer dose, except that we need a peak percent increase in cancer rate per rad for the specific organ under study, and the age-specific cancer mortality rates for that organ, rather than for the whole body. The latter value is readily available from vital-statistics data, so this poses no problem for us. However, the peak percent increase in breast cancer per rad (or lung cancer, stomach cancer, etc.) is quite another matter. We do not have the data to provide individual peak percent values for each and every cancer type. How shall we cope with this problem?

SECTION 1: THE EVIDENCE SUPPORTING A COMMON PEAK PERCENT FOR ALL KINDS OF CANCER

In 1969–1970, Gofman and Tamplin proposed a fundamental simplification in suggesting that the % excess in cancer rate per rad would be either the same for all kinds of cancer, or very close to the same. If this generalization is true, then our solution is straightforward: we simply use the peak percent values already obtained for cancers, overall, for each and every kind of cancer we wish to consider. So we must turn to the evidence which supports this idea that a single set of peak percent values is all that is required.

THREE GENERALIZATIONS ABOUT RADIATION CARCINOGENESIS

The generalization of Gofman and Tamplin described above was one of three generalizations, which follow:

Generalization 1: "All forms of cancer, in all probability, can be increased by ionizing radiation, and the correct way to describe the phenomenon is either in terms of the dose required to double the spontaneous mortality rate for each cancer or, alternatively, of the [percent] increase in mortality rate of such cancers per rad of exposure."

Generalization 2: "All forms of cancer show closely similar doubling doses and closely similar percentage increases in cancer mortality rate per rad." (Doubling doses are defined and discussed in section 7 of this chapter.)

Generalization 3: "Youthful subjects require less radiation to increase the mortality rate by a specified fraction than do adults." (1969a, pp. 663–4)

No serious student of the problem can overlook the mountain of evidence which indicates that all the major forms of cancer can be induced by ionizing radiation. New radiation-induced cancers have been added to the list with each passing year of study. It is also widely conceded that the other part of Generalization 1, the expression of risk as a % increase in mortality rate per rad—now known as the relative risk model—is at least one valid way of approaching the problem. Most scientific groups present cancer-risk data this way, either alone or along with the absolute risk method (see chapter 4). So Generalization 1 has stood the test of time. We shall show a little later in this chapter (and in chapter 9, in the material on uranium miners) that the absolute risk model is clearly not consistent with reality, and this demonstration will further strengthen Generalization 1.

Generalization 3 is so obviously supported by the growing evidence that few contest its correctness.

Generalization 2 has met with many types of criticism, and is still contested. Some claim, erroneously, that evidence against it has been found. This author believes that the evidence broadly *supports* Generalization 2, and that it is improper evaluation of the evidence which has led many investigators to doubt this generalization.

If Generalization 2 is correct, then we can use a single set of peak percents increase per rad for all forms of cancer, namely, the values we obtained in chapter 6. However, the author has no vested interest in Generalization 2. If it turned out that some cancers have different peak percent values than do other cancers, he would of course want to use the correct value for each kind of cancer. The methods of this book would make it extremely easy to accomplish such adjustments.

Generalization 2 did not arise out of thin air. Gofman and Tamplin made that generalization because powerful evidence in its favor already existed in 1969. At that time Gofman and Tamplin pointed out several reasons why scientists would be led astray unless they carefully scrutinized and analyzed the evidence in the literature.

THE DIRECT EVIDENCE THAT LED TO GENERALIZATION 2

The Stewart In Utero Data

In 1969–70, when Gofman and Tamplin proposed Generalization 2, evidence was available from the in utero irradiation studies of Stewart and Kneale (1968) that the % excess in mortality from a wide variety of childhood cancers and leukemias was almost the same, even though there was a large range of values for the spontaneous mortality rates for those cancers and leukemias. In effect, the Stewart studies indicate that if ionizing radiation increased the frequency of a rare cancer by 10%, for example, the same amount of ionizing radiation would also increase the frequency of a common cancer by 10%. This in turn means that the absolute number of cancers produced per unit of radiation is much greater for a common type of cancer than for a rare type, as would be predicted by Generalization 2. It was Stewart's work that originally suggested this generalization to Gofman and Tamplin.

The Stewart analysis, to be considered in detail in chapter 15 (which deals specifically with in utero irradiation), is based on a comparison of the frequency of maternal X-rays during pregnancy for children who develop cancer or leukemia, with the frequency of maternal X-rays during pregnancy for control children who do not develop these diseases. Obviously, if one is dealing with a small series of cases and controls for a particular cancer, sampling variation, our old nemesis, again presents itself. For most of the cancers and leukemias in the Stewart studies, the numbers of irradiated mothers are large enough so that sampling variation is not a problem. Recently, Bithell and Stewart (1975) presented an update of their findings, which are presented here in table 13.

TABLE 13: PERCENT EXCESS CANCER RISK IN CHILDREN FROM
MATERNAL RADIATION: A COMPARISON OF THE RISK FOR VARIOUS
CANCERS AND LEUKEMIAS*

Kind of Malignant Tumor	Number of Cases	% Excess Cancer Risk (for Diagnostic Radiation of approx. 1–2 rads)
Leukemias		
Lymphatic leukemia	2,007	54%
Myeloid leukemia	866	47%
Other leukemias, type not specified	1,179	43%
Solid Tumors		
Lymphomas	719	35%
Wilms' tumor	590	59%
Central nervous system tumors	1,332	42%
Neuroblastoma	720	46%
Other solid tumors	856	63%
Bone tumors	244	11%
Total Leukemias & Solid Tumors = 8,513 cases		47.6% = weighted average

*Data from Bithell and Stewart, 1975.

The findings in table 13 are remarkable indeed. With the exception of
bone tumors, all the percents excess per 1–2-rad dose cluster around a
weighted average % excess of 47.6%. No value except the bone-tumor value
is even 20 units away from the average value, which is consistent with their
all being the *same* in reality. The bone-tumor data come from the one group
consisting of a small total number: there were only 26 X-rayed mothers in
the case group, and only 22 X-rayed mothers in the control group. Sampling
variation could easily account for the fact that this *one* cancer is out of line.
Certainly, with the evidence as it now stands, the bone-tumor data by no
means constitute an argument against the generalization that the % excess
cancer risk per unit of radiation is the same for all cancers, or very close to
the same.

It should be noted that these data also provide strong confirmation of
Generalization 1, which proposes the relative risk model of radiation carcinogenesis. The absolute risk model would predict a fixed number of
excess cancers and leukemias per rad, regardless of the differing spontaneous rates of the various kinds of cancers. In table 13 we see instead closely
similar percents excess per rad over the spontaneous rates, for cancers with
widely differing spontaneous rates.

As the author will show in chapter 15, the work of Stewart and colleagues is widely accepted throughout the scientific community. Indeed, it

will be shown that the one possible basis for dissenting opinion—some studies from Japan—is no basis at all. One of the most elegant features of the Stewart studies is that all these irradiations were received in utero, and all were followed up between birth and the fourteenth year of life, so the studies are free from the common problems of differing ages and differing follow-up periods.

The Stewart series, except for the bone-tumor group (based on small numbers of cases and controls), affords us a remarkably powerful confirmation that grossly different types of cancers show very nearly the same % excess per unit of radiation.

The Ankylosing Spondylitis Series

In addition to the Stewart data, the early data of Court-Brown and Doll (1965) on the ankylosing spondylitis cases suggested to Gofman and Tamplin that the % excess risk per rad did not differ widely among the various cancers, if it differed at all. Those data have been superseded by the more recent data of Smith and Doll (1978), which cover only those patients who received a single course of therapy, and which therefore constitute a series much better controlled with respect to time of follow-up. The Smith and Doll data were analyzed in chapter 5. The values for the various cancers studied by Smith and Doll are reiterated here.

Kind of Cancer	Observed Cases	Expected Cases	Peak Percent per Rad
Bronchogenic Cancer	101	69.5	2.25
Cancer of Large Intestine	18	13.1	6.5
Cancer of Pancreas	12	7.5	6.6
Cancer of Stomach	36	24.6	5.8
Cancer of Esophagus	9	4.3	3.5
Lymphoma (Hodgkins Disease excluded)	13	6.59	3.1
Cancer of Kidney	7	3.12	26.5
Cancer of Urinary Bladder	8	5.98	10.8
Hodgkins Disease	0	2	0.0

When one considers the small-numbers problem plus the very real uncertainty of dosimetry for these cases, there is no way to prove that all these peak percent values are not truly identical. This series confirms Generalizations 1 and 2.

The Japanese Data: Gastrointestinal Cancers

In the BEIR-I report (1972), concern is expressed that the Japanese data for gastrointestinal neoplasms may be grossly out of line with Generalization 2.

The BEIR report admits that the Japanese data were at that time still thin in numbers. We have much more data now from Beebe, Kato, and Land (1978). In chapter 5, these data for the follow-up period 1950–1974 were analyzed in detail. In Bcebe's Table VII are presented the data for cancer of the digestive organs and peritoneum (ICD categories 150–159, and 197). Inspection of the O/E comparisons shows that for two age groups, the cancers of the digestive organs show slightly higher O/E values than do the cancers, overall; and for one age group, the cancers of the digestive organs show a slightly lower O/E value than do cancers, overall.

Taken together, these data provide no suggestion that cancers of the digestive system are less inducible by radiation than cancers, overall. So the original concern of the BEIR-I Committee, that digestive-organ cancer might be some eight times more difficult to induce by radiation than other cancers, has no foundation at all. Again, the data are perfectly consistent with a single % excess cancer risk per rad for all cancers.

The Japanese Data: Breast Cancers

For comparison, we will now bring together four sets of peak percents from chapters 5 and 6 (see table, p. 202). Our purpose is to explore whether the peak percents for breast cancer are different from the peak percents for other kinds of tumors.

At first glance, the comparisons appear to show that, internal to the Japanese series, breast cancer may have *higher* peak percents than cancers overall, while the *composite* peak percents for breast cancer (all studies combined) are often *lower* than the composite peak percents for cancers overall. With these opposite observations, we can say there is certainly no basis for jumping to the conclusion that breast tissue is either more, or less, sensitive to radiation carcinogenesis than other tissues.

However, let us be careful about comparing peak percents based largely on *incidence* (the breast-cancer series) with peak percents based largely on *deaths* (all types of cancers combined). Let us look more closely at the comparison internal to the Japanese data. That is the only series where we have enough data to answer the question, to what extent is the different peak percent for breast cancer caused by comparing incidence with death?

An analysis of incidence and death data shows that *no* disparity yet exists, internal to the Japanese series, between breast radio-sensitivity and the radio-sensitivity of all kinds of tissues combined. In this analysis, Japanese breast-cancer *deaths* were analyzed separately from all the other Japanese cancer deaths, and then compared with breast-cancer *incidence* in the same series. The peak percents increase for incidence turn out to be approximately twice as high as the peak percents increase for deaths, which explains the disparity noted in the summary above.

In chapter 8, our analysis of breast-cancer *incidence* data for Hiroshima-Nagasaki will show a supralinear relationship between % excess breast-cancer rate and radiation dose—i.e., the increase in cancer risk *per rad* goes

Japanese Breast-Cancer Incidence (chap. 5)		Japanese Overall Cancer Deaths (breast cancers included) (chap. 5, table 7)	
Age	Peak Percent	Age	Peak Percent
4.5	38.8	4.5	9.5
14.5	6.2	14.5	3.5
24.5	2.3	26.5	1.47
34.5	1.1	data did not fall into this age group	
44.5	0.0	42.0	0.82
55–60	1.7	50+	0.0

Combined Breast-Cancer Incidence (chap. 5)		All Tumors, All Studies Combined (largely death data) (chap. 6)	
Age	Peak Percent	Age	Peak Percent
0	no data	0	81.4
4.5	38.8	6.85	54.8
14.5	6.15	14.5	4.41
24.5	2.65	25.9	3.71
34.6	0.98	31.2	3.78
44.2	0.16	42.3	0.91
50+	1.4	50+	0.04

up as the dose goes down. The analysis of breast-cancer death data shows that supralinearity also characterizes the relationship between excess breast-cancer *deaths* and radiation dose.

The Japanese Data: Analysis by Jablon

Jablon presented a paper in 1973 summarizing his experiences with the Hiroshima-Nagasaki data, with which he has been closely associated over a period of many years. We quote Jablon's conclusions:

What kinds of solid tumors have been increased in the irradiated population? The largest relative risks were for lung cancer and cancer of the breast; only for cancer of the cervix and uterus was there no evidence of excess cancer mortality. On the other hand, as indicated by the width of the confidence intervals, the numbers are not so large as to yield very stable estimates, and, in fact, when these relative risks are tested as a set for heterogeneity, it turns out not to be significant. That is, despite the appearance of variations in relative risk and, in fact, some reasons for thinking that there should be heterogeneity, the data do not yet prove it to exist. (p. 28)

The English translation of Dr. Jablon's comments is, "The Japanese data are completely consistent, within their limits and numbers, with Generalization 2, namely, that the % excess risk per rad is the same for all forms of cancer."

SUMMARY OF CONSIDERATIONS OF GENERALIZATION 2

The data of Stewart and co-workers strongly support a single % excess per rad for all forms of solid cancer. No other data, including the Japanese data and the spondylitis data, provide any significant basis for requiring more than a single value.

The author retains the view that a single % excess per rad, *for a specified age at irradiation,* should be used in analyzing cancer induction in single organs, until some valid evidence is produced to suggest that the use of different values is appropriate.

It is worth reminding the reader that the peak percent increase per rad values come from the analysis of a large variety of cancers. For the major forms of cancer, it is therefore unlikely that any appreciable error will be introduced by using the peak percent values for cancers, overall in dealing with the specific types of cancer.

SECTION 2: CALCULATION OF VARIOUS INDIVIDUAL-ORGAN CANCER DOSES

We can now consider how to go about calculating a breast-cancer dose, a lung-cancer dose, a pancreas-cancer dose, etc.

Suppose we consider a specific organ, X, for which the age-specific cancer rates (spontaneously occurring, without added radiation) are one-tenth of the age-specific rates applying to cancers overall. The values that go into calculating the cancer dose would likewise be lowered to one-tenth of the value for cancers overall, including the sum of all radiation-induced cancers.

Now, since the cancer dose is calculated by dividing total person-rads by the total number of radiation-induced cancers, the cancer dose for cancer X must necessarily be *ten times higher* than the whole-body cancer dose. Instead of person-rads, we would use *organ-X-rads.* If we were studying breast cancer, we would use *breast-pair-rads,* since each individual has two breasts. If we were studying pancreatic cancer, we would use *pancreas-rads.*

We have, therefore, a simple rule, or equation, for converting whole-body cancer doses into specific-organ cancer doses. The first step is to ascertain *what fraction* of all cancer deaths is due to cancer in a specific organ. For any specific organ, we shall simply refer to this value as *the fraction.* Then we write the exceedingly simple equation:

$$\text{Specific-organ cancer dose} = \frac{\text{whole-body cancer dose}}{\text{the fraction}}$$

To illustrate, let us suppose that the fraction is 0.05, for a particular kind of cancer, that is, that 5% of *all* cancer deaths are deaths from cancer in that organ. Then we would write:

$$\text{Specific-organ cancer dose} = \frac{\text{whole-body cancer dose}}{0.05}$$

This converts directly into the statement that the cancer dose for *this* organ is 20 times the whole-body cancer dose.

For a particular age and sex, the specific-organ cancer dose is *always going to be higher* than the corresponding whole-body cancer dose. This is necessarily so since *the fraction* is always less than 1.0. If the fraction were 1.0, that would mean that the particular organ cancer was the *only* cancer causing death, and that situation simply never arises. Some readers may find it mysterious that the specific-organ cancer dose is always higher than the whole-body cancer dose. Intuition helps here. When the whole body is irradiated uniformly, or nearly so, there are some 60 to 70 organ sites that can develop a cancer. A cancer in *any* of these sites may by itself prove fatal. If only *one* site were irradiated, it is reasonable to expect that it would take *more* radiation to guarantee a fatal cancer than if we irradiated 60 sites. Very rare cancers have extremely high specific-organ cancer doses. The smaller *the fraction* is, the greater will be the disparity between specific-organ cancer dose and the whole-body cancer dose. Values of the fraction may vary from country to country.

The fraction will be the same whether the specific-organ cancer dose is being calculated for 0, 5, 10, 20, or 40 years of age at irradiation. But of course, just as whole-body cancer doses have different values for different ages, so do specific-organ cancer doses. Since there are so many types of cancers and so many ages to consider, a complete set of tables for specific-organ cancer doses would be a large volume by itself. Because it is so simple to get the specific-organ cancer dose from the fraction and our tables 10 and 11, we have no need for such a volume.

ACTUAL VALUES OF "THE FRACTION" FOR SPECIFIC CANCERS

The American Cancer Society publishes a very valuable "little journal" entitled *Ca-A Cancer Journal for Clinicians.* It is usually a gold mine of valuable information. One service it provides annually is an estimate of the number of cancer deaths for each type of cancer, for the entire country, by region. In tables 14 and 15, the 1980 data from Silverberg of the American Cancer Society are utilized to provide all the values for the fraction for both males and females in the United States. Also in tables 14 and 15 are the calculated specific-organ cancer doses for persons 25 years of age. This gives the reader a good idea of how these doses vary as one goes from a rare to a common cancer.

TABLE 14: VALUES OF THE "FRACTION" FOR U.S. MALES PLUS SPECIFIC-ORGAN CANCER DOSES ILLUSTRATED FOR 25-YEAR-OLD MALES, U.S.

Explanatory Notes for Legends and Methods of tables 14 and 15:

In the text, this chapter, the simple equation or rule for converting whole-body cancer doses to individual specific-organ cancer doses requires application of the "fraction," which is the specific-organ cancer death rate divided by the total death rate from cancer for the same country. We shall abbreviate, and refer to this as simply *fraction*. Then we write, as in the text:

$$\text{fraction} = \frac{\text{whole-body cancer dose}}{\text{specific-organ cancer dose}}$$

Estimates of 1980 deaths from individual specific-organ cancers and of total cancers are presented in "Cancer Statistics, 1980" in *Ca-A Cancer Journal for Clinicians*, Vol. 30, No. 1, January/February, 1980. These were prepared by Edwin Silverberg, Project Statistician, Dept. of Epidemiology and Statistics, American Cancer Society, New York, New York. These are the crucial data required for determining the fraction.

In tables 14 and 15 themselves, cancers are presented both in groups and as individual cancers. Thus, the category *digestive-organ cancers* is presented, and separately, such cancers as *esophagus, stomach,* etc. are presented. It is not appropriate to add numbers for a category to numbers for individual cancers, since the category numbers are already the sums of the numbers from the individual cancers making up the category.

Column 1:

The total number of estimated deaths from cancers, overall (leukemia excepted), is the first entry of this column. It is followed by entries for individual cancers and for groups of cancers.

Column 2:

The "fraction" is presented in this column. It is obtained, for each entry, by dividing the entry in column 1 by the lead entry in column 1, namely the total cancer death rate. As an illustration, cancer of the esophagus, in column 1, deaths = 5,500, and the lead entry, total cancer deaths, = 210,700. Therefore, the entry in column 2 = 5,500/210,700 = 0.0261.

Column 3:

These are the actual values for specific-organ cancer dose, calculated either for a single cancer or for a subgroup, e.g., digestive cancers. All values presented are for 25 years of age. The values at 25 years of age present a good view of the way in which specific-organ cancer doses vary among individual cancers. However, values of specific-organ cancer doses are needed for a variety of ages, and are as readily calculated as were those here for 25-year-olds. The "fractions" to be used *will not change with age*, for specific-organ cancer-dose calculations at various ages. The whole-body cancer dose does, of course, change with age, and is provided in tables 10 and 11 for all ages, in chapter 6. The simple "rule" above is the only other item required to get any specific-organ cancer dose for any age, male or female. The author has not provided all such values in tabular form because this would occupy some 100 pages.

Nomenclature of the specific-organ cancer doses: One should always remember that these values are for localized irradiation. Therefore,

TABLE 14 (CONTINUED)

Note for breasts and other bilateral organs: The only special point to note here is that, for bilateral organs, all calculations are based on the assumption that both bilateral organs were equally irradiated. This creates no problem if one treats data appropriately. Thus, if one breast was not irradiated, and one breast was irradiated with 100 rads, conversion into *breast-pair-rads* would require first averaging the 0 and 100 rads, to get 50 rads, and then stating that this individual received 50 breast-pair-rads.

person-rads per cancer seems inappropriate as a designation. This is why the author has chosen to use the organ-rad nomenclature, such as *pancreas-rads per cancer*, or *colon-rads per cancer*, etc.

TABLE 14: DATA AND CALCULATIONS

Organ or Category	COLUMN 1 *Total Deaths Estimated for 1980*	COLUMN 2 *"Fraction"*	COLUMN 3 *Specific-Organ Cancer Dose for Age 25 (organ-rads per cancer)*
Cancers, overall, leukemia excluded	210,700 (males)	1.0000	
Buccal cavity and pharynx:	6,100	0.0290	6,945
Lips	150	0.000712	282,900
Tongue	1,400	0.00665	30,290
Salivary glands	400	0.00190	106,000
Floor of mouth	400	0.00190	106,000
Other and unspecified sites in mouth	950	0.00451	44,660
Pharynx	2,800	0.01329	15,155
Digestive organs:	55,900	0.2653	759
Esophagus	5,500	0.0261	7,716
Stomach	8,400	0.0399	5,048

Small intestine	350	0.00166	121,300
Large intestine	20,500	0.0973	2,070
Rectum	4,800	0.0228	8,833
Liver & biliary passages	4,500	0.0214	9,411
Pancreas	11,100	0.0527	3,822
Other and unspecified digestive organs	750	0.00356	56,570
Respiratory organs:	*78,600*	*0.373*	*540*
Larynx	2,900	0.0138	14,594
Lung (really bronchi)	74,800	0.3550	567
Other and unspecified respiratory tissue	900	0.00427	47,170
Bone, connective tissue, and skin:	*5,400*	*0.0256*	*7,867*
Bone	1,000	0.00475	42,400
Connective tissue	800	0.0038	53,000
Skin (mainly melanoma)	3,600	0.0171	11,780
Breast-pair, male:	*300*	*0.00142*	*141,830*
Genital organs:	*22,500*	*0.1068*	*1,886*
Prostate	21,500	0.1020	1,975
Other and unspecified organs	1,000	0.00475	42,400
Urinary organs:	*11,800*	*0.0560*	*3,596*
Bladder	7,000	0.03322	6,063
Kidney and other urinary organs	4,800	0.02278	8,841
Eyes:	*200*	*0.00095*	*212,000*
Brain and central nervous system:	*5,400*	*0.02563*	*7,858*

TABLE 14 (CONTINUED)

Organ or Category	Column 1 — Total Deaths Estimated for 1980	Column 2 — "Fraction"	Column 3 — Specific-Organ Cancer Dose for Age 25 (organ-rads per cancer)
Endocrine glands:	600	0.00285	70,670
Thyroid	350	0.00166	121,325
Other endocrine glands	250	0.00119	169,240
Blood and lymph tissue cancers (other than leukemia):	10,800	0.05126	3,929
Hodgkins disease	1,100	0.00522	38,580
Multiple myeloma	3,300	0.01566	12,860
Other lymphomas	6,400	0.03037	6,629
All other and unspecified sites:	13,100	0.06217	3,240

All these specific-organ cancer doses are for cancer *deaths*, not for cancer incidence.
"Fractions" from this table are applicable for specific-organ cancer doses for males at *all* ages. A new set of fractions need not exist for each age at irradiation.

TABLE 15: VALUES OF THE "FRACTION" FOR U.S. FEMALES PLUS SPECIFIC-ORGAN CANCER DOSES ILLUSTRATED FOR 25-YEAR-OLD FEMALES, U.S.

Organ or Category	Column 1 — Total Deaths Estimated for 1980	Column 2 — "Fraction"	Column 3 — Specific-Organ Cancer Dose for Age 25 (organ-rads per cancer)
Cancers, overall, leukemia excluded	178,600 (females)	1.0000	

Buccal cavity and pharynx:	2,700	0.0151	16,662
Lips	25	0.00014	1,797,000
Tongue	600	0.00336	74,900
Salivary glands	250	0.0014	180,000
Floor of mouth	125	0.0007	359,000
Other and unspecified sites in mouth	500	0.0028	89,900
Pharynx	1,200	0.0067	37,550
Digestive organs:	50,950	0.2853	882
Esophagus	2,100	0.0118	21,300
Stomach	5,600	0.03135	8,025
Small intestine	350	0.00196	128,400
Large intestine	23,500	0.1316	1,912
Rectum	4,000	0.0224	11,230
Liver & biliary passages	4,800	0.0269	9,360
Pancreas	9,800	0.0549	4,583
Other and unspecified digestive organs	800	0.0045	56,200
Respiratory organs:	27,600	0.1545	1,628
Larynx	600	0.00336	74,880
Lung (really bronchi)	26,500	0.1484	1,695
Other and unspecified respiratory tissue	500	0.0028	89,900
Bone, connective tissue, and skin:	4,150	0.0232	10,840
Bone	750	0.0042	59,900
Connective tissue	800	0.0045	55,910
Skin (mainly melanoma)	2,600	0.0146	17,230
Breast-pair, female:	35,500	0.1988	1,266

TABLE 15 (CONTINUED)

Organ or Category	COLUMN 1 Total Deaths Estimated for 1980	COLUMN 2 "Fraction"	COLUMN 3 Specific-Organ Cancer Dose for Age 25 (organ-rads per cancer)
Genital Organs:	22,800	0.1277	1,970
Cervix uteri, invasive	7,400	0.0414	6,077
Corpus (endometrium) uteri	3,200	0.0179	14,060
Ovaries	11,200	0.0627	4,010
Other and unspecified genital organs	1,000	0.0056	44,920
Urinary Organs:	6,400	0.03583	7,022
Bladder	3,300	0.0185	13,600
Kidney and other urinary organs	3,100	0.01736	14,493
Eyes:	200	0.0011	228,700
Brain and central nervous system:	4,400	0.0246	10,228
Endocrine glands:	900	0.00504	49,920
Thyroid	700	0.00392	64,200
Other endocrine glands	200	0.00112	225,000
Blood and lymph tissue cancers (other than leukemia):	9,900	0.0554	4,542
Hodgkins disease	800	0.00448	56,200
Multiple myeloma	3,100	0.0174	14,460
Other lymphomas	6,000	0.0336	7,490
All other and unspecified sites:	13,100	0.0734	3,428

Explanatory notes for table 14 also apply for table 15.

USE OF "THE FRACTION": ANY ERROR INVOLVED?

The purist may suggest that the simple fraction should be used only if one is sure that the shape of the curve of age versus cancer death rate is exactly the same for the specific cancer as it is for cancers overall. The purist would be correct. However, the author doubts that differences in curve shapes will appreciably alter the values obtained by the simple method using the fraction. He invites other investigators to check out this point and satisfy themselves as to the great value of the simple method.

SECTION 3: PRACTICAL APPLICATIONS OF THE SPECIFIC-ORGAN CANCER DOSES

It is inevitable that the specific-organ cancer doses will, in the long run, be more widely used by readers of this book than the whole-body cancer doses, simply because most instances of radiation are of *partial-body*, rather than whole-body, radiation. On the other hand, it is unusual that only one organ will have been irradiated, although certainly possible. The most common partial-body radiation problems involve the radiation of a few organs in a region of the body, and we must learn to cope with risk estimates for such situations. Let us consider some practical problems.

QUESTION 1: *In the course of a series of diagnostic procedures it was finally estimated that 25 rads of X-radiation had been received by each breast of a 23-year-old woman. While some other tissues did receive radiation, this woman is concerned only with the problem of* breast-*cancer risk in her future. What is her risk?*

ANSWER: We will need two values: (a) the whole-body cancer dose for 23-year-old women, and (b) the fraction for breast cancer.

Value (a) is available in table 11, where whole-body cancer doses for females of all ages are presented. For a 23-year-old woman, the whole-body cancer dose is 250.5 rads. Value (b) is available in table 15, where the fraction is presented for all cancers developed by women. For breast cancer, the fraction is 0.1988. This number tells us, of course, that very close to 20% of all cancer deaths in women are due to breast cancer, as of 1980.

Now, applying our rule:

$$\text{Breast-cancer dose} = \frac{250.5}{0.1988} = 1{,}260.1 \text{ breast-pair-rads per cancer death.}$$

This woman received 25 breast-pair-rads. Since one breast-cancer dose guarantees *one* fatal cancer, her risk can be calculated as follows:

$$\text{Risk of breast-cancer death} = \frac{25 \text{ rads}}{1{,}260.1 \text{ rads}} = 0.0198$$

Given the various uncertainties, it is not at all unreasonable to round this figure off to 0.02, or 2%. Or, if the patient were unfamiliar with this form of stating risk, she could be informed that if there were 100 women in her situation, two of them, and we cannot say which two, would die prematurely of breast cancer.

This information is likely to lead to another important question.

QUESTION 2: *How does this woman's risk of dying of radiation-induced breast cancer compare with her "spontaneous" risk of dying of breast cancer?*

ANSWER: The radiation-induced risk at that dose at that age is not trivial, as we shall see. To ascertain the spontaneous risk of dying of *breast* cancer, we need two values: (a) the total risk of cancer death, and (b) the fraction for breast cancer. The second value is found in table 15, and the first value is found in table 17.

Since the reader may have many occasions to use the total risk of cancer at various ages of life, tables 16 and 17 have been prepared. They provide, for a given sex and a given age, the fraction of persons, from that age forward (up through the ninetieth year of life), who die of *some* form of cancer.

For women 23 years old, from table 17, the total future risk of death from cancer = 16.05%.

For all women, the fraction of cancer deaths which are breast-cancer deaths is 0.1988.

Therefore, the spontaneous risk of future breast-cancer death for a 23-year-old woman = (0.1988) × (16.05%), which is 3.19%, or, expressed as a fraction, 0.0319.

The radiation-induced risk was estimated to be 0.0198. Therefore, the total risk is 0.0319 + 0.0198 = 0.0517. And 0.0198/0.0517 = 0.383.

Thus, if a breast cancer does kill this woman, we can say that the chances are 38.3 out of 100 that radiation was the cause, and the chances are 61.7 out of 100 that radiation was not the cause.

Another way of putting this is that if we had a series of such 23-year-old women with the same radiation exposure, and if 100 breast-cancer deaths later occurred in such women, 38.3 of the breast-cancer deaths would be due to radiation, and 61.7 of the breast-cancer deaths would be due to other causes.

While the author prefers the clarity of the above statements to all other expressions of risk, one will often hear it said that something increases risk *by* a certain percentage. The doubling of this woman's risk of breast cancer would be expressed as "increasing her risk by 100%." Since a radiation-induced risk of 3.19% for breast-cancer death *would* increase her risk by 100%, it follows that a radiation-induced risk of 1.98% would increase her risk of breast-cancer death by (1.98/3.19) × (100%) = 62%.

TABLE 16: RISK OF DYING OF SPONTANEOUS CANCER BEFORE THE 91ST YEAR, AT VARIOUS AGES: MALES (U.S.)

Explanatory notes for tables 16 and 17:

For a variety of practical calculations with the whole-body cancer dose and the various specific-organ cancer doses, it is essential to know the risk of an individual dying of cancer, *without* added radiation. That is, we need the future risk of death from *spontaneous* cancer for all the ages at which irradiation has occurred or is contemplated. The steps toward obtaining this risk of spontaneous cancer death are very similar to those used in calculation of the whole-body cancer dose.

Columns 1 & 2:

We start with a population group. For each age (column 1), it is convenient to start with the number of survivors from 100,000 live births (column 2). Figures are given at 10-year intervals, as the percentage risk changes very little in that time.

Column 3:

We can ascertain the number of deaths from spontaneous cancer for each year beyond the survivors' present age. That number of cancer deaths is summed, and one entry is made for that age in column 3. So column 3 here is the cohort's spontaneous cancer deaths during its remaining life-span (or through the ninetieth year of age).

Column 4:

Since we know the number of survivors we started with for each age, and the cumulative sum of cancers out through the ninetieth year for that age group, we can obtain the risk of death from spontaneous cancer by simply dividing the sum of future cancers by the number of persons we started with. This is column 3 divided by column 2. If left as a quotient, we have the *fraction* of persons who die spontaneously of cancer. If multiplied by 100%, we have the *percent* of the surviving cohort who die of spontaneous cancer.

Beyond 50 Years of Age: The tables are carried through the fiftieth year, since irradiation studies will rarely concern themselves with more advanced ages. For those who desire them, the percentages for several additional age intervals are as follows:

Starting Age	% Dying of Cancer (males)	% Dying of Cancer (females)
55	18.86	14.70
60	18.34	13.72
65	17.41	12.53
70	15.85	10.99
75	13.61	9.16

TABLE 16: DATA AND CALCULATIONS

COLUMN 1 Age (years)	COLUMN 2 Survivors of 100,000 Live Births	COLUMN 3 Number of Members in the Surviving Cohort Who Will Die of Cancer Before Age 91	COLUMN 4 % of Group Who Will Die of Cancer by 91st Year
1	98,305 = cohort	18,130.0	18.44%
10	97,801	18,071.0	18.48%

TABLE 16: (CONTINUED)

20	96,900	18,006.2	18.58%
30	95,050	17,897.4	18.83%
40	92,897	17,650.1	19.00%
50	88,125	16,768.4	19.03%

TABLE 17: RISK OF DYING OF SPONTANEOUS CANCER BEFORE THE 91ST YEAR, AT VARIOUS AGES: FEMALES (U.S.)

COLUMN 1	COLUMN 2	COLUMN 3	COLUMN 4
Age (years)	Survivors of 100,000 Live Births	Number of Members in the Surviving Cohort Who Will Die of Cancer before Age 91	% of Group Who Will Die of Cancer by 91st Year
1	98,631 = cohort	15,782.6	16.00%
10	98,252	15,736.4	16.02%
20	97,868	15,692.5	16.03%
30	97,197	15,609.4	16.06%
40	96,070	15,322.1	15.95%
50	93,317	14,309.9	15.33%

Explanatory notes for table 16 also apply to table 17.

SECTION 4: ASSESSING RISK FROM MULTIPLE-ORGAN AND PARTIAL-ORGAN IRRADIATION

Instances exist of exposure virtually localized in a single organ. Far more common, however, are problems associated with a region of the body involving exposure of three or four organs. Such a situation would be treated just as we treated the breast-cancer examples, calculating the risk induced in each of the specific exposed organs separately. Then, the risks for all the organs can be summed to give the total risk to the individual. The difficult problem in many such instances is assessing the doses to the three or four organs involved (see chapter 13, on medical irradiation). For example, in a fluoroscopic examination of the *upper* gastrointestinal tract, some part of the large intestine gets irradiated, but it is difficult to assess just what fraction. The same might be true for liver and biliary passages, or for the pancreas. It is not good enough simply to state that these organs might have been in the X-ray beam, if a quantitative assessment of risk is desired. If a reasonable estimate of dose can be made, the data and methods of tables 14 and 15, and the typical problems we will solve here, can be used to assess risk.

ASSESSING RISK IN "PARTIAL" PARTIAL-BODY RADIATION

The author has encountered the erroneous impression that the *amount* of a specific tissue irradiated does not matter. In an assessment of risk, the amount of tissue irradiated makes all the difference in the world. We can illustrate this with a problem in *partial* partial-body irradiation.

QUESTION 3: *My son injured his left knee-joint in athletics. As a result, he had several X-rays of the knee, which finally received an exposure of 17 rads. He was 17 years of age at the time of this exposure. I have heard there is no safe amount of radiation. Does this mean my son is certain to get cancer from this exposure to X-rays?*

ANSWER: This is a classic illustration of the *partial* partial-body irradiation problem. It can also illustrate how cool, quantitative thinking can head off a hysterical reaction to radiation hazard.

We must first consider what tissues have been irradiated. Clearly, the tissues to consider are skin, bone, and connective tissue. To a very much smaller extent, we may wish to consider the blood and lymph tissue, which can generate such cancers as multiple myeloma, Hodgkin's disease, and lymphoma. (Leukemia will be considered separately, later in this book.)

From table 14, we obtain the fraction for bone plus connective tissue plus skin: 0.0256. For age 17 at irradiation, the whole-body cancer dose, from table 10, is estimated to be 190 person-rads per cancer death.

Therefore, applying our rule,

$$\text{Bone/connective-tissue/skin-cancer dose} = \frac{190}{0.0256} = 7{,}422 \text{ combined rads per cancer death}$$

Now, if this young man had received 17 rads to *all* of his bone, connective tissue, and skin, then we would calculate as follows: since 7,422 combined rads guarantee 1 cancer death, 17 combined rads guarantee 17/7,422 = 0.00229 cancer deaths. (By "combined" rads, we mean dose to skin plus connective tissue plus bone.) Expressed otherwise, this means there is a risk of 0.00229 of death due to cancer from such radiation *if* all bone, connective tissue, and skin were involved, and, of course, they certainly were not.

One knee-joint was involved in the irradiation out of all the bone, connective tissue, and skin of the body. A reasonable estimate would be that no more than 1/50 of all such tissue received radiation during the knee examinations. Therefore, the risk would be 1/50 of what we have estimated: 0.00229/50 = 0.000046, the final risk of cancer death. This risk can also be expressed as 4.6 chances in 100,000.

So the answer to the question raised by the mother of this young man is that it is far from certain that her son will develop a fatal cancer from the X-rays. Indeed, there are 99,995.4 chances out of 100,000 that he will *not* develop cancer from the irradiation. This is the personal-risk side of the problem. While the personal risk is very small indeed, we must not dismiss such amounts of radiation as unimportant. If 1,000,000 similar individuals received this diagnostic radiation exposure, 46 cancer deaths would result.

We mentioned above that it might be important to consider the possibility that multiple myeloma, Hodgkin's disease, or lymphoma may be induced by that knee-joint irradiation. Let us look more closely at that possibility. From table 14, *the fraction* for the blood and lymph tissues from which these disorders arise is 0.05126. So, the blood-lymph-tissue cancer dose = 190/0.05126 = 3,707 blood-lymph-rads per cancer death. The risk for 17 blood-lymph-rads would be 17/3,707 = 0.00459. This would be the case if *all* the susceptible blood and lymph tissue were irradiated. But in the knee-joint irradiation, virtually none of the lymphoid tissue of the body would have been irradiated, and it is hard to believe that 1/200 of the blood and bone-marrow tissue would have been irradiated. Considering both marrow and lymph together, it is doubtful that more than 1/500 of all these tissues in the body would have been irradiated. Therefore, the risk to these tissues is 0.00459/500 = 0.0000091. Since this is very small compared to the risk calculated above for bone/connective-tissue/skin irradiation, it is reasonable to neglect this part of the risk from the radiation.

It is important to answer questions such as the one raised by this mother as intelligently as we can. Although the risk to this young man is small, a slick assurance like, "Oh, a little X-ray never hurt anyone," is not appropriate in this or any other case. As we shall see in chapter 13, medical irradiation can kill.

SECTION 5: THE PROCEDURE FOR CHANGING CANCER DOSES IF FUTURE EVIDENCE REQUIRES

This book gives values for the whole-body cancer doses for all ages and both sexes in tables 10 and 11. Those values are based on the peak percents increase in cancer risk per rad developed from the consideration of all the human epidemiological evidence available at the time of writing of this book. (The peak percent increases can be read directly off figure 3.) Two questions must be raised and answered:

1. What if new evidence should suggest that the peak percent values need to be altered? How would we change the whole-body cancer doses in this book?

2. The specific-organ cancer doses are calculated by dividing the whole-body cancer doses by the value known as *the fraction*. What if it turns out that we should use separate peak percent increases per rad for each organ? How will we calculate the specific-organ cancer doses then?

CHANGING WHOLE-BODY CANCER DOSES

As a brief illustration, let us consider the situation for 25-year-old males. From figure 3, we find the peak percent increase in cancer rate to be 3.7% per rad. From table 10, we find the whole-body cancer dose to be 201.4 person-rads. But suppose, from new evidence, that it turns out the peak percent should be 5.2% instead of 3.7%. What will be the new whole-body cancer dose?

The equation for the solution of the problem is:

$$\frac{\text{Whole-body cancer dose}_{new}}{\text{Whole-body cancer dose}_{book}} = \frac{(\text{peak percent})_{book}}{(\text{peak percent})_{new}}$$

The subscript "new" designates the value we are seeking: the whole-body cancer dose as changed on the basis of new information. The subscript "book" indicates the values as calculated in this book.

Let us apply our equation. We are supposing that it has turned out that the peak percent should be 5.2% per rad instead of 3.7%. We write:

$$\frac{\text{Whole-body cancer dose}_{new}}{201.4 \text{ person-rads}} = \frac{3.7\% \text{ per rad}}{5.2\% \text{ per rad}} = 0.71$$

And clearing the 201.4 from the denominator, we have:

Whole-body cancer dose$_{new}$ = (201.4)(0.71) = *143.0 person-rads per cancer*

So, since initial values are available in this book, we can shift to new values in a moment by simply applying this equation. Obviously, the same principles would apply for any other age, or for females instead of males.

CORRECTING SPECIFIC-ORGAN CANCER DOSES

How would we correct specific-organ cancer doses if we wished to use a different peak percent than one used here? For example, suppose for stomach cancer, we had good reason to believe the peak percent value for 25-year-old males should be 2.5% per rad, instead of the 3.7% value used *for all cancers* in this book for that age at irradiation?

The equation for the solution of this problem is:

$$\frac{\text{Stomach-cancer dose}_{new}}{\text{Stomach-cancer dose}_{book}} = \frac{(\text{peak percent})_{book}}{(\text{peak percent})_{new}}$$

We can now apply this equation to the calculation of a new specific-organ cancer dose, for the stomach, for 25-year-old males. As noted above, our peak percent value is 3.7% per rad, for males 25 years of age at exposure. From table 14, the specific-organ cancer dose for males age 25, for the stomach, is 5,048 stomach-rads per cancer. Now we are supposing that some new evidence suggests that the peak percent value should be 2.5% per rad instead of 3.7%.

$$\frac{\text{Stomach-cancer dose}_{new}}{5,048 \text{ stomach-rads/cancer}} = \frac{3.7\%}{2.5\%} = 1.48$$

$$\begin{aligned} \text{Stomach-cancer dose}_{new} &= (1.48)(5,048 \text{ stomach-rads} \\ &\quad \text{per cancer}) \\ &= 7,471 \text{ stomach-rads per cancer} \end{aligned}$$

So, once all the work has been done, as it has been in the preparation of this book, it is a simple matter to obtain new cancer doses should the evidence suggest different peak percent values than those indicated by current epidemiological evidence.

SECTION 6: COMPARISON OF CANCER INCIDENCE RATES WITH CANCER DEATH RATES

Thus far, all calculations have been made for cancer deaths. Thus, a whole-body cancer dose describes the amount of radiation that guarantees a cancer *death*. The question arises, can we use such information to calculate the occurrence rate, or incidence rate, of various cancers? The answer is that we can readily make this conversion.

The estimates for 1980, prepared by Silverberg of the American Cancer Society, include estimates of incidence of new cases of cancer as well as estimates of mortality from cancer. Incidence versus mortality differs greatly from cancer to cancer, and is basically related to the fraction of cases of a particular type of cancer that result in death. Part of the great disparity may also result from diagnosis of cancer where none exists, followed by its "cure."

If cancer rates have not been changing drastically over some period of time, one can generally assume safely that the difference between incidence and mortality rates reflects cases that are either nonfatal in nature or are of the "cured" variety. However, when the *incidence* rate of a particular form of cancer is showing large increases, any corresponding increases in the mortality rate will necessarily occur only years *later,* since few cancers kill immediately after diagnosis. Since the ultimate ratio or disparity between incidence and mortality can be much lower than the early ratio, claims of a "high cure rate" based on the early ratio should definitely be regarded with skepticism.

The ratio, cancer incidence/cancer mortality, is presented in table 18. We shall call this ratio the *I/M ratio.* For the cancers in table 18, the absolute mortality values are available in tables 14 and 15.

As we know, for one whole-body cancer dose, one fatal cancer will ensue. But if, for example, the I/M ratio = 2, then the application of one whole-body cancer dose would cause two cancers, one of which would be fatal. Or, we could say that there would be an *incidence* of one cancer for a dose which is half the whole-body cancer dose.

We can, if we choose, define a whole-body cancer *incidence* dose by the following equation:

$$\text{whole-body cancer } \textit{incidence} \text{ dose} = \frac{\text{whole-body cancer (mortality) dose}}{\text{I/M}}$$

And, similarly for specific cancers:

$$\text{specific-organ cancer } \textit{incidence} \text{ dose} = \frac{\text{specific-organ cancer (mortality) dose}}{\text{I/M}}$$

Unless the I/M ratio is *unity* (1.0), it is evident that all cancer *incidence* doses are *lower* than corresponding cancer mortality doses.

Let it be re-emphasized that, in this book, if a cancer dose is not specifically designated as a cancer *incidence* dose, it must be understood to be a cancer *mortality* dose.

TABLE 18: THE RATIO, (CANCER INCIDENCE)/(CANCER MORTALITY), UNITED STATES, 1980 (I/M RATIOS)

Organ Site or Category	Males			Females		
	Cancer Incidence	Cancer Mortality	I/M Ratio	Cancer Incidence	Cancer Mortality	I/M Ratio
Buccal cavity and pharynx:	*17,900*	*6,100*	*2.93*	*7,600*	*2,700*	*2.81*
Lips	4,000	150	26.67	400	25	16.00
Tongue	3,200	1,400	2.29	1,600	600	2.67
Salivary glands						
Floor of mouth	5,600	1,750	3.20	3,700	875	4.23
Other and unspecified						
Pharynx	5,100	2,800	1.82	1,900	1,200	1.58
Digestive organs:	*95,800*	*55,900*	*1.71*	*90,500*	*50,950*	*1.78*
Esophagus	6,200	5,500	1.13	2,600	2,100	1.24
Stomach	14,000	8,400	1.67	9,000	5,600	1.61
Small intestine	1,200	350	3.43	1,000	350	2.86
Large intestine	36,000	20,500	1.76	43,000	23,500	1.83
Rectum	19,000	4,800	3.96	16,000	4,000	4.00
Liver & biliary passages	5,600	4,500	1.24	6,000	4,800	1.25
Pancreas	12,500	11,100	1.13	11,500	9,800	1.17
Other & unspecified	1,300	750	1.73	1,400	800	1.75
Respiratory system:	*96,000*	*78,600*	*1.22*	*34,700*	*27,600*	*1.26*
Larynx	9,000	2,900	3.10	1,700	600	2.83
Lungs (bronchi)	85,000	74,800	1.14	32,000	26,500	1.21
Other & unspecified	2,000	900	2.22	1,000	500	2.00
Bone, connective tissue, skin:	*10,500*	*5,400*	*1.94*	*10,000*	*4,150*	*2.41*
Bone	1,100	1,000	1.10	800	750	1.07
Connective tissue	2,500	800	3.13	2,000	800	2.50
Skin (melanoma only)	6,900	3,600	1.92	7,200	2,600	2.77

Breasts:	900	300	3.00	108,000	35,500	3.04
Genital organs:	71,000	22,500	3.16	75,500	22,800	3.31
Cervix (uterus), invasive only	—	—	—	16,000	7,400	2.16
Corpus (uterus), endometrium	—	—	—	38,000	3,200	11.88
Ovaries	—	—	—	17,000	11,200	1.52
Prostate	66,000	21,500	3.07	—	—	—
Other, male	5,000	1,000	5.00	—	—	—
Other, female	—	—	—	4,500	1,000	4.50
Urinary organs:	36,500	11,800	3.09	15,900	6,400	2.48
Bladder	26,000	7,000	3.71	9,500	3,300	2.88
Kidneys & other urinary	10,500	4,800	2.19	6,400	3,100	2.06
Eyes:	900	200	4.50	900	200	4.50
Brain and central nervous system:	6,600	5,400	1.22	5,300	4,400	1.20
Endocrine glands:	3,100	600	5.17	6,900	900	7.67
Thyroid	2,600	350	7.43	6,500	700	9.29
Other endocrine	500	250	2.00	400	200	2.00
Leukemia:	12,500	8,800	1.42	9,700	6,900	1.41
Other blood and lymph tissues:	20,800	10,800	1.93	18,400	9,900	1.86
Hodgkins disease	4,100	1,100	3.73	3,000	800	3.75
Multiple myeloma	4,700	3,300	1.42	4,400	3,100	1.42
Other lymphomas	12,000	6,400	1.88	11,000	6,000	1.83
All other and unspecified sites:	14,500	13,100	1.11	14,600	13,100	1.11

All basic data from Edwin Silverberg's "Cancer Statistics, 1980" in Ca, A Cancer Journal for Clinicians, Volume 30, No. 1, January/February, 1980.

SECTION 7: THE MEANING AND CALCULATION OF DOUBLING DOSES

Procedures for handling the knowledge of human radiation carcinogenesis have been "evolving" with that knowledge over the past decade. Whereas a decade ago (1969, 1970), this author made many references to *doubling doses* in his work, in this book most information is treated in terms of *cancer doses*. There is no conflict at all, and we will show in a moment how to convert a cancer dose into a doubling dose.

The doubling dose is defined as the amount of radiation required to add a frequency of cancer *equal* to the spontaneous frequency, during a specified period. In the treatment of cancer doses used in this book, *the applicable period for the spontaneous risk is the remaining life-span of the exposed.*

CALCULATION OF THE DOUBLING DOSE FOR WHOLE-BODY IRRADIATION

The way to calculate the doubling dose is from the whole-body cancer dose. The whole-body cancer dose confers 100% risk of death from cancer, or a probability of 1.0. Since the spontaneous lifetime risk of cancer death for men is approximately 18.5% at any age (see table 16), the doubling dose is that dose which would confer an 18.5% risk of death from *radiation-*induced cancer.

If we let *WBCD* stand for whole-body cancer dose in person-rads for a given age at irradiation, it follows that:

$$\text{Doubling dose in person-rads} = (18.5\%) \times (\text{WBCD})$$

We can make two general statements:

For men at a given age,
the doubling dose for $\qquad = (0.185)\ (\text{WBCD}_{\text{for given age}})$
whole-body irradiation

For women at a given age,
the doubling dose for $\qquad = (0.16)(\text{WBCD}_{\text{for given age}})$
whole-body irradiation

The reader has seen that we derive valid doubling doses from cancer doses. But he should not jump to the conclusion that he can derive a valid cancer dose by plugging any old doubling dose into the equation. For instance, the Hanford data (described in chapter 5, section 9) provide a doubling dose for that population sample for a *limited* follow-up period, from which we cannot derive a valid whole-body cancer dose, because the doubling dose and the k value (DD = 100/k) are applicable *only* for that limited period. The advantage of the cancer dose is that its derivation takes the *changing* post-irradiation k (% excess per rad) values into account. Thus, doubling doses derived from cancer doses also take the changing % excess per rad into account. Moreover, they tell us what is really of interest: the risk for the remaining life-span rather than for some arbitrary follow-up or 30-year plateau period.

THE DOUBLING DOSE FOR SPECIFIC-ORGAN CANCERS

The general rule is that for a particular age and sex, the doubling dose is the same for all individual kinds of cancers as for cancer overall.

We have noted that whole-body cancer doses are lowest at young ages, and increase progressively with increase in age. Doubling doses show exactly the same pattern of age variation as shown by whole-body cancer doses, provided one uses the right whole-body cancer dose for a given age at irradiation.

[CHAPTER 8]

THE NATURE OF
THE DOSE-RESPONSE
RELATIONSHIP

IN ALL THE ANALYSES MADE THUS FAR concerning radiation induction of human cancer, we have assumed the linear relationship, which states that the number of radiation-induced cancers is directly proportional to the dose of radiation delivered, down to the very lowest conceivable doses. *Directly proportional* means that the harm *per rad* does not vary between low doses and high doses. We said in earlier chapters that we would justify our use of the linear relationship in calculating the cancer doses, and this we will now do.

It is essential to be absolutely clear about what we mean by "directly proportional to dose." For any age, the relationship between dose and effect at irradiation can be written as follows:

Radiation-induced cancers =
   (S) the spontaneous cancer rate per 100,000 persons
× (K) the fractional increase in cancer rate over the spontaneous
     rate, per rad of radiation
× (D) the dose in rads

This relationship states that the only dose at which there are *no* radiation-induced cancers is D = 0. For all doses other than zero, some radiation-induced cancers occur; moreover, the number of radiation-induced cancers goes up directly in proportion to the increase in dose D.

If we have values for S and K, we can then calculate the number of radiation-induced cancers for any dose of D rads, where D can range from very small values, even 0.00001 rad, to high values, like 100 rads. If we were to plot radiation-induced cancers on the ordinate (vertical axis) and dose on the abscissa (horizontal axis), we would get a *straight line* that would originate where the two axes meet: at zero dose and zero effect (zero excess cancers). This is illustrated in figure 5a. Because this curve is a straight line we say that the relationship of radiation-induced cancers to dose in rads is *linear*.

Linearity between dose and effect means that if our group of 10-year-olds received 1,000 person-rads, as a group they would develop 1,000 times more excess cancer than if they received only 1 person-rad of exposure. Linearity also means that if individuals in the group received different doses, those who each received 1 rad would have 10 times the risk of developing radiation-induced cancer as those who each received 100 *millirads,* or 0.1 rad. And two or more individuals are not required to illustrate the point: the *same* child's risk would vary in direct proportion to varying doses. Thus a child would have a 10-fold higher risk from 1 rad than from 0.1 rad.

Linearity does *not* mean that if an adult received 1 rad, his/her risk would be 10 times greater than the risk of a child who received 0.1 rad. The reader will remember that adults are less at risk per rad than children. Although we cannot mix ages in *that* way when using the linear relationship, we can apply the linear relationship to a population of mixed ages in *this* way: if 10 person-rads to a population of mixed ages produced x cancers, then 100 person-rads to the *same* population (with the same mixture of ages) would produce 10x cancers.

IMPLICATIONS OF LINEARITY FOR NUCLEAR POWER AND MEDICAL IRRADIATION

Enthusiasts of nuclear power and of medical irradiation are forever hoping, quite understandably, that there will be found some *threshold*—a dose of radiation below which no harm would occur. A variation of this hope is that if one were to *divide* a radiation dose into many small doses (each below the alleged threshold), and then space such doses out over a period of time (that is, expose at a slow dose *rate*), even a high accumulated dose might be harmless. This hoped-for effect from slow delivery of radiation is called complete *protection by dose fractionation.*

If there *were* some threshold dose below which no harm would be done and above which the effect would be directly proportional to dose, the graph would look like figure 52b, instead of like 5a.

Figure 5c depicts a related but somewhat different hope of radiation enthusiasts, which we shall call *diminishing effects at low doses*—the hope that even if there is no harmless dose, the harm *per rad* might be less at lower doses than at higher doses, so that at very low doses the harm might be negligible.

Another hope, not depicted here, is for at least *partial* protection by fractionation—in other words, that dividing a dose into several exposures would *reduce* the harm per rad even if it would not eliminate it. In this case, the curve would still originate at the zero-dose/zero-effect intersect (rather than at some place to the right of the intersect on the abscissa), so any dose greater than zero would produce an effect.

From the point of view of nuclear-power and medical-irradiation enthusiasts, figure 5d is even worse than 5a. It depicts a *supralinear* effect, i.e., the effect per rad is even larger (more serious) at lower doses than at higher doses.

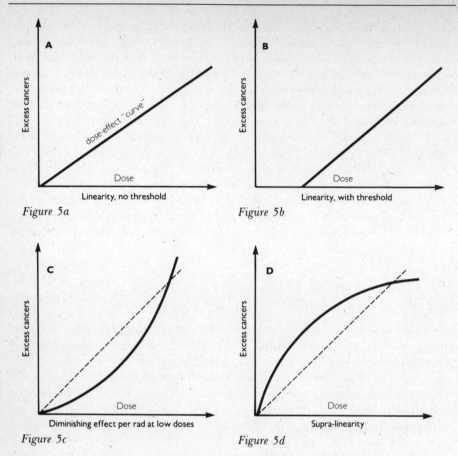

Figure 5a

Figure 5b

Figure 5c

Figure 5d

We shall discuss (1) linearity and supralinearity, (2) diminishing effect at low doses, (3) protection by dose fractionation, and (4) the threshold hypothesis, each in turn.

SECTION 1: LINEARITY AND SUPRALINEARITY

First, let us dispose of the issue of a linear dose-effect relationship from high LET radiation exposure, namely, irradiation by alpha particles (and perhaps neutrons). None of the calculations which preceded this chapter involved alpha-irradiation. As we will see in subsequent chapters, the dosimetry for alpha-irradiation is muddy at best. To the extent that the evidence on human cancer induction by alpha-irradiation is *able* to address the question of linearity, it supports linearity—for instance, the evidence from uranium miners (Archer et al. 1976; Sevc et al. 1976) and the evidence from ^{224}Radium injection (Spiess and Mays 1970). Indeed, the evidence concerning lung cancer in uranium miners supports supralinearity. (See chapter 9.)

Nuclear-power and medical-irradiation enthusiasts have focused most of their efforts on claiming that the effects of *low* LET radiation (X-ray, gamma-ray, and beta-particle) may be less serious than linear. By contrast, in all the calculations of previous chapters, we have assumed that the linear relationship is the correct one. Let us now consider the large body of human evidence, which shows that for low LET radiation a linear relationship or even a supralinear relationship holds from high doses right down to 250 millirads (¼ rad).

THE INCIDENCE OF BREAST CANCER IN THE WOMEN OF HIROSHIMA AND NAGASAKI

An analysis of the incidence of breast cancer in the bomb survivors of Hiroshima and Nagasaki was presented in chapter 5, as part of the evidence on radiation induction of breast cancer. However, we did not deal there with the cancer-induction rate per rad at low, intermediate, and high doses. Before describing the results of this analysis, based on the data of Land and McGregor (1979), we must again emphasize a potential error of serious proportions: use of a "zero" dose point for the Japanese data. In chapter 14 and in chapter 5, we describe evidence which supports the belief that the dose beyond 2.5 kilometers was not zero, but was several rads higher than the dose in the so-called 1–9-rad group. This causes us no difficulty in evaluating linearity or supralinearity in these data. Indeed, analyzing the breast-cancer data by dose interval affords an independent opportunity to test the concept of nonzero dose for those beyond 2.5 kilometers from the hypocenter of the bomb.

In analyzing the data for Hiroshima and Nagasaki combined, our objective is to derive values for K over the entire dose range for which we have data. Once we have the K values, we can find out what the dose-effect relationship is.

If the relationship is linear, we have pointed out that the % excess cancer risk per rad will remain the same at all dose levels. If the relationship is supralinear, the largest cancer-induction rate per rad will be found at the low end of the dosage scale, with a declining cancer-induction rate per rad as we go up the dosage scale. When a supralinear relationship is found, we do not know what mechanism accounts for it. One common proposal is that, at progressively higher doses, cells are inactivated or killed and therefore cannot participate in cancer induction. But we are not seeking to explain the mechanism here; we want only to know *from the evidence* whether the dose-effect relationship is supralinear, linear, or otherwise.

The behavior of the cancer-risk-per-rad value for a linear or supralinear relationship is totally different than for either a threshold or a diminishing-effects-at-low-doses relationship. In a threshold relationship, the cancer risk per rad must go to zero at the threshold. If we find the cancer risk per rad is going *up* as the dose goes *down,* we can say that the data do not support the concept of a threshold. In a diminishing-effects-at-low-doses relationship, we must expect a *decreasing cancer risk per rad* as we go to lower and lower doses. If we find the cancer risk per rad is constant or is increasing with decreasing dose, we can rule out that type of relationship.

Summary: Supralinearity in the Japanese Breast-Cancer Data

Analysis of the Land and MacGregor data yields the following tabulated values, obtained by comparing the cancer rates (breast cancers per 100,000 person-years) from progressively lower mean doses to the cancer rate from 2.9 rads.

Dose Group Considered	Mean Dose	K value	% Excess Breast Cancer per Rad
16.7 to 269 rads, inclusive	64.0 rads	0.0147	1.47% per rad
16.7 to 110 rads, inclusive	37.0 rads	0.020	2.0% per rad
16.7 to 54.3 rads, inclusive	25.07 rads	0.021	2.1% per rad
16.7 rads	16.7 rads	0.034	3.4% per rad

The only conclusion consistent with these data is that the behavior of breast-cancer risk versus radiation dose is *supralinear*: the risk of breast cancer per rad increases as the dose of radiation decreases. Moreover, the reliability of the risk values is best at the low end of the scale, because we are dealing with the largest numbers of breast-cancer cases in this dose region. There is simply no way to contort this valuable human evidence so that it would suggest a threshold relationship or a diminishing effect at low doses.

THE OCCURRENCE OF LEUKEMIA IN HIROSHIMA AND NAGASAKI

A few years ago, the dose-response curve for leukemia in the Nagasaki survivors caused a great to-do. It was said that the curvature was marked at low doses (indicating a lower leukemia incidence at low doses than would be expected from linearity), whereas the Hiroshima curve showed approximate linearity. Neutrons, more prominent in the Hiroshima dose, were supposed to explain the linearity of that curve. For the Nagasaki data, in which the gamma dose constituted almost the whole dose, the curve suggested a dose-squared relationship for the induction of leukemia by gamma rays (low LET radiation), according to Rossi and Kellerer (1974). That conclusion was entirely based on one low point, itself based on five cases of leukemia. And a virtual scientific edifice was built on that conclusion. As we will see in chapter 14, where leukemia in Japan is dealt with in detail, when the Nagasaki leukemia data are fully considered the evidence for curvature essentially disappears, taking the edifice with it. Both Beebe, Kato, and Land (1978) and the BEIR-III report (1979, p. 505) have conceded that the argument for a dose-squared relationship in the Nagasaki leukemia data cannot be taken seriously.

The findings for leukemia in the combined Hiroshima-Nagasaki series indicate a *supralinear* relationship between leukemia occurrence and radiation dose. The findings are *opposite* to those which would be expected for either a threshold or a diminishing-effect-at-low-doses relationship. So we see that both the Japanese breast-cancer data and the Japanese leukemia data strongly support at least linearity, and likely even supralinearity. We can now turn our attention to the largest body of cancer data—the cancer mortality data of Beebe, Kato, and Land.

LINEARITY IN OVERALL CANCER DEATHS IN THE HIROSHIMA AND NAGASAKI POPULATIONS

We have already analyzed the data on cancers, overall (from the publication of Beebe, Kato, and Land, 1978) in chapter 5, where we ascertained the peak percent increase in cancer rate per rad. Here we will analyze the relationship of cancer mortality to radiation dose at low doses versus high doses. The data for all forms of cancer, leukemia excepted, for all ages combined, and for the follow-up period 1950–1974, are based on the tabulations of Beebe, Kato, and Land. As with the Land and MacGregor breast-cancer data, we will simply summarize the results of the analysis here.

Summary: Supralinearity in the Japanese Cancer Deaths, Overall

Here we tabulate all the K values obtained through detailed analysis, in which we compared cancer rates (per 100,000 person-years) at progressively lower doses, to the cancer rate for the group that received 2.2 rads.

Dose Group Considered	Mean Dose	K value	% Excess Cancer Deaths per Rad
13.0 to 312.2 rads, inclusive	50.4 rads	0.00343	0.343% per rad
13.0 to 204.8 rads, inclusive	40.8 rads	0.00392	0.392% per rad
13.0 to 145.9 rads, inclusive	36.1 rads	0.00459	0.459% per rad
13.0 to 84.9 rads, inclusive	28.8 rads	0.00552	0.552% per rad
13.0 to 42.3 rads, inclusive	19.4 rads	0.00817	0.817% per rad
13.0 rads	13.0 rads	0.0125	1.25% per rad

The only conclusion consistent with this set of results is that the behavior of cancer death risk versus radiation dose is *supralinear*, i.e., the risk of cancer death per rad increases as the dose decreases. Moreover, the reliability of the risk values is best at the low end of the dose scale, because we are dealing there with the largest numbers of cancers. There is simply no way to contort this evidence so that it suggests a threshold relationship or a diminishing-effect-at-low-doses relationship. The observations are opposite to what either of those behaviors would require.

IMPLICATIONS OF SUPRALINEARITY

The implications of our analyses of the leukemia cases in Japan, the breast-cancer incidence cases, and the cancer deaths overall must now be considered. In all cases, the data indicate that a supralinear relationship describes the evidence best, in the range between 2.2 and 312.2 rads of absorbed dose. In practice, we are generally interested in the cancer risk produced by relatively low doses, say, less than 10 rads. For the individual cancers we have examined, we derived the cancer risk per rad from data based on doses of more than 10 rads, sometimes up to several hundred rads. We would have preferred, of course, to use data based on doses in the range in which we wish to make predictions. What the analyses of this chapter tell us is that we have *not been overestimating* the cancer risk per rad by assuming linearity. We have, indeed, been *underestimating* the cancer risk per rad, because the evidence shows that supralinearity describes the situation better than linearity.

This can best be illustrated by considering figure 6. Let us suppose the only data we had, from a cancer study, were for exposure at 150 rads. (The choice of 150 rads is arbitrary.) Now, we are plotting excess cancers versus radiation dose. The *true,* or supralinear, curve would be the solid curve. This would describe the number of excess cancers at all radiation doses below 150 rads. But, if we did not know about supralinearity, we would draw the dashed straight line, connecting the origin (0, 0 point) with the 150-rad point. The net result would be that, *for every dose lower than 150 rads all the way down to zero rads, we would underestimate the true cancer risk per rad.*

Therefore, the estimates of cancer risk per rad in this book are likely to be underestimates, rather than overestimates. It turns out that nuclear-power and medical-irradiation enthusiasts have all been going off in exactly the wrong direction. They have consistently suggested that linearity may overestimate the true cancer risk per rad. The real problem is that linearity underestimates the true cancer risk per rad, when one derives values from studies based on higher doses of radiation than the doses at which we wish to apply those values. At some later date, when a larger data base is available, the estimates of cancer risk per rad will in all likelihood have to be raised, to take into account the supralinear rather than linear relationship between cancer risk and dose.

THE IN UTERO IRRADIATION STUDIES OF STEWART AND CO-WORKERS

Thus far, in determining linearity and supralinearity, we have considered the dose range from approximately 2 rads to 300 rads. What happens below 2 rads?

As the dose (D) becomes smaller and smaller, larger and larger numbers of irradiated subjects are necessary to measure the number of radiation-induced cancers, and to be sure that the value obtained is statistically

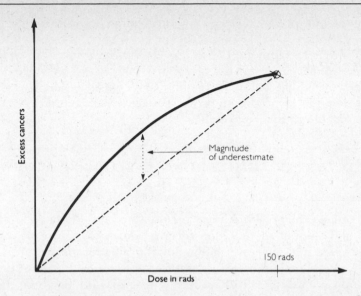

Figure 6: This depicts a study in which an excess cancer point is available only for 150 rads. If one did not know the true curve between zero rads and 150 rads to be supralinear (solid curve), and drew in a straight line between zero and the excess cancers at 150 rads, one would underesti-mate excess cancers per rad at all points below 150 rads. The magnitude of the underestimate is the distance between the curve and the straight line, as shown.

significant. However, if the effect per rad is quite large, even a modest number of cases will suffice.

In the case of in utero irradiation, where the effect per rad *is* large, Stewart was able to demonstrate that the linear relationship holds down to about 0.25 rads (250 millirads). In chapter 15, which deals with the in utero effects of radiation, we shall consider the controversy that has arisen around this claim. The prevailing opinion is that Dr. Stewart *has* proved this point, and the author concurs in this opinion, for reasons discussed in chapter 15.

But even if the linear relationship indisputably holds down to about 0.25 rads, the skeptic can still ask, where is the evidence for 0.20 rads, 0.15 rads, 0.1 rads, 0.001 rads (1 millirad)? One must readily concede that it would take studies of mammoth proportions, performed under exquisitely controlled conditions, to obtain direct epidemiological proof of the linear relationship. No such studies have been done, nor is it remotely likely that they ever will be done. But this is very different from saying that we cannot arrive at a scientifically reasonable conclusion without such studies. The author believes that the following sections will show that the existence of the linear relationship at very low doses is by far the most reasonable scientific conclusion.

Linearity and supralinearity in the ranges already considered certainly do not suggest that either a diminishing effect per rad or a threshold will suddenly appear below 250 millirads. Such a belief would require one to look at the data indicating that the effect per rad may grow *more* serious at lower doses, but claim that everything turns in the opposite direction under 250 millirads, and the effect per rad becomes *less* serious, or possibly nonexistent. There is certainly no law to prevent wishful thinkers from invoking unknown cellular mechanisms (gremlins) that would produce whatever curve they would like below 250 millirads. As we have said, it is not likely that anyone will *ever* be able to prove they are wrong. But it is not scientifically reasonable to invoke gremlins.

SECTION 2: DIMINISHING EFFECT PER RAD AT LOW DOSES?

In spite of the evidence for a linear relationship between radiation-induced cancers and amount of radiation received down to a dose of 0.25 rads, enthusiasts for nuclear power and medical irradiation persist in telling the public two falsehoods. The first is that we know quite a bit about the effects of radiation at levels above 100 rads, but we know nothing about the effects of low-dose radiation; the second, that to extrapolate from high doses to low probably exaggerates greatly the effect of low doses.

The reader perhaps now shares the author's amazement that the enthusiasts are willing simply to deny the evidence that we do know the effects of irradiation as low as a quarter-rad, and we do know that the effects are linear or supralinear.

When such "experts" disregard the evidence for linearity, they often claim, without basis in either evidence or logic, that the effect of radiation is proportional to the *square* of the dose, and not to the dose. Thus, they claim that the appropriate curve would be figure 5c instead of 5a. (When there is a squared term in such an equation, the resulting plot cannot be a straight line.)

Before we discuss the (dose)^2 term, a comment about this section is appropriate. Since the *evidence* shows linearity, the reader may wonder why the author should even bother to discuss arguments that require dismissing the evidence.

Whenever one is confronted with two (or more) sets of apparently contradictory evidence (observations, facts), a true scientist simply *must* "bother" to deal with them both (all). Indeed, the effort to reconcile apparently contradictory observations is often what leads to new insights and advances in knowledge. Since the proponents of dose-squared and other diminishing-effect-at-low-doses relationships have no data to offer, this is not a case of two or more conflicting sets of *observations*. It is a case of data versus wishful thinking. Nevertheless, we shall deal with these views because our discussion will introduce concepts that will be needed in sections 3 and 4. Furthermore, the reader will learn that even *if* the dose-response curve were not strictly linear, the author's use of the linear relationship still would not seriously exaggerate the effects of low doses.

THE ORIGIN OF THE DOSE-SQUARED TERM

The issue of whether a linear relationship or a quadratic relationship (containing a squared term) holds for doses between 5 rads and 100 rads (or more) pertains to those doses delivered acutely, that is, within seconds, minutes, or hours. This is so because the issue is whether a *single* event at the cellular level (or, probably, at the chromosomal level) produces the key lesion that leads to cancer, or whether two or more events must occur within a short distance from each other and within a short time period.

In chapter 3 the issue of *single-track* events versus *two-track* events was discussed. Much of the argument about whether a linear or a dose-squared relationship should hold for cancer production by radiation centers on the question whether two primary lesions must occur and interact with each other for cancer to result.

Simply stated, the dose-squared relationship assumes that all radiation-induced cancers originate from the interaction of two-track events at the cellular level. Linearity, on the other hand, assumes a relationship of direct proportionality between the radiation dose delivered acutely to an individual or a population and the probability of a cancer-producing event.

Both an analysis of the quantitative implications of the dose-squared term and an investigation of the possibility of another relationship, a combination of single-track and two-track events, result in dose-response curves that deviate significantly from the curve produced by plotting the linear relationship. It is not possible to say that the dose-squared and combined-mechanism hypotheses are incorrect in theory, but we can say with certainty that the evidence now available does not support either one.

In cellular biology observed linearity means that the crucial radiation events that initiate cancer are single events, or single-track events. Finding linearity does not tell us the exact nature of the crucial events. But we do know that the most plausible explanation for observed linearity is single-track events. We could, of course, invoke gremlins to account for the linearity, but that would be a violation of Occam's razor, the scientific maxim that counsels against concocting *many* explanations for a phenomenon that *one* adequately explains.

It is the author's opinion that the linear dose-effect curve resulting from the Japanese and the Stewart in utero data offers cancer researchers a clue worth some exploration. If radiation-induced cancer is increasing in proportion to (dose) rather than to $(dose)^2$, it suggests strongly that the primary relationship is to single-track events (perhaps deletions and chromosome imbalance) rather than to two-track events.

In any event, examination of both the dose-squared and the combined mechanisms shows that the linear relationship is in far better agreement with the evidence. Brown arrived at the same conclusion (1976). Indeed, his concern that linear extrapolation might *underestimate* the risk is confirmed by the supralinear results in section 1 of this chapter.

SUPRALINEARITY, DELETIONS, AND THE MECHANISM OF CARCINOGENESIS

The consistent finding of supralinearity in human cancer production by ionizing radiation may suggest that *deletions* deserve very serious consideration as the primary chromosomal event in human carcinogenesis. The general tendency among scientists is to lump deletions and translocations together as "chromosome aberrations." The author would like to suggest that this tendency may mislead.

The event necessary to produce deletions and translocations is a simple break in a chromosome arm. No one contests that there is a linear relationship between the *frequency of breaks* and the dose of ionizing radiation. If that simple, single break is never "healed," a terminal deletion in the chromosome is produced. As we consider genetic and chromosomally based diseases and disorders, we shall see what a serious matter the deletion of a single autosomal chromosome can be. (See chapter 15.)

Let us explore the possibility that such phenomena as translocations are really part of a natural mechanism that attempts to repair the serious injury which a deletion represents.

Suppose that deletion of some part of certain chromosomes were the primary carcinogenic event. In the very low dose range, we would expect to see a linear relationship between radiation dose and the frequency of radiation-induced cancers in humans. However, with increasing doses at acute dose rates, we would gradually move into dose regions where some of the single breaks disappear in the formation of translocations, *instead of remaining deletions*. So the higher we go in dose, the more prominent the two-track events would become, and hence the deletions *per rad* left over for carcinogenesis would steadily decrease, and cause a linear curve to "bend" into a supralinear curve. Therefore, with respect to *terminal* deletions versus dose, the curve would show supralinear behavior. And if the carcinogenic event at the chromosomal level were a simple terminal deletion, we would expect that *carcinogenesis* would also show a supralinear relationship with dose, when the dose rate is acute.

Supralinearity *is* the relationship observed in all the human evidence presented in this chapter and in chapter 14. However, the author by no means considers that the currently available evidence permits identification of any particular chromosomal lesion as the one primarily associated with carcinogenesis. To make such a claim, we would need very carefully analyzed data based on numbers of cases generally larger than are now available.

As the data base increases, as it inevitably will with time, we must ask the *meaning* of the dose-response curves, since certain curves are compatible with some mechanisms but not with others. Testing the deletion concept rigorously will require not only more data, but also some technological improvements in our ability to measure for terminal deletions.

THE ISSUE OF A CHANGING RBE

The most recent, fashionable way to attack the linear relationship of radiation dose with cancer induction arises from the misapplication of some findings of Kellerer and Rossi. These workers showed that for opacification of the lens of the eyes (cataract formation), RBE (see below) showed a trend toward higher and higher values at lower and lower doses, when neutron irradiation is compared with low LET gamma irradiation.

Let us review what RBE tells us and does not tell us. Recalling the definition of RBE (relative biological effectiveness), we know that RBE tells us the quantity of low LET radiation which must be delivered to produce the same biological effect as is produced by a given quantity of high LET radiation. For instance, *if* it took 10 rads of gamma radiation to produce the same biological effect produced by 1 rad of neutron radiation, then the RBE of neutrons would be 10. Stated another way, *if* neutrons had an RBE of 10 (and the evidence from Japan argues strongly against this, for carcinogenesis), then 1 rad of neutrons would do 10 times more biological damage than 1 rad of gamma rays. And if the linear dose-effect relationship holds for both neutrons and gamma rays (and the evidence argues that it does), then the RBE relating neutron and gamma radiation necessarily remains *constant* regardless of dose.

Although none of the Kellerer-Rossi findings have anything at all to do with human carcinogenesis, the astounding conclusion of some "experts," particularly the minority group of the BEIR-III Committee (Draft Report, May 1979), is that the Kellerer-Rossi findings show that low LET radiation must be less and less carcinogenic, per rad delivered, as the total dose is reduced—in other words, they claim the Kellerer-Rossi findings show that a diminishing effect per rad at low doses must exist for radiation carcinogenesis!

This is, at best, scientific nonsense. There is simply no justification for claiming that either the RBE value or the variation of RBE with dose is the same for one disease (lens opacification) as for another (cancer). To claim this is like saying that, having measured the relative effects of Virus A and Virus B on the respiratory system, we know their relative effects on the liver, or on the brain.

Furthermore, hypotheses *always* must come to terms with *evidence*. The evidence argues strongly for linearity or supralinearity of radiation carcinogenesis at low gamma doses—*not* for a diminishing effect per rad. Although such groups as the BEIR-III minority cannot by fiat abolish the facts, they can help to obscure the truth for a very long time.

SECTION 3: PROTECTION BY DOSE FRACTIONATION?

It has been claimed repeatedly by enthusiasts of nuclear power and medical irradiation that we do not have proof that several exposures to radiation are *cumulative* in their harmful effect. In other words, they deny the evidence that, if a person receives a single 5-rad exposure this year, a single 5-rad exposure next year, and a single 5-rad exposure the following year, that person will experience the risk associated with 15 rads.

They claim that the risk should be *less* than that associated with receiving 15 rads all at once, because of an alleged protection from slow delivery of the energy. In other words, they say the effect *per rad* should be weaker when the rads are delivered in three "small" doses than when they are delivered in one larger dose (a nonlinear dose-effect relationship).

It is easy to imagine a case in which the 15 rads (an amount chosen only for illustration) were divided into much smaller doses, delivered more frequently. Let us divide them into 1,095 daily doses (365 days/year, times 3 years), each 13.7 millirads. A situation of "chronic" irradiation can thus be regarded as just another type of dose fractionation.

Now, we shall consider both the human evidence and the physics of radiation exposure in order to show that there is no protection gremlin and no merit to the proposition that dose fractionation protects.

THE HUMAN EVIDENCE ON DOSE FRACTIONATION

First, let us consider the study of occupational radiation exposure of workers at the Hanford atomic facility in Washington State (Mancuso, Stewart, Kneale 1977; Gofman 1979). In that study, the radiation dose was accumulated very slowly, *averaging about 1 rad per year* in the group of persons who received more than 10 rads total in a 20-year period of employment. The % excess cancers induced per rad turned out to be surprisingly large (see chapter 5). It is a possibility that the effect per rad is *stronger* with slow delivery than with instantaneous delivery, although the author is not proposing that. However, the Hanford study surely shows that the cancer effect from slow delivery of radiation is *not weaker* than from instantaneous delivery. There is no way to interpret the Hanford data to mean anything other than that the cancer-producing effects of the doses accumulated.

We must also consider other major human studies, such as the breast-cancer studies. The two tuberculosis-fluoroscopy studies are based on 1.5 rads per exposure (in the Massachusetts study) and 7.5 rads per exposure (in the Nova Scotia study). If the cancer-producing effects of such exposures had *not* been cumulative, there is no way these two studies could have resulted in approximately the same percents excess per rad as did all the other studies, which were based on instantaneous doses of 30–100 rads per exposure. Perhaps the best summary statement on this problem is from Boice and co-workers (1979), who compared all the studies (not just the Japanese data) of human breast cancers induced by ionizing radiation. They state (with emphasis, in their paper):

The observation that multiple low-dose exposures did not produce significantly fewer cancers per unit dose than less highly fractionated larger exposures suggests that radiation damage is cumulative and that highly fractionated X-irradiation may be as effective in inducing breast cancer as single or less-fractionated exposures. (p. 593)

THE MYTH OF SLOW ENERGY TRANSFER

Over a period of years, this author has attended many sophisticated scientific meetings dealing with the cancer-producing effects of ionizing radiation. At least a dozen times, he has heard a scientist say the following, or a minor variation of the following: "I can understand how 100 millirads can produce a cancer effect when the dose is delivered instantaneously, but certainly the effect cannot be the same when the radiation is slowly introduced over a period of a year. One hundred millirads delivered over the course of a year is a rate of delivery 31,536,000 times slower than 100 millirads delivered in 1 second." Generally this statement is made in a tone suggesting the speaker has divulged gospel truth.

So we must ask ourselves whether it is true, at the cellular level, where the crucial events in cancer production occur, that one rate is really 31 million times slower than another. Application of the principles presented in chapter 2 will show that the rate of delivery of radiation at the cellular level is virtually the same whether 100 millirads are delivered in 1 second or over 1 year, astounding as that may seem.

When the cell is considered as a whole, the difference in the rate between acute and fractionated delivery at the cellular level is trivial: it is 5-fold (versus the 31,000,000-fold claimed). When 100 millirads are delivered over the course of a year, the 5 traversals of the cell may occur in January, March, June, August, and November. At 500 millirads (25 traversals per cell), a traversal will occur about once every two weeks.

Even "experts" have trouble keeping in mind that energy from ionizing radiation comes to cells in rather large packages. There is no way to spread out the 1 mev of energy of a primary beta particle over minutes, hours, days, or years. *It is not possible "slowly to introduce" ionizing radiation of any sort (beta particle, gamma ray, X-ray, alpha particle, neutron, or proton) into cells.* Either a cell receives an energy transfer or it does not; and when it does, the energy is all transferred in a fraction of a second.

This fact is what makes the following statement by a pronuclear "expert" (in a television debate) so irresponsible. He said, "Since we're not all dead from natural radiation, it means our bodies have learned to cope with radiation at slow dose rates."

SECTION 4: THE PROPOSITION THAT A THRESHOLD DOSE EXISTS

Those who refuse to accept the linear relationship between cancer induction and radiation dose have a favorite refrain: Repair mechanisms take care of injury at low doses.

Systems do indeed exist in the body which prevent permanent damage when certain sorts of injuries occur at a slow rate, but which are saturated when injuries occur at a fast rate. They cannot "keep up." A lethal dose of acute radiation exposure is a pertinent example: the rate at which cells die exceeds the rate at which they can be replaced by the body. Cell injuries from certain drugs and chemical poisons represent another example of such "threshold" phenomena, where no injury is observed *below* a certain dose because the repair, replacement, or removal mechanisms of the body "keep up" with the rate of injury.

But there is certainly no biological law which says that because *some* sorts of biological functions are threshold phenomena, *all* of them are. Nor is there a biological law that a repair mechanism even *exists* for each conceivable kind of injury.

Those who propose that repair mechanisms take care of radiation injury at low doses seem to go out of their way to suggest that both "laws" *do* exist. They often use an analogy which may mislead all but the really sophisticated: "The linear hypothesis means that giving one aspirin to each of 1,000 people will kill just as many people as giving 1,000 aspirin to one person." Since it is well known that large doses of aspirin can kill, but that there is a threshold dose below which aspirin cannot kill, this false analogy succeeds in convincing many people that the linear relationship is intrinsically ridiculous.

The assertion that repair mechanisms take care of radiation injury at low doses implies profound knowledge, and is surely an insult to all those in the vast field of cancer research who must labor patiently and ingeniously for years to gather even *small* bits of knowledge. It is interesting that such a statement can be made when we do not know *which* of the myriad possible effects on genes, chromosomes, the mitotic process, centrosomes, and still-unknown sites is responsible for cancer induction. How threshold proponents can be sure that repair takes care of a process that cannot even be identified is a mystery to this author.

There do exist several repair mechanisms that operate to correct certain kinds of defects in DNA, and these have been found to work within hours after injury. However, the genetic diseases provide abundant evidence that not all injuries to DNA get repaired. And if one considers all the genetic injuries that we never see because of spontaneous abortion (miscarriage), the fraction of DNA injuries which either do not get repaired, or for which no repair mechanism exists, may be significant.

Furthermore, simply using the word *repair* provides no information at all on the crucial issue, which is how well the alleged repair mechanism would operate as a function of radiation dose. In order to claim that low-dose radiation is repaired while high-dose radiation is not repaired, it would be necessary to show that at low doses, the repair mechanism worked well, whereas it worked progressively less well with increasing dose. No such demonstration has ever been made for carcinogenic damage. Indeed, we do not know that DNA injury is at the bottom of cancer development at all. There are many other candidates for that role, as was shown in chapter 3. So even if all DNA injuries were 100% repaired, we would still know nothing about a threshold dose for radiation carcinogenesis.

Possible repair of chromosomal injuries is even more problematical. We certainly have evidence (see chapters 3 and 15) that *not all* chromosomal injuries get repaired. It is clear that the pieces of a broken chromosome sometimes reattach to each other within hours after the break (Sax 1939; Wolff et al. 1956, 1958). Whether this represents complete repair is in doubt. Chromosome repair is in all probability even more complex than DNA repair, since chromosomes are not double strands of pure DNA, but also contain many proteins.

THE EVIDENCE PERTAINING TO EXISTENCE OF A THRESHOLD

Much attention has been focused in the press and in medical centers on a paper by Linos and co-workers (1980) of the Mayo Clinic (Departments of Medical Statistics and Epidemiology, and Diagnostic Radiology; Divisions of Therapeutic Radiology, and Hematology and Internal Medicine). It concludes:

No statistically significant increase was found in the risk of developing leukemia after radiation doses of 0 to 300 rads (3 Gy) to the bone marrow when these amounts were administered in small doses over long periods of time, as in routine medical care. (p. 1101)

This conclusion is not at all justified by the data which Linos and co-workers present; there are numerous extremely serious defects in the paper. Because the paper concerns leukemia, we will analyze it in chapter 14.

Another set of data that could be misinterpreted to support the existence of a threshold dose is the set from Hiroshima and Nagasaki. However, one will not be easily misled if one is aware of the increased dose received in the area beyond 2.5 kilometers from the hypocenter of the bomb. This issue is amply discussed in chapter 5, chapter 14, and earlier in this chapter.

Now, let us consider the other pertinent evidence. If we were to accept the idea that a threshold exists, we would naturally ask at what dose we would find it. In this section, the reader will notice some overlap with the evidence considered in the previous section. That is because one of the

hidden assumptions about protection by dose fractionation is that fractionation will place a greater share of any given dose below the alleged threshold,
where repair gremlins fix everything.

Let us recall (from chapter 5) the Modan series of children treated for
tinea capitis with scalp X-rays. During the treatment, their thyroids received
an estimated 7.5 rads, and the result was a significant excess of thyroid
cancer. This suggests there is no threshold above 7.5 rads.

Let us also recall (originally from chapter 5) the women of the Massachusetts tuberculosis-fluoroscopy study. Those women received only 1.5
rads with each fluoroscopy, and there was time for so-called repair before
the next fluoroscopy. Yet the peak percent increase per rad in their breast-
cancer rate is comparable to the peak percents, for example, of the series
of Japanese women who received instantaneous doses of 30–40 rads, of the
Rochester mastitis series in which the women received 50 or more rads per
dose, and of the Swedish series in which the women received in the neighborhood of 50 rads per dose. Apparently there was no functioning repair
mechanism available to the Massachusetts women when they received the
"low" dose of 1.5 rads per fluoroscopy. This suggests we will not find a
threshold above 1.5 rads.

The entire Japanese experience suggests that we will not find a threshold above about 2 rads.

The Hanford evidence is even more out of line with the repair concept.
The excess cancers that developed in those workers did so at an exposure
rate of about 1 rad per year, assuredly a low enough rate for those hypothetical repair mechanisms to operate to prevent carcinogenesis.

From the discussion in the previous section, the reader knows that 1 rad
delivered over the course of a year causes about 50 hits per cell. That means
1 hit per cell every 7 days, on the average. Such a rate provides plenty of
repair time. Is someone seriously going to propose that a *lower* dose—say,
at 100 millirads per year, or 1 hit per cell every 70 days—a repair mechanism
which cannot repair a single hit in 7 days is going to work? Or will it work
in 700 days, which is the interval between hits per cell at a dose of 10
millirads per year?

The Hanford evidence on irradiated adults is a powerful indication that
no threshold exists, or stated otherwise, that a threshold will be found at
no dose.

Corroborating the Hanford evidence in this respect is the Stewart evidence on in utero irradiation, where a linear dose-effect relationship was
found right down to 250 millirads. Let us indulge the threshold proponents
again; instead of considering 250 millirads, let us consider 500 millirads.

At 500 millirads (the equivalent of two separate films in the Stewart in
utero studies), there would be an average of 25 hits per cell. We estimated
in the original edition that, for 100 millirads, the crucial volume of the cell
would have only between 1 in 30 and 1 in 60 chances of being hit. For 500
millirads, the odds would be between 1 in 6 and 1 in 12. So only a fraction
of the cells would even have the crucial volumes hit *once*. This means that

the repair gremlins would rarely have to deal with more than 1 hit in the crucial volume of a given cell. It hardly seems reasonable that they could not cope with even this much damage.

Yet, for total in utero doses of between 0.25 and 1.5 rads, there was an increase in cancer and leukemia on the order of 50% per rad. Threshold proponents, who will grab at any straw, may claim that the repair mechanism may not be as good before birth as after birth. That is possible. But then how will they explain the Hanford evidence, which comes from men irradiated at an average age of 45–50 years?

THE LOGIC AGAINST THE EXISTENCE OF A THRESHOLD

Whether one considers the Stewart in utero infants or the Hanford workers, the evidence indicates that repair is either absent or incomplete *for the least possible damage* (no more than 1 hit in the crucial volume of a cell). It follows that when single hits occur from even lower doses or dose rates than those in these studies, repair will also be either absent or incomplete. Therefore, scientifically it is thoroughly reasonable to say that *cancer and leukemia induction by radiation is proportional to dose right down to the lowest conceivable doses.*

SECTION 5: PUBLIC-HEALTH IMPLICATIONS

The preceding sections explain why there is no safe dose of radiation.

Occasionally someone asks whether, if no dose is safe, *any* dose is lethal. The question implies that any dose is in one of two possible classes: lethal or harmless. This confusion may be widespread, for it is frequently nurtured by nuclear-power promoters, who remind us that most people never get cancer, even though everyone is exposed to low doses of natural-background radiation and many, many people receive medical irradiation. Thus they suggest that any dose to an individual below the dose which is *certain* to kill him is harmless. Exposure to any lower dose is belittled as only a risk, and it is pointed out that getting out of bed is risky too.

UNDERSTANDING THE WORDS "ONLY A RISK"

When we say that there is *no* harmless dose of radiation, we mean that every dose adds to one's *risk* of cancer. And risk means probability. A dose that virtually guarantees a radiation-induced cancer confers a risk of 100%, or a probability of 1, unity—in other words, certainty. Terms like *whole-body cancer dose, lung-cancer dose, breast-cancer dose,* and *brain-cancer dose* pertain to a risk of 100%. At lower doses than these, the risk of developing the cancer in question is less than 100%.

Suppose that an individual receives a dose which creates "only" a 10% risk. If he falls into the 10% that develop fatal cancers, he will not think that the radiation was harmless. But he has a 90% probability of *not* getting a radiation-induced cancer from that dose. Would he then announce that the dose he received is harmless? If he did, then, to be consistent, he would have to label as harmless any dose of any poison (or medicine, or germs, or stress) which did not kill him, even if that dose killed a multitude of others.

To belittle the importance of *risk* is to belittle a concept that is fundamental to disease and medicine in general: certainty seldom exists. For instance, not everyone who is exposed to *Mycobacterium tuberculosis* develops TB. Not everyone who is exposed to an influenza virus gets the flu. At various levels of exposure, one can observe that only some share of people (say, 10%, 25%, 60%) actually get the disease. The same uncertainty surrounds bad reactions to a medication: one may observe that perhaps 5% of patients will not tolerate a "safe" drug; then there is a 95% chance that any one patient *will* tolerate it.

So probability rather than certainty is fundamental to medicine. And no one in his right mind ever called the tubercle bacillus harmless because exposure to it does not *guarantee* death.

The situation is no different for radiation exposure. Not everyone who gets exposed to 100 millirads (or 0.1 rad) will develop a radiation-induced cancer. If we use 270 person-rads as the whole-body cancer dose for an equilibrium population of mixed ages (see chapter 6), we mean that if 2,700 people are each exposed to 100 millirads (an aggregate exposure of 270 person-rads), only *one* of them will get a radiation-induced cancer. The dose will be "safe" for 2,699, and lethal for one! If the dose is doubled to 200 millirads, the *risk* of every individual doubles from 1 chance in 2,700 (or an individual risk of 0.00037) to 2 chances in 2,700 (an individual risk of 0.00074).

The difference between risk considered from an individual's point of view and from the point of view of public health is striking. A "small" individual risk of 1 in 2,700 would translate into nearly 100,000 radiation-induced cancers if everyone in an equilibrium population of 250 million persons received a "low dose" of 100 millirads. That each of these 250 million individuals has *only a risk* of developing cancer does *not* mean that no one at all will be harmed.

OFFICIAL POLICY VERSUS REALITY

During the past decade, as the antinuclear movement burgeoned, pronuclear spokesmen in government and industry, and on quasi-governmental committees, which recommend "permissible" radiation doses, all assured the public and Congress that because of their deep concern for public health, they would always assume that the linear relationship holds right down to the lowest conceivable doses. One after another, individuals and groups in high positions stated that they would use this prudent assumption in calculating the risks imposed on people by nuclear power.

That was the message—until significant radiation releases occurred.

Then the officials and the scientists fell all over themselves shifting to the claim that the effects of very low doses of radiation were unknown. Gone were the assurances about using prudent public-health principles. Instead, we heard far and wide that the linear relationship probably exaggerates the cancer risk. And the public heard many, many statements following the accident at Three Mile Island, like "The average exposure was only about 20 millirads, and this is no more radiation than one gets in a chest film."

That comparison surely suggested to the public that the accident would not produce any cancers. Finally the "experts" declared that perhaps a fraction of one extra cancer might be expected "among 200,000 cancers which would occur anyway."

Yet if we consider the delivery from this accident of 20 millirads to 1 million people, we find this represents $(1,000,000) (0.020) = 20,000$ person-rads of exposure. And for a mixed population, our calculations (chapter 6) showed one cancer induced for every 270 person-rads of exposure. Therefore, *if* the accident at Three Mile Island initially exposed 1 million people to "only" an average dose of 20 millirads, then 74 cancer fatalities can be expected from just the initial release.

If the loss of 74 lives can be regarded as trivial simply because 200,000 of the 1 million people will die of cancer anyway, then why not put those 74 deaths into even "better perspective" by comparing them with the eventual deaths, from all causes, of all the 1 million residents of the area? No one gets out alive, in the end. This argument in favor of nuclear power has, in fact, been presented. A radiologist and member in 1970 of the quasi-governmental National Council on Radiation Protection testified in that year before the Pennsylvania State Legislature in defense of nuclear power for the country and for Pennsylvania in particular. Among his arguments was the remark that we all have to die sometime anyway.

That reasoning, to put it mildly, is inimical to the protection of the public health. It could justify even first degree murder. In the field of public-health protection, no one I know denies that we all have to die sometime anyway. Dying *prematurely* is the issue.

In the year following the accident at Three Mile Island (which occurred in late March 1979), it became abundantly clear that a powerful propaganda campaign was being mounted to repeat *ad nauseum* that the effects of low-dose radiation were unknown and would remain unknown for years. The scientists employed in various parts of the nuclear industry and its associated research establishments, in and outside universities, did not have to lie, because they could truthfully state that they were not aware of a single human study which showed cancer being produced at 20 millirads, or even at 50 or 100 millirads. They did not lie, but this chapter shows how they misled the public.

While a few scientists are becoming properly concerned about doses of 20, 50, or 100 millirads, the propagandists are attempting a truly bold maneuver. They are suggesting that there may be a safe threshold for radiation carcinogenesis at doses like 10 *rads*, not 10 millirads. The more daring among them suggest a safe threshold at even higher doses, such as 50 rads. No further back in history than 1969, one "expert" seriously proposed a safe threshold, with respect to carcinogenesis, at 1,000 rads (Evans et al., 1969).

The "experts" who are in charge of protecting the public health require careful watching. Of course, watching is futile as long as individuals are denied their *right* to stop the imposition of risk and injury upon themselves and future generations.

The author wishes to draw three conclusions to end this chapter. First, it is *scientifically* reasonable that the dose-effect relationship between radiation and cancer is linear, and that there is no threshold dose. This conclusion stands on its own merits and is totally independent of the next two statements, which summarize the author's philosophy with respect to public-health policy.

Second, it is a violation of the most fundamental human rights to impose risks (deaths) upon individuals without their consent. Human rights should not be sacrificed to the pursuit of "a healthy economy," affluence, progress, science, or any other goal. The whole "benefit versus risk" doctrine is a profound violation of human rights.

Third, if we did not yet know the effects of low-dose radiation as has been claimed, the human-rights issue would be the use of members of the public as experimental guinea pigs, whether or not they object. If guinea-piggery becomes an accepted policy, the danger of genocide is real: 10,000 pollutants, each of unknown toxicity, could finish the job in ten years if they turned out, on the average, to impose a "small risk" of 1 death per 100,000 infants or children per year.

[CHAPTER 9]

THE INTERNAL EMITTERS AND THEIR BIOLOGICAL EFFECTS

U P TO NOW we have been dealing chiefly with the health effects of
radiation absorbed through the skin from external sources such
as X-rays and atomic weapons. In this and following chapters, we
will investigate the nature and health effects of radiation from
internally deposited radionuclides, which are referred to as the internal emitters.

These fall into several groups, depending on the type of radiation
emitted (see chapter 2). Beta-particle emitters, such as tritium and some of
the gaseous products of nuclear-power reactors, are radionuclides that
decay by the emission of a beta particle (an electron released in the decay
of the radionuclide). The alpha-particle emitters decay by the emission of
alpha particles (the stripped nuclei of the element helium); they include
both natural radionuclides such as radium and man-made sources such as
plutonium. As we saw in chapter 2, alpha- and beta-particle emissions may
or may not be accompanied by gamma rays, a form of radiant energy with
a wavelength very close to that of X-rays. There are also some sources of
pure gamma-ray emission.

We will begin by considering the significant problems involved in measuring the biological impact of radiation from internally deposited sources;
the remainder of the chapter is devoted to analyzing the large family of both
natural and man-made alpha-emitters.

SECTION 1: HANDLING THE INTERNAL EMITTERS: DOSIMETRY AND APPLICATIONS

In chapter 2, we learned that there is no reason whatsoever to expect a
different cancer-producing effect from radiation emitted by a radionuclide
deposited *within* tissue than from any source of *external* radiation. This
statement, of course, carries two provisos:

1. Either we are speaking of radiations of equivalent LET values or we
have shown that LET is unimportant for the effect.

2. The rate of delivery of dose has been shown to be of negligible importance, as demonstrated in chapter 8.

A statement made earlier in this book deserves re-emphasis here. It is foolish to believe that an electron, generated from radioactive decay *inside* the body tissues, could produce an effect any different from that produced by an electron *of the same energy,* set in motion by the photoelectric or Compton effect, from X-rays or gamma rays originating *outside* the body tissues. And, of course, it is equally ridiculous to think a gamma ray generated inside the body by radioactive decay could produce a cancer effect different from the effect of a gamma ray that has penetrated from the outside.

For the same energy delivered, we can expect the same cancer consequences from internal radiation as from external radiation, corrected for any effect of LET. What this means is that whole-body cancer doses, specific-organ cancer doses, and the methods of applying them, *are all perfectly valid for the case of internal radiation by radionuclides.* What sets the case of internal deposition apart is that dosimetry is quite a bit harder to come by than is the case for external X-ray or gamma-ray exposures. Let us consider why this is so.

DOSIMETRY FOR INTERNALLY DEPOSITED BETA-EMITTING NUCLIDES

Let us consider a simple case: a single, orally administered dose of a beta-emitter in a 20-year-old woman.

The data we would need to have, in order to ascertain this woman's dose in rads to various organs, are:

1. What is the average energy of the beta particles emitted? Recall from chapter 2 that there is a spectrum of beta-particle energies, with the maximum energy being about three times the average energy. For dosimetry, it is the average energy of the beta particles that matters.

2. What fraction of the ingested dose gets absorbed, and what fraction is promptly excreted via the gastrointestinal tract?

3. Do gamma rays accompany the beta-particle emissions, and if so, of what energy are they, and how many accompany each beta emission?

4. What organs are the sites of deposition of the ingested radionuclide, and to what *extent* is the absorbed radionuclide deposited in these organs?

5. How long do the various organs continue to be irradiated by the radionuclide? This, in turn, has two determinants: (a) the radioactive-decay properties of the radionuclide, such as its half-life, and (b) its biological-elimination properties, including excretion and translocation to other body tissues.

The amount of information available for all the parameters will vary from radionuclide to radionuclide. For some, all the parameters will be accessible and reasonably well known. For others, many of the parameters will be poorly known, if any information at all is available. But this lack of information is of secondary importance. Those parameters which are not known now will, in the case of many of the radionuclides, become better known with time. What is important here is to learn *how* the information should be handled once it becomes available. Also, in many instances, some reasonable approximations can suggest to us at least the upper limits of a particular dose.

We shall begin *not* by asking what fraction of a beta-emitter is absorbed from the intestine and what fraction goes to each tissue or organ. We shall begin by assuming that *some* number of picocuries of a beta-emitter have been deposited in an organ which weighs 1,000 grams, and that the deposition is approximately uniform in that organ. Our objective is the determination of the dose to that organ in rads. We shall develop some exceedingly useful rules (or equations) that simplify matters enormously. (The beta-emitter could of course be deposited uniformly throughout the body as well as in just one organ.)

It is useful for many reasons to adopt a single convention for expressing concentration of a beta-emitter in tissue. Let us adopt the convention *picocuries per kilogram of tissue*. One picocurie (1 PCi) $= 3.7 \times 10^{-2}$ disintegrations per second (from chapter 2). One kilogram $=$ about 2.2 pounds. Let us further suppose that the average energy of the emitted beta particles is 0.5 mev each. What would be the dose delivered in rads *if* the level of the radionuclide were maintained at 1 PCi per kilogram of tissue *for a period of one year*? (Whether decay and excretion permit the nuclide to stay there for a whole year will be taken into account a little further on.) Dose, we recall, is measured in rads, or in this case in millirads, which prove to be more convenient.

After performing a calculation that takes into account all the factors above, we can write a general dose formula for *each* picocurie deposited in a kilogram of tissue:

Dose in millirads per year $= (18.68 \times 10^{-3}) \times$ (average energy in mev)

This relationship can be used for any beta-emitter. For deposits 100 times this quantity (in picocurie units), the dose will obviously be 100 times as great.

The reader will recall the set of assumptions made at the outset. The only concerns we have about the correctness of our answer are either that some of the beta-particle energy leaks out of this tissue and is lost to other tissues, or that more beta energy enters this tissue than is lost from it, causing more energy to be absorbed than we calculated. If the radionuclide is present *only* in the tissue for which we are calculating, the error will be very small, unless the organ is extremely thin or extremely small. The author would not like to use the simple relationship above for calculating dose to the tissues of a fetus, where both small and thin organs are still present. But for most adult tissues, the reader will certainly not go wrong, in any meaningful manner, by using the equation above *for every picocurie deposited per kilogram of tissue.*

DOSIMETRY FOR INTERNALLY DEPOSITED ALPHA-PARTICLE EMITTERS

Since the range of travel of alpha particles is far smaller than for beta particles, any energy either lost from the tissue or entering the tissue from surrounding tissues is virtually negligible under all circumstances. Therefore, the simple relationship of the previous section will hold well for alpha-emitters:

Dose in millirads per year = $(18.68 \times 10^{-3}) \times$ (average energy in mev) for each picocurie deposited per kilogram

The LET for alpha particles is, however, much higher than for beta particles, on the average. It is common to introduce a factor of 10 into the calculation, and to estimate that *rems* = $(10 \times rads)$ for alpha-particle radiation as it relates to cancer induction. While we would like to be far more certain of just how accurate that factor of 10 is, this author cannot suggest an alternative value to convert rads to rems. It represents a reasonable approximation at this time. Doses from specific alpha-emitters are considered in sections 2 and 3.

The short range of alpha particles' travel creates another problem of dosimetry for certain radioactive sources. If the particles bearing the alpha-emitting nuclide are of sufficient size, some of the alpha particles are actually stopped within the material itself, and hence they do no tissue damage. This is known as the phenomenon of *self-absorption* of alpha radiation. The net effect is that a smaller radiation dose is delivered to tissue than would be estimated without a correction for self-absorption.

DOSIMETRY FOR INTERNALLY DEPOSITED GAMMA-RAY EMITTERS

The same general principles apply for gamma-ray emission as for alpha- and beta-particle emission, except for one *major* difference. That difference resides in the *certainty* that some of the photons will escape from the tissue, and from the body, and *also* that some radiation will be delivered to the tissue from surrounding tissues if the nuclide is widely distributed in the body. For these reasons our simple assumptions for alpha- and beta-particle emitters do not apply. However, some very good approximations can be made. We shall treat two special cases:

1. The gamma-emitter is well distributed throughout the body, so there is loss of energy from the tissue and delivery of energy to the tissue from other tissues. The following approximate values, based on data in UNSCEAR (1977, Figure X1, p. 54), will be useful for estimating dose:

X-ray or Gamma-Ray Energy (mev)	Millirads/year/PCi/kilogram
0.1 mev	7×10^{-4}
0.2 mev	1.5×10^{-3}
0.5 mev	3×10^{-3}
1.0 mev	6×10^{-3}
1.5 mev	7.5×10^{-3}
2.0 mev	10×10^{-3}
2.5 mev	12×10^{-3}
3.0 mev	13×10^{-3}

2. The gamma-emitter is *not* well distributed throughout the body. In this case, it is difficult to estimate the dose. However, the *upper limit* of the dose can be taken from the tabulation above, since we are still losing energy *to* surrounding tissues, but getting none back from those tissues.

Coping with the Internal Gamma-Ray Problem in General

Virtually all the gamma-ray emitters encountered in internal dosimetry also emit beta particles or alpha particles. There are, however, some instances of pure gamma-ray emission.

In the case where gamma rays accompany alpha-particle emission, the bulk of the energy will come from the stopping of the alpha particle in the tissue, so any slight error in assessing the energy contribution of the gamma rays will hardly matter in dose estimation, in the first approximation.

In the case of either alpha-particle or beta-particle emission accompanied by gamma-ray emission, and when the emitting nuclide is fairly well spread throughout the body, we can use our equation for the alpha- or beta-emitter plus the tabulation above for the gamma-emitter.

The only remaining case of consequence is that of highly local deposition. Thereby, a particular radionuclide may be deposited in one small body organ but nowhere else in the body. Using our general equation for the alpha or beta emissions from such a nuclide will yield correct answers. However, calculating the gamma-ray contribution to the dose will present some difficulty, because radiation is escaping from the tissue but very little is being returned to it from other tissues. What little gamma radiation is returned is the result of the phenomenon of back-scattering. Since the gamma radiation will not represent a large share of the total dose when a beta or alpha particle also is emitted, a good approximation of gamma-ray dose would use one-half the dose listed in the tabulation above for gamma rays of various energies.

One Day Versus One Year

The reader will note that, in all these considerations, no questions were raised concerning whether the radionuclides were natural or artificial, whether they were long-lived, very long-lived, or relatively short-lived, whether they were nuclides of uranium, potassium, strontium, or some other chemical element. All these questions are irrelevant. Our equations and table are perfectly general and would not be altered by any answer to these questions.

It should be obvious that it would be hard to keep a short-lived nuclide in a tissue for a year, and our calculations apply to a one-year period. But even if the nuclide were in the tissue at 1 picocurie per kilogram for one day, the same equation would still apply if we simply added a sixth factor (1/365) to convert from one year to one day.

LIMITED PERIODS OF DEPOSITION OF INTERNAL EMITTERS

Our considerations thus far have not addressed the length of time that ingested or injected radionuclides will remain in the body or in a specific tissue. For a single dose, this length of residence will of course determine the dose received, according to the relationship just described.

When a fixed fraction of a radionuclide is *biologically* removed from a tissue per unit of time, we can speak of a biological *half-time*, just as we speak of a *half-life* for radioactive decay. Many biological removal processes, but not all, can be described in terms of biological half-times. One reason that the half-time concept may not pertain to some processes is that the nuclide may be in the tissue in different chemically bound forms, and each form may have its own characteristic removal process.

A biological half-time of 30 days means that one-half the material will be removed in 30 days, one-half the remaining material will be removed in another 30 days, and so on. This is *biological* removal, and is wholly independent of any radioactive decay. And we can express the mean, or average, residence time in the tissue as a rule similar to that for radioactive decay:

$$\text{Mean residence time} = \frac{\text{biological half-time}}{0.693}$$

Thus, for a 30-day half-time, the mean residence time is 30/0.693 = 43.3 days. This is the *key* value determining the dose. With deposition of 1 picocurie per kilogram of tissue of a beta-emitter of 0.5 mev, and a 30-day half-time, the material would remain in the tissue for 43.3 days, instead of one year, and the dose would be

$$\frac{43.3}{365} \times 9.34 \times 10^{-3} \text{ millirads} = 1.11 \times 10^{-3} \text{ millirads}$$

This method, utilizing the mean residence time, will take care of all very long-lived radionuclides.

However, if the radioactive half-life is not extremely long, calculation of the mean residence time is more complicated, since the radionuclide is disappearing both by biological removal and by radioactive decay. But this situation, as we shall shortly show, can be handled by very simple arithmetic, which permits the calculation of an average *effective* residence time. The term *effective* means that we have taken into account both biological removal and radioactive decay.

COMBINED RADIOACTIVE AND BIOLOGICAL LOSS FROM TISSUE

Any loss process in which a constant or fixed fraction of the remaining material disappears per unit time can be described with the help of a *half-time*, or $T_{\frac{1}{2}}$ (see chapter 2). The formula for obtaining the effective *half-time* of a radionuclide and its mean effective *residence* time, where effective half-time is expressed as $T_{\frac{1}{2}}$ effective, is:

$$T_{\frac{1}{2} \text{ effective}} = \frac{(T_{\frac{1}{2} \text{ radio.}})(T_{\frac{1}{2} \text{ biol.}})}{T_{\frac{1}{2} \text{ biol.}} + T_{\frac{1}{2} \text{ radio.}}}$$

This takes into account the loss of radionuclide by both radioactive decay and biological removal from the tissue. And, of course:

$$\text{Mean effective } \textit{residence} \text{ time} = \frac{\text{effective half-time}}{0.693}$$

A Practical Application of Dosimetry Calculation

PROBLEM: We wish to calculate the dose received by a tissue from a radionuclide deposited at a level of 1 picocurie per kilogram, where the following properties exist:

Average energy of the beta particles = 0.5 mev

$$T_{\frac{1}{2} \text{ biological}} = 5 \text{ days}$$
$$T_{\frac{1}{2} \text{ radioactive}} = 10 \text{ days}$$

Our equation is

$$T_{\frac{1}{2} \text{ effective}} = \frac{(T_{\frac{1}{2} \text{ radioactive}})(T_{\frac{1}{2} \text{ biological}})}{T_{\frac{1}{2} \text{ biological}} + T_{\frac{1}{2} \text{ radioactive}}}$$

$$= \frac{(10 \text{ days})(5 \text{ days})}{5 \text{ days} + 10 \text{ days}} = \frac{50 \text{ days}^2}{15 \text{ days}}$$

$$= \frac{50 \text{ days}}{15} = 3.33 \text{ days}$$

We know from prior statements that if $T_{\frac{1}{2} \text{ effective}} = 3.33$ days, then the mean, or average, effective residence time is

$$\frac{T_{\frac{1}{2} \text{ effective}}}{0.693} = \frac{3.33 \text{ days}}{0.693} = 4.81 \text{ days}$$

We showed earlier that for 0.5-mev beta particles, *in one year* of residence, 1 PCi per kilogram gives a dose of 9.34×10^{-3} millirads. But the combination of radioactive and biological loss makes the effective residence time only 4.81 days. Therefore,

$$\text{dose} = \frac{4.81}{365} \times 9.34 \times 10^{-3} \text{ millirads}$$

$$= 1.32 \times 10^{-2} \times 9.34 \times 10^{-3} \text{ millirads}$$

$$= 1.23 \times 10^{-4} \text{ millirads}$$

SUMMARY

A few simple rules and guidelines have been presented here for determining internal radiation doses, along with an example of their use. Once an internal dose has been calculated, it can be used just as any external dose is used in problems involving whole-body cancer-dose or specific-organ cancer-dose calculations, in estimating the risk of death from a cancer, or in any of the related problems discussed in this book.

In many cases, the problem will be to know such parameters as the fraction absorbed of a particular nuclide, and its mean residence time in tissue. The reader knows now how to deal with information about internal emitters once such parameters are made available.

The Society of Nuclear Medicine has a committee called the Medical Internal Radiation Dose Committee, which is constantly updating the information concerning biological residence times and related parameters. It therefore represents one good source of information. The Nuclear Regulatory Commission constantly uses such information, and is hence a potential source. For sound evaluation of values proposed for key parameters, the group at Heidelberg University should definitely be consulted (see chapter 11).

If one cannot get the proper information, one can still do "upper-limit" dose estimation by assuming that (1) the nuclide is totally absorbed from the intestines, (2) all of it is deposited in one organ of concern, and (3) the residence time is long—say, years. The true dose would certainly not exceed such upper-limit calculations, which could quickly provide some ballpark information when some perspective is needed in a hurry.

Section 2: Internal Alpha-Particle Emitters: Radium and Radon-Daughters

A number of important radionuclides decay by the emission of alpha particles (i.e., nuclei of helium, $^2_4$He). We shall endeavor here to analyze alpha-emitters in general, and shall take up specific points concerning several nuclides that deserve high public interest.

Referring to chapter 2 we learn that alpha particles either have a single energy when they are emitted from a particular radionuclide, or they have two or more discrete sets of energy, but never a continuum of energies. If they have more than one energy, then the alpha particles of lower energy are usually accompanied by gamma-ray emission, since the energy not carried off in the alpha particle is carried off in the gamma ray.

In the case of an external source of alpha emissions accompanied by gamma rays, the penetrating power of the alpha-emitter is really limited to its gamma rays. If we are dealing with a *pure* alpha-emitter, then there is no penetration to internal organs from an external alpha source. Cancer of the skin can be and has been caused by external alpha-emitting sources (Sevcova et al., 1978), but no internal cancer can be caused from an exterior source, since the alpha particles are stopped in a few cell diameters.

However, if any of the substances emitting alpha particles (e.g., radium, plutonium, thorium, neptunium, americium, curium) gain access to cells such as bronchial epithelial cells, bone-lining cells, or liver cells, they are potent carcinogens indeed.

We noted that in all the most useful studies of cancer induction by external radiation, the radiation was delivered instantaneously or over a short period of time. Then the follow-up period was devoid of radiation exposure. The treatment of such data we found to be straightforward, in chapter 5.

However, with the internal emitters, such as the alpha-particle emitters, it is rare to have such a clean situation for analysis. The chemicals emitting the alpha particles commonly have extremely long residence times in the body, so that, in effect, the irradiation period and the follow-up period overlap each other. Quantitative treatment of such data is difficult since we cannot be sure that all the radiation "counts." (This problem is less serious for lung-cancer induction by plutonium (section 3), because the residence time of plutonium in the lungs is relatively short.)

Suppose a cancer has been set in motion in bone cells from ^{226}Radium exposure, and yet the exposure continues for years beyond inception of the cancer. Since *we* do not know that the crucial event has already occurred, we may count the additional radiation as though it mattered, when in fact it is extraneous for that particular cancer.

As a result, the human epidemiological studies on alpha-emitters will be treated here as important individual sources of data; these data are hardly suitable, however, for building up "best" values of such parameters as whole-body cancer doses.

There is an additional problem in using alpha-emission data, namely, the problem of the LET of the radiation and the appropriate RBE factor to assign. It has been common for scientists to *assume* a value of 10 for the RBE of alpha particles, although there is precious little evidence to support that value. The reader who has followed the analyses made thus far in this book of the various human epidemiological studies will see immediately what a large undertaking it would be to find out what the RBE truly is. The requisite experiment is so difficult that we can be sure there will never be a direct answer to this question. The author feels that 10 is a reasonable value, looking broadly at all the experimental-animal evidence, although he would not *defend* that value. We must use some value, however, and provided we always remember the uncertainty in using 10, we can use it for now.

There is a third problem that makes analysis of alpha-emitters and cancer induction difficult. This concerns the uncertainty about how much of the alpha-irradiation actually gets to the vulnerable cells. The problem of radon and its daughter products is a classic case. As radon is inhaled, some of its daughter products deposit on the mucus-covered epithelial lining of the bronchi. Just how much of the alpha-particle radiation from either radon or its daughter products gets through the mucus and into the vulnerable cells of the bronchi, within the short half-lives of the daughter products, remains quite speculative.

Extensive efforts have been made over many years to estimate the dose in rads for such exposure, with even recent estimates ranging over a factor of 200 (BEIR-I, 1972, p. 148). The author feels there is little reason for confidence in these estimates and prefers to leave the exposure data in terms of the amount of radon and its daughter products inhaled.

CANCER PRODUCTION BY THE FAMOUS ^{226}RADIUM

Radium, of course, is a chemical element defined by its atomic number, 88. It has numerous radionuclides, but none so famous as ^{226}Radium, the one studied by Madame Marie Curie. ^{226}Radium was one of the first radioactive substances to produce a very convincing epidemiological story of cancer induction by ionizing radiation. Over a half-century ago, Martland published some now classic studies of the development of cancer in radium-dial painters.

Everyone is now familiar with the concept of luminizers—mixtures that glow in the dark. It was demonstrated long ago (and was even used as a measuring method) that ionizing radiation impinging on certain chemical substances would cause those substances to emit visible light. Zinc sulfide was early discovered to be such a substance. Many others are known today. Shortly after its discovery, radium began to be mixed with sensitive chemicals that were activated by the alpha particles of the radium, for the purpose of making luminous watch and clock dials. Today radium is still sometimes used for this purpose, although other nuclides, including tritium, are also used.

Martland (1931) reported that the young women who worked in this industry were developing bone cancers far in excess of expectancy. Spontaneous development of bone cancer is exceedingly rare. It turned out that because the women wanted a fine tip on the brushes which they dipped into the radium solution, so they could paint the numerals more accurately, they frequently put their brushes to their lips. As they repeatedly "tipped" their brushes, they steadily ingested radium into their bodies. Because of its similarity to calcium, the radium accumulated first on the surfaces of the bones and later in the matrix of the bone structure. The studies of Evans (1966), Rowland (1978), Hasterlik (1962), and others have abundantly confirmed Martland's original observations of bone cancer as "radium-dial painter's disease." Its story exemplifies the gruesome consequences of the philosophy of use first, learn later.

Once deposited in bone tissue, radium is very slowly removed from the body. Therefore, the dial painters continued to show radium in their bones for many decades after original ingestion. For individual cases, it is very difficult to know how the radium redistributed within the bone, or its true rate of elimination. Furthermore, the individuals did not come under observation immediately after ingesting radium.

As a result of these difficulties, the dosimetry for these individuals is of quite dubious reliability, although the efforts toward dosimetry have been valiant. Even if we did know the dosimetry accurately, there would still be the problem of how much of the radiation delivered over decades should be "counted" for production of bone cancer.

The author does not consider the radium-ingestion data suitable for attempting to estimate % excess cancer per rad, simply because the *rads* are in doubt. But we can use the radium data to estimate the number of cancers produced per unit of ^{226}Radium ingested. Unfortunately, the amounts ingested must be reconstructed from body burdens of radium estimated at later times, so there will be uncertainties, possibly severalfold, in those amounts.

Our estimates will nonetheless be of very great interest since they will provide a "ballpark" for estimating the consequences of environmental releases of radium, a large problem indeed.

Doses and Effects for ^{226}Radium Ingestion

Evans (1966) and, separately, Hasterlik (1962) published data for sizable groups of individuals who showed residual body burdens of from 1.0 to 10.0 microcuries of ^{226}Radium long after ingestion. Evans' work suggests that a reasonable factor for conversion of residual burden into initial ingestion is 20. Keeping in mind the crudeness of that factor, we shall use it here.

Evans reports that 14 out of 40 persons (in the group showing 1.0 to 10.0 microcuries residual body burden) developed bone cancer, and that the *median* residual burden was 5.5 microcuries (mean value was not presented).

Spontaneously occurring, such bone cancers are so very rare (approximately 60 per 100,000 persons in the United States would have been expected in the comparable time period) that it can be stated with considerable confidence that all 14 cancers were the result of the radium ingestion.

Therefore, for people who have a residual 5.5 microcuries of ^{226}Radium, the bone-cancer rate is 14 cancers/40 persons = 0.35 cancers per person. To calculate the rate per person if the residual radium was only 1.0 microcurie, we divide: 0.35/5.5 = 0.064 cancers per person per residual microcurie.

If we use the approximation that the initial ingestion is 20 times the residual body burden, we can say that 0.064 bone cancers per person is the rate per initial ingestion of 20 microcuries per person. To obtain the bone-cancer rate per person if the initial ingestion was only 1.0 microcurie, we divide: 0.064/20 = 0.0032 cancers per person per initially ingested microcurie. To describe this figure as *at least* 0.0032 would be safer, because it is based upon studies that are incomplete. However, the radium-dial painters were studied for four or five decades (or more), so the observed cancers probably represent a very large fraction of all the cancers that ever will occur in these exposed painters. Certainly the number observed is the minimum number of cancers they will develop. If we do assume we have counted the total yield of bone cancers, we can estimate the bone-cancer dose by a shortcut method.

We ask, if ingesting 1 microcurie of ^{226}Radium gives an individual a bone-cancer risk of 0.0032, what dose would give a bone-cancer risk of 1.000? The answer is 1.000/0.0032 = 312.5 microcuries. Since the dose that guarantees 1 cancer is the cancer dose, 312.5 person-microcuries is the bone-cancer dose for ^{226}Radium. And as usual, we can say that 312.5 person (or bone)-microcuries guarantees 1 fatal bone cancer no matter how many persons share this radium. If 10 persons each ingest 31.25 microcuries of ^{226}Radium, there will develop 1 fatal bone cancer among them, but we cannot say in which person.

Analysis of Hasterlik's data leads to an almost identical result. Here the bone-cancer dose is 322.6 microcuries, which is very close indeed to the value of 312.5 microcuries determined from the Evans data.

We shall average these two values, and use 317.5 microcuries ingested ^{226}Radium as the bone-cancer dose for women approximately 25 years of age at exposure—the age of the radium-dial painters and others who were the subjects of these studies. We already commented on the difficulty of knowing the true age of effective exposure due to the long persistence of radium in the body.

The Bone-Cancer Dose at Other Ages

There is every reason to believe that the effects of radium as a carcinogen will show the same age-related behavior as demonstrated in chapter 5 for cancers in general, although the evidence for ^{226}Radium simply is inadequate to test for this in any rigorous manner. The author suggests that, until some human data suggest otherwise, we apply the age trends already observed for cancers in general. These trends are reflected in the whole-body cancer doses in tables 10 and 11.

The change with age of the bone-cancer dose for ^{226}Radium from 317.5 bone-microcuries (for 25-year-old women) can best be handled by the relationship:

$$(\text{bone-cancer dose})_{\text{age x}} = (317.5) \times \frac{(\text{whole-body cancer dose})_{\text{age x}}}{(\text{whole-body cancer dose})_{\text{age 25}}}$$

It is clear that this equation produces the correct direction of change with age, lower whole-body cancer dose going with lower bone-cancer dose, and higher whole-body cancer dose going with higher bone-cancer dose.

Practical Problems Involving Exposure to ^{226}Radium

The history of the lack of care employed in dealing with ^{226}Radium in industrial practice in the United States is a sorry one indeed. With an approximate bone-cancer dose now available, we can appreciate that lack of care. We must now turn our attention to some of the facts concerning amounts of ^{226}Radium in existence, where it comes from, what we do with it, and what the consequences have been and are likely to be.

While there once was a radium industry, as such, of consequence, it is probably quite fair to say that in recent decades, the ^{226}Radium problem has arisen as a by-product of the nuclear-weapons and nuclear-power industries. These two industries necessitate the mining and milling of uranium-bearing ores, and this inevitably means bringing to the surface of the earth large quantities of ^{226}Radium which would otherwise never have been brought to the surface in a distributable form.

^{226}Radium is in the mainline chain of radioactive decay in the uranium series, which starts with ^{238}Uranium. The "parent" in this chain is $^{238}_{92}$U, a form of uranium of extremely long half-life, 4.5 billion years. A half-life of this duration means that half the uranium in this form will still be around at the time some people estimate the sun will burn out. $^{238}_{92}$U decays to $^{234}_{90}$Th, a radionuclide of the element thorium (atomic number 90), which has a half-life that is very, very short by comparison, 24.1 days. $^{234}_{90}$Th decays by emission of a beta particle to the element protoactinium (atomic number 91), in the form of the radionuclide $^{234}_{91}$Pa. And so on until, three steps later in the chain, we get ^{226}Radium.

In nature, where uranium has been undisturbed for millions of years and more, this chain of radioactive decay has attained what is known as *secular equilibrium* with respect to all the products down to ^{222}Rn (radon) and beyond. For now, we shall just consider the chain down to ^{226}Radium. Later we shall consider the radon problem separately.

This state of secular equilibrium essentially describes a state of equilibrium between the rate of production and the rate of decay of a given radionuclide. Its effect, which is the central point here, is that the number of curies of every single member of the decay chain, in undisturbed uranium ore, is exactly the same as the number of curies of $^{238}_{92}U$ itself. Our objective in this discussion is to ascertain the amount of $^{226}_{88}Ra$. Now we know that the amount of $^{226}_{88}Ra$ *in curies* must be exactly the same as the amount of $^{238}_{92}U$ *in curies*. From first principles, it can be shown that a kilogram of uranium (which is 99.3% $^{238}_{92}U$) represents 3.3×10^{-4} curies (considered in terms of alpha-particle disintegrations). Therefore, we can say that, in perfectly undisturbed ore, there must be 3.3×10^{-4} curies of $^{226}_{88}Ra$ present in that ore for every kilogram of uranium present. The same is true for the number of curies of every other member of the uranium decay chain.

Now, when we bring this ore to the surface of the earth and treat it to remove the uranium (a process 85–90% successful), what remains includes all those members of the decay chain that are also present in the ore. So, if the residue from the milling of 1 kilogram of uranium is dumped into so-called tailings ponds, there is no escaping the fact that present in those tailings ponds are 3.3×10^{-4} curies of $^{230}_{90}Th$, with its half-life of 80,000 years, and 3.3×10^{-4} curies of $^{226}_{88}Ra$, with its half-life of 1,602 years.

Gofman (1977b) estimates that a one-year supply of fuel for a 1,000-megawatt light-water reactor (such as those in the United States), if it operates at approximately 70% capacity, requires the extraction of roughly 160 tons of uranium from ore (exact value depends on assumptions made). Let us now estimate how much $^{230}_{90}Th$ and $^{226}_{88}Ra$ must be left over in tailings ponds from the fueling of one reactor for one year. By 70% capacity, we mean that a reactor rated at 1,000-megawatts capacity puts out 700 megawatts of electrical power, on the average. We estimate:

$$(160 \text{ tons}) \times \frac{(1{,}000 \text{ kilograms})}{\text{ton}} \times \frac{(3.3 \times 10^{-4} \text{ curies})}{\text{kilogram}} = 52.8 \text{ curies}$$

per fueling. This means that 52.8 curies of $^{230}_{90}Th$ and 52.8 curies of $^{226}_{88}Ra$ are left over in tailings ponds. For the equivalent of 50 plants, each of 1,000 megawatts, each operating at 70% of capacity (a good estimate of 1980 U.S. installed nuclear capacity), $(50) \times (52.8) = 2{,}640$ curies of each nuclide are dumped into tailings ponds every year, even if no fuel is prepared for additional reactors.

The federal Energy Research and Development Administration reported in 1974 that some 13,950 curies of radium were already in tailings ponds and piles from mining. This, of course, includes military and civilian uses of uranium. It is obvious, with about 2,640 curies of each nuclide being dumped *per year,* we are now creating this particular variety of nuclear refuse at a greatly accelerated rate.

The reader will appropriately ask, since the $^{230}_{90}Th$ and $^{226}_{88}Ra$ already existed in nature, how can they possibly do harm simply because they have been moved into tailings ponds and piles? That excellent question has its answer built in. The key word is *moved.* So long as those nuclides were decaying deep in the bowels of the earth, without access to surface waters, they were doing no harm. But now that they have been moved to the surface of the earth and converted into a form much more accessible to water, now that they do get into water supplies, they *can* and *do* harm our health significantly. Let us examine some of the facts.

Levels of $^{226}_{88}$Ra in Surface Waters

Wagoner (1979) cites data for the period before the advent of widescale uranium mining, indicating that the natural or background concentration of $^{226}_{88}$Ra in surface waters of the western United States generally was lower than 0.1 PCi per liter. According to Wagoner, the few times that levels as high as 0.8 to 1.0 PCi per liter were found, they were associated with small-scale, local uranium-mining activities. In contrast, according to Wagoner, during the heyday of serious uranium mining and milling activities in the United States (pre-1960), $^{226}_{88}$Ra concentrations as high as 88 PCi per liter were detected at locations downstream from uranium mills. This provides a good idea of the care that was taken in handling the by-products of the mining and milling.

In addition, measurements of the $^{226}_{88}$Ra content of sediments from streams of the western United States (not affected by the milling of uranium) showed an average of 1.3 PCi $^{226}_{88}$Ra per gram of dry sediment. Wagoner points out that with the advent of large-scale mining and milling of uranium, concentrations of $^{226}_{88}$Ra as high as 2,100 PCi per gram were reported in one river. In another river, the Animas River, concentrations of $^{226}_{88}$Ra were 800 PCi per gram of mud immediately below the mill site and 100 PCi per gram some *40 miles downstream*. At Churchrock, New Mexico, in 1979, a dam gave way and dumped thousands of tons of tailings into the Rio Puerco River, and thus enormously enhanced the prospects for human ingestion of radium and other nuclides.

The Personal and Public-Health Consequences of $^{226}_{88}$Ra Ingestion

UNSCEAR (1977, pp. 59–60, and Table 17) presents considerable evidence from around the world that the average intake of $^{226}_{88}$Ra comes to about *one* PCi per day per person. There are some rare locales with high background radiation where the intake is greater, but it is reasonable to use 1 PCi as a rough average intake around the world. We shall estimate the bone-cancer consequences of this level of exposure, and then consider the unfortunate individuals whose water supply may be so contaminated that they receive doses on the order of 10 to 100 PCi *in each liter* of water they drink.

For an equilibrium population of 250,000,000 people, if everyone ingested 1 PCi per day, 288 bone cancers would be produced each year. This estimate converts to 0.12 bone cancer fatalities per 100,000 persons per year, a rate which is not very far below the values found in the vital-statistics tables for bone cancers in the United States. This may suggest that radium represents an appreciable cause of current bone-cancer deaths.

For 1 PCi ingested per day over a year, the added risk to each individual of bone-cancer death is 1.15×10^{-6}. It is readily seen that if surface waters were contaminated to levels of 10 to 100 picocuries of $^{226}_{88}$Ra per liter, the radium intake of persons using such waters could reach 3,650 to 36,500 picocuries per year and more. The personal risks of bone-cancer fatalities would go up to 1.15×10^{-5} for the 10-PCi-per-day exposure, and to 1.15×10^{-4} for the 100-PCi-per-day exposure. These are not enormous added risks, but one wonders whether anyone should have to take such additional risks because of sloppy handling of residue from the mining and milling of uranium.

To this point we have discussed the consequences of exposure only to $^{226}_{88}$Radium. We have seen how the bone-cancer dose for $^{226}_{88}$Ra can provide us with *quantitative* estimates of the consequences of dumping radium. When a "spill" such as the Churchrock accident occurs, such quantitative estimates should be publicized, as a rational basis for discussion, instead of such standard public-relations statements as that a spill has occurred but it will cause no harm to the public health. The harm *will* accrue in *direct proportion* to the increased intake of $^{226}_{88}$Radium by the people who are in the vicinity and who use water taken from the affected river for quite a distance downstream. The harm should neither be minimized nor exaggerated; rather, it should be honestly explained.

BONE CANCER FROM $^{224}_{88}$RADIUM, ANOTHER RADIUM NUCLIDE

Medicine, as already indicated in chapter 5, has been one of the major sources of cancer cases induced by radiation or by radionuclides. Spiess and Mays (1970) reported on one disastrous experience resulting from the treatment of some 2,000 German patients with injections of $^{224}_{88}$Ra, another alpha-emitter, during the years 1944–1951. These patients suffered from ankylosing spondylitis, tuberculosis of the bone and soft tissues, and some other diseases. The duration of the injections varied from a few weeks to a few years. We quote Spiess and Mays on the cessation of this treatment in children: "The injection of ^{224}Ra into children was stopped in 1951 when it became obvious that ^{224}Ra was completely ineffective in the treatment of tuberculosis" (pp. 713–14).

The special importance of the studies of Spiess and Mays is that they provide evidence on human cancer induction from a radium nuclide which has a very short half-life, 3.64 days, in contrast to the half-life of ^{226}Radium, which is 1,602 years. The dose is therefore delivered in a time that is short compared with standard follow-up periods for the development of cancer, making the case material more suitable for epidemiological examination than is the case for ^{226}Radium ingestion.

However, a reliable RBE value for alpha-particle irradiation is not available, so the author has not incorporated these ^{224}Radium studies into the composite sample in chapter 5. There are other difficulties too. The conversion of the ingested quantity of ^{224}Ra into dose in rads, averaged over the vulnerable bone-lining cells, is no small task. Spiess and Mays attempted it, but it is hard to say just how good their estimates really are. Another difficulty is that firm data for the unirradiated population in Germany are not available; we have only the statement, "The natural incidence rate for this kind of cancer is extremely low (in the order of 1 bone sarcoma per 100,000 persons per year)" (p. 719).

But the effect of ^{224}Ra in inducing bone cancer in these cases is clear and deserves examination. In an addendum to their paper, Spiess and Mays present an updated set of results, tabulated below.

A crude analysis is possible with these data, even though good values for the true expected cancer rates are unavailable, and even though the age at irradiation is not available for the adults. We can approximate the age of the adults at irradiation by using the average age at irradiation of those who *did* later develop bone sarcoma: 32.9 years.

Approximate Data for the "Therapy" with $^{224}_{88}$Ra

Group Treated	Observed Cancers per 100 Rads of Bone Dose	Corresponding Observed Cancer Rate per 100,000 Persons per 100 Rads of Bone Dose
212 juveniles (11.1 years of age at treatment)	1.51% of subjects	1,510
642 adults (32.9 years of age at treatment)	0.90% of subjects	900

For the juveniles, the analysis yields a % excess per rad of 70.9% for the limited follow-up period of 0 through 21 years.

For the adults, the result is a % excess per rad of 49% for the limited follow-up period of 0 through 18 years.

Appropriate Handling of the Bone-Sarcoma Data

Ordinarily, for a solid cancer, we would have converted the values just determined into peak percents per rad, using the conversion factors of table 2. However, in a recent publication, Mays, Spiess, and Gerspach (1978) report that there was a definite tapering off in the occurrence rate of new bone sarcomas after 1969 in this series, and that it is possible that by 30 years post-exposure the bulk, if not all, of the radiation-induced cases will have occurred. If subsequent follow-up confirms this, it would appear that bone-sarcoma induction by radiation behaves more like leukemia induction by radiation than it does like the majority of solid cancers studied (see chapter 14 on leukemia induction). Bone sarcoma and leukemia are both of "connective-tissue" origin.

If this is indeed the pattern of bone-sarcoma evolution induced by radiation, then there is no basis for predicting any appreciable increase in % excess per rad over the recorded values for the limited follow-up period, since the bulk of the cases has already been seen. The values 70.9% per rad for the juveniles and 49% per rad for the adults, after correcting by an RBE factor of 10, become 7.09% and 4.9%. These values are not out of line with other observations on cancer induction by radiation.

It is to be hoped that follow-up and study of this exposed population will continue. Refinements in dose assessment are needed, along with careful checking that the effect truly does seem to be over within 30 years after irradiation. My recent research shows that the reason for the earlier occurrence of bone sarcomas is because the radiation was alpha-irradiation, *not* because of the connective-tissue origin of bone sarcoma. This is a major observation, and I believe it holds for all solid cancers induced by alpha-particle radiation.

The Bone-Cancer Dose for $^{224}_{88}$Ra

If we accept that the bone-sarcoma induction from exposure to $^{224}_{88}$Ra is largely over by 25–30 years post-exposure, we can make a preliminary estimate of the bone-cancer dose for this nuclide. Let us assume that the ultimate number of bone sarcomas will increase over those listed above by only 10%. Using the standard procedure for calculating specific-organ doses, we arrive at a dose of 6,020 bone-rads per sarcoma for the juveniles, and 10,100 bone-rads for the adults. These doses to bone that produce a sarcoma are comparable to the doses to bone marrow (chapter 14) that produce a leukemia.

Fractionation of the Dose Increases the Bone-Sarcoma Risk

One of the routine, though never documented, claims of those who downplay radiation risks is that fractionation of the dose may protect against cancer induction. This claim was dealt with in detail in chapter 8, where we showed that it has no substance. The findings of Mays and Spiess are even more embarrassing to the promoters of this idea. Mays, Spiess, and Gerspach (1978) found that the induction of bone sarcoma was *increased* if a particular dose of ^{224}Ra was administered over a period of time rather than all at once.

The Embryological Origin of Bone Sarcoma

We noted above that bone sarcoma and leukemia are both of connective-tissue origin, meaning that embryologically they originate from the *mesodermal layer*, the layer that gives rise to connective tissues. It will be of great interest to see whether tumors of connective-tissue origin have generally different time-frames of occurrence following irradiation than do epithelial cancers, which constitute the bulk of solid cancers.

Radon Carcinogenesis: Lung Cancer in the Uranium Miners

It has been known for centuries that miners who work in uranium mines in Europe show a great excess of death from lung disease compared to other workers. Prior to atomic fission, uranium was used for such purposes as pigment and glaze manufacture.

Wagoner (1979) cites a source from as early as 1546 which indicates that miners of uranium-bearing ores in the Erz Mountains of Central Europe showed an unusually high frequency of fatal lung disease. In 1879 Harting and Hesse demonstrated both clinically and anatomically that the real nature of the pulmonary disorder among uranium miners of Schneeberg, Germany, was malignancy of the lung. Subsequent reports indicated that both for this area and for Joachimsthal, Czechoslovakia, approximately 50% of uranium miners died of lung cancer, which is a considerably higher rate than would have been expected in the population at large.

Uranium is quite widespread in the earth. And when other metals are mined with uranium present, the miners risk exposure to radon and radon-daughter products, and subsequently, the development of lung cancer in the miners is possible. Excess lung cancer has occurred in iron, lead, and zinc miners in Sweden, in fluorspar miners in Newfoundland, and in uranium miners in several locations (BEIR-I 1972, p. 146).

In the 1930s, the separate publications of Pirchan and Sikl (1932) and of Peller (1939) pointed strongly to the possibility that airborne radioactive substances in uranium mines were the reason for the excess lung-cancer mortality in uranium miners. This airborne radioactivity turned out to be radon and its daughter products in the uranium decay chain. In spite of the fact that this causal association was recognized before World War II, uranium mines in the United States were worked during and after that period with poor ventilation, and hence with high concentrations of radon and its daughter products. Indeed, so poor was the ventilation that a tragic epidemic of lung cancer occurred among the miners. Nevertheless, until recently working conditions remained the same despite the persistent and elegant work of Archer, Wagoner, Lundin, and their colleagues in the Public Health Service in documenting the consequences.

Radon and Its Daughter Products

In our considerations of radium, we carried the $^{238}_{92}$U decay chain down as far as $^{226}_{88}$Ra. The next product in the chain after ^{226}Radium is the nuclide $^{222}_{86}$Rn, or radon, which in turn is parent to seven daughter products. The last of these, $^{206}_{82}$Pb (a stable nuclide of lead), terminates the decay chain.

One very important feature of radon, in this case of the nuclide $^{222}_{86}$Rn, is its gaseous nature. It is a natural member of the group of elements known as *noble gases,* so named because of their extreme unreactivity with other chemical elements. As soon as a radium atom decays by alpha-particle emission, it becomes a radon atom, and that atom "behaves" like the noble gas it is.

While all the decay products of uranium up to that point "want" chemically to behave like solids at room temperature, radon "wants" to behave like a gas, and does. Therefore, radon gets inhaled, while radium does not.

The short-lived intermediate products between $^{222}_{86}$Rn and $^{210}_{82}$Pb are nuclides of the elements polonium, bismuth, and lead (Pb). As generated in the radioactive decay of radon gas, they do not "want" to remain gaseous, but to become solid or to attach themselves to dust particles, droplets, or other surfaces in the vicinity. What they end up doing in particular circumstances depends on factors like humidity.

Unfortunately, this tendency of the bismuth, lead, and polonium daughter products of radon to attach themselves to various surfaces also manifests itself in the pulmonary airways. When air containing radon, in secular equilibrium with its daughter products, is breathed in, some of the daughter atoms are free in air, some are attached to droplets in the air, and some are attached to dust particles in the air. Where in the pulmonary tree (the bronchi or elsewhere) these daughter products will lodge is uncertain and condition-dependent. Particular characteristics of an individual's bronchial epithelium may well influence the extent of deposition of daughter products.

In any case, when radon and its daughter products are breathed in, much of the daughter-product "load" of the air is retained in the lung and finally decays in the lung, while the radon itself is there only for the few seconds required for an average gas exchange in breathing (UNSCEAR 1977, p. 68). Then a new breath is taken, again containing radon in partial or complete equilibrium with its daughter products, and again the daughter products are largely retained to decay in the pulmonary airways, and the radon is breathed out, except for a small quantity that goes via the blood to fatty tissues.

So, to the extent that the daughter products are retained in the airways while the radon is breathed out, *the radiation dose is delivered primarily from the daughter products of radon rather than from the radon itself.* The important alpha-particle-emitting daughter products are the short-lived $^{218}_{84}$Po and $^{214}_{84}$Po. And of primary importance is the extent to which the daughter-product alpha particles get to the sensitive cells of the intermediary bronchi, the vulnerable sites for lung-cancer induction. The works of Bale and of Shapiro show the significance of the radon daughter products.

The Working Level: A Unit to Cope with Radon Daughter Products

Because the dose from exposure to radon depends on the behavior of its daughter products, which in turn varies with humidity and with dust-particle type and concentration, a measuring unit was introduced based, not on the radon concentration itself, but on the concentration of the daughter products that were expected to be harmful on inhalation. That unit has come to be known as the *working level* (abbreviated WL). One working level (1 WL) is defined as the amount of any combination of short-lived radon daughter products which, during their decay all the way to $^{210}_{82}Pb$, result in a total emission of 1.3×10^5 mev of alpha-particle energy.

The reader may wonder why we are focusing on the alpha particles when beta particles and gamma rays are also emitted. To be sure, the beta particles and gamma rays are also injurious, exactly to the extent we discussed in chapter 5. But here we are concerning ourselves with lung cancer developing from particulates or gases in the bronchial airways. The cells likely to develop cancer represent a *very* thin layer near the air-tissue interface. The alpha particles expend virtually all their energy in the sensitive region. The beta-particle energies are expended over a much larger range of tissues, in structures that are not sensitive to the development of lung cancer. And the gamma rays expend their energy over a still larger range of tissues, most of which have nothing to do with lung-cancer development. Therefore, with respect to lung cancer as a consequence of inhalation of radon and its daughter products, the energy delivered to the sensitive cells is very largely energy from alpha-particle decay.

While we would prefer to discuss the health impacts of exposure to radon and its daughter products in terms of rads, there is considerable uncertainty about the translation from working levels to rads delivered, for example, to the bronchial lining cells (epithelium). There is more than a 200-fold difference in suggested conversion factors (BEIR-I 1972, p. 148). The author feels it would be a mistake to accept any of the conversion factors, and therefore will treat lung-cancer induction by radon and its daughter products in terms of working-level units. Many other scientific investigators hold this view, which is evident from the use of WL units rather than rads in their publications.

The literature describing the effects of exposure to radon always provides dose in terms of working levels. If a person in an industrial setting (a mine, for example) works in air that shows 1 WL of radon daughter products, and if he remains there for 170 hours, he is said to have received a total exposure of 1 *working-level-month* (1 WLM). This, of course, reflects the practice of considering 170 hours a work-month.

We shall handle the problem of continuous exposure of a population somewhat differently, later in this discussion.

Lung-Cancer Induction and Working-Level-Month Exposures

Archer, Lundin, Wagoner, and others have published a number of classic papers on their investigations of lung-cancer development in U.S. miners on the Colorado Plateau. The most up-to-date summary of their findings in this ongoing follow-up study is presented by Archer and co-workers (1976). We shall consider the quantitative aspects of those studies. Separately, Sevc and co-workers (1976) published similar findings of lung-cancer development in uranium miners in Czechoslovakia.

While the two studies are alike in presenting overwhelming evidence for the production of lung cancer by exposure to radon daughter products, the peak percents increase in lung cancer per WLM are quite different in the two studies. This may well be due to dosimetry differences, but we cannot now be sure of this. We shall average the results of the two studies since we do not have good reason to choose one or the other.

The Experience of the U.S. Miners: Combining all miners of uranium (both smokers and nonsmokers of cigarettes), and combining all categories of WLM exposure, Archer and co-workers report 142 observed cases of lung cancer occurring in the follow-up period from 5 years through approximately 29 years after initiation of mining. The expected number of lung-cancer cases for the number of person-years of exposure risk is 27.9. (In numerous prior papers, Archer and co-workers demonstrated that such factors as cigarette smoking had been taken into account in calculating the expected value.)

The peak percent increase in lung-cancer rate, based on an estimated mean WLM for the entire group, is *1.14% per WLM*. Note that the data can be handled just as if we were dealing with rads; and we are using the WLM unit simply because we are not sure how to convert it to rads.

The Czechoslovakian Uranium Miners: The data of Sevc, Kunz, and Placek can be used for a calculation that will permit comparison with the findings of Archer and co-workers.

From the data for the age distribution of these miners, we very roughly estimate a mean age of about 33 at the start of uranium mining. Again, assigning a value for the estimated mean age at exposure is difficult because we do not have WLM per year for each age group. We will approximate the mean age at exposure as 34 years for this group as we did for the Archer group.

We obtain 5.88% per WLM as the peak percent value for the Czechoslovakian miners, compared to 1.14% for the U.S. miners. Averaging these two values, we arrive at a final estimate of 3.51% as the peak percent increase in lung cancer per WLM for males approximately 34 years of age at exposure.

Each of the studies involved over 3,000 miners, followed for over 20 years, so there is little difference between them in sample size or length of follow-up. Sevc and co-workers suggest that dosimetry may be better in the Czechoslovakian study than in the American study, but no objective evidence is presented to support that claim. The author considers WLM dosimetry crude at best. Further, there is overlap (discussed in this chapter) between exposure and follow-up. Neither study provides the years the miners worked. All these considerations mean that no one should be surprised to find that the peak percent values for these two studies differ from each other by a factor of 5. The values do provide us, however, with a reasonable base for estimating the effects on the population of radon dispersal in the environment.

Smokers Versus Nonsmokers Among the Uranium Miners

There have been many efforts to becloud the issue, of lung-cancer causation in uranium miners by radon daughter products, with the question, how do you know the whole effect is not due to cigarette smoking? This issue was resolved quite adequately in 1965 by Wagoner and co-workers. Even with the most generous allowance for any effects due to cigarette smoking, it is clear that exposure to radon daughter products did cause lung cancer. Sevc and co-workers point out that the percentage of cigarette smokers among the Czechoslovakian miners (about 70%) was the same as in the general male population of Czechoslovakia. This statement is based on several repeated investigations made by Sevc and co-workers of random groups of 700 uranium miners each. Moreover, Sevc points out that *within* the group of smoking miners, cigarette consumption did not go up with radiation dose.

The author considers that any confounding effect proposed for cigarette smoking has been adequately disposed of by both the American and the Czechoslovakian studies.

While there is no reason at all to *blame* cigarettes for the lung cancers produced by radon and its daughter products, cigarette smoking does play an important role in the development of these cancers. Archer and co-workers (1976) provide lung-cancer rates for nonsmokers and for various classes of smokers among the uranium miners. It is very clear from the data presented that cigarette smoking grossly accentuates the number of lung cancers occurring due to exposure to radon daughter products. Saccomanno (1978), who collaborated in many of these studies, made the following analysis, based on 280 Colorado miners who died of lung cancer:

Lung-Cancer Death Rates per 100,000 per Year

Nonsmokers, non-uranium-miners	12.5
Nonsmokers, uranium miners	20.0
Heavy smokers, non-uranium miners (2 packages cigarettes/day)	265.0
Heavy smokers, uranium miners	700.0

One notes that among the nonsmokers, uranium mining increased the lung-cancer death rate by 7.5 per 100,000 per year (20 minus 12.5). Many governmental bodies and committees have continued to use such absolute rates in calculating radiation-induced cancer effects (see chapter 5). It is no accident that the use of absolute rates continues; this method gives the lowest possible risk estimates, since the follow-up time is almost always too short to reveal more than a fraction of the total number of excess cancers which will appear. Moreover, when there is a synergistic relationship between radiation and some other agent (e.g., cigarettes), the absolute risk method *can* be applied in a way that will be misleading regardless of follow-up considerations. This can be clearly shown in an analysis comparing the absolute risk and relative risk methods.

Lung Cancer Among the Native American Uranium Miners

In the early phases of the U.S. Public Health Service studies of the uranium miners of the Colorado Plateau, the numbers of lung cancers were smaller than they are now, and a test for association between uranium mining and lung cancer in the Native American miners produced results below the level required for statistical significance. This was an example of the small-numbers problems, *not* proof of no effect. Because statistical significance was lacking, the Native American miners were usually denied workmen's compensation when they developed malignant lung disease (Wagoner 1979).

However, now it is quite clear that there is a highly significant excess of lung-cancer deaths among the Native American uranium miners, just as among the white uranium miners. The actual data for the Native Americans are as follows:

Entire Follow-up Period, 1950–1974

Observed lung-cancer deaths   11
Expected (based on matching)   2.6
Difference significant at $p < 0.01$ (Archer et al., 1976)

Archer and co-workers point out that the reason it took so long to obtain definitive evidence for the Native Americans lies in their low consumption of cigarettes. The following was the distribution of their smoking histories at the time of examination:

Smoking History	*Number of Cigarettes Smoked*
(Native American miners of uranium)	(1950–1974)
256 current smokers	5.8 cigarettes per day
32 former smokers	5.1 cigarettes per day (when they smoked)
487 nonsmokers	0 cigarettes per day

OTHER RESPIRATORY DISEASES AND RADON EXPOSURE

The work of Archer and co-workers (1976) represents one of the studies in which it has been possible to prove a noncancer chronic, somatic effect of ionizing radiation. Among the white uranium miners, there were 80 deaths due to nonmalignant respiratory disease (in ICD categories 470–527); the expected number was 24.9. At first glance, one might be suspicious about these extra deaths being attributed to exposure to radon daughter products, since there is a deficit in reported heart-disease deaths among the uranium miners. Congestive heart failure can be hard to differentiate from obstructive lung disease, and indeed the two commonly coexist, so one might wonder about a bias in death certification toward obstructive lung disease.

However, Archer and his colleagues show a consistent increase in obstructive lung-disease deaths with increasing WLM exposure to radon daughter products. It would require quite a stretch of the imagination to believe that death-certificate bias could be proportional to dose in WLM, when the dose in WLM was not even known to the signers of the death certificates.

The question is still open whether some chemical exposure in the miners, which increased with WLM exposure, could account for the excess of "other respiratory disease deaths." If there is nonmalignant injury to the lungs from alpha-particle irradiation at occupational levels, this would be important to know. Archer expresses no definite opinion concerning the possible mechanism by which exposure to radon daughter products might cause the excess nonmalignant injury. He does suggest that this injury might be due to pulmonary insufficiency resulting from diffuse radiation injury to the lung parenchyma (body of lung), leading to later fibrosis and emphysema.

Radon and Radon-Daughter-Product Exposure in the General Population

Several important questions have arisen in the past few years concerning the effects of exposure to radon and radon daughter products on the public at large.

For instance, there is the well-documented fact that radon regularly escapes from the earth into the atmosphere, a process wholly unassociated with uranium mining. We shall examine the lung-cancer risks associated with such exposure.

Second, there is no doubt whatsoever that certain building materials contain *radium,* and hence such materials exude radon and its daughter products. Since there is a concerted effort to conserve energy and to block air leaks in some climates, we shall examine whether such practices can increase risk, and by how much.

Third, there is the important and hotly debated issue of the mountains of tailings left over from the mining and milling of uranium for both the military and the civilian nuclear programs. Pohl (1976) and Kepford (1979) have written about the long-term lung-cancer problem posed by this aspect of the nuclear fuel cycle. Since this issue raises profound ethical as well as medical questions, we shall consider it last.

Two other sources of exposure, which we shall only mention, are the combustion of natural gas, which is variably contaminated with radon, and the use of certain fertilizers originating from phosphate deposits fairly rich in uranium.

Converting Lung-Cancer Doses to the Person-WLM Units

The first step in assessing the impact on the general public of various sources of radon exposure is to convert our values for peak percent increase in lung-cancer deaths per WLM into lung-cancer doses in person-WLM units, just as we did previously for person-rad units. The key factors that enter into this conversion are (1) adjusting the lung-cancer dose to an average age; (2) estimating the person-WLMs per lung cancer for smokers and nonsmokers (including children); and (3) evaluating exposure for a 24-hour day rather than for a working day.

Based on these adjustments, this author agrees with other observers that it is reasonable to use a rounded figure of 25 WLM per year of continuous population exposure to 1 WL of radon daughter products.

Natural Ambient Exposures to Radon and Its Daughter Products

Wholly aside from any of our activities, we are exposed to radon and its daughter products as a result of the emanation of radon from the earth.

The chemical element of atomic number 86 has numerous radionuclides. The best-known one is called radon ($^{222}_{86}Rn$), formed in the main-line of radioactive decays from natural uranium ($^{238}_{92}U$). The chemical element, thorium, occurs in nature, its most prominent nuclide being $^{232}_{90}Th$. In the mainline of radioactive decays that start with $^{232}_{90}Th$, there is formed a radionuclide of element 86, and this nuclide, $^{220}_{86}Rn$, is known as *thoron*. The thoron, being gaseous also, emanates from the thorium of the earth. It is estimated that thoron and its daughter products probably contribute a radiation dose equal to that contributed by radon and its daughter products. It has become customary to refer to $^{222}_{86}Rn$ as "radon," but we must remember that thoron ($^{220}_{86}Rn$) is chemically also a form of radon.

Because of the contribution to dose from thoron and its daughter products, we should estimate that the *total* dose received is approximately double that received from "radon" ($^{226}_{86}Rn$) and its daughter products.

Of course, no one knows the concentration and the kind of dust and vapor particles in the air, on the average, everywhere on earth, so no one can know what fraction of radon daughter products stay airborne by attaching themselves to such surfaces. For simplicity, we shall assume that the radon daughter products are in full equilibrium with the radon in breathed air. This would mean that air containing radon at 100 PCi/liter exposes our lungs to 1 WL of radon daughter products.

Based on estimates by Wilkening and co-workers (1972), UNSCEAR (1977, p. 71) calculates the total [222]Radon emanation from all the land areas of the globe to be about 50 curies per second. The oceans contribute much less, approximately 1 to 10% of this emanation.

Over continental land, at ground level, the radon concentrations are estimated (UNSCEAR, p. 73) to be approximately 0.1 PCi per liter of air, which we shall use in this book as the average exposure on land.

Let us now assume the population to be 250 million and estimate the annual population exposure to radon and radon daughter products. The necessary calculations yield the following values for person-WLMs:

Male smokers: 5.95×10^5 person-WLMs
Male nonsmokers: 2.38×10^6 person-WLMs
Female smokers: 6.55×10^5 person-WLMs
Female nonsmokers: 2.62×10^6 person-WLMs

The deaths from radon inhalation can now be calculated with the aid of the various lung-cancer doses:

$$
\begin{aligned}
\text{Male smoker deaths} &= 2,100 \text{ deaths} \\
\text{Male nonsmoker deaths} &= 840 \text{ deaths} \\
\text{Female smoker deaths} &= 763 \text{ deaths} \\
\underline{\text{Female nonsmoker deaths}} &= \underline{305 \text{ deaths}} \\
\textit{Total deaths per year} &= 4,008 \text{ deaths}
\end{aligned}
$$

Let us round this off as 4,000 deaths *per year* in a population of 250 million persons from inhaling radon daughter products at the ambient level. If we use UNSCEAR's estimate (p. 72) that in the first few meters above ground level, thoron activity equals radon activity, these deaths should be doubled, becoming 8,000 per year. Failing full equilibrium of the daughter products, the number of deaths will be less than estimated here; these values can be taken as upper limits.

A Note on Certain "Health Spas": The UNSCEAR report (1977, p. 79) points out that, in certain special areas, radon concentration in water can be very high. Cited are some highly radioactive spas at Badgastein (Austria), whose so-called thermal galleries have been used for many years as part of *radon-inhalation treatment.* UNSCEAR estimates that the release of radon into the air from such waters leads to concentrations of approximately 1 PCi per liter in open air, approximately 10 PCi per liter in room air, and 3,000 PCi per liter in the air of one of the thermal galleries. This last is some 30,000 times the ambient air concentration around the world. It is the firm opinion of the author of this book that the only effect a patient could expect from such "therapy" would be a greatly increased risk of lung-cancer death.

Building Materials, Ventilation, and Exposure to Radon and Radon Daughter Products

The primary determinant of radon exposure *indoors* is the composition of the building materials used in construction. Wood is generally lowest in radium content and hence in radon emanation. But if concrete or other material containing radium is used in construction, then the ventilation rate becomes the most crucial variable determining the radon content of the air indoors. UNSCEAR (p. 75) calculates some reasonable conditions that could lead to a radon concentration of 0.15 PCi per liter of air, a 50% increase over ambient levels outdoors. The conditions included the concentration of radon per gram of concrete and its rate of emanation, and the volume of the room. They assumed a ventilation rate of one air change per hour.

Clearly, the higher the rate of ventilation, the lower will be the ^{222}Rn content of the air. In the limiting case of *no ventilation at all,* the only way the radon is removed is by its own radioactive decay. In such a case, the radon concentration would be closer to 20 PCi per liter of air. Such an exposure is serious indeed, and definitely to be avoided.

Let us estimate the risk for male smokers, the group which would be at highest risk, for both the 0.15 and the 20 PCi per liter levels of exposure to radon and its daughter products. For one man, the risk of fatal lung cancer, incurred in 1 year from ambient ^{222}Rn levels, is 8.8 chances per 100,000. At the 0.15 level of exposure, the risk goes up to 13.1 chances per 100,000. Lastly, for one man, in an unventilated situation—a concrete building, for example—the risk of fatal lung cancer incurred in 1 year from exposure at the 20 PCi level is 1.77 chances per 100. And each additional year of exposure would *add* to the risk. This is quite a high risk.

All these considerations, of course, relate to exposure to the same level 24 hours per day, which is seldom the case for indoor exposures. Nonetheless, the calculations point out that the choice of building materials has health consequences. Wood is the best material for avoiding supplemental radon exposure, a statement that says nothing about the potential disadvantages of wood—flammability, etc. More important, the calculations point out that decreasing ventilation in an effort to conserve fuel deserves careful evaluation, since a sizable increase in radon exposure can occur. Circulation of the air through some type of filter system may help reduce exposure to radon daughter products. There is little doubt that the nature of construction materials and ventilating systems will receive increasing attention in the future as a public-health issue.

The Grand Junction Fiasco: In the early 1970s, the United States public learned about the scandalous mismanagement of the tailings from uranium mining and milling. Tailings are a sandlike residue remaining after removal of approximately 85% of uranium from ore. Tailings were actually used (especially in the 1950s) as a construction material to build homes and a variety of other buildings in towns such as Grand Junction, Colorado. Tailings were used as "fill" for building foundations, and sometimes as an ingredient in concrete and mortar. Wagoner (1979) cites Axelson and Edling (1979) as having recently demonstrated a significant association between lung-cancer risk and living in homes having elevated levels of radon and its daughter products. While the author has not yet examined that evidence, it would indeed be surprising if a serious excess of lung cancer did *not* accompany living in residences built with materials containing high levels of [226] Radium.

UNSCEAR (Table 27, p. 75) suggests that uranium-mill tailings used as a building material would emanate at a rate 40 times the rate of concrete. Let us consider the effect such a dose would have on a male smoker, for whom the lung-cancer dose is 283.2 person-WLMs. If he spent all his time in such contaminated buildings, his risk of *radiation*-induced lung cancer would be 5.3 chances per 1,000—after only *one* year of exposure. Clearly, the risk associated with living for a long time in dwellings made of uranium-mill tailings is not trivial. The risk to specific classes of individuals would require adjustments for sex and changing age during irradiation. Children will suffer the greatest consequences from radon exposure, all other factors being held constant.

THE LONG-TERM RADON-EXPOSURE PROBLEM ASSOCIATED WITH NUCLEAR POWER

To date, most of the tailings from uranium mining and milling have been left uncovered ("unstabilized"); leaving them exposed, eroding and steadily exuding radon, is cheaper than any remedy. Because the volume of the tailings increases during the ore processing, it is not possible simply to return all the tailings to the mines. Pohl (1976) and Kepford (1979) have expressed considerable concern about the lung-cancer implications of this part of the nuclear-power fuel cycle. Recently, the U.S. Nuclear Regulatory Commission proposed measures for decreasing the radon emissions from U.S. tailings (see *Federal Register*, 44FR 50012).

The Magnitude of the Hazard: Lung-Cancer Estimates

Pohl has presented some rough estimates. Using these, the author has calculated the radon levels that would result from tailings piles in a fully developed "nuclear economy." Further calculations show that such levels should lead to 3.9 lung-cancer deaths per year in an equilibrium population of 250 million.

This number, 3.9 lung-cancer deaths per year, seems small compared to natural radon-induced lung-cancer deaths, indeed just about 1/1,000 of the natural rate. But we must ask another question. How long will the radon piles continue to emanate radon? *If* we assume that *all* the uranium is removed in the milling of the uranium, then the radon emissions are maintained by the longest-lived member of the decay chain of uranium. That member is $^{230}_{90}$Th, with a half-life of 80,000 years. This thorium nuclide continues to replenish the radium, and the radium continues to produce the radon. The *average* life of a radionuclide is equal to its half-life/0.693. Therefore, the average life of the [230]Thorium is 80,000/0.693 = 115,440 years. The pile can be treated as though it were at its initial strength for a period of 115,440 years, and of zero strength thereafter. (This is a mathematical equivalent of the real situation, in which the surface emanations decline gradually and continue far, far longer than 115,440 years.) Therefore, if the radon source produces 3.9 lung-cancer deaths per year, then the total cancers produced during the 115,440 years are (115,440) $\times$ (3.9) = 450,000 fatal lung cancers, rounded off. Radon-induced cancer deaths result from the very beginning of the fuel cycle, before the reactors have operated at all.

It is rare to hear from the nuclear-power industry that the operation of a full nuclear-power program would guarantee 450,000 future lung-cancer deaths, accumulated over a very long period, for *each year of operation* even if everything else in the entire fuel cycle went perfectly. On the other hand, this toll would be significantly reduced to the extent that plutonium is substituted for uranium as fuel. But then we would have the problems associated with plutonium (see chapter 10).

It is important to emphasize that all these calculations assume that the tailings piles remain undisturbed and in the same configuration for the entire average life of the ^{230}Thorium. If the pile were spread around by wind erosion, gopher erosion, or water, it is possible that the emanation would increase rather than decrease. On the other hand, if any of the disturbed tailings fell into water, the radon emanation would decrease. Since it is uncertain, to say the least, where a tailings pile will migrate during the next 115,000 years, we can reasonably speculate that it will remain unchanged.

The Profound Ethical Question

The supporters of the nuclear electricity industry are quick to point out that, during the time interval when the tailings piles would kill 450,000 persons from lung cancer, natural radon emissions will kill 1,000 times as many people from lung cancer. According to this reasoning, no ethical problem exists.

Pohl and Kepford have asked the question in another way: What right do current electricity users have to inflict 450,000 lung-cancer deaths on future individuals, for *each year* of use of nuclear electric power, and this from only one small part of the nuclear fuel cycle?

The nuclear industry's justification is essentially that something else kills more people; therefore, there should be no concern about lung-cancer deaths from the tailings piles. But when has society ever agreed that homicide is justified provided *natural* disasters kill people at a higher rate?

The radon issue is ethically profound, and we should carefully think through the implications of taking one position or the other, on it and on many similar issues.

The calculations become even more grotesque if we consider that some 10–15% of the uranium is lost into the tailings piles. This uranium, with its half-life of 4.51×10^9 years, will keep renewing the thorium and the thorium will keep producing the radium and the radium will keep producing the radon, for periods much longer than 115,000 years. But if the people of this society cannot come to a reasonable decision about the production of 450,000 lung-cancer deaths per year of operation of a full nuclear-power economy, it is doubtful that a more grotesque calculation will influence them appreciably.

THE LUNG-CANCER HAZARD FOR LOCAL RESIDENTS IN THE VICINITY OF TAILINGS PILES

It is reasonable that concern has been expressed concerning the lung-cancer hazard to individuals in the vicinity of a major tailings pile. It turns out that the hazard is not large on a relative scale.

We can begin by estimating the *maximum* hazard which could exist, even under unrealistic conditions, and then close in on more realistic conditions.

If the entire country were totally covered with tailings piles, the risk can be calculated (based on data from Pohl) to be 5.3 lung-cancer deaths. This means each person at risk would have 5.3 times the risk required to kill him of lung cancer, a certain death warrant. But of course, a country covered with tailings piles is a gross exaggeration. The true risk must be much less, as we shall now see.

Let us consider a severe situation: a community living in a region 1 km by 1 km, with a tailings pile in the center of the region. The natural radon emitted in such a community would be 4.2×10^5 PCi per second. Let us compare the natural emission rate in such a community with the emission rate from its tailings pile, which is 5×10^7 PCi/second based on Pohl's estimate of the radon emanation from the average tailings pile. The tailings pile puts 119 times as much radon into the community as does the natural radon emanating from the earth.

But now we must consider the fate of the radon from the two sources, once emitted. For the natural radon, if the wind blows new air into the community, it brings with it just as much radon, on the average, as the displaced air takes away, since we are assuming that natural radon is emitted everywhere (on land, at least). However, the new air does not bring radon from another tailings pile under credible circumstances. Therefore, to the extent that air moves out of the region, it is replaced by air free of tailings-pile radon.

The worst situation would exist if there were no air exchange at all. In that case, the risk would be 119 times the risk from natural radon. For an adult male cigarette smoker in this hypothetical community that risk would be just about 1 out of 2.

But this is an unrealistic upper limit, since there certainly would be appreciable air exchange. A more realistic situation would be *at least* one full air exchange with new air per hour, on the average. There would undoubtedly be even more frequent exchange under virtually all circumstances.

The average life of a radon atom is 132.2 hours. Regardless of whether a natural radon atom stays in one place or moves and is replaced by another, people will be exposed for 132.2 hours per average atom released (except near oceans). However, the situation is totally different for the *tailings-pile radon.* Radon is radon, of course, but the tailings-pile radon is *not* replaced when the wind blows it away from the community, because the new air does not come from a region with a tailings pile. We assumed that the tailings-pile radon stays in the vicinity only one hour, and even that is really an exaggeration since exchange will in all likelihood be more frequent than every hour.

Therefore, the effectiveness of the tailings-pile radon is reduced by a factor of 1/132.2 compared to natural radon. Our calculation of lung-cancer death risk must also be reduced by this factor. Thus, for the male cigarette smoker, the lung-cancer death risk is reduced to $(1/132.2) \times (0.53) = 0.004$, or 4 chances out of 1,000 for 50 years residence in this hypothetical community. This would appear to be a maximal risk, since air exchange is likely to clear the region more than once per hour. The more the air is cleared by winds from outside, the more the risk will decrease below the estimates just calculated.

None of these calculations even tries to address the problem of children who actually play on such tailings piles—a spectacle shown in a recent television documentary on the uranium industry. At the surface of such tailings piles, with little opportunity for their emanations to have become diluted by admixture with outside air, the radon levels could be quite high indeed. And children are the most sensitive to cancer induction. It would seem to be the height of folly for tailings piles to be accessible to children, but that appears to have occurred.

It must be emphasized that there are two additional hazards of the presence of a tailings pile in the community, over and above the radon in ambient air. First, the wind can blow dust from such a tailings pile into the community, with a resultant accumulation in and around houses. Second, there is always the hazard that people will use the tailings-pile material as a construction material. These two prospects can indeed add to the health risk for individuals in such a community.

Some Cautions Concerning the Lung-Cancer Dose in Person-WLMs

The author feels it is essential to point out two reasons why the true risk from radon exposure may be *underestimated* here. First, there is the problem of knowing how much of the dose received really counts toward cancer induction. The reader must be aware that the estimates of lung cancer in miners are for exposure over many years, in most cases. So the exposure period and the follow-up period can overlap. The net effect is that we may be counting some radiation which occurred after the cancer was induced.

Second, in an early analysis, Tamplin and Gofman (1970b) dealt with the data for the U.S. uranium miners which were then available. Although the number of cases was smaller, the data were consistent with a supralinear relationship between lung-cancer production and WLMs of exposure. BEIR-III (1980, p. 384) presents an update of the experiences of the U.S. uranium miners. While a detailed analysis of supralinearity versus linearity is not possible, the data clearly are consistent with *supralinearity*.

By our usual procedures, we can convert these data to excess lung-cancer rates per WLM:

Cumulative WLM Mean	O/E Value	Percent Increase in Lung-Cancer Rate	Percent Increase in Lung-Cancer Rate per WLM
155.8	2.25	125%	0.80%/WLM
585.9	4.71	371%	0.63%/WLM
2,388.2	10.32	932%	0.39%/WLM

These findings, consistent with supralinearity and based upon the extensive data now available, both confirm the original findings of Gofman and Tamplin and are consistent with all the findings of supralinearity in the Hiroshima-Nagasaki data (chapters 8 and 14).

In the evaluation of radon carcinogenicity in this chapter, we used Archer's overall data, and these data are for a mean cumulative exposure of 876.9 WLMs. But in evaluating exposures of the general public, we are really interested in much lower radon daughter exposures; we must realize that using the Archer data without correction for supralinearity will definitely underestimate the cancer hazard from radon. Therefore, all the estimates of radon-induced lung cancers in this chapter are, in all probability, underestimates of the true lung-cancer hazard. The data presented above suggest that the magnitude of the underestimate is on the order of a factor of 2 or 3. But without data for the very low WLM categories, the author does not feel that a definitive estimate of the factor should be made.

SECTION 3: THE MAN-MADE EMITTERS: PLUTONIUM AND OTHER TRANSURANICS

The advent of the nuclear era has presented society with a new class of alpha-particle-emitting radionuclides of the greatest importance and concern—nuclides of plutonium (element 94) and other transuranic elements (those with atomic numbers beyond 92).

Plutonium is the most prominent source element for several reasons. One radionuclide of plutonium, $^{239}_{94}$Pu, which was used in the bomb that devastated Nagasaki, is formed in great quantities in ordinary nuclear reactors, such as in light-water reactors in the United States, and is expected to be the fuel for one version of the proposed *breeder* reactors.

Any time that a nuclear chain reaction is maintained by neutrons, and some $^{238}_{92}U$ (also called uranium-238) is also present, the production of $^{239}_{94}Pu$ is inevitable. This sequence of reactions has one intermediate product, $^{239}_{93}Np$, which is a radionuclide of the element neptunium, of atomic number 93. The $^{239}_{94}Pu$ decays by alpha-particle emission and has a half-life of 24,400 years.

In biological terms, there are two general ways of describing the persistence of toxic radionuclides:

1. The time required for the radioactivity to decrease by a factor of 1,000, and by a factor of 1,000,000. For a factor of 1,000 (actually 1,024), 10 half-lives of radioactive decay are required. For a factor of 1,000,000, 20 half-lives are required. Thus, for $^{239}_{94}Pu$, 10 half-lives = (10) (24,400) = 244,000 years, and 20 half-lives = (20) (24,400) = 488,000 years.

2. The average life of a plutonium atom. For any radioactive substance, this can be shown to be the half-life/0.693. Therefore, for $^{239}_{94}Pu$, the average atomic life is equal to 24,400/0.693 = 35,209 years.

Either of these measures is quite sobering when we contemplate the escape of $^{239}_{94}Pu$ into the environment, from which it can gain access to the biosphere. And the problem is far more complex than just the generation of long-lived $^{239}_{94}Pu$. In the nuclear reactor generating $^{239}_{94}Pu$ from the reaction of neutrons with $^{238}_{92}U$, there are several other inevitable reactions, some generating additional radionuclides of the element plutonium, and others generating radionuclides of other transuranic elements. The total burden of health concern is thereby grossly amplified, as we shall see.

PRODUCTION OF THE PLUTONIUM RADIONUCLIDES

It is the $^{235}_{92}U$ and $^{238}_{92}U$ nuclides of natural uranium which provide the original source material for generation of all the plutonium radionuclides. The key reaction in the generation of new nuclides is one in which a neutron is captured and a gamma ray is emitted. The other essential reaction is radioactive decay.

The series of reactions from either $^{235}_{92}U$ or $^{238}_{92}U$ give rise to radionuclides of the following transuranic elements: Americium, curium, neptunium, and plutonium. In a nuclear reactor these various transuranic elements are produced in quantities that depend in part on the nature of the reactor, and in large part on how long the fuel elements have been in the reactor. The quantities can be described in terms of weights or numbers of curies.

UNSCEAR (1977, p. 204) presents the following data for production

of the major plutonium radionuclides from spent, high burn-up fuel in
reactors:

Nuclide	Weight Percent
^{239}Pu	60
^{240}Pu	22
^{241}Pu	12
^{242}Pu	4.5
^{238}Pu	1.5

Also from UNSCEAR, we have data for the production in curies of
radionuclides from light-water reactor fuel. *Burn-up* is the term that describes how much of the usable, fissionable material has actually fissioned.
The units to describe burn-up are megawatt-days (thermal) per ton of fuel
metal (uranium or plutonium). The tabulations that follow are the curies
present at 150 days after the fuel rods are removed from the reactor, after
high burn-up. The reason it has become customary to look at the quantities
at 150 days is that, when the reprocessing of nuclear fuel was expected to
be usual, 150 days was to have been the cooling-off period before reprocessing began. The data are presented in table 19 (based on UNSCEAR, Table
25, p. 202, and ORNL-4451).

TABLE 19: PRODUCTION OF TRANSURANIC RADIONUCLIDES IN LIGHT-WATER REACTOR FUEL

(Burn-up. 33,000 megawatt(thermal)-days per ton. 150 days cooling.)

Element	Radio-nuclide	$T_{1/2}$	Curies per mwyr (electrical)	Curies for 1,000 Reactors, each 1,000 mwyr
Neptunium	$^{239}_{93}$Np	2.33 days	0.6	6×10^5
Plutonium	$^{238}_{94}$Pu	92 yrs	94.0	9.4×10^7
Plutonium	$^{239}_{94}$Pu	24,400 yrs	11.0	1.1×10^7
Plutonium	$^{240}_{94}$Pu	6,580 yrs	16.0	1.6×10^7
Plutonium	$^{241}_{94}$Pu	14 yrs	3,850.0	3.85×10^9
Americium	$^{241}_{95}$Am	475 yrs	6.7	6.7×10^6
Curium	$^{242}_{96}$Cm	162 days	503.0	5.03×10^8
Curium	$^{244}_{96}$Cm	19 yrs	84.0	8.4×10^7

While ^{239}Pu dominates in weight percent among the various plutonium
nuclides, it is far from dominant in terms of radioactivity at 150 days. Let
us just consider the alpha-particle emitters ^{238}Pu, ^{239}Pu, and ^{240}Pu. Their
respective numbers of curies per megawatt (electrical)-year are 94:11:16. So
^{239}Pu constitutes only $(11/121) \times 100\% = 9.1\%$ of the alpha radioactivity
from plutonium.

^{241}Pu is a beta-particle emitter with a 14-year half-life. The relatively large number of curies of ^{241}Pu makes it important to our health even if alpha particles are more effective per unit of energy than beta particles. But what is even more important in the long run is that ^{241}Pu converts almost totally in about 70 years to ^{241}Am, an alpha-emitter, and the number of curies of ^{241}Am finally produced is close to $3,850 \times (14/475) = 113.5$ curies. This is so because, when a short-lived substance decays into a long-lived one, the number of curies is reduced by the ratio of their respective half-lives.

So, we must face the fact that in the transuranic "mixture," after 70 years or so, the amount in curies of Americium-241, an alpha-emitter, is *greater* than the total amount in curies of ^{238}Pu, ^{239}Pu, and ^{240}Pu combined. Any plutonium source, with ^{241}Pu present, is always generating ^{241}Americium. (Note that, in 70 years, much ^{238}Pu decays.)

All the relationships in curie strength among the transuranic species change with the passage of time. After a few hundred years, ^{238}Pu is no longer prominent compared to the combination of ^{239}Pu and ^{240}Pu. And still later, from 5,000 years onward, ^{239}Pu becomes dominant—increasingly dominant, because ^{240}Pu is being lost much more rapidly than ^{239}Pu.

HEALTH CONSIDERATIONS: THE TRANSURANICS AS A GROUP

The various plutonium radionuclides will in general show identical biological behavior with respect to distribution, since they are nuclides of the same chemical element. The one possible exception is the case of pure particles of a short-lived nuclide versus pure particles of a long-lived nuclide, where solubility differences might relate to the radioactivity itself. But this is a very rare problem in practice.

The transuranic elements have many chemical properties in common, and their similarity is considered to be due in large measure to the fact that they are members of an *actinide* group of elements, sharing properties in the same way the rare-earth elements between atomic numbers 57 and 71 do. Certainly, the behaviors of particulates containing oxides of the transuranic elements will be quite similar. And, as we shall see, particulates containing transuranic elements in insoluble form present one of the most serious problems associated with these elements—the problem of induction of human lung cancer.

We shall begin our considerations of health effects by focusing on ^{239}Pu, for simplicity. Then we shall consider the health consequences of exposure to mixtures of the plutonium nuclides ^{238}Pu, ^{239}Pu, and ^{240}Pu. Such plutonium mixtures produced in reactors are known as *reactor-Pu,* and they have a level of alpha activity greater than that of pure ^{239}Pu. The reason for the greater alpha activity is that some of the plutonium nuclides have half-lives shorter than that for pure ^{239}Pu. The ratio of plutonium nuclides will vary somewhat in used ("spent") fuel according to the exact burn-up time per ton and the kind of reactor in which the fission occurred. However, no large errors will be introduced by considering only the data for light-water-reactor fuel after high burn-up and 150 days of cooling.

It is calculated that plutonium in spent light-water-reactor fuel has an alpha-particle activity 5.4 times that of pure ^{239}Plutonium. Therefore, in all subsequent discussions we shall say that reactor-Pu is 5.4 times as serious a health hazard as pur ^{239}Plutonium.

HEALTH HAZARDS OF ^{239}PLUTONIUM AND OF REACTOR-PU

Aside from accidental wounding, the two major routes of entry of plutonium into the human being are inhalation and ingestion. Until recently, the ingestion route was considered relatively unimportant, particularly by nuclear scientists ever hopeful of demonstrating a low toxicity for plutonium. The reason given was that, in general, it was anticipated that any ingestion was likely to be mainly of the highly insoluble oxide of plutonium PuO_2, and there is very little absorption of this compound from the intestine.

Recent evidence (Larsen and Oldham 1978) indicates that this may have represented a rash dismissal of a very serious aspect of plutonium exposure. Mechanisms are now known to exist that make plutonium more accessible to plants than previously thought to be the case, and more readily absorbed from the gastrointestinal tract than had been thought possible.

At this point, we wish to consider in detail the very serious consequences that ensue from the insolubility of plutonium oxides. The insolubility of PuO_2 means that, after inhalation and once the compound is lodged in various structures in the pulmonary tree, it is only very slowly cleared from the lungs. This long residence-time means a high degree of radiation of pulmonary structures per unit of deposited plutonium.

For X-radiation and gamma radiation, we have direct studies of the induction of lung cancer (the ankylosing spondylitis series for X-radiation, and the Hiroshima-Nagasaki survivors for gamma-plus-neutron radiation). The reader may well think that by now, considering all the workers who have been involved in military and civilian plutonium processing, an excellent study would have been conducted to ascertain the health effects of plutonium exposure.

The situation as of 1975, over 30 years after major quantities of plutonium began to be handled, is well described by Dr. George Voelz, medical director of the Los Alamos Scientific Laboratory (New Mexico):

Formal studies for delayed effects from these exposures have not been reported, so it is only possible to state that no cases of acute human pathology following plutonium exposures have been reported to date. Most of these workers have been followed with regular periodic medical examinations during their employment with AEC contractors. After termination of employment most workers have not been followed by medical examinations for the specific purpose of determining possible clinical effects from plutonium (or any other hazardous materials they may have encountered in their work). (1975, p. 554)

And in the same paper, Voelz also states:

It would be nice to be able to report that the long-term studies on plutonium workers have been practiced faithfully throughout the industry. Unfortunately, the follow-up of workers following termination of their employment in plutonium work has been limited to only a few special situations. (p. 555)

Very few people realize the scantiness of any efforts to find out what has happened to plutonium workers over the past three decades. It is to Voelz's credit that he has pressed vigorously for more effective and extensive follow-up efforts in this field.

In the light of Voelz's statements, the reader will understand why it has remained possible for nuclear promoters to proclaim that they are not aware of any studies showing a serious health effect of plutonium on human beings. Technically, that statement is correct. Technically, it would be correct even if one billion people had died of plutonium toxicity, as long as no one had ever set up the epidemiological study required to demonstrate the association of those deaths with plutonium.

The reader would do well to remember the history of cigarette smoking's demonstration as a causal factor in human lung cancer. The author recalls many statements by medical authorities that they were not aware of any evidence for harmful effects in health caused by smoking. In spite of tens of thousands of deaths, such false reassurances were not *lies* until the requisite epidemiologic studies were done.

It can be stated with considerable certainty that it is impossible for plutonium inhalation *not* to cause human lung cancer. Plutonium-239, and other alpha-emitting nuclides, produce precisely the same *physical* radiation as do radon daughter products. It would require a miracle of physics for the alpha particles from radon daughter products to produce lung cancer in man, which they assuredly do (see section 2), and for the alpha particles from plutonium not to produce lung cancer.

So, what is at issue is not whether plutonium will produce human lung cancer, but precisely how many lung cancers it will produce per unit inhaled.

This becomes a question of how much radiation will be delivered per unit of plutonium inhaled, which itself is a question of where in the pulmonary tree the plutonium will lodge and what its residence time will be.

LUNG-CANCER PRODUCTION BY PLUTONIUM NUCLIDES

Related to the question of the site of deposition of the plutonium is the question of the *type* of lung cancer produced. The predominant form of lung cancer is the one called *bronchogenic cancer of the lung*; a form of cancer about one-tenth as common is known as *bronchiolo-alveolar cancer of the lung*.

The airways leading finally to the pulmonary alveoli (where the air-gas-blood exchanges really occur) start with the trachea, which divides into the major bronchi. In turn, each bronchus divides and subdivides many, many times, this branching process creating tubes of smaller and smaller diameter, until finally we have what are called *terminal bronchioles* and *bronchiolo-alveolar junctions.*

Bronchogenic cancer rarely occurs in the trachea or the major primary bronchial branches. This form of cancer is also very rare in the very small bronchioles. This means that bronchogenic cancer, the overwhelmingly predominant form of lung cancer, must originate in the intermediate bronchi, called *segmental bronchi.* The crucial tissues within the segmental bronchi are the *epithelial-layer cells.* We shall be interested in learning the extent of plutonium deposition in these tissues.

Bronchiolo-alveolar cancer, the less prominent form of lung cancer (approximately 10% of all cases), arises in the junctional region between the terminal bronchioles and the pulmonary alveoli (air sacs). So we shall also be quite interested in the deposition of plutonium in this region and, as it turns out, in the factors that may alter the relative distribution between this region and the segmental bronchi.

Estimates for Bronchiolo-alveolar Cancer of the Lung

It is possible to make some indirect estimates for human bronchiolo-alveolar cancer based on experimental studies of this form of cancer in the beagle dog. Generally speaking, we should prefer to rest *no* human estimates upon data from other animal species, because we cannot be sure whether human beings are more sensitive than, as sensitive as, or less sensitive than the other species. However, for the pressing and serious problem of plutonium-inhalation hazard, the absence of a direct series of observations on human beings makes it worthwhile to *initiate* estimation of plutonium-induced human lung cancer by considering the beagle-dog data.

In the beagle dog, inhaled particulates of plutonium dioxide, which do get into the deep lung tissues, lodge themselves largely in the bronchiolo-alveolar regions. The lung cancers that develop are virtually all bronchiolo-alveolar cancers. Obviously, then, any extrapolation from the beagle dog to man would, at best, describe only the expected bronchiolo-alveolar lung-cancer rate in man per unit of deposition of plutonium in the bronchiolo-alveolar region.

However, any *bronchogenic* cancer of the lung would necessarily be *in addition* to the estimated bronchiolo-alveolar cancers produced by plutonium deposition. Stated otherwise, the estimated bronchiolo-alveolar cancers produced by plutonium would represent the *minimum* total number of lung cancers from the deposition of plutonium. Such a floor estimate would be extremely useful. It should be understood that this floor estimate would be based on the assumption that man and beagle dog are equally sensitive to the induction of *bronchiolo-alveolar* cancer of the lung by plutonium inhalation.

Bair and Thompson (1974) induced bronchiolo-alveolar cancers of the lung in beagle dogs with [239]Plutonium oxide inhalations. From their experiments, it is possible to estimate only the *minimum* hazard, because the carcinogenicity of plutonium was initially underestimated, with the result that bronchiolo-alveolar cancer of the lung developed in essentially 100% of the beagles, *even at the lowest doses of plutonium tested.* A dose of 0.049 micrograms of [239]Plutonium deposited per gram of bloodless lung produced bronchiolo-alveolar cancers in 100% of the dogs.

If we scale up to man, with 570 grams of bloodless lung as a reasonable estimate, and assume equal sensitivity of man and dog, a deposited dose of $(570) \times (0.049) = 28.0$ micrograms of [239]Plutonium should yield 100% incidence of bronchiolo-alveolar cancer. Note that the true dose required, even based on this extrapolation, is probably less than 28 micrograms because the beagle experiment was inadvertently a saturation experiment. It is highly probable that the true dose of [239]Pu required for 100% bronchiolo-alveolar lung cancer in the beagle is less than the accidentally chosen 0.049 micrograms/gram lung. How much less should be learned from some ongoing experiments at lower doses on the beagle dog. (See the work of R. O. McClellan and colleagues, 1979, cited in the Bibliography.)

At this time, we can use 28 micrograms as the upper limit of [239]Plutonium *deposition* which is required to provoke 100% incidence of bronchiolo-alveolar cancer of the lung in human beings. And since the dose that produces 100% incidence of fatal lung cancer is the lung-cancer dose, we can say that 28 micrograms of *deposited* [239]Plutonium is the upper limit of the bronchiolo-alveolar lung-cancer dose for human beings.

Inhaled Versus Deposited Plutonium: There is one item the reader should check in any literature report concerning the carcinogenicity of plutonium. Some papers report the amount of plutonium *inhaled,* whereas others report the amount of plutonium *deposited* for long-term retention. In these considerations of plutonium deposition we are excluding large particles (above 10 microns in diameter) that do not get through the nasopharyngeal regions to the bronchi. One mode of reporting is not more correct than another, but in order to compare reports, the modes must be the same.

In his own earlier papers, the author used the amount of plutonium deposited in the lung, rather than the amount inhaled. Throughout this book, he has changed to the use of the amount inhaled. There is a difference of approximately a factor of 4 between the two uses. This means that approximately *one-fourth* of the respirable particles inhaled are retained for long periods.

Thus, we must convert the 28 micrograms of deposited plutonium to $(4) \times (28) = 112$ micrograms of *inhaled* plutonium as the upper limit of the bronchiolo-alveolar lung-cancer dose for human beings.

Now let us recall that the plutonium produced in nuclear-power plants is not pure [239]Plutonium, but is rather a mixture of plutonium radionuclides which has an alpha-particle radioactivity some 5.4 times that of pure [239]Plutonium. Since the energies of the alpha particles emitted from the various plutonium radionuclides are closely similar, it can be stated that it should take 1/5.4 as much reactor-Pu to produce the same carcinogenic effect as is produced by any quantity of ^{239}Plutonium. Therefore, the bronchiolo-alveolar lung-cancer dose for reactor-Pu would be $(1/5.4) \times (28) =$ 5.2 micrograms *deposited* in human lungs, which converts to 20.8 micrograms *inhaled* into human lungs.

For plutonium, as for any other radiation source, we treat the cancer effect as proportional to dose (extensively justified in chapter 8). Therefore, 20.8 micrograms inhaled into human lungs would guarantee one fatal bronchiolo-alveolar lung cancer, no matter how it is distributed. If 1,000 persons each inhaled 0.0208 micrograms of reactor-Pu into their lungs, the total inhalation would be 20.8 micrograms, and, we would expect *one* fatal bronchiolo-alveolar cancer to occur, but we would not know in which person.

The Question of Bronchogenic Lung Cancer Induced by Plutonium

Thus far we have addressed only the rare form of lung cancer, bronchiolo-alveolar cancer. Of potentially much greater importance is the question of the production of *bronchogenic* lung cancer by plutonium in man. This would, as we have said, require the deposition of plutonium in the epithelial cells of the vulnerable intermediate bronchi.

The first question we might have raised has already been answered. If plutonium *does* deposit in the vulnerable bronchi of man, will bronchogenic cancer be produced? Yes, since plutonium alpha particles can and will do in the bronchi what alpha particles from radon daughter products have been shown to do, namely, induce bronchogenic lung cancer. The only question really open is *how many* bronchogenic cancers will be produced. This requires us to determine the fraction of plutonium that can be expected to deposit in the vulnerable bronchi, plus the average residence time of that plutonium.

Erroneous Thinking Concerning Plutonium Deposition in Bronchi:

Unfortunately, it has been widely assumed, on the basis of grossly inadequate experiments, that insoluble particles (e.g., particles of plutonium dioxide) will not be retained in or on the bronchial epithelium for any significant length of time. The Task Group on Lung Dynamics of The International Commission on Radiological Protection (ICRP) suggests a model (1966) for the physiologic clearance of insoluble particulates from various parts of the tracheo-broncho-pulmonary tree. That model *assumes* essentially *zero* long-term retention of plutonium-oxide particles in the bronchial epithelium; all long-term retention of these particles is supposed to occur in the terminal bronchioles and the alveoli.

It is of utmost importance to understand the reasoning behind the ICRP Task Group's model predicting *no* retention of such particulates in the bronchial epithelium. The Task Group makes the assumption that a combination of mucus secretion and ciliary action would propel any plutonium deposited in the segmental bronchi back up to the nasopharynx within a day, with subsequent gastrointestinal excretion. The Task Group completes its scenario by stating that the reason for the very long half-times, e.g., 500 days, of insoluble particulates (such as plutonium dioxide) in the deeper (bronchiolo-alveolar) region is that *the cells of this region do not have cilia.*

This reasoning is consistent with the occurrence in beagle dogs of bronchiolo-alveolar lung cancer from plutonium exposure, rather than bronchogenic carcinoma of the lung.

In 1975 Gofman challenged this set of assumptions as possibly very seriously in error for the human case, particularly, but not exclusively, for the approximately 35–50% of people who smoke cigarettes. The consequences of error may include drastic underestimation of the lung-cancer risk to human beings from plutonium exposure, particularly the risk of bronchogenic cancer of the lung.

Cilia are short hairlike projections present on specialized cells. These projections are in motion, so that they create a true propelling effect on material on the surface of cells to which they belong. Healthy cells of the bronchial epithelium are richly endowed with cilia. However, numerous studies have been published which demonstrate that cigarette smoking causes serious injury to cilia of the bronchial cells. The injury is twofold. First, there is actual denudation of the cilia in a large fraction of the lining cells. Second, the remaining cilia do not function normally in terms of propulsion action (Auerbach et al. 1961).

Ide and co-workers (1959) demonstrate that 30% of the ciliated cells in cigarette smokers are denuded of their cilia. Thus, the bronchi will have sizable regions with no cilia—and the cilia represent, for the ICRP Task Group, the mechanism for clearing particulates rapidly from the bronchi. So the very mechanism that according to the ICRP keeps the bronchi free from long-term retention of plutonium-oxide particulates can, when nonfunctional, *guarantee* long-term retention—retention on the order of 500 days. It is reasonable, if one agrees with the ICRP that the 500-day half-time of plutonium in bronchiolo-alveolar regions is due to the absence of cilia, that one should assume a 500-day half-time for other bronchial regions denuded of cilia, as a result of cigarette smoking or other injury to ciliated cells.

Powerful experimental confirmation of Gofman's suggestion of delayed clearance of particulates in cigarette smokers recently appeared in the work of Cohen, Arai, and Brain (1979). These workers utilized nonradioactive iron-oxide particles (Fe_3O_4) as tracers for studying the long-term clearance of particulates from cigarette smokers and nonsmokers. A method of magnetization of the particles was used for measuring the residual content of the originally inhaled particulates. The results were unequivocal in demonstrating—reliably, in this author's opinion—the grossly longer retention time of particulates in the broncho-pulmonary trees of cigarette smokers compared to nonsmokers (in studies approximately one year in duration).

While the Cohen, Arai, and Brain studies cannot pinpoint the exact location of excessive retention of particulates in the broncho-pulmonary trees of smokers, the implications of their results are self-evident. No evidence has appeared which would refute the concept that bronchi with ciliary injury will retain particulates for periods of time comparable to the retention times for originally unciliated portions of the lung.

We shall now explore the implications of these concepts and findings in evaluating the induction of bronchogenic cancer of the lung by plutonium-containing particulates.

Estimation of the Plutonium Dose to Cancer-Prone Bronchial Cells:
Two steps in estimating the plutonium dose to the cancer-prone bronchial epithelial cells are essential if we are to assess the bronchogenic-cancer potential of plutonium:

1. Estimation of the fraction of the total tracheo-bronchial region which is relevant for development of bronchogenic cancer

2. Estimation of the true extent of retention of plutonium-oxide particles by bronchial epithelium with impaired ciliary function

The Relevant Part of the Tracheo-bronchial Region: There are three parts of the tracheo-bronchial region to consider: (1) the trachea and large bronchi, which are not major sites for bronchogenic cancer; (2) the segmental bronchi, which *are* major vulnerable sites; and (3) the very small bronchi and bronchioles, which are not vulnerable sites. We wish to know what mass of epithelial cells is present in each of these three regions, for any plutonium retained in the bronchi for long-term clearance will be dispersed in these masses of epithelial cells.

Calculations yield the following results:

Compartment	Name	Epithelial Cell Mass (grams)
I	Trachea + large bronchi	0.527
II	Segmental bronchi	1.062
III	Smaller bronchi through terminal bronchioles	1.966
	Total mass of epithelial cells	3.555

Any plutonium retained for a long period because of ciliary injury in the bronchi will be retained in one or more of these three compartments and will irradiate the mass of epithelial cells shown for these compartments.

Fraction of Plutonium Retained Long-Term: In the ICRP model it is assumed that: 25% of inhaled plutonium deposits in the deep pulmonary tissue beyond the bronchi, namely, in bronchiolo-alveolar and alveolar regions; and 8% of inhaled plutonium deposits in the tracheo-bronchial tissue.

Further, the ICRP model suggests that, for the deep pulmonary tissue, 40% of deposited plutonium is released within a few days, by going back up the respiratory tract, whereas 60% is retained for long-term clearance.

So, if one microcurie of plutonium were inhaled, $0.60 \times 0.25 \times 1.0$ = 0.15 microcuries would be retained in the deep pulmonary tissues.

For the tracheo-bronchial region, the ICRP model suggests that all 8% of the deposited plutonium is released rapidly, with no long-term retention. This is where the ICRP fails to take into account destroyed and impaired cilia. The reasonable assumption to make is that the 30% of the tracheo-bronchial tree unciliated in the cigarette smoker will behave as does the unciliated part of deep pulmonary tissue; the ICRP's own reasoning supports this assumption.

Therefore, of the 8% of inhaled plutonium deposited in the tracheo-bronchial tree, we would calculate that 60% would be retained long-term in the 30% of the area denuded of cilia. So, $0.08 \times 0.6 \times 0.30 = 0.0144$ of the plutonium would be retained for clearance according to a 500-day half-time. Of 1 microcurie of plutonium inhaled by a cigarette smoker, 0.0144 microcuries would be retained for long-term clearance.

But there is one additional source of plutonium retention in the bronchi, namely, the plutonium coming back up from the deep pulmonary tissues. We reported above, from ICRP, that 40% of the original 25% deposited in deep tissues comes back up quickly. So for 1 microcurie inhaled, 0.10 microcuries must come back up through the bronchial channels. This amount has a 60% chance of being retained in the unciliated regions of the bronchi, which are 30% of the total. So, $0.6 \times 0.3 \times 0.1 = 0.018$ microcuries would be retained in this way.

The total amount of plutonium retained in the tracheo-bronchial tree for long-term clearance would be $0.0144 + 0.018 = 0.0324$ microcuries out of 1 microcurie inhaled, in cigarette smokers.

We know that there are three compartments among which this plutonium must be distributed. We shall make the reasonable assumption that the three compartments receive plutonium in proportion to the masses of their epithelial tissue. So in the vulnerable region (the segmental bronchi), $(1.062/3.555) \times (0.0324)$ microcuries = 0.00968 microcuries would be retained for clearance according to a half-time of 500 days. This 0.00968 microcuries would be distributed in a mass of 1.062 grams of epithelial cells. We shall assume that such plutonium would be in or on the cells directly, rather than in any mucus layer. The absorption of any plutonium alpha energy in mucus would, of course, lower the dose to the bronchial cells.

The Radiation Dose from the Retained Plutonium: We can calculate these doses from section 2 and first principles from basic physics.

Summarizing, we have the following doses per microcurie of *inhaled* plutonium:

Vulnerable bronchi, smokers	17,134 rems
Vulnerable bronchi, nonsmokers	857 rems
Bronchiolo-alveolar and alveolar cellular mass (smokers and nonsmokers)	2,256 rems

For many purposes, it is preferable to provide these doses in rems per *microgram* of ^{239}Plutonium instead of per microcurie. It takes 16.3 micrograms of ^{239}Plutonium to represent 1 microcurie. Therefore, the above doses per *microgram* of inhaled ^{239}Plutonium are:

Vulnerable bronchi, smokers	1,051.2 rems
Vulnerable bronchi, nonsmokers	52.6 rems
Bronchiolo-alveolar and alveolar cellular mass (smokers and nonsmokers)	138.4 rems

Bronchogenic Cancer in Cigarette Smokers Versus Nonsmokers: It is widely estimated that approximately 90% of all human bronchogenic cancers occur in smokers of cigarettes. It is also estimated that in the United States approximately 35% of adult males are currently cigarette smokers and 65% are not. The percentage of cigarette smokers has been dropping appreciably in recent years.

In any calculations of lung-cancer dose, we would wish to correct the observed rates of lung cancer to the appropriate rates for smokers and nonsmokers. In table 14, the lung-cancer dose for 25-year-old U.S. males is given as 567 person-rads. From all previous considerations, we know that the higher the spontaneous lung-cancer rate, the lower will be the calculated lung-cancer dose, for a specified peak percent increase per rad. And since we assume that the peak percent increase per rad is the same for cigarette smokers and nonsmokers, we can now get separate lung-cancer doses for smokers and nonsmokers.

These doses, based on current percentages of smokers and nonsmokers, are calculated to be 236.3 person-rads (smokers) and 2,363 person-rads (nonsmokers).

Final Translation of Plutonium Doses into Lung-Cancer Doses in Micrograms: *The Male Cigarette Smoker* (bronchogenic cancer of the lung): It takes 236.3 person-rads to guarantee 1 lung-cancer death. One microgram of ^{239}Plutonium inhaled gives 1,051.2 rems to 1 person, or 1,051.2 person-rems. Therefore, the lung-cancer dose in micrograms = 236.3/1,051.2 = 0.225 micrograms of inhaled ^{239}Plutonium.

The Male Nonsmoker (bronchogenic cancer of the lung): It takes 2,363 person-rads to guarantee one lung-cancer death. One microgram of ^{239}Plutonium inhaled gives 52.6 rems to 1 person, or 52.6 person-rems per microgram. The lung-cancer dose in micrograms = 2,363/52.6 = 44.9 micrograms of inhaled ^{239}Plutonium.

Bronchiolo-alveolar Cancer: Since this type of cancer seems to be as influenced by cigarette smoking as other types, we can use the direct ratios of its frequency to get lung-cancer doses.

For male cigarette smokers, since bronchiolo-alveolar cancer is roughly 1/10 as frequent as bronchogenic cancer, the lung-cancer dose must be

236.3 $\times$ 10 = 2,363 person-rads. We showed above that each microgram of inhaled [239]Plutonium delivers 138.4 rems to the bronchiolo-alveolar and alveolar tissues. Therefore, the lung-cancer dose is 2,363/138.4 = 17.1 micrograms of inhaled [239]Plutonium.

For male nonsmokers, the lung-cancer dose must be 2,363 $\times$ 10 = 23,630 person-rads, or 23,630/138.4 = 170.7 micrograms of inhaled [239]Plutonium.

For females, the risk of lung cancer is approximately 1/3 that for males. Therefore, all lung-cancer doses for females can be obtained by multiplying appropriate male values by a factor of 3.

Bronchogenic Cancer Induction by Reactor-Plutonium: Earlier it was shown that reactor-Pu is approximately 5.4 times as alpha-radioactive as is pure [239]Plutonium because of the admixture of shorter-lived nuclides of plutonium. Therefore, it will necessarily require 1/5.4 as much reactor-Pu to produce a given health effect as is required of [239]Plutonium. Thus, we can write the following bronchogenic lung-cancer doses for reactor-Pu.

For male cigarette smokers, the bronchogenic lung-cancer dose for inhaled reactor-Pu = 0.225/5.4 = 0.042 micrograms.

For male nonsmokers, the bronchogenic lung-cancer dose for inhaled reactor-Pu = 44.9/5.4 = 8.3 micrograms.

Age Corrections for Lung-Cancer Doses from Plutonium: For nonsmokers there is no problem converting the lung-cancer doses just obtained here for 25-year-old males to values for any other age, since we know that specific-organ cancer doses behave like whole-body cancer doses. The relationship is as follows:

$$(\text{plutonium lung-cancer dose})_{\text{age x}} =$$
$$(\text{lung-cancer dose}_{25}) \times \frac{(\text{whole-body dose})_x}{(\text{whole-body dose})_{25}}$$

With smokers the conversion becomes complicated if there is plutonium exposure in the period before smoking starts. We really do not know how the two effects interact. For this case, the author suggests using the same type of relationship as above, with the understanding that the lung-cancer dose may thereby be underestimated. Converting the lung-cancer dose for smokers irradiated *after* age 25 does not have this complication, because most smokers have started their smoking by then.

The Question of Respirable Particles and Insoluble Particles: All the calculations in these discussions of induction of lung cancer by plutonium are predicated on the assumption that the particle size of the plutonium dioxide (or other compound of insoluble character) is such that the particles actually do get to the deep lung tissues. If insoluble particles are too large in size, they are rejected quite high in the respiratory tree, and cannot even be considered relevant here. Particles in the general range of less than 5 microns in diameter are considered *respirable,* meaning they will pass the upper respiratory airway and may be deposited in segmental bronchi, bronchioles, and alveolar tissues.

It is of interest that in the nuclear fuel cycle, when plutonium oxide is prepared for the purpose of making fuel rods, the particle sizes of insoluble plutonium compounds are in the 1-micron range, perfectly suited for respiratory toxicity.

We must also consider the question of insolubility of the inhaled compounds. A long retention time (a 500-day half-time, in the ICRP model) is predicted for highly insoluble compounds, which are known as the Class Y compounds. Plutonium oxide generally qualifies as Class Y. If wet, fresh plutonium oxide were prepared and somehow dispersed in very fine particulates, it might be more readily dissolved and acted upon by biological compounds. It might then qualify as a Class W compound, for which a retention half-time of 50 days is suggested by the ICRP Task Group.

We can say that the lung-cancer dose will necessarily go up with a decrease in the half-time of particulates in the vulnerable regions of the bronchial epithelium. Thus, if a particular plutonium compound were inhaled in particulate form, and the solubility were sufficient to indicate that the retention time would be only 50 days instead of 500 days, then the bronchogenic lung-cancer dose would be *10 times* as high as is reported here. This should be intuitively evident. A higher solubility would mean a shorter period of irradiation of the cancer-prone cells, meaning a smaller dose would be delivered per microgram inhaled. Therefore, it would take more micrograms to guarantee a fatal lung cancer.

Are the Estimates Presented Here Too High or Too Low? It is evident to the reader that certain key parameters of human physiological function, relating to plutonium behavior in the lung, are simply not available through direct experimental evidence. For example, we do not have a direct measure of the relationship between cilia loss and retention of plutonium particulates in the crucial bronchial regions, so we estimated here that the denuded areas behave like areas never covered with cilia. That is an approximation. One day we would like to know this quantitatively.

The 500-day half-time for retention of highly insoluble particles is an estimate from a model. It may be too long a time, and it may be too short. More data will allow us to know retention time more closely.

We may well have underestimated the serious extent to which cigarette smoking causes retention of plutonium in the pulmonary tree. The striking difference in long-term retention noted in the Cohen-Arai-Brain studies for smokers versus nonsmokers is quite consistent with the possibility that we have here seriously underestimated the dose to the vulnerable bronchi from retained plutonium, and thus the real hazard of plutonium as a lung-cancer producer.

On the other hand, three factors may contribute to a possible overestimate here of the dose to the vulnerable bronchi. One, already mentioned, is the absorption of some of the alpha-particle energy in the mucus layer covering the epithelial cells. Another is the "self-absorption" of some of the alpha-particle energy in the insoluble particulates themselves. Last, cells near the alpha-particle source may die but remain in place and absorb some of the alpha-particle energy. Each of these possibilities is difficult to evaluate.

But in the absence of a valid and meaningful epidemiological study, we are faced with the necessity of making estimates and approximations. It is particularly sad that this should be necessary for plutonium, since a sufficiently large number of persons have been exposed to plutonium and an epidemiological study should by now have been completed. Unfortunately for human health, there are powerful reasons why a delay in getting firm answers concerning plutonium toxicity is extremely useful to the nuclear industry. In the next chapter we will discuss the existing inadequate studies.

The Lung-Cancer Effects of the Other Transuranic Nuclides

Insoluble particles of americium or curium oxides, or of other compounds of either americium or curium, would produce upon inhalation the same risk as does plutonium, after correction for the number of microcuries per microgram of radionuclide. The more soluble these americium or curium compounds, the weaker their effect in the bronchi, just as we discussed for the differential solubility of plutonium compounds.

Other Physiologic Parameters Deserving Consideration

While nuclear promoters will naturally be concerned that these estimates of the carcinogenic properties of plutonium and other transuranics are too high, the author thinks there are cogent reasons to believe that the estimates may really be much too low.

First of all, our estimate of retention in the vulnerable bronchial regions is based on the ICRP model, which suggests 8% initial deposition in the entire tracheo-bronchial region. When we examine the approximately 5-fold slower clearance of Fe_3O_4 particles in cigarette smokers, we must seriously wonder whether the bronchial deposition may not be considerably greater in smokers than we have estimated here, and considerably greater than the 8% suggested in the ICRP model.

Second, we have not yet considered some additional serious changes that go on in the bronchial epithelium of cigarette smokers, over and above ciliary injury and destruction, such as the total change in the character of the lining cells (*metaplasia*) and the new growth of additional layers of cells (*hyperplasia*), with some regions showing four, five, or more cells in the epithelial layer, rather than the normal one cell.

We must ask whether this injured and altered epithelial tissue has an increased concentration of *phagocytic cells* (cells that engulf foreign particles, including bacteria), causing the tissue to take up unusually high quantities of PuO_2 particulates. From what we know of the general physiology of injured or inflamed tissue, we would expect a large increase in phagocytic activity. Any such increase would make the plutonium carcinogenicity more severe than we calculated.

On the other hand, with the increased thickness of the bronchial epithelium in the metaplastic-hyperplastic areas of the bronchi, it is possible that some of the plutonium alpha radiation does not reach the cancer-prone cells. The microdistribution of plutonium is simply not known for such regions. In this case, we would need to reduce the estimated carcinogenicity of inhaled plutonium.

Early in this section we made a ballpark estimate of the bronchiolo-alveolar lung-cancer dose from the beagle-dog experiments, assuming we knew the scaling factor from dog to man. That estimate was an inhaled dose of 112 micrograms of ^{239}Plutonium. Since the beagles were of course nonsmokers, we should compare that value of 112 micrograms with our calculated estimate of the bronchiolo-alveolar lung-cancer dose for non-smokers—170.7 micrograms. This is very reasonable agreement. Our estimate depends on the mass of bronchiolo-alveolar tissue into which the plutonium is deposited, and on the ICRP Task Group estimate of both the fraction retained and the half-time for clearance from this region of the lung. The figure from the beagle-dog experiment may be too high, because the experiment was a "saturation" experiment.

Readers who are not familiar with this area of research may think these estimates, 112 and 170.7 micrograms, are far apart. But the very fact that the two estimates are in the same ballpark is heartening indeed; it suggests we are not far from discovering the true value. To be within a factor of two (or even five) from the actual value would be very good, in advance of any *human* evidence.

Calculated Versus Observed

No one should be happy or satisfied that our estimates of the lung-cancer toxicity of plutonium and other transuranic nuclides rest on calculations rather than observations. It is not that the author is suggesting that a deliberate experiment should have been done: that would be barbaric. Rather, he is expressing his dismay that numerous people *were* exposed, and that the responsible officials are some 25 years late in realizing that there existed some obligation to find something out about how those people were affected.

But that cannot be remedied now, so what we face is the following. Either we use the toxicity estimates as presented here (or as modified, if some valid, scientific criticism suggests the estimates are too high or too low), or we simply operate in the dark. Certainly, scientific criticism of each and every aspect of these estimates is most welcome, so that we can improve the calculational basis of estimation.

And we do have, even though belatedly, some ongoing studies of exposed workers (Voelz 1978) to draw from in the future. In time, the occurrence or nonoccurrence of lung cancer in those workers as a function of their plutonium dose will begin to provide a reality-check for our calculations. If toxicity has been overestimated here, the nonoccurrence of the required number of lung cancers will tell us very clearly that this is the case, provided we analyze the data in a meaningful manner. If toxicity has been underestimated, the extra lung-cancer cases will also notify us that we have underestimated certain crucial parameters.

The next ten years, if a meaningful effort is made to follow up exposed workers, should help materially to set some reasonable bounds on estimates of the true toxicity of plutonium compounds and other transuranics as pulmonary carcinogens.

One point is certain: it is simply absurd for anyone to suggest that plutonium may turn out *not* to cause human lung cancer. That is an impossibility, if one assumes that any plutonium at all gets to the bronchi.

CHAPTER 10

PLUTONIUM INHALATION AND LUNG CANCER

SECTION 1: LUNG CANCERS ALREADY PRODUCED BY PLUTONIUM INHALATION

It is commonplace to hear from the nuclear promotional community that there has not been a single documented case of plutonium-induced lung cancer. The uninitiated would certainly interpret this to mean that *no* lung cancer fatalities have been caused by plutonium-particle inhalation. Certainly, the intelligent public would have every right to think that the statement above means that a valid, meaningful search has been made for a "documented" case of plutonium-induced lung cancer, and that search has demonstrated such a case *does not exist*. The simple truth is that no such search has been made.

This section will present the basis for the author's estimate that plutonium particulates have already committed approximately 950,000 persons worldwide to a lung-cancer death, and that more will be so committed in the future, *even* if no more plutonium is dispersed in the environment. At this juncture, there are two crucial points to be made:

1. The absence of an adequate epidemiological study is worlds apart from the absence of a major effect of plutonium.

2. There is one fact about cancer which *must* be understood, if one is to understand the field of environmentally and industrially caused cancers. Once a cancer has been produced, it does not carry any flag telling us the specific agent that caused it. There is at present no direct examination of patients, either living or dead, which can tell us the particular cause of a particular cancer.

At present, over 100,000 lung-cancer fatalities occur annually in the United States. Let us suppose, for the sake of illustration, that 10,000 of these cancers are caused by plutonium that has been environmentally dispersed. Would it be possible for us to discover that fact? Even though the plutonium-induced cancers carry no special marker? Yes. If we knew the dose from the plutonium exposure, and if, from other sources of information, we knew the consequences of such a dose, we could figure out the number of lung cancers produced by the environmental dispersal of plutonium. This is true even though we could not point to a single case and say, "That is a plutonium-induced cancer."

Statements that no case of plutonium-induced lung cancer has been documented reveal either a total ignorance of public-health science or a desire to mislead people.

THE CONSEQUENCES FROM ATMOSPHERIC BOMB-TESTING FALLOUT

The United States, the Soviet Union, and the United Kingdom detonated large numbers of plutonium-containing nuclear weapons in the atmosphere during the late 1940s, the 1950s, and the early 1960s. Inevitably, some of the plutonium in such weapons does not itself get fissioned (plutonium either originally present in the atomic weapon, or produced by neutrons generated in fission and captured by uranium nuclides). So, in such an explosion, plutonium gets dispersed into the atmosphere.

Particularly when weapons are detonated in the air, most of this "unburned" plutonium goes into the stratosphere, from which it is dispersed worldwide. The air from the Northern and Southern Hemispheres mixes very slowly, so most of the plutonium dispersed into the Northern Hemisphere remains in that hemisphere. Over a period of years, the plutonium descends into the troposphere and finally to the surface of the earth.

Virtually all the plutonium injected into the atmosphere through 1962 has now returned to the earth. The best estimate of the total global dispersion and fallout of ^{239}Pu-equivalent plutonium is 320,000 curies (Hardy 1974). We use the term ^{239}Pu-equivalent because this dispersed plutonium is a mixture of plutonium radionuclides. Unless a careful analysis is made for specific nuclides, the alpha activity from plutonium is all lumped together and estimated in curies. It can then be expressed as that amount of ^{239}Pu which would produce the number of curies of alpha activity found.

For most calculations, this procedure is satisfactory, since the alpha-particle energies of the various plutonium nuclides are closely similar. However, it would not be appropriate if we were endeavoring to consider effects 20,000 years from now, at which time the shorter-lived nuclides of plutonium would have decayed. In that case, we would need a specific analysis for each plutonium radionuclide present in the fallout.

As all the plutonium from the nuclear testing descended through the atmosphere, attached to a variety of particulates, it was available for inhalation by human beings, particularly in the Northern Hemisphere. This is the reason that virtually every human being on earth now has plutonium in his or her body.

We showed in chapter 9 that plutonium inhalation seriously increases lung-cancer risk. Here we will evaluate how many lung-cancer fatalities are currently being caused by inhaled plutonium fallout, and estimate how many cases are to be expected in the future.

Determining the Inhaled Dose

We have already developed the method for assessing the number of lung cancers produced per unit plutonium as the result of inhalation of insoluble dusts containing plutonium. What remains to be assessed here is the average quantity of plutonium inhaled by human beings from the fallout.

In an elegant treatment of the problem, Bennett (1974) provides the estimate that the cumulative intake through 1972 was approximately 42 picocuries (picocuries, not microcuries) per person (particles 0.4 micron in diameter).

Bennett points out that analysis of the tissue burdens of plutonium suggested that the plutonium-containing particulates in fallout probably behaved like plutonium dioxide, PuO_2. If we applied the terminology of the ICRP Task Group, plutonium fallout would consist of *Class Y* compounds (highly insoluble particles), which would be expected to clear from the lungs according to a half-time of 500 days.

The first step is conversion of picocuries to micrograms. Since the picocurie levels are expressed in ^{239}Pu equivalents, we can use the conversion, 1 picocurie represents 16.3 picograms of ^{239}Pu-equivalent. Since there is $1/1,000,000$ (or 10^{-6}) microgram per picogram, the quantity of plutonium inhaled per person can be calculated to be 6.85×10^{-4} micrograms per person.

Lung Cancer in U.S. Men from Plutonium Fallout

The males in the United States in the early 1960s receiving the fallout were of a spectrum of ages, ranging from infancy to advanced age. A refined estimate of the cancers caused by this plutonium would involve separate estimates for each age group, appropriately adjusted for the fraction of the population in each age group in the early 1960s. While this could be done, the author believes a reasonable approximation can be achieved by calculating the expected number of cancers as though the average male were 25 years old in the early 1960s.

At that time, a higher proportion of men smoked cigarettes than is the case at present. We shall use the approximation that 50% of males were cigarette smokers in the early 1960s; since children did not smoke, we are assuming that over 50% of male adults did. The total U.S. population at that time was approximately 2×10^8 people, roughly half men and half women. Therefore, in the 1960s there were about 10^8 total males, of which 5×10^7 were smokers and 5×10^7 were nonsmokers. Each of these two major groups inhaled (6.85×10^{-4} micrograms per person) $\times$ (5×10^7 persons) = 34,300 micrograms of plutonium.

For male smokers of cigarettes, the bronchogenic lung-cancer dose was estimated (in chapter 9) to be 0.225 person-micrograms. Therefore, the total number of bronchogenic lung-cancer doses received by male smokers was 34,300/0.225 = 152,400.

For male nonsmokers of cigarettes, the bronchogenic lung-cancer dose is 44.9 person-micrograms of ^{239}Plutonium. Therefore, the total number of doses received by male nonsmokers was 34,300/44.9 = 764.

Total bronchogenic lung-cancer doses to
males = 152,400 + 764 = 153,164

We must make one essential correction. The lung-cancer doses utilized here are based on spontaneous lung-cancer rates in the 1980 period. They are appropriate for assessing hazard of exposure in the 1980 period. However, there has been a large increase in the spontaneous lung-cancer rate since the early 1960s. American Cancer Society estimates for the early 1960s show a lung-cancer death rate 0.61 times that for 1975. A reasonable correction, therefore, is that the number of lung cancers produced by fallout will be 0.6 times the estimate above. (Radiation-induced cases are always taken to be proportional to spontaneous cases—see chapter 8.) Therefore, lung-cancer fatalities induced in the U.S. male population by the plutonium fallout = (0.6) × (153,164) = 92,000 (rounded off).

We have made the assumption here that the spontaneous rate *at the time of irradiation* is what counts. Lung cancer is unusual since it is the one cancer in the United States that has shown a steeply rising age-specific death rate over the past three decades. It is possible that we have underestimated lung-cancer deaths from plutonium fallout by using the lower spontaneous rate from the time when the plutonium exposure occurred, but we have no basis in evidence for raising the estimate because of a post-radiation rise in the spontaneous rate.

Lung Cancer in U.S. Women from Plutonium Fallout

As shown in tables 14 and 15, the bronchogenic lung-cancer dose in *person-rads* for 25-year-old males is 567 person-rads, and for 25-year-old females is 1,695 person-rads. All lung-cancer doses in person-*micrograms* for plutonium and other transuranics will have the same *relative* values for males versus females.

Therefore, the bronchogenic lung-cancer dose for 25-year-old women who are cigarette smokers is (0.225 person-micrograms) × (1,695/567) = 0.673 person-micrograms of ^{239}Plutonium.

The bronchogenic lung-cancer dose for 25-year-old women who are nonsmokers is (44.9 person-micrograms) × (1,695/567) = 134.2 person-micrograms of ^{239}Plutonium.

Using the above procedure (but with a different proportion of female smokers to nonsmokers) we can estimate the number of lung-cancer deaths for women from plutonium fallout = 12,460.

Summary for U.S. Men and Women

The total deaths due to plutonium-induced lung cancer in men and women are estimated to be 92,000 + 12,460 = *104,460 lung-cancer deaths.*

This value, however, takes into account only the plutonium breathed during its first descent through the atmosphere to earth. Any future resuspension of deposited plutonium, with subsequent inhalation of plutonium by human beings, would add to the total number of lung-cancer deaths.

Anticipated Worldwide Plutonium-Induced Lung-Cancer Deaths

The plutonium fallout from atmospheric weapons testing was worldwide in scope; however, the Northern Hemisphere received much more than the Southern Hemisphere. Bennett's calculation (1974) of 42 picocuries as the average inhalation of plutonium is based on data for New York. There is no reason to doubt that this is a very reasonable approximation of the inhaled plutonium everywhere in the Northern Hemisphere, on the average.

The other item of information needed to assess worldwide plutonium-fallout deaths is the spontaneous lung-cancer death rate in Northern Hemisphere countries besides the United States. Based on World Health Statistics, the spontaneous lung-cancer death rate, age-adjusted, for 1968–1969, and averaged over 33 countries of the Northern Hemisphere, is 33.3 per 100,000—compared with 44.0 per 100,000 in the United States for the same time period. Therefore, all calculated lung-cancer rates based on U.S. data must be reduced by a factor of 33.3/44.0 = 0.76, to be applicable to other Northern Hemisphere countries. The population of the Northern Hemisphere was approximately 10 times that of the United States. Therefore, the total number of lung-cancer deaths caused in the Northern Hemisphere by plutonium fallout is (104,460) × (10) × (0.76) = 794,000, in addition to the number in the United States, which is 104,460. The total, rounded off, is 900,000.

The population of the Southern Hemisphere will suffer approximately an additional 5% of this number, or 45,000 additional deaths, if the population was 25% of that of the Northern Hemisphere and the fallout was about 20% as great.

So overall, we are dealing with a worldwide lung-cancer death commitment in the neighborhood of 950,000 from plutonium, and this is without any consideration of additional deaths from possible inhalation of resuspended plutonium in the future.

When Will These 950,000 Worldwide Plutonium-Induced Deaths Occur? It is possible to estimate how many of these deaths are occurring now and how many will occur sometime in the future. The first step in making such an estimate is to choose an approximate time for the exposure. Actually the exposure occurred over several years. But a high fraction of the total plutonium inhaled was inhaled during 1962–1964. Since the intake for the years before that period exceeded the intake for the years after it, it is reasonable to take 1962 rather than 1963 as the "average" time of inhalation.

As an example, let us consider 25-year-old males irradiated with 1 rad to the lungs.

Using the approximation that everyone was irradiated at 25 years of age, the number of worldwide plutonium-fallout-induced lung-cancer deaths in each year beyond 1962 is estimated in table 20.

The reader is aware, of course, that many uncertainties necessarily entered into the estimate of 950,000 lung-cancer deaths from the plutonium fallout. Key parameters remain undetermined. However, the reader has available every approximation made in the absence of hard data, and he has also the method to enable him to recalculate the estimates when more information is available.

The author thinks the reader has ample reason, in the meantime, to reject misleading statements of the following type, this one from Bair, Richmond, and Wachholz (1974):

There has been no recorded instance of cancer in man resulting from the internal deposition of any plutonium isotope in the more than three decades that plutonium has been used. The excellent record has resulted from extremely effective control methods. (p. 25)

TABLE 20: THE TIME DISTRIBUTION OF THE PLUTONIUM-INDUCED LUNG-CANCER DEATHS FROM WORLDWIDE FALLOUT*

Calendar Year (exposure at 1962)	% of Ultimate Lung-Cancer Deaths which have occurred by stated year	Number of Plutonium-Induced Lung-Cancer Deaths which are estimated to have occurred by stated year
1965	0	0
1970	0	0
1975	0.0445%	423
1980	0.3945%	3,748
1985	1.8410%	17,490
1990	6.6593%	63,263
1995	18.6362%	177,044
2000	37.25 %	353,875
2005	59.61 %	566,295
2010	80.56 %	765,320
2015	93.69 %	890,055
2020	98.77 %	938,315
2025	99.92 %	949,240

*950,000 lung-cancer deaths in toto.

ONGOING STUDIES OF TWO SETS OF WORKERS EXPOSED TO PLUTONIUM

The proponents of nuclear energy have suggested that the concern over plutonium carcinogenicity is excessive. As evidence, they point to two studies of workers who were exposed to plutonium, but who have not yet shown any lung-cancer deaths. We must examine both of these negative studies very carefully to ascertain whether they do indeed indicate that plutonium carcinogenicity has been overestimated. The first such group is represented by 25 workers who received significant lung burdens of [239]Plutonium in the course of a fire in 1965 at the Rocky Flats, Colorado plutonium-handling facility. The second is represented by 26 Manhattan Project workers exposed in the mid-1940s to plutonium in unknown form at the Los Alamos Laboratory.

The Workers Exposed at Rocky Flats, Colorado

The data for the Rocky Flats workers are quite good. Measurements were made by *body counting* within a short period after the inhalation exposure during the fire.

If a radionuclide emits either an X-ray or gamma ray in its decay scheme, this radiation can be detected from outside the body of the person in whom the radionuclide is present. In this way, certain alpha-particle emitters can be detected, even though none of the alpha particles can themselves be detected from outside the body. The technique is known as *body counting*. Of course, body counting is not possible for any alpha-particle emitter that does not have accompanying emission of X-rays or gamma rays. Another technique for estimating body burden years after the exposure uses urinary plutonium excretion. This method yields very rough estimates.

We know from Mann and Kirchner (1967) that the exposure at Rocky Flats was to PuO_2 in particulate form. Class Y behavior (that for insoluble compounds) is expected; hence we use ICRP's $T_{1/2}$ of 500 days for clearance of deposited material. The data for individual exposures were provided by the Rocky Flats management and are presented in table 21. The mean value for deposition (body burden) in the 25 workers, expressed by Rocky Flats management as a time-weighted average over the 12 months following exposure, is 31.6 nanocuries, or 0.032 microcuries, of [239]Plutonium equivalent. It is most unfortunate that Rocky Flats was unable to provide any data concerning the smoking habits of these workers. The mean age of the workers at the time of exposure was 43.6 years.

Conversion of 0.032 microcuries to micrograms gives $(0.032) \times (16.3)$ = 0.52 micrograms as the average amount present in each worker's body at examination. A reasonable factor for correcting to inhaled dose, on the average, is 4, giving 2.08 micrograms as the average *inhaled* dose. For 25 workers, the total inhaled quantity of [239]Plutonium is 52 micrograms.

The next step is to ascertain the correct lung-cancer dose for males exposed at 43.6 years of age. The appropriate calculations and corrections yield a dose of 1.52 micrograms of [239]Pu (for smokers), and 302.9 micrograms (for nonsmokers).

Since information on the workers' smoking habits was not available, we will approximate that 50% of the workers smoked cigarettes and 50% did not. Using this distribution of smoking habits, we assign 26 micrograms as

TABLE 21: PLUTONIUM EXPOSURES FOR 25 EMPLOYEES IN THE
1965 ROCKY FLATS FIRE

"Following is a list of employees by age and their respective plutonium exposures. The amount in the lungs (chests) of the 25 employees is a time-weighted average over the 12 months following the exposure."

"We have no records of individual's smoking habits."

—*H. E. BOWMAN, General Manager, Dow Chemical Company, Rocky Flats Division, June 23, 1975*

Age	Plutonium (nCi)*		Age	Plutonium (nCi)
24	13		44	7
24	16		45	12
24	19		46	11
29	15		49	20
33	56		52	100
33	12		53	140
38	8		56	130
39	14		56	12
39	23		59	34
39	18		59	59
40	18		60	10
42	9		64	24
42	11			

*The nCi is the nanocurie. There are 10^3 nanocuries in one microcurie.

The author expresses his appreciation to Mr. Bowman and the Dow Chemical Company for prompt provision of all this information upon letter request.

the total inhaled by smokers and 26 micrograms as the total inhaled by nonsmokers.

The *lifetime* expectation of lung cancer caused by plutonium in the smokers is $26/1.52 = 17.1$ lung-cancer deaths. The lifetime expectation of lung cancer in the nonsmokers is $26/302.9 = 0.086$. The latter number means there is about 1 chance in 11 that *any* plutonium-induced lung cancers would occur in the whole group of nonsmokers. However, the former number, 17 lung cancers, expected in 12 or 13 supposed smokers, is a very serious one. A careful follow-up should definitely be able to find such an excess of lung cancers.

But what is exceptionally interesting is that at the time (1975) that the nuclear community was citing this group of workers as not having developed lung cancers from plutonium exposure, the *total elapsed time* since exposure was 9 years. One thing we have emphasized in this book is that there is no use looking for radiation-induced cancers *before* they are expected to occur.

From everything developed in this book (see especially chapters 4 and 5), 9 years post-irradiation is still too early for radiation-induced cancers to begin showing up, and even when they do begin, the rate of their appearance is very low compared to what it will be later. Thus, if one chooses an observation time too early in the latent period for most exposed persons, one may observe zero excess cancer even though the ultimate cancer burden may be devastating.

At the present time the case of the Rocky Flats workers cannot help us decide whether the bronchogenic lung-cancer dose estimates presented here are too high, correct, or too low.

Further follow-up of these 25 workers is very important: it should extend over their full life-spans. It is hard to believe that the Department of Energy and the Rocky Flats management cannot ascertain the cigarette-smoking history of these workers. Often the technique used in industry to prevent acquisition of such information is to resort to the claim that it is an invasion of the privacy of the workers even to *ask* if they smoked cigarettes.

This is not the only group of workers that has received body burdens of plutonium, although it is a very important group. The Department of Energy claims that an effort is currently being made to ascertain the health status of additional workers exposed to plutonium. The reader should remember that these studies are under the auspices of a government department with a tremendous vested interest in finding that plutonium has a low toxicity.

But it is also important to give credit where credit is due. The Department of Energy sponsors the work of Dr. Roger McClellan and his associates at the Lovelace Foundation. The work of Dr. McClellan and associates on the development of plutonium-induced lung cancers in the beagle dog is outstanding work. Overall, the work of this group on plutonium is excellent.

The Manhattan Project Workers

Hempelmann and co-workers (1973) reported on the 26 Manhattan Project workers who were apparently exposed in the mid-1940s at the Los Alamos Laboratory. The extent of plutonium inhalation by these workers is poorly known, simply because neither inhalation data nor any early body counts are available.

The main problem in the study of the Manhattan Project workers is estimating *initial* lung deposition from a plutonium body burden estimated from 10 to 27 years after the exposure. The amount of plutonium remaining in the workers is sufficiently small to press the efficacy of body counting to its limits. These difficulties alone would make it foolhardy to rest conclusions about plutonium carcinogenicity on these cases. Moreover, whether these workers were exposed to *any particulates* containing plutonium is not at all certain. The circumstances were such that the exposure may have been to *dissolved* plutonium in aerosol droplets. Nevertheless, these cases do deserve analysis, since they represent part of the accumulating evidence concerning plutonium and health.

Gofman (1975a, 1976a) criticized the conclusion that the absence of lung cancers in this group in any way suggests a lesser lung carcinogenicity for plutonium than outlined in chapter 9. We quote the 1976 statement:

I have considered the doses to these workers in detail, and based upon that analysis, the estimate is that 0.2 of a lung cancer should have occurred by now for this exposure. The occurrence of zero cancers by this time is in accord with this estimate and in no way mitigates the lung carcinogenicity of plutonium. (pp. 285–6)

At that time, Gofman pointed out two problems: (1) that the plutonium body burden had been overestimated by Hempelmann and co-workers; and (2) that the smoking history was not provided for these workers. As the reader is aware, the estimate of the carcinogenicity of plutonium for non-smokers is grossly lower than for smokers, so a smoking history is essential.

Recently, Voelz, Hempelmann and co-workers (1979) published the results of an extension of the follow-up on the Manhattan Project workers. The body burdens are lowered in that paper to a value between their former value and the one suggested by Gofman, and a detailed smoking history is provided. So we can now assess lung carcinogenicity in this group.

We can summarize the group exposures as follows:

10 nonsmokers cumulative burden (1977) = 0.508 person-microcuries
5 smokers cumulative burden (1977) = 0.359 person-microcuries
8 quitters cumulative burden (1977) = 0.397 person-microcuries
2 became smokers cumulative burden (1977) = 0.220 person-microcuries
1 history unknown cumulative burden (1959) = 0.023 person-microcuries

We shall combine the quitters and the two subjects who became smokers into a single category of 10 persons with a total burden of $(0.397 + 0.220)/2 = 0.309$ person-microcuries.

There is still considerable reason to retain some skepticism about how well the body burden is estimated from the urinary plutonium assays. Voelz and co-workers consider that the data are improving in this regard. We shall, for purposes of this analysis, accept the body-burden estimates presented by Voelz and co-workers. The next question is the translation of current body burdens into initial lung inhalation of plutonium. After correcting for various factors, we obtain the following summary of inhaled doses of plutonium for each group:

10 nonsmokers $(6.67 \times (0.635) = 4.24$ microcuries inhaled
5 smokers $(6.67) \times (0.449) = 2.99$ microcuries inhaled
10 quitters plus new smokers $(6.67) \times (0.386) = 2.57$ microcuries inhaled
1 history unknown $(6.67) \times (0.029) = 0.19$ microcuries inhaled

Estimation of the Appropriate Lung-Cancer Dose for 1945 Exposure: A few additional corrections enter into our final calculation of the Manhattan Project workers' lung-cancer doses. The corrections are for the solubility characteristics of the inhaled plutonium and for the spontaneous lung-cancer death rates in 1945.

For cigarette smokers 25 years of age (very close to the age of the Manhattan Project workers at exposure), the corrected bronchogenic lung-cancer dose is 5.38 person-micrograms of [239]Plutonium.

For 25-year-old nonsmokers, the corrected bronchogenic lung-cancer dose is 1,074.5 person-micrograms.

With these values in hand, we are in a position to estimate the *lifetime* expectation of lung cancer for the various described categories of Manhattan Project workers. From there we shall go on to estimate how many lung cancers should have been expected during the 32-year follow-up reported on by Voelz and co-workers.

Lifetime Expectation of Lung Cancer in the Manhattan Project Workers: Our final calculations reveal a lifetime estimation of lung cancer in the nonsmoking group of 0.064 of a case of lung cancer induced by plutonium. Therefore, the odds are overwhelming that we would *not* see a single radiation-induced lung-cancer death from plutonium in the nonsmokers in their whole lifetime, nor, certainly, in the 32-year follow-up period. Thus, we can say that the absence of lung cancer in the nonsmokers is precisely as would be expected from the carcinogenicity estimates in this book. The claim that the toxicity of insoluble plutonium is exaggerated is therefore in no way justified by the nonoccurrence of lung cancer in this group.

Among the cigarette smokers, the lifetime expectation of lung cancer is 9.05 lung cancers. These 5 persons have an average expectancy of more than 1 lung cancer per person, though of course one can only die once of lung cancer. This estimate is the *lifetime* expectancy, not the expected number during the 32-year follow-up.

For the combined group of quitters and new smokers, we obtain 7.79 lung cancers as a *lifetime* expectation. It is hard to know whether we are overestimating the risk for these 10 men or not.

Lung-Cancer Cases Expected in the 32-Year Follow-up: The question we must ask, now that we have a 32-year follow-up of these workers, is, what fraction of the lifetime plutonium-induced cancers should we have expected within the 32-year period, for exposures at approximately 25 years of age? Not only is this an answerable question, but it is the kind of estimate one must commonly make in problems of radiation exposure. In cases of potential radiation injury, it is of the utmost importance to avoid "looking" for cases before they are truly expected to occur.

We have calculated that, of the group of 5 smokers, 1.42 cases of lung cancer should be expected within the 32-year follow-up period. At this point they would be 57 years old (age 25 at irradiation + 32). In addition, such smokers each have an elevated *spontaneous* lifetime risk of lung cancer of 12%, or 0.12, which means that the lifetime risk for the group of 5 is 0.6. By age 57, however, only 20% of their lifetime spontaneous risk is manifest, which means that only 0.12 case of spontaneous lung cancer would be expected by 1977 in this group of 5 smokers. The combined spontaneous and plutonium-induced lung cancers expected are therefore 1.42 + 0.12 = 1.54 cases. Zero lung cancers were observed as of 1977. With 1.54 cases expected, observing zero cases is a reasonable probability (p = 0.21).

A similar calculation for the 10 quitters and new smokers is made, which yields 1.22 expected radiation-induced lung cancers during the 32 years of follow-up. The members of this group also have the risk of spontaneous lung cancer; we shall assign them half the risk of habitual smokers. Since this group is twice the size of the true-smokers group (10 versus 5), the number of spontaneous lung cancers expected by 1977 is the same: 0.12 case. The total expectation is therefore $1.22 + 0.12 = 1.34$ lung cancers. None were observed. The probability of observing zero cases with 1.34 cases expected is $p = 0.26$. It must be acknowledged that the probability of observing zero cases for *both* the smokers and the quitters is lower than the probabilities calculated above.

Interpretation of the Result for the Manhattan Project Workers: For the observed *absence* of lung cancer in the 26 Manhattan Project workers as of 1977, two types of interpretations can be made. One is that the dose was overestimated, and the other is that this author has overestimated the carcinogenicity of inhaled, insoluble plutonium particulates (chapter 9). Let us consider first the issue of dose.

If these workers truly were exposed to highly soluble plutonium delivered in aerosol form, as the Voelz et al. description so strongly suggests, then the data on the Manhattan Project workers simply would never be *relevant* as a reality-check for the estimated toxicity of either Class W or Class Y plutonium in the lungs. The formula we used in calculating exposure, which was heavily weighted toward the insoluble Class W compounds and posited an average half-time of 95 days for clearance from the lung, would have enormously overstated the dose. The average clearance half-time for *dissolved plutonium ions* (which is highly dependent on what other ions were present) might be a few days, or even much less. The average half-time simply cannot be known for the Manhattan Project workers' exposure.

In view of the high probability that our formula for the proportions of soluble and insoluble compounds may seriously overestimate the dose and therefore the number of radiation-induced lung cancers expected, to draw any conclusions from the absence of observed lung cancers in this group would be scientifically foolish.

On the other hand, this author has no desire to pretend that his estimated lung-cancer doses for inhaled insoluble plutonium particulates are firm. He is eager for reality-checks that will help close in on the truth. The important thing, in his opinion, is not to move *away* from the truth by making unexamined and possibly false assumptions about the lung dose received by the 26 Manhattan Project workers. Unless the uncertainty about their real lung dose can be substantially reduced, not much can be determined even from lifetime follow-up of these workers. The author hopes that follow-ups of other workers, whose lung dose and smoking histories can be determined, will yield data that are scientifically more useful. No one should be happy about currently having only a calculational basis for assessing plutonium's lung-cancer toxicity in humans.

SECTION 2: PLUTONIUM-INDUCED LUNG CANCERS IN A PLUTONIUM-ENERGY ECONOMY

In chapter 11, the author will calculate how well fission products from the nuclear fuel cycle must be contained if we wish to avoid a major cancer and leukemia epidemic in a full-scale nuclear-power economy. Here we take up the issue of *plutonium* containment or noncontainment, and its lung-cancer consequences, in a fully developed *plutonium-energy economy*, which is still the dream of the community that promotes nuclear energy. Plutonium is receiving separate attention because it is *not* a fission product; it is not one of the fragments from a split atom.

The plutonium dispersal from weapons testing, and its subsequent deposition in humans, make it possible to address certain implications of a future plutonium economy with some realistic numbers. *Of a given weight of plutonium fallout, we know how much is inhaled by humans (section 1).*

We cannot know the magnitude of the plutonium dispersed into the atmosphere and the rest of the environment from a future nuclear fuel cycle. We do know that the handling of plutonium has been often sloppy in the past. Instead of guessing the magnitude of future plutonium releases, we can assess the consequences of various degrees of containment of the plutonium handled. We think this approach is without bias, and is in the best, rational tradition of asking, when making decisions, what would be the consequences if . . ? Incidentally, it was as the result of making the kinds of calculations which will be presented in this and in the next chapter that the author became "antinuclear" in 1969.

In contrast to this approach, the nuclear promoters much prefer to predict virtually perfect control of the plutonium they will have to handle, in an industry they have never before operated, namely, a commercial fast-breeder and fuel-reprocessing industry. From the *assumption* of perfect control, of course, it follows that there will be no releases and therefore no consequences to discuss! The public, however, may wish to think over that assumption, examine the performance record of the existing nuclear industry, and ponder the possibility that industrial containment may not be perfect.

CONTAINMENT: SOME MEASURING AND MONITORING PROBLEMS

It is certainly true that, if plutonium were never released to the atmosphere in particles small enough to get into the bronchi or the alveolar regions of the lung, there would never be any plutonium-induced lung cancers. The promoters of a plutonium economy scoff at the prospect that a plutonium-based nuclear-energy cycle would ever release much plutonium, particularly in the hazardous form of small particles of plutonium dioxide or other comparably insoluble plutonium particulates.

They seem to forget, or overlook, the fact that in the preparation of fuel rods for the nuclear cycle, they have already handled plutonium oxide in the form of 1-micron particles, either alone or admixed with uranium oxide. It would be hard to find a more dangerous form of plutonium to handle, with respect to lung cancer.

They seem to forget, as they suggest that plutonium is "too heavy" to become airborne, that between ¼ and ½ pound of plutonium (100–200 grams) leaked out of some barrels containing plutonium millings in solvents, reached the ground, and finally ended up in small particles carried aloft by winds and transported for tens of miles, to be redeposited to the east of the Rocky Flats plant in Colorado.

These promoters seem to overlook the fact that the Kerr-McGee Company could not account (at the Karen Silkwood trial) for some 40 pounds of plutonium at its Cimarron facility, where fuel rods for reactors were being prepared.

They seem to forget, as they promise perfect plutonium containment, that they have never been able to do better than to account for 98 to 99% of the plutonium already handled in military and civilian programs. If they do not even know whether they have released 1% of the plutonium they have handled, one wonders how they can claim they will not release 0.00001% of the plutonium they will handle in the future.

Assuredly they have an accounting problem. It is true that it is difficult to tell where all 100 grams out of an initial 100 grams are. It is true that 1 gram lost may not be lost into the uncontrolled environment; it may be kicking around in the pipes somewhere, as is often claimed.

But there is another side to this truth—which nuclear promoters seldom have the honesty to discuss publicly—namely that, since the method of accounting for the plutonium is so very poor, we simply do not have the foggiest notion of whether 1 gram out of every 100 grams is or is not lost into the environment in some way or other. The nuclear industry is simply unable to speak to the issue of 99.9% containment, much less 99.9999% or better.

Why, then, do serious engineers assure us of an ability to contain plutonium to 1 part in 1 million, or 1 part in 10 million? An example from real experience may shed light on this problem.

At Rocky Flats, the engineers place monitors in certain exhaust stacks. These monitors were intended to intercept any plutonium released from the facility, even during a fire. So, with ultimate confidence in these monitors, it is not surprising that the engineers at that facility stated, following a major fire in 1969, that less than 1 milligram of plutonium could have come out of the Rocky Flats facility. Yet Dr. Edward Martell (1970) found that between ¼ and ½ pound of plutonium of Rocky Flats origin had escaped to the surrounding environment, as far away as 10 miles and more.

The engineers were dumbfounded when Dr. Martell's work was confirmed by Atomic Energy Commission scientists. How could their monitors have misled them? And they found the answer: plutonium, stored at the plant in thousands of leaking barrels, right out in the open, had leaked into the ground. The wind had picked up the plutonium and carried it for miles.

It is ever thus. The leaks do not know where the engineers have placed their monitors, and so they go ahead and leak, and the monitors are never the wiser.

It is the author's considered opinion—as a chemist with long experience in handling radioactive materials, and observing their handling, day in, day out, with burps, spills, leaks, puffs, human error, and machine error—that it is absurd to believe plutonium containment will be better than 99.9%, better than 99.99%, better than 99.999%, better than 99.9999%. Because no committees, commissions, or expert bodies can know what degree of plutonium containment will actually be achieved, every person who considers the question of a plutonium economy must decide for himself (herself) what is likely to be achieved. The author cannot, and would not, want to make this decision for the reader. *There is one major contribution this book can make to the reader's deliberations—that is to calculate the health consequences of various degrees of plutonium containment.*

How Will the Plutonium Releases from a Plutonium-Energy Economy Compare in Nature to Those from Weapons Testing?

We know from direct evidence (see section 1) that weapons testing in the atmosphere most certainly did put plutonium into the atmosphere in a very treacherous form—particles with a solubility comparable to that of plutonium oxide, and of approximately 0.4 microns in diameter.

There is no way to know whether the particles in nuclear-power releases will be identical in nature with those from weapons testing. The particles may be more hazardous, equally hazardous, or less hazardous. In the absence of information, and with no desire to exaggerate, we shall assume the particles to be equally hazardous, in terms of access to the lungs.

The British, the French, and the Japanese have already taken the fateful step of reprocessing spent nuclear-fuel rods to recover plutonium and uranium for reincorporation into new fuel rods. The United States has, at this time, suspended commercial fuel reprocessing, but goes ahead toward a breeder economy based on plutonium or related fuels.

In reprocessing used fuel rods and fabricating new ones, we introduce the largest hazard involved in the handling of plutonium. The plutonium must finally be converted to a powder of plutonium dioxide, either pure or mixed with uranium oxide. Such powder, in the form of particles in the general size range of 1 micron, is exceedingly treacherous because, upon dispersion in the air, the particles can readily gain access to bronchial and pulmonary structures.

A fully developed nuclear-energy economy in the United States would mean 1,000 or more large nuclear plants of the breeder variety, fueled mainly by plutonium. An average breeder reactor would have about 3 tonnes (3,000 kilograms) of plutonium in it, and about one-third of this would have to be reprocessed and refabricated into new fuel rods, annually. Therefore, for 1,000 such plants, 1,000 tonnes, or 1,000,000 kilograms, of plutonium would be handled annually through reprocessing and fuel-fabrication steps.

Bennett's data (1974) for New York City show that the cumulative deposition of plutonium from weapons testing through 1972 was 2.65 millicuries per kilometer^2 in that area. If we assume that the *average* deposition for the United States was not very different from that for New York, then for the coterminous 48 states of the United States, with an area of 7.6 $\times$ 10^6 km^2, the total deposition of plutonium was (7.6 $\times$ 10^6) $\times$ (2.65) = 2.01 $\times$ 10^7 millicuries of ^{239}Pu equivalent. The conversion factor from millicuries to milligrams is 16.3. Therefore,

$$\text{Total deposition in coterminous U.S.} = 2.01 \times 10^7 \times 16.3$$
$$= 3.28 \times 10^8 \text{ milligrams}$$
$$= 328 \text{ kilograms deposited}$$
$$\text{through 1972.}$$

We estimated (section 1) that such deposition would produce 104,460 fatal lung cancers. Therefore, 1 kilogram ^{239}Pu distributed in the United States would produce 104,460/328 = 318 lung cancers. This estimate was based on a population of 200 million persons. In the future we can reasonably expect the population to be 250 million. Many of the calculations in this book are made for an equilibrium population of 250 million, and we shall use that estimate here. If the U.S. population increases, the same deposition of plutonium will increase the number of lung cancers in proportion to the population increase. Our estimate is (250/200) $\times$ 318 = 398 lung cancers produced for one kilogram ^{239}Pu distributed in the United States.

Having this value as a reference point for distribution of plutonium in this country, we can ask what would be the consequences of releasing upon the U.S. land area various fractions of the breeder plutonium that would be handled here.

ESTIMATED LUNG-CANCER CONSEQUENCES OF A PLUTONIUM ECONOMY

The 398 lung cancers produced by every 1 kilogram ^{239}Pu distributed in the United States is based on the spontaneous lung-cancer rates prevailing in 1962. But those spontaneous rates were 0.6 of the 1980 rates. Therefore, for future considerations, we must correct the estimate to (398) $\times$ (1.0/0.6) = *663 lung cancers produced per kilogram ^{239}Pu distributed in the United States.*

In table 22 are presented the estimates of lung-cancer fatalities per year from various degrees of containment of the 1,000,000 kilograms of plutonium that would be handled in a full plutonium energy economy.

It is self-evident that plutonium released from various parts of the nuclear fuel cycle would not be as evenly distributed in the United States as was the fallout from weapons testing. However, the population is also not uniformly distributed, so it would be hard to say whether there would be a greater or lesser average dose per person for fuel-cycle plutonium fallout than for weapons-testing fallout. We shall assume the doses to be the same, for the same amount of plutonium distributed per kilometer^2.

The estimates of table 22 do *not* in any way require that the dispersal of plutonium be uniform throughout the United States. The reader must always remember that 1 microgram of plutonium inhaled by 100 persons will give the same number of lung cancers as 0.1 microgram inhaled by 1,000 persons.

Entry into a plutonium-based energy economy means subjecting the citizens of this society to a gigantic game of roulette. No one can know in advance what degree of containment is going to be achieved. If the ever-optimistic engineers are correct in their vision of perfection, and the plutonium containment is good to one part in one billion, virtually no lung cancer will result. However, if the reality of the future is like the reality of the past, there will be a major lung-cancer epidemic in a plutonium-based energy economy.

TABLE 22: LUNG-CANCER DEATHS PRODUCED ANNUALLY
BY VARIOUS DEGREES OF ^{239}PLUTONIUM CONTAINMENT AND
DISPERSION*

(for equilibrium population of 250 million persons: 663 lung-cancer deaths per kilogram Pu dispersed)

% Containment	^{239}Plutonium Dispersed (in kilograms)	Lung-Cancer Deaths per Year
99%	10,000	6,630,000
99.9%	1,000	663,000
99.99%	100	66,300
99.999%	10	6,630
99.9999%	1	663
99.99999%	0.1	66

*1,000,000 kilograms of Pu handled per year.

Since all these calculations are for ^{239}Plutonium handled in quantities of 1,000,000 kilograms per year, the number of lung-cancer deaths would be increased by 5.4-fold for each entry if the admixture of other radionuclides of plutonium increased the alpha-particle activity by a factor of 5.4, which is close to the actual case for light-water reactor-Pu. In a breeder economy, a factor of 5.4 is probably too low. See final section of this chapter.

A containment of 99.999% means that one part in 100,000 of the plutonium handled is dispersed to the environment in a form as readily inhaled as weapons-fallout plutonium. This table does not speculate on the chance that such containment will be achieved. It reports the consequences of various containments, defined in a specific manner.

Because future smoking habits of men and women cannot be predicted, the author has made no adjustment to the assumption that 50% of American males smoke, and 20% of American females smoke.

If Plutonium Is Really So Toxic, Why Aren't We All Dead?

The author has been asked the question, if plutonium is really so toxic, why aren't we all dead?, at some 25 or 35 meetings at which he has spoken. It is a good question, and has a straightforward answer. Once one has thought the question and answer through, one realizes a great deal about the tricks that can easily confuse people who have not gone through the logic and exercises in this book.

We have stated that 328 kilograms of ^{239}Plutonium-equivalent were released upon the coterminous United States through 1972 as a result of fallout from atmospheric weapons testing. And we presented bronchogenic lung-cancer doses for inhalation of plutonium in 1962: 0.375 micrograms for male smokers, and 74.8 micrograms for male nonsmokers. Let us consider the smokers first. If 328 kilograms were released, and it takes only *0.375 micrograms* to cause a fatal cancer, then there must be enough plutonium distributed to cause $328 \times 10^3 \times 10^6/0.375 = 8.75 \times 10^{11}$ lung cancers. This is 875 billion lung cancers!

The reason all the smokers did not die is, of course, evident: they simply did not inhale very much of the plutonium that came through the atmosphere and was deposited on the ground. Very fortunately, most of the plutonium ended up on the ground and not in our lungs. Otherwise, we would have suffered consequences far graver. Let us go through the arithmetic.

From Bennett's datum (1974) of 42 picocuries inhaled per person, we calculated that each person inhaled 6.85×10^{-4} micrograms of ^{239}Pu. So, 200,000,000 people inhaled 1.37×10^5 micrograms, or 0.137 grams of ^{239}Plutonium, out of 328,000 grams dispersed in the United States. One part of 2,394,000 parts actually entered human lungs; the bulk of it fell to the ground without being inhaled.

That is precisely why we are still alive, in spite of all the plutonium dumped on us. And that is why, while the toxicity of plutonium is very severe indeed, we have not all been killed by it.

These calculations address only the lung-cancer consequences of the plutonium in its descent through the atmosphere to the earth. Very little is known of the long-term fate of the plutonium that is on the ground. For example, there is a serious question about the possible interaction of plutonium with organic compounds in soil, which may make the plutonium available to human beings via the food chain. To the extent that such plutonium becomes available, there will be an additional burden of cancers in the future. And there is also the problem of resuspension of plutonium dioxide from the earth, with subsequent inhalation, which can add to the lung-cancer toll in the future.

CONTAINMENT REQUIREMENTS AS AFFECTED BY
PLUTONIUM OTHER THAN ^{239}PU AND BY CURIUM AND
AMERICIUM

The correspondence between various degrees of containment and various rates of human lung cancer is based on pure ^{239}Pu in table 22. As pointed out in the notes to table 22, all lung-cancer calculations would be immediately increased by a *factor of 5.4* if the admixture of other radionuclides of plutonium was just as it is in spent light-water-reactor fuel.

But the situation may be considerably worse in a fast-breeder reactor based on ^{239}Plutonium. Because of the high speed of neutrons in such a breeder, the reaction $^{239}_{94}$Pu (n, 2n) $^{238}_{94}$Pu, is more productive than in a light-water reactor, which extensively moderates the speed of neutrons. The production of ^{238}Pu is especially distressing in this regard, since its 92-year half-life means that its specific activity (alpha-particle emission per unit weight) will be very high. Therefore, it is quite likely that the requirements for containment of plutonium in a fast-breeder economy will be even more severe than would be calculated based on the composition of the plutonium nuclides in a light-water reactor.

The radionuclides of americium and curium must be carefully contained as well. The curium nuclides, ^{242}Cm and ^{244}Cm, represent alpha activities, at 150 days of cooling of light-water-reactor fuel (see table 19), some six times greater than the alpha activities of the plutonium nuclides combined. To be sure, ^{242}Curium, decaying according to a half-life of 162 days, becomes less of a problem in a few years, but its alpha activity is still in the neighborhood of the combined plutonium activities even after a year. ^{244}Curium remains as intense an alpha-particle emitter as about three-fourths of the combined plutonium nuclides for a very long period.

^{241}Plutonium must not be neglected either, for it is a potent producer of ^{241}Americium, and as we calculated in chapter 9, the ultimate ^{241}Americium alpha activity just from ^{241}Plutonium decay is on the order of the alpha activity of the combined plutonium nuclides.

All these considerations suggest that containment may really have to be as much as one order of magnitude (10-fold) better than shown in table 22 to keep lung-cancer production at a specific level. If the production by fast neutrons of ^{238}Pu is serious enough, containment requirements may have to be even more stringent.

"Coping" with Plutonium: LICAM-C Compounds

It is not surprising that people are eager to hear of some solution which will make the plutonium problem less ominous. Just recently there has been a great deal of newspaper and media comment on a discovery by Drs. Kenneth Raymond and Frederick Weitl of the Lawrence Berkeley Laboratory of a chemical compound that binds plutonium ions tightly.

Certain of the chemicals that bind ions are known as *chelating compounds* (*chelate* is from the Greek for "crab's claw"). Weitl and Raymond (1980) synthesized an organic chemical known as LICAM-C (known chemically as *linear catechoylamide carboxylate*), which appears, according to a news announcement from the laboratory (September 11, 1980), to bind plutonium relatively specifically. The researchers have some evidence that injections of the compound into mice result in the binding of any plutonium in the mouse tissues, with subsequent urinary-tract excretion of the plutonium. The general approach of using chelating chemicals to treat accidental wounds containing plutonium is not new. What is new is the claim that, so much more *specific for plutonium* is LICAM-C, that it reduces the danger of chelating some of the body's normal and desirable trace metal elements.

Unfortunately, the media accounts would suggest that this discovery "solves the plutonium problem." This is a cruel bit of nonsense. The author thinks that the new compound may have a very limited usefulness: in the event of an accident in which soluble forms of plutonium gain access to the body, particularly through wounds. The truly serious plutonium problems are those arising from the inhalation of insoluble plutonium compounds (such as plutonium dioxide) into the lungs. It is extremely doubtful that LICAM-C would be of any use in clearing such *insoluble* plutonium compounds from the lung tissues. Hence the "plutonium problem" remains unsolved.

Another claim has been made for LICAM-C in some of the press accounts, namely, that it may solve the radioactive-waste problem. *One* of the concerns about radioactive waste is that it may contain plutonium compounds. It is suggested that LICAM-C could be used to extract this plutonium. This is ludicrous as a "solution." What one would be doing is dividing the waste into two piles, one containing no plutonium, and the other containing plutonium chemically combined with LICAM-C. How converting the waste into two piles instead of one solves anything escapes this author. Indeed, the plutonium in the pile with the LICAM-C might be in a form more readily accessible to the biosphere and therefore more dangerous than it was originally. The LICAM-C work is interesting, but it hardly suggests the solutions which have been claimed for it in the popular reports.

CHAPTER 11

LIKELY RADIATION DOSES AND THEIR EFFECTS IN A NUCLEAR-POWER ECONOMY

PERHAPS NO SUBJECT has caused more confusion among members of both the public at large and the scientific community than the subject of radiation doses delivered by the nuclear-power industry. It must be emphasized that what we will deal with here are the likely doses of radiation that will be received even if no major accidents occur.

It will be shown in this chapter that estimation of these doses is a very complex matter, that industry and government estimates are hardly worth the paper they are written on, and that the public can take a common-sense approach that will produce more worthwhile estimates than those offered by most scientific committees and commissions.

THE DOSES PROMISED BY THE NUCLEAR INDUSTRY

It should come as no surprise that the doses predicted and projected by the nuclear industry and by governmental promoters of the nuclear industry may be seriously questionable. One does not promote a product by predicting that it is likely to cause serious epidemics of leukemia, cancer, and genetic diseases.

First we must consider the size of any installed nuclear-power industry, for doses and effects are intimately tied to size. As of 1980, in the United States, the installed capacity of nuclear electric-power production was approximately 50 gigawatts, which is the *equivalent* of 50 large plants, each with an electrical capacity of 1,000 megawatts (1 gigawatt = 1,000 megawatts). While the most ambitious sights of the nuclear industry have been somewhat lowered since the Three Mile Island accident, there is no doubt that serious nuclear planners are still looking forward to an operating capacity of 1,000 gigawatts, in the form of roughly 1,000 plants, most of which plants would have some type of breeder reactor.

One hears, and sees in print, a variety of estimates both of the dose of radiation currently being delivered in the United States from the installed nuclear-electricity industry (approximately 50 gigawatts installed capacity from about 72 total plants), and of the radiation dose that would be received if we had an installed capacity of 1,000 plants, each of 1,000 megawatts electrical output. A common number bandied about is less than 0.003 millirems per person per year, on the average, from existing plants and all parts of the nuclear fuel cycle combined (BEIR-I 1972, p. 19). It is also promised that when the full number of 1,000 nuclear plants are operating, the average dose per person per year will be no more than 0.4 millirems (McCormack 1975). And more loosely, the average dose suggested by others is 0.1 millirems per year.

The author suggests that, if there were any chance that these estimates of radiation dose were correct or too low by a factor of 10, there would hardly be much reason for public concern about the radiation effects of nuclear power, aside from major accidents. But there are, unfortunately, very good reasons for doubting that these estimates bear any relationship to present or future reality.

If these predictions of dose did bear *some* relationship to reality, we would have to wonder about some glaring inconsistencies in the behavior of governmental and industrial nuclear-promotional agencies and individuals. For example, for an industry endeavoring to repair a totally shattered public credibility, there could be no better avenue of *objective* reassurance than a demonstration that it really believes what it says about likely future radiation doses in a nuclear-power economy, namely, that the average radiation dose to the public will not exceed 0.1 millirems per year, even with 1,000 nuclear plants in operation.

That reassurance would be forthcoming if the electric utility industry would request that the federal standards for permitted radiation doses to the public (all stated in equivalent whole-body dose) somehow be brought into line with the promoters' own dose predictions. If the utility industry really believes it will operate in a manner such that the public will not receive more than 0.1 millirems per year, *on the average,* the industry might demand that the permissible standard be set at 1 millirem, on the average. This standard should provide an enormous "cushion," since it would be ten times higher than the dose predicted by many industry people.

The behavior of the industry and its governmental sponsors is, and has been, quite different from that just proposed. For the past 10 years, they have fought with vigor and determination every effort to reduce the permissible public exposure. Through December 1979, the applicable standard (originally set by the Federal Radiation Council over a decade ago) was an average of 170 millirems per year per person from various "peaceful" atomic uses. This 170 millirems is over and above radiation received from natural and medical sources.

If the doses from the nuclear-power industry are not going to exceed 0.1 millirem per year *ever,* even with a 20-fold increase in the size of the industry, then why, it repeatedly has been asked, do we need a permissible dose some 1,700 times higher? This is obviously not a moderate cushion, but a mountain of cushions. Certainly the persistence with which the nuclear industry has fought to maintain the high permissible dose is hardly a prescription for generating confidence on the part of the public.

A classic exchange that occurred in the halls of Congress in 1970 bears directly on this issue. Congressman Craig Hosmer (of the then-extant Joint Committee on Atomic Energy) asked then-AEC Commissioner Theos Thompson this question: "I am not talking about an average. I am talking about an average plus a reasonable cushion and asking if size 99 to 100 is a reasonable cushion or wouldn't size 25, for example, be a reasonable cushion?" To which Commissioner Thompson replied: "Mr. Hosmer, we don't have at the moment any way to set a reasonable cushion. There is not that sort of experience. So we should not move and make that cushion smaller until such experience exists" (p. 203). *At the very moment* that Commissioner Thompson was making his forthright admission (which can be found in Hosmer 1970), the nuclear industry and its scientific supporters were loudly proclaiming the ability of the industry to keep the U.S. population dose below 0.1 millirems per year, a dose 1,700 times lower than that which the commissioner was stating to be essential as a federal standard because the industry simply did not know what it could really do, in terms of actual performance.

CONSEQUENCES OF VARIOUS DOSES

People are indeed interested in and have the right to know what the probable health price of nuclear power is going to be. From the methods developed in several prior chapters of this book, we can readily estimate the *cancer fatality price* if we know the dose to the public. Let us recall the simple steps in such an estimation.

1. If we know the average dose of radiation received per person, and we know the population size, we can calculate the aggregate population dose per year in person-rems (or person-rads).

2. We have provided (chapter 6) the whole-body cancer dose, which applies as an average value for an equilibrium population of 250,000,000 persons.

3. We then simply divide aggregate population dose in person-rads by whole-body cancer dose, and get the estimate of fatal cancers per year at the specified dose level.

It will be instructive to go through this exercise for several of the numbers we have been discussing:

a. 0.003 millirems per person per year—a common claim of the existing nuclear-power industry.

b. 0.1 millirems per person per year—a common claim for the 20-fold larger industry projected.

c. 170 millirems per person per year—the standard in force for over a decade. On December 1, 1979, a new, lower EPA standard replaced it, despite vigorous resistance from the nuclear industry.

d. 25 millirems per person per year—the new, halfhearted EPA standard that went into force on December 1, 1979. The author calls this standard halfhearted because it applies to nuclear power under "normal, planned operations." A violation of this standard for doses delivered in an "unplanned" manner will be granted a variance "to insure orderly flow of electricity." In effect, the new EPA standard is a wishy-washy permit to deliver just about *any* dose of radiation to the public.

e. 1,000 millirems per person per year—a dose level which, as we shall see in later discussions in this chapter, is not a remote possibility given a fully developed nuclear industry with 1,000 plants in operation (see table 24). A good case can be made for looking at even higher exposure levels. Since this one is a round number, the reader can quickly make the estimates for higher exposure levels.

All the estimates are presented in table 23.

The consequences of these "possible" doses in a nuclear-power economy are, to say the least, enormously different from each other. There is certainly ample reason for the public to wonder—to wonder seriously—what dose of radiation nuclear power will really give us.

TABLE 23: PREDICTED CANCER CONSEQUENCES FOR DELIVERY OF VARIOUS DOSES FROM NUCLEAR POWER

Equilibrium Population: 119 million males; 131 million females
Whole-body cancer dose: Males: 235 person-rads
Females: 300 person-rads

Annual Dose (millirads)	Person-Rads, Males	Cancer Deaths per year (males)	Person-Rads, Females	Cancer Deaths per year (females)	Total Cancer Deaths per year
0.003	357	1.52	393	1.31	2.83
0.1	11,900	50.6	13,100	43.7	94.3
170	20,230,000	86,085.1	22,270,000	74,233.3	160,318.4
25	2,975,000	12,659.6	3,275,000	10,916.7	23,576.3
1000	119,000,000	506,400.0	131,000,000	436,700.0	943,100.0

HOW DO WE KNOW (OR FIND OUT) WHAT THE REAL DOSE IS FROM NUCLEAR POWER?

To determine the public's actual dose from nuclear power, the logical procedure would seem to be to go out and *measure* it. Straightforward though that seems, however, obtaining a meaningful answer by measurement is an enormously complex and difficult undertaking. Why?

First of all, the nuclear fuel cycle (which includes *all* steps involved in the generation of nuclear power) is itself complex. There are the mining and milling of uranium; the enrichment of uranium; the fabrication of fuel rods; the normal and abnormal releases from the nuclear-power plant itself; the removal, transport, and storage of various contaminated materials (including tools, filters, chemicals, shoes, gloves, clothing, etc.); the handling of used fuel rods, either by storing the rods somewhere indefinitely, or by dissolving the rods to recover unused uranium and plutonium from the residual, extremely high-level radioactive waste; interim storage of that waste somewhere; the transport of high-level waste to so-called final storage; and its storage. Each of these steps is accompanied by deliberate, "small" releases of radioactivity, and each provides ample opportunity for unintentional additional releases.

For now, we shall neglect the doses to people who work directly in the nuclear industry. Their doses are over and above those received by the population at large, and shall be treated elsewhere (chapter 12).

Doses to the public will come mostly from products of the nuclear-fission process itself, rather than from gamma rays emanating from reactor buildings. Also, there will be little chance of public exposure to neutrons.

Fission Products and Activation Products of the Nuclear Fuel Cycle

When uranium (or plutonium) fissions in a nuclear reactor, hundreds of different kinds of radioactive by-products are formed in two major ways:

1. As direct "leftovers," or fragments from the fissioned atom itself.
2. As substances formed (created) by the capture of neutrons in uranium or plutonium, or in a variety of construction materials or chemicals in the reactor milieu itself. We are already familiar (chapter 9) with the creation of the transuranic elements through the capture of neutrons by ^{235}U and ^{238}U.

The Fission Products: In this class of substances are such familiar radionuclides as radioiodine (^{131}I) with $T_{1/2} = 8$ days, radiostrontium, (^{90}Sr) with $T_{1/2} = 28.5$ years, and radiocesium (^{137}Cs) with $T_{1/2} = 30.1$ years. *Several hundred* different radioactive species are produced in the fissioning of uranium and plutonium. Some have half-lives of fractions of a second, some of seconds, minutes, hours, days, or years, and some have half-lives of centuries or much longer.

Neutron-Activation Products: In this class of substances, created by neutron capture in materials inside and nearby the reactor vessel itself, are another host of important radionuclides. The transuranic nuclides of plutonium, americium, and curium are all neutron-activation products, originating from neutron capture in uranium nuclides (not from the fission of these nuclides). Some others are such extremely important substances as

[14]Carbon, [3]H (tritium, which is also made during fission itself), [55]Fe (iron), [54]Mn (manganese), [65]Zinc, [58]Co and [60]Co (cobalt). The membership of this group depends to a large extent on the materials in the vicinity of the nuclear-reaction area.

Physicists and nuclear chemists can do, and have done, a very good job of measuring precisely how much of every one of the many hundreds of radionuclides is created for every unit of heat produced by the fissioning; the heat, in turn, can be expressed in terms of kilowatt-hours of electricity. Such calculations are all relatively easy, but they are only the first step of a tremendously long journey—to determining what radiation dose an individual receives from nuclear-power generation.

For if we are to know the true dose received by the average person (and it will vary, for many reasons, from person to person), we will have to determine what dose, if any, is delivered to people from *each* of several hundred separate radionuclides. Then we would have to add up the separate doses to obtain the final dose in millirads, or in any other exposure unit. To illustrate the complexities involved, let us consider some of the problems that arise for just one of the radioactive fission products of the nuclear fuel cycle, [90]Strontium.

Gaseous Emissions

[90]Strontium is made in the nuclear-fission reaction by at least three independent routes. We must recall that when a $^{235}_{92}$Uranium nucleus splits in fission, there are 92 protons that must be distributed among the fission products. One hundred forty-two neutrons must also be distributed among the fission products.

Numerous combinations of neutrons and protons can occur in these fission products, but there are only three for which the sum of protons and neutrons equals 90. They are [90]Kr (of the element krypton), [90]Rb (rubidium), and [90]Sr (strontium). All three have a total mass of 90 units; they differ from each other in their proportion of protons to neutrons.

When these substances are made, they are located in the fuel pellets of uranium oxide; the pellets, in turn, are encased in very long tubes containing many pellets stacked next to each other. These tubes are clad with an alloy of the element zirconium (called *Zircalloy*). If the cladding were perfect, and therefore impermeable, all three substances, [90]Kr, [90]Rb, and ^{90}Sr, would be retained within the reactor-fuel rod. But the cladding is not perfect, and the nuclear industry expects and states that a certain number of pinholes exist. So some fraction of all three nuclides gets into the primary cooling water that bathes the fuel rods in a light-water reactor.

Gaseous radionuclides move even more readily through the holes into the cooling water. If they remain gases long enough, they do in time end up in the atmosphere. In the case of intentional releases of gases, sometimes the gases are stored for a specified period before release, so that additional decay can occur. In the case of unintentional releases ("puffs"), the storage time is shorter or nonexistent. In addition, gases may escape through leaks whose location is not even known to the operators of the plant.

Let us suppose that one is concerned about radiation doses from ^{90}Strontium in the vicinity of a nuclear plant. One might ask the nuclear-plant owners whether any ^{90}Sr is escaping in the exhaust gases from the plant. Their perfectly sincere answer could be, "Of course not. ^{90}Sr is *not* a gas, and therefore it does not escape from the plant." But let us look at the three products of atomic mass 90 listed above. We find that *some* of the ^{90}Sr is not made *directly*, but arises as a product of the decay of ^{90}Kr. A rubidium nuclide, ^{90}Rb, is the intermediate product. ^{90}Krypton is a noble gas (inactive chemically; a member of the same family as helium and radon).

No one denies that noble gases do indeed escape from the exhaust stacks of nuclear plants. But in this special case, nature has been kind in that ^{90}Krypton has a very short half-life: 32.3 seconds. Therefore, by the time ^{90}Krypton has escaped through a pinhole in the zirconium cladding, and then from the cooling water into an exhaust somewhere in the plant, many minutes at least, on the average, will have elapsed. If a substance has a half-life of 32.3 seconds, it will decay to 1/1,000 of its original amount in 10×32.3, or 323 seconds. Thus 999/1,000 of the original ^{90}Kr will have been converted to ^{90}Rb in those 323 seconds (approximately 5 minutes) and hence will no longer be a gas and will not be able to escape as a gas.

So when 5 minutes elapse between the creation of ^{90}Kr and its escape, only a tiny fraction of it *will* escape. But there can be circumstances under which 5 minutes do not elapse. Whatever ^{90}Kr gets out of the plant and into the environment *must* become ^{90}Strontium.

When doses are estimated for each of the nuclides, the dose of ^{90}Strontium may be based on the *assumption* that none of the ^{90}Kr gets out of the plant, or that some specific fraction gets out. That assumption may simply be wrong for a particular plant at a particular time. It is crucial for the reader to know that for the case of ^{90}Sr arising from ^{90}Kr, the dose estimates made by industry or government are *not* the result of *measurement*, but are speculations about how much ^{90}Kr should be getting out (or not getting out) if everything were working as designers thought it ought to—which may or may not be the case.

Other similar chains of nuclides—with a gaseous nuclide as one precursor—are not so benign. For example, ^{89}Krypton decays with a half-life of 3.18 minutes to ^{89}Rubidium, which decays with a half-life of 15.4 minutes to ^{89}Strontium. ^{89}Strontium is particularly important because it is a beta-particle emitter with a half-life of 50.5 days. Once in the environment, it has ample opportunity to get through the food chain into the human body, where it can deliver sizable radiation doses—in proportion, of course, to the quantity taken in by each person.

Similarly, ^{135}Xenon, also a noble gas, has a half-life of 9.17 hours. With this long half-life, it has ample opportunity to escape from a nuclear plant before it is converted to ^{135}Cesium, a nongaseous form. ^{135}Cesium has a half-life of 3,000,000 years, and decays by beta emission. Fortunately, 1 curie of ^{135}Xe produces only 0.349 *nanocuries* of ^{135}Cesium.

On the other hand, ^{135}Cesium introduced into the environment by man *can accumulate,* because of its long half-life. The operators of a nuclear plant, if asked about any escape of ^{135}Cesium, could say, "No, cesium is not a gas. It does not escape from the plant in the gaseous stream." Correct! But the answer omits the fact that ^{135}Xenon is going into the environment, and it inevitably becomes ^{135}Cesium, which will persist in the environment virtually forever.

Nature has been kind to us in the case of ^{133}Xenon, the noble gas with a half-life of 5.27 days. Large quantities of ^{133}Xenon did escape at Three Mile Island and irradiate people in the form of beta and gamma emissions (though only the gamma rays were of consequence for internal dosage to organs other than the lungs). But ^{133}Xenon decays to ^{133}Cesium. And ^{133}Cesium is stable; it does not decay at all. Hence it produces no radiation dose.

Liquid Emissions

Liquids containing dissolved radionuclides also are discharged from nuclear plants on both a routine and an "abnormal" or unplanned basis. An effort is made to prevent primary cooling water from escaping without prior treatment, because this water is contaminated with a complex mixture of radionuclides as the result of pinholes in the fuel cladding and of activation products generated in, or dissolved in, the water. But inevitably, some primary cooling water does escape, and carries a variety of radioactive species into the environment.

Even when operations are normal, and the liquid is first treated with ion-exchangers (chemicals which will take up the ionic forms of many radioactive substances), the ion-exchanged solids must at some point be packaged up, transported to some dumpsite, and deposited there. Radioactive substances have spread from these dumpsites into the environment. In other words, if a plant is clean, it is only because it has moved its poisons somewhere *else.*

The Meaning of a Low Dose at the "Fence-Line"

While we are not concerned here with just how much of each of the radionuclides enters the environment via known and unknown releases, it should be evident that the unknown distribution of the various nuclides, into leaks (gaseous or liquid) or into solid wastes spilled in transport or migrating from burial sites, makes dose estimates necessarily very uncertain.

And if we wish to understand the true complexity of ascertaining dose, we can take one nuclide and follow it through its travels, once it is released from the nuclear fuel cycle, at the plant or elsewhere. Consider ^{137}Cesium, one of the truly important nuclides.

If originally airborne, ^{137}Cesium can deposit on land or in water. For example, rainfall is efficient in washing aerosols out of the atmosphere and onto the ground. From the ground surface, ^{137}Cs can directly irradiate people with its gamma rays.

Whether deposited into a river, onto land, or into the ocean, ^{137}Cs becomes available to participate in what is called the *food chain*. Cesium can be directly incorporated into the tissues of freshwater or saltwater fish, or into a variety of crops directly consumed by human beings. We eat a myriad of crop species; ^{137}Cs is incorporated in each in a specific way. Or, cesium can get into forage crops eaten by cattle or hogs and thus get into either the meat or the milk of such animals. The milk, moreover, may be converted to cheeses, still incorporating a large part of the ^{137}Cesium, and the cheeses may be shipped halfway around the world and irradiate people who never heard of nuclear-power plants. Thus, ^{137}Cs is incorporated into human tissues, indeed into virtually all human tissues, in the case of this nuclide.

So it is truly absurd to consider the problem of escaped ^{137}Cesium as one local to the power plant itself. The dose from nuclides spread into the food chain can simply dwarf the gamma-ray dose to someone standing next to the fence-line of the plant. Moreover, a fuel-reprocessing plant may distribute into the environment a much larger fraction of the radionuclides from the power plant than the fraction released by the power plant itself. This, too, indicates the absurdity of narrowly focusing on doses to people in the neighborhood of the plant.

Nuclear-plant officials are delighted to keep the focus very narrow, and to tell the public about a very low gamma-ray dose received by someone at the fence-line of a normally operating nuclear plant. With enough steel and concrete between a person and a gamma-ray source, it is no miracle that the dose received from direct gamma radiation is very small. The fence-line gamma dose *has* to be trivial if the workers inside the plant are going to avoid acute radiation sickness.

And at the very moment that a low gamma dose is being measured at the fence line, liquid effluents can be spreading radionuclides into regions tens and hundreds of miles away. At the same time, a reprocessing plant can be spreading nuclides into the environment, or a leaking waste shipment or a leaking burial site can be spreading nuclides into the food chain.

But it is very effective public relations to point to a low gamma dose at the fence-line of a nuclear plant and to say, falsely, "If nuclear power is delivering such a low dose at the fence-line, think of how low the dose must become as we go progressively further away." That is absolutely correct for the gamma dose, and absolutely irrelevant to the vastly more important problem of the spread of radionuclides produced in nuclear-power plants.

Why Not Solve the Dose-Estimation Problem by Monitoring?

One may quite sincerely ask, why not monitor all foodstuffs for all the hundreds of radionuclides that can potentially be released, and do so for all crop seasons and for all nuclear installations? Then, one may reason, we would at least know how much we are taking in, although that knowledge is only the beginning of calculating the dose in rads to our tissues, as we shall see.

Monitoring every food for every radionuclide for all facilities is simply out of the question, unless we are seriously considering diverting a fair share of our national labor effort to this monitoring. The best approach we have seen so far is spot monitoring for a few radionuclides in a few foods.

Because comprehensive monitoring is not at all feasible, the predicted doses from the nuclear industry represent estimates based on the *presumed* travels of such substances as ^{137}Cesium through food chains, once these substances have been released. As we shall see, we are in trouble not only with respect to knowing the amount released but also with respect to the basis for estimating what fraction of that amount ends up in food.

Transfer Factors from Soil to Crops: Let us suppose (and this supposition requires a great stretch of the imagination) that for each nuclear plant, someone could provide us with good measurements of the amount of ^{137}Cesium which escapes from all parts of the nuclear fuel cycle, and of its distribution on the surrounding land in all directions for a radius of 50 or 100 miles. Let us even suppose the measurements tell us how much ^{137}Cesium is present per gram of soil in which crops are grown. Do we now have everything we need to estimate dose? No, we have only a little of the necessary information.

The estimate of the dose in rads received by human beings depends on many more items of information:

1. The transfer factor, which is equal to PCi per kilogram of fresh plant/PCi per kilogram of soil. A separate transfer factor is needed for each crop. Moreover, the factor for a single crop can vary with the type of soil, its mineral and water content, its pH, and its biological activity. It can also depend on the form in which ^{137}Cesium is presented to the crop.

2. Other crucial factors, such as

a. The fraction of ^{137}Cesium, ingested in plant form, which gets absorbed from the gastrointestinal tract into the blood.

b. The average length of time that any ^{137}Cesium deposited in an organ *remains* in that organ, and where the cesium goes when it is removed from that organ. Some substances are excreted; others are translocated.

It is self-evident that both a. and b. will have everything to do with dose determination even after we know the content of ^{137}Cesium per kilogram of food crop.

If we are concerned with the ingestion of milk or meat containing ^{137}Cesium, we must know other transfer factors as well. For milk, we need to know what fraction of ^{137}Cesium ingested by the cow is transferred to the milk, or PCi per liter of milk/PCi per day intake. And for meat, we need to know the value of PCi per kilogram meat/PCi per day intake.

So, the chain of information required to go from a particular release of ^{137}Cesium to the dose to man is indeed complex. The accuracy of a calculation of the dose received is no better than the accuracy of the various transfer factors and parameters used in the calculation.

And this is what is required for each and every radionuclide of concern —perhaps 50 or 100 radionuclides.

In view of the enormous complexity of going from curies released to rads absorbed, one can only marvel at the self-assurance of those who confidently state the dose that the public is receiving or will receive from nuclear-power generation. One may marvel at the self-assurance, but there is virtually no reason to believe the figures.

A.COMMON-SENSE APPROACH TO ESTIMATING LIKELY DOSES FROM NUCLEAR POWER

Evaluating the public's radiation dose from the release of even *one* radionuclide (^{137}Cesium) is an enormously complex problem, as explained above. The uncertainties are simply multiplied when one attempts to evaluate the dose from 50 or more major radionuclides.

It would make good sense to dismiss as essentially worthless those claims that nuclear power is delivering a population dose of 0.003 millirems per year, and to remember that such doses have *not* been measured, they have been calculated. Calculation is a valid way to obtain such information only when the calculations *begin* with some basis in reality. It should be evident that such calculated doses cannot be meaningful at present since the amounts of the initial releases are so very poorly known, and the measured transfer factors for a single nuclide (e.g., ^{137}Cesium) in a single type of transfer (e.g., from soil to plant) vary by as much as a factor of 8,000, or even 20,000.

The author believes the problem can be approached in a common-sense way by simply bypassing most of the arguable details and minutiae, and by asking whether it is reasonable to believe that the dose *could* be kept below some particular level, a level for which an estimate of consequences in cancer fatalities can be made. The reader saw a similar approach used for plutonium pollution in chapter 10.

It is not coincidental that both chapters 10 and 11 make use of data provided by weapons fallout. These data have some basis in reality. One of the purposes of science is to find valid ways to use available information from past experience to comprehend potential future experience.

Underlying Principles of the Common-Sense Method

In its essence, the common-sense method the author proposes has the following components:

1. The quantity of radionuclides produced, which is readily determined.

2. The dose delivered to human beings from a specified environmental distribution of at least *one* major radionuclide. This information is available from the data for weapons fallout.

3. The containment requirement corresponding to various doses to human beings from this one nuclide, and the cancer consequences thereof.

4. The relationship of the likely dose to the dose from the one nuclide.

It will be noted that even this method depends (in point 2) on the numerous biological transfer factors from soil all the way to human tissue for the specific radionuclide studied. But if we use the values recommended by official sources, it is likely that we will not overestimate the doses.

In the unabridged edition of this book is a table including figures for the amount of radioactivity in curies present at 150 days for one megawatt-year of nuclear-power generation, and for the amount present at 150 days for a full-fledged "Nuclear America"—namely, for 1,000 plants, each generating 1,000 megawatts per year. This is the type of information needed for point 1 above.

Using data for the radionuclides still present in the spent-fuel rods of light-water reactors (U.S. type) 150 days (of cooling time) after their removal from the reactors, the author has performed a sample calculation to determine the radiation dose to the public from the release of ^{137}Cesium in a fully developed nuclear economy. We can compare this estimate with official estimates of the current radiation dose received by the public of ^{137}Cesium from weapons-testing fallout.

The Dose from ^{137}Cesium in a Fully Developed Nuclear Economy

The radiation dose to the U.S. public from ^{137}Cesium from weapons testing is estimated (both by the author and by UNSCEAR) to be 0.66 millirads per person, if the ^{137}Cesium were dispersed uniformly at a concentration of 1 millicurie per km^2.

By contrast, if all the ^{137}Cesium in a year's worth of spent nuclear fuel were dispersed over the coterminous United States each year, each person in the United States would receive a dose on the order of 3.08×10^5 millirads, or about *300 rads*, per person. This is based on the amount of ^{137}Cesium in spent fuel from the nuclear generation of 1,000 gigawatt-years (or 1,000 plants producing 1,000 megawatts each per year); in other words, a fully developed nuclear economy.

Of course, this inventory is not all going to escape, but this calculation provides the author and the reader with the ability to calculate the dose and consequences for *any* estimated fraction which might really escape:

Degree of Containment of ^{137}Cesium	Percent of ^{137}Cesium Escaping	Dose in Millirads (whole-body exposure) Per Year for Each Person in U.S. Population
99 %	1.0000%	3.08×10^3 millirads/yr
99.9 %	0.1 %	3.08×10^2 millirads/yr
99.99 %	0.01 %	3.08×10 millirads/yr
99.999 %	0.001 %	3.08 millirads/yr
99.9999%	0.0001%	3.08×10^{-1} millirads/yr

These are very sobering numbers indeed. If the doses in a "Nuclear America" are to be in the promised realm of 0.1–1.0 millirads per year, then ^{137}Cesium will have to be contained better than 99.999% perfectly, and absolutely no amount of the several hundred other fission products and transuranic elements can be released at any point in the entire nuclear fuel cycle.

In the place of computer print-outs for a mythically operated nuclear fuel cycle, this common-sense approach substitutes a simple question, which each person can answer as a sensible expert: Do you believe that fallible men and machines are going to contain ^{137}Cesium better than 99.999% perfectly, and are going to contain every other radionuclide absolutely perfectly? Those who can answer this question in the affirmative will probably not have any concern about nuclear power, aside from mammoth accidents, bomb proliferation, terrorism, cost, and unreliability.

But ^{137}Cesium Is Hardly the Entire Problem

The quantities of other nuclides such as ^{95}Zr, ^{103}Ru, ^{140}Ba, ^{141}Ce, ^{144}Ce, ^{106}Ru, and ^{134}Cs are by no means negligible in the mixture of nuclides present in spent fuel that has cooled 150 days. Every one of these nuclides will add to the external gamma dose. So the dose contributed by ^{137}Cs will be supplemented by doses from whatever fractions of these additional nuclides escape confinement.

The radionuclides still present at 150 days cooling constitute a small fraction of the total radioactivity of fuel in curies at times shorter than 150 days. It hardly seems likely that *no* dose is going to be delivered from any of the shorter-lived nuclides, but certainly the chance is smaller that such nuclides will escape from relatively intact fuel rods than that long-lived nuclides will escape from fuel rods subjected to fuel reprocessing at some time after 150 days.

It seems inevitable that the dose received by people from fission products will be appreciably higher than the dose delivered by ^{137}Cesium alone. Yet to consider pollution by this *one* radionuclide gives us ballpark values that indicate the various degrees of containment which would be necessary in a full nuclear-power economy.

The Distribution of Cesium from Nuclear Power Versus from Fallout

It is difficult to predict just how the cesium will be distributed in the environment during the nuclear fuel cycle; that is, whether distribution will be via liquid effluents or other pathways of loss. The author suspects that liquid effluents and solid wastes would be the most likely pathways of loss.

It is not possible to prove that each millicurie of ^{137}Cesium from the nuclear fuel cycle will end up delivering the same dose of radiation as did each millicurie deposited on land by weapons-testing fallout. The actual nuclear-power dose might be higher than, equal to, or less than the dose from the atmospherically distributed ^{137}Cesium. In the absence of data on which to base an answer to this question, it is reasonable to assume that the doses from the two forms of distribution will be comparable.

Another point must be made. The calculations of dose in millirads for various degrees of containment of ^{137}Cesium assume that all the cesium will be restricted to the 48 coterminous United States. This is probably a rather good assumption for the circumstances under which the ^{137}Cesium is likely to be dispersed from the nuclear fuel cycle. Moreover, the cesium that may migrate outside the 48 states might well be replaced by losses from nuclear-power facilities in other countries.

PROBABLE CANCER CONSEQUENCES OF THE NUCLEAR FUEL CYCLE

Even when we restrict our dose estimates to radiation delivered by one nuclide (out of hundreds) in the nuclear fuel cycle, we find, as we found above, that containment requirements are stringent if a high average dose of radiation is to be avoided. It is worthwhile to examine the cancer consequences of various degrees of containment of this one nuclide for the projected nuclear fuel cycle (i.e., 1,000 plants each generating 1,000 mega-watt-years per year). These cancer consequences, for an equilibrium population, are presented in table 24.

The Question of Incremental Dose from the Burial of Radioactive Waste

The public is appropriately concerned about the management of the radioactive waste left over from the nuclear fuel cycle, including the mountainous quantities of so-called low-level waste, the spent fuel rods that remain if reprocessing does not take place, or the high-level waste if reprocessing does take place. To be sure, whatever method is used to store such materials, above or below ground, we should be concerned about leakage into the environment, which can expose people to radiation.

But the leakage of radioactivity into the environment from storage and burial places is not likely to be the major problem leading to human exposure. The real problem occurs long before any burial of wastes is achieved: in all the losses of radioactive materials on the *surface* of the earth during a myriad of steps. We have shown above that 99.99% containment is not good enough, even if we artificially restrict our concern to just one radionuclide, ^{137}Cesium. If containment is only 99.99% perfect, tens of thousands of extra cancer deaths will occur each year in a fully developed nuclear-power economy.

If we cannot guarantee the achievement of nearly perfect containment during the various processes that must be accomplished *before* the "final" burial of radioactive waste, then nuclear power will introduce a reversal of advances in public health even *without* any later leaks from buried radioactive waste. In this sense, the concern over the burial of radioactive waste is a diversion from the very real and very serious problem that should be the

TABLE 24: ESTIMATED CANCER FATALITIES PER YEAR IN AN EQUILIBRIUM POPULATION OF 250 MILLION WITH VARIOUS DEGREES OF CONTAINMENT OF ^{137}CESIUM IN A FULL NUCLEAR-POWER ECONOMY*

% of ^{137}Cs Contained	Whole-Body Dose, millirads/yr	Person-Rads, Males	Cancer Deaths, Males (yearly)	Person-Rads, Females	Cancer Deaths, Females (yearly)	Total Cancer Deaths per Year for Nuclear Fuel Cycle (for ^{137}Cs)
99	3080	3.66×10^8	1,560,000	4.03×10^8	1,343,000	2,903,000
99.9	308	3.66×10^7	156,000	4.03×10^7	134,300	290,300
99.99	30.8	3.66×10^6	15,600	4.03×10^6	13,430	29,030
99.999	3.08	3.66×10^5	1,560	4.03×10^5	1,343	2,903
99.9999	0.308	3.66×10^4	156	4.03×10^4	134	290
99.99999	0.0308	3.66×10^3	15.6	4.03×10^3	13.4	29

*1,000 gigawatt years per year (1 gigawatt = 1,000 megawatts will put out a total of 1,000 megawatt-years per year, or 1 gigawatt-year per year. The equilibrium population is expected to comprise 119 million males and 131 million females.

The calculations here are totally over and above cancers due to transuranic elements associated with the same nuclear fuel cycle. For the additional cancers from transuranic elements, see chapter 10, table 22.

The tabulations are made using 235 person-rads as the whole-body cancer dose for males in an equilibrium population and 300.2 person-rads as the whole-body cancer dose for females in an equilibrium population.

The estimated cancer fatalities can be easily adjusted by simple proportionality to correspond to assumptions of either a greater or lesser number of operating nuclear-power generators.

first order of business, namely, the degree of perfection of containment from day to day, *now*.

If nuclear power were rejected as an energy source, the problem would nevertheless remain of how to manage the radioactive garbage already accumulated, both from the nuclear-power industry and from the military program. This problem is complex; its best solution is as yet undetermined.

"WE HAVE SO MUCH RADIOACTIVITY FROM THE MILITARY PROGRAM—WHY WORRY ABOUT THE CIVILIAN NUCLEAR-POWER PROGRAM AT ALL?"

A curious notion often encountered is that the radioactive waste from the military program is so huge that the nuclear-power program is not even worth worrying about. This is dangerous, and possibly *sponsored*, nonsense! A few simple calculations will demonstrate the absurdity of this notion.

The military waste arises from the operation of nuclear reactors (almost all without associated electrical-power generation) for the production of two substances, plutonium and tritium. The average reactor used in these endeavors is not as large as a 1,000-mw(e) reactor, but for the purposes of *exaggerating* the military-waste problem, we shall assume that the military reactors are equivalent in power to 1,000-mw(e) civilian reactors. On the average, fewer than ten such military reactors have been operating each year in the United States for approximately 35 years (1945–1980). Therefore, the radioactive waste generated by the military program, in toto, would be that generated by 10 reactors × 35 years, or 350 reactor-years.

The current civilian nuclear-power program in the United States consists of the equivalent of 50 plants of 1,000-mw(e) capacity (this capacity is actually distributed into 72 plants of lower average capacity). Therefore, each year there are 50 reactor-years of waste generation to contend with. Since these civilian plants have operated some 5 years, on the average, the total generated waste is 250 reactor-years' worth. But in the proposed "nuclear economy" 1,000 large nuclear plants would be on line, generating waste at a rate of 1,000 reactor-years of waste generation *per year*. Thus, a full-scale civilian program would, *in each year of operation*, generate an amount of radioactive waste exceeding by 3-fold the waste generated by the entire military program in its 35 years of operation.

What Does Experience Show the Level of Containment of [137]Cesium to Be?

A UNSCEAR report (1977) estimates the [137]Cesium present in fuel rods at 150 days of cooling to be *3,550 curies per megawatt-year (electrical)*. This is a valuable reference point for examining some of the reported experiences at reprocessing plants, sites of expected major releases of radioactivity from the nuclear fuel cycle.

Windscale Reprocessing in the United Kingdom reported (UNSCEAR

1977, p. 201) a release rate for 1972 of 13.9 curies of ^{137}Cs per megawatt-year (electrical). This amounts to a loss of $13.9/3,550 \times 100\% = 0.39\%$ via the liquid-effluent pathway, and corresponds to a containment of 99.61%, *if* we assume no other pathways of loss. If future experience were to match this Windscale experience, pollution from ^{137}Cesium alone, and from the reprocessing step only, would result in major increases in the cancer death rate.

In New York State, the Nuclear Fuel Services Plant, now shut down, reported ostensibly better ^{137}Cs containment for 1971, the one year for which the data seem adequate. In that year, 10 curies of ^{137}Cs were released in liquid effluents for 720 equivalent megawatt-years of electricity generated. Taken at face value, this report would suggest that the percent released was 0.0004%. That would be impressive indeed compared to the Windscale experience, since it would suggest that 99.9996% containment was achieved.

However, when one looks a little closer at the NFS containment, the picture is not nearly so optimistic. The UNSCEAR report states:

Liquid wastes from NFS were passed through a series of three small lagoons before discharge to the stream. This system provided a 30–60 day hold-up of the liquids and, in addition, removed considerable amounts of activity by sedimentation. (p. 203)

This information alters the picture considerably. One can hardly regard ^{137}Cs dumped into an open lagoon as having been contained. The ^{137}Cs at NFS seems to have been about as well contained as the chemicals dumped into the Love Canal in the Niagara area.

Moreover, there remains the question how much ^{137}Cs will be lost at Windscale and at Nuclear Fuel Services during interim storage on site. The half-life of ^{137}Cs is 30.2 years, so the story does not end in the year in which reprocessing takes place.

There soon will be considerably more information available, from the reprocessing plants which are in operation, concerning the loss rate for nuclides such as ^{137}Cs. Let us hope it proves possible to acquire this information in unadulterated form. And let us hope further that effluents are not diluted and divided among numerous exits, each exit "monitored" by instruments of insufficient sensitivity to *detect* any losses occurring at such dilute rates. For under such circumstances, one could even release "the whole ball of wax" into the environment, and nevertheless report (because the monitors always did read zero) that detected losses indicated better than a 99.999999% level of containment. And who could ever show otherwise?

Lastly, while this chapter has not considered serious accidents with attendant large releases, one simple fact is worth pointing out. If the fuel reprocessor were operating with 99.99% containment of such fission products as ^{137}Cs—a containment which would be rather poor considering the high price of cancer deaths which would go with it (see table 24)—the occurrence of just one serious accident at a reprocessing facility, releasing 10% of the inventory, say, would release the same amount of radioactivity as would be released in 1,000 years of operation at 99.99% containment.

[CHAPTER 12]

IONIZING-RADIATION EXPOSURES FROM NATURAL SOURCES, CONSUMER PRODUCTS, AND PARTICULAR OCCUPATIONS

"WHY WORRY ABOUT RADIATION from nuclear power? It's only a small dose compared to natural radiation,"

"It's no more radiation than a chest film gives."

"Diagnostic radiation hasn't killed anyone."

"Just being in Grand Central Station will give you more radiation than being at the fence-line of a normally operating nuclear-power plant."

"I hear color television sets give you more radiation than nuclear power."

"You get irradiated from the potassium-40 in your wife's body while you are in bed."

These are typical of some of the statements with which the public continues to be bombarded, and which have thoroughly confused some members of both the technical community and the nontechnical public. The probable doses and cancer effects from nuclear power were presented in chapters 10 and 11. Medical irradiation will be considered in chapter 13. Here we will examine some other sources of radiation exposure, and the magnitude and cancer consequences of the radiation they emit.

SECTION 1: NATURAL SOURCES OF IONIZING-RADIATION EXPOSURE, AND THEIR EFFECTS

It is absolutely true that there are natural sources of ionizing radiation and radioactivity totally independent of any human activity. Of course, we have seen that man, by disturbing nature (for example, by mining and milling uranium ore), can greatly increase his exposure to particular natural sources of radiation.

From the large body of evidence presented or summarized in this book, we have good reason to believe that cancer and leukemia induction by ionizing radiation is proportional to the dose received over a wide range of doses. There is absolutely no reason to exempt natural radiation sources from this generalization.

The fact that radon and its daughter products are "natural" sources of ionizing radiation did not prevent tragic lung-cancer deaths in the uranium miners. The fact that ^{226}Radium is a "natural" source of radiation did not prevent the horrible fate of the radium-dial painters.

Furthermore, there exists no reason whatsoever to dismiss as negligible any radiation dose from a man-made source simply on the grounds that the dose it delivers is lower than the dose from some combined sources of natural radiation. Most natural sources of ionizing-radiation exposure cannot be avoided by man, as we shall see when we consider the origins of natural radiation. Natural radiation takes its toll in health and life, quantitatively to the extent we shall examine below. It would hardly make sense, however, to suggest that man-made sources of radiation are acceptable because they do not necessarily add *quite* as much misery and death as do natural sources. Adding doses of man-made radiation equal to the total received from natural sources is *public health in reverse.*

WHERE DO THE NATURAL RADIATION EXPOSURES COME FROM?

Natural radiation exposures come from two broad classes of sources, terrestrial and extraterrestrial (cosmic). Both are important.

The Cosmic Sources of Ionizing Radiation

The cosmic sources, which are thought to be mostly stars, provide radiation in three ways: (1) creation of radionuclides from the interaction of neutrons (produced from cosmic rays) with elements in the atmosphere; (2) direct ionizing radiation from collision of cosmic radiation with human tissue, where electrons are set in motion; and (3) neutron exposure. We shall consider these groups in sequence.

Cosmic Sources of Radionuclides: Two very well-known radionuclides to which humans are exposed have been produced for millions of years by neutrons that owe their origin to cosmic radiation. They are tritium (^3_1H) and carbon-14 ($^{14}_6C$). It is estimated (UNSCEAR 1977, p. 54) that the world inventory of tritium from the cosmic source is some 34 megacuries of tritium, of which 99% is in the form of tritiated water, and most of this is in the oceans. Ocean water is estimated to have had a natural (meaning cosmic) level of 3 PCi of ^3_1H per liter, before nuclear explosions and nuclear reactors started producing this nuclide. Fresh water, which received the tritium from air sources before the ocean did, is estimated to have had a natural level of 6–24 PCi per liter. Since these reactions have been going on for millions of years, and since all the equilibration processes on earth are of far shorter time spans, the levels of tritium of cosmic origin have not changed for millions of years.

The radiation dose from natural tritium is quite low, estimated (UNSCEAR, p. 55) at approximately 1 microrad, or about 0.001 millirad, annually.

^{14}Carbon, with a half-life of 5,730 years, has been formed on the earth for millions of years; its natural level is 6.1 PCi per gram of the element carbon. Every compound in the human body has ^{14}Carbon built into it. All carbon dioxide contains ^{14}Carbon. One interesting point about fossil-fuel carbon is that, having had its organic carbon laid down at a time very long ago compared with the half-life of ^{14}Carbon, it is very low in ^{14}C, since much of the ^{14}C has decayed. Thus, as we inject CO_2 into the atmosphere from the burning of fossil fuels, the specific activity, or the PCi of ^{14}C per gram of carbon, actually decreases (not a good reason for burning excesses of fossil fuel!).

The dose of ionizing radiation from ^{14}Carbon is estimated at approximately 1.3 millirads per year to the whole body (UNSCEAR, p. 56).

Other cosmogenically produced nuclides include ^{7}Be, ^{22}Na, and ^{24}Na, plus a host of very short-lived nuclides. Even combined, these others are not appreciable contributors to the dose of radiation, giving less than one-tenth the dose given by ^{14}Carbon (UNSCEAR, p. 56).

In summary, the dose from radionuclides produced on earth from cosmic radiations is largely the dose from ^{14}Carbon, about 1.3 millirads per year.

The Total Cosmic-Ray Dose and the Cancer Price: Cosmic ionizing radiation, producing direct ionization in tissues without the intermediacy of any radionuclides, is responsible for approximately 28 millirads per year of tissue-absorbed dose to humans at sea level (UNSCEAR, p. 40). This dose definitely goes up at higher altitudes, and is estimated to be 50 millirads per year at Denver, Colorado (altitude 1,600 meters) and about 125 millirads at Leadville, Colorado (3,200 meters).

The third form of cosmic radiation is direct exposure to neutrons. At sea level, this dose is estimated (UNSCEAR, p. 41) to be approximately 0.35 millirads per year. Even if a sizable RBE were assigned to neutron radiation (and the evidence does not favor this for cancer induction—see chapter 5), the neutron component of cosmic radiation would be small compared to the direct ionizing component.

For sea-level exposure, we would add together 28 millirads from the ionizing component, 0.35 millirads from the neutron component (if RBE is 1), 1.3 millirads from ^{14}Carbon, plus about 0.2 millirads for short-lived cosmogenic nuclides, yielding a final per capita dose of 29.85 millirads per year. This we can round off to 30 millirads annual whole-body absorbed dose due to cosmic radiation. For an equilibrium population of 250,000,000 persons, the following would be the doses and cancer prices per year, for the United States.

For males, $(1.19 \times 10^8$ persons$) \times (0.030$ rads$) = 3.57 \times 10^6$ person-rads. For females, $(1.31 \times 10^8$ persons$) \times (0.030$ rads$) = 3.93 \times 10^6$ person-rads. For males, the whole-body cancer dose applicable for an equilibrium population is 235 person-rads; for females, it is 300.2 person-rads (tables 23 and 24). Therefore, in an equilibrium population of 250,000,000 persons, annual cancer deaths from cosmic radiation would be (for males) 15,200 cancer deaths, and (for females) 13,100 cancer deaths.

The United States is *not* an equilibrium population at 250,000,000 at this time. The adults who are developing cancer today were born into a much smaller population. The cancer deaths at this time from cosmic radiation are probably close to one-half of the equilibrium estimate, or approximately 14,000 per year. So this is the consequence of just *one* kind of natural radiation, which some use as a model to assure us that low doses of radiation (like 30 millirems per year) do not deserve any real concern. It would seem that 28,300 extra cancer deaths per year would not be considered a trivial matter.

The Terrestrial Sources of Ionizing Radiation

Part of our natural radiation exposure comes from sources right on the earth, and which have been on earth in all likelihood, since its formation. These sources can be divided into those which irradiate us from outside our bodies, and those which irradiate us internally.

External Terrestrial Radiation Doses: The prime sources of external terrestrial radiation are gamma rays emitted from what are called the *primordial* nuclides. These include ^{40}Potassium ($^{40}_{19}$K), ^{87}Rubidium ($^{87}_{37}$Rb), the members of the uranium decay chain which begins with the nuclide $^{238}_{92}$U, the members of the $^{232}_{90}$Th decay chain, plus (and to a much lesser extent) the members of the decay chain which begins with $^{235}_{92}$U. These nuclides and their daughter products, where daughter products exist, are by no means spread uniformly over the earth. Hence exposure can vary a great deal according to location.

$^{40}_{19}$Potassium and $^{87}_{37}$Rubidium are of especial interest for two reasons. First, it is rare among the naturally occurring nuclides for elements of such low atomic numbers (19 and 37) to be unstable. Second, potassium ions are the most prominent positive ions inside human cells. The $T_{1/2}$ value for ^{40}K is 1.26×10^9 years, and for ^{87}Rb is 5×10^{10} years. Of course, if their $T_{1/2}$ values were not so long, these primordial nuclides would long ago have disappeared from the earth and have been converted into other elements. These two nuclides contribute to both the external and internal radiation doses.

The decay scheme for ^{40}K is important, inasmuch as the decay of this nuclide accounts for a large part of the terrestrial natural radiation dose. ^{40}K decays in two ways. Eighty-nine percent of its decays are by the *emission* of a beta particle, to produce ^{40}Calcium. And 11% are by electron capture plus the emission of a gamma ray, to produce ^{40}Argon. Both ^{40}Argon and ^{40}Calcium are stable nuclides. ^{40}Potassium is unstable, and decays partly to the argon nuclide and partly to the calcium nuclide.

Those who belittle the hazard from radiation by telling us that our spouses irradiate us in bed (from ^{40}K) really do not understand their physics very well. Since only 11% of ^{40}K decays with a gamma-ray emission, and only a small part of any gamma rays emitted from one person can possibly reach another, the dose from another person's gamma rays is *minuscule* compared with the dose from our *own* ^{40}K beta-particle emissions.

Although the external gamma dose can be quite different from region to region, we can approximate the average absorbed tissue dose per year. It is noteworthy that the indoor dose can be quite different from the outdoor dose. If one lives in a wooden building, or spends much time in one, the indoor dose is in the neighborhood of 0.7 times the outdoor dose; the indoor dose is lower simply because of shielding and distance from the outdoor source of radiation. However, if one lives in a building made of materials of the composition of local soils, then the dose is higher indoors than outdoors, by a factor of about 1.3, on the average, because the same materials which would produce irradiation outdoors are closer to the inhabitant indoors (see UNSCEAR, pp. 49–51).

An average value of approximately 32 millirads per year absorbed tissue dose is given (UNSCEAR, p. 52) for exposure in the United States to external (to the body) terrestrial nuclides.

Internal Terrestrial Radiation Doses: ^{40}K is by far the leading source of internal exposure from terrestrial primordial radionuclides, ^{87}Rb making a smaller contribution. The estimated concentrations and annual dose are as follows:

Nuclide	Activity PCi/kg of tissue	Whole-Body Dose, average, per year millirads
^{40}K	1600	17
^{87}Rb	230	0.4

(Source of data is UNSCEAR, Table 13, p. 57.)

Internal exposure also results from ingestion of the numerous members of the decay chains of uranium and thorium. The situation for radon and radium has been discussed in chapter 9. As for all the other nuclides, including those of thorium, uranium, polonium, bismuth, and lead, the total dose under usual conditions is small compared with the external dose plus the internal dose from ^{40}K and ^{87}Rb. (Excluded from this consideration is the inhalation of uranium or thorium nuclides, which will be treated separately later.) It would be about right to add 1 millirem per year for the other nuclides listed above to the contribution from external terrestrial radiation plus internal dose from ^{40}K and ^{87}Rb.

External plus Internal Terrestrial Dose and Cancer Price: Total natural dose of terrestrial radiation from all sources is 50.4 millirads per year.

For an equilibrium population of 250,000,000, the whole-body doses would be (for males) 6.00×10^6 person-rads/year, and (for females) 6.60×10^6 person-rads/year.

Annual cancer deaths from internal plus external terrestrial radiation would be (for males) 25,500 cancer deaths, and (for females) 22,000 cancer deaths, for a total of 47,500. These deaths are in addition to the 4,000 from inhaled radon, the 288 from ingested radium, and the roughly estimated 4,000 deaths from inhaled thoron and its daughter products (see chapter 9).

Combined Dose from Cosmogenic and Terrestrial Natural Radiation

Summing up the natural radiation sources, including both the cosmogenic and the terrestrial sources, we have the average total whole-body dose = $30 + 50.4 = 80.4$ millirads per year. Total extra cancer deaths due to all forms of natural radiation (excluding inhalation dose and radium dose), calculated for an equilibrium population of 250,000,000 people, = 28,300 + 47,500 = 75,800. When we add the inhalation cancers from radon and thoron (4,000 each), we arrive at an estimate of 83,800 cancer deaths.

However, the current annual toll has to be lower, because those who are developing cancer now grew out of a much smaller population. The probable number of such cancer deaths per year from natural radiation sources in the early 1980s is about 42,000, or about one-half the eventual rate.

An eventual toll of about 83,800 cancer deaths per year from unavoidable natural radiation can hardly be regarded as a benchmark of acceptability for other radiation doses. It would be foolish indeed for the population to accept even a "low" dose of 5% of the natural dose without an exceedingly good reason for doing so. In an equilibrium population of 250 million, such a dose could add $(0.05) \times (83,800) = 4,200$ extra cancer deaths per year for each year it was maintained.

Will Home Building Materials Become an Issue?

It is quite clear that the incorporation of natural terrestrial radionuclides into building materials can cause appreciably higher indoor doses than are suffered in wooden buildings. The extent to which the dose is increased depends of course on the content of ^{40}K, the ^{238}U series, and the ^{232}Th series in local soils and rock materials. When the content of such nuclides is high, doses double those received in wooden buildings could occur. However, it should be noted that the dose from *direct* cosmic radiation (averaging 28 millirads per year) is higher in wooden structures than in stone, brick, or cement structures. So one must consider the total picture.

"Should We Move Everyone Out of Denver Because of Cosmic Rays?"

The author has heard discussed many times the relocation of populations to safeguard them from natural radiation. No matter what the hazard of cosmic rays at Denver or anywhere else, "we" have no right to consider forcibly moving *anyone anywhere*. Individuals have the right to decide where they will live.

But provision of information on which voluntary action can be based is quite another matter. We stated earlier that the cosmic-ray dose is higher in Denver than at sea level, by approximately 22 millirads per year. In fact, there is also some increase in terrestrial radiation in that region because of the higher-than-average uranium content of the soil. But we shall just consider the cosmic-radiation component.

Suppose we consider a population of approximately 1 million in an area such as Denver, with an incremental annual dose of 22 millirads. The increment in person-rads per year would be 1,000,000 persons multiplied by 0.022 rads, or 22,000 person-rads. As an approximate value, averaged for both sexes, we can say that the whole-body cancer dose is 270 person-rads. Therefore, additional cancer deaths per year in Denver due to the cosmic-ray increment would be 22,000/270 = 81. This would represent an increase of 3.3% in the risk of cancer death.

Some Inhalation Problems with Naturally Occurring Radionuclides

The problem of radon and radon-daughter-product inhalation was treated in chapter 9, as was the problem of inhalation of nuclides of plutonium and other transuranics. Here we shall examine carcinogenesis by inhalation of such natural materials as ^{238}Uranium and ^{232}Thorium, when such materials are in the form of insoluble particles. The principles we need to handle this problem are the same as the ones we used in discussing the carcinogenicity of plutonium.

The author has calculated (based on UNSCEAR data) that the average annual ^{238}Uranium inhalation per person $= 0.511$ picocuries. From both this and the plutonium lung-cancer doses in chapter 9, lung-cancer doses of ^{238}Uranium can be calculated. For male cigarette smokers, the lung-cancer dose for ^{238}U is 0.0156 microcuries.

Therefore, 0.511 picocuries of ^{238}U (the annual inhalation at urban dust concentrations) would represent 3.28×10^{-5} bronchogenic lung-cancer doses. Clearly the annual inhalation of ^{238}U at the levels described poses a very small lung-cancer risk to cigarette-smoking males—3.28 chances out of 100,000. The risk is even lower for female smokers. For a male nonsmoker, the lung-cancer risk from the annual inhalation of ^{238}U is 1.64 chances per 10,000,000. Again, because of the higher lung-cancer doses for women than for men, the nonsmoking female's risk is lower still.

UNSCEAR (p. 58) suggests that ^{232}Th dust concentrations are about the same on the average as ^{238}U concentrations. Since the alpha-particle energies are nearly the same, all the results for ^{238}U would apply for ^{232}Th, when risk is expressed per microcurie. The combined risk would be twice the risk for one of the nuclides alone.

When solid, insoluble uranium compounds are spilled on highways (as has occurred with "yellowcake," U_3O_8), a point of reference is that the amount of ^{238}U per lung-cancer dose for male smokers is 0.0156 microcuries, and for male nonsmokers, 200 times as much. A key question in such accidents is the size of the escaping particles: the respirable sizes are under 5 microns in diameter. (Note also that 1 kilogram of ^{238}U represents 3.3×10^{-5} curies.)

PERSONAL VERSUS PUBLIC-HEALTH RISK: THE GENOCIDAL POTENTIAL OF "SMALL RISKS"

We must always keep in mind that even when something creates a risk that is small *per individual,* it will lead to a sizable number of deaths in a population if *many* individuals are put at that risk. The aggregate effect of many, widespread, small risks—each considered trivial on a personal basis—can be huge. We shall illustrate the effect of just one "trivial" risk by calculating the approximate number of lung-cancer deaths that would result if the whole U.S. population were to breathe ^{238}U and ^{232}Th at the levels just outlined.

For the United States, in 1980, we shall estimate *roughly* that 2×10^7 males smoke. (The current estimates are that about 35% of males smoke, and we must make some correction for those too young to have started smoking, out of a population of 1.1×10^8 males.) Therefore, $(2 \times 10^7) \times (3.28 \times 10^{-5}) = 656$ lung-cancer deaths per year from ^{238}Uranium inhalation.

For nonsmokers (estimating that roughly 9×10^7 males, including those at young ages, are nonsmokers), the number would be $(9 \times 10^7) \times (1.64 \times 10^{-7}) = 14.8$ lung-cancer deaths. The total number of deaths would be doubled if we took the ^{232}Th contribution into account. So the total number of deaths annually, just for U.S. males, would be $2 \times (656 + 14.8) = 1,342$.

This example suggests the insidious character of separate risks that each appear small from a personal point of view. Considered separately, each one appears like "a risk I'm willing to take." But if we knowingly and unknowingly accept *thousands* of small risks, or impose them on others, the *aggregate* risk could be of suicidal or genocidal proportions. And as long as there is no discussion about valid methods to calculate risks, and little education about the aggregate and delayed nature of their consequences, how many people will sense the danger in time?

The combined risks from numerous sources of ionizing radiation and from numerous chemical poisons may *reverse* public health advances before anyone realizes the cause—especially in the face of well-funded countereducation that urges people to keep "very, very small risks in perspective," or ridicules calculated health effects as "unreal" and "merely statistical."

If someone had predicted in 1968 that in 1978, 375,000 Americans would die of cancer (as was the case in 1978), would that prediction have been ridiculed for being a "mere calculation"? Of course not. Public-health science is ridiculed only when it associates negative effects with some specific activity, product, or enterprise having powerful backers.

EFFORTS TO MEASURE CANCER AND LEUKEMIA PRODUCED BY NATURAL RADIATION

Over a period of years many people have asked why no one has directly measured the cancers and leukemias produced by natural radiation simply by observing the cancer death rates in regions that differ in natural background. This is an excellent question, and we shall address it here. We shall consider (a) the fundamental requirement for such studies and (b) the published evidence from studies of this kind that have attempted to make the measurement directly.

In discussions in chapters 4 and 5 it was pointed out that the validity of an epidemiological study of radiation effects depends on the comparability of the exposed and the unexposed in all respects other than the radiation. If the two groups are not comparable, there must be a way to correct for the differences, or the study is essentially meaningless. And it is precisely here that the difficulty arises in the effort to make a direct measurement of the induction of cancer and leukemia by natural radiation. In the United States the regions of relatively high background radiation are at higher altitudes than the regions with relatively low background radiation. But altitude is only one problem. There are other differences between those living in the high-altitude, high-background regions and those living in the low-altitude, low-background regions which make such studies exceedingly difficult to accomplish in any meaningful manner.

How Large an Effect Would Be Anticipated?

It is possible, in the United States, to find regions that differ from each other by 100 millirads per year in individual exposure to natural background radiation. Let us estimate the *expected* difference in cancer death rates between two regions that differ in natural exposure by 100 millirads of whole-body radiation per year, assuming all other features are identical.

The necessary calculations tell us that we can expect a difference of 16.1% in cancer death rate for a population with an extra 0.1 rad per year in natural radiation compared with the cancer death rate for a population, otherwise equivalent, but without that extra 0.1 rad per year. So, if our vital statistics are good enough to detect a 16.1% difference in cancer death rates, we should be able to measure the effects of 0.1 rad per year difference in natural background radiation.

Frigerio and Stowe (1976) attempted this sort of measurement by examination of natural background radiation in all the 50 United States and the vital statistics data for cancer death rates by state. Frigerio and Stowe stated the following in their abstract: "Observation of the populations at risk showed not only no increment in malignant mortality with increasing background, but a consistent and continuous decrement" (p. 385). They did not examine their own data closely enough, however, for the data do not support their conclusion. It is true that the data indicate that the cancer death rate is lowest for the 14 states with the highest natural background radiation. But the data do not support the "consistent and continuous decrement" claimed by Frigerio and Stowe. Had they separated the data for the remaining 36 states, they would have noted that their claim does not stand up. The actual data are as follows:

	Highest 14 States	Middle 22 States	Lowest 14 States
Natural Background (mrem/year)*	170	130.4	118
White Population	16,897,000	81,471,000	59,683,000
Cancer Death Rates, age adjusted, per 100,000/year	132.2	155.1	146.8

*Note that these background values include radon and thoron exposure, whereas the 80.4 millirems per year (in the text) do not include these exposures.

Comparison of the 14 states with the highest background (170 millirems/year) with the 22 states (the middle group) with 130.4 millirems/year shows a higher cancer death rate for the latter group, the group with the lower background. This is in accord with Frigerio and Stowe's conclusion. But this is only part of the story. Comparison of the middle group with the 14 states with the lowest background shows a higher cancer rate for the middle group, the group with the higher background, an effect exactly the opposite of—and of about the same magnitude per millirem as—that noted by Frigerio and Stowe. So the evidence is *anything but consistent.* When this sort of finding is made, one must suspect that factors other than radiation are operative, and are of sufficient magnitude to obscure the true effect of the radiation differences between regions. Some of these other factors might include cultural lifestyles that affect disease rates, the ratio of physicians to persons in each region, and industrialization.

The lesson of interest is that we must respect fundamental requirements in such studies. When it is obvious that something other than background radiation has a predominant effect in determining cancer rates in the population under study, we simply have not fulfilled the essential conditions for a valid study.

The Studies of the High Background Radiation Research Group, China

In August 1980, a study appeared, authored by the High Background Radiation Research Group, China. This study describes an effort to measure chromosomal aberrations, cancer and leukemia rates, and genetic-chromosomal diseases in a region of China (Yangjiang County in Guangdong Province) where the background radiation levels are approximately two to three times higher than they are in surrounding regions. Unfortunately the total population in the high-background region is small—on the order of 80,000—which severely limits the vital-statistics data.

The following items were evaluated for the population samples in the high-background and control regions:

1. Cytogenetic alterations in the chromosomes
2. Cancer mortality rates for the period 1970–1974
3. Spontaneous abortion rates for the period 1963–1975
4. Incidence of Down's syndrome (see chapter 15)
5. Frequency of 31 kinds of "hereditary diseases and congenital deformities of children"

Unfortunately, all the studies suffer seriously from inadequate numbers of cases, making the conclusions of very dubious significance.

"TECHNOLOGICALLY ENHANCED NATURAL-RADIATION EXPOSURES"

When the author first encountered the term *technologically enhanced natural-radiation exposure,* the masterpiece of "doublespeak" in the nuclear era, he was unbelieving. While it sounds like something no one would want to do without, it is not meant to be something favorable. Gesell and Prichard (1975) define it as exposure to natural sources of radiation (that is, naturally occurring radionuclides and cosmic radiation) which would not occur without (or is increased by) some technological activity not expressly designed to produce radiation. We shall consider several of these "technological enhancements."

The Dose from Air Travel, the Result of Altitude

There is, as was pointed out earlier in this chapter, an increase in cosmic radiation with an increase in altitude. UNSCEAR (p. 82) suggests, for subsonic flights under average solar conditions (absence of flares), an absorbed dose of approximately 0.3 millirads per hour of flight. It is estimated (UNSCEAR, p. 82) that in 1975, the annual distance flown worldwide (excluding data from China) by all passengers on such flights was 0.676×10^{12} passenger-kilometers. Since average speed is about 600 kilometers per hour, a total of approximately 10^9 passenger-hours were spent in such travel per year, as of 1975. The collective dose was, therefore, 3.4×10^5 passenger- or person-rads.

If we consider the flying population as a sort of equilibrium population and use the average of the male and female whole-body cancer dose (U.S.) to describe the average risk, the number of cancer deaths caused by cosmic radiation (the technological enhancement associated with passenger flying) was 3.4×10^5 person-rads/270 person-rads per cancer death = 1,260, the worldwide yearly price of subsonic air travel.

People should know about these risks. The author doubts that many would thereby be deterred from air travel. This type of cancer induction, voluntarily accepted by individuals in exchange for the convenience of air travel, requires no control whatsoever by society. It is simply not society's business.

The Problem of Airline Crews: UNSCEAR (p. 257) makes some of its estimates of cosmic-radiation dose to airline crew members on the basis that the average crew member flew 1,000 hours per year. Let us use this estimate along with 0.3 millirads per hour as the incremental radiation dose. The annual dose increment per crew member was, therefore, 300 millirads. If we assume that the average crew member was 25 years of age, we calculate the *incremental* risk of cancer per year as follows:

The whole-body cancer dose for 25-year-old males = 201.4 person-rads. The whole-body cancer dose for 25-year-old females = 251.6 person-rads. (Both values are from tables 10 and 11.)

Personal Risk to Female Flight Personnel: Annual increment was 0.3/251.6 = 0.00119. This means an added 1.19 chances per 1,000 of developing a fatal cancer as a result of a year of such work. Stated otherwise, of 1,000 female personnel, 1.19 would have incurred a fatal premature cancer from each year of work.

Personal Risk to Male Flight Personnel: Annual increment was 0.3/201.4 = 0.00149, or 1.49 chances per 1,000 of developing a fatal cancer.

The Radiation Dose from Coal-Fired Electric Power Plants as Compared with Nuclear Plants

It is commonly stated that the burning of coal in electric-power plants causes the release of radioactivity into the environment because uranium and its decay products, and sometimes thorium and its decay products, are present in the coal. (The content of such uranium and thorium series in coal is quite variable from region to region.) This is a valid illustration of "technologically enhanced natural radiation": if we did not burn the coal, we would not be releasing the extra uranium and decay products of uranium into the environment.

However, this entire issue has been grossly distorted as part of a promotional endeavor to persuade people that nuclear power is clean. It is widely claimed that coal-fired power plants release more natural radioactivity to the environment than do nuclear plants. This claim is fraudulent. After looking at the problem realistically, we find that nuclear-power generation puts 35 to 81 times more of the naturally radioactive nuclides on the surface of the earth than does coal power. This ratio is, of course, exclusive of the man-made (unnatural) radionuclides created by nuclear-power plants. Pohl (1975) reached similar conclusions.

If one wished to know how much natural radioactivity is brought to the environment by the nuclear-power cycle versus the coal-power cycle, it is self-evident that one would compare *all* parts of the nuclear cycle that put natural radioactivity into the environment with *all* parts of the coal cycle that put natural radioactivity into the environment. Sadly, failure to do this is commonplace in nuclear promotion.

A detailed analysis of this issue shows that it is *impossible* for the coal cycle ever to bring as much natural radioactivity to the environment as does the nuclear fuel cycle.

This does not *necessarily* mean the dose from the natural nuclides associated with nuclear power will be 35–81 times higher than the dose from coal. The dose ratio may be inside that range or higher or lower, depending on several unknowns, including the actual migration and reconcentration of these nuclides in the biosphere, and the likelihood of human irresponsibility, such as using uranium tailings for major building projects (in Colorado), or damming uranium mill ponds with dams that break easily, to name two real examples.

SECTION 2: INDUSTRIAL AND CONSUMER PRODUCTS WITH RADIONUCLIDES

LUMINOUS-DIAL WRISTWATCHES

Historically, the *consumer* products that have irradiated the public in the most widespread manner have been wristwatches and clocks with luminous dials. The nuclide ^{226}Radium, occurring in nature, was admixed with a chemical called the *scintillator,* which would glow upon exposure to the alpha particles from the radium or its decay products. Such watches are still sold on a worldwide basis, although in the United States the use of radium has been replaced by the use of tritium and [147]Promethium, both of which are soft beta-particle emitters and hence are expected to deliver a lower dose than [226]Radium, which is a source of gamma rays as well as alpha particles.

The amount of [226]Radium in a wristwatch will be less than 0.1 microcurie, *if* recommendations made for safety reasons by the International Atomic Energy Agency (IAEA) are followed. It is estimated (UNSCEAR 1977, p. 96) that the wearer of a wristwatch containing 0.1 microcurie would receive a gonadal dose of approximately 6 millirads per year. The wearer of a *pocket watch* containing the same amount would receive 8 millirads per year.

It is interesting that society so often attempts to solve its problems in ways that make matters worse rather than better. In the endeavor to reduce the gamma-ray doses from wristwatches, ^{3}H and [147]Promethium have been used instead of [226]Radium. It is estimated (UNSCEAR, p. 96) that to get the same average brightness as is produced with 1 microcurie of [226]Radium over the assumed five-year life of the watch, it would take 11,000 microcuries of ^{3}H or 390 microcuries of [147]Pm.

The consequences that might follow from the handling of large quantities of these two nuclides do not appear to have been considered, as has been the case with all such uses of radionuclides. The ludicrous suggestion has been made that people will voluntarily return devices containing radionuclides to some central place, such as the factory, once the devices are no longer useful *but still radioactive.* In fact, no one has the foggiest notion what dump heap, or what fire, such devices will end up in. We can expect that most radionuclides used in consumer products will simply end up contaminating the surface of the earth.

Sometimes even the immediate purpose of making improvements is subverted. The reader will recall from chapter 2 that whenever electrons in motion are slowed down (as in a high-voltage tube), X-rays will be emitted. An analogous event occurs with a pure beta-particle emitter. When the beta particles are slowed down, for instance, by components of the watch case itself, we have the emission of photon radiation, called *bremsstrahlung,* which is X-radiation. It has been estimated that the substitution of [147]Promethium for radium would still give a gonadal dose of 0.3 millirads per year, *if* the recommended promethium limit were observed, from such bremsstrahlung radiation. If we really want to eliminate unnecessary sources of radiation, we might consider simply eliminating the luminous-dial watch.

UNSCEAR (p. 97) cites the Moghissi-Carter estimate that the total dose from radioluminous timepieces in the United States during 1973 was a minimum of 6,100 man-rads. Using a rough average value of 270 person-rads per cancer death, this dose would produce about 23 extra cancer deaths per year—in exchange for the privilege of using radioluminous timepieces.

TWO ETHICAL ISSUES

While the author is not concerned about the cancer risk voluntarily incurred by knowledgeable users of radioluminous timepieces, two very troublesome ethical points do arise from that use. First, there is the question of the genetic injury to be felt by future generations as a result of this practice. Second, there is the injury to be felt by someone, somewhere else, because these radioactive sources ultimately will be dumped in one way or another into the general environment. Someone who did not choose to have the "benefit" of the device will later feel the resulting hazard—cancer. These ethical questions are not peculiar to radiation sources; they also arise with the distribution of certain *chemicals* in millions and billions of consumer products that also will eventually be discarded into the environment.

PROLIFERATING PRODUCTS (A PARTIAL LISTING)

Industrial and consumer devices incorporating radionuclides are proliferating about as fast as inventors and entrepreneurs can dream them up. Supply of the radionuclides is hardly a problem, since most are by-products of the nuclear industry. In principle, the use of radionuclides in industrial and consumer products is the opposite of the way we would be proceeding if our objective were to keep radioactive poisons out of the biosphere.

The UNSCEAR report provides a long list of commercial products containing radionuclides (pp. 95–99). Radioluminous products with the nuclide in paint or plastic include timepieces, aircraft instruments, compasses, instrument dials and markers, thermostat dials and pointers, automobile lock illuminators, automobile shift quadrants, bell pushes, fishing lights, and spirit levels. The nuclides include ^{9}II, in quantities ranging from 0.3 millicuries to 10 curies, ^{147}Pm, in quantities ranging from 60 microcuries to 0.75 curies, and ^{226}Radium, in quantities of from 0.1 to 20 microcuries.

Radioluminous sources in sealed tubes are found in the following: timepieces, ordinary compasses, marine compasses, marine navigational instruments, markers, signs and indicators, exit signs, step markers, mooring lights and buoys, public-telephone dials, light-switch markers, bell pushes, and miniature light sources. The nuclides include ^{3}H, in quantities between 0.2 and 30 curies, and ^{85}Krypton, in quantities of approximately 0.25 curies.

Electronic and electrical devices containing radionuclides include electronic tubes, glow-discharge tubes, voltage-discharge tubes, cold-cathode tubes, fluorescent-lamp starters, gas-discharge lamps (high-pressure mercury-vapor lamps), vacuum tubes, glow lamps, spark-gap tubes, high-voltage protective devices, and low-voltage fuses. Tritium, ^{3}H, is present in some of these devices in amounts ranging from 1 microcurie to 10 millicuries. ^{137}Cesium is sometimes present in amounts of 5 microcuries, ^{226}Radium in amounts of 1 microcurie. Other nuclides present are natural thorium, [63]Nickel, [60]Cobalt, [85]Krypton, [147]Promethium, all generally in amounts in the microcurie range.

Antistatic devices containing radionuclides include lightning rods, various instruments, antistatic brushes, and precision balances. The radionuclides include [226]Ra, in amounts of from 10 microcuries to 1 millicurie, [241]Americium, in amounts of from 2 to 700 microcuries, ^{3}H, in amounts of 1 millicurie, and [210]Polonium, in amounts of from 0.05 to 0.5 millicuries.

Gas and aerosol (smoke) detectors, now numbering in the millions, contain [241]Americium in amounts of between 1 and 100 microcuries, [226]Radium in amounts of between 0.01 and 15 microcuries, and [238]Plutonium in amounts of 20 microcuries.

Lest the reader think that many of these sources of radioactivity are far away from him, a few other uses of radionuclides will be of interest. Both thorium and uranium have been used in the manufacture of optical lenses. UNSCEAR (p. 98) cites the work of Wrixon and Webb to the effect that some optical lenses contain up to 30% by weight of uranium or thorium, and that these lenses can deliver appreciable doses to the lens of the wearer's eyes. McMillan and Horne (1973) report that the absorbed dose rate (in air) at the surface of a lens containing 18% thorium by weight was found to be (using thermoluminescent dosimeters) *one millirad per hour*.

Dental porcelains, in the majority of instances, contain a combination of uranium and cerium compounds for the purpose of simulating the fluorescence of natural teeth in daylight and artificial light. The studies of O'Riordan and Hunt (1974) on the uranium content of dental porcelains led to the estimate that the absorbed dose in the basal layer of the epithelium of the mouth could be on the order of *3 rads per year*. The government of the United Kingdom recommended cessation of the use of radioactive fluorescers in dental porcelain following these studies.

Ceramics (e.g., dinner plates) and glassware are reported (in UNSCEAR, Table 45, p. 96) to contain as much as 10% uranium or thorium.

As a final point the reader should note this statement in the UNSCEAR report ("activities" refers to curies):

The radionuclides and the approximate range of activities used are also given in Table 45. It must be pointed out, however, that accurate information on the activities contained in the consumer products and on the number of products manufactured is sometimes difficult to obtain. (p. 96)

One wonders why manufacturers are so reluctant to be straightforward on this issue.

The UNSCEAR report concludes its discussion of the use of radionuclides in consumer and industrial products with the estimate that the likely annual average gonadal dose from consumer products is less than 1 millirad per person, almost entirely due to radioluminous timepieces. The discussion ends with the statement, "However, in view of the growing number and diversity of consumer products, it is important to ensure that proper control is maintained over their use and disposal" (p. 99). Has the reader ever found a better example of unrealistic wishful thinking?

The Color-Television Problem

The color-television problem is part of a more general problem. As the reader knows from chapter 2, any time electrons are allowed to fall through a potential difference, the stage is set for the production of X-rays when the electrons are stopped. This is, of course, how X-rays are generated in an X-ray tube. A variety of electronic equipment may contain some part showing a voltage difference of 10, 20, 30, 40 kilovolts or more. To the extent that any current flows through such potential differences, X-rays will be formed. Sometimes, the electronic gear as normally operated does not have a high kilovoltage, but on repair or adjustment, the kilovoltage is raised. The higher the kilovoltage, the more serious the problem, in all cases, simply because the chance that the X-rays will have enough energy to penetrate the case is enhanced.

As general advice, the author suggests that when a question exists about a piece of equipment, a test should be made with film badges or an X-ray-sensitive measuring device. This is the sure way to determine the dose from the device. Who knows when some manufacturer is going to put a 50-kv potential difference somewhere in circuitry? As an illustration of an instrument in which X-rays are generated because of high-voltage electrons used for another purpose, we can consider the electron microscope. The author has been personally involved in cases where significant X-ray doses were received by operators of electron microscopes because this problem was not appreciated.

The UNSCEAR report states that "it is likely that the x-ray emission from recently built colour television receivers is negligible under conditions of normal operation and servicing" (1977, p. 99). The International Atomic Energy Agency's Safety Series No. 9 (1967) recommends that the dose rate at any readily accessible point, 5 cm from the surface of a television set, should not exceed 0.5 milliroentgens per hour under normal working conditions.

Wang (1975) made an experimental study of the ionizing radiation (low-energy X-rays) from 28 randomly chosen color-television home receivers of the kind commonly purchased in Taiwan in about 1973. Such brands as Sony, Hitachi, National, Sanyo, Sharp, Toshiba, Victor, and Admiral were represented, and picture-tube sizes ranged from 12 through 25 inches. Thermoluminescent dosimeters were used for the measurements. The measurements were made with the dosimeters close to the center of the front glass surface of the face of the sets, and with the dosimeters close to the surface of both sides of the sets. Exposure rates at the sides were found to be almost equal in average value. The average values found ranged from 0.010 to 0.042 milliroentgens/hour, when measured in front of the set, and from 0.002 to 0.016 milliroentgens/hour at the side of the set. There was no direct correlation between screen size and dose.

The dose per year at the face of the set, in front, would be 193 milliroentgens/year. The dose per year at the side of the set would be 56 milliroentgens/year. But it is hardly likely that anyone would remain this close to a television set 24 hours a day. A conservative estimate would be that the effective distance from the source to Wang's dosimeters was approximately 10 centimeters. (A television set is not a perfect point source.) Now let us suppose the viewer would ordinarily be 2 meters, or 200 centimeters, from the set, on the average. Then the dose would be reduced by a factor of approximately 400.

Therefore, the dose per year, from constant viewing 24 hours per day, would be 193 mR/400 = 0.48 mR per year. Since the milliroentgen is so close to the millirad, we can say that the dose per year would be close to 0.5 millirads, a very small dose, especially considering that one would have to watch television 24 hours a day to receive it.

We should be concerned that the kilovoltages on the tubes are not raised, since this would increase the penetration power of the X-rays produced, and hence raise the dose. This used to occur in early repair work, when servicemen found that raising the voltage helped to correct certain problems.

SECTION 3: OCCUPATIONAL EXPOSURES TO IONIZING RADIATION AND THEIR EFFECTS

The UNSCEAR report (1977) is an excellent source of detailed summaries from around the world of the average doses being received by workers in a variety of occupations, including those occupations involving major opportunities for radiation exposure, such as in the nuclear-power industry, industrial radiography, and various aspects of the practice of medicine, including diagnostic and therapeutic uses of radiation. By and large, there is probably some validity in the levels of radiation exposures reported around the world. But whenever people are exposed, and at all occupational levels—from the exposed individual up through the managerial chain—employees recognize that they cannot possibly make themselves more popular by reporting (or having reported for them) overexposures. Self-interest thus leads to lowering the exposure levels reported.

The author has personally witnessed, in leading laboratories, the practice of setting a film badge or other monitoring device away in a "safe" place while a "dirty" radiation operation is performed. The author mentions this not as grounds for mountains of regulations and controls, but rather as a caution to those who are considering using reported exposure data for serious scientific purposes. It would be fair to state that the true occupational exposure is not likely to be less than the reported exposure. In most instances it is simply impossible to predict how much higher the true dose may be. In the case of nuclear power, to be considered below, we do have an estimate of a large number of unreported exposures—of those workers known as *jumpers* or *human sponges*.

SOME PRINCIPLES CONCERNING OCCUPATIONAL EXPOSURE

The author does not share the widespread view that what we need to control occupational exposure is an increase in regulations or a lower permissible dose. With one important caveat, the author believes that a well-informed worker has a right to decide whether he or she wishes to take a job that involves a radiation-induced excess risk of cancer. What is really needed is some honesty about what the levels of exposure really are, and what their health effects are likely to be. Fair treatment is at least the absence of deception about both dose and effect. But overall fairness in industrial uses of radiation has been absent so far.

The caveat mentioned above is the question of the genetic effects of radiation. When a worker receives a dose of ionizing radiation that reaches his gonads, this dose is genetically significant for the entire population, since the worker is part of the entire procreational pool. To the extent that genetic injuries are proportional to dose received (see chapter 15), a relatively large dose to a limited number of workers can have the same effect on future generations as a smaller dose distributed widely in the population. So harm of this sort is by no means limited to the worker who receives the radiation.

A profound ethical question arises here. It concerns the right of the worker to undertake hazardous work if he so chooses, versus the right of the yet unborn to inherit their genetic informational systems intact. The genes that are at risk now are the same genes on which future generations' very health and capabilities depend. How this problem of justice should be resolved deserves very serious discussion and concern. The radiation-associated technologies are hardly the only ones causing injury to genes or chromosomes; there is no doubt that certain chemicals cause such injuries. If each worker has the right to do whatever work he chooses, how will genetic and chromosomal "plagues" be avoided?

Clearly, among the minimal steps to be taken is to let workers *know* what they may be doing to future human beings. And we need to examine the possibility that willful genetic injury is morally equivalent to child abuse, a monstrous application of "might makes right," and the ultimate in the bullying of the defenseless by those with power.

SOME ACTUAL DOSES REPORTED FOR VARIOUS MAJOR INDUSTRIES

If we assume that the doses reported by industry reflect reality to some extent, we can make some interesting observations and calculations.

The Nuclear-Power Industry

For the nuclear industry, after examining reports from many countries, UNSCEAR finally reaches the following summary of exposures (p. 242). In looking at this summary, the reader must be aware that temporary workers (to be discussed below) are not included, so the listed exposures are to be regarded as minimum exposures.

Part of the Nuclear Fuel Cycle	Dose per Megawatt-Year (electrical) (whole-body dose in man-rads/mwyr)
Uranium mining, milling, fuel fabrication, and transport of irradiated and unirradiated fuel	0.2
Nuclear reactor operations	1.0
Fuel reprocessing (based on U.K.)	1.2
Research and development in support of nuclear-power industry	1.4
Total occupational exposure, all phases, (waste disposal not considered)	3.8 man-rads/mwyr

There are many ways one could quarrel with these summary numbers, and the UNSCEAR report considers most of them. For example, there is large variability from reactor to reactor, from year to year. There is the claim that many of these data were acquired during the "learning curve" for nuclear power, and that doses will be lower in the future. And, concerning the assignment of research-and-development exposures to the nuclear fuel cycle, it is suggested that in a more mature industry these exposures will not occur at the same level. All these claims have some validity.

Nonetheless, we have here a ballpark estimate of occupational exposure per megawatt-year electrical. We must remember that reactors become more radioactive with age, and that the exposures resulting from maintenance operations go up with reactor age. And we have not yet added in the "jumpers."

Let us assess the consequences of a fully developed nuclear industry, in a country like the United States, with 1,000 plants each delivering 1,000 megawatt-years of electricity per year. In such a nuclear-power economy, breeder reactors would have to be in operation, and one can only speculate whether that would mean increased doses or decreased doses at the reactor phase. Certainly it would mean that reprocessing would be part of the cycle.

Presented in table 25 are the whole-body cancer doses and the expected cancer consequences for a fully developed nuclear-power industry, including only the *occupational* cancer deaths per year. The total energy output per year would be 10^6 megawatt-years. Since we do not know what the average age of the workers would be, the annual consequences for several possible mean ages have been calculated.

Table 25: Estimated Cancer Deaths Among Those Occupationally Exposed in a Fully Developed Nuclear-Energy Economy (10^6 megawatt-years(e) per Year)

Assumed Average Age of Workers (in years)	Whole-Body Cancer Dose in Person-Rads (males)	Person-Rads Delivered	Cancer Deaths per year, Occupational*
20	200.1	3.8×10^6	18,990
25	201.4	3.8×10^6	18,865
30	234.2	3.8×10^6	16,225
35	327.6	3.8×10^6	11,600
40	537.5	3.8×10^6	7,070
45	1,232.5	3.8×10^6	3,085

*One should *not* add all the cancer deaths in the final column. The number of deaths are estimated, as though the average age of nuclear employees were the age in column 1. It is evident that the younger the workers are, the higher the cancer price of such occupational exposure.

All calculations are based upon the whole-body cancer doses of table 10. Similar calculations could be made for an all-female work force, using table 11. But since the calculations are illustrative, not definitive for obvious reasons, those additional calculations have not been made here.

Supplement to Table 25

The Temporary Workers ("Human sponges" or "jumpers")

Since the evidence indicates that the "human sponges" take a dose about equal to that taken by regular workers, it would be appropriate to multiply all numbers in this table by a *factor of 2* as a reasonable way to estimate more honestly and seriously what the true number of cancers is likely to be.

Thus, if we calculate illustratively for the 25-year-old worker, the true number of cancers is more likely to be approximately 37,500 than the 18,865 listed above. The industry may suggest it will stop the use of "jumpers," but this would not alter the calculation one bit, for if the "jumpers" do not take their dose, someone else will have to do their work and take their dose.

The Temporary Workers—the "Jumpers": Franklin (1979) has done a fine job of investigative journalism reporting on a side of the nuclear industry that its promoters might prefer never to have mentioned. It would be hard to describe the "jumpers" better than Franklin has, so we quote him:

Jumpers are unskilled, short-term employees who expose themselves to quick doses of relatively high radiation for relatively high pay, often for only minutes of work.

Chosen at the "body shop" for their size which enables them to crawl through the 18-inch-wide passageways of mammoth steel reactor pressure vessels, they may do no more than turn a bolt. But in a workplace giving off as many as 25 rems an hour of radiation, it must be done in seconds.

Franklin estimates, based on data from the Nuclear Regulatory Commission, that by 1979, 50% of the total dose received occupationally in the nuclear-power industry was received by jumpers. This means that whatever number of cancers we estimate for regular workers, whose doses we use in our tabulations, the true number of cancers is probably *on the order of twice as large.* So the estimates in table 25 should be multiplied by 2.

The Medical "Industry"

Reports exist of average doses received by workers who perform various tasks associated with the medical "industry." We shall use data accumulated by UNSCEAR (1977, pp. 242–246):

1. In the United Kingdom, to an estimated 20,000 workers involved with radiation, the average dose in 1974 was 0.21 rads/worker.

2. Klement's survey, based on U.S. data between 1965 and 1970, indicates an annual average dose of 0.32 rads per nonfederal X-ray worker, a value which Klement and co-workers suggest can be applied to 194,541 medical workers.

3. A survey of nuclear-medicine departments in 47 hospitals in the United States, 1968 through 1973, gives average annual doses per worker of 0.38 rads (1968), 0.37 rads (1969), 0.45 rads (1970), 0.45 rads (1971), 0.49 rads (1972), and 0.48 rads (1973).

4. A survey of doses in Canada for 1974 shows highest average exposures in rads per person of 0.19 rads for radiologists in therapeutic work, 0.15 rads for isotope technicians, and 0.14 rads for radiologic technicians involved in therapy. All other values are lower, ranging down to 0.01 for dentists.

5. A survey of doses in Denmark for 1974 shows employees of radium (therapy) centers averaging 0.29 rads per person annually, dermatologists averaging 0.14 rads annually, X-ray-department employees averaging 0.07 rads annually, and employees of all other departments averaging less.

6. A survey of doses to 20,517 medical workers in France, for 1975, shows that the highest values were 0.36 rads per worker, annual average, in conventional radiotherapy centers, and 0.20 in Curie Centers. Hospital radiodiagnostic centers showed average values of 0.18 rads per worker versus 0.15 to 0.22 rads for private radiodiagnostic centers.

All these values provide a reasonable picture of the exposures now encountered, *on the average,* in medical work. The average dose does not matter much to the unfortunate worker who gets a radiation dose well *above* the average; but such workers are relatively few in number.

As an illustration of *average*-exposure consequences, we might evaluate the cancer price of the exposures reported by Klement, for the United States during the 1965–1970 period, of 194,541 medical workers who each received an average dose of 0.32 rads. This amounts to a yearly exposure of 62,253 person-rads. If we use a rough average value for whole-body cancer dose in an equilibrium population of approximately 270 person-rads, then 62,253/270 = 230 deaths would be anticipated per year from this sort of exposure if the number of medical X-ray workers remained at 194,541.

The "Permissible Dose"

An early recommendation by the International Commission on Radiological Protection (ICRP) was that the permissible dose for occupational exposure should be calculated according to this formula:

Dose accumulated at a particular age = (5) × (age minus 18) rems

Let us assume that a person went to work in a radiation-associated industry at age 18. By the time that first year of work was over, he would be "permitted" to have accumulated $(5)(19 - 18) = 5 \times 1 = 5$ rems of radiation. Suppose this worker received the full permissible dose in the first year, but received only 1 rem per year in the next 5 years. The total accumulated was 10 rems. However, the ICRP formula would permit this worker, now 24 years of age, to have accumulated $(5)(24 - 18) = 30$ rems. So, in a sense, he has accumulated a "bank account" of 20 unused rems. Neither the ICRP nor anyone else has ever suggested that workers should be exposed up to the permissible limit. But there is a way this worker's "bank account" may get used. Suppose the plant that employs him has a "dirty" job to do. The authorities may feel it is all right to draw on his bank account, provided he receives no more than 12 rems per year, and of that dose, no more than 3 rems per quarter. So instead of receiving a maximum dose of 5 rems per year, this worker is allowed to draw on his bank account until his exposure is again limited by the (5)(age − 18) rule. Thereafter, his limit is again 5 rems per year.

It is evident that this formula would permit a 30-year-old *new* worker, with no prior occupational exposure, to receive a total of $(5)(30 - 18) = 60$ rems. This new worker could receive 12 rems per year for a number of years before his exposure would have to come down to 5 rems per year.

In fact, there is not a shred of scientific substance behind this elaborate minuet of 5-rem and 12-rem annual doses. Nor is there any basis for the 3-rem-per-quarter limitation. In the author's opinion the reason for all these variations of permissible dose is to make it *appear* to the worker that someone somewhere must know what he is doing in setting dose limits.

The real issue is the use of the term *permissible*. Workers are encouraged directly and indirectly to believe that *permissible* means *safe*. The reader of this book knows by now that there is no evidence whatever for *any* safe dose of ionizing radiation with respect to cancer induction: cancer is expected to be in excess in proportion to the dose received. There is some hope on the horizon, however.

Johnson and Trimel (1978) report on an interview with Drs. Robert Minogue and Karl Goller of the Office of Standards Development of the U.S. Nuclear Regulatory Commission. Dr. Minogue (director of that office) was asked his opinion about the idea that there exists a level of radiation—a threshold—below which exposure is not harmful. And Dr. Minogue is alleged to have replied, "What we have found is, by God, there ain't no threshold. There are some diehards who still believe in it, but it's a myth that there is a threshold." Dr. Goller, who is director of the Commission's Division of Siting, Health, and Safeguards Standards, is alleged to have stated, "Workers must be informed that no radiation is good radiation. The specialized workers who are picking up higher doses will have to determine whether it is worth it. It is their choice."

Such candid, straightforward, scientifically honest statements are so rare from a government bureau that the author felt he had better see if Drs. Goller and Minogue would confirm that they had indeed made them. In reply to a letter from the author, Drs. Minogue and Goller stated:

However, we feel that the authors have made a fair and generally successful effort to present the main thrust of what we said. Although much of the material in quotation marks is in fact a summary of a rather long discussion, we don't feel that what was said is misrepresented, recognizing that a writer must have some latitude in reducing a long interview to an article of reasonable length.

Drs. Minogue and Goller provided some additional material in their letter which is important and to the point:

One point we discussed was the importance of an informed decision by radiation workers to accept exposure, and this is undoubtedly the basis for the somewhat paraphrased quote attributed to Goller. The evidence mounts that, within the range of exposure levels encountered by radiation workers, there is no threshold, i.e., a level which can be assumed as safe in an absolute sense. We have found in discussions with people both in the power industry and in the nuclear medicine field that many people in these fields honestly believe that the low levels of exposure permitted are without risk, which reflects that somehow the wrong message has been delivered, in spite of the fact that our regulatory program has been based on the prudent policy assumption that any amount of radiation has a finite probability of inducing a health effect, e.g., cancer. We brought out in the interview our concern that in the past the way the regulations were written and regulatory programs were established may be responsible for creating the impression among many workers that the levels of exposure permitted are completely without risk. We felt it should be made clear to workers that there is some risk.

A fine statement.

OCCUPATIONAL-RISK CALCULATIONS FOR WORKERS, LAWYERS, AND COMPENSATION-COURT JUDGES

Two questions come up repeatedly in occupational-exposure situations:

1. What risk of future cancer do I incur at the permissible level of radiation?

2. If I develop a cancer, what is the chance that my occupational radiation exposure was its cause?

Both questions are important, and both will be answered. The first is the simpler one.

1. The Future Risk of Cancer from Exposure at the "Permissible" Dose

One point of a medico-legal nature needs clarification first. When a person is exposed to ionizing radiation, the *injury* occurs at the time of exposure, at the cellular or chromosome-gene level. The clinical *manifestation*, in the form of cancer, appears many years later. The author has seen courtroom situations in which it has not been understood clearly that the irreversible injury increasing the risk of cancer occurred at the time of irradiation. If the irradiation was protracted over a period of time, as in occupational settings, *injury was accumulated* over that period of time.

We shall concern ourselves here with the *lifetime* risk of cancer development which results from occupational radiation exposure, and would not occur without that exposure. In answering question 2, we shall deal with the chance that a cancer which occurs by *a specified age* is due to radiation exposure versus the chance that it is "spontaneous."

Table 26 provides the information necessary for answering question 1. If the exposures are less than those permissible (here we shall use 5 rads per year of whole-body radiation as the permissible dose), then the risk estimates will be proportionately lower than those presented in table 26. Since the risk incurred is different for different ages at irradiation, table 26 is based on 10 years of work, and 5 rads of exposure per year, and the data are treated as though all the exposure occurred at the midpoint of the 10-year interval. This is a simplified approach compared with calculating the risk for each year of work and summing those risks, which is the strictly correct approach. We shall do one sample calculation comparing our simplified approach with the strictly correct one, to ascertain how much error we introduce. The estimates for various ages at exposure are presented in table 26.

Longer Periods of Employment: Suppose that someone worked for two 10-year intervals, one with a midpoint at age 25 and the other with a midpoint at age 35. What is the risk of cancer death from total exposure to 100 rads, of which 50 rads was received in each of the two intervals?

For the first interval, the cancer-death probability due to radiation = 0.248 (from table 26). For the second interval, the probability = 0.153. The total radiation-induced cancer-death probability = 0.248 + 0.153 = 0.401 (4 chances out of 10).

Exposures Lower Than 5 Rads per Year: If someone were exposed to 1 rad per year for 10 years instead of 5 rads per year, the risk of radiation-induced fatal cancer would be, for a midpoint at age 25, 10/201.4 = 0.0497, which is exactly ⅕ of the risk for 5 rads per year. Reminding the reader how a risk of 0.05 (rounding off) is interpreted, it predicts that 5 out of every 100 workers—we cannot say which 5—will die prematurely of cancer somewhere in the body.

TABLE 26: LIFETIME CANCER RISKS ASSOCIATED WITH
PERMISSIBLE OCCUPATIONAL DOSES (MALES)

BASIS: *10 years of employment; 5 rads per year, received at different ages.
Age listed is the midpoint of employment period.*

COLUMN 1	COLUMN 2	COLUMN 3
Midpoint of Employment Period (age in years)	*Whole-Body Cancer Dose (person-rads per cancer death)*	*Probability of Cancer Death as a Result of Exposure Occupationally to 5 Rads per Year*
25	201.4	0.248
30	234.2	0.213
35	327.6	0.153
40	537.5	0.093
45	1,232.5	0.041

Column 2 provides the whole-body cancer doses from table 10.

Column 3 is obtained as follows: For 10 years of work at 5 rads per year, the accumulated total for 1 person is 50 person-rads. If 201.4 person-rads guarantee 1 cancer death, then 50 person-rads give a probability of 50/201.4, or 0.248 of a fatal cancer, which is entered in column 3.

The calculations would proceed in an entirely analogous fashion for women receiving radiation occupationally, except that the column 2 entries would be obtained from table 11.

The Simplified Calculation Versus the Refined Calculation: We will test our simplified method versus the strictly correct method for 10 years of exposure and a midpoint at age 25. For the strictly correct approach, we look up in table 10, the whole-body cancer dose for every age in our interval, starting with age 20, and calculate the cancer-death risk for 5 rads per year, using those whole-body doses, for each year in the interval. Then all the risks are summed, as in the table below.

In table 26, our simplified approach yielded 0.248 as the risk, which is not appreciably different from the value obtained by the strictly correct approach, 0.24413 (less than 2% difference).

2. The Probability That a Cancer in a Previously Exposed Worker Is Occupational in Origin

This question requires more detailed consideration than question 1. It comes up over and over again in medico-legal situations. We have already shown how to calculate the *lifetime* risk of cancer from occupational radiation exposure (table 26). We now ask if a cancer occurs at age 45 in a worker who was exposed to ionizing radiation at age 25, what is the probability that the *radiation,* rather than spontaneous causes, accounts for the cancer? In a more general way, we want to know for any age of *occurrence* of cancer and any age at *irradiation,* what the probability is that the radiation is responsible for the cancer.

Let us consider a very simple case. A man is exposed at age 25 and develops a cancer at age 28. Since we have based all our calculations on the

Age (years)	Whole-Body Cancer Dose (person-rads/cancer death)	Cancer Death Risk for 5-Rad Exposure in Stated Year
20	200.1	0.02499
21	200.2	0.02498
22	200.4	0.02496
23	200.6	0.02493
24	200.9	0.02489
25	201.4	0.02483
26	203	0.02463
27	208	0.02404
28	214	0.02336
29	222	0.02252
	Total	0.24413

evidence that essentially no radiation-induced cancers will show up within 3 years after exposure, we would conclude that there is almost a zero probability that radiation is the cause of this cancer. We have developed a set of factors that enable us to estimate, for a specified amount of radiation exposure, what the number of radiation-induced cancers will be for every post-exposure year up to age 90.

What we need now is a group of figures, calculated from those factors, that covers every possible age at irradiation and both sexes; then we would be in a position to answer the probability question under all possible circumstances. The preparation of such an enormous volume of tabular material would be impractical, but a solution just about as useful is the preparation of tables for 5-year age intervals, with two entries in each table:

1. Spontaneous number of cancer deaths
2. Radiation-induced cancer deaths, for 1 rad of radiation given at a stated age

Table A, which constitutes an appendix to this book, presents such information for males and females. The entries were obtained by calculating from the same factors as were used in chapter 6 to calculate whole-body cancer doses. One point must be noted. For each age at irradiation, the population sample at risk is the number of survivors from 100,000 live-born. It turns out to be much simpler to do all the calculations on this basis. It really does not matter how many persons are in the initial sample, since the key comparison is *between spontaneous cancer deaths and radiation-induced cancer deaths*.

Use of Table A to Answer the Question of the Probability of Radiation Causation: We can answer question 2 for the case of a man exposed at age 25 to 5 rads per year who develops a fatal cancer at age 45. Several possibilities will be considered.

a. Suppose the man had worked only 1 year and had received a total of 5 rads of whole-body radiation.

From part f, table A, we have the following:

91 cancer fatalities, spontaneous, for an initial population of 95,943 persons.

1.11 cancer fatalities, radiation-induced *per rad,* for that same initial population.

Therefore, from 5 rads delivered at age 25, (5) $\times$ (1.11) = 5.55 fatal cancers would result. The total cancer deaths in such a population sample would be the sum of the radiation-induced plus the spontaneous cancer deaths, or 91.0 + 5.55 = 96.55 cancer deaths. The fraction due to radiation = 5.55/96.55 = 0.057. Therefore, we can say that the probability that radiation caused this man's cancer is 0.057, or that there are 5.7 chances out of 100 that radiation was the cause.

Let us now consider the same exposure circumstances, but ask about a cancer that develops at age 60 instead of at age 45. From part f, table A, we have the following:

410 cancer fatalities, spontaneous, for an initial population of 95,943 persons.

14.1 cancer fatalities, radiation-induced *per rad,* for that same initial population.

Therefore, for 5 rads delivered at age 25, (5) $\times$ (14.1) = 70.5 fatal cancers would result. Total cancer deaths in this population sample would be 410 + 70.5 = 480.5. The fraction due to radiation = 70.5/480.5 = 0.147. Therefore, we can say that the probability that radiation caused this man's cancer is 0.147, or that there are 14.7 chances out of 100 that radiation was the cause. Since we cannot ever hope to tell which cancers are radiation-induced and which are not, the author prefers to describe the findings slightly differently; he considers it appropriate to say that the causation of 14.7% of this man's cancer must be assigned to radiation. In saying this, we will be wrong in some specific instances, but on the average we will be correct.

b. Let us now consider the case of the worker who worked for 10 years and received 5 rads per year. We shall assume that he worked from age 20 to age 30, so that the midpoint of his exposure was at age 25.

We shall ask the same two questions. First, what is the probability of radiation causation of a fatal cancer at age 45, and second, what is the probability of radiation causation of a fatal cancer at age 60?

The Case of a Fatal Cancer at Age 45: From part f, table A, values are obtained as before for fatal cancers at age 45, namely, 91 spontaneous cancer fatalities, and 1.11 cancer fatalities *per rad.* But we now have 50 rads of total exposure (10 years of work at 5 rads per year). For 50 rads, the expected cancers = (50) × (1.11) = 55.50. Total cancers, spontaneous plus radiation-induced, = 55.5 + 91 = 146.5. The fraction due to radiation = 55.5/146.5 = 0.379. The probability that radiation was the cause of the fatal cancer is 0.379, which is the same as saying there are 37.9 chances out of 100 of radiation causation.

The Case of a Fatal Cancer at Age 60: Values from part f, table A, for 60 years of age are 410 spontaneous cancer fatalities and 14.1 cancer fatalities per rad. For 50 rads total exposure, the expected cancers = (50) × (14.1) = 705. Total cancers, spontaneous plus radiation-induced, = 410 + 705 = 1,115 fatal cancers. The fraction due to radiation = 705/1,115 = 0.632. The probability that radiation was the cause of the fatal cancer is 0.632, which is the same as saying that there are 63.2 chances per 100 that radiation was the cause of the worker's cancer. The author prefers to say that 63.2% of the cancer was caused by radiation.

The reader may wonder why the fraction of cancers due to radiation is higher for the worker at 60 years of age than at 45. A review of the diverging O and E curves in chapter 4 will clarify this matter completely.

Other Ages, Other Doses of Radiation

We have already demonstrated how to handle different radiation doses. The entries in table A are at 5-year intervals of age-at-exposure. Suppose one wished to make a calculation for someone exposed at an age between two ages listed in table A. One would make the appropriate calculation for the 5-year entries on either side, and interpolate between the answers to get the correct answer for the intermediate age. The error in any probability value so obtained will be very small.

APPLICABILITY OF TABLE A TO NONOCCUPATIONAL ISSUES

Table A provides data that permit calculations for exposures at ages all the way back to infancy, so that it is useful for medico-legal issues besides those involving workers.

[CHAPTER 13]

IONIZING-RADIATION EXPOSURES FROM MEDICAL IRRADIATION

There can be no question at all that the diagnostic and therapeutic uses of ionizing radiation in medicine represent a major source of exposure of the general public. There is also no reason to challenge the statement that today medical radiation is the largest *man-made* source of exposure of the public at large, and, from all indications, is still a growing source of per capita exposure. For now, medical radiation is right behind natural sources of radiation as the largest source of human exposure. We have separately considered the prospect that a growing nuclear-power industry could one day usurp this leading position from medical radiation. So far it has not.

In 1970, the Bureau of Radiological Health (U.S. Department of Health, Education, and Welfare) estimated that, during that year, 130 million out of 200 million persons had one or more X-ray examinations. It is estimated that the use of diagnostic X-ray examinations has increased since then (Work Group on Radiation Exposure Reduction 1979).

In addition to this major source of *external* ionizing radiation, a whole variety of radiopharmaceutical agents are used internally both in diagnosis and in therapy. The 1977 UNSCEAR report comments (p. 331) that the 1972 UNSCEAR report had said diagnostic use of radiopharmaceuticals was doubling every three years, and that, at the writing of the 1977 report, such use was still increasing.

A most interesting question—not an easy one to study or to answer—is whether this increasing use of medical radiation is making a positive contribution to human health, or is causing deaths at a faster rate than it is working to improve health.

At the time when mammography (a radiological procedure for seeking out breast cancer) was being widely promoted, the dose to the breast was in the neighborhood of 10 rads (much more in some clinics), *not* millirads. Finally the whistle was blown on this procedure (Bailar 1976; 1978) when the question was raised whether more breast cancers were being *induced* than curable breast cancers were being *found*. More recently, the procedure is being revived at grossly lower radiation doses, less than 0.1 rad.

Mammography is a reminder that one must always ask, is this medical procedure doing more good than harm, or is it the other way around? This question is asked all too rarely. Certainly in the light of our knowledge today that the cancer risk of radiation is much greater than was thought 10 to 15 years ago, it is appropriate for both professionals and patients to question seriously, at least, the wisdom of using medical X-rays with great frequency.

It is also important to point out that an individual and his (her) physician must have the right, a right not to be infringed on by anyone, to decide whether having a particular X-ray examination offers more to gain than to lose. No bureau, no committees, should be involved in this decision.

Excluded from this chapter are two major studies on the induction of leukemia by medical irradiation (the Tri-State study and the Mayo Clinic study), because those studies are analyzed in chapter 14, which deals with radiation induction of leukemia in general.

Section 1: X-rays: Uncertainties About the Doses Received

An individual can make an intelligent decision about whether to undergo a particular X-ray examination only if he (she) is provided with the facts. Some of the questions involved are the value of the diagnostic information to be provided, whether less hazardous procedures can provide the same or even better information, and the dose to be received by the patient. As we shall see, it is virtually in the lap of the gods, even in advanced countries like the United States and Canada, what dose one will receive from standard X-ray examination procedures from hospital to hospital, from clinic to clinic, and even at the same institution from one time to another.

It escapes this author how a patient, together with his physician, can make an intelligent decision whether an X-ray procedure should be accepted when the physician has not the vaguest idea what dose the patient will receive as a result of that examination. And the dosage situation, right up to the present, is far from encouraging.

Many factors account for the inability of physicians to provide patients with meaningful estimates of the doses particular procedures will produce. Equipment performance can be and is very spotty, so that a physician's estimate may be nullified by the poor performance of equipment. As we shall see, equipment performance is particularly poor in the case of fluoroscopic procedures. Doses given, for a particular X-ray examination, are lower when the examination is made by a radiologist than when made by other physicians.

How Well Do X-ray Equipment and Operators Perform?

In the United States, the Food and Drug Administration (FDA) has responsibility for the development and promulgation of performance standards for the manufacture of radiation-emitting electronic products. The performance standards for diagnostic medical and dental X-ray components became effective on August 1, 1974, and apply to products manufactured after that date.

Field test data (p. 93, Report of the Work Group on Radiation Exposure Reduction 1979) showed a noncompliance rate of over 30%, primarily due to problems in the assembly of equipment. This has led to more stringent testing programs and to more stringent enforcement of the requirements on the assemblers of equipment. It is reported that since the standards became effective, 72 recalls of medical and dental X-ray systems, involving more than 38,000 noncompliant products, have occurred. Under the defect provisions of the Health and Safety Act of 1968, which applies to all diagnostic X-ray equipment manufactured after October 18, 1968, 26 recalls, including more than 35,000 products, have been initiated. And there is *no* regulatory control over equipment manufactured before October 1968.

Perhaps the best evidence for the real difficulty in knowing what dose one is getting from a particular X-ray procedure comes from an important recent study made by Taylor and colleagues in Canada (1979).

The Canadian Studies of X-ray Doses

The seriousness of the variability in dose from the same X-ray procedure makes it rather meaningless to assign an "average" dose to a particular procedure. Taylor and co-workers decided to investigate just how serious such variability is in the current performance of several major, common procedures, some involving fluoroscopy and some involving only radiography. They measured the X-ray dose to patients in 30 different X-ray facilities in the city of Toronto, Canada. Certainly Toronto can be regarded as a center of rather advanced medical practice. Some of their findings follow:

Chest X-rays (in 3 separate facilities): Dose in roentgens at skin, for postero-anterior views, ranged from 20 to 60 milliroentgens; for lateral views, from 24 to 150 milliroentgens.

Barium Meal (examination of upper gastrointestinal tract) (in 3 separate facilities): Total exposures, including radiographs plus fluoroscopy:

- □ First facility, dose   = 1.6–4.8 roentgens at skin
- □ Second facility, dose = 12.8–15 roentgens at skin
- □ Third facility, dose   = 50–90 roentgens at skin

(Any time a range is quoted, at least three patients were studied in each facility.) These data indicate a difference from the "best" examination facility to the worst of a factor *on the order of 20.* Taylor, in a masterful understatement, writes about the facility that gave the doses of 50–90 roentgens at the skin, "The former (doses) are very high exposures for an examination carried out on men and women, often of reproductive age, who commonly are found to have no serious disease" (p. 8).

One might add, parenthetically, that while such patients had no serious disease before they underwent the X-ray examination, by undergoing an examination at these dose levels they accrued a serious risk of future disease.

Barium Enema (examination of lower gastrointestinal tract):

- ☐ First facility, dose   = 16–20 roentgens at skin
- ☐ Second facility, dose = 56–128 roentgens at skin

Taylor's comment on the doses of 128 roentgens: "The total exposures in Room 8 of up to 128 R must be a cause for considerable concern, since our studies show that similar situations could and do arise in many X-ray departments" (p. 9).

We must observe *why* doses in this one examination room were as high as 128 R (skin dose). It turned out that the major feature of the machine in this room was a very high fluoroscopic exposure rate of 12 R per minute. This was its *maximum* output, and was in use because the contacts of the potentiometer (which automatically controlled the exposure rate) had been bent into contact with each other *in order to get the cover on the machine.* Interestingly, when this was repaired and the exposure rate was reduced to 3 R per minute, the radiologists using the machine did not notice the reduction and did not comment on any poorer image quality resulting from it.

Intravenous Pyelogram (examination of kidney and upper urinary tract):

- ☐ First facility, dose   = 3–7 roentgens at skin
- ☐ Second facility, dose = 41 roentgens at skin
- ☐ Third facility, dose   = 1.3–1.5 roentgens at skin
- ☐ Fourth facility, dose = 16 roentgens at skin

Note that there is approximately a 30-fold range in dose.

Gall-Bladder Examination:

- ☐ First facility, dose   = 4–5 roentgens at skin
- ☐ Second facility, dose = 41–48 roentgens at skin

It was found that this entire difference of a factor of 10 was due to a 10 times higher fluoroscopic exposure rate in the second facility.

Efforts to Improve the Situation of These Gross Differences in Dose

After the evaluation was completed, Taylor and co-workers worked on reducing the doses in the examination facilities giving the highest doses. Two major actions made a large difference:

1. Reducing the excessive fluoroscopic exposure rates until they were all less than 3.5 R per minute for an average patient

2. Doubling the speed of the films used

Taylor points out that all this was done without any noticeable change in image quality either for fluoroscopy or for radiography. There were no complaints from radiologists regarding the reductions, and mostly they did not notice that changes had been made. Following the changes the doses were examined for the period between June 1977 and February 1978, and it was found that total doses had been reduced by a factor of between 2.0 and 3.6, the larger reductions in the cases with higher proportions of fluoroscopy.

Taylor makes a very important point, namely, that in order to maintain the lower fluoroscopic exposure rates, the rates must be monitored regularly—at monthly intervals, for example. He states that the equipment to do this is simple, easy to use, and readily available. If this is not done, Taylor found that fluoroscopic exposure rates start to creep up with time, as equipment is serviced or adjusted.

One additional point made by Taylor is that the literature indicates that in exposures of patients from X-ray examinations, from one facility to another, outside Canada, dose varies by as much as a factor of 10 from one X-ray machine to another.

It would be fair to state that the first step in improving the ability of the patient and the physician to decide whether a particular procedure, with its potential benefits, constitutes an unacceptable *risk,* is to make available to them some better evaluation of its *dose.*

AN EARLY GOAL FOR PHYSICIANS AND PATIENTS

Most people look to governmental bureaucracy to improve this dismal dosimetry situation. And some government departments do indeed try very hard to do a good job of testing machines, inspecting machines. But universally they claim they are grossly understaffed, and this means that inspections are nominal rather than meaningful.

The author does not think that the solution is to pour great sums of money into further buildup of regulatory agencies. Rather he believes that the solution has to come through determined *insistence* by physicians and potential patients in a particular area that institutions and private clinics determine the dose from radiologic procedures in some reliable manner. This means giving one's business only to radiologists who provide a dose estimate for the procedures they do, and who permit some sort of independent consultant system to test and certify the dose ranges they claim.

No doubt some radiologists will be offended at the idea that physicians and patients who use their services should be so brash as to request evidence that the doses are as claimed. That is just fine. Radiology is a business, and assuredly some radiologists will be pleased to provide the desired service by having the appropriate measuring equipment and skills to determine what doses they are really giving in various procedures, and by allowing independent testing to verify the doses. No one is worrying about 10% differences between claimed and actual doses, but we should be very concerned about differences of a *factor of 10*. Those radiologists who will provide dose estimates, and who can show that they deliver the lowest range of doses consistent with the state of the art, are the ones likely to get referrals from physicians and to get business from patients.

The patients, or potential patients, of a region can voluntarily subscribe to some testing service that will satisfy their desire to know which radiology offices overdose and which do not. Nongovernment consumer-testing services are nothing new in the United States. If enough people value certain kinds of information, a business will usually spring up to provide that information.

The idea is currently common that if the government provides a service it is "free." On the contrary, governmental services are *far* from free. They ultimately are paid for out of tax dollars, and the costs are probably considerably higher than would be the case for well-operated private services.

Of course, the objection will be raised that certain people cannot afford private services. But there is no reason at all that a service cannot be "shared" by those who do buy it with less fortunate people who cannot afford it. The author thinks that this would be preferable to adding to the practice of medicine yet one more layer of inspectors, sets of regulations, and forms to fill out.

Probably the reason this service has not existed sooner in radiology is that people, *including physicians,* have simply not realized that doses from medical-diagnostic radiation are by no means low *even under the best of circumstances* for many common procedures, and that the cancer risk of radiation is much more serious than they have been led to believe.

Let us now consider some of the doses received in the course of common X-ray procedures. Appropriate skepticism here would mean that when we see "usual" doses for procedures, we keep in mind that in a particular institution the doses *may* be 5, 10, or even 30 times higher.

DOSE TO ORGANS: HOW MANY? WHICH ONES? HOW OFTEN?

In some of our prior discussions, the doses given were *skin* or *entrance* doses in roentgen units. This is the dose in air at the surface of the body, and does not tell us the dose to the various organs irradiated by the passage of the X-ray beam through the body. The familiar problems in assessing internal dose which we have talked about exist as before: attenuation of the beam as it passes through tissue; back-scattering of radiation from deeper tissues to more superficial ones; variation in the kilovoltage being used by a particular operator; differing filtration of the beam. All these factors determine the dose at various depths in the body.

If our concern is increase in the risk of cancer from radiographic procedures—and that certainly should be our concern—it is the actual dose delivered to organs like the pancreas and colon, not the skin dose, which we
really want to know.

In chapter 2, it was pointed out that it is sometimes no easy matter to
determine the dose from a particular X-ray setup at a particular voltage, and
that health physicists and radiation physicists sometimes resort to the use
of tissue phantoms, and sometimes to elaborate calculations, to determine
the true dose to specific organs.

Ascertaining the true dose to one organ—for example, to the stomach
in an upper gastrointestinal series of X-rays and fluoroscopic examinations
—is a good first step. But it is only a first step. In no X-ray examination is
just one organ irradiated. A number of organs are in the examination field,
except under the rarest of circumstances.

We learned in chapter 7 how to calculate *specific-organ cancer doses* and
how to use them to estimate the risks of inducing a future fatal cancer
associated with delivering different doses to a specific organ. If we are
realistically to evaluate the risk of cancer from a particular type of X-ray
procedure, we must add up the risks for all the organs that get irradiated.
Certain abdominal examinations can involve irradiation of the gall bladder,
part of the liver, part of the stomach, part of the small intestine, part of the
large intestine, part of the pancreas, some bone marrow, some of the lymphatic tissue, part of the kidneys, and possibly still other significant tissues.

The author does not wish to underestimate the difficulty of the problem. Anatomical differences from person to person can mean that more or
less of a particular organ is included in the X-ray beam of a particular
examination. We should start by attempting to get an estimate of doses for
an "average" anatomical configuration.

As a physician himself, the author would be highly skeptical about
blithely accepting someone's advice that an X-ray examination of one of the
types in the Taylor study be done, in which 100 roentgens (surface) dose
are delivered to several organs high on the list of sites of spontaneous
cancer. (Recall from chapter 2 that 1 roentgen = approximately 1 rad.) The
organs will not receive 100 rads of absorbed dose when the surface dose is
100 R, but depending on circumstances, voltage, filtration, etc., it is certain
that doses like 5 to 20 rads *will* be received by deep organs.

A deep-tissue dose of 5 to 20 rads, even to a limited number of organs
(depending on *which* organs), is no small matter at all, in terms of the risk
of later cancer.

And what is of even more concern is that X-ray procedures are often
done repeatedly. A physician may wish to ascertain the progression of some
disease, or alleged disease, or the response to a therapeutic measure. Soon
a patient has had not one upper gastrointestinal series but three or four. If
those examinations are given in the wrong room of Taylor's studies, the risk
may be far more serious than the disease, or alleged disease, for which they
were ordered in the first place.

The author has even seen a procedure such as an upper gastrointestinal series (Taylor's barium-meal study) ordered as part of an "executive check," and repeated every year or every few years. Some radiology institutions *can* do this procedure with a relatively low dose, but how many do? Here again we would welcome radiologists providing a reliable estimate of the dose their particular institution gives, on the average, for various procedures commonly ordered by referring physicians.

INFORMED CONSENT AND MUTUAL RESPECT

Physicians and the public have the right to insist on the patient's right to know just what dose will be received and what risk will be taken with radiologic procedures. The doses from some common procedures are not at all low; they carry a sizable future cancer risk; and a patient should certainly have the opportunity to discuss with his physician whether he stands to gain more than he loses by having the procedure. We should seriously ask how often such procedures can simply be eliminated.

There will, of course, be an outcry from some physicians that "scaring the patient" is not going to result in better health care. So far as the author is concerned, if a physician wishes to recommend a procedure that carries a risk of, say, 1 chance in 100 of inducing a fatal cancer, it is elementary decency to inform the patient of the risk. A first-class physician should be able to point out the risk of a procedure to a patient and, at the same time, to point out his best estimate of the risk of *not* doing the procedure. Obviously, there must be some medical situations in which the risk of not doing a particular radiologic procedure far outweighs the risk of doing it. An intelligent human being will make the right decision if the facts are pointed out to him. But the crucial question is, how often are procedures done that are of no real consequence for the health of the patient? Certainly, a discussion of the risk of these procedures is the best way to initiate an evaluation of how many of them we could forgo, thereby reducing one source of needless cancer deaths.

Some physicians will undoubtedly be incensed at a patient who has the nerve to ask about the hazards of an X-ray examination. But since there are many, many physicians in practice, patients can choose the ones to whom they give their business.

SECTION 2: HOW PHYSICIANS AND PATIENTS CAN COPE WITH UNCERTAINTIES

It will be a while before most clinics, offices, and hospitals are prepared to give patients and physicians good estimates of the dose to each organ irradiated in particular radiological procedures. This should already be commonplace, state-of-the-art procedure, but the author doubts that a sensible answer could be obtained from 1 out of 100 installations. And beyond that, the reader has seen that, depending on circumstances, it is possible to get a dose 10–30 times the average dose by selecting the wrong institution or being examined in the wrong room on the wrong day.

In the interim, before radiologists begin to inform the referring physicians and the public, some method of approximating dose and risk is essential. A method is provided by the author, with the necessary warnings about approximations.

THREE FACTORS INVOLVED IN THE ORGAN DOSE

It has been pointed out before in this book that the *skin* or *entrance* dose is not the dose that determines the risk of cancer to a particular organ from a radiological procedure. To determine the risk of cancer of the pancreas induced by radiation, one would need to know *the absorbed dose in rads to the pancreas.* Knowing the entrance dose in roentgens is a long way from knowing the true absorbed dose in rads to a specific organ. Let us review some of the physical factors involved in the organ dose.

1. *The kilovoltage on the X-ray tube.* When we are trying to estimate pancreas dose, for example, from skin dose, it makes all the difference in the world whether we are dealing with X-rays from a machine operating at 60 kv or from one operating at 100 kv. The amount by which the X-ray beam is attenuated (decreased) in going through the tissues before reaching the pancreas is much greater for 60-kev X-rays than for 100-kev X-rays. And the same is true for the beams accompanying 60-kev beams as compared to the beams accompanying 100-kev beams. So, unless one knows the actual operating voltage in a particular facility, one cannot know what correction to apply to skin dose to get depth dose to the pancreas (or to any other organ, of course).

2. *The amount of filtration of the X-ray beam.* Operators of X-ray machines are often eager to get rid of at least part of the low-energy X-rays (the so-called soft X-rays, and the less useful rays in diagnostic work), since all they do is deliver a dose to the skin and the relatively superficial tissues. The technique they often use is to insert a filter of aluminum or copper in the X-ray beam, the thickness differing from one institution to another. Unless one knows what the filtration is, one can make an error in estimating the dose to a tissue from a skin dose.

3. *Intervening tissues.* The amount and kind of tissue through which an X-ray beam must pass after going through skin and before reaching the tissue of interest can make a very large difference in the dose received by the tissue of interest. The reader may recall from chapter 5 descriptions of various studies of the induction of breast cancer. There it was shown that in fluoroscopies of women with tuberculosis, the X-ray dose to the breasts was 1.5 rads for women with their backs to the X-ray tube, versus 7.5 rads for women facing the X-ray tube. Since the fluoroscopies were attempting to get about the same picture of the lungs, we can presume that the entrance doses were not far apart.

Another illustration is the case where bony tissues intervene between the skin and the organ of interest. For example, if X-rays need to go through the bony pelvis, as in a postero-anterior beam (going from back to front), the ratio of skin dose to the dose to an organ in the pelvis will be much higher than the ratio for an antero-posterior beam, which does not go through bone on its way to the organ of interest.

As a result of these uncertainties, it is difficult to arrive at a factor for translating skin dose to absorbed dose in rads to a particular deep tissue. Moreover, one needs to know how deep the tissue of interest lies with respect to the skin. Here the biological variables of amount of fat, muscularity, and body features can also alter the factor.

For organs lying near the skin surface, the appropriate correction factor may be between 0.8 and 1.0. For organs lying about one-half of the way through the body from the surface, the correction factor may be on the order of 0.25. For organs still farther away from entrance beam, the correction factor may be as low as 0.1, meaning that the tissue-absorbed dose is 0.1 the skin dose. And remember that all these estimates are sensitive to the voltage on the tube and the filtration.

TWO RECOMMENDED MEANS OF APPROXIMATION

The author suggests two procedures for approximating organ doses, for those patients and referring physicians without the services of a radiology institution that provides reliable organ doses. Approximating organ doses by these two procedures is suggested when only vague statements about skin-dose level are offered, and when one cannot even ascertain whether the skin dose cited is one which is usually measured at the facility in question or is some value supposedly applying throughout the country.

Approximation 1: Use the approximation that the organ dose is one-fourth of the skin dose. This is likely to produce a somewhat low estimate of the organ dose and thus may tend to underprotect the patient. Then the second approximation helps.

Approximation 2: Having reduced the organ dose to one-fourth of the skin dose, *multiply* the new organ dose by 10. The reason for this is simple: you will generally not have the vaguest idea whether the radiology facility being used is at the upper or the lower end of the dose ranges known to exist.

When both approximations have been applied to the skin dose, the approximate risk of cancer from the X-ray procedure can be calculated. If you are a patient and the risk based on the approximations does not seem excessive to you, then you may deem the procedure acceptable. If the cancer risk based on approximation 1 seems reasonable to you, but the risk based on approximation 2 seems quite unacceptable, then you and your physician ought to consider very carefully whether the procedure should be done. It is this second situation, resulting from an unnecessary lack of information, which makes the author feel that radiologists should move rapidly to provide the actual doses received, so that approximations and gross uncertainty are not necessary. A third situation exists: the true dose provided by the radiologist indicates an estimated cancer risk that is deemed significant. Then you and your physician must ask, is this X-ray procedure really necessary?

A GALL-BLADDER EXAMINATION: IRRADIATION OF MULTIPLE ORGANS

The UNSCEAR report (1977, p. 311) includes some tabulations of "Typical Skin Doses in the Primary Beam in Diagnostic X-ray Examination." We shall want to make use of some of those typical doses, but before we can, we must understand an additional gross inadequacy of the information provided by radiologists. We really need to know *all* the organs receiving major amounts of radiation in the X-ray diagnostic procedure, if we are to obtain a *meaningful* cancer risk estimate.

This point can be illustrated well by considering a gall-bladder examination (cholecystogram). This X-ray procedure is one of the most common. In this procedure, even if we know the entrance exposure, and are willing to use Approximations 1 and 2, we do not know which organs will receive radiation. That depends to a large extent on whether the radiologist uses a wide beam, covering a large part of the abdomen, or whether he cones the beam down, so that as little as possible of the abdomen receives radiation. The width of the beam is highly variable from radiologist to radiologist, and from institution to institution.

It makes a whole lot of difference if we consider a gall-bladder X-ray examination to irradiate the gall bladder, or if we consider it to irradiate the following:

□ The gall bladder
□ ⅓ of the stomach
□ ⅕ of the small intestine
□ ⅓ of the pancreas
□ ¼ of the liver
□ some fraction of the lymph nodes
□ ⅕ of the large intestine
□ ¼ of the kidneys
□ ¼ of the esophagus

Is this far-fetched? Not at all. Procedures such as gall-bladder examinations or upper gastrointestinal series can very definitely result in the irradiation of many abdominal organs, and sometimes can involve chest-organ irradiation too.

It is precisely with this type of listing that the radiology profession could provide us for each of its procedures. Everyone realizes that such a listing would not be perfect, simply because the anatomical differences between people would not permit perfection, even if the radiological data were perfect. But a reasonable approximation is vastly superior to the total absence of such a listing, which is the situation today. The author, who despises bureaucratic forms and regulations, thinks that the provision of crucial information—information that pertains to life-and-death decisions—is quite a different matter from regulation. It would be a service paid for by those who value such information. And it would be a large step forward if attention now wasted on forms and regulations were given to worthwhile endeavors, such as finding out which organs receive what doses in common (but not low-dose) X-ray procedures.

Calculation of the Risk of Cancer for a Specific Diagnostic Procedure

UNSCEAR (1977) presents the following data for examination of the upper gastrointestinal tract (barium meal):

Skin dose in rads, for entire examination, including fluoroscopy: Range of average values = 6 to 25 rads.

We really do not know just which organs will be in the beam during such an examination, so for illustrative purposes we shall use the list given above for gall-bladder examination. To be sure, different radiologists will tell us that in their practice certain organs on this list may receive less or more radiation, that certain organs should be removed from and certain organs added to the list. Nonetheless, this calculation will be very instructive.

Approximation 1 suggests that we use ¼ of the entrance dose for the organ doses. We will make this correction, and then correct each organ dose for *the fraction* of the organ irradiated.

For skin doses (given above) of 6–25 rads, the ¼ correction gives us organ doses of about 1.5–6 rads. Now we shall correct the dose to each

Organ	Fraction irradiated (estimated, for illustration)	Dose to Organ, corrected for fraction irradiated
Gall bladder	$^1/_4$	0.37 to 1.50 rads
Stomach	$^1/_3$	0.5 to 2.00 rads
Small intestine	$^1/_5$	0.3 to 1.20 rads
Pancreas	$^1/_3$	0.5 to 2.00 rads
Liver	$^1/_4$	0.37 to 1.50 rads
Lymph nodes	$^1/_{20}$	0.075 to 0.3 rads
Large intestine	$^1/_5$	0.3 to 1.20 rads
Kidneys	$^1/_4$	0.37 to 1.50 rads
Esophagus	$^1/_4$	0.37 to 1.50 rads

organ supposed to be affected by the procedure by the fraction of that organ estimated to be irradiated. We will assume ¼ of the gall bladder to be irradiated in this exam.

Approximation 2 would lead us to multiply every dose estimate in the last column by 10, to take care of real-world contingencies concerning the doses one definitely could get in certain radiology facilities. For the stomach, for example, the Approximation 2 values would be 5.0 to 20 rads instead of 0.5 to 2.0 rads. As we estimate cancer risks, we shall use both Approximation 1 and Approximation 2 values.

We must now use our specific-organ cancer doses (table 14). We shall make our calculations for males 25 years old at irradiation, and point out *how* to make calculations for females and for other ages at irradiation. All the requisite data and information are presented in table 27.

The results obtained show a total range of risk (from the optimistic results of Approximation 1 to the pessimistic results of Approximation 2) of values from 0.000519 to 0.021. The higher figure is not an unrealistic one. The reader will realize this by returning to Taylor and co-workers' studies of various X-ray facilities in Toronto, in which it was reported that at one facility the skin dose for a barium-meal examination was 50 to 90 roentgens, which is several times the "range of average values" (6–25 rads) given in the UNSCEAR report. In selected facilities, therefore, risks of cancer from barium-meal examinations well in excess of those calculated here could occur, since these calculations are based on doses of 6–25 rads.

It would certainly seem there should be a very good medical indication for a procedure that could increase the risk of fatal cancer by 0.02. (In medicine the word *indication* means *reason.*) If a radiologist can show that (a) in his facility the total dose is much less than the dose that produces such a risk and (b) in his facility the beam does not irradiate as much of the various organs as listed, then the risk of using his facility would be correspondingly reduced. All that is required is that the patient and referring physician be convinced by objective evidence that these claims are true. When the radiology profession starts providing the essential information on doses to the organs involved in a specific procedure, the necessary approximations will be fewer and the risk estimates better.

RISK FOR WOMEN AND RISK AT DIFFERENT AGES

The entire set of calculations in table 27 can be made for females, using the specific-organ cancer doses for females in table 15, in precisely the same way as for males.

The second issue is the variation in risk with age at irradiation. Since the specific-organ cancer doses come from the whole-body cancer doses (see chapter 7), it follows that correction of all specific-organ doses will be made in proportion to the ratio of whole-body doses at two ages, for example, 25 years and some other age. And since the risk estimated in table 27

TABLE 27: DEMONSTRATION OF CALCULATION OF CANCER RISK FROM MEDICAL X-RAY PROCEDURES

MALES AT 25 YEARS OF AGE

Organ	Specific-Organ Cancer Dose in Organ-Rads per Cancer	Dose in Rads by Approximation 1	Dose in Rads by Approximation 2	Risk of Cancer Death, Based on Approximation 1 Dose	Risk of Cancer Death, Based on Approximation 2 Dose
Gall bladder and liver together	9,430	0.37 to 1.50	3.7 to 15.0	0.0000392 to 0.00016	0.000392 to 0.0016
Stomach	5,051	0.50 to 2.00	5.0 to 20.0	0.000099 to 0.00040	0.00099 to 0.0040
Small intestine	121,250	0.30 to 1.20	3.0 to 12.0	0.000002 to 0.00001	0.00002 to 0.0001
Pancreas	3,823	0.5 to 2.00	5.0 to 20.0	0.00013 to 0.00052	0.0013 to 0.0052
Lymph nodes	3,930	0.075 to 0.30	0.75 to 3.0	0.000019 to 0.000076	0.00019 to 0.00076
Large intestine	2,070	0.30 to 1.20	3.0 to 12.0	0.00014 to 0.00058	0.0014 to 0.0058
Kidneys	8,841	0.37 to 1.50	3.7 to 15.0	0.000042 to 0.00017	0.00042 to 0.0017
Esophagus	7,717	0.37 to 1.50	3.7 to 15.0	0.000048 to 0.00019	0.00048 to 0.0019
Total cancer death risk From the Upper Gastrointestinal X-ray Exam:				**0.000519 to 0.0021**	**0.00519 to 0.021**

This calculation is based on the reasonable approximation that irradiation of ¼ of an organ gives ¼ the cancer risk as irradiation of the entire organ. There could be situations where this does not hold rigorously because one part of an organ is much more cancer-prone than another part. A classic illustration of an exception to the general rule would be the segmental bronchi versus the alveolar region of the lung. The segmental bronchi are much more cancer-prone, so an evaluation based only on fraction of total lung mass would be in error in that case.

The calculation of risk of cancer death has been demonstrated in several places in this book. Let us simply demonstrate it once again, using the first entry in the table for dose, 0.37 rads in the Approximation 1 column. For 1 person, the organ-rads = (1) × (0.37) = 0.37 (for gall bladder plus liver). From here, it is a simple problem of proportionality. If 9,430 organ-rads guarantees 1 fatal cancer of liver plus gall bladder, then 0.37 organ-rads would guarantee (0.37/9,430) = 0.0000392 of a fatal cancer. That is the entry in the risk of cancer column for the very first calculation.

would go *down* if the specific-organ cancer dose went up, it follows that all estimates made for risks at age 25 would be corrected as follows:

$$\text{Risk at age x} = (\text{risk at age 25}) \frac{\text{whole-body cancer dose}_{\text{age 25}}}{\text{whole-body cancer dose}_{\text{age x}}}$$

Let us apply this relationship, using the data in table 27 for the upper-gastrointestinal-tract, X-ray, fluoroscopic examination, to calculate the cancer death risk for men irradiated at age 45 rather than at age 25. The whole-body cancer doses for males at various ages are presented in table 10. These are 201.4 person-rads at age 25 and 1,232.5 person-rads at age 45.

Therefore, if we take the highest estimate of cancer death risk from an upper gastrointestinal examination of 0.021 at age 25, the corresponding risk at age 45 = (0.021) × (201.4/1,232.5) = 0.0034. The risk from receiving this X-ray examination, therefore, goes down with increasing age at examination. This is fortunate, of course, since many of the common procedures involving high doses are more frequently performed on people who are much older, on the average, than 25.

The inverse problem should be taken very seriously. The inordinate sensitivity of children to radiation induction of cancer, as expressed in the much lower whole-body cancer doses in tables 10 and 11 for children, means that we should always be more reluctant to perform X-ray examinations on children than on adults.

On the other hand, we must remember that the diseases or problems of diagnosis that bring physicians to prescribe X-ray procedures are probably more serious for children than for adults, (dental X-rays excepted). It would be tragic if an acute problem with a 50/50 chance of leading to a child's death, unless diagnosed accurately, were left undiagnosed because a parent refused to permit an X-ray examination that would result in a 0.01 risk of later cancer.

This is precisely the responsibility of the physician and radiologist: to assist in the assessment of the radiation risk, so that the family of the child can make a reasonable decision. The author doubts that many parents would withhold an X-ray procedure carrying a 0.01 risk of later cancer death if they knew that the risk of going without the procedure could be 0.1, 0.3, or 0.5.

Some special radiological procedures produce quite sizable radiation doses in such regions as the chest, which contains organs of high spontaneous susceptibility to cancer, such as the lungs, breasts, and to a lesser extent the lymph nodes and esophagus.

Gough and co-workers (1968) cite a skin dose (mean) of 47 rads to a group of 85 patients undergoing cardiac catheterization, with a maximum value in one case of 140 rads. These are very disturbing doses, particularly if they are delivered in youth or childhood. But on the other hand, it is indeed unusual for cardiac catheterization to be performed at young ages. Some serious disease, itself representing major risk, is generally the reason for the procedure. The relative risks must, of course, be clearly pointed out in discussions with patients and families of children who are patients.

It must be noted that in a small child, who has a much lower body thickness than an adult, the average tissue-absorbed dose will be much closer to the skin dose than in an adult. For infants or small children, the absorbed dose to most tissues should be between 50 and 90% of the skin dose. In considering the risk of cardiac catheterization, this must be borne in mind, and one could adjust Approximation 1 by using ½ rather than ¼ of the entrance dose.

IS THERE SUCH A THING AS A MEANINGFUL AVERAGE DOSE FOR X-RAY PROCEDURES?

No doubt many physicians and others reading this book would like to have a table of doses received for various X-ray procedures. Nothing would please the author more than to provide *information* on this subject, but nothing is more important than avoiding *misinformation*. Enough has been said, with the Taylor studies and technical factors as a background, to warn the reader that any such tabulations are likely to be deceptive. However, the physician or patient armed with Approximations 1 and 2 above, and fully aware of the fact that these approximations may still underestimate the dose, may find the following listing useful, based on data in the 1977 UNSCEAR report.

The X-ray procedures are listed as *high, medium,* or *low* with respect to the skin dose of the *primary beam.* The reader of this chapter will immediately realize the *limited* value of such a listing for calculating cancer risk. Though the organs that provoke the procedures are specified, the additional organs that are exposed are not named. Yet irradiation of these organs may contribute more to the cancer risk than irradiation of the primary organ.

Procedures Giving "High Skin Dose" (range per examination, 3–26 rads): Barium meal (upper gastrointestinal fluoroscopy), barium enema (lower gastrointestinal fluoroscopy), whole-chest examination (fluoroscopic), lumbosacral spine, lumbar spine. Also listed with this group is cardiac catheterization, mentioned above.

Procedures Giving "Medium Skin Dose" (range per examination, 0.3–5.0 rads): Head, cervical spine, clavicle and shoulder, dorsal spine, thorax, cholecystography (gall-bladder exam), abdomen, abdomen-obstetric, urography (from kidney down), urography retrograde (from bladder up), salpingography (Fallopian-tube fluoroscopy), placenta, cystography (bladder exam), pelvis, hip and upper femur, dental, angiography-head, angiography-abdomen, tomography (chest), mass survey of chest. These last chest examinations are far higher in dose than a simple chest film.

Procedures Giving "Low Skin Dose" (range per examination, 0.07–1.7 rads): For arm and hand, values as high as 1.7 rads are listed.

Chest X-ray (*not* fluoroscopy) is listed as giving 0.07–0.15 rads. Femur (lower two-thirds), leg, and foot are listed as giving 0.3–0.4 rads.

The reader should note that all these listings are for the entire X-ray examination as usually practiced, which may involve several X-ray films.

DENTAL X-RAYS AND BRAIN CANCER

Tests have shown that only a negligible amount of the scattered radiation from dental X-rays reaches distant organs. It appears to the author that the place to which one should direct serious attention, in the case of dental X-rays, is the dose to the brain itself. The following values are given for specific-organ cancer doses for males and females in tables 14 and 15.

Specific-Organ Cancer Dose (organ-rads/cancer death)

Organ	Males at age 25	Females at age 25
Brain and central nervous system	7.860	10,228
And for comparison:		
Eyes	212,000	227,000
Thyroid	121,325	64,200

Many people are considerably concerned about thyroid doses and thyroid cancer from dental X-ray procedures. The brain is of far more concern *per rad delivered,* as these specific-organ cancer doses demonstrate. Eyes *are* of concern, for example, with respect to cataract or corneal injury, but are of far less concern than the brain with respect to cancer death risk.

Dental examinations are often performed on children *repeatedly.* We must emphasize that the specific-organ cancer doses will be some four times lower for very young children than the values listed above, or on the order of 2,000–2,500 organ-rads.

Let us do a simple calculation to assess the meaning of delivering 1 rad to the brain of a young child. If a young male child receives 1 rad to the brain, he receives 1 brain-rad. If it takes 2,000 brain-rads to guarantee 1 fatal brain cancer, then the delivery of 1 brain-rad gives him a risk of fatal cancer of 0.0005, or 5 chances in 10,000. Stated otherwise, 5 out of every 10,000 male children given 1 rad to the brain will eventually die of brain cancer.

One rad to the brain constitutes a high risk, in the author's opinion, in exchange for the benefits of dental X-rays in general. So does 0.2 rad to the brain, which means that 1 out of every 10,000 children so "examined" will die of brain cancer. Given that techniques are very different from office to office and locale to locale, we should not be surprised at all to find a 100-fold range in brain exposure from dental X-rays.

There are undoubtedly good reasons for dental examinations; the decision is up to the individual adult or the family of the individual child. But the dental profession has an obligation to provide some serious estimate of brain radiation dose for the procedures and equipment being used. The public should demand this information.

WHY DO WE HAVE SO MANY DENTAL AND MEDICAL X-RAY EXAMINATIONS?

It would certainly be comforting to believe that we are enjoying better health in some direct relationship to the quantity of X-ray examinations we receive. There is a considerable body of opinion, however, in which the author shares, which holds that many of the examinations performed do not contribute to the health of the population but do contribute to the number of cancer deaths in the population.

Why do we have so many X-ray examinations over and above those really necessary for solving crucial diagnostic problems, or for essential evaluation of the progress of certain diseases under treatment? There are several causes, some of which are listed and discussed below.

Repetition of Unnecessary X-rays

In cases of accidents, commonly automobile accidents but also others, insurance companies are often to blame for the unconscionably excessive use of X-rays. The person injured or ostensibly injured in an accident gets X-rays taken during his acute care. If he has an attorney, the attorney wants medical opinions from "experts" who can testify on behalf of his client. Generally these experts will want their own sets of X-rays, rather than those taken as part of the acute event. Then there is the question of following the progression or lack of progression of the supposed injury. More X-rays! And finally the insurance company wants experts to examine the subject too, and these experts of course want the "best" X-rays they can get, either taken by them or by a radiologist in whom they have confidence. It may be well worth considering whether the harm from all the X-rays does not itself exceed the injuries from the accident.

Third-Party Payment

Most people think that when an insurer pays for a procedure, such as a medical X-ray, there is no cost to the individual. This is, of course, naive, since the cost of the insurance is directly related to the number of procedures ordered. Curiously, a fair number of people feel that "free goods" should be accepted, even if those "free goods" will kill them. But this is largely the result (in the case of X-ray examinations) of decades of promoting "checkups" and failing to inform the public of the hazard of the X-ray examinations. It is not too surprising, therefore, to find that people commonly feel they have not been properly examined by a physician unless he has ordered a number of X-rays. And if they are covered by "third-party" payments through insurance or some employment plan, they feel positively defrauded if X-rays are not ordered.

The easy path for the physician is to accede to the general wishes of the public and order more X-rays than are necessary. There is no doubt that some physicians resist this pressure on the principle that they would refuse to do any unnecessary or harmful procedure, but we can wonder what fraction of physicians they represent. So, this is an illustration of the public acting against its own best interests with a modest assist from the medical profession.

Protection Against Medical Malpractice Suits

Attorneys, of course, often put on their "righteous indignation" clothes when they discuss the awful things done to patients by the medical profession. They are absolutely correct that medical malpractice does exist, that the culpable individuals should be brought to justice, and that compensation should reach those who have been harmed by malpractice.

However, it is a well-known fact that in medical and dental malpractice cases, plaintiffs' attorneys commonly request that the X-rays be produced. If the physician has not taken *all* the X-rays one could think of taking, the plaintiff's attorney raises his eyebrows in the courtroom to show his skepticism that anything but poor medical practice could have been the reason why additional X-rays were not taken. Through the school of hard knocks, dental and medical practitioners have learned that if they wish to avoid losing malpractice suits, *no matter what the merit of the cases may be,* they simply had better have all the X-rays that could conceivably be asked for in court.

Attorneys have played upon the ignorance of juries concerning such matters. It sounds very reasonable to a juror that the doctor *should* have taken all the "necessary" X-rays. But there is the rub. The difference between what a clever attorney may try to convince a juror was necessary, and what was really necessary to the care of that particular patient, may be the difference between night and day.

The "function" of attorneys is to win lawsuits for their clients; furthermore, their fee in a malpractice case is a percentage of the "take." The "function" of dental and medical practitioners is to protect themselves from costly malpractice judgments. The jurors sit in the middle, and can be conned by effective attorneys. The losers, of course, are the thousands of victims of fatal radiation-induced cancers that result from this outrageous situation.

Of course, a physician or dentist who does not take an X-ray that is really needed by a particular patient should be sued for malpractice. That would be just, on an elementary basis. But, in the author's opinion, something needs to be done to curb zealous attorneys who endeavor to mislead jurors about the necessity of particular X-rays in particular cases. They should be forced by the court to show positive proof that the X-ray in question was necessary.

Remedy Through Understanding

As part of his general philosophy, the author feels that the overuse of X-rays is a problem that cannot be well solved by laws and regulations, imposed on people "for their own good" but destined to create costly armies of unnecessary bureaucrats. A better solution, consistent with liberty and dignity, lies in the widespread education of the medical community, the legal profession, patients, and jurors (the general public) about the hazards of ionizing radiation.

Then jurors would no longer be taken in by the nonsense that the absence of an X-ray automatically constitutes malpractice. And the more the medical and legal professionals understand, the more likely it will be that physicians can find competent defense attorneys for malpractice suits in which the absence of X-rays is an issue.

Another result of public education is that, in time, some patients will sue for malpractice on the grounds that unnecessary X-rays were performed by both dental and medical practitioners. In other words, once people recognize that there is a problem with overuse, they will already have the means to stop it, without more laws and regulations.

SECTION 3: THE USE OF RADIOIODINE IN NUCLEAR MEDICINE

Nuclear medicine is without a doubt one of the most rapidly growing sources of ionizing-radiation exposure of the public. The Work Group on Radiation Exposure Reduction (1979) estimates that approximately 6.7 million in vivo nuclear-medicine procedures were performed in 1975 in the United States alone. (An *in vivo* procedure requires that a radionuclide be put inside a person, rather than be used in some laboratory procedure.)

In general, the use of radionuclides in nuclear medicine does not provide whole-body radiation, so there is no single, simple procedure for estimating doses. The nature of calculating risk, if one knew the doses to specific organs, would be very similar to the procedure used in table 27 for an X-ray procedure involving the irradiation of several organs. It is always a matter of adding up the *risks* to the organs, rather than the *doses* to the organs.

Much of the information concerning the doses received by various organs from procedures involving radionuclides will be crude, simply because the key parameters needed for dose estimation, such as the average residence time of the nuclide (in the form used in the nuclear-medicine procedure), are either not well known or entirely unknown. The problem of dealing with such nuclides in a general way was discussed in chapter 9.

For special cases, the reports of the Medical Internal Dose Committee (MIRD reports) represent a good effort to provide likely doses. This work is continually updated as new information becomes available concerning the biochemistry and physiology of the handling by the body of some nuclides.

RADIOIODINE AND THYROID DISORDERS

The radionuclide ^{131}Iodine (formally $^{131}_{55}$I) is undoubtedly the most prominent one in the history of the medical use of radiopharmaceuticals. It has been used extensively both in diagnostic work on the thyroid gland and its functional state, and in therapeutic work for the treatment of hyperthyroidism and some forms of thyroid cancer. This book is not about the history of the uses of radionuclides, so we will not spend time telling the story of ^{131}I. But we are concerned with misuses in the past, and even more acutely with misuses likely to occur in the future, if present trends and opinions are followed by the medical profession.

In chapter 2 it was pointed out that physics teaches us that radionuclides delivering their energy internally from beta particles can be expected to produce the same effects as external X-rays, provided the same quantity of ionizing-radiation energy is delivered to a specific tissue or organ at the same age. The small effect of differing linear energy transfer among the various beta-particle emitters or X-ray sources of electrons will not alter that generalization in any significant manner.

Unfortunately, physicians are still not widely aware of the physics of these matters, an awareness of which would alter their fantasy that certain radionuclides delivering an internal dose will not do harm.

In particular, the author believes that the situation of radioiodine is fraught with danger to the health of many thousands, perhaps ultimately hundreds of thousands of persons, if current medical "wisdom" prevails. It will not be the first time that medicine has caused an epidemic of a specific type of cancer; some of the epidemics are described in this book.

^{131}I is taken up by the thyroid gland because of the general physiological avidity of the thyroid gland for the element iodine, which the gland uses in the synthesis of hormonal products, which in turn actually contain iodine atoms. Therapeutically, there are two leading uses of ^{131}Iodine:

1. For treatment of hyperthyroidism
2. For treatment of some cases of thyroid cancer

Before considering these therapeutic uses, it is very important to inform the reader of what the administration of ^{131}Iodine does in addition to irradiating the thyroid gland. A major effect of ^{131}I, in the cases where sizable doses to the thyroid gland are delivered, is also to deliver sizable doses of *whole-body* irradiation via the blood. This fact is very well documented and well known among physicians.

In one of two recent studies, ^{131}Iodine was used to treat 51 hyperthyroid patients; in the other study, 40 patients with a form of thyroid cancer were treated. The estimated mean dose to the hyperthyroid group can be set at 10.0 rads, and the dose to the thyroid-cancer group at 47 rads. The consequences of such dose levels of whole-body radiation would be (using the whole-body cancer dose for 25-year-old males): a risk of fatal cancer of 0.05 for the 10-rad group, and a risk of 0.24 for the 47-rad group.

If one knew absolutely nothing else about iodine, thyroid disease, or the treatment of thyroid disease, one would know that there should be an overwhelmingly strong medical reason to give medication that itself creates a 5% chance or a 24% chance of cancer death.

Most physicians would agree that a medication having 5 chances out of 100 of killing a patient is to be used with the greatest discretion, only under the most unusually threatening conditions. Many physicians would find it hard to believe that any thyroid disease would warrant such therapy. The author would certainly like to have some powerful evidence of benefit to the patient before advising medication inducing this level of risk. Yet we find that some medical writers are recommending more aggressive use of [131]Iodine in therapy.

The researchers who conducted both the studies mentioned above have recommended in their published reports that the use of [131]Iodine in treatment of the thyroid be increased. The author has analyzed these studies and several others in considerable detail, and concludes that any proved benefits of such therapy are overshadowed by the risks involved. These analyses indicate that the calculated risk of cancer death from whole-body radiation received in the course of [131]Iodine therapy is *by no means small.*

Whether [131]Iodine really reduces any risk from thyroid cancer itself remains unknown. Are medical practitioners justified in aggressively sponsoring [131]Iodine therapy for thyroid cancer? This author believes there is a real hazard of creating a physician-induced rash of future cancer deaths with no offsetting benefit to the thyroid-cancer patient. Nothing is contributed to the resolution of this issue by unsupported, meaningless statements that the theoretical *risks* of [131]Iodine therapy have not materialized. What we need now is evaluation of the therapy's presumed *benefit* for thyroid-cancer patients.

The Goal of Medicine Is, Above All, to Do No Harm

This author is concerned about the burgeoning use of radionuclides in medicine. Many unanswered questions remain about the therapeutic use of [131]Iodine; they do not reassure us that a proper evaluation of the risks and benefits of this therapy has been made. One wonders whether the diagnostic and therapeutic applications of *other* radionuclides are being made with a better scientific approach. Certainly, unless a patient stands to gain significantly from the diagnostic or therapeutic use of a radionuclide, its use is not justified.

The methods and principles of this book make it possible to estimate the cancer death risks associated with radionuclide use. It is to be hoped that some serious attention will be given to the issue of whether current medical practice with radionuclides is doing people more harm than good.

[Chapter 14]

Induction of Human Leukemia by Ionizing Radiation

L EUKEMIA WAS EARLY RECOGNIZED TO BE a major health consequence of ionizing radiation. It was actually a combination of "quirks" which led to the recognition of the leukemogenic effect of radiation and away from the full appreciation of the much larger problem of solid-cancer induction by ionizing radiation. And, while cancer is a dread disease in the public's mind, it is probably true that leukemia is feared even more.

In both of the major sources of human evidence concerning ionizing radiation and malignant disease, the data from Hiroshima and Nagasaki and the ankylosing spondylitis series, leukemia was the malignancy that became apparent earliest. Why leukemia begins to manifest itself as a radiation-induced lesion 3 to 5 years post-irradiation remains unknown. In contrast, as we have already seen, most solid cancers begin to be detectable in excess only at 10 years post-irradiation.

Another difference between the findings on leukemia induction and those on solid-tumor induction is that little excess leukemia is likely to appear after the thirtieth year post-irradiation. The leukemia data do not rule out the possibility, however, that up to 10% of the cases may occur after that time. Both the spondylitis and the Japanese series are in agreement on the limited duration of the leukemia effect, although the spondylitis follow-up does not extend beyond irradiation as long as the Japanese follow-up.

In the analyses here, we shall assume that 10% of the leukemia deaths will occur after the twenty-ninth year post-irradiation, which is the latest follow-up year for the Hiroshima-Nagasaki survivors for which we have data. The *observed* leukemia deaths among the Japanese will be multiplied by 1.10 to take into account cases "yet to come." It is doubtful that the total leukemia effect will thereby be seriously underestimated; it is also doubtful that it can be meaningfully overestimated.

For the quantitative analysis of leukemia, we shall utilize the Hiroshima-Nagasaki data alone, for one reason. It represents the only data where the entire story is essentially in, so we do not have to make the kind of forward estimates required in the case of the solid cancers. In time, the data from the spondylitis series will also be available in "complete" form.

A few other sources of information on leukemia induction exist, but we shall not use them as prime sources. First, there are the patients who received the alpha-emitting, thorium-containing *Thorotrast,* used as a medical contrast medium (see Mole 1978a). Estimation of the radiation dose to those patients would be difficult at best, and there is the question of possible chemical effects over and above radiation effects. Second, there are the studies of Lyon (1979), which will not be considered because dosimetry is absent. The studies of Bross (1979) will be treated under "retrospective" studies. The Japanese data are not likely to mislead us in any significant manner on the radiation-leukemia question, if properly handled.

Section 1: The Japanese Bomb Survivors

Age Trends in Human Leukemia Induction by Ionizing Radiation

The data for leukemia deaths in Japan are presented by Beebe, Kato, and Land (1978). These data are given in T-65 dose categories, and must be corrected to the true doses absorbed by the leukemia-vulnerable cells. We shall consider that the dose to bone marrow most closely approximates the dose of consequence for leukemia induction. After converting T-65 doses to absorbed doses, using the procedures described in chapter 5, we arrive at the corrected doses tabulated below. In all calculations, the data for Hiroshima and Nagasaki will be combined.

In our analyses of the leukemia data, we shall use the same principle as we used in our analyses of the solid-cancer data, namely, the assumption that radiation-induced leukemia occurrence rates are proportional to radiation dose received. Separately, we shall comment on the issue of whether or not the leukemia data are consistent with linearity.

Summary of Hiroshima-Nagasaki Leukemia-Relevant Doses and Age Trends

Age Group (age at exposure)	Mean Absorbed Dose in Rads	% Excess Leukemia Deaths per Rad
0–9	19.8	11.5
10–19	28.7	9.4
20–34	26.6	8.7
35–49	24.1	2.9
50+	20.3	18.0

In the table above are presented data on age trends in leukemia induction by radiation in Hiroshima and Nagasaki. Note that the trend is toward a lower and lower % excess in the leukemia death rate per rad as one moves from early ages at exposure to ages 35–49 at exposure. There is a marked rise in the % excess per rad for the 50+ age group. The magnitude of the percent increase is startling, and at least part of it does not seem trustworthy. The leukemia death rate for the *unexposed* persons 50+ years of age is unusually low, and constitutes a trend reversal, which the author finds dubious. Certainly in the United States the spontaneous leukemia death rate is higher in the 50+ age group than in the 35–49 age group. But even with this questionable expected value, it still appears that the 50+ age group is quite sensitive to the leukemogenic effect of radiation. The Hiroshima-Nagasaki data are the only data we are likely to have on this situation in the early future, so we must use them even with their limits.

The expression of leukemia excesses as % excesses per rad is of limited value, since the % excesses are determined by the length of the follow-up period. The situation for leukemia is very different from that for solid cancers, where the cancers are induced for periods comparable with the lifetimes of the exposed individuals. Essentially all the radiation-induced leukemias which are ever going to occur *have* occurred within 30 years of irradiation. Therefore, if we should prolong the follow-up period from, say, 30 years to 60 years, the *number* of radiation-induced leukemias would not increase at all, but the number of leukemias not radiation-associated would more than double. The result would be that the *percent* excess leukemia deaths per rad would decrease with an increase in the length of the follow-up period. But the numbers themselves are of interest, in that they show radiation to increase the leukemia death rate by such values as 3 to 18% per rad, based on the 29-year follow-up.

The reader will encounter discussions of leukemia occurrence in Hiroshima and Japan based on the use of the T-65 doses rather than true absorbed doses. Of course, using the larger T-65 doses makes the radiation effect look smaller than it truly is. There can be no good reason for a scientist still to base analyses on T-65 doses. We cannot object, obviously, to performing calculations with T-65 doses when data are presented in that form, but the last step in such calculations should be conversion of all findings to absorbed doses, the only meaningful form.

THE "WHOLE-BODY LEUKEMIA DOSE"

As was also the case for the analyses of solid cancers, the analyses of leukemia should really be based on the *whole-body leukemia dose,* which gives us the number of person-rads that will guarantee one fatal leukemia. The results from Hiroshima and Nagasaki are taken, of course, to represent whole-body radiation. The reader is quite familiar with the imperfections of that assumption of uniformity of dose over the whole body, but we will proceed on it, since no better estimate can be made.

Procedure for Calculating Whole-Body Leukemia Dose

We shall utilize the Hiroshima-Nagasaki data. Starting with the data for the group 0–9 years of age at the time of bombing, we have the following:

Leukemia deaths per 10^6 person-years, exposed = 103.0

Leukemia deaths per 10^6 person-years, nonexposed = 31.5

Difference, i.e., leukemia deaths per 10^6 person-years due to the radiation exposure = 71.5

For the whole-body leukemia dose we need person-rads, but our data are presented in the form of person-years. Although every person was not followed for 24 years (the follow-up began at 5 years post-irradiation), we can regard 1,000,000 person-years accumulated in 24 years as being in every calculational way identical with 1,000,000/24, or 41,666.7 persons each followed for the full 24 years. So, whenever we want a person-rad value to go with the 1,000,000 person-years, we shall simply multiply 41,666.7 persons by mean dose in rads.

Since the mean dose for this age group is 19.8 rads, the person-rads are $(19.8) \times (41,666.7) = 825,000.7$. This exposure produced an excess of 71.5 leukemia deaths per 10^6 person-years. The correction for leukemia deaths "yet to come" raises this to $(1.10) \times (71.5) = 78.7$ leukemia deaths per 10^6 person-years years of follow-up observation.

Therefore, the whole-body leukemia dose = 825,000.7 person-rads/78.7 leukemia deaths = *10,483 person-rads per leukemia death.* Actually, the 825,000.7 person-rads are per 10^6 person-years, and the 78.7 leukemia deaths are per 10^6 person-years, so we simply left the 10^6 person-years out of the calculation.

The whole-body leukemia dose for the remaining age groups is calculated in exactly the same way. The results are tabulated below:

Age Group (age at exposure)	Whole-Body Leukemia Dose (in person-rads)
10–19	16,540
20–34	11,473
35–49	16,962
50+	5,616

Summarizing All the Leukemia Doses for Japan

For these subjects, we have a range of leukemia doses from 5,616 person-rads to 16,962 person-rads. The author is concerned about essentially all of these values resting upon a small number of leukemia cases in the unexposed groups, which introduces a statistical instability. There is no way to improve this situation, and the Japanese data are the best we have. Considering these data, the author suggests the leukemia dose to be on the order of 5,000 or 15,000 person-rads per leukemia death. There is no clear trend associated with age at exposure.

Conversion of the Japanese Leukemia Doses to Doses Applicable to the United States and Other Countries

As discussed in chapter 8, our best estimate is that radiation increases malignant disease in proportion to the spontaneous occurrence rate of the disease, for a specified quantity of radiation delivered. There is no reason known to the author why leukemia should be excluded from this generalization. Using this generalization, we would anticipate that the leukemia dose for the United States would be much lower than that for Japan, because leukemia rates are appreciably higher in the United States than in Japan (see table 12). The actual data for 1974 show the following (Silverberg 1980):

Leukemia Death Rates per 100,000

	Males	Females
United States	6.9	4.3
Japan	4.2	3.1

The factor of increase for the United States, for males, is 1.64, and the factor for females is 1.39. Averaging the factors for both sexes, we can say that the leukemia rate is 1.52 times higher in the United States than in Japan (at least for 1974).

Therefore, the appropriate leukemia doses for the United States would be in the range of 5,000/1.52 to 15,000/1.52 = 3,289 to 9,868 person-rads. Given all the uncertainties, we should round this off to 3,000–10,000 person-rads. We are not likely to know these numbers, nor their age trends, very much better in the next decade or so.

WHOLE-BODY RADIATION VERSUS PARTIAL-BODY RADIATION

All the estimates for leukemia are based on the assumption that *all* vulnerable tissue has been irradiated. Since bone marrow is believed to represent the largest source of leukemias, making that assumption is tantamount to saying that all the bone marrow has been irradiated. It is certain that some part of the leukemia total must arise from lymphatic tissues, inside or outside the bone marrow. For calculational purposes, one should attempt to estimate the fraction of the bone marrow that has been irradiated in order to estimate leukemia risks. Thus, if one-half the marrow has been irradiated, we should regard the leukemia dose as 6,000–20,000 person-rads, instead of 3,000–10,000 person-rads. So if one-half the marrow received 100 rads of ionizing radiation, the risk of development of a fatal leukemia would be between 100/6,000 and 100/20,000, or between 0.0167 and 0.005.

THE COMPARATIVE SERIOUSNESS OF THE LEUKEMIA AND SOLID-CANCER EFFECTS OF RADIATION

When we recall that the rough average value of whole-body cancer dose for an equilibrium population is 270 person-rads, whereas the leukemia doses are on the order of 3,000–10,000 person rads, it becomes very clear that the solid-cancer consequences of *whole-body* radiation are far greater than the leukemia consequences. This in no way denigrates the gravity of the production of fatal leukemia by ionizing radiation. Rather, it re-emphasizes the seriousness of solid-cancer production by radiation.

Additionally, one very important feature of the leukemia deaths must be noted: since they occur well within 30 years after exposure to ionizing radiation, whereas a large proportion of the solid-cancer deaths occur well beyond 30 years after exposure, the average loss of life expectancy is far higher per leukemia fatality than per solid-cancer fatality. If one wishes to compare the impacts from whole-body irradiation, this greater loss of life-span from leukemia tends to offset the greater total number of deaths from solid cancers.

IS THE PRODUCTION OF LEUKEMIA IN HUMANS PROPORTIONAL TO RADIATION DOSE?

It will be useful to repeat here a paragraph from chapter 8, dealing with the issue of linearity between dose and response in leukemia in Japan:

A few years ago, the dose-response curve for leukemia in the Nagasaki survivors caused a great to-do. It was said that the curvature was marked at low doses (indicating a lower leukemia incidence at low doses than would be expected from linearity), whereas the Hiroshima curve showed approximate linearity. Neutrons, more prominent in the Hiroshima dose, were supposed to explain the linearity of that curve. For the Nagasaki data in which the gamma dose constituted almost the whole dose, the curve suggested a dose-squared relationship for the induction of leukemia by gamma rays (low LET radiation). That conclusion was entirely based upon one low point, itself based upon five cases of leukemia. And a virtual scientific edifice was built upon that conclusion. When the Nagasaki leukemia data are fully considered, the evidence for curvature essentially disappears, taking the edifice with it. Both Beebe, Kato, and Land (1978) and the BEIR-III report (1979, p. 505) have conceded that the argument for a dose-squared relationship in the Nagasaki leukemia data cannot be taken seriously.

The author has examined the Nagasaki evidence to show, first, how the proponents of the dose-squared interpretation arrived at their faulty conclusions, and second, how the Nagasaki data are correctly interpreted. One of the key errors in the faulty analyses was the reliance on a small sample of data with low statistical reliability. An unbiased scientist will recognize the dangers inherent in such misplaced reliance but, as we have noted previously, it must be realized that in the field of radiation induction of cancer or leukemia there is enormous pressure on scientists to find that the dose-response curve is *less steep than linear.*

Additional follow-up on the Hiroshima-Nagasaki survivors, available since the publication of the unabridged edition of this work, is even more conclusive in discrediting the gamma-ray-versus-neutron effect and the dose-squared hypothesis. Indeed, Mendelsohn and Loewe of the Livermore National Laboratory have demonstrated (1982) that the neutron dose at Hiroshima was *grossly* lower than the T-65 doses previously reported. The final result is to invalidate all the dose-squared proposals (already discredited by other evidence presented in the unabridged edition) made by those who "hope" to minimize the seriousness of radiation effects.

SECTION 2: EXCESS LEUKEMIA IN SOLDIERS EXPOSED TO NEVADA TEST "SMOKY"

Caldwell and co-workers (1980) published their observations on the occurrence of leukemia among participants in military maneuvers at a nuclear bomb test in 1957 at the Nevada Test Site. The findings can best be summarized by the following statements made in the abstract accompanying the Caldwell publication:

Preliminary studies indicate that nine cases of leukemia have occurred among 3,224 men who participated in military maneuvers during the 1957 nuclear test explosion "Smoky." This represents a significant increase over the expected incidence of 3.5 cases. They included four cases of acute myelocytic leukemia, three of chronic myelocytic leukemia, and one each of hairy cell and acute lymphocytic leukemia. At the time of diagnosis, patient ages ranged from 21 to 60 years (mean, 41.8 years) and the interval from time of nuclear test to diagnosis from two to 19 years (mean, 14.2 years). Film-badge records, which are available for eight of the nine men, indicated gamma radiation exposure levels ranging from 0 to 2,977 millirems (mean, 1,033 millirems). Mean film-badge gamma dose for the entire Smoky cohort was 466.2 millirems. (p. 1575)

Caldwell and co-workers point out that further efforts are needed to try to reconstruct exposure levels from sources other than the film-badge records, particularly because the circumstances of the military maneuvers were such that radionuclides could have been inhaled or ingested, providing a dose additional to the external gamma-ray dose measured on the film badge. This reasoning is certainly sound. As matters now stand, all that can be said is that the external dose recorded can be taken to represent only the *minimum* value for the true exposure of these men.

It is of interest that none of the cases of leukemia is of the chronic lymphocytic variety, the one leukemia for which radiation induction has not yet been provable. Of further interest is the observation that follow-up has been possible for only 2,459 members of the cohort of 3,224 men (or 76%), so that it is possible that additional cases of leukemia will still be discovered among members of the cohort.

While this leukemia series cannot be appropriately used in the evaluation of the leukemia risk from ionizing radiation, primarily because only a minimum estimate of dose is available, it does raise some serious questions. If the results are analyzed as they currently are reported, there is an excess of 157% in leukemia from a mean dose of 0.466 rems (O/E is 9/3.5, or 2.57, which means an excess of 157%). Therefore, the % excess per rem is 157%/0.466 rems, or 337% per rem. This is *grossly* higher than the result just analyzed for the Hiroshima-Nagasaki survivors. Since there is a very real possibility that the men of the "Smoky" cohort received an additional internal dose, judgment must be reserved concerning the real meaning of the % excess per rem. Additionally, since we are dealing with a total of 9 cases of leukemia, the confidence we can place in the O/E ratio is still quite limited.

Caldwell and co-workers report that at the time of analysis there was no provable increased mortality from any form of cancer other than leukemia. They state, appropriately, "Since follow-up of the Smoky cohort is incomplete, final analysis of cancer incidence and mortality is not possible" (p. 1578). The author would add that further follow-up is *essential*, because cancers other than leukemia are known to occur later, on the average, than leukemia—and the "Smoky" cohort is just entering the period when an appreciable excess of cancers other than leukemia would be expected, if, indeed, an excess is to occur. Since the true dose received by these soldiers is unknown, the number of cancers to be expected is difficult to predict.

The Dosimetry Problem in the "Smoky" Cohort

It is evident that a careful effort to assess the total dose received by military personnel who participated in this test operation was not made. One wonders why a careful program of cytogenetic studies of members of the cohort is not instituted now. The crucial issue is whether or not the true dose (including internal dose) might be appreciably greater than that measured on film badges. Such studies, which seek out chromosome aberrations, can help greatly in reconstructing doses even several *decades* in the past.

Possibly such studies are planned for the "Smoky" group, and for several other sets of military personnel exposed to atomic tests and fallout. Assuredly such studies *can* be done. The authorities, who failed in their responsibility to make good measurements in the first place, can perhaps redeem themselves by taking responsible actions *now*.

SECTION 3: RETROSPECTIVE STUDIES OF
LEUKEMIA INDUCTION BY RADIATION

In most of the studies reported in this book, the evidence for human carcinogenesis or leukemogenesis was obtained by a *prospective* follow-up,
meaning that a group of persons who had been irradiated was observed for
the incidence of malignant disease, cancer or leukemia. To the extent that
their control group is matched in all respects other than the irradiation, such
studies are preferred as a reliable way of acquiring information. There is no
problem of "recall" of information, and the doses for the various individuals
are determined in advance of knowing who develops cancer or leukemia.
Such prospective studies are by no means perfect. For example, for the
survivors of Hiroshima and Nagasaki, legitimate questions have arisen about
confounding effects of postwar conditions and nonradiation injury from the
bombing.

THE NATURE OF RETROSPECTIVE STUDIES

There is a wholly separate way of acquiring information concerning radiation carcinogenesis and leukemogenesis, known as the *retrospective* method.
In this method one identifies a group of individuals with a disease and then
a group without it, comparable with respect to as many variables as possible,
except for radiation dose, to serve as the *control* group for the study. Then, with
radiation the variable of interest, one attempts to ascertain how much radiation on the average the disease group and the control group each received
in the past. Or, one might ask what fractions of the disease group and of the
control group each received certain radiation exposures.

   If radiation increases the risk of the disease, those with the disease will
be found, on the average, to have received *more* irradiation, since those with
the greatest irradiation most often "select themselves out" of a population
to get the disease.

   The retrospective method of ascertaining evidence for carcinogenesis
is a valid method, provided one understands its limitations. It is always
possible that one may determine an association between radiation and cancer or leukemia production, but that the association is not necessarily a
causal one. For example, suppose the persons in the cancer group had
certain symptoms that led them to get more X-rays than the persons in the
control group. The extra X-rays could then simply reflect some effect of
disease or some constitutional characteristic which led to the disease. We
would find an increased X-ray exposure in the history of those with the
disease, but that exposure would not be the *cause* of the disease. It is largely
because of this problem that we prefer evidence based on prospective studies rather than retrospective studies. But we are not barbarians, so we do
not set up prospective studies by irradiating some people and not others.
The circumstances of medical exposure or atomic bombing sometimes set

up prospective studies that were not intended, and then we do make use of the information they provide.

If we can demonstrate that the radiation was not related to the constitution of the person or to medical features of the disease from which he is suffering, then we can interpret the excess radiation exposure in a retrospective study as causal and can work out the mathematics for determining the increase in risk per rad of exposure. The retrospective method is often available to us when no prospective study is available.

In chapter 15, the retrospective method of Stewart and co-workers for demonstrating the effect of in utero radiation in causing childhood cancers and leukemias is described. In the particular case of in utero radiation, as we shall see in chapter 15, one prospective study is available (Kato 1971) which has defects so serious that we prefer the results of the retrospective study. Ordinarily, however, a properly conducted prospective study is scientifically preferable.

The Choice of Control Group and the Handling of Evidence

We are shortly going to consider several retrospective studies of the question of radiation causation of leukemia in human beings. Before examining the studies we must give attention to some serious potential pitfalls of the retrospective method. Anytime we endeavor to choose a control group, we may introduce a *bias* in our choice of controls and in the handling of the evidence. Such a bias, often exceedingly subtle and totally unintentional on the part of the investigators, can completely subvert the study and lead to erroneous conclusions. Let us illustrate how this can happen.

Suppose we have 300 patients with leukemia and we wish to ask whether medical diagnostic radiation may have been responsible for causing some or all of those leukemia cases. We shall try to ascertain this by comparing the prior X-ray exposure history of the leukemia cases with the prior X-ray exposure history of the controls. Suppose we think of two possible mistakes we might make in choosing a control group. The first might be choosing as controls individuals from a higher economic stratum than the leukemia cases. The second error might be choosing controls from a lower economic stratum than the leukemia cases.

In the first case, the economically privileged would have received more medical care, and hence a larger number of X-ray examinations. We would "discover" that the leukemia cases had had fewer X-rays than the controls, and we could draw the totally unwarranted conclusion that X-rays protect against leukemia.

In the second case, the economically underprivileged would have received less medical care, and hence a smaller number of X-ray examinations. We would "discover" that the leukemia cases had had more X-rays than the controls, and we could draw the unwarranted conclusion that X-rays cause leukemia.

Since our objective is to derive conclusions that will stand up, we must avoid such errors in the choice of control groups. So the proper choice of a control group is of supreme importance. We can go through the most meticulous, elegant, statistical analysis, prove that there is less than one chance in a million that the results could be due to chance, and the whole study would still be worthless, and worse, because it would be *deceptive*. All our effort would have been wasted because of the poor choice of a control group.

Sometimes the bias of the investigator can doom the study in advance without anyone, including the investigator, realizing that bias is operative. Indeed, the investigator might be horrified if he (she) realized that bias on his (her) part was even conceivably present. Let us consider the way such a bias might enter, again in the choice of controls.

A radiologist in a large medical center administers radiation in diagnostic procedures to many patients in the course of a busy practice. Any human being would feel terrible if he thought that his career work had induced many cases of leukemia or cancer or both. Even if this person were the most honest and objective scientist imaginable, there would still exist a powerful psychological desire (possibly not at the conscious level) to find that diagnostic radiation *cannot* cause leukemia or cancer. But because the person considers himself a concerned, objective scientist, he decides to launch a large-scale retrospective investigation of leukemia and diagnostic radiation. He decides to use as controls patients who came to the medical center but who did *not* develop leukemia. He intends to match sex, age, and residence area case by case, one control for each leukemia case. Somebody has to examine the chart records of those controls to see that they are "suitable" for inclusion in the study. And there's the rub!

In this hypothetical study, the key finding that would "prove" that diagnostic radiation causes leukemia would be more frequent X-rays in the leukemia group than in the control group. The key finding that would "exonerate" radiation would be more frequent or equally frequent X-rays in the control group. Now, the person who chooses the control group will find some chart records satisfactory for inclusion and others not satisfactory. Inevitably some records will show extensive histories of X-ray examinations; here, subconscious bias can enter the study. A person with an extensive history of X-ray examination may be "found" to be perfectly suitable for inclusion in the control series, whereas other persons with no history of X-ray examination may be "found," for a variety of reasons, *not* suitable for inclusion. The ball game is over, so far as the results are concerned. The study will contain a built-in "proof" that the controls received as much radiation as the leukemia cases, or more. And diagnostic X-radiation will be exonerated without a true test.

If one were to suggest that the investigator had allowed personal and professional bias to affect the selection of the controls, the investigator would be shocked and offended! Biasing the study would be the last thing he (she) *intended* to do. But the annals of medical history are replete with such biased studies. Thousands of pharmaceutical agents have been "proved" to produce beneficial results in patients, only to have repeat studies fail to confirm the result. The initial result was based, in all likelihood, on a biased choice of cases.

Another subtle form of bias can operate. We have discussed the situation in which a radiologist conducts a study that could determine he has harmed his patients. Let us consider a bias in the opposite direction. It happens to be a fact that reputations are made and people get advancements by discovering *positive* things, not negative things. In fact, it is quite a bit harder to get a paper published that presents a negative result. Suppose an ambitious scientist decides to investigate whether diagnostic radiation causes leukemia. When *this* scientist goes to the archives to pick out his series of control cases, the unconscious bias operating is to choose those records with very few X-ray entries. These just happen to be "suitable" for inclusion as controls in his study. The final result is that the average X-ray exposure is found to be greater in the leukemia cases than in the controls, and the scientist "discovers" that diagnostic X-rays cause leukemia.

It is regrettable that such potential biases exist, but it would be scientific naiveté of the worst kind simply to try to wish them away.

Biases also enter in during the handling and procurement of the data themselves, independent of the choice of controls. In one major study we shall consider, the method of ascertaining past X-ray history was by interview, followed by checking of medical records to see if the interview had indeed provided accurate information. The investigators, trying to be super-objective, did not tell the interviewer whether a particular household was that of a leukemia case or a control, in order to insure that the interviewer would try just as hard to obtain information about radiation exposure in the leukemia cases as in the controls. As the reader has no doubt guessed, in a high proportion of the interviews the interviewer could tell the leukemia cases from the controls. To interview extensively a person with leukemia or the family of someone who has died of leukemia yet not feel the presence of the disease is almost impossible. So in spite of a commendable intention to prevent bias in this phase of the study (the Tri-State study of Gibson and co-workers), the *opportunity* for it to enter existed nevertheless.

Beyond the interview stage there is still large potential for bias. Graham and co-workers, who conducted the Tri-State leukemia survey, point out that, based on a sample of 200 subjects out of their total study, they found the following:

a. The informants (during the interview) failed to recall or mention many of the diagnostic X-ray films.

b. Of films taken in physicians' or dentists' offices, 79.6% were not mentioned in the interview.

c. Of films taken in hospitals, 66.5% were not mentioned in the interview.

Graham and co-workers point out, appropriately, that verification of records was a most important study component. But what they do not point out is that the verification procedure is itself subject to hidden biases. It is no simple task to examine hospital and physicians' records of radiation exposure, particularly of exposure many years in the past. Diligence in seeking out the radiation history of the leukemia cases in such records must equal the diligence in seeking out the radiation history of the control cases. We must always ask if equal diligence was applied. If it was not, then the results of the investigation can have little or nothing to do with the relationship of X-rays and leukemia.

The reader may be asking, "But since control groups must be used in prospective studies too, why isn't bias also a major problem there?" In prospective studies, mistakes in choosing control groups are a greater hazard than bias. The issue of appropriate control groups for the ankylosing spondylitis study and for additional prospective studies was discussed in chapter 5.

But in prospective studies, the problem of bias is grossly reduced because the investigator makes a commitment to report on what happens to each member of at least two groups (for example, an irradiated group and an unirradiated one) at a time when their fates are utterly unknown. No investigator is capable of selecting cases that will turn out to support his bias or of excluding cases that will turn out to refute it. Even in a study such as the Hanford death study (chapter 5), where the "story" (death from cancer versus death from some other cause) is complete by the time the investigator enters the scene, the investigator has no choice, no discretion as to who becomes part of the study. Like it or not, he is stuck with his samples, as is every other prospective investigator. The dose-disease relationship has been determined by nature without his influence, and recorded in the raw data for all to see. If such an investigator starts actually tossing out the particular results that do not support his bias, he has a much harder time fooling himself, and others, than does a retrospective investigator, whose bias can creep in in less obvious ways.

The author would not like to leave the impression that the retrospective method is so fraught with potential biases as to be useless. It can be a powerful method of investigating important problems where other methods, such as prospective studies, are simply unthinkable. But there is no point in failing to realize that the retrospective method has serious potential pitfalls.

For leukemia induction by radiation, we have a tremendously powerful base of evidence in the Hiroshima-Nagasaki *prospective* study. Moreover, the radiation effects shown in that study, analyzed in section 1 of this chapter, are consistent with the results of an equally powerful prospective study of ankylosing spondylitis patients, although the latter study is omitted here because it is based on very high doses to the bone marrow. One should be extremely reluctant to take seriously any retrospective study that challenges those results. In science there is ultimately only one truth, and eventually. we must become able to ferret out reasons for apparent discrepancies.

The author suggests that bias should be carefully looked for when a retrospective study challenges the result from a well-conducted prospective study which has itself been carefully scrutinized for possible errors in method.

THE TRI-STATE STUDY OF LEUKEMIA FROM MEDICAL IRRADIATION

Gibson and co-workers (1972), Graham and co-workers (1966), and Bross and co-workers (1979) all published reports based on the original Tri-State survey. In one part of this survey, the relationship between adult leukemia and diagnostic medical irradiation was examined in 1,414 adult leukemia cases from upstate New York and the Minneapolis and Baltimore metropolitan areas, and in 1,370 adult controls labeled as "comprising a probability sample" of the same areas. In order to minimize any possibility of interviewer bias, Gibson and co-workers use only those data derived from verified information from hospitals and medical practitioners.

The principle used in these studies is that one obtains a measure of dose from the number of X-ray films. If radiation is related to leukemia induction, the leukemia cases should show a history of more medical X-ray exposure than the control cases. If no relationship exists, the history of medical X-ray exposure should be the same in the leukemia cases as in the controls.

The number of X-ray films is the basis for the report of Gibson and co-workers. A much more satisfactory measure would be the actual radiation dose received. While it is difficult to measure the true bone-marrow dose from records of number of films taken, Bross and co-workers suggest a rough translation of number of films into skin dose in rads. Bross suggests that:

$$(\text{skin dose})_{\text{rads}} = (0.167)(\text{number of chest X-rays})$$
$$+ (0.790)(\text{number of abdomen X-rays})$$

The Gibson study does not segregate thorax, abdominal, and pelvic X-rays; these are lumped together under the heading *trunk films*. Since we do not know whether a specific case received radiation to the thorax or the abdomen, we shall use a value halfway between the values Bross gives, in order to describe dose in the Gibson study. Thus, $\frac{1}{2}(0.167 + 0.790) = \frac{1}{2}(0.957) = 0.48$. Let us round this off to 0.5 rads to the *trunk* per X-ray film. The true mean marrow dose is much less than this skin dose to the trunk. We must emphasize that the doses are very rough and are used only because they are preferable to leaving the doses in terms of number of films.

Gibson and co-workers studied the relationship of radiation to the following types of leukemia: acute myelogenous plus monocytic leukemia, acute lymphatic leukemia, chronic myelogenous leukemia, chronic lymphatic leukemia, and leukemia unspecified with respect to cell type. The results follow.

Acute Myelogenous plus Monocytic Leukemia:

MALES:

Trunk Films	Dose in Rads	Percent Exposed Cases	Percent Exposed Controls	Probability	Relative Risk
11 or more	5.5 rads or more	26.20	18.12	0.05	1.72
21 or more	10.5 rads or more	13.36	6.83	0.025	2.23
41 or more	20.5 rads or more	7.93	1.08	0.0001	6.78

FEMALES: For this comparison, Gibson and co-workers state that there was no significant increase in the relative risk of the irradiated population.

Gibson's interpretation is as follows. Those who received 5.5 rads or more, for example, of trunk radiation from medical X-rays have 1.72 times the risk of leukemia as those who received fewer than 5.5 rads of trunk radiation, and the chance that the effect is not real is 0.05 (1 in 20). The rise in relative risk with increase in dose supports the relationship between radiation and leukemia.

Chronic Myelogenous Leukemia:

MALES:

Trunk Films	Dose in Rads	Percent Exposed Cases	Percent Exposed Controls	Probability	Relative Risk
11 or more	5.5 rads or more	33.06	18.70	0.001	2.22
16 or more	8.0 rads or more	23.92	12.57	0.003	2.33
21 or more	10.5 rads or more	18.82	6.92	0.0003	3.26
41 or more	20.5 rads or more	9.15	1.30	0.0001	7.14

FEMALES:

Trunk Films	Dose in Rads	Percent Exposed Cases	Percent Exposed Controls	Probability	Relative Risk
11 or more	5.5 rads or more	22.79	20.28	0.58	1.29
16 or more	8.0 rads or more	16.18	14.41	0.66	1.32
21 or more	10.5 rads or more	10.80	9.54	0.71	1.43

For Males: The association demonstrated between medical X-ray exposure and leukemia is powerful, and the increasing relative risk with increasing dose strongly supports the association. The statistical probabilities make chance a very remote explanation of the findings.

For Females: While the direction of the evidence is toward a higher percent of leukemia cases exposed than controls, in no case does the association approach statistical significance. The relative risks listed are *not* statistically significant. The inability to prove an association for the females does not appear to be due to a lack of cases. The relationship is simply not nearly as strong as for the males, if a relationship exists at all. Gibson and co-workers are unable to provide any explanation for the male-female difference.

Acute Lymphatic Leukemia:

MALES:

Trunk Films	Dose in Rads	Percent Exposed		Probability	Relative Risk
		Cases	Controls		
11 or more	5.5 rads or more	20.62	15.34	0.31	1.63
16 or more	8.0 rads or more	13.19	9.47	0.38	1.75

FEMALES:

11 or more	5.5 rads or more	27.00	31.50	0.54	0.89

While the direction of the data for the males indicates an association between medical X-ray exposure and acute lymphatic leukemia, the relative risks cannot be proved to be significant statistically within this study. For the females, even the direction is wrong for an association, but not significantly so.

Chronic Lymphatic Leukemia:

MALES:

Trunk Films	Dose in Rads	Percent Exposed		Probability	Relative Risk
		Cases	Controls		
11 or more	5.5 rads or more	18.36	18.82	0.89	1.03
16 or more	8.0 rads or more	14.09	12.45	0.56	1.25
21 or more	10.5 rads or more	12.45	7.01	0.02	2.03

FEMALES:

11 or more	5.5 rads or more	18.19	24.33	0.37	0.84

These results are analyzed separately below.

Leukemia, Cell Type Unspecified: For 234 cases no histologic (cell-type) studies had been done. Gibson and co-workers do not present tabular data, but instead make the statement, "We found no significant differences in the risk of leukemia of unspecified type for males and females with irradiation to all sites or to the trunk" (p. 308).

Comparison of These Results with Those in Prospective Studies

The Gibson and co-workers' results are consistent with all other studies in showing that chronic myelogenous leukemia and acute myelogenous leukemia are induced in males by ionizing radiation. The Gibson study is at variance with general findings in that it was unable to prove that either of these forms of leukemia was induced in females.

Gibson and co-workers' results also differ from those of other studies in the inability to prove a relationship between radiation and acute lymphatic leukemia in either males or females. In the opposite direction, the finding of an association in one dose group of the chronic lymphatic leukemia series of males is at variance with all other studies, which report no association. The other studies show no association for females, and neither does the Gibson study.

The findings for both acute and chronic myelogenous leukemia in the males are statistically highly significant, but no explanation is available for the failure to find an association for the females.

The Graham paper (1966) is not treated separately here. Gibson was a co-author of that study, as Graham was a co-author of the Gibson paper (1972); the Bross study, which is considered below, uses the Gibson/Graham data. To the extent that any bias operated in the collection and assembly of the Tri-State data, the validity of all three studies suffers. The opportunities for bias in that study have already been discussed; they include possible variation in the diligence of verification of exposure records for the leukemia cases, as opposed to that for controls.

Myelogenous Leukemia in the Tri-State Study Compared with the Hiroshima-Nagasaki Studies

Bross has continued to analyze the Tri-State findings in more detail. From one of his recent papers (Bross, Ball, and Falen 1979), it is possible to derive a % excess per rad and a doubling dose, and to compare the results with those from Hiroshima and Nagasaki, already presented in this chapter.

To summarize, we find that the K values (% excess per rad) from the Bross and co-worker studies range from 0.095 to 0.154, for five groups of males over 65 years of age receiving doses of less than one rad to 20 rads. The doubling doses range from 10.5 rads to 6.5 rads.

From the Hiroshima-Nagasaki data for deaths from leukemia in the $50+$ age group, we have calculated (see the unabridged edition of this book) that the K value was 0.180 per rad, which would correspond to a doubling dose of $1/0.180 = 5.6$ rads.

The Bross analyses are based on corrected doses to the trunk, and we really do not know precisely how Bross's trunk dose compares with the bone-marrow dose in the Japanese data. It is certain that 1 rad of trunk dose is equal to much less than 1 rad to the marrow, on the average. If this is true, the doubling dose based upon the Tri-State data would be lower than in the 6.5–10.5-rad range. It is clear that the order of the doubling dose estimated from the Tri-State data is close to that estimated from the Hiroshima-Nagasaki leukemia data. And given the uncertainties in both studies, asking for better than a general order of magnitude agreement would be asking for too much. We may conclude from the analysis of the Tri-State leukemia data that medical irradiation with X-rays produces the same type of leukemia effect per rad as does atomic-bomb radiation given in one dose. We are left, if we do that, with no explanation at all for the absence of a provable leukemogenic effect of medical irradiation upon the *women* in the Tri-State study, and no explanation for the apparent positive association between medical irradiation and excess chronic lymphatic leukemia in *one* of the male groups.

The findings from the Tri-State data appear internally inconsistent. This may be the consequence of some undetected and undetectable bias introduced long ago, when the data were collected and assembled.

THE LINOS AND CO-WORKERS STUDY OF LEUKEMIA FROM MEDICAL IRRADIATION

Recently Linos and co-workers (1980) published a paper, the abstract of which concludes the following:

No statistically significant increase was found in the risk of developing leukemia after radiation doses of 0 to 300 rads (3 Gy) to the bone marrow when these amounts were administered in small doses over long periods of time, as in routine medical care. (p. 1101)

Since this conclusion differs so drastically from the Japanese experience for leukemogenesis in the 0–300-rad region, we must examine the paper carefully. Unfortunately, the paper is most unusual as medical papers go in this field, for it is devoid of any data with which the reader could examine the findings. It is totally devoted to giving the conclusions of its authors and does not provide the reader with any meaningful ability to draw his (her) own conclusions. It is rare for editors to permit the publication of a paper so totally lacking in the crucial data upon which the conclusions are based. A letter to the senior author of the paper from the author of this book, requesting the basic information missing in the paper, was simply ignored.

Within the small body of information that the authors do provide, there are a great many flagrant errors of method, and any one of them provides more than sufficient reason to discount the results as any serious contribution to the literature on radiation-induced leukemia. Here we shall simply describe the nature of these errors briefly.

First, one is immediately struck, in this paper, by the curious labeling of 0–300 rads as "low-dose radiation"—a concept drastically at variance with virtually all other scientific views. Second, the paper states that 7 leukemia cases involving exposure to more than 300 rads were arbitrarily excluded from the study; the inclusion of these cases would certainly have altered the results of the study. Third, the Linos data are heavily weighted in favor of data on chronic lymphocytic (lymphatic) leukemia, the one form of the disease for which, in all other studies, no association with radiation has been found. Fourth, the use in this study of "lifelong" radiation experience—which at first might appear desirable—turns out to be faulty. As we pointed out earlier, the leukemogenic effect of radiation seems to be almost totally spent in 25–30 years after irradiation; therefore, radiation received more than 25 years before the diagnosis of leukemia (such data are used by

Linos et al.) is either totally irrelevant or, at best, minimally relevant. Fifth, there are in the paper a number of overt misstatements of the findings of other studies, a serious matter indeed. Sixth, the Linos study is highly vulnerable in the area of bias in screening for the controls. Finally, this study (like others) persists in claiming that little is known about exposure to low doses of radiation over long periods of time. We have dealt with this view in chapter 8 and elsewhere and showed how unreasonable it is; yet this is how the Linos study proposes to exonerate "doses of 0 to 300 rads to the bone marrow when these amounts were administered over long periods of time."

If the paper of Linos and co-workers did not have the vulnerabilities pointed out above, and had Linos and co-workers at least given the reader the opportunity to see the data on which the conclusions are based, then the author of this book would have treated this study just as he has treated other studies with "negative" findings in this book.

If this author seems to be particularly hostile to the paper by Linos and co-workers, it is because he *is,* on strictly scientific grounds. It was the lead article in one of the foremost medical journals, and will therefore have an enormous impact on the medical community—especially since it puts forth a message the medical community longs to hear. In fact, the author knows directly of its impact on several large medical centers within three weeks of its appearance. Countless future patients could suffer the consequences of the erroneous reassurance in this paper concerning medical irradiation in the dose range of 0–300 rads. The author makes no apologies for his antipathy.

It will be sad indeed if acceptance of this totally vulnerable study leads to complacency in the medical profession about the cancer and leukemia hazards of diagnostic radiation.

[CHAPTER 15]

CONGENITAL AND GENETIC EFFECTS OF IONIZING RADIATION

W E MUST CONSIDER THREE broad types of health effects in evaluating the health effects of ionizing radiations:

1. Effects on the *individual* receiving the radiation, at any time *after birth*. These effects are widely referred to as the *somatic* effects of radiation. In earlier chapters we considered two major somatic effects in detail and quantitatively: cancer and leukemia.

2. Effects on the *descendants* of the individual receiving the radiation. Under these circumstances the radiation is received *before conception* of the descendant. We are concerned with radiation delivered days or centuries before the conception of the descendant. While such effects are broadly referred to as *genetic,* we mean either effects on the single-gene molecule or effects of a variety of sorts on the chromosomes that carry the DNA (gene) molecules.

3. Effects on the individual, *already conceived but as yet unborn,* irradiated while the individual is in utero. All such effects are commonly referred to as *congenital,* or *teratogenic,* effects, rather than genetic effects. The term *congenital* really refers only to the time of irradiation, rather than to the mechanism of effects. We do indeed believe that a large proportion, if not all, of the irradiation effects on the individual in utero are effects on the DNA (gene) molecule or on the chromosomes bearing the genes. So, in terms of *mechanism,* as opposed to *time* of irradiation, the genetic and congenital effects can be regarded as highly similar. We will see that excess childhood leukemia and cancer are among the congenital effects of in utero irradiation.

Let us clarify further. For our purposes here, any effects occurring after the fertilization of the ovum by the sperm will be regarded as congenital, or in utero, effects, even though the fertilized ovum may not yet be *implanted* into the uterine wall. Any effects occurring in the sperm (or its precursor cells) or the ovum before, even soon before, fertilization will be regarded as genetic effects. Some might prefer a different definition, but as long as we are consistent in usage, the exact definition is not of great importance.

"Stochastic" Versus "Nonstochastic" Congenital Effects of Radiation

Certain effects fall into the category of "all or none" effects, in which a given amount of radiation confers a probability, or chance, of developing the effect. These are known as *stochastic* effects of ionizing radiation. The severity of the effect is not at issue; rather, the probability that the effect will occur at all is what we may relate to radiation dose. Two outstanding examples of stochastic effects of radiation are cancer and leukemia, whether that radiation is delivered in utero or at any other period of life. One does not develop a "little bit" of cancer or leukemia, although it is true that certain cancers are far more rapidly lethal to their hosts than others. (For example, lung cancers kill early; thyroid cancers kill only after decades, if at all, in most cases.) The radiation increases the probability of developing the cancer, but does not influence the severity of its clinical manifestations.

Practically all other effects that occur in utero, or in genetic material passed on to generations as yet not conceived, are *nonstochastic* in nature. There is every reason to believe that they can vary from exceedingly mild effects to exceedingly severe effects, the degree being in some way related to the amount of radiation.

We shall start our considerations of in utero effects by considering the nonstochastic developmental effects that can vary in severity. Thereafter, we shall turn our attention to the two important stochastic effects of in utero radiation: cancer and leukemia. The final sections of this chapter will examine what is known about the genetic and chromosomal effects on future generations.

Section 1: The Nonstochastic (Nonmalignant) Effects on Embryo Development

---

Possible Developmental Effects

A simple rule in medicine and biology is, "If you can visualize something that can go wrong, it probably will, somewhere, sometime." Certainly the developing embryo shows us the validity of that rule. Virtually every organ system can and does undergo deviations from the normal in structure or function, or both, during the in utero period. If the alterations of structure or function are sufficiently severe, there is spontaneous abortion, or even failure long before there is an embryo to abort. A very early "lesion" in a fertilized ovum can lead to failure of implantation in the uterus, so that no embryo develops at all. No doubt a large proportion of abnormalities are never apprehended because a pregnancy is not known to have existed.

But we can now consider potential damage to structure or function which is not embryo-lethal, and which can ultimately give rise to a live-born child with defects ranging from very mild to very severe. No organ system is "immune" to malformation and maldevelopment during the gestation period. Let us consider some of the main malformations or defects that can lead to major malfunction.

1. A host of central-nervous-system defects, most of which lead to mental retardation in the live-born child, from moderate to extremely severe. These central-nervous-system defects can include failure of development of some segment of the brain itself, and associated abnormalities of skull development, including small head circumference, elongated shape of the skull, and others.

2. A host of different abnormalities of the sensory organs, such as defects in the structure of the ears, the ear canals, the eyelids, the eye muscles, the iris, and the eyes themselves.

3. Virtually every form of heart and great vessel defect. Indeed, the recognition that such lesions may be induced during embryogenesis is the reason we refer to them as part of "congenital heart disease."

4. Cleft palate, a common deformity, with or without cleft lip, which can be part of a variety of malformation events occurring in utero.

5. Congenital dislocation of the hip, and a variety of other skeletal abnormalities, including the malformation and even absence of such structures as the patella (kneecap).

6. Polydactyly, or an abnormal number of fingers or toes, and a host of other deformities of fingers and toes that can occur even if the number of fingers and toes is normal. (*Poly-* means "many," or "extra.")

7. Serious defects in the gastrointestinal canal, such as failure of perforation of the anal opening.

8. A variety of the so-called aplasias and dysplasias. The aplasias are failures of certain organs to develop at all. The dysplasias are maldevelopment of certain organs, structurally or functionally. For example, a variety of aplasias and dysplasias are sometimes found in the urinary system, including anomalous development of the kidneys themselves, the ureters, and the bladder.

9. Cryptorchidism, or the failure of the testes to descend, a very common abnormality, which can occur in conjunction with a variety of different in utero abnormalities.

10. Major deformities in the vertebral column and ribs.

11. Failure to thrive. This is a functional description of many children born with serious malformations. While they survive the embryonic and fetal stages and are live-born, they simply do not develop normally in early infancy.

12. Hernias, either inguinal or umbilical.

A very, very long list could be made of other abnormalities that arise during the in utero period.

QUANTITATIVE ASPECTS OF DEVELOPMENT OF IN UTERO ABNORMALITIES

One of the serious difficulties in knowing the frequency of spontaneous development of in utero abnormalities is that the same abnormalities can be the result of genetic inheritance. In fact, the author considers that it would be quite hard, and probably not rewarding at all at this time, to try to ascertain what fraction of abnormalities are genetic versus congenital. This makes it difficult to appraise the quantitative aspects of radiation induction of in utero defects. Even if we knew that radiation could double the frequency of some event, we would need to know the frequency of the spontaneous event in order to assess the total price of radiation injury.

But even though we are not sure of the spontaneous frequency of in utero causation of some of the anomalies found, we can analyze the mechanisms and possible mechanisms for production of the anomalies, and for some of the mechanisms we can state specifically the extent to which ionizing radiation can increase the frequency.

THE CHROMOSOMAL MECHANISM OF CONGENITAL ABNORMALITY FORMATION

The evidence is overwhelming that a very large proportion of all the major anomalies of in utero development can be traced to *an abnormal chromosomal constitution of the embryo.* And we shall develop reasons for believing that chromosomal abnormalities which are not appreciated, because of limitations of technique, probably account for a large number of additional abnormalities of in utero development. To the extent that ionizing radiation produces some of the various chromosome lesions, there is every reason to believe that in utero abnormalities based on such chromosome lesions are increased by radiation exposure.

Trisomy and the In Utero Production of Mosaic Humans

In normal human somatic cells each autosomal chromosome class is represented in duplicate, one member of the class having come from the father and one from the mother. Such normal cells are referred to as *disomic.* If, by one or another error, three chromosomes of a class are present in a cell (or in all the somatic cells of a human being), that cell (or that human being) is referred to as *trisomic. Trisomy* is the state of having cells that are trisomic.

One of the common errors in cell division is the distribution of both chromatids of a chromosome pair to one daughter cell in the process of mitosis, yielding one daughter cell with 47 chromosomes and one with 45 chromosomes. A similar error in meiosis results when both homologues (the maternal and paternal representatives of a particular automsomal chromosome) go to one daughter cell instead of one to each daughter cell. The result is a sperm or ovum with 24 chromosomes which, on mating with a normal gamete containing 23 chromosomes, produces a fertilized ovum with 47 chromosomes. Several such matings can produce a viable offspring. However, since events that occur in gamete formation, either to sperm or ovum, really fall into the category of genetic-chromosomal disorders, we shall not consider them until later in this chapter.

Separately, an important part of the story of trisomy formation is of direct concern as an in utero effect: the phenomenon of *mosaicism,* or *mixoploidy.* A human being is said to display mosaicism if there are present in his (her) body more than one type of cell. Normal people have 46 chromosomes per cell. Some abnormal people, for example those with Down's syndrome, have 47 chromosomes, each cell having an extra chromosome. Mosaic humans have some cells with 46 chromosomes and some with another number, most frequently (but not exclusively) 47. These persons are also said to exhibit mixoploidy, because they have more than one "ploidy," or number of chromosomes per cell.

We shall see why it is possible that mosaicism may be the most *underrated* basis for in utero anomaly formation. We shall also see why it is difficult to verify this experimentally.

Production of Mosaicism In Utero: For a mosaic to form in utero after a fertilized ovum has begun with the normal 46 chromosomes, an abnormal mitosis must occur. This results in one daughter cell getting 47 chromosomes and one getting 45 chromosomes. This is a very important occurrence in utero, possibly of much greater frequency than is now thought to be the case.

Unfortunately, there are just about no data worth considering that tell us anything about the quantitative aspects of radiation effects in causing the *mitotic errors that can lead to cells with 47* and 45 chromosomes in utero in the human being. Indeed, as we shall see later in this chapter, the data concerning the production of trisomy via the abnormal *meiosis* mechanisms are very contradictory as well. It is widely held, but has been by no means proved, that ionizing radiation is not very effective in producing mitotic errors that lead to 47- or 45-chromosome cells. The author considers that the evidence is so poor, and so thin, that the question of the magnitude of any effects of ionizing radiation on this mitotic error mechanism must remain open. Certainly the question is open as far as the crucial errors that may occur in mitoses in the *early* stages of development of the embryo are concerned.

At the very early stages, when the entire embryo is constituted of two to eight or so cells, certain types of errors in chromosome distribution can produce exceedingly serious results. Let us consider some of these.

The name we give to one process of improper distribution of chromosomes in a mitotic cell division is *nondisjunction.* This occurs when both chromatids go to one daughter cell rather than one to each daughter cell. In theory we know of no reason why nondisjunction cannot occur in *any* of the autosomes or sex chromosomes in a cell. We may never see the results of a nondisjunction in certain of the autosomes simply because the daughter cells produced are not viable.

Nondisjunction Leading to Trisomy E-18: In this case we start with a presumably normal fertilized ovum with 46 chromosomes (23 from the sperm and 23 from the ovum). If in the first cleavage there is nondisjunction of an autosome, e.g., the autosome known as E-18, then the products of that mitosis are a cell with 45 chromosomes, with one E-18 missing, and a cell with 47 chromosomes, with three E-18 chromosomes.

It is widely believed (see Zellweger and Simpson 1977, pp. 29–30) that cells with an autosome missing, such as the above-mentioned cell with one E-18 missing, are of very low viability and not likely to proliferate a clone of viable cells. This point could use some further proof, but it is true that one does not see reports of children showing many cells with 45 chromosomes, missing one autosome.

The other cell, with 47 chromosomes and a trisomy of chromosome E-18, can go on to develop an embryo and produce a live-born infant. Every cell in that infant's body will have 47 chromosomes, each cell being trisomic for chromosome E-18. We shall later consider the enormous range of defects in virtually every organ system that can occur in trisomy-E-18 embryos and infants, and the very short life-span of those that are live-born. But here we have a different objective, namely, getting at the question of mosaicism.

Suppose we consider the possibility of a *normal* first cleavage, yielding a two-cell stage in which both cells have 46 chromosomes and a normal chromosomal distribution. Now in the second division of each of these cells, let us assume the following:

a. One of the cells divides normally, yielding two cells, each with 46 chromosomes.

b. The other cell undergoes nondisjunction for the E-18 chromosome, yielding one cell with 45 chromosomes, missing an E-18 chromosome, and one cell with 47 chromosomes, trisomic for E-18.

We shall assume here that the cell with 45 chromosomes, missing one E-18 chromosome, is not viable.

If the chance of subsequent successful cell division is exactly the same for the cells with 46 chromosomes as for the cells with 47 chromosomes, then we would expect that, in the final individual produced, 33% of the cells would contain 47 chromosomes (with three E-18's), and 67% of the cells would contain 46 chromosomes (with two E-18's). Do such individuals exist? The answer is yes.

If nondisjunction had occurred at some later cell division than the second one after fertilization, the final embryo produced would have something less than 33% cells with 47 chromosomes (trisomy-E-18) and something more than 67% normal cells with 46 chromosomes.

When an individual has an appreciable fraction of cells showing deviation from the normal 46-chromosome complement, we refer to that individual as a *mosaic:* his chromosome picture is a mosaic of two different chromosome pictures. Now we must consider how we come to realize that such a situation exists. Then we shall understand how incomplete our knowledge is.

The Likelihood of Undetected Trisomies: If *all cells* in an embryo have 47 chromosomes and trisomy-E-18, it is a very serious matter indeed. Most such embryos are spontaneously aborted. Just about every kind of congenital abnormality one can think of occurs in a fair proportion of such embryos. If a live-born infant results, his life expectancy is very short: over half die before the age of 2 months, and survival beyond the age of 1 year is rare. Zellweger states that few persons with trisomy-E-18 have reached an age of 10 years or more. It is the clinical appearance of a child, his clinical abnormalities, that leads us to realize we have an infant with trisomy-E-18.

But what has been found is that a number of these infants with clinical disease characteristic of E-18 trisomy are instead mosaics. The clinical disease is known as *Edwards' syndrome.* Hamerton (1971) reviewed 146 cases of Edwards' syndrome from the literature. Of these, 119 cases (82%) appeared to have *monoclonal* trisomy-E-18, which simply means that no one could find cells with other than 47 chromosomes, and that each cell did show the E-18 trisomy. But Hamerton also found that 14 of the 146 cases (9.6%) were definitely mosaics. The mosaics had some cells with 46 chromosomes, no trisomy present, and some with 47 chromosomes, showing the E-18 trisomy.

In those instances where mosaicism is picked up as a result of noting the clinical features of a disease, it can be quite difficult to prove that mosaicism exists. The reader may not realize that we have only a limited number of sites in a living person from which to obtain cells for a determination of chromosome constitution. We have the peripheral blood, we have the fibroblasts from connective tissue, we have the cells of the bone marrow but that is nearly the end of the list. So even if we suspect a chromosome abnormality in the cells which gave rise to part of the interventricular septum of the heart, there would be little or no chance of ever confirming it. Even in clinical cases of flagrant Edwards' syndrome, it can be difficult to discover that a mosaic exists and that some of the body cells are truly trisomic for the E-18 chromosome.

This means that *lesser* degrees of trisomy-E-18 may very well not be detected at all. Thus, if the mitotic error should occur at a slightly later stage of embryogenesis, the final number of cells in the body which are trisomic for E-18 may be a very small part of the total number of cells. But if the trisomic cells are among the cells producing a specific tissue organ during embryogenesis, *that local region may suffer from its trisomy-E-18 just as much as it would if all body cells were trisomic.* This provides a potential mechanism for producing a host of more localized congenital abnormalities, in contrast to the widespread abnormality of many organ systems in a full trisomy-E-18.

The Various Human Trisomies and Their Clinical Features: Thus far, in our discussion of trisomies and mosaics, we have only mentioned chromosome E-18. This was because viable infants with E-18 trisomy do exist, and also because it was useful for illustrative purposes. Several other autosomal trisomies produce viable infants: trisomies of D-13 (Patau's syndrome), of G-21 (Down's syndrome), of G-22 (formerly called *cat-eye syndrome* or *Schmid-Fraccaro syndrome*—Zellweger 1976). These are trisomies for which full-term infants are born with a total trisomic complement of an autosomal chromosome. In Zellweger and Simpson's *Chromosomes in Man* (1977), no cases are described in which full-term infants are born with a total trisomic complement of any other autosome. It would appear therefore that no trisomy of any other autosome, producing *only* cells with 47 chromosomes and that trisomy, is compatible with the development of a live-born infant. Or, and this is unlikely, such cases remain to be discovered.

One of the truly striking features of the various trisomies is the overlap in certain abnormalities among the various syndromes. For example, studies have shown that congenital heart defects are present in the majority of cases of all of the trisomies mentioned. This affords strong support for the concept that chromosome *balance* has a great deal to do with normal development. It argues against the concept that a specific chromosome necessarily determines the development of a specific structure.

The list of congenital defects for such trisomies as E-18, D-13, and G-22, covering virtually every organ system of the body, which occur with a higher frequency than in the population at large, is a very long one.

Developmental retardation is a feature of virtually all of the trisomies, but the specific anatomical brain defects may vary considerably from case to case, even for one of the trisomies.

Why Mosaicism May Be a Most Important Cause of Congenital Anomalies: For each of the major trisomies that have been recognized from their clinical manifestations as occurring in full form (all the cells of an individual showing 47 chromosomes and the trisomy)—E-18, D-13, G-21, and G-22—mosaics with full-blown clinical manifestations have also been found, with an appreciable proportion of cells showing 47 chromosomes and the trisomy (Zellweger and Simpson). We must seriously consider the implication of these findings.

It is only because of obvious clinical manifestations that such cases are discovered to be mosaics. Had these not presented external gross features in many organ systems, it is very doubtful that they would ever have come to chromosomal study, particularly study as sophisticated as trying to search out a "hidden clone" of cells with 47 chromosomes. Indeed, if a specific, isolated congenital lesion were caused by a nondisjunction producing a trisomy in a localized region of the body, it is highly unlikely that either a blood lymphocyte study *or* a study of skin fibroblasts would reveal cells with 47 chromosomes and the trisomy.

The author considers it reasonable to propose that a fair fraction of congenital anomalies might arise by nondisjunctional errors occurring in utero, but occurring after there are sufficient numbers of cell divisions that the trisomy produced is not widespread in all tissues. The more limited the region involved, the less severe would be the overall impact on health, and the less bizarre would be any anatomical features. Most likely such a case would just get passed off as "another congenital defect."

Just how large a role ionizing radiation could play in the causation of such nondisjunctional errors in embryogenesis remains unknown. One should not be fooled by the statement that trisomy is not much influenced by radiation. First of all, that statement is generally made in connection with trisomies that result from *meiotic* errors leading to gametes with 24 chromosomes instead of 23. There is no reason at all to assume that mitotic errors in the early-developing embryo are even related to such meiotic errors. The two are separate phenomena. Indeed, the mechanics of the meiotic process are grossly different from the mechanics of the mitotic. But the statement is not well grounded, wholly aside from the meiosis-mitosis differences, as we shall see later in this chapter.

We must leave open the possibility that localized mosaicism for trisomic cells (and not necessarily only for those autosomes already described) may represent a common basis for congenital (in utero) defects. And we must state that the role of radiation in producing such mosaicism has simply not been evaluated.

Deletions, Congenital Abnormalities, and Radiation Effects

From earlier discussions (chapter 3), the reader is familiar with the fact that deletions are one of the best-studied chromosome alterations produced by ionizing radiation. Indeed, as we shall note here in our quantitative development, deletions are induced exceedingly easily by ionizing radiation, the doubling dose for humans being very, very low.

Do Deletions Produced In Utero Cause Congenital Defects? That deletions of a part of a chromosome can produce severe abnormalities in the human being is without question. What fraction of the deletions that cause abnormalities occurs in utero is a more difficult question to answer. A deletion can occur in an autosome of the spermatogonial cells and be carried through spermatogenesis, or it can occur in the development of the ovum. In either case, all the cells of the developing embryo would be expected to show the deletion. If a deletion occurred in utero, *after* the first cell division of a fertilized ovum, then only some fraction of the cells of the embryo would show the deletion. That fraction would depend on how many cell divisions of the zygote had already occurred, and on the relative viability of cells with and without the deletion.

There is every reason to believe that mosaics for deletions of one or another chromosome do indeed occur as a result of in utero breakage of chromosomes. If mosaics occur for trisomies of various kinds, there would be no logical reason why mosaics for deletions would not occur.

Why Are So Few Deletion Syndromes Reported? Hamerton and co-workers (1975) assembled the data from several surveys of newborns, involving 46,150 newborns in all, and found that 130 had trisomies but only

2 had deletions. This would suggest that deletions might not be very important as a source of congenital abnormalities. The author doubts that this is
the case. Unless a newborn presents severe clinical abnormalities, there is
little chance that a deletion will be looked for in the laboratory. And, second,
our technical ability to find small deletions is exceedingly poor, even with
the advent of the banding techniques for studying chromosomes. The combination of mildness of clinical effects with smallness of deletions can make
it appear that deletion syndromes are rare, when they may be very common
indeed.

The Prominent Deletion Syndromes and Their Manifestations: The
most common deletion syndrome is characterized by a *5p deletion,* meaning
that a part of the short arm of one chromosome 5 is missing in all the cells.
This was also the first deletion syndrome described: in 1963 Lejeune and
his co-workers described four patients who showed psychomotor retardation, growth failure, microcephaly, low-set ears, and a strange cry that came
to be called a *mewing cry* or *cri-du-chat.* All four patients showed a partial
short-arm deletion of chromosome B-5. This disorder is severe indeed.
Mental deficiency and retardation in most cases are profound.

Other major deletion syndromes include the one known as *Wolf* or
Wolf-Hirschhorn syndrome, in which a deletion of 10–80% of the short arm of
chromosome B-4 occurs. The clinical features indicate how severe the
consequences can be of deletion of a small piece of a single chromosome.
Some of the characteristic features of this syndrome include delay in psychomotor development, severe mental handicap, both prenatal and postnatal growth failure, and multiple malformations. It is important to note that
the malformations, as was the case for most of the trisomies, are not specific
to the particular chromosome abnormality, but appear to reflect chromosome imbalance. It is inconceivable to this author that deletions of the 4p
type do *not* occur in utero; he considers it highly likely that such deletions
occur at some stage in early cleavage or in the embryo, produce a localized
clone of cells carrying the 4p deletion, and produce localized congenital
abnormalities. Such abnormalities go unrecognized because neither peripheral blood studies nor studies of fibroblasts need show any cells with the 4p
deletion at all.

One particular deletion syndrome is of special relevance to our consideration of cancer. Some children are born with a deletion of a part of the
long arm of chromosome 13. Aside from its other serious effects, a remarkable finding in the 13q deletion syndrome is that 20% of all the recognized
cases developed the serious cancer, retinoblastoma. The retinoblastoma
occurred in one eye or in both eyes; the tumors showed up in infancy or in
early childhood. A genetic disorder does exist in which retinoblastoma
occurs, but this disorder does not show abnormalities of chromosome 13.
The cases of 13q deletion that involve retinoblastoma also involve delayed
psychomotor development or mental deficiency; the genetically caused
cases of retinoblastoma do not show these other features. It has been specu-

lated that there may be a relationship between the gene-caused disease and the deletion-caused disease, but the relationship remains obscure (Zellweger and Simpson, p. 155).

The direct finding of a chromosome deletion that causes inordinate susceptibility to a specific kind of cancer is, however, clear. And it is of special interest with respect to radiation and its relationship to cancer. Ionizing radiation has been observed to cause deletions in general, so there is every reason to suppose it can cause the 13q deletion specifically. To what extent the observed 13q deletions were caused by ionizing radiation and to what extent they were caused by "spontaneous" (meaning unknown) causes remains to be learned. In considering the relationship of radiation to chromosomes and to cancer, we must always keep in mind that two separate phenomena are involved. One is direct injury to the chromosomes of a cell, which may put that cell on the path to cancer. The other is chromosome injury that can be passed on and become manifest in every cell of a person's body, and which, by mechanisms as yet unknown, can make the individual inordinately likely to develop certain forms of cancer. In such instances, the chromosome constitution of the cancer cells themselves remains to be described.

The Quantitative Aspects of Radiation Production of Deletions in Human Beings: The author's opinion is that small deletions occurring in utero produce mosaicism that will prove to be an important basis for congenital abnormalities. This is an opinion, not a fact. It is a fact that the technology for studying this question is not currently available. It is to be hoped that researchers will be stimulated to seek out new methods for examining this and similar questions.

Ionizing-radiation induced deletions in the human being have been studied quantitatively over a long period of time. Although the studies were not done with in utero material, we may still learn a great deal from them about the quantitative aspects of deletion formation by ionizing radiation.

An analysis of the work of Brewen, Preston, and co-workers (1973) suggests a range of 3.8 to 13.2 rads as the doubling dose for *deletion* production in human cells from irradiations under 100 rads. As Evans and co-workers (1979) point out, in vitro chromosome aberration yields are in good accord with in vivo yields, so the results obtained in cultures are definitely relevant for human irradiations.

Sasaki employed the same general method as did Brewen, Preston, and co-workers for measuring deletions in human cells before and after irradiation. The results of this study, when converted to a common base with the Brewen-Preston work, yield a doubling dose of 16.4 rads.

There is reasonable agreement between the two studies. They place the doubling dose for deletion formation in human lymphocytes between about 3.8 and 20 rads. The values at either end of this range are very sobering. Some workers might suggest that the higher doubling doses of Sasaki are the result of a lesser effectiveness (due to lower LET) of the cobalt gamma rays compared to the lower energy 250-kv X-rays in the Brewen, Preston, and co-workers study.

Radiation Health Cost Implications of the Doubling Dose for Deletions: While the author believes that deletions have been grossly underestimated as a source of ill health in general, we shall restrict our considerations at this point to the issue of in utero radiation effects. We have already stated that we do not know the extent to which in utero deletion events (resulting in a mosaic human, some cells having the deletion, some not) occur and are responsible for "spontaneous" congenital abnormalities. The author can *assure* the reader that no one knows this answer.

Since we do not know the extent to which such deletional events are important, let us consider some reasonable possibilities. Overall the incidence of congenital abnormalities is given as several percent (up to 10%). It is not possible to know which of these are genetic, and which are produced in utero. We can be sure some originate from both sources. Let us consider the implications for society if the following incidences of in utero deletional causes of congenital abnormalities were correct:

From: 1.0% of all live births (meaning that a spontaneous incidence of deletional events in utero causes 10,000 congenital abnormalities per million live births).

To: 0.1% of all live births (meaning that a spontaneous incidence of deletional events in utero causes 1,000 congenital abnormalities per million live births).

This is certainly a modest range, and no data exist anywhere in the world which would contradict the possibility that these numbers may be correct. We shall use the range of 3.8 to 16.4 rads for the doubling dose for deletion production (the extremes of the values from the Brewen and the Sasaki studies) to estimate the potential effects of 1 rad delivered to an embryo in utero during early stages of implantation and embryogenesis. The calculations are presented in table 28.

One might wish to use the calculations of table 28 to estimate the personal risk to the child of a pregnant woman who underwent some ill-advised radiological procedures very early in a gestation. Of course, the calculations only address the deletion problem, but they illustrate a method for approaching other injury mechanisms.

If the woman received 1 rad to the developing embryo, the risk that she would have a child with one or another congenital abnormality would be between 6.1 chances per 10,000 and 26.3 chances per 10,000, if the spontaneous incidence were 10,000 per million. On the other hand, if the spontaneous incidence were at the other end of the range, at 1,000 per million, then her risk would be between 6.1 chances per 100,000 and 26.3 chances per 100,000.

It is evident from these calculations that we need to know such data as the spontaneous incidence of deletionally induced congenital abnormalities

TABLE 28: POTENTIAL RADIATION-INDUCED CONGENITAL ABNORMALITIES BASED ON DELETIONS*

Assumed spontaneous incidence of deletional events in utero per million live births	Number of congenital abnormalities produced per rad delivered early in gestation per million live births	
	Using 3.8 rads as doubling dose	Using 16.4 rads as doubling dose
10,000 per million	2,632	610
5,000 per million	1,316	305
2,500 per million	658	153
1,000 per million	263	61

*The calculations are for 1 rad delivered early in the relevant pregnancy, not 1 rad per generation.

and the doubling dose for radiation-induced deletions if practical applications are to be made.

Translocations As a Basis for Congenital Abnormalities

A number of chromosome translocations have been demonstrated to be associated with serious congenital deformity. For example, some cases of Down's syndrome are due to a translocation trisomy of G-21 chromosomal material. But such translocations are really genetic, in that they are transmitted through either sperm or ovum. We shall discuss these later in this chapter.

Whether there exist mosaic humans who show cells that have a normal chromosome complement and cells that have either a balanced or an unbalanced translocation is simply not known. Logically, one would certainly expect such mosaics to occur. If the translocation occurred only in a local region, a congenital abnormality could be based on it, and it would be undetectable by peripheral blood or fibroblast study. If such mosaicism did occur spontaneously, there is every reason to expect that ionizing radiation would increase it, and for doses up to the order of 50–100 rads or so and down to the lowest conceivable doses, we would expect a linear dose-response relationship (see chapter 8).

Prominent Abnormalities Associated with Embryonic Chromosome Damage

As one reviews the findings for the various trisomies, deletion syndromes, and translocation syndromes, it is hard not to be impressed with the fact that the central nervous system rarely escapes prominent involvement. This also tends to be true of organs that are developmentally part of the central nervous system, such as the eye. Perhaps defects in central-nervous-system function are more readily noted by the observer than are defects in internal organs such as the pancreas or liver. Or, a reason why central-nervous-system abnormalities of structure and function are so prominent may be related to the finicky requirements of this highly developed system for exactly the correct chromosome balance.

Since so many different chromosome derangements are potentially associated with central-nervous-system abnormalities, we would expect, following irradiation of a population sample, to see the effects of many separate types of chromosomal injuries. One particular chromosome abnormality, for example, a localized trisomy of a particular chromosome, might occur in only 1 out of 1,000 irradiated subjects. But there are tens or hundreds of potential chromosome injuries, each of which might have serious central-nervous-system effects. If one looked at the irradiated population for evidence of central-nervous-system injury, one would, in a sense, be integrating several different types of radiation injuries.

One is also impressed, on examining the clinical features of the various trisomies, deletions, and translocations, with the prominence of serious cardiovascular-system injuries. One finds that a high proportion of individuals with certain trisomies and of individuals with deletions of pieces of certain chromosomes demonstrate serious congenital heart disease. Too much of several types of chromosomal material seems to produce the same heart lesions as too little of certain other chromosomal material. Further, too much or too little of the *same* chromosomal material can produce the same type of congenital heart disease. A classic illustration of this is the high percentage of congenital heart defects found both in trisomy-D-13 and in the 13q deletion syndrome. (Details are in Zellweger and Simpson 1977, pp. 88 and 156.)

The lesson to be learned from all this is the very urgent requirement, at least during gestation, for minimum disruption of the balance of total chromosomal material, irrespective of the issue of mutation of specific genes. When one considers deletion alone as a prominent effect of ionizing radiation, linear in dose response, and effective down to the lowest conceivable doses, one realizes the desirability of keeping irradiation of early developing embryos to an absolute minimum.

Let us now turn to the evidence we do have concerning the effects of ionizing radiation on infants in utero, and let us consider the shape of the dose-response curve for such irradiation. The data we have are for the survivors of Hiroshima and Nagasaki.

THE HIROSHIMA AND NAGASAKI EVIDENCE

Several reports, beginning with Plummer's in 1952, have demonstrated the increased prevalence of small head circumference and of mental retardation in persons who were in utero at the time of bombing and were close to the hypocenter in either Hiroshima or Nagasaki. Miller and co-workers (1972, 1976) and Wood and co-workers (1967) materially extended the observations both on head size and mental retardation, so that it is now possible to look at the quantitative aspects of both problems in some detail.

In their 1972 paper, Miller and Blot presented detailed dose estimates relating to small head size. The important finding was that the relationship of reduced head size to radiation dose held, for Hiroshima, down to doses of 10–19 rads (T-65 dose) for those exposed during the first 17 weeks of gestation. The reader will be quite familiar with the necessity for correcting T-65 doses to true absorbed doses. For in utero radiation, an appropriate correction would be division by about 2. Therefore, when Miller and Blot state that the reduction in head circumference holds down to doses of 10–19 rads, it really holds down to 5–9 rads absorbed dose to the fetus. Miller and Blot acknowledge this with their statement: "The abnormality was found in excess among children whose mothers received as little as 10–19 rads in Hiroshima. The dose to the fetus or embryo may be still less, because to some extent the mother's body shielded the child" (p. 786). Miller and Blot state further: "Intrauterine radiation exposure induced small head circumference at very low doses—the lowest yet known to produce a grossly detectable effect in man" (p. 786). There is one serious difficulty with this statement. The reader may get the impression that a very large number of people exposed to radiation were examined for the whole host of possible congenital defects described in this chapter, and very low doses were found *not* to have produced other defects than small head circumference. That is simply untrue. The correct statement would be that there *had not been an adequate study* to ascertain the rate of production of a variety of other congenital abnormaliteis as a function of radiation dose. It is the prominence of abnormal central-nervous-system development that makes it possible to demonstrate the effect even at very low doses. Of course the central-nervous-system effects are extremely important, and we are fortunate to know how serious the effect of low-dose radiation is on this vital system.

Miller and Blot point out:

The main stimulus to skull growth is brain growth. Radiation apparently causes general cell depletion of the developing brain, with secondary small head circumference. When depletion is great enough, mental retardation ensues. With less depletion, intelligence is within normal range, but may be reduced as compared with the child's full potential had he not been irradiated. It seems, therefore, that even small intrauterine exposures may deprive the individual of some intelligence. (p. 786)

This is a key paragraph, which the reader must appreciate fully. So many people comment on the Japanese data on "small head size" as though small head size were a cosmetic problem, like a short or long nose or small or large feet, when in truth, as Miller and Blot emphasize, it is a reflection of the most serious of developmental abnormalities, *the failure of the brain to develop fully!* In subsequent discussions of head size, the reader should constantly keep in mind its relation to brain development.

Radiation Dose and Small Head Circumference in Hiroshima and Nagasaki

The key points of an analysis of the data of Miller and Blot can be summarized. First, there is little reason to doubt the conclusion of Miller and Blot that the effects of radiation on brain and head development are much more severe in the first 17 weeks of gestation than afterward. This indication of the importance of gestational age in determining effects is in accord with a large body of experimental literature.

On another point, the author's interpretation of the data differs from that of Miller and Blot. In comparing the results from Hiroshima and Nagasaki, Miller and Blot conclude that in Hiroshima there were effects from doses all the way down to 10–19 rads (T-65 dose, not absorbed dose) *because* of neutrons, but that effects in Nagasaki are demonstrable, without neutrons, only above 150 rads.

Over and over again, the investigators of the effects of the Hiroshima and Nagasaki bombings have wanted to ascribe any peculiar differences between the data of the two cities (often based on grossly inadequate sample sizes) to the fact that there were more neutrons in the mixture of radiation at Hiroshima than in the mixture of radiation at Nagasaki, where the dose was virtually all from gamma radiation. This well-known explanation has been steadily failing as more data have become available. The recent findings of a virtual absence of neutrons in the Hiroshima radiation have finally laid to rest the "neutron explanation" for apparent differences in congenital effects between Hiroshima and Nagasaki, just as the neutron explanation for breast cancer in the two cities died once the data became adequate (see chapter 6), and just as the neutron explanation evaporated for the leukemia data (see chapter 14).

The conclusions of the Miller and Blot study also are questionable because they are apparently based on statistics that have been stretched a little too much: that is, the group available for study in Hiroshima was much larger than that for Nagasaki. Rather than consider the two groups separately, as Miller and Blot did, this author feels that the appropriate treatment is to combine the results for both cities, using the proper correction factors. The final results are presented in table 29.

Within the goodness of the data, it would be difficult to rule out a linear dose-response relationship between small-head-circumference development, implying inadequate brain development, and absorbed dose in rads. The effect was *severe* even in the lowest dose group: an average of 5 rads absorbed dose produced a 19.4% per rad increase over the spontaneous rate. This would make the doubling dose 5.2 rads. The author does not think that the *apparent* very steep rise to 45.4% per rad for the 13.7-rad group should be taken as more than a small-numbers problem. As is obvious from these data, there is no suggestion whatsoever of any threshold below which this severe developmental failure of the head (really developmental failure of the *brain*) is not seen.

In a more recent paper, Miller and Mulvihill (1976) present a histogram relating dose to percent small head size, using Hiroshima data alone (citing the work of Blot). For their 10–19-rad range (T-65 dose) they show approximately 12% small heads, compared with approximately 4% for zero dose. This is a 200% excess for an *absorbed* dose of 14.5/2 = 7.25 rads, or a % excess of 27.6% per rad. This is in excellent accord with the results presented above, based on table 29 calculations.

Direct Studies of Severe Mental Retardation

As explained by Miller, the development of a small head is itself evidence of the development of a small brain, since brain development is the chief stimulus to skull development. Severe mental retardation was also studied directly in the Hiroshima and Nagasaki children who were exposed in utero. Detailed studies were made by Wood and co-workers (1967).

It is understandable that one attempts to study a phenomenon under circumstances most likely to produce a positive result. Thus, if one has shown marked mental retardation to result from radiation exposure, at a high level of statistical significance, one has proved a point. But one may also have left a grossly erroneous impression in the minds of those who read about the work. In the case of mental retardation as an effect of ionizing radiation in utero, it would be sad indeed if our concern were only for those who are so seriously retarded as to meet the criteria of the Wood and Blot-Miller studies. Those criteria are the inabilities of a subject "to perform simple calculations, to carry on a simple conversation, to care for himself," or complete unmanageability, or institutionalization at any time (Blot and Miller 1973, p. 617). If we do not concern ourselves with radiation until these effects are present, there will likely be no human beings left who can care for themselves.

Obviously we should really be concerned about grossly smaller effects than those looked for in the Hiroshima and Nagasaki infants exposed in utero. It is true that testing is difficult, but with the numbers of cases available at Hiroshima and Nagasaki who received doses above 50 rads (T-65 dose)—actually 135 cases and a control group of 1,076—it seems as though some more sophisticated study of mental development could have been made that would have given meaningful information about lesser degrees of mental retardation.

Blot and Miller analyzed the 30 children in the in utero sample (exposed plus unexposed) which met Wood and co-workers' criteria for mental retardation. Twenty-one of these subjects did receive *some* exposure; the remaining 9 were in the not-in-the-city or distal groups, both of which groups are presumed to have received no radiation.

The mental retardation of some of the cases was due to apparently identifiable causes other than radiation, for example, Down's syndrome. It appears legitimate to exclude those cases from the total. After such exclusions, the final numbers are 5 cases of mental retardation in the unexposed

TABLE 29: PERCENT EXCESS SMALL HEAD DEVELOPMENT PER RAD FOR HIROSHIMA AND NAGASAKI COMBINED

Dose Group (T-65 dose)	True Absorbed Dose in Rads	Small Heads	Total Group	Small Head Development Rate (number per 1,000)	O/E	% Excess Small Heads per Rad
Distal, unexposed	0	41	1010	40.6	—	—
0 to 19 rads	5	10	125	80.0	1.97	97% for 5 rads, or 19.4%/rad
20 to 39 rads	13.7	12	41	293	7.22	622% for 13.7 rads, or 45.4%/rad
40 to 99 rads	31.7	12	46	261	6.43	543% for 31.7 rads, or 17.1%/rad
100+ rads	121	15	28	536	13.2	1,220% for 121 rads, or 10.1%/rad

Dose Calculation: The doses were calculated taking into account numbers of persons at each dose, and then summing person-rads and dividing by persons. This is illustrated for the 40–99-rad group as follows:

$$\frac{(17 \text{ persons})(44.5 \text{ rads}) + (29 \text{ persons})(74.5 \text{ rads})}{46 \text{ persons}} = \frac{756.5 + 2,160.5}{46} = \frac{2,917.0}{46} = 63.4 \text{ rads}$$

But this dose, 63.4 rads, is a T-65 air dose. Multiplying by 0.5 gives 31.7 rads, absorbed dose. The dose for the 100+-rad group is taken from Beebe, Kato, and Land (1978), who give approximately 242 rads for the 100+-rad group in the Life Span Study. Multiplying by 0.5 to convert to absorbed dose gives 121 rads.
Percent Excess Calculation: This method of calculation is used in extenso in chapter 5 in calculation of % excess cancer deaths per rad. The principles are identical for use of this method here.

and 16 cases in the various groups of exposed, for T-65 doses from 0 to over 300 rads.

Combining the Blot and Miller data on mental retardation with the data for Hiroshima and Nagasaki, we arrive at the following estimates of % excess mental retardation per rad from in utero exposure:

For a group receiving a mean absorbed dose of 13.7 rads, the % excess per rad = 9.8%.

For a group receiving a mean absorbed dose of 121 rads, the % excess per rad = 28.5%.

When we consider the small numbers of mentally retarded cases these estimates are based on, it would be hard to prove that the % excess per rad is really different for the high-dose group than for the low-dose group. In either case, *the effect is large per rad of an in utero exposure.* There is no evidence that suggests any threshold for this effect.

The effects reported here include effects from exposures well beyond the seventeenth week of gestation. The effects may well have been larger, expressed as % excess per rad, had the data for just the most sensitive period of gestation been analyzed.

The Importance of Gestational Age for Radiation Effects

The Hiroshima-Nagasaki experience itself demonstrates that the time during gestation at which irradiation occurs is important in determining the effects of the radiation.

In the early discussions of this chapter, the problem of an abnormal clone developing at various *early* states post-zygotically was considered. Obviously the development of a chromosomally abnormal cell clone that represents 33% of all the cells of the embryo is significantly different from the development of a chromosomally abnormal cell clone that represents 0.1% of all the cells of the embryo.

Beyond all this, there is an important question to address concerning possible "critical periods" for causation of congenital abnormalities. The abnormalities considered to be gross malformations (or "monstrosities") are likely to develop during the in utero period of major organogenesis. There is no sharp dividing line between parts of the in utero period, but broadly we speak of a pre-implantation period of about a week in the human being, of a major organogenesis period following implantation into the uterus lasting until about six weeks after conception, and thereafter of a fetal growth period lasting until term delivery of the infant. The transition from major organogenesis to fetal growth is not a sharp one, and indeed the transition from fetus to infant is not sharp either, since many processes of growth initiated in utero continue after birth.

For decades the concept has been promulgated that "critical periods" exist in organogenesis, and that injuries during those critical periods determine the specific kind of defect produced. In fact, such periods are not absolute. There is overlap between the critical periods for, say, a specific structure in the eye and a specific skeletal structure. But it is true that at certain periods, in many experimental species, the dose of radiation required to produce a specific abnormality is definitely lower than it is either before or after that period. We simply cannot overlook this fact; it requires explanation.

There is every reason to believe that the abnormalities produced are due to events in chromosomes, and to the viability and behavior of cells in which chromosomal injuries occur. But we must make another point here. The trend in embryogenesis, beyond the earliest stages during which one cell can replace another that is injured or lost, is toward loss of totipotency of cells and development of differentiation of cells. Since we know that all cells in a normal embryo have 46 chromosomes, it is self-evident that some major changes must occur with respect to activation or inactivation of regions of chromosomes or the genes within them in the shift from totipotency to differentiation. We really know very little about what changes take place in the chromosomes during this shift, in combination with active cell division. What this combination means for sensitivity to radiation is not known, and it represents a major challenge for the future. Very likely it is indeed something about the combination of differentiation and further cell mass increase by cell division which makes a particular period a "critical period." But not much more can be said now about this very intriguing and important problem.

SECTION 2: STOCHASTIC IN UTERO EFFECTS: CANCER AND LEUKEMIA INDUCTION

We stated earlier that cancer and leukemia are major illustrations of radiation effects for which the probability of occurrence is proportional to the dose of radiation. There is no such thing as a partial cancer. Either an injury initiates a cancer or it does not.

From everything we have observed about human irradiation from near birth to quite advanced age (see chapter 5), it would be surprising indeed if in utero radiation did not produce cancer or leukemia. And from the fact that a higher % excess risk of cancer of various types per rad results from irradiation in early childhood than at any later period, we would expect irradiation in utero to be quite effective in increasing the risk of cancer. Let us now consider the work of Stewart and colleagues (1956–1975), which demonstrates the cancer and leukemia effects of irradiation in utero. We shall consider criticism of this work as well.

THE STUDIES OF DR. ALICE STEWART AND CO-WORKERS

There is a strong tendency to forget how primitive medicine is today in its appreciation of the problems caused by low doses of radiation. Some of the cancers produced in the course of the practice of medicine are amply described in this book. If we go back in history approximately three decades, we find that medical practitioners had truly primitive ideas about radiation effects.

In the 1950s medical science labored under a major delusion about ionizing radiation. Essentially, it was held that doses of ionizing radiation under 100 rads would not harm anyone, particularly if the dose was received in fractions or slowly over time. The basis for this delusion was that the wrong effects were being considered. It certainly is true that the doses required to produce sterility, blood-count depression, nausea, and vomiting are generally over 50 rads, and even those must be delivered rapidly. Most radiation effects of these types depend on the extent to which cells are depleted in critical organs. If the regeneration rate can stay ahead of the depletion rate, as is the case with slow delivery of radiation, the health effects listed above simply do not materialize. But what was not appreciated during this period was that subtle changes do indeed occur in individual cells, changes that later, much later, manifest themselves as cancer or leukemia. Indeed, the very cells (often called stem cells) that replace those cells injured or killed by radiation themselves may suffer the subtle genetic or chromosomal damages leading to cancer or leukemia. Yes, they replace functional cells, and prevent a blood-count drop, but they also suffer delayed effects totally hidden from view.

This delusion lingers, in spite of a mountain of scientific evidence, and the reader will still encounter a fair number of physicians who say, "A little radiation like X-ray diagnostic radiation never hurt anybody."

Think of the situation in 1956 when a British physician-researcher, Dr. Alice Stewart, published her landmark paper, which stated that diagnostic radiation on the order of 1 to 2 rads, delivered to the fetus in utero, provoked about a 50% increase in the frequency of a variety of childhood cancers and of childhood leukemia. In particular, though not exclusively, Dr. Stewart was referring to the procedure known as diagnostic pelvimetry, which is an X-ray procedure used to determine pelvic dimensions. At that time, diagnostic pelvimetry was used almost routinely in some obstetric practices, and only when concern existed about the prospects for a normal vaginal delivery in other practices. Since the doses involved were in the diagnostic range of 1–2 rads, which is considerably lower than doses from several other X-ray and fluoroscopic procedures, physicians were simply incredulous at Dr. Stewart's suggestion that the procedure could provoke a 50% increase in childhood cancer and leukemia.

Numerous criticisms have been made of the Stewart work, which we shall consider below, including studies that might appear to present different results. But large studies have also been made that confirm the Stewart findings. The argument is hardly about the findings any more, but rather about the interpretation of the findings. Steadily, many of the earlier doubters have one by one conceded that the data do indeed point to a large percentage increase in cancer and leukemia in childhood from small doses of radiation in the diagnostic category of 1–2 rads (see Mole 1974 and Pochin 1976). In the light of the much larger body of information from around the world now available, this author is surprised only that the cancer and leukemia effects of radiation in utero are not somewhat larger than they are.

In essence, what Dr. Stewart did was to compare the history of radiation exposure in utero of children who died of cancer or leukemia in childhood, with the comparable history of children matched for age, sex, and region who had no malignant disease. Dr. Stewart found that some 10% of the mothers of the healthy children had diagnostic radiation during the relevant pregnancy, whereas some 15% of the mothers of the children who died of cancer or leukemia had radiation. Stewart correctly interpreted such data as consistent with roughly a 50% increase in the risk of cancer or leukemia from diagnostic radiation delivered during pregnancy. It is not immediately obvious that the incidence of X-irradiation can be translated into risk of cancer or leukemia, but it can be proved with simple arithmetic. At this point, one issue should be settled. Dr. Stewart never stated that ionizing radiation is the only cause of cancer and leukemia in childhood. Even in the women whose children did develop cancer or leukemia there was only a 15% incidence of diagnostic radiation during the relevant pregnancy. So diagnostic radiation in pregnancy cannot possibly be blamed for 85% of the cases of cancer or leukemia in the offspring, because those children received no medical radiation at all. This confuses people, so let us emphasize that a specific agent can be considered a potent carcinogen without having imposed upon it the foolish requirement that it must be responsible for *all* cases of cancer or leukemia.

SOME CRITICISMS AND REBUTTALS OF THE STEWART WORK

Among the early criticisms of the Stewart work were two major ones:

1. Since Dr. Stewart found out irradiation history by questioning the mothers, the possibility exists that the mothers of the children with cancer or leukemia might have been prone to "over-remember" any possible radiation exposure, compared with the mothers of the healthy children.

2. The suggestion was made that perhaps the women who did get irradiated had some underlying constitution or disease (though the critics could not specify which constitution or disease) that *simultaneously* led them to get X-rays during pregnancy and led their offspring to have a higher risk of cancer or leukemia within the first 10 years of life. According to this criticism (it does not deserve the term *hypothesis*), there is no relationship whatsoever between the radiation dose to the child and the subsequent development of cancer or leukemia. The radiation and the child's disease have a common cause but have no causal relationship to each other.

All questions seriously raised about important problems such as the production of cancer or leukemia by small doses of radiation given in utero deserve very careful consideration. These criticisms did receive very careful consideration, and are by now widely recognized to be without validity. Very few scientists doubt that Stewart's work demonstrates the production of cancer and leukemia by diagnostic radiation during pregnancy, although there are some diehards who, though they cannot explain the findings away, still say they are skeptical.

Let us now consider some of the ancillary evidence that has pretty well demolished the criticisms described. Dr. Stewart herself long ago studied the question of mothers "over-remembering" radiation exposure if they had a child with cancer or leukemia, and she found that such "over-remembering" could not possibly account for the findings. MacMahon (1962) did an independent study of the type that Dr. Stewart had done, and confirmed the general findings, including their magnitude. He relied on hospital records for the evidence concerning the number of X-rays received, so mothers "over-remembering" was not an issue.

This does not mean that MacMahon is himself totally convinced that causality was the relationship between diagnostic radiation in utero and the development of cancer or leukemia in the children. In 1972 he was still raising the possibility of a "constitutional" basis (see above) for the results. He does make a valid point: the best kind of study to prove beyond a shadow of a doubt that the relationship is causal would be a very large study of children whose mothers received diagnostic X-rays as part of a routine work-up, rather than for medical or obstetric reasons, coupled with a follow-up of a sufficiently large number of children whose mothers were not irradiated, so that adequate cancer and leukemia statistics could be obtained. It would take quite a large study to accomplish this result, and it would certainly be unethical to irradiate pregnant women with X-rays in the light of our overall knowledge of the problem.

The "constitutional" question appears to have been laid to rest effectively in a later set of studies by Stewart and Kneale (1970). In these studies, the risk of cancer plus leukemia in the offspring was tested as a function of the number of X-ray films taken during the relevant radiographical examination. As Stewart and Kneale point out, the determinants of the numbers of X-ray films taken of the mothers were either technical factors, relating to X-ray examination itself, or were the physicians' choices; the determinants were *not* the constitutions of the mothers nor any diseases of the mothers. The result of the studies, which had the mothers divided into groups of those who had one, two, three, four or more X-ray films taken, is that the cancer-leukemia risk in the offspring *went up with an increasing number of films taken.* On any rational basis, this finding would have silenced the "constitutional" adherents once and for all; and to a large extent most scientists have become convinced that the Stewart and Kneale study relating the number of X-ray films to cancer-leukemia risk does indeed prove causality.

Stewart and Kneale point out that the rise in cancer-leukemia risk with each additional film is consistent with a linear relationship between number of films (at 200–400 millirads per film) and cancer-leukemia risk. Since the dose to the fetus is directly proportional to the number of films, these data would support the statement that risk of radiation-induced cancer or leukemia is directly proportional to radiation dose in the range of a couple of hundred millirads up to a couple of thousand millirads, small doses indeed. This finding is consistent with all the evidence and concepts outlined in this book for cancer induction by radiation.

While conceding that the relationship between number of films and risk of cancer or leukemia is strong evidence against the "constitutional" concept and for causality, there are some who still refuse to accept that the data are good enough to prove a linear relationship between dose and effect.

Newcombe and McGregor (1971) re-analyzed all the Stewart data independently and quantitatively, and they concluded: "The correlation conforms closely to a simple linear relationship with dose, and argues against the idea of a safe threshold for juvenile cancer" (p. 1152).

Holford (1975), in a separate and independent study, goes further with the analysis of the data than Newcombe and McGregor do. Holford's point is that even though the Newcombe-McGregor analysis indicates a linear relationship, the nature of the Newcombe-McGregor statistical tests is not sufficiently powerful to exclude all relationships other than a linear relationship. The Holford statistical analysis leads to two major conclusions about the Stewart-Kneale data:

1. Powerful statistical methods indicate that a hypothesis showing no relationship of cancer risk to dose was more than 1,400 times *less* likely than the hypothesis of a linear relationship.

2. One rad of radiation to the fetus (in late pregnancy) increases the risk of cancer-leukemia by between 50 and 100%.

Trimester of Exposure

Initially Stewart indicated that the sensitivity of the fetus to radiation-induced malignancy is greater in the first trimester of pregnancy than later, with no provable difference between second and third trimesters. Later, Stewart and Kneale presented evidence that in their earlier study the *dose* was higher in the first trimester, and hence they retracted the claim of greater sensitivity in the first trimester than in the third trimester (1970b).

The Evidence Said to Be Against the Stewart In Utero Findings

Those who do not accept the Stewart findings always refer to one set of data as evidence that Stewart and colleagues must have overestimated the risk of in utero radiation: the data obtained on in utero irradiation in Hiroshima and Nagasaki, as reported by Kato (1971).

The reader saw in chapter 5 that the author is perfectly happy to accept and include scientifically adequate studies that do not show any effect from radiation. What troubles him about the Kato study on in utero cancer effects is not the apparent absence of effect, which would be good news, but rather the doubtful scientific validity of the findings.

All others things being equal, the author would consider a prospective study like the Kato study to be more reliable than a retrospective study like the Stewart study. However, all other things are certainly not equal. Not only are the Stewart findings based on *hundreds* of childhood cancers (versus a total of 8 cases at issue in the Kato study), but there are very serious, confounding variables in the Kato study which good science requires us to consider.

The author hopes that readers with strong personal or professional interests in this issue will refer to the complete discussion in the unabridged edition of this book. In the meantime, be certain that it would be poor science to reject the Stewart findings on the basis of the highly questionable Kato findings.

INFANT MORTALITY AND IN UTERO IONIZING RADIATION

A great deal has been said and written popularly about the subject of in utero radiation as a cause of infant mortality. In particular, Sternglass (1977) has published a summary of his findings linking radiation releases to ostensible increases in infant mortality. Unfortunately, for almost none of the situations in the Sternglass reports can the dose received by the population be determined, with the exception of the claim that weapons-testing fallout (where dose estimation *is* possible) produced a great increase in infant mortality. By infant mortality most authors mean deaths occurring in the first year of life, a fair proportion of them in the first week of life. When the deaths are in the very early postnatal period, they are referred to as *perinatal deaths*.

The absence of dose estimates makes it impossible to handle the Sternglass studies in this book. Also, by their very nature, his studies can compare infant mortality rates before and after some radiation releases, but they cannot provide a control group. Therefore, this author would not be able, to his own satisfaction, to distinguish the seasonal, cyclical, and statistical fluctuations in mortality rates from possible radiation-induced changes in the rates.

The only set of data including dose estimates and infant mortality rates is the set of data from Japan presented by Kato. While we can and should have severe reservations about any conclusions requiring a *diagnosis* in the Kato data, we can probably use the data to give us an estimate of the likely magnitude of any excess infant mortality per rad. Infant mortality requires no further diagnostic description; it simply refers to deaths within the first year.

In the Kato data, there were 60 total deaths in the group that received a median dose of 0 rads, the unexposed group. The total number of persons at risk in this group was 795. Therefore, the infant mortality rate was 75.5 per 1,000, which is quite a high rate. However, we must remember that this rate applies for Hiroshima-Nagasaki in the first year after the bombing, when conditions were indeed poor, so its magnitude is not so surprising. The infant mortality for all exposed groups combined was 43 cases out of a total of 471 persons, corresponding to a rate of 91.3 per 1,000. The mean dose, *in absorbed dose units,* not T-65 dose units, for the exposed group was 39.1 rads. $O/E = 91.3/75.5 = 1.21$, or an excess of 21% in infant mortality rate for 39.1 rads. The % excess infant mortality rate per rad is 21%/39.1 rads = *0.54% per rad.*

This value requires major caveats, since it is the % excess per rad only for a very special area, post-bombing Hiroshima-Nagasaki, where overall infant mortalities were high compared with most areas of the world for which we might want to use the value. So, we can only state that if the relative effects of radiation are the same at generally low total infant mortality rates as at high rates, then the estimate of 0.54% per rad may be valid. There is no way comparability of effects can be proved or disproved with the evidence currently available to us.

The data of Kato indicate that the effects on infant mortality that did materialize were more pronounced for radiation in the third trimester of pregnancy than for radiation in either of the two earlier trimesters. There are free-floating opinions that the effect should be much larger in the first trimester than in later periods of pregnancy, but these opinions are simply not supported by Japanese findings.

Implications of the Infant Mortality Findings

If the data of Kato from Hiroshima and Nagasaki for overall infant deaths could be relied upon, and we are concerned about this because of the apparent unreliability of specific diagnoses, then the value of about 0.5% increase in infant mortality per rad would argue strongly against claims of huge effects from very low doses. Thus, if someone found 100% increases from doses far below 1 rad (call this Situation A), we would have to note that such findings are orders of magnitude from the 0.5% per rad value. There are, of course, two possible explanations, assuming the actual infant mortalities were correctly measured:

1. The Japanese data are deceiving us badly.
2. The radiation dose in Situation A is *much* higher than reported.

Lastly, we must discuss the correct measurement of infant mortalities. All sorts of measurements in the vital statistics show variability, particularly when a small geographical region is being considered and the total number of deaths is very small—5, 15, or 25. We must remember that the statistical error for such numbers is roughly their square root. So a measured value of 5 has an error band of about 2.2; a measured value of 15 has an error band of about 3.8; and a measured value of 25 has an error band of about 5. Before believing in a massively greater effect per rad than older evidence would suggest, it would be well to make sure a meaningful measurement of infant mortality rate was used.

SOME USEFUL WARNINGS FROM THE UNSCEAR REPORT

By now the sophisticated reader of this book has absorbed sufficient evidence to realize the nonsense of the claim that radiation effects on humans do not occur below 100 rads. We have discussed here the evidence concerning microcephaly in Japan, where effects were observed from absorbed doses down to 0–10 rads.

The human evidence is not broad, for which we must really be grateful, not sorry. While we wish to avoid relying on experimental-animal data as a general rule, there is some merit in considering what a very large experience with induction of teratogenic effects in experimental animals has taught, particularly in order to evaluate that old refrain of no effects below 100 rads. The UNSCEAR report (1977) includes a particularly cogent paragraph on this issue:

Regarding the possible existence of thresholds in dose-effect relationships there is consistent evidence showing that doses as low as 5 rads may still be effective in inducing selected malformations. Direct experimental tests of the absence of thresholds in this dose region would tend to exclude their existence at even lower doses. *Theoretically, the possibility does exist that thresholds might occur at even lower doses, but experiments of sufficient precision to reveal them would be technically difficult or even impossible for statistical reasons. (p. 709; emphasis added)*

There is reason to believe that some redundancy exists in a variety of tissues, in terms of a larger-than-needed supply of cells to carry on a particular function. So, it is possible that the function will not be noticeably impaired if there is some cell loss, say, by radiation injury. On the other hand, loss of any part of such a *functional reserve,* particularly in nonreproducing cells such as those in the central nervous system, is itself an injury, although it will not be detected by existing tests of cerebral and psychological function.

SECTION 3: THE GENETIC AND CHROMOSOMAL EFFECTS OF IONIZING RADIATION: INTRODUCTION

We have considered the *somatic* hazards of ionizing radiation (the effects directly experienced by the individual receiving the irradiation at any time after birth), and the *teratogenic* effects of radiation (effects on the individual irradiated while in utero). Now we will turn our attention to the effects produced by ionizing radiation in the descendants of the individuals irradiated. These effects are broadly grouped under the heading *genetic effects of ionizing radiation.*

In many respects, the information base concerning genetic and chromosomal injury to the human being from ionizing radiation is far less adequate than is the information base for cancer and leukemia as a whole. As a result, we shall not be able to make the kinds of quantitative estimates that have been possible throughout this book for many problems involving the risk of cancer and leukemia from ionizing radiation. It is important to know when we do have quantitative information and when we do *not.* We shall see that sufficient evidence is available to make some ballpark estimates of the role of ionizing radiation in producing one or another of the various gene or chromosomal lesions that together make up the so-called genetic effects of radiation. What is important is to present the evidence, to identify the places where evidence is lacking, and to predict possible pitfalls in interpreting data.

The Use of Logic to Extend Incomplete Data

At this stage of human knowledge, the belief that ionizing radiation induces genetic (inherited) injuries, such as mental and physical disabilities, is necessarily based on logical deduction from the observations listed below, all of which will be discussed in this section:

a. We observe that, in spite of "nature's filters," not all injuries to genetic materials are eliminated; we observe that some such injuries are passed from generation to generation; it may turn out that a large share of genetic alterations is passed along, but at present no one knows how large is the heritable share.

b. We observe that certain specific diseases and disabilities are caused by specific genetic injuries; year by year, we discover more of them; it may turn out that most biologically based afflictions have a genetic basis, but no one knows at present how many do.

c. We observe that some of the types of genetic injuries that cause specific afflictions can be caused by ionizing radiation; future data may show that *all* such injuries to genetic material can be caused by ionizing radiation.

Based on the three sets of observations above, we can deduce that ionizing radiation *must* add to inherited afflictions, and in fact, everyone in the field of radiobiology (including the BEIR and UNSCEAR committees) has reached this conclusion.

However, for reasons that will be discussed in this section, it is extremely difficult to prove the conclusion by counting inherited radiation injuries in a sample of irradiated human beings, even in as large a sample as the approximately 17,000 children of parents irradiated by the atom bombings in Japan. So, when it comes to reliable *quantitative* estimates of genetic effects per rad of exposure, present human knowledge is very thin indeed.

In this section, we shall survey and analyze what is known at this time.

Some Discrepancies Between Studies

It will be found, in considering the evidence in section 6 of this chapter, that there are some glaring and gross discrepancies in apparent results from one study of human beings to another. So serious are some of these discrepancies that they have a large effect on estimates of the health costs of certain amounts of radiation exposure. The discrepancies will be presented, the evidence on both sides will be presented, and an effort will be made to interpret the evidence as it stands. In several important instances it is not possible to resolve the discrepancies.

Where there are unresolved discrepancies, and no real reason exists for choosing one set of data over another, the author's position is that one should carefully consider the public-health implications of both choices. It is simply irresponsible to say that a particular genetic effect has not been proved, so let's act as though it does not exist. It is hard to think of a reason for acting differently, when there is an open question on a health issue, from when an effect has been established beyond doubt. If these two situations are handled differently, then there can be no doubt that a willingness to experiment on human beings is present.

"Good" and "Bad" Genetic Alterations

It follows from the theory of evolution that some fraction of genetic alterations must be beneficial. Wags routinely use this fact to suggest, for example, that an industry has a right to irradiate the population, because, "you know, there are *good* mutations too." Let us contrast such statements with the conventional wisdom that, when such alterations are made at random (as they are by ionizing radiation), an overwhelming number of them are injurious. For example, the BEIR-I report (1972) offers the following statement:

In every species studied by geneticists, the overwhelming majority of mutations that have effects large enough to be readily observed are deleterious. . . . The Subcommittee is convinced that any increase in the mutation rate will be harmful to future generations. (p. 49)

The author has no personal quarrel with people who challenge that conventional wisdom. He has himself often challenged conventional wisdom on other matters, but always on the basis of clearly stated logic and evidence and never on the basis of wishful thinking. Those who talk to the public about "good" mutations and belittle the genetic consequences of radiation exposure have so far demonstrated only utter ignorance of the subject, and that is why the author dismisses their remarks as worthless. The subject of possibly beneficial genetic alterations is certainly not taboo with him. On the contrary, future studies of beneficial as well as injurious genetic alterations are bound to improve human understanding of the still largely mysterious processes of life, its replication, and the evolution of its diversity.

The Use of Certain Terms

Since the chromosomes are the structures that carry almost all our genetic materials, injury to the chromosomes is injury to our genetic materials. Therefore, it seems sensible to use the term *genetic injury* to cover heritable chromosomal aberrations (both structural and numerical) as well as heritable DNA alterations.

Alterations in the bases of DNA molecules are commonly called *mutations* (a word that simply means "changes"). The author will often call these mutations *chemical mutations*, in order to distinguish them from mutations of the chromosomes. Readers should not think the author means mutations caused *by* chemicals; what he means is *mutations of the chemical bases of DNA molecules (genes), regardless of cause.*

Some readers may be unclear about bases, but everyone knows something about acids (which are chemically neutralized by bases), thanks to the bad news about the "acid rain" (partly sulfuric acid) poisoning lakes and the evacuation of towns after the derailment of trains carrying tank cars of hydrochloric acid, and thanks to television advertisements about cures for excessive "stomach acid" and so forth. The four common bases in our DNA molecules are named adenine, guanine, cytosine, and thymine. These bases are like a four-letter alphabet in which all the genetic information of the human species (and of most other species too) is "written." Alteration of a base can garble the information, just as the word *cat* can be garbled to *ctt* by changing the middle letter.

The *loss* of a gene (or tens or hundreds of genes), through deletion of part of a chromosome, is every bit as much a mutation, in the broad sense of the word, as is the chemical alteration of one of the four bases in the DNA gene molecule. When a DNA gene molecule is so chemically altered that it no longer codes properly for the production of an enzyme or other protein, we commonly refer to that change as a mutation (chemical mutation); because of the mutation, the individual is deprived of the product (the enzyme or other protein) whose production that gene would have directed. A person will also be deprived of the functional product of that particular gene if the gene is positioned on a piece of chromosome that is lost by deletion. The reader will find that the meaning which various writers assign to the word *mutation* varies, ranging from exclusively a base change in a single DNA molecule, up through inclusion of translocations, deletions, and trisomies. As long as we specify which type of mutation we are referring to, there should be no reason for confusion.

What Are the Dimensions of the Problem of "Genetic Effects"?

There are several parts to our ultimate problem of quantitatively evaluating the genetic effects per rad of ionizing radiation:

1. Identification of the disabilities, diseases, and deformities that have a genetic or chromosomal origin, whose occurrence could be increased by ionizing radiation.

2. Estimation of the spontaneous incidence of these problems, without which we cannot determine the doubling dose of radiation.

3. Estimation of the quantitative relationship between the mutation rate and the spontaneous incidence. Spontaneous incidence can be very much greater than the rate of new mutation. Moreover, the ratio between the mutation rate and the accumulated incidence of mutations in a population can vary enormously from one disease to another.

Unless attention is given to each of these parts of the issue, it is impossible to make scientifically valid use of whatever "experimental" evidence now exists or may exist in the future.

SECTION 4: TYPES OF GENETIC INJURIES

The genetic effects of exposure to ionizing radiation encompass more, and very likely a great deal more, than base changes in single DNA molecules (chemical mutations). The reader will easily see how this statement relates to other analyses of genetic effects (for instance, by the BEIR and UN-SCEAR committees) if the author uses the same classifications of genetic diseases as are used by the quasi-official committees, so the author will do so, although other classifications would be valid too. The classifications that the BEIR and UNSCEAR committees use are as follows, and their meanings will be made clear in this section:

☐ Chromosomal diseases
☐ X-linked diseases
☐ Autosomal dominant diseases
☐ Recessive diseases
☐ Irregularly inherited diseases

CHROMOSOMAL DISEASES: MONOSOMY AND TRISOMY

All normal cells receive *two* copies of each gene via two copies of each autosomal chromosome (chapter 3, section 3). *Disomy* is the name for this proper condition.

The genetic injury that results in the transmission of only *one* autosomal chromosome per cell to an "intended" descendant is called *monosomy*. We must say "intended" descendant because no case has been described of a human being living with an entire autosomal chromosome completely missing. Grossly abnormal human beings are known to survive birth and live for some years with a part of an autosome missing (the major deletion syndromes), but no case is recorded of a human being surviving with a 45-

chromosome complement in all cells, with one autosomal chromosome missing. So, rather obviously, not having the genes to code for whatever most of the genes of any single autosome code for is very serious, even though each of those genes is represented on the other autosome of the pair. Quantitatively, either one copy of the genes belonging to that autosome is not enough for normal cell function, or several of the genes are abnormal in the remaining autosome and hence cannot provide adequate function.

But it is also extremely serious for a person to be trisomic for one of the autosomes, that is, for his cells to contain three copies of an autosomal chromosome instead of two copies. We know (from section 1) of the serious defects present in individuals who survive birth in spite of trisomy. Down's syndrome is one of the most serious and common chromosomal disorders, and is characterized by cells that have *three* G-21 chromosomes, and thus three instead of two copies of the genes carried on that chromosome.

CHROMOSOMAL DISEASES: DELETIONS AND TRANSLOCATIONS

As noted in our discussions of cellular mechanisms of radiation injury (chapter 3), chromosome breaks are regarded as one of the most common injuries caused by ionizing radiation. If a chromosome break results in the loss of a piece of chromosome (containing anywhere from a few to several hundred genes), we refer to this injury as a *deletion,* and we have discussed some of the serious disorders now known to be deletion syndromes (section 1). Following simple breaks in two chromosomes or in two parts of one chromosome, pieces can be interchanged. This form of ionizing radiation injury to the hereditary material is called *translocation,* and is widely regarded to be a major mode of genetic radiation injury.

With respect to both deletions and translocations, the author would like to warn the reader about a very poor practice in a great deal of the medical and scientific literature. The technology for recognizing and measuring relatively small deletions and translocations is most appropriately described as primitive, even after taking the new banding techniques into account. The large majority of small deletions and translocations cannot possibly be recognized with the use of available technology. Yet many authorities simply treat these injuries as though they simply did not occur.

But there are still more difficulties associated with detecting the true frequency of deletions or translocations. Just why and how does one go about searching for evidence of a small deletion (or even a fairly large one)? If a newborn shows no grossly abnormal characteristics, no one will be alerted to search with extreme care in many, many cells for an abnormality such as a deletion in one chromosome. And newborns can appear normal and behave perfectly normally while harboring one or more of a whole variety of lesions in one organ system or another, lesions that will later show up as a mild to severe handicap not suspected of being the result of a chromosome deletion. The reader will wish to keep this in mind when the genetic effects of the bombing of Hiroshima and Nagasaki are discussed later in this chapter.

So the fact that known deletion syndromes are limited to the cri-du-chat syndrome (5p deletion), the Wolf-Hirschhorn syndrome (4p deletion), the 13q deletion (also known as *partial monosomy-13 syndrome*), the 18p or 18q deletions (also known as *partial monosomy-18 syndrome*), and some other rarities reported from time to time, only tells us that these deletions produce effects which are so obvious that they call themselves pleadingly to the attention of the people doing the chromosome analyses. Once one finds a cri-du-chat case with a fairly large piece of the short arm of chromosome 5 missing; then the next time a cri-du-chat case shows up clinically, one may, by careful looking, be able to discern even a 10% loss of the short arm of chromosome 5. But just try to look for 5% losses or 2% losses in cases where no clinical features have demanded explanation.

A whole host of human handicaps, very probably the overwhelming majority of them, are not of the bizarre and blatant kind that signal themselves even in the nursery. Although they are far less blatant, these handicaps may be responsible for much ill health and incomplete development of human potential. What cytogeneticist or geneticist would be so brash as to say that a 2% deletion in chromosome A_2 or C_8 is not the basis for a learning difficulty that shows up in a child in the third or fourth grade and handicaps that child for life? What cytogeneticist or geneticist would be so brash as to say that a 1% deletion in chromosome A_1 is or is not the basis for development of diabetes in certain persons? Our available technology in this field simply precludes certainty on such issues.

We shall return to some of the quantitative aspects of the deletion and translocation problems later, particularly to the probable extent to which the relation of such genetic effects to radiation and other agents has been grossly underestimated.

Lest the reader be confused into thinking that a loss of 1, 2, or 5% of an autosomal chromosome is not much of a loss and is hence unlikely to produce much of an effect on a human being, let us remember that although we do not know the precise number of human genes in a cell, numbers in the ballpark of 25,000 to 100,000 are not unreasonable. Since there are normally 46 chromosomes, if we assign to each an equal number of genes, each chromosome has roughly 500 to 2,000 genes. Actually it is unreasonable to assume that each chromosome has an equal number of genes, since long chromosomes, such as the A_1, A_2, and A_3 chromosomes, must have much more genetic material than short chromosomes, such as the D, E, F, and G chromosomes. For example, an A_1 chromosome could have 1,000 to several thousand genes. The loss of 1%, 2%, 5% of genetic material from that chromosome could represent the loss of between *10 and several hundred genes.*

One has to be very brave indeed to insist, without knowing anything about these genes, that the loss of 10 to several hundred genes is without effect. Yet that is what one claims when one cavalierly says something about the rarity of deletions as a basis for hereditary abnormalities—deletions one cannot even measure with current technology.

Translocations, Balanced and Unbalanced

Translocations are a well-known and prominent effect of ionizing radiation, as observed in cultures of blood lymphocytes and fibroblasts. Translocations can very definitely be transmitted over many generations, and certain of them seriously affect human health.

It is crucial that the reader understand the difference between the implications of translocations in cells that are going to undergo only mitosis, and the implications of translocations for the process of gametogenesis, fertilization, implantation, embryogenesis, and finally birth. (*Gamete* is a term for either an ovum or a sperm, each of which has only 23 chromosomes.)

Translocations and Mitosis: When a symmetrical translocation occurs in a cell with a full complement of 46 chromosomes, all the chromosomal material is still present in the cell. We must keep in mind that genes may be split by translocations, and also that there may be injury in the neighborhood of the breaks in the chromosomes which is not repaired fully when the chromosome parts are rejoined. We will discuss this reservation later. For now, however, we are primarily concerned with the question of the bulk of the genetic material in the arms or parts of chromosome arms that are being translocated.

Let us consider the well-known radiation effect called *reciprocal translocation.* This process involves two chromosome breaks, plus the rejoining of part of each chromosome to the bulk of the other, and vice versa—an exchange of genetic material, in other words. Aside from possible injury in the region of the breaks, or associated with the rejoining process, all genetic material is preserved in the cell.

When the cell containing the translocated chromosomes undergoes *mitosis* (simple cell division), the daughter cells each receive their complement of genetic material in rearranged form, but without any of the material missing. And this will be true after any number of successive mitoses. Therefore, so long as we are dealing with mitoses, reciprocal translocations that do not involve dicentric chromosomes will continue to result in perfectly balanced chromosomal material. We do *not* say that such cells are perfectly normal, for there are three ways in which they can have been injured genetically. The first is that some material may have been altered or lost in the original break and rejoining. The second is that genes are now in new positions, and there may be a position effect of consequence for their functioning. The third is a possible split in a gene molecule at the break. The key point is that there is, in mitosis, no *gross* loss of chromosomal material with a reciprocal translocation.

Translocations and Meiosis: When we come to spermatogenesis, we have a wholly different situation. In the process of meiosis, the existence of balanced translocations can definitely produce trouble, and some of the products of the meiosis may not be viable.

Experimental evidence indicates that the presence of translocations can prevent some cells from going into meiosis at all; that is, the cells are somehow prevented from accomplishing the first meiotic division. From the point of view of potential future offspring, this difficulty experienced by spermatogonial cells bearing reciprocal translocations in even entering meiosis is probably a very fortunate thing indeed, since it is one of the many filters nature has devised to weed out defective procreative material.

But in spite of this filter inhibiting meiosis itself, some of the cells bearing translocated chromosomes do accomplish the first meiotic division and become primary spermatocytes (the first stage of sperm formation). It is at the next stage, the secondary meiotic division, that the real seeds of trouble for the embryo are planted. In this division, there are many opportunities for the product cells to receive unbalanced genetic material—pieces of translocated chromosomes that do not add up to the full complement of genetic material. This is in contrast to what happens in mitosis, and the effects on the embryo of such *unbalanced translocations* are nearly always severe.

The Reasons for Serious Concern Even About the Balanced Translocations: The conventional wisdom about balanced translocations is that the persons involved do not suffer. It is indeed true that such persons do not in general show severe overt stigmata of disease or deformity. But we will recall some reasons why the conventional genetic wisdom should be viewed with suspicion, and then discuss the direct evidence that it is incorrect.

In a balanced translocation, *two* breaks have occurred in chromosome arms, and the position of some genetic material has grossly changed vis-à-vis other DNA material. We can only speculate as to what damage has been sustained during the breaking and rejoining process. There is certainly no reason to dismiss the potential effects of changes in position, especially in view of the large quantity of DNA material that is present in the chromosomes, which does not appear to code for the production of proteins but must have some function. One wonders whether simply moving the coding genes away from the other DNA they are normally close to can be without effect. The effect of splitting a gene in the course of a translocation is most likely to be the same as the effect of deleting that gene.

As for the direct evidence that the conventional wisdom is not correct about the implications of balanced translocations, the author refers the reader back to the discussion in chapter 3 of the recent work of Cohen and co-workers (1979) on the role of balanced translocations between the short arm of chromosome 3 and the long arm of chromosome 8 in conferring an enormous increase in risk of kidney carcinoma. None of the members of the family under study showed *unbalanced* translocations, so presumably these were not viable (to adulthood, at least).

Some of the Well-Known Diseases Resulting from Unbalanced Translocations in Human Beings: Down's syndrome, discussed in section 1, is due to a trisomy of chromosome G-21, in 95% of the cases. About 4% of the cases are due to a translocation of a chromosome G-21 long arm to another chromosome, most frequently a D or G group chromosome. About 50% of the G to D translocations and about 90% of the G to G translocations (according to Zellweger and Simpson 1977, p. 43) are the result of de novo translocations, with parents showing normal karyotypes. (When we say that a translocation is *de novo,* we mean that it occurred in either the sperm or the ova of the immediately preceding generation.) The remaining cases of G to D and G to G translocation cases had a parent with that same translocation present in all body cells in balanced form. Approximately 1% of Down's syndrome cases are mosaics (see section 1).

Patau's syndrome, or trisomy-13 (see section 1), is due to a translocation rather than to a true trisomy in between $\frac{1}{5}$ and $\frac{1}{6}$ of the cases, according to Zellweger and Simpson. Mixoploidy accounts for $\frac{1}{10}$ of cases, and the remainder are true trisomies. While most cases of translocation-trisomy-13 are de novo, some 10% are said to be inherited from a parent with a balanced D to D translocation.

For Edwards' syndrome, or trisomy-18, Zellweger and Simpson report that 4% are translocations: chromosome 18 material is translocated to chromosomes of the B, D, E, and G groups. While most are de novo cases, some have been described as arising from balanced translocations in the parents.

Effect of Radiation on Translocation Rates: Information from studies by Brewen and Preston (1975) and by Jacobs and co-workers (1972) on the effects of radiation in the formation of translocations can be used to suggest that a dose of 2.1 rads per generation is sufficient to produce a 100% increase in the translocation frequency. (Stated otherwise, 2.1 rads is the doubling dose for translocation induction.) While this range for translocation induction is indeed sobering, we must raise the lower limit to 3 rads, since that is the lowest possible with a natural-radiation dose of 3 rads per generation.

The general view in the literature would lead us to downplay the importance of translocations in the total volume of genetic-chromosomal injury which is potentially induced by ionizing radiation. The opinion often expressed is that the "screen"—comprising failure to go through spermatogenesis, failure of fertilization, failure of implantation, and failure to produce a full-term viable infant—will reduce the translocation frequency much more than is indicated by the Brewen-Preston calculation, a calculation the present author considers to be quite a reasonable one for dealing with the evidence at our disposal. It would be helpful if those who doubt the calculation would produce some evidence in support of their position.

It is reasonable to estimate that Jacobs and co-workers missed about as many translocations in their study of spontaneous rates as did Brewen and Preston in their study of radiation-induced rates. For this reason, the author suggests that a doubling-dose range of 3 to 17 rads for human beings is probably quite good.

Very likely a large number of translocations of smaller pieces of chromosomes were not measured in either study. This number of translocations is some unknown number of times larger than the measured number. The health impact of the translocation we do not measure must also remain unknown for now, but it is important information to seek in the future. If there is such a body of unrecognized translocations, larger, say, by a factor of 10 than the recognized ones, the spontaneous rate would be 4,000 per 1 million live-born children (1 per 250) instead of Jacobs' 400 per million. A radiation dose of between 3 and 17 rads per person per generation would then produce an additional 4,000 such humans per 1 million births, with their associated defects, instead of 400. This would hardly be a minor matter.

THE SEX CHROMOSOMES AND THE X-LINKED DISEASES

As the reader knows (from chapter 3, section 3), in the male there is only one copy of all the genes that are on the X-chromosome. The Y-chromosome is considered to have very few genes at all. In the female, there are two copies of all the genes carried on the X-chromosomes, since there are two X-chromosomes, although, as suggested by Lyon (1961, 1962), it is likely that only one gene copy is active for most of the genes on the X-chromosome in the female.

It is the absence of the extra copy of the X-chromosome genes which makes the human male subject to some particular and serious defects and diseases. If a particular gene carried on the X-chromosome is needed for avoidance of a disease, and if the one gene copy in the male undergoes a chemical mutation and can no longer function normally (or possibly is deleted), then the male does not have the end product(s) of that gene. The female will not suffer from such a mutation provided one copy of the normal gene is enough, and in many cases it is. A male with a mutation of an X-chromosome can experience mild trait differences, such as color-blindness, or serious life-threatening diseases, such as hemophilia. The diseases known as *sex-linked* or *X-linked* diseases have in common the loss of a normal gene on the X-chromosome in the male, who then has no copy of the normal, functioning gene.

THE AUTOSOMAL DOMINANT DISEASES

Each gene that is carried on one or another of the 22 autosomal chromosomes is represented in duplicate. Of those genes carried on the X-chromosome (a sex chromosome), there is only one gene in the male, and two in the female.

The biochemical evidence would indicate that a particular gene can code for some maximal production of a particular protein, an enzyme for example, when that gene is in no way suppressed. Therefore, if one had two normal genes of a particular type, the total production capacity for that protein would be twice what it would be if only one of the two genes were normal, or if only one of the two genes were present at all. The reader should recall that deletion of a piece of a chromosome bearing a gene can produce effects similar or identical to chemical mutation of that gene.

Homozygous Versus Heterozygous Genes

If both genes of a particular type are present (one on each autosome of the pair), and if both genes are normal and unaltered, we say that the person is *homozygous normal* for that gene. If one gene is of the normal variety and one is altered (mutated), we say the person is *heterozygous* for that gene. A person can be heterozygous for a particular gene by having one mutated copy of the gene or by having lost one copy entirely, such as by the loss of an autosome or a deletion on an autosome.

When a heterozygous state exists, there are three major possible cases:

1. The production capacity for the particular protein is only half what it would be with two normal genes (one on each autosome). The mutant gene we shall assume produces either no protein or an *inactive* protein. For many genes, indeed for a large number, it appears that 50% production capacity is sufficient to prevent the appearance of severe ill health or serious abnormality. *This does not mean that 50% capacity is satisfactory,* nor does it mean that subtle defects or ill health are not present. An enormous amount remains to be learned about the effects of 50% versus 100% production capacity for certain proteins.

2. The production capacity for a particular normal protein is only 50% of what it could be with two normal genes (one on each autosome); in addition, the abnormal gene shifts 50% of the potential production capacity into production of an abnormal protein that produces signs of disease ranging from mild to severe.

3. The other gene is simply missing, as would be the case with a monosomy, or a deletion. So, there is neither an inactive nor a disease-producing protein being produced, and in this case, too, the production capacity of the normal protein is only 50%.

Case 2 is illustrated by the situation involving the gene for hemoglobin production. A specific change in that gene can produce a variant form of hemoglobin (one amino acid is substituted for another in the hemoglobin molecule) known as *sickle hemoglobin.* If only one of the two genes for hemoglobin production has been so altered, while the gene on the other autosome is normal, the person has 50% capacity for producing normal hemoglobin molecules, and 50% capacity for producing sickle hemoglobin molecules. In this heterozygous state, the person is said to be characterized by *sickle cell trait*. Some mild to moderate disabilities are caused by up to 50% of the hemoglobin being of the sickle variety. However, such disabilities are simply trivial when compared to the *homozygous abnormal* state, when both genes code for the production of sickle hemoglobin, and no normal hemoglobin is produced. This homozygous state defines the disease known as *sickle cell anemia*, which is severe in its manifestations, and can be fatal.

Heterozygotes: Dominant Versus Recessive Behavior

Whenever we injure a gene by chemical mutation or lose it by deletion, there are two clinical possibilities for the first generation of affected offspring:

1. No deleterious effect is noted at all. In this case, we have either produced an allele of the gene (a closely related DNA molecule) which does no harm, or, if there has been a deletion, we have produced no harm because the remaining gene (on the other autosome of the same class), with 50% capacity to do whatever that gene does, is perfectly adequate for the metabolic and health needs of the individual. This absence of a noticeable effect of a mutant or missing gene is called *recessive* behavior.

2. Harmful effects, mild or severe, are produced. In this case, we can properly say that the mutant gene (or missing gene) is demonstrating *dominant* behavior. The meaning of dominance has nothing to do with the severity of the abnormality but rather with the fact that the abnormality is perceived in the *heterozygous state*, namely, where only *one* of the pair of genes is affected.

There are two ways in which the heterozygous state can be said to demonstrate dominant behavior. The first way is for one gene to be inactive or to produce an inactive protein, or for the gene to be missing. If 50% production capacity is *not* adequate for normal health, signs of disease will be apparent, and we will say that dominant behavior exists.

The second way is for the production of 50% normal protein and 50% abnormal protein to lead to ill health. Depending on its nature, a particular abnormal protein can have very deleterious effects even when much of the normal protein is produced. In this case, dominance is the result of the production of an abnormal protein rather than the absence of sufficient quantity of a normal protein.

The reason for the term *dominant* is that biochemical, physiological, and anatomical abnormalities can be severe even when the normal protein product is being produced (in reduced amount). The term *recessive*, strictly used, means that heterozygosity is causing *no* harmful effects. Why, then, will the reader soon encounter the term *recessive diseases*? Isn't there a contradiction within that term? In a moment, we will define many terms as they are currently used in the literature, because some are not used in the way one might expect.

The problem begins with the fact that dominant and recessive conditions are by no means as black-and-white as they were once thought to be. Dominance or recessivity is partly determined by how hard one looks. In the sickle cell trait, for instance, we still refer to the abnormal state with one normal gene and one abnormal gene as a heterozygous *recessive* state, but this is confusing now that we know there *are* some health effects from the heterozygous state. When there are health effects from heterozygous states, we *should* say that abnormality is dominant.

A legitimate question is whether there ever exists a justification for the use of the term *recessive*. A mutation that reduces production of a certain enzyme, for example, may not be obvious; indeed, its effects may show up in the individual only under metabolic or infectious stress. But when one decides to classify a particular mutation as having no effect in the heterozygous state, one can almost never be sure that one has looked for the effect in the right way, biochemically and physiologically. However, if one looks hard and finds *no* effect from the heterozygous state, it is correct to say provisionally that the abnormal gene shows recessive behavior.

Perhaps the situation for *heterozygotes* can best be described as a continuum:

Total Dominance ← Shades of Gray → Total Recessivity
(severe effects in the   (no effects in the
heterozygous state)   heterozygous state)

Whenever heterozygotes exist in a population, there is the possibility that they will mate with each other and that some of their children will be *homozygous abnormal,* and may or may not survive. We have already mentioned homozygous abnormals with respect to sickle cell hemoglobin.

Another illustration of interest, because it pertains to heart disease, involves the genes that control one aspect of cholesterol and fat metabolism. This genetic disorder elevates blood cholesterol levels, and is very serious indeed, since a major result is grossly premature coronary artery atherosclerosis and coronary heart attacks and deaths.

If one of the genes involved in this aspect of cholesterol-fat metabolism is the abnormal gene, we have the heterozygous state. The effect of 50% of the capacity of the pair of genes going into the production of the abnormal gene product (or the effect of 50% of the production capacity of a needed gene product lacking altogether) is serious. So, the abnormal gene produces effects in the heterozygous state, and can be called dominant for that reason.

However, there is a far more serious state—the homozygous abnormal state—in which this particular abnormal gene is present in *both* autosomes. In this case, 100% of the genes' capacity is for the abnormal product, resulting in enormously elevated blood cholesterol levels with very early coronary heart disease. The effects of this state are far more severe than are the "dominant" effects of the heterozygous state. This situation must not be confused with the so-called recessive diseases (defined below), which also require the homozygous abnormal condition.

DEFINITIONS: DOMINANT, RECESSIVE, AND IRREGULARLY INHERITED DISEASES

A Dominant Disease (also called *autosomal dominant disease*) is a disease caused by an abnormal or missing gene on *one* member of a pair of autosomal chromosomes. In such cases, the effect is even more severe when the corresponding genes on *both* autosomes are abnormal or missing (the homozygous abnormal state).

An X-Linked Disease is a disease caused by mutation or deletion on an X-chromosome.

A Recessive Disease is a disease that shows up only in the homozygous abnormal state (no manifestation of it has been noted in the heterozygous state).

The Irregularly Inherited Diseases are a group of disorders that clearly have a hereditary aspect but that are not transmitted numerically in a way consistent with causation by single-gene dominant mutations. It is thought that these diseases possibly result from involvement of more than one gene, so they are sometimes provisionally called *multigene* or *polygene* diseases. This group of diseases occurs far more frequently in the population than single-gene diseases. For instance, this category includes some common *degenerative* and *constitutional* diseases, as well as *congenital anomalies* and *anomalies expressed later.*

CHROMOSOME LOSS VERSUS ABNORMAL GENE

For those dominant traits which are manifest because of loss of function of one of the two genes in a pair, it is very difficult to tell whether chemical gene mutation or a chromosome deletion has occurred. *Undoubtedly some proportion of so-called dominant mutations are really cases of chromosome deletions.* This is one of the ways that deletions are underestimated as a source of disease or abnormality. With more and more knowledge about the chromosomal position of various genes, including the identities of neighboring genes, it will become possible in the future to differentiate between chemical mutation and deletion as a basis for dominant genetic disease in a specific case.

Why Bother About Distinguishing Chemical Mutations from Chromosome Deletions?

We have reasoned that at least for some genes the same effect can be produced by a chemical mutation as by a deletion of a part of a chromosome. Ionizing radiation has been unequivocally proved to be capable of causing chemical mutation of one of the bases of the DNA molecule into another base (Freifelder 1965, 1968). Additionally, and importantly, ionizing radiation causes production of deletions in chromosomes.

But there is nothing *a priori* which suggests that the quantitative aspects of the production of these two types of lesions are at all similar. For this reason alone it would be important to establish, for dominant alterations that could be caused by either of the two mechanisms, which *is* the cause; our predictions of effect per rad would depend on this knowledge.

There is an additional reason for asking which is the cause. The chemical- or radiation-induced mutation of a single gene has effects limited to that gene. The deletion of a piece of a chromosome will eliminate a particular gene, and can mimic the dominant effect of mutation of that gene. But the deletion can also eliminate 5, 10, or hundreds of additional genes, so that the overall effect can be far more serious (and variable) than the elimination of the one gene whose dominant effects are under study.

SECTION 5: QUANTITATIVE IMPORTANCE OF GENETIC AND CHROMOSOMAL DISEASES

For the current spontaneous incidence of genetic diseases, the BEIR Committee has presented two estimates (one in BEIR-I, 1972, and one in BEIR-III, 1979), and UNSCEAR (1977) has recently presented an estimate also. We shall compare the recent BEIR estimate with the UNSCEAR estimate.

The UNSCEAR estimates are as follows (from their Table 50, p. 539):

Disease Classification	Current Incidence per Million Live-Born Individuals
Autosomal dominant and X-linked diseases	10,000
Recessive diseases	1,100
Chromosomal diseases	4,000
Congenital anomalies Anomalies expressed later Constitutional and degenerative diseases	90,000
Total	105,100

In its Draft Report, BEIR-III, the BEIR Committee presents the following incidence figures for "Genetic Effects" (p. 129):

Type of Genetic Disorder	Current Incidence per Million Live-Born Individuals
Autosomal dominant and X-linked	10,000
Recessive	1,100
Chromosomal aberrations	6,000
Irregularly inherited	90,000
Total	107,100

The two reports differ from each other very little, although that does not mean either one should be taken as correct (see also BEIR-I, p. 54).

WHY THE OFFICIAL ESTIMATES MUST BE TOO LOW

The autosomal dominant diseases have been increasingly recognized with the passage of time and with careful work, and there is every reason to believe that their numbers will grow still further in the future, possibly partly as a result of transfer of some diseases from the *irregularly inherited* category. And it will grow because both the BEIR Committee and UNSCEAR simply neglected some diseases that do not become clinically apparent until adulthood. But for now, we can utilize the figure of 10,000 per million if we keep in mind that it is too low.

The recessive diseases deserve special comment. In these tabulations the committees are not referring to the incidence of recessive heterozygotes per million persons, but to the incidence of homozygotes per million who have developed the full-blown disease. The former incidence is much higher than 1,100 per million persons. The author has no reason to challenge the latter incidence.

The estimates of 4,000 and 6,000 for the chromosomal diseases or "aberrations" (numerical and structural) represent fairly soft estimates, since there is variation in reported incidences from one part of the world to another. But of far greater importance is that neither estimate really takes into account the possibility that deletions and translocations are far more prevalent in society than is generally recognized. It is, therefore, possible that the estimates for chromosomal disorders are grossly too low.

Major Omissions from the Largest Category

The last category, that of irregularly inherited diseases, or according to UNSCEAR's designation, of the combination of congenital anomalies, later anomalies, and constitutional and degenerative diseases, undoubtedly represents a very serious underestimate by both the UNSCEAR and BEIR reports. Neither UNSCEAR nor BEIR tries to defend its estimate very seriously, and the evidence they both present indicates that they have obviously left out a large part of the genetic problem. The major source of information on which the estimate of 90,000 persons per million is based is a study in British Columbia (Trimble and Doughty 1974) which endeavored to find out incidences for persons up through 21 years of age. Therefore, disorders that first become manifest after 21 years of age are totally missed in this accounting.

Indeed the BEIR-I report (1972) flatly states about its *arbitrary* choice of 1.5% for the incidence of constitutional and degenerative diseases:

This figure is taken to be 1.5%, but is quite arbitrary, depending upon what diseases are included. Anemia, diabetes, schizophrenia, and epilepsy, for example, are included.

Heart disease, ulcer, and cancer have not been included, although there is known to be a genetic component in each. (p. 56)

It is difficult to understand why these committees, ostensibly trying to find the current incidence of genetic-chromosomal disease so that they could estimate how much each unit of radiation exposure would increase the incidence, would leave out what is probably the largest part of the problem. There are varying estimates of the fraction of all known diseases which have a genetic aspect (see BEIR-I, p. 55 and p. 59). Few are lower than 25%; some are well above 50%.

One disorder alone, atherosclerosis of the arteries, underlies the occurrence of coronary heart disease, cerebral thrombosis, most obstructive arterial diseases of the lower extremities, and some forms of kidney disease. Together, these major consequences of atherosclerosis cause over 50% of premature deaths in the United States. "Environmental factors" are definitely involved in this disease, if we consider diet and cigarette smoking broadly as "environmental," as opposed to genetic, in nature. But it would seem rash indeed, at this stage of our knowledge, to suppose that *less* than one-half of atherosclerotic disease is genetic in origin. Since the precise inheritance mechanism is not clear, atherosclerosis is best considered as a member of the group of irregularly inherited diseases. Since atherosclerosis accounts for over 50% of all premature mortality in the United States, it is reasonable to say that the irregularly inherited diseases (via atherosclerosis alone) must account for approximately 25% of *all* premature mortality. This provides some perspective on the *underestimation* of the importance of the irregularly inherited diseases.

And this says nothing of all the other diseases that become apparent only after 21 years of age and may well have a serious genetic aspect. The author believes that 90,000 per million as an estimate of irregularly inherited diseases must be *at least a factor of 3 too low. It would not be surprising if further information indicates that this figure is a factor of 5 too low. In the meantime, it would be highly reasonable, whenever these committees estimate the genetic effects of radiation exposure, derived largely from the spontaneous incidence of the irregularly inherited diseases, to multiply such estimates by a factor of 3.*

The Question of the "Mutational Component" of Irregularly Inherited Diseases

The inheritance pattern for the irregularly inherited diseases is not clear, not only because it is irregular, but because it has hardly been studied at all for some diseases. One should therefore exercise great caution in saying very much about the specific role of mutation rate in such diseases. Yet the BEIR Committee and UNSCEAR concluded that the "mutational component" of such diseases cannot be over 5–50%, that is, that these diseases cannot be caused by genetic mutation in more than 5–50% of cases. UNSCEAR likes the figure of 5%; the BEIR-III report uses the range of 5–50%.

The author of this book considers that the case for a mutational component between 5% and 50% made by these committees is very weak indeed, hardly better than sheer, unsupported speculation. It is truly amazing, for a set of disorders about which we have very little solid information, that these committees are willing to go out on a limb with a proposition which arbitrarily reduces the genetic effects of radiation by a factor of between 2 and 20 for the preponderant category of diseases, the "irregularly inherited" ones.

In the final section of this chapter, the author will propose a possible explanation for the irregular nature of the inheritance patterns and clinical manifestations of these diseases. However, at present, we *all* share a great ignorance about the inheritance of these disorders, and the most reasonable approach would be to eliminate the poorly documented concept of a 5–50% mutational component. Of course, doing so would raise the committees' estimates of radiation-inducible irregularly inherited disease by 2- to 20-fold. The protection of public health argues for the reasonableness of this suggestion.

A Summary of Our Present Ignorance

We have now explored two kinds of considerations necessary to give meaning to any quantitative *data* provided by various studies of the genetic effects of ionizing radiation on human beings. We have looked at the kinds of problems that have a genetic basis, and at the existing incidence of such problems in the population. A third consideration—the quantitative relationship of the existing incidence to the rate of *new* genetic injuries—is examined in the unabridged edition of this work but is not critical to our purposes here. All three areas, we know, are characterized by gross uncertainties and ignorance.

In the next section of this chapter, we shall consider the existing studies of the genetic effects of ionizing radiation on humans. The reader may be astonished to find that only *two* kinds of genetic disorders have been studied in much depth so far: one is very early death (by age 17), and the other is Down's syndrome, or trisomy-21.

Section 6: The Human Evidence on Genetic Effects

Early Death in the Descendants of the Atom-Bomb Survivors

Neel, Kato, and Schull (1974) reported the latest results of an ongoing set of studies in Hiroshima and Nagasaki which seek to discover any effects of ionizing radiation on the children of those actually exposed. These effects, which exclude effects on children in utero at the time of exposure, would be, by definition, genetic or chromosomal effects. These studies were reported by Kato, Schull, and Neel in 1966; the 1974 report includes an additional eight years of observation.

Rationale of the Study

The studies of Neel and co-workers are based on a straightforward premise. They searched out the number of deaths *before maturity* (17 years of age, on the average) in the offspring of persons irradiated in the Hiroshima and Nagasaki bombings, and contrasted those deaths with the deaths of offspring of individuals presumably unexposed but present during the bombings, and with the deaths of offspring of individuals who were not in the cities at all during the bombings. (In their 1966 study, Kato, Schull, and Neel used death-before-age-9 in the offspring as the manifestation of dominant disorders.)

There is certainly good reason to believe that whenever dominant disorders are produced, some of them will be serious enough to cause death before maturity. If dominant disorders were produced genetically in Japan (either by direct chemical mutation or by chromosomal mechanisms), one manifestation of some, at least, of the dominant disorders would be extra deaths before the age of 17. And if one could measure the doubling dose of radiation for early death, the doubling dose could be provisionally applied to most other human dominant disorders.

While all this is reasonable, there are also serious problems in the Japanese studies. One difficulty is that, if a doubling dose is to be calculated, we must have a value for the Japanese of the *spontaneous* rate of dominant mutations that cause death by age 17. That is essential. But no such datum could possibly emerge from these Hiroshima-Nagasaki studies. So Neel, Kato, and Schull concocted such a value by "guesstimate." The author of this book does not object to that, provided that everyone realizes that the derived doubling doses carry the same relative uncertainty as exists in the spontaneous rate "guesstimated" by Neel, Kato, and Schull.

Neel, Kato, and Schull state in both their first and second papers that there is good reason to believe, "on the basis of both theoretical and enumerative" considerations, that 0.005 of a cohort of live-born children will die before age 9 as a result of mutation in the preceding generation. In their 1974 paper, they elect to keep this estimate, 5 per 1,000, as the number of live-born children (in a cohort) who will die before age 17 as a result of mutation in the preceding generation. This nonadjustment is appropriate provided there are not very many deaths between 9 and 17 years of age. The 0.005 figure means that 1 out of every 200, or 5,000 out of every million, live-born children will die before age 17 of a dominant disorder that is the result of a mutation in the preceding generation. It does not mean that this is the total death rate which will be observed out to age 17, since deaths other than those due to dominant disorders will be admixed, as will be some "carryover" cases of the dominant disorders.

Just how good the 0.005 estimate may be is hard to say. Neel, Kato, and

Schull later qualify their estimate by saying they doubt that it could be lower than 0.003, which gives a pretty good idea of how confident they are in it. We shall proceed to consider the Japanese studies utilizing the Neel, Kato, and Schull guesstimate.

It is a reasonable proposition that this method of study represents one valid way of searching for evidence of radiation-induced dominant disorders in first-generation offspring of irradiated persons. But it will also be shown later in the discussion that the nature of this particular study makes it hard to ascertain positive findings.

Let us now consider the technical aspects of the Neel, Kato, and Schull studies. It is worthy of note that Neel and co-workers point out, correctly, that they would have no way of knowing whether effects observed in the form of early mortality were truly chemical genetic effects or one of the several forms of chromosomal aberrations of structure or number.

The Hiroshima-Nagasaki Findings

Neel, Kato and Schull studied three groups of subjects:

Group 1: Either or both parents (of the offspring) were within 2,000 meters of the hypocenter at the time of the bombing.

Group 2: Neither parent was within 2,000 meters, but either or both were in one of the cities at distances greater than 2,500 meters.

Group 3: Neither parent was in the city at the time of the bombing.

The great majority of the births of offspring (in this study) occurred between 1948 and 1953. The radiation doses received by the parents are those estimated in T-65 units. The reader knows from reading prior chapters that Neel and co-workers should *not* have used those doses in conclusions, since the doses seriously overstate the true doses absorbed by the gonads of the exposed parents. Thus, every calculation made by Neel, Kato, and Schull of effects per rad is an underestimate of the true effects because of this failure to convert to absorbed dose to tissue.

Neel, Kato, and Schull credited neutron exposure as having an RBE of 5 compared with gamma rays, for the purpose of this study. They state, "In this complex situation we will for now set the average RBE at 5 for the types of genetic damage (point mutations, small deletions, unbalanced translocations, nondisjunction) which we may assume are being measured in this study" (1974, p. 314). There is no reason to quibble with the choice of 5 for the RBE, inasmuch as no one really knows what the correct value should be.

The data obtained, from an average 17-year follow-up of offspring of exposed persons, raise several questions. One of the first one might ask is whether an effect can be shown from paternal radiation versus from maternal radiation. A large body of experimental-animal data suggests that females may be sensitive to the mutational effects of radiation for only a limited period of time, although this has not been proved for the human female. Neel, Kato, and Schull did separate extensive statistical analyses for paternal and maternal radiation, and we shall consider these below. But for now, we can do a simple analysis to get an idea of how large any effects might be.

There is a major lesson to be learned from the data. In spite of the large number of people in Hiroshima and Nagasaki at the time of the bombing, when we come to searching out a genetic effect, we find that we are dealing with numbers like 20, 16, 17 persons in crucial categories of exposure. While the appropriate reaction is an appreciation of the difficulty of studying the genetic effects of radiation on human beings, the wags claim that if we cannot find a genetic effect in two whole cities that had been bombed, the effect must surely be small. That is an ignorant and scientifically foolish reaction, for, as will be shown a little later in this section, the nature of the search in Hiroshima-Nagasaki for genetic effects has a built-in feature that could obscure even large effects.

Paternal Radiation and Excess Deaths in Offspring: We can compare the results for all the persons whose fathers were irradiated, irrespective of the exposure of their mothers, with the results for the unexposed.

Deaths per 1,000 persons, for paternally exposed = 67.09
Deaths per 1,000 persons, for paternally unexposed = 63.09
Deaths per 1,000 person-years, for paternally exposed = 3.56
Deaths per 1,000 person-years, for paternally unexposed = 3.36

While in both tests (deaths per 1,000 persons and per 1,000 person-years) the tendency is toward a larger death rate for the offspring of exposed versus the offspring of unexposed, the differences, in this crude test that lumps all exposures together, cannot be proved significant at the 5% statistical level. However, Neel, Schull, and Kato performed and reported a careful statistical analysis by the regression method which takes size of dose into account, and which takes into account the mother's dose, year of birth, and sex of child.

It should be noted that rather large effects of birth year and sex of child were found. Whenever *several* variables in a study are "bouncing around," it becomes increasingly difficult to show a statistically significant difference in *one* variable (for instance, exposure of the father to radiation). We shall return to the reasons why the Japanese studies are unfavorable for testing for radiation-induced mutations. Indeed, in the face of the difficulties, it is all the more remarkable that Neel found a positive relationship between paternal radiation exposure and offspring death before age 17.

The Doubling Dose Suggested by This Study

We can appreciate why the Japanese data are far from ideal for demonstrating even a very serious effect of ionizing radiation on genes and chromosomes by first considering the doubling dose they suggest.

From the regression analysis of Neel and co-workers, the coefficient of regression for death within 17 years among live-born infants after paternal radiation was found to be 0.000029 per rem of exposure. This means that if 1 million fathers were exposed to 1 rad, there would be 29 deaths in their offspring by age 17 (for this Japanese population), if we assume that the value of 0.000029 holds up in further studies.

Now, what we are really interested in is the doubling dose for genetic and chromosomal mutations, or, expressed otherwise, in the percentage by which the spontaneous mutation rate is increased from 1 rad (or rem) of radiation. The study of deaths before age 17 serves to suggest the magnitude of this doubling dose, which is presumed to be about the same for a whole variety of dominant disorders, many, many times more numerous than the specific genetic injuries that lead to death by age 17.

Neel and co-workers admit that it is very difficult to know the spontaneous rate of new dominant mutations that cause death by age 17. Let us accept their values for spontaneous new mutations, 0.005 as the best value and 0.003 as the lowest value, and determine their implications. Also, we will use the correction of these rates recommended by Neel and co-workers for dealing with only *paternal* radiation. The corrected values for the spontaneous rates, according to Neel and co-workers, are 0.0025 as the best value, and 0.0015 as the lower limit, for the fraction of live-born infants who will die before maturity as a result of spontaneous mutation *in the father* in the immediately preceding generation.

So 2,500 per million will die before maturity as a result of spontaneous mutation in the father in the preceding generation. We stated above that the regression data led Neel and co-workers to an estimate that 29 deaths per million would occur per rem. The doubling dose would therefore be 2,500/29 = 86 rems, *if* Neel and co-workers' regression results hold up.

But let us look a little further at the true doses absorbed by the gonads. All the Neel, Kato, and Schull calculations are based on T-65 kerma dose in air, which is significantly different from absorbed dose to tissue. The correction from T-65 dose to dose received by the male gonads is probably not very different from the correction from T-65 dose to bone-marrow dose, or approximately 0.55. One must consider the direction of the gonads vis-à-vis the bomb radiation: in most cases the radiation would have had to penetrate the body before reaching the gonads. Certainly a reduction factor of 0.6 is not an exaggeration. Applying this factor to the estimate of 86 rems, we have the corrected value for gonadally absorbed dose = (0.6)(86) = 52 rems as the doubling dose for genetic and chromosomal effects.

Let us also take the value of 0.0015 suggested by Neel and co-workers as the lower limit of the spontaneous rate for paternal mutations. This corresponds to 1,500 spontaneous deaths before maturity per million. Dividing this by 29 deaths per million per rem, we get 1,500/29 = 52 rems as the doubling dose. Multiplying by 0.6 to correct for conversion from kerma dose to absorbed tissue dose, we arrive at (0.6)(52) = 31 rems as the lower limit for doubling dose based on the Neel, Kato, and Schull findings for paternal irradiation in the Hiroshima-Nagasaki data.

We agree with Neel, Kato, and Schull, who, referring to one of their own doubling-dose calculations, state that the estimation of the spontaneous rate is "the most vulnerable aspect of this calculation." And we do not overlook the fact that the finding of an effect from paternal irradiation is at the 5% level of statistical significance.

But the results from the Neel, Kato, and Schull studies are very different from the message being spread by certain special interests to the effect that the Japanese studies show that radiation has no effect in producing mutations in human beings. Instead of dismissing the grave effect found by Neel and co-workers, we should express it clearly as a serious warning to the human community about the possible magnitude of the effect of ionizing radiation in producing genetic and chromosomal mutations.

Problems with the Circumstances of This Study

Many people who think about "experiments" to ascertain the doubling dose for radiation erroneously believe that it ought to be easy to see an effect that doubles the spontaneous mutation rate, and to see it in the first generation. What they fail to realize is that there exists a large background of deaths present *in addition to* the deaths caused by new mutations. In postwar Japan the childhood death rate was high, no doubt due partially to conditions there and partially to the carry-over of spontaneous mutations built up in the population.

This large background of non-radiation-induced deaths hurts the Neel, Kato, and Schull study badly, because the relatively small number of extra deaths due to radiation-induced mutations cannot be proved statistically significant against this large background. So, even with a serious doubling dose like 52 rads, it is difficult, in the sample size used by Neel, Kato, and Schull, to demonstrate an effect.

THE PROBLEM OF RADIATION-INDUCED TRISOMIES IN HUMAN BEINGS

Trisomy formation is a very important phenomenon among human chromosomal errors; it exacts a high price in human suffering. And the information concerning its induction by radiation is neither clear nor consistent. There are reports of human studies that would indicate doubling doses for trisomy formation in the neighborhood of a few rads; there are others that would suggest that the doubling dose could not possibly be as low as 50 rads. We shall consider all the evidence.

Two Types of Trisomies

There are really two types of trisomies that concern us:

1. Trisomies occurring in mitotic cells
2. Trisomies occurring in meiotic cells

In our discussion of congenital anomalies (developing in utero), we referred to the formation of embryo mosaics, some of the cells of which have 46 chromosomes and some 47. Mosaicism can either have very widespread effects throughout the body of the developing embryo, or milder effects on a single region if mosaic formation occurs somewhat later in embryogenesis. We stated earlier in this chapter that such mosaics are formed post-zygotically (the fertilized ovum begins, correctly, with 46 chromosomes). Therefore, trisomic mosaic formation in embryogenesis (very likely of far greater importance than is now recognized) must be due to events occurring in mitotic, not meiotic, processes.

The information on mitotic nondisjunction, as related to radiation, is exceedingly thin, which is unfortunate. Nondisjunction may represent a major mechanism of radiation injury, particularly in the production of mosaic disomic/trisomic embryos in utero. Moreover, it may turn out that mitotic nondisjunction in a father's germ cells, as well as meiotic errors in the germ cells of either parent, can account for some totally trisomic embryos.

If a spermatogonial cell were to undergo a nondisjunction of one particular chromosome, it would produce one cell with 47 chromosomes and one with 45 chromosomes. Most experts in this field would insist that few, if any, of the cells with 45 chromosomes would survive if the missing chromosome were an autosome, and they may or may not be correct about this. But it is the other cell we are concerned with—the spermatogonial cell that acquired 47 chromosomes as a result of the nondisjunction. Such a cell could divide innumerable times while still a spermatogonial cell, and all its descendant cells would also have 47 chromosomes with one chromosome in trisomic form.

Sooner or later, these trisomic spermatogonial cells would go into meiosis, on the way to producing spermatozoa. We do not know at present of any reason why they would have particular difficulty in managing either the first or second meiotic division; on the other hand, remembering the inhibition of meiosis by translocations (discussed in section 4 of this chapter), we can speculate that trisomy might cause a similar problem. But if a trisomic spermatogonial cell were to complete meiosis successfully, half the resulting sperm would have 23 chromosomes and half would have 24 chromosomes. And if one of the sperm with 24 chromosomes should fertilize a normal ovum with 23 chromosomes, the result would be a totally trisomic embryo or individual, with 47 chromosomes in every cell.

Experimental Production of Trisomy in Mitotic Human Cells

Uchida and co-workers (1975) conducted experiments to ascertain the radiation-induced frequency of nondisjunction in mitotic cells, by using human lymphocytes in culture. The cells were irradiated in vitro (after removal from the body) by [137]Cesium gamma rays, at 29 roentgens/minute, for a total dose to the cells of 50 roentgens, which is approximately 50 rads. An additional purpose of these experiments was to determine whether the lymphocytes from the mothers or fathers of children with trisomy-21 were more likely to show nondisjunction than were the lymphocytes from controls matched for age and sex who had no family history of trisomy-21.

A higher frequency of hypermodal cells (with more than 46 chromosomes) was reportedly found in the irradiated cells (both from the parents of children with Down's syndrome and from the control parents) than in the unirradiated cells (also from both groups). The reported frequency of hypermodal cells was 29 out of 28,000 cells examined, or 0.1%, versus 0.025% in the unirradiated cells.

The same investigators also report that unirradiated lymphocytes put into irradiated blood serum showed the same frequency of hypermodal cells, 28/28,000. If the effect is real, it is indeed interesting. It might suggest that, via the blood serum, exposure to radiation can have a genetic impact even if the germ cells are not themselves irradiated. There is no doubt that chemically active radicals and other unstable, reactive molecules are produced by radiation, but before anyone goes off the deep end with the implications of the reported result (equal effect of irradiated serum and irradiated cells), the author thinks the result should be independently replicated.

With respect to the other purpose of this study, it turned out that the lymphocytes of neither the fathers nor the mothers of trisomy-21 children showed a greater "sensitivity" than did those of the control group. However, of the total number of 57 hypermodal cells examined, 12 of them came from 2 individuals; so $1/5$ of the hypermodal cells came from $1/14$ of the subjects. This evidence *suggests* that there may be some differences in the susceptibility of individuals to nondisjunction.

Considering the importance of this subject, one would hope that a large research effort would be made to pursue the interesting leads of Uchida and co-workers. The Uchida work, taken at face value, would indicate a 4-fold increase in somatic nondisjunction (0.1% versus 0.025%) from a dose of 50 rads. This is a 300% increase from 50 rads, or 6%/rad, which corresponds to a doubling dose of 16.7 rads. This would have severe implications for such phenomena as mosaic formation in utero as a base for congenital anomalies.

Maternal and Paternal Radiation and Trisomic Offspring

Fundamentally there are two ways in which we can search for a relationship, epidemiologically, between the radiation of parents and the development of a trisomy in their offspring.

The first is the retrospective method, the type of method used by Dr. Alice Stewart in demonstrating the association of maternal irradiation during pregnancy with cancer and leukemia in the offspring. Dr. Stewart compared the history (either verbal or recorded) of radiation exposure in the mothers of a group of children with cancer or leukemia, and the history of radiation exposure in the mothers of a group of matched control children. This method of study has been applied several times to the question of parental radiation and trisomy in offspring, with quite varying results.

The second way of studying the question is to compare the occurrence rate of trisomy in the offspring of parents whose radiation history has already been determined. This is the so-called prospective method. This method has also given mixed results.

Readers who have skipped chapter 14 on leukemia will want to refer to section 3 of that chapter, where the methods and pitfalls of retrospective and of prospective studies are compared.

Mother's Age and Spontaneous Rate of Occurrence of Down's Syndrome

By far the most common trisomy that gives rise to live-born infants is Down's syndrome, or mongolism, which shows trisomy of chromosome G-21. For trisomy-21, a pronounced effect of maternal age at the time of birth has been shown. Since this age effect may turn out to be an important variable in determining the possible role of radiation in inducing trisomy, it is important to appreciate it fully:

Maternal Age Group	Frequency of Down's Syndrome (data of Penrose and Smith 1966)
under 25 years	1 in 1,600 births
between 25 and 30 years	1 in 880 births
between 30 and 35 years	1 in 290 births
above 40 years	1 in 95 births

Stevenson and co-workers (1970) indicate that these age-related rates seem to be applicable all over the world for Down's syndrome.

The Retrospective and Prospective Studies of Uchida and Co-workers

The study that set off the controversy about the history of radiation exposure in the parent and mongolism in the offspring was the study of Uchida and Curtis in Canada in 1961. This retrospective study compared the history of radiation exposure in 81 mothers of children with Down's syndrome with the history of two "control" groups: the first was composed of mothers of children with cleft lips and palates, matched for economic background, place of residence, and maternal age; and the second was 71 mothers of neighboring children. Essentially this study was based on the mothers' recall of prior X-ray history. Significantly more mothers (actually 4 times as many) of Down's syndrome cases fell into the exposed category (4 or more medical X-ray exposures, or fluoroscopies, or both) than did mothers from either of the control groups.

But other studies were done in this general time period, some before the Uchida study. One study was Lunn's, done in Scotland (1959). It was based on interviews with the parents of 117 children with Down's syndrome, and with parents who had given birth to a live-born normal child in the same year. The results showed no significant difference between the mothers of Down's syndrome cases and control mothers: 30 of the Down's mothers versus 28 of the control mothers had a history of "significant X-ray exposure." Among the fathers, 6 of the Down's group and 12 of the control group had a history of "significant X-ray exposure." The difference for the fathers, which was not "statistically significant," was in an unexpected direction.

Carter and co-workers (1961), in England, also published a negative retrospective study, based on interviews of 51 mothers of children with Down's syndrome, and using mothers of children with congenital heart disease, congenitally dislocated hips, and central-nervous-system malformations as the control group. More of the *control* mothers showed a history of 4 or more X-rays or fluoroscopies than did mothers of the mongoloid children. However, the author of this book cannot take the Carter study seriously because the choice of control group was so poor. *All* the children of *all* the mothers suffered from injuries that may be radiation-inducible! Much more evidence is needed on the potential association between parental radiation history and the incidence of congenital anomalies such as those studied by Carter. One must consider the possibility that radiation may have been as heavily involved in the problems of the control group as in the trisomy-21 group (if at all, in either group), and possibly even more heavily involved.

All this controversy prompted Uchida and her colleagues to undertake a prospective study, in an attempt to eliminate objections about the goodness of the recall of pre-pregnancy exposure to radiation by the mothers in the retrospective study, a problem Uchida freely admitted should be of concern.

In the prospective study of Uchida and colleagues (1968), the irradiated subjects were chosen by searching the files of the department of radiology of the Winnipeg General Hospital for all married women under 60 years of age who had had abdominal radiological examinations. Out of an initial 6,062 women, 2,200 women were finally located and interviewed. And finally, based on the interviews, the number was reduced to 861 mothers. One must presume, if the studies are to be taken seriously, that no bias was introduced in going from the 6,062 potential subjects to the 861 who "survived" the initial screening.

Part of the interview procedure was designed to discover any X-ray exposure additional to that received at the Winnipeg Hospital. Uchida and co-workers did attempt to check out the records of extra-hospital exposures.

The 861 irradiated mothers included in the study provided 972 offspring for the post-irradiation group, and there were 972 offspring in the control group. Some of the control children were children of unirradiated mothers, and many were the *pre*-irradiation children of the mothers whose *post*-irradiation children were in the other group. No pre-irradiation child served as a control for his own post-irradiation sibling, however; control children were matched according to the age of their mothers when they were conceived.

While the selection procedure for the controls was not simple in this study, it does not appear that any appreciable bias was introduced at this stage, although this is an admittedly tricky area. However, the author of this book finds some additional information provided by Uchida and co-workers to be disturbing in this regard:

Six cases of clinically diagnosed Down's Syndrome were omitted from the study (1 born after the 1965 time limit, 2 mothers not available for or refused interview, 3 [cases] allocated to control group but interview revealed previous radiation exposure of mother). Three of these were proven trisomic [by karyotyping]. (p. 1048)

We shall return to this information shortly.

The findings from this study are summarized in table 30.

The difference in offspring with chromosome trisomies between the irradiated mothers and the unirradiated mothers was statistically significant.

TABLE 30: NORMAL AND ABNORMAL BIRTHS IN POST-IRRADIATION AND CONTROL GROUPS (THE WINNIPEG STUDY)*

Classification of Offspring (normal or abnormal)	Children from Post-irradiation Mothers	Children from Control Mothers
Apparently normal	892	889
Stillbirths	20	34
Neonatal deaths	18	19
Congenital anomalies	31	29
Chromosomal aberrations	11	1
Totals	**972**	**972**

*Uchida and co-workers.

Of the chromosomal aberrations, clinical diagnosis of trisomy was made in 10 of the post-irradiation children. Of these 10, 8 were clinically Down's syndrome and 2 were clinically trisomy-18 (see section 1).

The difference in stillbirth frequencies between irradiated and control mothers was significant at the p = 0.05 level, and the direction was opposite to that for the trisomies. One might seriously doubt that the radiation protected against stillbirths. More likely this is a lesson about the small numbers of cases in small-scale prospective studies. And that lesson should be considered to apply also to the positive results for the trisomy cases here. The statistics of small numbers can be treacherous.

The difference in stillbirth frequencies between irradiated and control mothers was significant at the p = 0.05 level, and the direction was opposite to that for the trisomies. One might seriously doubt that the radiation protected against stillbirths. More likely this is a lesson about the small numbers of cases in small-scale prospective studies. And that lesson should be considered to apply also to the positive results for the trisomy cases here. The statistics of small numbers can be treacherous.

Of those with karyotyping proof of trisomy, the values were 7 cases and 0 cases, respectively.

However, we are dealing with numbers of cases only as large as 7, 10, and 11 after 6 cases of clinically diagnosed Down's syndrome were thrown out of the study. One always should worry when reasons are found for throwing out such a high proportion of the data.

From the author's long experience in handling such material and in observing other scientists handling it, he knows of the subtle, probably unrecognized and unintended biases that can be introduced. One must wonder just how unbiased the procedure was when 3 control mothers with Down's syndrome children demonstrated in later interviews that they had received significant radiation exposure. Uchida and colleagues may well have made this exclusion with perfect justification. Nevertheless, the author of this book is concerned about it.

Percent Increase per Rad: Taking the studies at face value and as unbiased, we can go on to examine the doses of radiation received by the women who gave birth to the 11 children with chromosomal aberrations. The gonadal dose was estimated by Dr. M.K. Kiernan, radiologist at Winnipeg General Hospital, for various types of examinations, and from these estimates, plus the examination record of the mothers, the gonadal doses were estimated for those who gave birth later to trisomic children.

One must always wonder if a few cases who received an *abnormally* high radiation dose account for much of the result. These data show that problem did not occur, and are reassuring on that account. From Table II of the original paper, it is possible to estimate that the mean gonadal dose to the 972 mothers who constitute the "irradiated" group was 1.335 rads. No estimate was provided for the dose to the "unirradiated" group; let us assume it was essentially negligible compared to 1.335 rads. From table 30, the O/E value is 11.0, which means there was a % excess occurrence of chromosome aberrations of 1,000% from a mean dose of 1.335 rads, or 749% per rad. (If the mean dose to the "unirradiated" group were more than zero, the % excess per rad would be even higher.)

This is an astronomical value, as far as radiation effects go. Even if we were to assume that more chromosome aberrations truly occurred in the *control* group than were perceived, and even if we were to raise the 1 case in the control group to 5 cases on the assumption that 4 were "missed" in this statistical sampling—and the author would not play fast and loose with the data in that way—even then the O/E ratio would be 11/5 or 2.20. That would be an excess of 120% from 1.34 rads, or 89.6% per rad, which is still a very high value.

This sort of % excess per rad for chromosome aberrations, the large majority of which are trisomy formations, stretches this author's imagination quite a bit. It is not possible to say that the result is *wrong;* it is simply hard to believe. Therefore, one would want to look very carefully for possible biases and one would seek a great deal of independent confirmation.

There are those who are always critical of this type of study on the grounds that possibly the women who are "constitutionally" disposed to have mongoloid or other trisomic children are also "constitutionally" disposed to develop illnesses in the years before conceiving their abnormal children, such illnesses requiring much X-ray diagnostic exposure. This criticism cannot be ruled out.

Maternal Age and Radiation Exposure in Producing Trisomy: The variation in risk of having a Down's syndrome child with maternal age was discussed above. From the Penrose-Smith data, for women 40 years or older at the time of conceiving, the rate is 1 mongoloid child per 95 births, or 10.5 cases per 1,000. In the Uchida series 5 children with chromosomal aberrations were born to 81 irradiated women over 40 years of age, a rate of 61.7 cases per 1,000.

Even if one case was not a trisomy-21, it appears that the over-40 group with the irradiation history showed an excess over expectancy. Although the numbers are somewhat small for one to be able to place much confidence in them, Uchida and co-workers point out that the apparently larger effect of prior irradiation of mothers who became pregnant after 40 years of age is consistent with their *earlier* findings (in their retrospective study). Another study (Alberman and co-workers), which we shall also review, also shows this relationship of the interaction of radiation and maternal age at pregnancy.

The Retrospective and Prospective Studies of Stevenson and Co-workers

In an early study, Stevenson and co-workers, at Oxford, found a negative result for radiation association with Down's syndrome, based on the retrospective questioning of 197 mothers of Down's syndrome children and matched controls. This report was of course at variance with the positive retrospective results of Uchida and co-workers. The positive results in the Uchida *prospective* study stimulated Stevenson and colleagues to do a prospective study of their own (1970).

From a search of X-ray registers, 3,267 women were ascertained to have had one of several types of X-ray examinations. Finally this search yielded 630 mothers who bore a total of 1,052 live-born children after they received radiation. The best estimate of the mean dose to their ovaries was approximately 0.9 rads.

Three trisomy-21 children with clinical mongolism were found in the birth group. Using the maternal ages and the number of mothers at each maternal age, plus the Penrose and Smith spontaneous frequencies of trisomy-21 by maternal age, Stevenson and co-workers estimated that there should have been 2.14 mongoloids among their children if there had been *no* radiation effect. Stevenson acknowledges that the series he and his colleagues report is too small to be definitive, and that they cannot deny the findings of Uchida and co-workers. The Stevenson findings could be consistent, statistically, with as much as a 2- or 3-fold higher rate of trisomies in the children of irradiated mothers than in those of unirradiated mothers.

The "Collaborative Project": A Retrospective Study by Marmol and Co-workers

Some sixteen institutions pooled their data in a retrospective evaluation of radiation dose to the mothers of 61 mongoloid infants. These women were part of a group of 55,932 pregnant women who registered for prenatal care at these institutions. From the same group a matched control group of 224 mothers of normal children was also formed.

The estimate of radiation exposure was quite crude. It was based only on the mother's interview recollection of X-ray procedures, not on any radiology records. Only abdominal and pelvic X-ray procedures were considered.

The results were as follows: 61 mothers of Down's syndrome children reported 37 X-ray procedures; and 224 mothers of normal children reported 97 X-ray procedures. Conversion to X-ray procedures per 1,000 shows that for the mothers of the Down's syndrome cases the rate was 606 procedures per 1,000, whereas for the mothers of normal children the rate was 433 procedures per 1,000. The direction of these data is consistent with a causal relationship between X-ray exposure and the risk of bearing a mongoloid child. However, the numbers are so small that, by itself, this study provides no confirmation at the 5% level of statistical significance. Marmol and co-workers (1969) are correct in their modest conclusion: "However, we must emphasize that it would be inappropriate to construe these data as conclusive evidence that such factors [as ionizing radiation exposure] may not play an important role in the etiology of Down's syndrome" (p. 542).

An Aggregation of Small Studies

The author must comment on the meaning of a series of studies, many of which give results in a single direction, but which individually are too small to provide statistically significant results. If one finds a whole series of studies consistent in one direction, and the various studies allow only for conclusions with probability values of 0.1 or 0.2, it is important to remember that combining these studies can itself provide a result of higher statistical significance than any of the individual studies can provide.

The Johns Hopkins Retrospective Studies by Sigler and Co-workers

In a carefully conducted and well-described study, Sigler and his colleagues (1965) reported a large retrospective study of 216 cases of Down's syndrome and 216 matched controls. The study is notable for its demonstration that the "recall" of the mothers or fathers could not possibly have influenced the results, since their "recall" was tested against hospital records, and this was done "blind" as far as the investigators themselves were concerned while the study was in progress.

The final conclusion of the study (the details of which we shall examine) was as follows:

The conclusion derived from the present study is that Mongolism is statistically associated with maternal radiation. The likelihood that the radiation association is a causal relationship is considerably enhanced by the evidence—experimental and other kinds— which has already been reviewed. (p. 396)

And, separately:

It should therefore be emphasized that although a causal interpretation does not mean radiation must be implicated in every case, the results do suggest that certain physical energy sources, such as ionizing radiation, are involved in the pathogenesis of some cases of Mongolism. (p. 396)

The results of this study vary according to the type of radiation exposure (diagnostic, fluoroscopic, and therapeutic).

Employment in Medicine or with Radar: Occupational exposure was also considered as a possible source. It did turn out that 7.9% of the mothers of children with Down's syndrome worked in a professional or technical capacity in medical fields, whereas only 3.3% of the mothers of control children had such a work record. The difference proved to be significant at the $p = 0.05$ level.

One unexpected finding came out of the occupational-exposure interview data for the fathers of the Down's syndrome cases. There was no relationship of paternal participation in a medical occupation with the frequency of Down's syndrome offspring, but there was a relationship, significant at the 2% level, between frequency of Down's syndrome offspring and father's intimate contact with radar, in and out of the armed forces. Eighteen of the 216 fathers of Down's syndrome children had such contact, whereas 7 of the 216 fathers of control children had such contact. If this association between paternal exposure to radar and mongoloid children is confirmed by further testing, accounting for it will be an interesting challenge. As noted in chapter 2, radar radiation is definitely not energetic enough per photon to produce ionization.

The Magnitude of the Maternal Ionizing-Radiation Effect: There is clearly a statistically significant relationship between the mothers' exposure to ionizing radiation in the past and the bearing of Down's syndrome children, in the study by Sigler and co-workers. Less subject to evaluation are the quantitative aspects of the relationship. Both fluoroscopy and therapy *can* represent doses one or more orders of magnitude greater than diagnostic radiation. So it is possible that we are dealing with doses in the tens of rads and possibly higher. But since there are no measurements available for any of the doses in the Sigler studies, we are not able to present any quantitative analysis of the risk of having a Down's syndrome child as a result of radiation exposure, aside from the statement that the risk is enhanced if the exposure involves fluoroscopy or therapy.

The British Studies of Alberman and Co-workers at Guy's Hospital

Alberman and colleagues published twin papers (both in 1972) on two important aspects of the association of radiation with genetic-chromosomal lesions in offspring. One paper deals with the relationship of maternal radiation history to the chromosomal abnormalities found in spontaneous abortions, and the other, with the relationship of maternal radiation history to the chance of bearing a Down's syndrome child. Some positive effects were found in both studies, although they were thin in the study of Down's syndrome. Still, the consistency between the two studies would appear to lend additional credibility to the relationship of low-dose radiation to genetic-chromosomal effects.

The findings on Down's syndrome, in addition to supporting the importance of maternal age as a factor in general, seem to confirm Uchida's results—that for mothers over age 40, a very large effect of radiation is an increase in the risk of having a Down's syndrome child. The results, although inconclusive, are certainly suggestive and deserve further testing.

The results of studies on the relationship of radiation exposure to chromosomal abnormalities in spontaneously aborted fetuses are quite striking; they demonstrate an increasing incidence of abnormalities with higher radiation exposures. In a breakdown of abnormalities by type, the largest number of cases involved autosomal trisomies, followed by X-chromosome monosomy and triploid embryos. Like the Sigler and Uchida studies, the Alberman studies on chromosomally aborted fetuses are consistent with large effects from very small doses, of 100 to several hundred millirads to the ovaries, delivered years earlier than the pregnancy.

The Hiroshima-Nagasaki Studies of Schull and Neel

Probably the strongest negative study of the possible association of ionizing radiation with nondisjunction and the development of trisomy-21, or clinical Down's syndrome, is the prospective study by Schull and Neel (1962) of the Hiroshima and Nagasaki survivors.

These workers report that during the period between 1948 and 1954, 76,628 infants born to survivors of the atomic bombing were examined shortly after birth. Schull and Neel acknowledge that, in this very early examination, some cases of Down's syndrome may have been missed. However, 21,788 infants had a second examination about nine months after birth, and Schull and Neel's report on Down's syndrome is based on this second examination, at the time of which, they presume, greater accuracy of diagnosis could have been achieved. We shall return to this issue of diagnostic accuracy after examining the data, for all is not necessarily straightforward where the Japanese data are concerned.

Schull and Neel present the data for the occurrence of Down's syndrome as a function of *maternal* radiation exposure, utilizing only those matings where the father was *not* exposed, for this analysis. They present the following results:

	Mother Unexposed	Mother Exposed	Total
Number of Children, Normal	9,440	5,579	15,019
Number of Children, Down's Syndrome	12	3	15
Total Number of Children	9,452	5,582	15,034
Down's Syndrome Frequency per 1,000 Children	1.27	0.54	1.00

The findings of Schull and Neel show *fewer* cases per 1,000 persons in the exposed group (0.54) than in the unexposed group (1.27), although this difference is at the borderline of significance. But it is clear that there was certainly no *excess* of Down's syndrome cases in the exposed group of Schull and Neel.

In view of the enormous effect suggested by the other studies from just a few hundred millirads, the immediate question is, naturally, what was the dose to the exposed mothers in the Japanese study?

By *exposed* Schull and Neel simply mean (and we quote their exact words) "present in the city at the time of the bombings." At the time they published their paper, in 1962, they referred to the estimation of the dose as "so far insurmountable." They speculated that the possible dose to the "exposed" was "very roughly" 36 rads, without a correction from kerma to absorbed dose. After making this correction, and adjusting doses per more recent data from Beebe, Kato, and Land (1978), we can estimate that the corrected absorbed mean gonadal dose to the population of individuals characterized as exposed (by Schull and Neel's definition) was 16.1 rads. This is hardly different from the original Schull-Neel "very rough" estimate, when that estimate is corrected from kerma to absorbed dose.

On the other hand, as the reader can ascertain for himself, a great deal of the average dose to the exposed group was contributed by those mothers who were in the two highest dose groups. For the purpose of illustrating a scientific point only, let us suppose that the mothers in the two highest dose groups did not—or could not—reproduce at all. In that event, it would be absurd to include these dose categories in a calculation of the average dose. In reality, reproduction rates per dose group could have ranged from total nonreproduction to more-than-average reproduction. If one were trying accurately to assess the true dose to the exposed mothers who brought their children in for the second examination, it would be essential to know in this study whether the high-dose groups contributed the same number of off-spring per 100 mothers as did the low-dose groups.

Of course, such information would not resolve the large discrepancy with respect to Down's syndrome between the Schull-Neel study and the studies by Uchida, Sigler, Marmol, and Alberman. For even if all the children of exposed mothers belonged to mothers who were in the lowest dose groups, the average dose would still be far higher in Japan than in the positive studies.

Could it turn out that the magnitude of the Japanese dose would actually account in some way for the negative results with respect to Down's syndrome? And were all the children examined either "normal" or "Down's," or was there also a class of children (not reported) with *other* kinds of abnormalities?

We cannot answer these questions. We can only report that there is an obvious discrepancy between the Japanese study on Down's syndrome and several others. It is interesting to note that the Japanese data yield the lowest effects per rad of ionizing radiation, compared with other studies, not only on Down's syndrome but also on cancer induction overall, and on cancer induction in those exposed in utero. What this trend means is simply not clear at this time.

The final question one must ask about the negative Schull-Neel study of Down's syndrome is, are there any reasons why we should be skeptical about their study? There are some reasons why we *must* be skeptical about their data. It may be that their ostensibly negative result should be given much less weight than the studies already reported here.

Reasons for Caution: Just as the author of this book worries about a possible bias operating in Uchida's positive prospective study, so does he worry about a possible bias operating in the negative Schull-Neel study. There is good reason to wonder whether, on that second examination nine months after birth, a truly unbiased sample of exposed ("present in the city") mothers brought their children in for examination.

It is very well known that in Japan there is a social stigma attached to having been irradiated in the atom-bombing. Whether that stigma operated in the early years of 1948–1954, when the Schull-Neel data were collected, is not clear, but we must surely consider this, and insist on receiving some rather good assurance from Schull and Neel that this was not the case.

Sztanyik (1978) recently commented on the prejudice that would cause people not to wish to register themselves as *hibakusha* (meaning A-bomb survivors). A mother who was in the city at the time of the bombing *and* who had an abnormal child would probably have been especially concerned about being stigmatized. One must wonder if she would appear at an official agency to show her abnormal child.

This could constitute a severe potential bias toward Schull and Neel *missing* cases of Down's syndrome children born to the exposed mothers. If this bias truly operated on their data, it could have obscured an appreciable excess of Down's syndrome cases. It is interesting that Schull and Neel did not address this serious question.

In addition to that concern, we must again be very concerned about diagnosis in the early period after the bombing, in the cases where the dose to the mother was high. We have previously analyzed the Kato data on children exposed in utero and found a severe and bizarre effect, highly significant statistically. The effect was such that if the dose to the mother was high, there was a low chance of diagnosing the reason for infant death, whereas if the dose to the mother was low, this difficulty did not exist. This exceedingly strange finding may suggest some sort of socio-cultural problem in families who both received a high radiation dose and bore an abnormal or ill child. Whether this effect carried over to 1948–1954, we do not know. It may, however, have become a more serious problem with time, rather than a less serious one.

Because these serious unanswered questions exist in the Hiroshima-Nagasaki study, it would certainly be unjustifiable to conclude that the study provides strong counterevidence for the association of ionizing radiation of the mother with the development of Down's syndrome in the offspring.

Summary on Down's Syndrome

Overall, the existence of and the magnitude of any causal relationship between radiation of the mother and Down's syndrome in later offspring must remain moot. The various studies have been presented. There are problems with just about every one of them. None can be considered definitive. We must leave open the possibility that numerical chromosome aberrations, such as trisomy-21, may yet be conclusively shown to increase appreciably with each rad of maternal radiation.

Some of the data suggest that there may be a co-action between maternal age and radiation in the past. It is unfortunate, in addition to its other defects, that the Schull and Neel report makes no breakdown of mothers by maternal age and radiation.

One reminder: in the human female, by the time of her own birth, all the oocytes that will later give rise to ova have already gone into the early stages of the first meiotic division. Therefore, any radiation effect in adulthood would be an effect on meiotic cells, not mitotic cells. In contrast, in the adult male, effects on spermatogonial cells are primarily mitotic effects, since these cells persist throughout fertility as cells with 46 chromosomes and undergo many, many mitotic divisions before going to meiosis. With respect to numerical chromosomal aberrations such as trisomy-21, none of the evidence suggests any effect of paternal ionizing radiation exposure.

Section 7: An Alternative Explanation for Irregularly Inherited Disorders

---

A little historical perspective nudges the author into presenting an alternative hypothesis to explain the irregularly inherited diseases (section 5)—an alternative that does not require the unwarranted assumptions often made in this field.

THE BIGGER PICTURE COULD LITERALLY NOT BE SEEN

Mendelian inheritance was extensively studied long before 1950, and by 1953, Watson and Crick had published their now-classic description of the chemical and physico-chemical nature of DNA, the chemical which is essentially the gene. Recessive and dominant diseases, explained on the basis of gene behavior, were described in all college genetics courses. Today, McKusick (1978) lists over 700 diseases as autosomal dominant diseases, most of which are thought to be single-gene diseases. Their frequency is estimated to be 10,000 per million live births. And for each of the separate single-gene diseases, the average estimated "spontaneous" mutation rate is thought to be in the range of 1 in 100,000 to 1 in 1,000,000 (UNSCEAR 1977, p. 520).

But 100 years before Watson and Crick discovered the nature of the gene, Seguin (1846) published his first monograph describing a syndrome called *lowland cretinism,* to distinguish it from the disorder *cretinism,* which was endemic in the Swiss Alps due to thyroid deficiency. His second monograph in English was published the same year as J. H. Langdon Down's article (1866) on the same syndrome, which has now come to bear his name in most quarters. But at the time of the enormously sophisticated studies by Watson and Crick on the gene and DNA, the cause of Down's syndrome still remained a mystery.

In the early 1950s certain technical developments were occurring which were to revolutionize an area of hereditary research in which very little progress had been made, namely, the study of the chromosomes. Two technical discoveries made it possible to do enormously better studies of human chromosomes. First, there was the use of a mitotic inhibitor, such as colchicine, to arrest cells in the metaphase, when chromosomes are most easily studied. And second, there was the fortunate discovery that lowering the salt content of solutions bathing mitotic cells would swell them so that the chromosomes became better separated. By 1956, these advances made it possible for Tjio and Levan to establish conclusively for the first time that the diploid number per cell in the normal human being is 46 chromosomes.

Within just three years, thanks to the new techniques permitting investigators to count chromosomes, Lejeune and co-workers in France, and Jacobs and co-workers in England, discovered an extra chromosome in patients with Down's syndrome. These were the discoveries (1959) which led to the knowledge of trisomies. Down's syndrome, of course, is trisomy-21. It occurs everywhere in the world. By itself it accounts for between 1,000 and 1,250 cases per million live births. Thus, in the United States, and probably in many other countries, a single hereditary disorder—a trisomy —is responsible for as many cases per million live births as *all recessive disorders put together,* or for as many cases per million live births as *one-tenth of all 700 dominant diseases combined.*

What Does All This Have to Do with the Irregularly Inherited Diseases?

Among the features of the irregularly inherited disorders and diseases which are said to be hard to account for are (1) the high frequency of their occurrence in the population, and (2) the lack of a dominant mode of inheritance.

Why do we not take a leaf from the book of experience with Down's syndrome, and look at the chromosome side of the picture, where we observe events with frequencies like 1 per 100 (in mothers over 40 years of age) and 1 per 1,000? These rates are about 1,000-fold higher than the estimated de novo mutation rates for the separate diseases thought to be single-gene diseases.

And a likely place to look would be at the two chromosomal lesions, deletions and translocations. We know full well that deletions of huge chunks of major chromosomes cannot be what we are looking for, since if these were present, and explained many of the irregularly inherited diseases, this would most likely have been noted some time ago. But that in no way argues against deletions (and possibly small translocations also) as a potential cause of many of these disorders. The technique and technology for testing this concept have just not been available or applied.

Could Translocations and Small Deletions Be Consistent with the Evidence?

First of all, we must emphasize that the measured deletions and translocations must be a very small part of those which actually occur. Thus, when Bender and Gooch (1962) report a frequency of deletions of 1.1 per 1,000 cells per roentgen of radiation, they are reporting the deletions they can observe under the microscope *grossly*. Deletions of 1% to 10% of chromosome-arm length simply would not have been picked up in those studies, nor would small interstitial deletions, no matter where on the chromosome they occurred. So the author feels confident that deletions cannot be ruled out, on the basis of a too low frequency, as an explanation for the irregularly inherited diseases.

The true frequency of deletions per rad remains unknown. For translocations in germ cells, again where small aberrations are not even noted, we have the Brewen-Preston (1975) estimate of 3 to 17 rads as the doubling dose for human beings, a very low doubling dose indeed. The true frequency of translocations, as previously discussed, is undoubtedly higher than measured.

A small deletion *is* a polygene change. And from case to case of a deletion in a single chromosome, the clinical picture might very well not be "neat," since the variation in the size of the deletion would mean variation in the number of genes lost, which could result in variation in clinical features among patients.

Nondominant transmission—namely, to fewer than one-half the off-spring—is not a problem if we try explaining the irregularly inherited diseases by deletions or translocations. Although we know next to nothing about possible filtering out of injuries in the female germ cells, we are well aware of the filtration occurring in various stages of spermatogenesis, fertilization, and implantation, all of which can operate to decrease the fraction of offspring with the disorder below the 50% expected for the "dominant diseases." And for any particular disease, the filtration rate could vary from individual to individual according to the severity of the chromosomal injury.

WHY WOULD IT BE IMPORTANT TO KNOW THE MECHANISM?

It is always important, of course, to understand mechanisms for reasons intrinsic to human knowledge. But in this instance, the implications of understanding particular mechanisms are very great for the integrity of the human genetic-chromosomal heritage. So long as committees persist in assuming, without any proof, that the largest categories of human heritable diseases do not have more than a 5% "mutational component," we have a built-in *reduction factor of 20* in the possible hazard from ionizing radiation. If the committees can ever provide some evidence for their position, that would be fine. But the naked assumption, with a possible 20-fold denigration of radiation hazard, should not be taken lightly by the public.

HOW SCIENTISTS GENERALLY THINK

It would be fair to state that scientists, with some exceptions, generally think in a manner controlled by the techniques and technologies available to them at a given time. The reason given by scientists for eschewing any other thinking is that it is a waste of time, since it is not subject to experiment. Now, there is some merit in that thinking, since it is true that one cannot experiment without the requisite tools. But occasionally, thinking outside the currently available techniques may help provide the breakthroughs that make new techniques available.

It is absolutely fantastic that a technique permitting us merely to *count* the number of chromosomes in a human cell accurately did not materialize until 1956. Yet, with that technique available, three short years later, the causation of a disorder equal in impact to all recessive diseases combined, or to one-tenth of the autosomal dominant diseases combined, was identified as a disorder involving one too many chromosomes.

Today scientists scoff at the importance of small deletions. Such deletions are hardly ever mentioned, even though they involve tens or hundreds of genes at a time. Why? The techniques for studying small deletions in a quantitative way are not yet well developed. It seems to this author that scientists should think about the anomalous situation in the early 1950s, when the most elegant, sophisticated ideas of the structure of the gene were being effectively explored by Watson and Crick, because X-ray diffraction was by then very well developed—while at the same time, in the field of genetics, one could not even *count* the chromosomes that carry essentially all the human genes.

APPENDIX

TABLE A1 : SPONTANEOUS AND RADIATION-INDUCED CANCER DEATHS AT VARIOUS AGES FOR IRRADIATION WITH 1 RAD WHOLE-BODY RADIATION AT SPECIFIED AGE (MALES)

PART A: IRRADIATION AT 0 YEARS OF AGE (100,000 PERSONS)

Age (years)	Spontaneous Cancer Deaths	Cancer Deaths Induced by 1 Rad at Age 0	Age (years)	Spontaneous Cancer Deaths	Cancer Deaths Induced by 1 Rad at Age 0
1	6.2	0.0	38	36.2	15.9
2	6.2	0.0	39	41.0	18.4
3	6.4	0.0	40	46.5	21.2
4	6.7	0.0	41	51.4	23.5
5	6.9	0.0	42	56.3	25.2
6	6.9	0.0	43	68.9	30.3
7	6.9	0.0	44	80.5	34.6
8	6.7	0.0	45	91.0	38.7
9	6.4	0.0	46	105.0	43.7
10	5.7	0.052	47	112.5	45.2
11	5.4	0.098	48	127	49.9
12	5.3	0.145	49	142	53.3
13	5.6	0.204	50	160	56.4
14	6.1	0.276	51	175	58.4
15	6.4	0.383	52	191	59.5
16	7.0	0.545	53	212	61.0
17	7.3	0.634	54	237	62.9
18	7.8	0.786	55	266	65.8
19	8.4	0.901	56	293	67.2
20	8.7	1.12	57	316	66.4
21	9.2	1.39	58	349	65.2
22	9.6	1.61	59	379	64.0
23	9.9	1.86	60	410	61.9
24	10.5	2.20	61	436	55.8
25	11.0	2.53	62	460	52.5
26	11.5	2.84	63	491	49.6
27	12.1	3.22	64	513	44.5
28	12.9	3.71	65	532	41.3
29	13.3	4.15	66	556	33.0
30	14.5	4.83	67	570	26.0
31	15.2	5.34	68	590	21.6
32	16.9	6.32	69	606	16.6
33	18.9	7.43	70	621	11.4
34	21.7	8.72	71	626	5.7
35	24.5	10.2	72	631	0
36	27.7	11.8	73	632	0
37	30.9	13.3	74	628	0

TABLE.A1 (CONTINUED) (MALES)

PART A: IRRADIATION AT 0 YEARS OF AGE (100,000 PERSONS)

Age (years)	Spontaneous Cancer Deaths	Cancer Deaths Induced by 1 Rad at Age 0	Age (years)	Spontaneous Cancer Deaths	Cancer Deaths Induced by 1 Rad at Age 0
75	615	0	83	358	0
76	601	0	84	316	0
77	579	0	85	279	0
78	557	0	86	236	0
79	531	0	87	195	0
80	502	0	88	155	0
81	451	0	89	113	0
82	403	0	90	74	0

PART B: IRRADIATION AT 5 YEARS OF AGE (98,002 PERSONS)

Age (years)	Spontaneous Cancer Deaths	Cancer Deaths Induced by 1 Rad at Age 5	Age (years)	Spontaneous Cancer Deaths	Cancer Deaths Induced by 1 Rad at Age 5
6	6.86	0	30	14.46	2.29
7	6.85	0	31	15.18	2.57
8	6.66	0	32	16.86	3.10
9	6.36	0	33	18.90	3.76
10	5.67	0	34	21.69	4.62
11	5.38	0	35	24.47	5.51
12	5.28	0	36	27.70	6.62
13	5.57	0	37	30.92	7.76
14	6.05	0.04	38	36.24	9.31
15	6.44	0.08	39	41.01	10.91
16	7.02	0.12	40	46.45	12.63
17	7.31	0.17	41	51.39	14.08
18	7.78	0.23	42	56.30	15.76
19	8.35	0.32	43	68.93	19.71
20	8.72	0.43	44	80.52	23.51
21	9.19	0.51	45	91.00	26.57
22	9.55	0.61	46	105.00	30.03
23	9.92	0.72	47	112.5	31.50
24	10.48	0.86	48	126.9	34.77
25	11.03	1.06	49	142.1	38.65
26	11.49	1.24	50	160.3	42.64
27	12.14	1.46	51	174.8	44.92
28	12.88	1.73	52	191.4	48.04
29	13.33	1.95	53	211.7	50.60

PART B: IRRADIATION AT 5 YEARS OF AGE (98,002 PERSONS)

Age (years)	Spontaneous Cancer Deaths	Cancer Deaths Induced by 1 Rad at Age 5	Age (years)	Spontaneous Cancer Deaths	Cancer Deaths Induced by 1 Rad at Age 5
54	237.4	53.42	73	632.1	11.06
55	266.2	56.70	74	628.3	7.35
56	293.4	58.39	75	614.9	3.57
57	316.2	58.18	76	600.5	0.0
58	348.9	58.96	77	579.1	0.0
59	378.5	59.80	78	556.8	0.0
60	410.0	59.86	79	530.7	0.0
61	435.6	58.37	80	501.6	0.0
62	460.3	55.24	81	450.6	0.0
63	490.8	53.01	82	403.0	0.0
64	512.5	49.20	83	358.3	0.0
65	532.0	43.62	84	316.4	0.0
66	555.7	40.55	85	278.8	0.0
67	569.5	36.45	86	235.8	0.0
68	589.7	32.43	87	195.4	0.0
69	605.9	30.05	88	154.9	0.0
70	620.8	23.59	89	112.6	0.0
71	625.6	18.27	90	73.9	0.0
72	631.2	14.77			

PART C: IRRADIATION AT 10 YEARS OF AGE (97,801 PERSONS)

Age (years)	Spontaneous Cancer Deaths	Cancer Deaths Induced by 1 Rad at Age 10	Age (years)	Spontaneous Cancer Deaths	Cancer Deaths Induced by 1 Rad at Age 10
11	5.38	0	26	11.49	0.36
12	5.28	0	27	12.14	0.44
13	5.57	0	28	12.88	0.53
14	6.05	0	29	13.33	0.61
15	6.44	0	30	14.45	0.78
16	7.02	0	31	15.18	0.91
17	7.30	0	32	16.85	1.13
18	7.78	0	33	18.90	1.42
19	8.35	0.03	34	21.69	1.78
20	8.72	0.06	35	24.47	2.15
21	9.19	0.09	36	27.70	2.63
22	9.55	0.12	37	30.91	3.18
23	9.92	0.16	38	36.25	4.02
24	10.48	0.22	39	41.00	4.88
25	11.03	0.31	40	46.45	5.85

TABLE A1 (CONTINUED) (MALES)

PART C: IRRADIATION AT 10 YEARS OF AGE (97,801 PERSONS)

Age (years)	Spontaneous Cancer Deaths	Cancer Deaths Induced by 1 Rad at Age 10	Age (years)	Spontaneous Cancer Deaths	Cancer Deaths Induced by 1 Rad at Age 10
41	51.39	6.89	66	556.1	41.71
42	56.27	7.88	67	569.5	38.16
43	68.91	9.85	68	589.7	35.38
44	80.50	11.91	69	605.9	32.72
45	91.03	13.84	70	620.8	28.56
46	105.04	16.07	71	625.5	25.65
47	112.5	17.55	72	631.2	22.72
48	126.9	20.31	73	632.1	19.60
49	142.1	23.16	74	628.3	17.59
50	160.3	26.13	75	614.7	12.91
51	174.8	28.00	76	601.1	9.62
52	191.3	28.94	77	579.1	7.53
53	211.7	32.39	78	556.8	5.46
54	237.4	36.08	79	530.6	3.45
55	266.3	39.41	80	501.2	1.65
56	293.4	41.96	81	451.3	0.0
57	316.2	44.27	82	403.4	0.0
58	348.9	46.75	83	358.2	0.0
59	378.2	47.65	84	316.5	0.0
60	410.2	48.81	85	278.8	0.0
61	435.6	48.35	86	235.8	0.0
62	460.3	47.41	87	195.4	0.0
63	491.0	46.65	88	154.9	0.0
64	512.5	45.10	89	112.6	0.0
65	532.1	43.63	90	73.9	0.0

PART D: IRRADIATION AT 15 YEARS OF AGE (97,586 PERSONS)

Age (years)	Spontaneous Cancer Deaths	Cancer Deaths Induced by 1 Rad at Age 15	Age (years)	Spontaneous Cancer Deaths	Cancer Deaths Induced by 1 Rad at Age 15
16	7.02	0	23	9.92	0
17	7.30	0	24	10.47	0.01
18	7.78	0	25	11.03	0.03
19	8.35	0	26	11.49	0.04
20	8.72	0	27	12.14	0.06
21	9.19	0	28	12.88	0.08
22	9.55	0	29	13.33	0.10

PART D : IRRADIATION AT 15 YEARS OF AGE (97,586 PERSONS)

Age (years)	Spontaneous Cancer Deaths	Cancer Deaths Induced by 1 Rad at Age 15	Age (years)	Spontaneous Cancer Deaths	Cancer Deaths Induced by 1 Rad at Age 15
30	14.45	0.15	61	435.3	22.98
31	15.18	0.17	62	460.3	23.75
32	16.86	0.22	63	491.0	24.16
33	18.90	0.28	64	512.5	23.68
34	21.69	0.36	65	532.0	23.30
35	24.47	0.49	66	555.7	22.67
36	27.70	0.62	67	569.6	21.53
37	30.92	0.76	68	590.2	20.54
38	36.24	1.00	69	605.9	19.63
39	41.01	1.23	70	620.8	18.62
40	46.45	1.51	71	625.6	17.27
41	51.39	1.79	72	630.7	15.52
42	56.27	2.13	73	632.1	14.03
43	68.93	2.81	74	628.3	12.44
44	80.50	3.53	75	614.9	10.33
45	91.03	4.21	76	600.5	9.01
46	105.0	5.17	77	579.7	7.65
47	112.5	5.81	78	557.3	6.35
48	127.0	6.71	79	530.6	5.41
49	142.1	7.76	80	501.6	3.91
50	160.3	8.95	81	450.6	2.70
51	174.8	9.86	82	403.0	1.93
52	191.4	11.03	83	359.0	1.29
53	211.7	12.45	84	316.5	0.76
54	237.4	14.24	85	278.1	0.33
55	266.2	15.97	86	235.8	0.0
56	293.2	17.24	87	195.4	0.0
57	316.2	18.21	88	154.9	0.0
58	348.9	19.68	89	112.6	0.0
59	378.2	21.10	90	73.9	0.0
60	410.2	22.40			

PART E: IRRADIATION AT 20 YEARS OF AGE (96,900 PERSONS)

Age (years)	Spontaneous Cancer Deaths	Cancer Deaths Induced by 1 Rad at Age 20	Age (years)	Spontaneous Cancer Deaths	Cancer Deaths Induced by 1 Rad at Age 20
21	9.19	0	24	10.47	0
22	9.55	0	25	11.03	0
23	9.92	0	26	11.49	0

TABLE A1 (CONTINUED) (MALES)

PART E : IRRADIATION AT 20 YEARS OF AGE (96,900 PERSONS)

Age (years)	Spontaneous Cancer Deaths	Cancer Deaths Induced by 1 Rad at Age 20	Age (years)	Spontaneous Cancer Deaths	Cancer Deaths Induced by 1 Rad at Age 20
27	12.14	0	64	512.5	20.50
28	12.88	0	65	532.0	20.75
29	13.33	0.01	66	555.7	21.12
30	14.46	0.03	67	569.5	21.07
31	15.18	0.04	68	589.2	20.62
32	16.86	0.06	69	605.9	19.99
33	18.99	0.08	70	620.2	19.23
34	21.69	0.12	71	625.6	18.14
35	24.47	0.18	72	631.2	17.04
36	27.70	0.23	73	632.1	15.80
37	30.92	0.29	74	628.3	14.45
38	36.24	0.39	75	614.9	13.22
39	41.01	0.49	76	600.5	11.89
40	46.45	0.65	77	579.1	10.19
41	51.39	0.82	78	556.8	8.91
42	56.27	0.99	79	530.7	7.43
43	68.91	1.36	80	501.1	6.01
44	80.50	1.73	81	451.3	4.87
45	91.00	2.09	82	403.0	3.83
46	105.0	2.63	83	358.2	2.94
47	112.5	3.04	84	316.5	2.31
48	126.9	3.68	85	278.8	1.56
49	142.1	4.41	86	235.8	1.01
50	160.3	5.29	87	195.4	0.67
51	174.8	6.12	88	154.9	0.40
52	191.4	7.08	89	112.6	0.19
53	211.7	8.04	90	73.9	0.06
54	237.3	9.25			
55	266.3	10.65			
56	293.4	11.85			
57	316.1	12.96			
58	348.9	14.65			
59	378.5	16.28			
60	410.0	17.63			
61	435.6	18.30			
62	460.3	18.87			
63	490.8	19.83			

PART F: IRRADIATION AT 25 YEARS OF AGE (95,943 PERSONS)

Age (years)	Spontaneous Cancer Deaths	Cancer Deaths Induced by 1 Rad at Age 25	Age (years)	Spontaneous Cancer Deaths	Cancer Deaths Induced by 1 Rad at Age 25
26	11.7	0	65	532	19.7
27	12.1	0	66	556	20.2
28	12.9	0	67	570	20.2
29	13.3	0	68	590	20.5
30	14.5	0	69	606	20.8
31	15.2	0	70	621	20.9
32	16.9	0	71	626	20.4
33	18.9	0	72	631	20.0
34	21.7	0.02	73	632	19.2
35	24.5	0.04	74	628	17.9
36	27.7	0.06	75	615	16.6
37	30.9	0.09	76	601	15.1
38	36.2	0.13	77	579	13.5
39	41.0	0.20	78	557	12.0
40	46.5	0.29	79	531	10.6
41	51.4	0.36	80	501	9.3
42	56.3	0.46	81	451	7.7
43	68.9	0.64	82	403	6.1
44	80.5	0.84	83	358	4.9
45	91.0	1.11	84	316	3.9
46	105	1.44	85	279	2.9
47	113	1.71	86	236	2.2
48	127	2.16	87	195	1.6
49	142	2.63	88	155	1.1
50	160	3.21	89	113	0.71
51	175	3.76	90	74	0.36
52	191	4.46			
53	212	5.33			
54	237	6.40			
55	266	7.59			
56	293	8.88			
57	316	10.1			
58	349	11.4			
59	378	12.8			
60	410	14.1			
61	436	15.2			
62	460	16.3			
63	491	17.8			
64	512	19.0			

TABLE A1 (CONTINUED) (MALES)

PART G: IRRADIATION AT 30 YEARS OF AGE (95,050 PERSONS)

Age (years)	Spontaneous Cancer Deaths	Cancer Deaths Induced by 1 Rad at Age 30	Age (years)	Spontaneous Cancer Deaths	Cancer Deaths Induced by 1 Rad at Age 30
31	15.2	0	68	589.2	17.32
32	16.9	0	69	605.9	18.18
33	18.9	0	70	620.2	18.61
34	21.7	0	71	625.6	18.39
35	24.5	0	72	631.2	18.18
36	27.7	0	73	632.1	17.83
37	30.9	0	74	628.3	17.53
38	36.2	0	75	614.9	16.79
39	41.0	0.03	76	600.5	15.85
40	46.5	0.06	77	579.1	14.94
41	51.4	0.09	78	556.8	13.70
42	56.3	0.14	79	530.7	12.26
43	68.9	0.21	80	501.1	10.97
44	80.5	0.31	81	451.3	9.21
45	91.0	0.46	82	403.0	7.62
46	105.0	0.60	83	358.2	6.23
47	112.5	0.74	84	316.5	5.13
48	126.9	0.95	85	278.8	4.18
49	142.1	1.19	86	235.8	3.25
50	160.3	1.59	87	195.4	2.40
51	174.8	1.94	88	154.9	1.72
52	191.4	2.35	89	112.6	1.11
53	211.7	2.92	90	73.9	0.62
54	237.3	3.56			
55	266.3	4.31			
56	293.4	5.11			
57	316.1	5.97			
58	348.9	7.12			
59	378.5	8.29			
60	410.0	9.47			
61	435.6	10.72			
62	460.3	11.88			
63	490.8	12.96			
64	512.5	13.99			
65	532.0	14.84			
66	555.7	15.67			
67	569.5	16.40			

Part H: Irradiation at 35 years of age (94,119 persons)

Age (years)	Spontaneous Cancer Deaths	Cancer Deaths Induced by 1 Rad at Age 35	Age (years)	Spontaneous Cancer Deaths	Cancer Deaths Induced by 1 Rad at Age 35
36	27.70	0	75	614.86	13.53
37	30.92	0	76	601.10	12.98
38	36.24	0	77	579.08	12.22
39	41.01	0	78	556.79	11.53
40	46.45	0	79	530.66	10.88
41	51.39	0	80	501.25	10.03
42	56.27	0	81	451.26	8.75
43	68.93	0	82	403.39	7.62
44	80.52	0.04	83	358.25	6.45
45	91.00	0.08	84	316.45	5.35
46	104.98	0.14	85	278.77	4.49
47	112.50	0.20	86	235.84	3.54
48	126.95	0.28	87	195.36	2.72
49	142.08	0.41	88	154.88	1.98
50	160.34	0.60	89	112.64	1.34
51	174.80	0.73	90	73.92	0.81
52	191.39	0.93			
53	211.68	1.16			
54	237.44	1.46			
55	266.17	1.93			
56	293.23	2.39			
57	316.22	2.85			
58	348.87	3.52			
59	378.24	4.16			
60	410.22	4.88			
61	435.28	5.57			
62	460.28	6.40			
63	490.96	7.36			
64	512.46	8.25			
65	531.96	8.99			
66	555.24	9.99			
67	569.60	10.77			
68	589.24	11.43			
69	605.88	12.12			
70	620.86	12.73			
71	625.51	12.95			
72	631.24	13.32			
73	632.10	13.65			
74	628.06	13.82			

TABLE A1 (CONTINUED) (MALES)

PART I: IRRADIATION AT 40 YEARS OF AGE (92,897 PERSONS)

Age (years)	Spontaneous Cancer Deaths	Cancer Deaths Induced by 1 Rad at Age 40	Age (years)	Spontaneous Cancer Deaths	Cancer Deaths Induced by 1 Rad at Age 40
41	51.39	0	66	555.7	4.83
42	56.27	0	67	569.5	5.38
43	68.91	0	68	589.2	6.01
44	80.50	0	69	605.9	6.63
45	91.00	0	70	620.2	7.16
46	105.0	0	71	625.6	7.69
47	112.5	0	72	631.2	8.14
48	126.9	0	73	632.1	8.34
49	142.1	0.04	74	628.3	8.61
50	160.3	0.10	75	614.9	8.58
51	174.8	0.16	76	600.5	8.47
52	191.4	0.23	77	579.1	8.34
53	211.7	0.32	78	556.8	8.18
54	237.3	0.46	79	530.7	7.96
55	266.3	0.68	80	501.1	7.52
56	293.4	0.84	81	451.3	6.63
57	316.1	1.04	82	403.0	5.80
58	348.9	1.31	83	358.2	5.05
59	378.5	1.59	84	316.5	4.42
60	410.0	2.03	85	278.8	3.81
61	435.6	2.42	86	235.8	3.11
62	460.3	2.83	87	195.4	2.52
63	490.8	3.39	88	154.9	1.91
64	512.5	3.84	89	112.6	1.30
65	532.0	4.31	90	73.9	0.81

PART J: IRRADIATION AT 45 YEARS OF AGE (91,032 PERSONS)

Age (years)	Spontaneous Cancer Deaths	Cancer Deaths Induced by 1 Rad at Age 45	Age (years)	Spontaneous Cancer Deaths	Cancer Deaths Induced by 1 Rad at Age 45
46	105.0	0	54	237.4	0.04
47	112.5	0	55	266.2	0.09
48	126.9	0	56	293.2	0.14
49	142.1	0	57	316.2	0.20
50	160.3	0	58	348.9	0.28
51	174.8	0	59	378.5	0.39
52	191.4	0	60	410.0	0.56
53	211.7	0	61	435.6	0.66

PART J: IRRADIATION AT 45 YEARS OF AGE (91,032 PERSONS)

Age (years)	Spontaneous Cancer Deaths	Cancer Deaths Induced by 1 Rad at Age 45	Age (years)	Spontaneous Cancer Deaths	Cancer Deaths Induced by 1 Rad at Age 45
62	460.3	0.81	77	579.1	3.98
63	491.0	0.98	78	556.8	3.92
64	512.8	1.15	79	530.7	3.86
65	532.0	1.40	80	501.6	3.73
66	555.7	1.65	81	451.3	3.39
67	569.6	1.87	82	403.0	3.10
68	589.7	2.17	83	358.3	2.81
69	605.9	2.42	84	316.4	2.53
70	621.3	2.68	85	278.8	2.23
71	625.6	2.90	86	235.8	1.85
72	631.2	3.18	87	195.4	1.50
73	632.1	3.44	88	154.9	1.17
74	628.3	3.67	89	112.6	0.84
75	614.7	3.79	90	73.9	0.54
76	600.5	3.94			

PART K: IRRADIATION AT 50 YEARS OF AGE (88,125 PERSONS)

Age (years)	Spontaneous Cancer Deaths	Cancer Deaths Induced by 1 Rad at Age 50	Age (years)	Spontaneous Cancer Deaths	Cancer Deaths Induced by 1 Rad at Age 50
51	174.8	0	71	625.6	0.23
52	191.4	0	72	631.2	0.26
53	211.7	0	73	632.1	0.29
54	237.3	0	74	628.3	0.31
55	266.3	0	75	614.9	0.33
56	293.4	0	76	600.5	0.35
57	316.1	0	77	579.1	0.37
58	348.9	0	78	556.8	0.38
59	378.5	0.01	79	530.7	0.39
60	410.0	0.02	80	501.1	0.39
61	435.6	0.03	81	451.3	0.38
62	460.3	0.04	82	403.0	0.35
63	490.8	0.05	83	358.2	0.32
64	512.5	0.07	84	316.5	0.29
65	532.0	0.09	85	278.8	0.26
66	555.7	0.11	86	235.8	0.22
67	569.5	0.13	87	195.4	0.19
68	589.2	0.15	88	154.9	0.15
69	605.9	0.17	89	112.6	0.11
70	620.2	0.21	90	73.9	0.07

TABLE A2 : SPONTANEOUS AND RADIATION-INDUCED CANCER DEATHS AT VARIOUS AGES FOR IRRADIATION WITH 1 RAD WHOLE-BODY RADIATION AT SPECIFIED AGE (FEMALES)

PART L: IRRADIATION AT 0 YEARS OF AGE (100,000 PERSONS)

Age (years)	Spontaneous Cancer Deaths	Cancer Deaths Induced by 1 Rad at Age 0	Age (years)	Spontaneous Cancer Deaths	Cancer Deaths Induced by 1 Rad at Age 0
1	5.23	0	37	35.71	15.36
2	5.42	0	38	42.40	18.61
3	5.52	0	39	49.06	21.98
4	5.51	0	40	55.72	25.46
5	5.41	0	41	62.34	28.49
6	5.31	0	42	71.39	31.98
7	5.11	0	43	81.18	35.64
8	4.52	0	44	93.35	40.16
9	4.23	0	45	104.5	44.4
10	4.03	0.04	46	118.4	49.3
11	3.93	0.07	47	129.9	52.2
12	3.93	0.11	48	141.7	55.7
13	4.03	0.15	49	153.7	57.6
14	4.12	0.19	50	167.9	59.1
15	4.32	0.26	51	178.4	59.6
16	4.51	0.35	52	190.4	59.2
17	4.90	0.43	53	202.2	58.2
18	5.00	0.51	54	219.4	58.1
19	5.09	0.58	55	236.2	58.3
20	5.19	0.66	56	256.2	58.7
21	5.38	0.81	57	277.6	58.3
22	5.76	0.97	58	291.4	54.5
23	6.45	1.21	59	306.6	51.8
24	7.12	1.50	60	317.8	48.0
25	8.00	1.83	61	330.5	42.3
26	8.87	2.19	62	341.2	38.9
27	10.32	2.73	63	354.1	35.8
28	12.26	3.53	64	366.1	31.8
29	13.82	4.30	65	377.2	29.3
30	15.55	5.19	66	387.8	23.0
31	17.48	6.15	67	397.8	18.2
32	19.89	7.46	68	412.9	15.1
33	22.59	8.88	69	427.8	11.7
34	25.17	10.12	70	436.2	7.98
35	28.04	11.66	71	448.4	4.08
36	31.88	13.55	72	457.4	0.0

PART L: IRRADIATION AT 0 YEARS OF AGE (100,000 PERSONS)

Age (years)	Spontaneous Cancer Deaths	Cancer Deaths Induced by 1 Rad at Age 0	Age (years)	Spontaneous Cancer Deaths	Cancer Deaths Induced by 1 Rad at Age 0
73	474.0	0.0	82	427.0	0.0
74	488.7	0.0	83	395.5	0.0
75	494.8	0.0	84	363.8	0.0
76	503.9	0.0	85	331.2	0.0
77	503.2	0.0	86	297.5	0.0
78	504.5	0.0	87	265.0	0.0
79	496.8	0.0	88	233.3	0.0
80	489.0	0.0	89	201.6	0.0
81	458.2	0.0	90	168.0	0.0

PART M: IRRADIATION AT 5 YEARS OF AGE (98,392 PERSONS)

Age (years)	Spontaneous Cancer Deaths	Cancer Deaths Induced by 1 Rad at Age 5	Age (years)	Spontaneous Cancer Deaths	Cancer Deaths Induced by 1 Rad at Age 5
6	5.31	0	31	17.48	2.95
7	5.11	0	32	19.89	3.66
8	4.52	0	33	22.59	4.50
9	4.23	0	34	25.17	5.36
10	4.03	0	35	28.04	6.31
11	3.93	0	36	31.88	7.62
12	3.93	0	37	35.71	8.96
13	4.03	0	38	42.40	10.9
14	4.12	0.02	39	49.06	13.1
15	4.32	0.05	40	55.72	15.2
16	4.51	0.08	41	62.34	17.1
17	4.90	0.12	42	71.39	20.0
18	5.00	0.15	43	81.18	23.2
19	5.09	0.19	44	93.95	27.3
20	5.19	0.26	45	104.5	30.5
21	5.38	0.30	46	118.4	33.9
22	5.76	0.37	47	129.9	36.4
23	6.45	0.47	48	141.7	38.8
24	7.12	0.58	49	153.7	41.8
25	8.00	0.77	50	167.9	44.7
26	8.87	0.96	51	178.4	45.8
27	10.32	1.24	52	190.4	47.8
28	12.26	1.64	53	202.2	48.3
29	13.82	2.02	54	219.4	49.4
30	15.55	2.46	55	236.2	50.3

TABLE A2 (CONTINUED) (FEMALES)

PART M: IRRADIATION AT 5 YEARS OF AGE (98,392 PERSONS)

Age (years)	Spontaneous Cancer Deaths	Cancer Deaths Induced by 1 Rad at Age 5	Age (years)	Spontaneous Cancer Deaths	Cancer Deaths Induced by 1 Rad at Age 5
56	256.2	51.0	74	488.7	5.72
57	277.6	51.1	75	494.8	2.87
58	291.4	49.2	76	503.9	0.0
59	306.6	48.4	77	503.2	0.0
60	317.8	46.4	78	504.5	0.0
61	330.5	44.3	79	496.8	0.0
62	341.2	40.9	80	489.0	0.0
63	354.1	38.2	81	458.2	0.0
64	366.1	35.1	82	427.0	0.0
65	377.2	30.9	83	395.5	0.0
66	387.8	28.3	84	363.8	0.0
67	397.8	25.5	85	331.2	0.0
68	412.9	22.7	86	297.5	0.0
69	427.8	21.2	87	265.0	0.0
70	436.2	16.6	88	233.3	0.0
71	448.4	13.1	89	201.6	0.0
72	457.4	10.7	90	168.0	0.0
73	474.0	8.30			

PART N: IRRADIATION AT 10 YEARS OF AGE (98,252 PERSONS)

Age (years)	Spontaneous Cancer Deaths	Cancer Deaths Induced by 1 Rad at Age 10	Age (years)	Spontaneous Cancer Deaths	Cancer Deaths Induced by 1 Rad at Age 10
11	3.93	0	25	8.00	0.22
12	3.93	0	26	8.87	0.28
13	4.03	0	27	10.32	0.37
14	4.12	0	28	12.26	0.50
15	4.32	0	29	13.82	0.64
16	4.51	0	30	15.55	0.84
17	4.90	0	31	17.48	1.05
18	5.00	0	32	19.89	1.33
19	5.09	0.02	33	22.59	1.69
20	5.19	0.03	34	25.17	2.06
21	5.38	0.05	35	28.04	2.47
22	5.76	0.08	36	31.88	3.03
23	6.45	0.11	37	35.71	3.68
24	7.12	0.15	38	42.40	4.71

PART N: IRRADIATION AT 10 YEARS OF AGE (98,252 PERSONS)

Age (years)	Spontaneous Cancer Deaths	Cancer Deaths Induced by 1 Rad at Age 10	Age (years)	Spontaneous Cancer Deaths	Cancer Deaths Induced by 1 Rad at Age 10
39	49.06	5.84	65	377.2	30.9
40	55.72	7.02	66	387.8	29.1
41	62.34	8.35	67	397.8	26.7
42	71.39	9.99	68	412.9	24.8
43	81.18	11.61	69	427.8	23.1
44	93.35	13.82	70	436.2	20.1
45	104.5	15.88	71	448.4	18.4
46	118.4	18.1	72	457.4	16.5
47	129.9	20.3	73	474.0	14.69
48	141.7	22.7	74	488.7	13.68
49	153.7	25.1	75	494.8	10.39
50	167.9	27.4	76	503.9	8.06
51	178.4	28.5	77	503.2	6.54
52	190.4	29.7	78	504.5	4.94
53	202.2	30.9	79	496.8	3.23
54	219.4	33.3	80	489.0	1.61
55	236.2	35.0	81	458.2	0.0
56	256.2	36.6	82	427.0	0.0
57	277.6	38.9	83	395.5	0.0
58	291.4	39.0	84	363.8	0.0
59	306.6	38.6	85	331.2	0.0
60	317.8	37.8	86	297.5	0.0
61	330.5	36.7	87	265.0	0.0
62	341.2	35.1	88	233.3	0.0
63	354.1	33.6	89	201.6	0.0
64	366.1	32.2	90	168.0	0.0

PART O: IRRADIATION AT 15 YEARS OF AGE (98,129 PERSONS)

Age (years)	Spontaneous Cancer Deaths	Cancer Deaths Induced by 1 Rad at Age 15	Age (years)	Spontaneous Cancer Deaths	Cancer Deaths Induced by 1 Rad at Age 15
16	4.51	0	24	7.12	0.01
17	4.90	0	25	8.00	0.02
18	5.00	0	26	8.87	0.03
19	5.09	0	27	10.32	0.05
20	5.19	0	28	12.26	0.07
21	5.38	0	29	13.82	0.11
22	5.76	0	30	15.55	0.16
23	6.45	0	31	17.48	0.20

TABLE A2 (CONTINUED) (FEMALES)

PART O: IRRADIATION AT 15 YEARS OF AGE (98,129 PERSONS)

Age (years)	Spontaneous Cancer Deaths	Cancer Deaths Induced by 1 Rad at Age 15	Age (years)	Spontaneous Cancer Deaths	Cancer Deaths Induced by 1 Rad at Age 15
32	19.89	0.26	69	427.8	13.86
33	22.59	0.34	70	436.2	13.09
34	25.17	0.42	71	448.4	12.38
35	28.04	0.56	72	457.4	11.25
36	31.88	0.71	73	474.0	10.52
37	35.71	0.88	74	488.7	9.68
38	42.40	1.17	75	494.8	8.31
39	49.06	1.47	76	503.9	7.56
40	55.72	1.81	77	503.2	6.64
41	62.34	2.17	78	504.5	5.75
42	71.39	2.70	79	496.8	5.07
43	81.18	3.31	80	489.0	3.81
44	93.95	4.09	81	458.2	2.75
45	104.5	4.83	82	427.0	2.05
46	118.4	5.83	83	395.5	1.42
47	129.9	6.70	84	363.8	0.87
48	141.7	7.48	85	331.2	0.40
49	153.7	8.39	86	297.5	0.0
50	167.9	9.37	87	265.0	0.0
51	178.4	10.06	88	233.3	0.0
52	190.4	10.97	89	201.6	0.0
53	202.2	11.89	90	168.0	0.0
54	219.4	13.16			
55	236.2	14.17			
56	256.2	15.06			
57	277.6	15.99			
58	291.4	16.43			
59	306.6	17.11			
60	317.8	17.35			
61	330.5	17.45			
62	341.2	17.61			
63	354.1	17.42			
64	366.1	16.91			
65	377.2	16.52			
66	387.8	15.82			
67	397.8	15.04			
68	412.9	14.37			

PART P: IRRADIATION AT 20 YEARS OF AGE (97,868 PERSONS)

Age (years)	Spontaneous Cancer Deaths	Cancer Deaths Induced by 1 Rad at Age 20	Age (years)	Spontaneous Cancer Deaths	Cancer Deaths Induced by 1 Rad at Age 20
21	5.38	0	60	317.8	13.67
22	5.76	0	61	330.5	13.88
23	6.45	0	62	341.2	13.99
24	7.12	0	63	354.1	14.31
25	8.00	0	64	366.1	14.64
26	8.87	0	65	377.2	14.71
27	10.32	0	66	387.8	14.74
28	12.26	0	67	397.8	14.72
29	13.82	0.01	68	412.9	14.45
30	15.55	0.03	69	427.8	14.12
31	17.48	0.05	70	436.2	13.52
32	19.89	0.07	71	448.4	13.00
33	22.59	0.10	72	457.4	12.35
34	25.17	0.14	73	474.0	11.85
35	28.04	0.20	74	488.7	11.24
36	31.88	0.26	75	494.8	10.63
37	35.71	0.34	76	503.9	9.98
38	42.40	0.46	77	503.2	8.86
39	49.06	0.59	78	504.5	8.07
40	55.72	0.78	79	496.8	6.96
41	62.34	1.00	80	489.0	5.87
42	71.39	1.26	81	458.2	4.95
43	81.18	1.61	82	427.0	4.06
44	93.35	2.01	83	395.5	3.24
45	104.5	2.40	84	363.8	2.66
46	118.4	2.96	85	331.2	1.85
47	129.9	3.51	86	297.5	1.28
48	141.7	4.11	87	265.0	0.91
49	153.7	4.76	88	233.3	0.60
50	167.9	5.54	89	201.6	0.35
51	178.4	6.24	90	168.0	0.14
52	190.4	7.04			
53	202.2	7.68			
54	219.4	8.56			
55	236.2	9.45			
56	256.2	10.35			
57	277.6	11.38			
58	291.4	12.24			
59	306.6	13.18			

TABLE A2 (CONTINUED) (FEMALES)

PART Q: IRRADIATION AT 25 YEARS OF AGE (97,551 PERSONS)

Age (years)	Spontaneous Cancer Deaths	Cancer Deaths Induced by 1 Rad at Age 25	Age (years)	Spontaneous Cancer Deaths	Cancer Deaths Induced by 1 Rad at Age 25
26	8.87	0	63	354.1	12.85
27	10.32	0	64	366.1	13.55
28	12.26	0	65	377.2	13.96
29	13.82	0	66	387.8	14.08
30	15.55	0	67	397.8	14.12
31	17.48	0	68	412.9	14.37
32	19.89	0	69	427.8	14.72
33	22.59	0	70	436.2	14.70
34	25.17	0.02	71	448.4	14.62
35	28.04	0.04	72	457.4	14.55
36	31.88	0.07	73	474.0	14.36
37	35.71	0.11	74	488.7	13.93
38	42.40	0.16	75	494.8	13.36
39	49.06	0.24	76	503.9	12.70
40	55.72	0.35	77	503.2	11.72
41	62.34	0.44	78	504.5	10.85
42	71.39	0.58	79	496.8	9.94
43	81.18	0.75	80	489.0	9.05
44	93.35	0.97	81	458.2	7.79
45	104.5	1.27	82	427.0	6.49
46	118.4	1.62	83	395.5	5.42
47	129.9	1.97	84	363.8	4.44
48	141.7	2.41	85	331.2	3.44
49	153.7	2.84	86	297.5	2.74
50	167.9	3.36	87	265.0	2.15
51	178.4	3.84	88	233.3	1.63
52	190.4	4.44	89	201.6	1.27
53	202.2	5.10	90	168.0	0.81
54	219.4	5.92			
55	236.2	6.73			
56	256.2	7.76			
57	277.6	8.83			
58	291.4	9.50			
59	306.6	10.33			
60	317.8	10.93			
61	330.5	11.50			
62	341.2	12.11			

Part R: Irradiation at 30 years of age (91,797 persons)

Age (years)	Spontaneous Cancer Deaths	Cancer Deaths Induced by 1 Rad at Age 30	Age (years)	Spontaneous Cancer Deaths	Cancer Deaths Induced by 1 Rad at Age 30
31	17.48	0	61	330.5	8.13
32	19.89	0	62	341.2	8.80
33	22.59	0	63	354.1	9.35
34	25.17	0	64	366.1	9.99
35	28.04	0	65	377.2	10.52
36	31.88	0	66	387.8	10.94
37	35.71	0	67	397.8	11.46
38	42.40	0	68	412.9	12.14
39	49.06	0.03	69	427.8	12.83
40	55.72	0.07	70	436.2	13.09
41	62.34	0.11	71	448.4	13.18
42	71.39	0.17	72	457.4	13.17
43	81.18	0.24	73	474.0	13.37
44	93.35	0.36	74	488.7	13.63
45	104.5	0.53	75	494.8	13.51
46	118.4	0.67	76	503.9	13.30
47	129.9	0.86	77	503.2	12.98
48	141.7	1.06	78	504.5	12.41
49	153.7	1.29	79	496.8	11.48
50	167.9	1.66	80	489.0	10.71
51	178.4	1.98	81	458.2	9.35
52	190.4	2.34	82	427.0	8.07
53	202.2	2.79	83	395.5	6.88
54	219.4	3.29	84	363.8	5.89
55	236.2	3.83	85	331.2	4.97
56	256.2	4.46	86	297.5	4.11
57	277.6	5.25	87	265.0	3.26
58	291.4	5.94	88	233.3	2.59
59	306.6	6.71	89	201.6	2.00
60	317.8	7.34	90	168.6	1.42

Part S: Irradiation at 35 years of age (96,737 persons)

Age (years)	Spontaneous Cancer Deaths	Cancer Deaths Induced by 1 Rad at Age 35	Age (years)	Spontaneous Cancer Deaths	Cancer Deaths Induced by 1 Rad at Age 35
36	31.88	0	39	49.06	0
37	35.71	0	40	55.72	0
38	42.40	0	41	62.34	0

TABLE A2 (CONTINUED) (FEMALES)

PART S: IRRADIATION AT 35 YEARS OF AGE (96,737 PERSONS)

Age (years)	Spontaneous Cancer Deaths	Cancer Deaths Induced by 1 Rad at Age 35	Age (years)	Spontaneous Cancer Deaths	Cancer Deaths Induced by 1 Rad at Age 35
42	71.39	0	67	397.8	7.52
43	81.18	0	68	412.9	8.01
44	93.35	0.04	69	427.8	8.56
45	104.5	0.09	70	436.2	8.94
46	118.4	0.16	71	448.4	9.28
47	129.9	0.23	72	457.4	9.65
48	141.7	0.31	73	474.0	10.23
49	153.7	0.44	74	488.7	10.75
50	167.9	0.63	75	494.8	10.89
51	178.4	0.75	76	503.9	10.88
52	190.4	0.92	77	503.2	10.62
53	202.2	1.11	78	504.5	10.44
54	219.4	1.35	79	496.8	10.18
55	236.2	1.71	80	489.0	9.78
56	256.2	2.09	81	458.2	8.89
57	277.6	2.50	82	427.0	8.07
58	291.4	2.94	83	395.5	7.12
59	306.6	3.37	84	363.8	6.15
60	317.8	3.78	85	331.2	5.33
61	330.5	4.23	86	297.5	4.46
62	341.2	4.74	87	265.0	3.68
63	354.1	5.31	88	233.3	2.99
64	366.1	5.89	89	201.6	2.40
65	377.2	6.37	90	168.6	1.85
66	387.8	6.98			

PART T: IRRADIATION AT 40 YEARS OF AGE (96,070 PERSONS)

Age (years)	Spontaneous Cancer Deaths	Cancer Deaths Induced by 1 Rad at Age 40	Age (years)	Spontaneous Cancer Deaths	Cancer Deaths Induced by 1 Rad at Age 40
41	62.34	0	48	141.7	0
42	71.39	0	49	153.7	0.05
43	81.18	0	50	167.9	0.10
44	93.35	0	51	178.4	0.16
45	104.5	0	52	190.4	0.23
46	118.4	0	53	202.2	0.30
47	129.9	0	54	219.4	0.43

PART T: IRRADIATION AT 40 YEARS OF AGE (96,070 PERSONS)

Age (years)	Spontaneous Cancer Deaths	Cancer Deaths Induced by 1 Rad at Age 40	Age (years)	Spontaneous Cancer Deaths	Cancer Deaths Induced by 1 Rad at Age 40
55	236.2	0.60	73	474.0	6.26
56	256.2	0.73	74	488.7	6.70
57	277.6	0.92	75	494.8	6.90
58	291.4	1.09	76	503.9	7.10
59	306.6	1.29	77	503.2	7.25
60	317.8	1.57	78	504.5	7.42
61	330.5	1.83	79	496.8	7.45
62	341.2	2.10	80	489.0	7.34
63	354.1	2.44	81	458.2	6.74
64	366.1	2.75	82	427.0	6.15
65	377.2	3.06	83	395.5	5.58
66	387.8	3.37	84	363.8	5.08
67	397.8	3.76	85	331.2	4.52
68	412.9	4.21	86	297.5	3.93
69	427.8	4.68	87	265.0	3.42
70	436.2	5.04	88	233.3	2.87
71	448.4	5.52	89	201.6	2.33
72	457.4	5.90	90	168.6	1.85

PART U: IRRADIATION AT 45 YEARS OF AGE (94,996 PERSONS)

Age (years)	Spontaneous Cancer Deaths	Cancer Deaths Induced by 1 Rad at Age 45	Age (years)	Spontaneous Cancer Deaths	Cancer Deaths Induced by 1 Rad at Age 45
46	118.4	0	62	341.2	0.60
47	129.9	0	63	354.1	0.71
48	141.7	0	64	366.1	0.82
49	153.7	0	65	377.2	1.00
50	167.9	0	66	387.8	1.15
51	178.4	0	67	397.8	1.30
52	190.4	0	68	412.9	1.52
53	202.2	0	69	427.8	1.71
54	219.4	0.04	70	436.2	1.88
55	236.2	0.08	71	448.4	2.08
56	256.2	0.12	72	457.4	2.31
57	277.6	0.18	73	474.0	2.58
58	291.4	0.23	74	488.7	2.85
59	306.6	0.32	75	494.8	3.05
60	317.8	0.43	76	503.9	3.31
61	330.5	0.50	77	503.2	3.46

TABLE A2 (CONTINUED) (FEMALES)

PART U: IRRADIATION AT 45 YEARS OF AGE (94,996 PERSONS)

Age (years)	Spontaneous Cancer Deaths	Cancer Deaths Induced by 1 Rad at Age 45	Age (years)	Spontaneous Cancer Deaths	Cancer Deaths Induced by 1 Rad at Age 45
78	504.5	3.55	85	331.2	2.65
79	496.8	3.62	86	297.5	2.33
80	489.0	3.64	87	265.0	2.04
81	458.2	3.45	88	233.3	1.75
82	427.0	3.28	89	201.6	1.50
83	395.5	3.10	90	168.6	1.23
84	363.8	2.91			

PART V: IRRADIATION AT 50 YEARS OF AGE (93,317 PERSONS)

Age (years)	Spontaneous Cancer Deaths	Cancer Deaths Induced by 1 Rad at Age 50	Age (years)	Spontaneous Cancer Deaths	Cancer Deaths Induced by 1 Rad at Age 50
51	178.4	0	75	494.8	0.27
52	190.4	0	76	503.9	0.29
53	202.2	0	77	503.2	0.32
54	219.4	0	78	504.5	0.34
55	236.2	0	79	496.8	0.36
56	256.2	0	80	489.0	0.38
57	277.6	0	81	458.2	0.38
58	291.4	0	82	427.0	0.37
59	306.6	0.01	83	395.5	0.35
60	317.8	0.01	84	363.8	0.33
61	330.5	0.02	85	331.2	0.31
62	341.2	0.03	86	297.5	0.28
63	354.1	0.04	87	265.0	0.25
64	366.1	0.05	88	233.3	0.23
65	377.2	0.06	89	210.6	0.20
66	387.8	0.07	90	168.6	0.17
67	397.8	0.09			
68	412.9	0.10			
69	427.8	0.12			
70	436.2	0.14			
71	448.4	0.17			
72	457.4	0.19			
73	474.0	0.22			
74	488.7	0.24			

BIBLIOGRAPHY

ABRAHAMSON, S., AND WOLFE, S. 1976. Re-analysis of radiation-induced specific locus mutations in the mouse. *Nature* **264:**715–719.

ALBERMAN, E., POLANI, P.E., FRASER ROBERTS, J.A., SPICER, C.C., ELLIOTT, M., AND ARMSTRONG, E. 1972. Parental exposure to X-irradiation and Down's Syndrome. *Annals of Human Genetics, London* **36:**195–208.

ALBERMAN, E., POLANI, P.E., FRASER ROBERTS, J.A., SPICER, C.C., ELLIOTT, M., ARMSTRONG, E., and DHADIAL, R.K. 1972. Parental X-irradiation and chromosome constitution in their spontaneously aborted foetuses. *Annals of Human Genetics, London* **36:**185–194.

AMERICAN CANCER SOCIETY 1975. Cancer statistics, 1975. *Ca—A Cancer Journal for Clinicians* **25:**10–11.

ANTOKU, S., AND RUSSELL, W.J. 1971. Dose to the active bone marrow, gonads, and skin from roentgenography and fluoroscopy. *Radiology* **101:**660–678.

ARCHER, V.E., GILLAM, J.D., AND WAGONER, J.K. 1976. Respiratory disease mortality among uranium miners. *Annals of the New York Academy of Sciences* **271:**280–293.

ARCHER, V.E., AND LUNDIN, F.E. JR. 1967. Radiogenic lung cancer in man: exposure-effect relationship. *Environmental Research* **1:**370–383.

AUERBACH, O., STOUT, A.P., HAMMOND, E.C., AND GARFINKEL, L. 1961. Changes in bronchial epithelium in relation to cigarette smoking and in relation to lung cancer. *New England Journal of Medicine* **265:**253–267.

AUSTIN, D.F. 1980. A study of cancer incidence in Lawrence Livermore Laboratory employees. *Report #1, Malignant Melanoma.* Department of Health Services, Resource for Cancer Epidemiology Section, State of California, Sacramento.

AUXIER, J.A., HAYWOOD, F.F., JONES, T.D., et al. 1975. Dosimetry for human exposures. *Oak Ridge National Laboratory Report* **ORNL-5056:**79–82.

AXELSON, O., AND EDLING, C. 1979. Health hazards from radon daughters in dwellings in Sweden. In *Proceedings of Conference on Health Implications of New Energy Technology,* Society for Occupational and Environmental Health, in press.

BAILAR, J.C. III 1976. Mammography: a contrary view. *Annals of Internal Medicine* **84:**77–84.

————. III 1978. Radiation hazards of X-ray mammography. In *Late Biological Effects of Ionizing Radiation,* proceedings of a symposium, March, 1978. International Atomic Energy Agency, Vienna. **Vol. 1:**251–261.

BAIR, W.J., RICHMOND, C.R., AND WACHHOLZ, B.W. 1974. A radiobiological assessment of the spatial distribution of radiation dose from inhaled plutonium. WASH-1320. United States Atomic Energy Commission, Superintendent of Documents, U.S. Government Printing Office, Washington, D.C. 20402.

BAIR, W.J., AND THOMPSON, R.C. 1974. Plutonium: biomedical research. *Science* **183:**715–722.

BALE, W.F. 1951. Hazards associated with radon and thoron. Unpublished Memo to the U.S. Atomic Energy Commission.

BALE, W.F., AND SHAPIRO, J.V. 1955. Radiation dosage to lungs from radon and its daughter products. In *Proceedings of the United Nations International Conference on*

Peaceful Uses of Atomic Energy, August, 1955. **Vol. 13**:233–236. New York: United Nations, 1956.

BARAL, E., LARSSON, L., AND MATTSSON, B. 1977. Breast cancer following irradiation of the breast. *Cancer* **40**:2905–2910.

BECK, H.L., AND DE PLANQUE, G. 1968. The radiation field in air due to distributed gamma-ray sources in the ground. *U.S. Atomic Energy Commission Report* **HASL-195.** New York.

BECKER, D.V. 1979. The role of radioiodine treatment in childhood hyperthyroidism. *Journal of Nuclear Medicine* **20**:890–894.

BEEBE, G.W. 1980. *What knowledge is considered certain regarding human somatic effects of ionizing radiation?* Issue Paper No. 1, Clinical Epidemiology Branch, National Cancer Institute.

BEEBE, G.W., KATO, H., AND LAND, C.E. 1978. Studies of the mortality of A-bomb survivors: 6. Mortality and radiation dose, 1950–1974. *Radiation Research* **75**: 138–201.

BEIERWALTES, W.H. 1978. The treatment of hyperthyroidism with Iodine-131. *Seminars in Nuclear Medicine* **8**:95–103.

BEIR COMMITTEE (The Advisory Committee on the Biological Effects of Ionizing Radiation) 1972. BEIR-I: *The effects on populations of exposure to low levels of ionizing radiation.* Division of Medical Sciences, the National Academy of Sciences, National Research Council, Washington, D.C. 20006. (Generally known as the *BEIR Report.*)

———. 1979. BEIR-III: *The effects on populations of exposure to low levels of ionizing radiation.* Draft Report. Division of Medical Sciences, Assembly of Life Sciences, National Research Council, National Academy of Sciences. (Generally known as the *BEIR-III Report.*)

———. 1980. BEIR-III: *The effects on populations of exposure to low levels of ionizing radiation.* Final Report. Division of Medical Sciences, Assembly of Life Sciences, National Research Council, National Academy of Sciences. (Generally known as the *BEIR-III Report, Final.*)

BENDER, M.A., AND GOOCH, P.C. 1962. Types and rates of X-ray-induced chromosome aberrations in human blood irradiated *in vitro. Proceedings of the National Academy of Sciences* (U.S.) **48**:522–532.

BENNETT, B.G. 1974. Fallout [239]Pu Dose to Man. In *Fallout Program Quarterly Summary Report,* Health and Safety Laboratory, USAEC Report **HASL-278**:41–66.

BITHELL, J.F., AND STEWART, A.M. 1975. Pre-natal irradiation and childhood malignancy: a review of British data from the Oxford survey. *British Journal of Cancer* **31**:271–287.

BLOT, W.J. AND MILLER, R.W. 1973. Mental retardation following *in utero* exposure to the atomic bombs of Hiroshima and Nagasaki. *Radiology* **106**:617–619.

BLOT, W.J., AND SAWADA, H. 1972. Fertility among female survivors of the atomic bombs of Hiroshima and Nagasaki. *American Journal of Human Genetics* **24**: 613–622.

BOICE, J.D., JR., AND LAND, C.E. 1979. Adult leukemia following diagnostic X-rays? (review of report by Bross, Ball, and Falen on a tri-state leukemia survey). *American Journal of Public Health* **69**:137–145.

BOICE, J.D., JR., LAND, C.E., SHORE, R.E., NORMAN, J.E., AND TOKUNAGA, M. 1979. Risk of breast cancer following low-dose radiation exposure. *Radiology* **131**: 589–597.

BOICE, J.D., JR., AND MONSON, R.R. 1977. Breast cancer in women after repeated fluoroscopic examinations of the chest. *Journal of the National Cancer Institute* **59**: 823–832.

BOREK, C. 1979. Neoplastic transformation following split doses of X-rays. *British Journal of Radiology* **50**:845–846.

BOREK, C., AND HALL, E.J. 1973. Transformation of mammalian cells *in vitro* by low doses of X-rays. *Nature* **243**:450–453.

———. 1974. Effect of split doses of X-rays on neoplastic transformation of single cells. *Nature* **252**:499–501.

BOVERI, T. 1929. *The origin of malignant tumors.* Baltimore: Williams and Wilkins (translation into English of the original German Edition, first issued in 1914).

BRANDOM, W.F., BLOOM, A.D., ARCHER, P.G., ARCHER, V.E., BISTLINE, R.W., AND SACCOMANNO, G. 1978. Somatic cell genetics of uranium miners and plutonium workers: a biological dose-response indicator. In *Late Biological Effects of Ionizing Radiation,* proceedings of a symposium, March, 1978. **Vol. 1:**507–518. International Atomic Energy Agency, Vienna.

BRESLOW, L., THOMAS, L.B., AND UPTON A.C. 1977. Final reports of the National Cancer Institute Ad Hoc Working Groups on Mammography in screening for breast cancer, and A summary report of their joint findings and recommendations. *Journal of the National Cancer Institute* **59**:468–541.

BREWEN, J.G., AND PRESTON, R.J. 1975. Analysis of X-ray-induced chromosomal translocations in human and marmoset spermatogonial stem cells. *Nature* **253**:468–470.

BREWEN, J.G., PRESTON, R.J., JONES, K.P., AND GOSSLEE, D.G. 1973. Genetic hazards of ionizing radiations: cytogenetic extrapolations from mouse to man. *Mutation Research* **17**:245–254.

BRINKLEY, D., AND HAYBITTLE, J.L. 1969. The late effects of artificial menopause by X-radiation. *British Journal of Radiology* **42**:519–521.

BROSS, I.D.J., BALL, M., AND FALEN, S. 1979. A dosage response curve for the one rad range: adult risks from diagnostic radiation. *American Journal of Public Health* **69**:130–136.

BROSS, I.D.J., NATARAJAN, N. 1980. Cumulative genetic damage in children exposed to preconception and intrauterine radiation. *Investigative Radiology* **15**:52–64.

BROWN, J.M. 1976. Linearity versus non-linearity of dose-response for radiation carcinogenesis. *Health Physics* **31**:231–245.

———. 1977. The shape of the dose-response curve for radiation carcinogenesis: extrapolation to low doses. *Radiation Research* **71**:34–50.

BUREAU OF RADIOLOGICAL HEALTH, F.D.A. 1970. Population exposure to X-rays —U.S. 1970. *Food and Drug Administration* 73–8047.

CALDWELL, G.G., KELLEY, D.B., AND HEATH, C.W. 1980. Leukemia among participants in military maneuvers at a nuclear bomb test: A preliminary report. *Journal of the American Medical Association* **244**:1575–1578.

CARTER, C.O., EVANS, K.A., AND STEWART, A.M. 1961. Maternal radiation and Down's Syndrome (mongolism). *Lancet* **2**:1042.

COHEN, A.J., LI, F.P., BERG, S., MARCHETTO, D.J., TSAI, S., JACOBS, S.C., AND BROWN, R.S. 1979. Hereditary renal-cell carcinoma associated with a chromosomal translocation. *New England Journal of Medicine* **301**:592–595.

COHEN, D., ARAI, S.F., AND BRAIN, J.D. 1979. Smoking impairs long-term dust clearance from the lung. *Science* **204**:514–517.

CONARD, R.A. AND COLLEAGUES 1975. A twenty-year review of medical findings in a Marshallese population accidentally exposed to radioactive fallout. *Brookhaven National Laboratory* BNL-50424, New York.

CONTI, E.A., PATTON, G.D., CONTI, J.E., AND HEMPELMANN, L.H. 1960. Present health of children given X-ray treatment to the anterior mediastinum in infancy. *Radiology* **74**:386–391.

COOK, D.C., DENT, O., AND HEWITT, D. 1974. Breast cancer following multiple chest fluoroscopy: the Ontario experience. *Canadian Medical Association Journal* **111**:406–412.

COURT-BROWN, W.M., AND DOLL, R. 1965. Mortality from cancer and other causes after radiotherapy for ankylosing spondylitis. *British Medical Journal* **2**:1327–1332.

CREAGAN, R., AND RUDDLE, F.H. 1977. New approaches to human gene mapping by somatic cell genetics. In *Molecular Structure of Human Chromosomes,* chap. 4, 89–142. Edited by J.J. Yunis. New York: Academic Press.

CURTIN, C.T., MCHEFFY, B., AND KOLARSICK, A.J. 1977. Thyroid and breast cancer following childhood radiation. *Cancer* **40**:2911–2913.

DELARUE, N.C., GALE, G., AND RONALD, A. 1975. Multiple fluoroscopy of the chest: carcinogenicity for the female breast and implications for breast cancer screening programs. *Canadian Medical Association Journal* **112**:1405–1413.

DOLPHIN, G.W. 1968. The risk of thyroid cancers following irradiation. *Health Physics* **15**:219–228.

DOWN, J.L.H. 1866. Observation on an ethnic classification of idiots. *London Hospital Report* **3**:259–262.

EDWARDS, J.H., HARNDEN, D.G., CAMERON, A.H., CROSSE, V.M., AND WOLFF, O.H. 1960. A new trisomic syndrome. *Lancet* **1**:787–790.

EGLI, F., AND STALDER, G. 1973. Malformations of the kidney and urinary tract in common chromosomal aberrations. *Humangenetik* **18**:1–15.

ENVIRONMENTAL PROTECTION AGENCY (U.S.) 1975. *Draft environmental statement for a proposed rule-making action concerning environmental radiation protection requirements for normal operations of activities in the uranium fuel cycle.* Office of Radiation Programs, E.P.A., Washington, D.C. 20460.

EVANS, H.J., BUCKTON, K.E., HAMILTON, G.E., AND CAROTHERS, A. 1979. Radiation-induced chromosome aberrations in nuclear-dockyard workers. *Nature* **277**: 531–534.

EVANS, R.D. 1966. The effect of skeletally deposited alpha emitters in man. *British Journal of Radiology* **39**:881–895.

EVANS, R.D., KEANE, A.T., KOLENKOW, R.J., NEAL, W.R., AND SHANAHAN, M.M. 1969. Radiogenic tumors in the radium and mesothorium cases studied at M.I.T. In *Delayed Effects of Bone-Seeking Radionuclides,* 157–194. Edited by C.W. Mays et al., Salt Lake City: University of Utah Press.

FABIA, J., AND DROLETTE, M. 1970. Life tables up to the age of 10 for mongols with and without congenital heart defect. *Journal of Mental Deficiency Research.* **14**: 235–242.

FAVUS, M.J., SCHNEIDER, A.B., STACHURA, M.E., ARNOLD, J.E., YUN RYO, U., PINSKY, S.M., COLMAN, M., ARNOLD, M.J., AND FROHMAN, L.A. 1976. Thyroid cancer occurring as a late consequence of head- and neck-irradiation: evaluation of 1056 patients. *New England Journal of Medicine* **294**:1019–1025.

FORD, C.E., SEARLE, A.G., EVANS, E.P., AND WEST, B.J. 1969. Differential transmission of translocations induced in spermatogonia of mice by irradiation. *Cytogenetics* **8**:447–470.

FRANKE, B., KRÜGER, E., STEINHILBER-SCHWAB, B., VAN DE SAND, H., TEUFEL, D. 1979. *Radiation exposure to the public from radioactive emissions of nuclear power stations; critical analysis of the official regulatory guides.* A report from the IFEU (Institut für Energie- und Umwelt-forschung), Im Sand 5, 6900 Heidelberg, West Germany.

FRANKLIN, B.A. 1979. Nuclear plants hiring stand-ins to spare aides radiation risks. *The New York Times,* p. 1, July 16, 1979.

FREIFELDER, D. 1965. Mechanism of inactivation of coliphage T 7 by X-rays. *Proceedings of the National Academy of Sciences,* U.S. **54**:128–134.

————. 1968. Physicochemical studies on X-ray inactivation of bacteriophage. *Virology* **36**:613–619.

FREITAS, J.E., SWANSON, D.P., GROSS, M.D., AND SISSON, J.C. 1979. Iodine-131: optimal therapy for hyperthyroidism in children and adolescents? *Journal of Nuclear Medicine* **20**:847–850.

FRIGERIO, N.A., AND STOWE, R.S. 1976. Carcinogenic and genetic hazard from background radiation. In *Biological and Environmental Effects of Low-level Radiation,* 385–393. Vienna: International Atomic Energy Agency.

FURCINITTI, P.S., AND TODD, P. 1979. Gamma Rays: further evidence for lack of a threshold dose for lethality to human cells. *Science* **206**:475–477.

GESSEL, T.F., AND PRICHARD, H.M. 1975. The technologically enhanced natural radiation environment. *Health Physics* **28**:361–366.

GIBSON, R., GRAHAM, S., LILIENFELD, A., SCHUMAN, L., DOWD, J.E., AND LEVIN, M.L. 1972. Irradiation in the epidemiology of leukemia among adults. *Journal of the National Cancer Institute* **48**:301–311.

GOFMAN, J.W. 1959. *Coronary Heart Disease.* Springfield, Illinois: Charles C. Thomas.

———. 1960. Medical aspects of radiation. In *Modern Nuclear Technology: A Survey for Industry and Business,* chap. 15. Edited by M.M. Mills, A.T. Biehl, and R. Mainhardt. New York: McGraw-Hill.

GOFMAN, J.W. 1975. The cancer hazard from inhaled plutonium. *Congressional Record* **121**:S14610–14616.

———. 1975b. Estimated production of human lung cancers by plutonium from worldwide fallout. *Congressional Record* **121**:S14616–14619.

———. 1976. The plutonium controversy. *Journal of the American Medical Association* **236**:284–286.

———. 1977a. Testimony for the GESMO hearings: general response to all critiques of John W. Gofman's estimates of the lung cancer hazard of plutonium. Submitted by Public Interest Research Group, Washington, D.C. 20036. Also as *CNR Report* 1977, Committee for Nuclear Responsibility, Box 11207, San Francisco, California, 94101.

———. 1977b. Cancer hazard from low dose radiation. Docket No. RM-50-3. Statement before the Hearing Board of U.S. Nuclear Regulatory Commission, submitted by the Sierra Club, Box 123, Market Station, Buffalo, New York, 14203. Also as *CNR Report* 1977–9, address as above.

———. 1977c. Gross energy available through light water reactors. *CNR Report* 1977–2, Committee for Nuclear Responsibility, address as above.

———. 1979. The question of radiation causation of cancer in Hanford workers. *Health Physics* **37**:617–639.

GOFMAN, J.W., GOFMAN, J.D., TAMPLIN, A.R., KOVICH, E. 1972. Radiation as an environmental hazard. In *Environment and Cancer* (a collection of papers presented at the 24th Annual Symposium on Fundamental Cancer Research, 1971, at the University of Texas M.D. Anderson Hospital and Tumor Institute at Houston):157–186. Baltimore: Williams and Wilkins.

GOFMAN, J.W., RUBIN, L., McGINLEY, J., AND JONES, H.B. 1954. Hyperlipoproteinemia. *American Journal of Medicine* **17**:514–520.

GOFMAN, J.W., AND TAMPLIN, A.R. 1969–70. Low dose radiation and cancer. Presented at the 1969 Institute for Electrical and Electronic Engineers Nuclear Science Symposium, October, 1969. Published in *IEEE Transactions on Nuclear Science,* Part I, **Vol. NS-17**:1–9, February, 1970.

———. 1969a. Federal Radiation Council guidelines for radiation exposure of the population-at-large—protection or disaster? Testimony presented to the Senate Committee on Public Works, November 18, 1969. In *Environmental Effects of Producing Electric Power,* Hearings before the Joint Committee on Atomic Energy, 91st Congress, First Session, Part I, October and November, 1969:655–683.

———. 1969b. Studies of radium-exposed humans: the fallacy underlying a major foundation of NCRP, ICRP, and AEC guidelines for radiation exposure to the population-at-large. Supplement to above testimony, November 18–19, 1969. Ibid.:695–706.

————. 1970a. Studies of radium-exposed humans II: further refutation of the R.D. Evans claim that the linear, non-threshold model of human radiation carcinogenesis is incorrect. Supplement to above testimony, November 18–19, 1969. In *Underground Uses of Nuclear Energy,* Hearings before the Subcommittee on Air and Water Pollution of the Committee on Public Works, U.S. Senate, 91st Congress, First Session, on S.B. 3042, Part I, November 18–19, 1969:326–350.

————. 1970b. Radiation-induction of human lung cancer. Supplement to testimony, January 28, 1970. Ibid.:389–399,

————. 1970c. The mechanism of radiation carcinogenesis. Supplement to testimony, January 28, 1970. Ibid.:400–418.

————. 1970d. Major fallacies in the AEC staff comments on the Gofman-Tamplin papers and Congressional testimony. Supplement to testimony, January 28, 1970. Ibid.:426–433.

————. 1970e. Radiation-induction of breast cancer in the rat; a validation of the linear hypothesis of radiation carcinogenesis over the range 0–600 rads. Supplement to testimony, January 28, 1970. Ibid.:434–441.

————. 1970f. A proposal for at least a ten-fold reduction in the Federal Radiation Council guidelines for radiation exposure to the population-at-large; supportive evidence. Testimony before the Joint Committee on Atomic Energy, January 28, 1970. Ibid.:319–325.

————. 1970g. 16,000 cancer deaths from FRC guideline radiation (Gofman-Tamplin) vs. 160 cancer deaths from FRC guideline radiation (Dr. John Storer): A refutation of the Storer analysis. Testimony before the Joint Committee on Atomic Energy, February 9, 1970. In *Underground Uses of Nuclear Energy,* Hearings before the Subcommittee on Air and Water Pollution of the Committee on Public Works, U.S. Senate, 91st Congress, Second Session, on S.B. 3042, Part II, August 5, 1970:-1382–1386.

————. 1970h. The cancer-leukemia risk from FRC guideline radiation based upon ICRP publications; complete consistency with Gofman-Tamplin estimates. Supplementary testimony to the Joint Committee on Atomic Energy, February 20, 1970. Ibid.:1465–1475.

————. 1970i. Fluoroscopic radiation and risk of primary lung cancer following pneumothorax therapy of tuberculosis. *Nature* **227**:195–196.

————. 1970j. The question of safe radiation thresholds for alpha emitting bone seekers in man. *Health Physics* **21**:47–51.

————. 1971. Epidemiologic studies of carcinogenesis by ionizing radiation. In *Proceedings of the Sixth Berkeley Symposium on Mathematical Statistics and Probability:*235–277. Berkeley: University of California Press.

GOUGH, J.H., DAVIS, R., AND STACEY, A.J. 1968. Radiation doses delivered to the skin, bone marrow, and gonads of patients during cardiac catherization and angiocardiography. *British Journal of Radiology* **41**:508–518.

GRAHAM, S., LEVIN, M.L., LILIENFELD, A.M., SCHUMAN, L.M., GIBSON, R., DOWD, J.E., AND HEMPELMANN, L. 1966. Preconception, intrauterine, and postnatal irradiation as related to leukemia. In *National Cancer Institute Monograph No. 19: Study of Cancer and Other Chronic Diseases:*347–371.

GRAY, H. 1936. *The Anatomy of the Human Body* [Gray's Anatomy], 23rd edition. Edited by W.H. Lewis. Philadelphia: Lea and Febiger. Chapter on trachea and bronchi:1075–1090.

GREGG, E.C. 1977. Radiation risks with diagnostic X-rays. *Radiology* **123**:447–453.

GUNZ, F.W., AND ATKINSON, H.R. 1964. Medical radiations and leukemia: A retrospective survey. *British Medical Journal* **1**:389–393.

HAMERTON, J.L. 1971. *Cytogenetics, Volume 2, Clinical Cytogenetics.* London: Academic Press.

HAMERTON, J.L., CANNING, N., RAY, M., AND SMITH, S. 1975. A cytogenetic survey of 14,069 newborn infants. 1. Incidence of chromosome abnormalities. *Clinical Genetics* **8**:223–243.

HARDY, E.P. JR. 1974. Worldwide distribution of plutonium. In *Plutonium and Other Trans-Uranium Elements,* U.S. Atomic Energy Commission Report WASH-1359.

HARDY, E.P., KREY, P.W., AND VOLCHOCK, H.L. 1973. Global inventory and distribution of fallout plutonium. *Nature* **241**:444–445.

HARLEY, N.H., ALBERT, R.E., SHORE, R.E., AND PASTERNACK, B.S. 1976. Follow-up study of patients treated by X-ray epilation for tinea capitis. Estimate of the dose to the thyroid and pituitary glands and other structures of the head and neck. *Physics in Biology and Medicine* **21**:631–642.

HARTING, F.H., AND HESSE, W. 1879. Der Lungenkrebs, die Bergkrankheit in den Schneeberger Gruben. *Viertelj für Gerichtl. Med. u. offen. Sanitats* **30**:296–308. Ibid. **31**:102–132 and 313–337.

HASTERLIK, R. 1962. In *Radiation Standards, Including Fallout,* Hearings of the Joint Committee on Atomic Energy, 87th Congress, Part 1, June 4–7, 1962:325–331.

"The Heidelberg Studies" (Radioecological Assessment of the Wyhl Nuclear Power Plant.) 1978. Dept. of Environmental Protection of the University of Heidelberg, University of Heidelberg, 6900 Heidelberg, Im Neuenheimer Feld 360. Available in English as *NRC Translation 520* (TIDC 520), U.S. Nuclear Regulatory Commission. This is a collaborative study involving the following authors: Bruland, W., Erhard, T., Franke, B., Grupp, H., v.d. Lieth, C.W., Matthis, P., Moroni, W., Ratka, R., v.d. Sand, H., Sonnhof, U., Steinhilber-Schwab, B., Teufel, D.

HEMPELMANN, L.H., HALL, W.J., PHILLIPS, M., COOPER, R.A., AND AMES, W.R. 1975. Neoplasms in persons treated with X-rays in infancy: fourth survey in 20 years. *Journal of the National Cancer Institute* **55**:519–530.

HEMPELMANN, L.H., LANGHAM, W.H., RICHMOND, C.R., AND VOELZ, G.L. 1973. Manhattan Project plutonium workers: a twenty-seven year follow-up study of selected cases. *Health Physics* **25**:461–479.

HIGH BACKGROUND RADIATION RESEARCH GROUP, China. 1980. Health survey in high background radiation areas in China. *Science* **209**:877–880.

HIRSCHHORN, K., AND COOPER, H.L. 1961. Apparent deletion of short arm of one chromosome (4 or 5) in a child with defects of midline fusion. *Human Chromosome Newsletter* **4**:14.

HOLFORD, R.M. 1975. The relation between juvenile cancer and obstetric radiography. *Health Physics* **28**:153–156.

HOSMER-THOMPSON EXCHANGE IN CONGRESS 1969. In *Environmental Effects of Producing Electrical Power,* Hearings before the Joint Committee on Atomic Energy, 91st Congress, First Session, Oct. 28–31, Nov. 4–7, 1969. Part 1:203–205.

HOWARD, R.O., BREG, R., ALBERT, D.M., AND LESSER, R.L. 1974. Retinoblastoma and chromosome abnormality. *Archives of Ophthalmology* **92**:490–493.

HSU, T.C., AND POMERAT, C.M. 1953. Mammalian chromosome in vitro: II. A method for spreading the chromosomes of cells in tissue cultures. *Journal of Heredity* **44**:23–29.

HUBERT, J.P., KIERNAN, P.D., BEAHRS, O.H., McCONAHEY, W.M., AND WOOLNER, L.B. 1980. Occult papillary carcinoma of the thyroid. *Archives of Surgery* **115**:394–398. (Includes discussion at the presentation of this paper at the 87th Annual Meeting of the Western Surgical Association, November, 1979.)

ICHIMARU, M., ISHIMARU, T. 1975. Leukemia and related disorders. *Journal of Radiation Research* **16** (supplement): 89–96.

IDE, G., SUNTZEFF, V., COWDRY, E.V. 1959. A comparison of the histopathology of tracheal and bronchial epithelium in smokers and non-smokers. *Cancer* **12**:473–484.

IKNAYAN, H.F. 1975. Carcinoma associated with irradiation of the immature breast. *Radiology* **114**:431–433.

ISHIHARA, T., KUMATORI, T. 1966. Polyploid cells in human leukocytes following in vivo and in vitro irradiation. *Cytologia* **31:**59–68.

ISHIHARA, T., SANDBERG, A.A. 1963. Chromosome constitution of diploid and pseudodiploid cells in effusions of cancer patients. *Cancer* **16:**885–895.

JABLON, S. 1973. Late mortality effects of radiation in man. In *Health Physics Society Seventh Midyear Topical Symposium: Health Physics in the Healing Arts:* p. 28. Food and Drug Administration, Department of Health, Education, and Welfare.

JABLON, S., AND MILLER, R.W. 1978. Army technologists: 29-year follow-up for cause of death. *Radiology* **126:**677–679.

JACOBS, P.A., BAIKIE, A.G., COURT-BROWN, W.M., AND STRONG, J.A. 1959. The somatic chromosomes in mongolism. *Lancet* **1:**710.

JACOBS, P.A., FRACKIEWICZ, A., AND LAW, P. 1972. Incidence and mutation rates of structural rearrangements of the autosomes in man. *Annals of Human Genetics* **35:** 301–319.

JANOWER, M.L., AND MIETTINEN, O.S. 1971. Neoplasms after childhood irradiation of the thymus gland. *Journal of the American Medical Association* **215:**753–756.

JOHNSON, L., AND TRIMEL, S.M. 1978. Radiation roulette? Exposure limits: Studies cast doubt on adequacy. *The Day*, New London, Connecticut, Friday, June 30, 1978.

JONES, T.D., AUXIER, J.A., CHEKA, J.S., AND KERR, G.D. 1965. In Vivo Dose Estimates for A-Bomb Survivors Shielded by Typical Japanese Houses. *Health Physics* **28:**367–381.

JUNIS, J.J., TSAI, M.Y., AND WILLEY, A.M. 1977. Molecular organization and function of the human genome. In *Molecular Structure of Human Chromosomes*, chap. 1:1–33. Edited by J.J. Yunis. New York: Academic Press.

KAKATI, S., OSHIMURA, M., AND SANDBERG, A.A. 1976. The chromosomes and causation of human cancer and leukemia: XIX. Common markers in various tumors. *Cancer* **38:**770–777.

KAN, K., SANTEN, B.C., VELTHUYSE, H.J.M., AND JULIUS, H.W. 1976. Exposure of radiologists to scattered radiation during radiodiagnostic examinations. *Radiology* **119:**455–457.

KATO, H. 1971. Mortality in children exposed to the A-bombs while in utero, 1945–1969. *American Journal of Epidemiology* **93:**435–442.

KATO, H., SCHULL, W.J., AND NEEL, J.V. 1966. A cohort-type study of survival in the children of parents exposed to atomic bombings. *American Journal of Human Genetics* **18:**339–373.

KEPFORD, C. 1979. *In response to the de minimus theory and ALAB-509.* Docket No. 50-320 and Docket Nos. 50-277 and 50-278, United States Nuclear Regulatory Commission, before the Atomic Safety and Licensing Appeal Boards, February 19, 1979.

KLEMENT, A.W., MILLER, C.R., MINX, R. P., AND OTHERS 1972. Estimates of ionizing radiation doses in the United States 1960–2000. *U.S. Environmental Protection Agency Report* **ORP/CSD 72-1.**

KNEALE, G., STEWART, A., MANCUSO, T. 1978. Reanalysis of the data relating to the Hanford study of the cancer risks of radiation workers (1944–1977 deaths). In *Late Biological Effects of Ionizing Radiation*, proceedings of a symposium, March, 1978. **Vol. 1:**387–412. International Atomic Energy Agency, Vienna.

KNUDSON, A.G. JR. 1971. Mutation and cancer: statistical study of retinoblastoma. *Proceedings of the National Academy of Sciences (U.S.)* **68:**820–823.

———. 1973. Mutation and Human Cancer. *Advances in Cancer Research* **17:** 317–352.

———. 1976. Genetics and the etiology of childhood cancer. *Pediatric Research* **10:**513–517.

KNUDSON, A.G., JR. MEADOWS, A.T., NICHOLS, W.W., AND HILL, R. 1976. Chromosomal deletion and retinoblastoma. *New England Journal of Medicine* **295:** 1120–1123.

KREY, P.W., AND HARDY, E.P. JR. 1971. *Plutonium in soil around the Rocky Flats plant.* USAEC Report HASL-235.

LAND, C.E., AND McGREGOR, D.H. 1979. Breast cancer incidence among atomic bomb survivors: Implications for radiobiologic risk at low doses. *Journal of the National Cancer Institute* **62:**17–21.

LARSEN, R.P., AND OLDHAM, R.D. 1978. Plutonium in drinking water: Effects of chlorination on its maximum permissible concentration. *Science* **201:**1008–1009.

LEEPER, R.D. 1973. The effect of ^{131}I on survival of patients with metastatic papillary or follicular thyroid carcinoma. *Journal of Clinical Endocrinology and Metabolism* **36:**1143–1152.

LEJEUNE, J., GAUTIER, M., AND TURPIN, R. 1959. Le mongolisme, premier exemple d'aberration autosomique humaine. *Comptes Rendus Hebdomadaires des Séances de l'Académie des Sciences de Paris* **259:**1721–1722.

LEJEUNE, J., GAUTIER, M., VIALATTE, J., BOESWILLWALD, M., SERINGE, P., AND TURPIN, R. 1963. Trois Cas de délétions du bras court d'un chromosome 5. *Comptes Rendus Hebdomadaires des Séances de l'Académie des Sciences de Paris* **257:**3098–3102.

LELE, K.P., PENROSE, L.S., AND STALLARD, H.B. 1963. Chromosome deletion in a case of retinoblastoma. *Annals of Human Genetics* **27:**171–174.

LEVINE, H. 1971. *Clinical cytogenetics.* Boston: Little, Brown, and Co.

LINOS, A., GRAY, J.E., ORVIS, A.L., KYLE, R.A., O'FALLON, W.M., AND KURLAND, L.T. 1980. Low-dose radiation and leukemia. *New England Journal of Medicine* **302:** 1101–1105.

LUNDIN, F.E. JR., LLOYD, J.W., SMITH, E.M., ARCHER, V.E., AND HOLADAY, D.A. 1969. Mortality of uranium miners in relationship to radiation exposure, hard rock mining, and cigarette smoking—1950 through September, 1967. *Health Physics* **16:** 571–578.

LUNDIN, F.E. JR., WAGONER, J.K., AND ARCHER, V.E. 1971. *Radon daughter exposure and respiratory cancer: Quantitative and temporal aspects.* NIOSH-NIEHS Joint Monograph No. 1, U.S. Department of Health, Education, and Welfare. (NIOSH = National Institute of Occupational Safety and Health; NIEHS = National Institute of Environmental Health Sciences.)

LUNN, J.E. 1959. A survey of mongol children in Glasgow. *Scottish Medical Journal* **4:**368–372.

LYON, J.L., KLAUBER, M.R., GARDNER, J.W., AND UDALL, K.S. 1979. Childhood leukemias associated with fallout from nuclear testing. *New England Journal of Medicine* **300:**397–402.

LYON, M.F. 1961. Gene action in the X-chromosome of the mouse (Mus Musculus L). *Nature* **190:**372–373.

———. 1962. Sex chromatin and gene action in the mammalian X-chromosome. *American Journal of Human Genetics* **19:**135–148.

———. 1974. Evolution of X-chromosome inactivation in mammals. *Nature* **250:** 651–653.

MACKENZIE, I. 1965. Breast cancer following multiple fluoroscopies. *British Journal of Cancer* **19:**1–8.

MACMAHON, B. 1962. Prenatal X-ray exposure and childhood cancer. *Journal of the National Cancer Institute* **28:**1173–1191.

———. 1972. Susceptibility to radiation-induced leukemia? *New England Journal of Medicine* **287:**144–145.

MAKINO, S. 1975. *Human Chromosomes.* Amsterdam: North-Holland Publishing Company. (Reference concerning chromosomes in cancer is on p. 429, chapter on neoplasia.)

MANCUSO, T., STEWART, A., AND KNEALE, G. 1977. Radiation exposures of Hanford workers dying from cancer and other causes. *Health Physics* **33**:369–384.

MANN, J.R., AND KIRCHNER, R.A. 1967. Evaluation of lung burden following acute inhalation exposure to highly insoluble PuO_2. *Health Physics* **13**:877–882.

MARMOL, J.G., SCRIGGINS, A.L., AND VOLLMAN, R.F. 1969. Mothers of mongoloid infants in the collaborative project. *American Journal of Obstetrics and Gynecology* **104**: 533–543.

MARTELL, E., Colorado Committee for Environmental Information, Subcommittee on Rocky Flats 1970. Report on the Dow Rocky Flats fire: implications of plutonium releases to the public health and safety. Boulder, Colorado.

MARTLAND, H.S. 1931. The occurrence of malignancy in radioactive persons: A general review of data gathered in the study of the radium dial painters, with special reference to the occurrence of osteogenic sarcoma and the interrelationship of certain blood diseases. *American Journal of Cancer* **15**:2435–2516.

MATANOSKI, G.M., SELTSER, R., SARTWELL, P., DIAMOND, E., AND ELLIOT, E. 1975. The current mortality rates of radiologists and other physician specialists: Specific causes of death. *American Journal of Epidemiology* **101**:199–210.

MAYS, C.W., SPIESS, H., AND GERSPACH, A. 1978. Skeletal effects following [224]Ra injection into humans. *Health Physics* **35**:83–90.

MAZZAFERRI, E.L., YOUNG, R.L., OERTEL, J.E., KEMMERER, W.T., AND PAGE, C.P. 1977. Papillary thyroid carcinoma: The impact of therapy in 576 patients. *Medicine* **56**:171–196.

MCCLELLAN, R.O. 1979. *Annual report of the Inhalation Toxicology Research Institute operated for the United States Department of Energy by the Lovelace Biomedical and Environmental Research Institute, Inc.* October 1, 1978–September 30, 1979. LF-69: UC-48, December, 1979. (This volume and several for previous years provide a wealth of data on inhalation experiments with plutonium in the beagle dog. In particular, the current volume provides "Status Report: Toxicity of Inhaled Alpha-Emitting Radionuclides." Authors: Muggenburg, B.A., Mewhinney, J.A., Hahn, F.F., Boecker, B.B., Guilmette, R.A., Hobbs, C.H., Mauderly, J.L., McClellan, R.O., Merickel, B.S., Lundgren, D.L., Pickrell, J.A., and Stalnaker, N.D.)

MCCORMACK, U.S. CONGRESSMAN MIKE 1975. Nuclear Power: The Nation's Salvation. *The New Engineer*, October 29–31, 1975.

MCGREGOR, D.H., LAND, C.E., CHOI, K., TOKUOKA, S., LIU, P.I., WAKABAYASHI, T., AND BEEBE, G.W. 1977. Breast cancer incidence among atomic bomb survivors, Hiroshima and Nagasaki, 1950–69. *Journal of the National Cancer Institute* **59**:799–811.

MCKUSICK, V.A. 1978. *Mendelian inheritance in man: Catalogs of autosomal dominant, autosomal recessive, and X-linked phenotypes.* 5th ed. Baltimore: The Johns Hopkins University Press.

MCMILLAN, R.C., HORNE, S.A. 1973. Eye exposure from thoriated optical glass. In *Proceedings of the Third International Congress of the Radiation Protection Association:* 882–888. Washington, D.C.

METTLER, F.A. JR., HEMPELMANN, L.H., DUTTON, A.M., PIFER, J.W., TOYOOKA, E.T., AND AMES, W.R. 1969. Breast neoplasms in women treated with X-rays for acute post-partum mastitis; a pilot study. *Journal of the National Cancer Institute* **43**: 803–811.

MIGEON, B.R., AND MILLER, C.S. 1968. Human-mouse somatic cell hybrids with single human chromosome (Group E): Link with thymidine kinase activity. *Science* **162**:1005–1006.

MILLER, R.W., AND BLOT, W.J. 1972. Small head size after in-utero exposure to atomic radiation. *Lancet* **2**:784–787.

MILLER, R.W., AND MULVIHILL, J.J. 1976. Small head size after atomic irradiation. *Teratology* **14**:355–358.

MINKLER, J.L., GOFMAN, J.W., AND TANDY, R.K. 1970a. A specific common chromosomal pathway for the origin of human malignancy. *British Journal of Cancer* **24**:726–740.

———. 1970b. A specific common chromosomal pathway for the origin of human malignancy-II: Evaluation of long term human hazards of potential environmental carcinogens. In *Advances in Biological and Medical Physics* **13**:107–151. New York: Academic Press.

MINOGUE, R.B., AND GOLLER, K.R. September 11, 1978. Letter to J.W. Gofman from Drs. Minogue and Goller of the U.S. Nuclear Regulatory Commission.

MIRD COMMITTEE (Medical Internal Radiation Dose) 1975. Summary of current radiation dose estimates to humans for ^{123}I, ^{124}I, ^{125}I, ^{126}I, ^{130}I, and ^{132}I as sodium iodide (Dose Estimate Report No. 5). *Journal of Nuclear Medicine* **16**:857–860. (One of a series of extremely useful reports issued by the MIRD Committee of the Society of Nuclear Medicine.)

MITELMAN, F., and LEVAN, G. 1976. Clustering of aberrations to specific chromosomes in human neoplasms II. A survey of 287 neoplasms. *Hereditas* **82**:167–174.

MITELMAN, F., LEVAN, G., NILSSON, P.G., AND BRANDT, L. 1976. Nonrandom karyotypic evolution in chronic myeloid leukemia. *International Journal of Cancer* **18**:24–30.

MITELMAN, F., NILSSON, P.G., LEVAN, G., AND BRANDT, L. 1976. Nonrandom chromosome changes in acute myeloid leukemia. Chromosome banding examination of 30 cases at diagnosis. *International Journal of Cancer* **18**:31–38.

MODAN, B., BAIDATZ, D., MART, H., STEINITZ, R., AND LEVIN, S.G. 1974. Radiation-induced head and neck tumors. *Lancet* **1**:277–279.

MODAN, B., RON, E., AND WERNER, A. 1977. Thyroid cancer following scalp irradiation. *Radiology* **123**:741–744.

MOGHISSI, A.A., AND CARTER, M.W. 1975. *Public health implications of radioluminous materials.* U.S. Department of Health, Education, and Welfare publication DHEW (FDA) 76-8001.

MOLE, R.H. 1974. Antenatal irradiation and childhood cancer: Causation or coincidence? *British Journal of Cancer* **30**:199–208.

———. 1978a. The radiobiological significance of the studies with ^{224}Ra and Thorotrast. *Health Physics* **35**:167–174.

———. 1978b. The sensitivity of the human breast to cancer induction by ionizing radiation. *British Journal of Cancer* **51**:401–405.

MYRDEN, J.A. 1972. Personal communication to the BEIR-I Committee. BEIR-I (see *BEIR Committee* in this bibliography):141.

MYRDEN, J.A., AND HILTZ, J.E. 1969. Breast cancer following multiple fluoroscopies during artificial pneumothorax treatment of pulmonary tuberculosis. *Canadian Medical Association Journal* **100**:1032–1034.

NATIONAL CANCER INSTITUTE 1975. *Third National Cancer Survey.* Monograph 41. U.S. Dept. of Health, Education, and Welfare, Government Printing Office, Washington, D.C.

NATIONAL CANCER INSTITUTE AD HOC WORKING GROUPS ON MAMMOGRAPHY: see Breslow, L.

NATIONAL COUNCIL ON RADIATION PROTECTION AND MEASUREMENTS 1979. *Tritium and other radionuclide labeled organic compounds incorporated in genetic material.* NCRP Report No. 63.

NEEL, J.V., KATO, H., AND SCHULL, W.J. 1974. Mortality in the children of atomic bomb survivors and controls. *Genetics* **76**:311–326.

NERO, A.V. JR. 1979. *A Guidebook to Nuclear Reactors.* Berkeley: University of California Press.

NEWCOMBE, H.B., AND McGREGOR, J.F. 1971. Childhood cancer following obstetric radiography. *Lancet* **2**:1151–1152.

NIEBUHR, E. 1972. Localization of the deleted segment in the cri-du-chat syndrome. *Humangenetik* **16**:357–358.

NISHIYAMA, H., ANDERSON, R.E., ISHIMARU, T., ISHIDA, K., II, Y., AND OKABE, N. 1973. The incidence of malignant lymphoma and multiple myeloma in Hiroshima and Nagasaki atomic bomb survivors, 1945–1965. *Cancer* **32**:1301–1309.

NOWELL, P.C. 1976. The clonal evolution of tumor cell populations. *Science* **194**: 23–28.

NOWELL, P.C., AND HUNGERFORD, D.A. 1960. A minute chromosome in human chronic granulocytic leukemia. *Science* **132**:1497.

NUCLEAR REGULATORY COMMISSION (often listed as U.S. Nuclear Regulatory Commission), Office of Nuclear Material Safety and Standards 1979. *Draft generic environmental impact statement on uranium milling* NUREG-0511, **Vol. II,** appendix G-5: Inhalation dose conversion factors for radon daughters. Dose calculations for individuals, p. G-44. **Vol. II,** Appendix G-1: Source term estimation for the radon emission from tailings piles: p. G-13. Washington, D.C. 20555.

———. 1979. Uranium mill tailings licensing: Final regulations with request for comments. *Federal Register* **44,** No. 166, August 24, 1979.

OAK RIDGE NATIONAL LABORATORY 1970. Sitting of fuel reprocessing plants and waste management facilities. Oak Ridge National Laboratory Report, ORNL-4451.

OHKITA, T., TAKAHASHI, H., TAKEICHI, N., AND HIROSE, F. 1978. Prevalence of leukemia and salivary gland tumors among Hiroshima atomic bomb survivors. In *Late Biological Effects of Ionizing Radiation,* proceedings of a symposium, March, 1978. **Vol. 1**:71–81. International Atomic Energy Agency, Vienna.

O'RIORDAN, M.C., AND HUNT, G.J. 1974. Radioactive fluorescers in dental porcelains. National Radiological Protection Board Report, NRPB-R25. Harwell, England.

PALMER, J.P., AND SPRATT, D.W. 1956. Pelvic carcinoma following irradiation for benign gynecological diseases. *American Journal of Obstetrics and Gynecology* **72**:497–505.

PARKER, L.N., BELSKY, J.L., YAMAMOTO, T., KAWAMOTO, S., AND KEEHN, R.J. 1974. Thyroid carcinoma after exposure to atomic radiation: A continuing survey of a fixed population, Hiroshima and Nagasaki, 1958–1971. *Annals of Internal Medicine* **80**:600–604.

PATAU, K., SMITH, D.W., THERMAN, E., INHORN, S.L., AND WAGNER, H.P. 1960. Multiple congenital anomaly caused by an extra autosome. *Lancet* **1**:790–793.

PATTERSON, J.T., BREWSTER, W., AND WINCHESTER, A.M. 1932. Effects produced by aging and X-raying eggs. *Journal of Heredity* **23**:325–333.

PELLER, S. 1939. Lung cancer among mine workers in Joachimsthal. *Human Biology* **11**:130–143.

PENROSE, L.S., AND SMITH, G.F. 1966. *Down's anomaly.* Boston: Little, Brown.

PIRCHAN, A., AND SIKL, K. 1932. Cancer of the lung in the miners of Jachymov. *American Journal of Cancer* **16**:681–722.

PLUMMER, G.W. 1952. Anomalies occurring in children exposed in utero to the atomic bomb in Hiroshima. *Pediatrics* **10**:687–692.

POCHIN, E.E. 1976. Radiology now: Malignancies following low radiation exposures in man. *British Journal of Radiology* **49**:577–579.

POHL, R.O. 1975. *Nuclear energy: Health effects of Thorium-230.* A report prepared in answer to *Environmental analysis of the uranium fuel cycle,* published by the U.S. Environmental Protection Agency, October, 1973. (Dr. Pohl's address: Department of Physics, Cornell University, Ithaca, New York.)

———. 1976. Health effects of radon-222 from uranium mining. *Search* **7**:345.

RICCARDI, V.M., SUJANSKY, E., SMITH, A.C., AND FRANCKE, U. 1978. Chromosomal imbalance in the aniridia-Wilms' tumor association: 11p interstitial deletion. *Pediatrics* **61**:604–610.

ROSSI, H.H. 1977. The effects of small doses of ionizing radiation: Fundamental biophysical characteristics. *Radiation Research* **71**:1–8.

ROSSI, H.H., AND KELLERER, A.M. 1974. The validity of risk estimates of leukemia incidence based on the Japanese data. *Radiation Research* **58**:131–140.

ROWLAND, R.E., STEHNEY, A.F., BRUES, A.M., LITTMAN, M.S., KEANE, A.T., PATTEN, B.C., AND SHANAHAN, M.M. 1978. Current status of the study of ^{226}Ra and ^{228}Ra in humans at the Center for Human Radiobiology. *Health Physics* **35**:159–166.

ROWLEY, J.D. 1973. A new consistent chromosomal abnormality in chronic myelogenous leukaemia identified by Quinacrine fluorescence and Giemsa staining. *Nature* **243**:290–293.

RUSSELL, L.B., AND RUSSELL, W.L. 1952. Radiation hazards to the embryo and fetus. *Radiology* **58**:369–377.

RUSSELL, W.L. 1977. Mutation frequencies in female mice and the estimation of genetic hazards of radiation in women. *Proceedings of the National Academy of Sciences* (U.S.) **74**:3523–3527.

SACCOMANNO, G. 1978. Comments on lung cancer in cigarette-smoking and non-smoking uranium miners. In Radioactivity and the biological effects of radiation with reference to existing standards, chap. 3 of *Final Report: Cluff Lake Board of Inquiry*: 61. Saskatchewan Department of the Environment, Regina, Saskatchewan.

SAFA, A.M., SCHUMACHER, O.P., AND RODRIGUEZ-ANTUNEZ, A. 1975. Long-term follow-up results in children and adolescents treated with radioactive iodine (^{131}I) for hyperthyroidism. *New England Journal of Medicine* **292**:167–171.

SANDBERG, A.A., YAMADA, K., KIKUCHI, Y., AND TAKAGI, N. 1967. Chromosomes and causation of human cancer and leukemia. III. Karyotypes of cancerous effusions. *Cancer* **20**:1099–1116.

SARKAR, S.D., BEIERWALTES, W.H., GILL, S.P., AND COWLEY, B.J. 1976. Subsequent fertility and birth histories of children and adolescents treated with ^{131}I for thyroid cancer. *Journal of Nuclear Medicine* **17**:460–464.

SASAKI, M.S. 1975. A comparison of chromosomal radiosensitivities of somatic cells of mouse and man. *Mutation Research* **29**:433–447.

SASAKI, M.S., AND MIYATA, H. 1968. Biological dosimetry in atomic bomb survivors. *Nature* **220**:1189–1193.

SAX, K. 1939. The time factor in X-ray production of chromosome aberrations. *Proceedings of the National Academy of Sciences* (U.S.) **25**:225–233.

SCHULL, W.J., AND NEEL, J.V. 1962. Maternal radiation and mongolism. *Lancet* **1**:537–538.

SCIENCE WORK GROUP OF THE INTERAGENCY TASK FORCE ON IONIZING RADIATION 1979. Biological effects of ionizing radiation. Draft Report, February 20, 1979.

SEARLE, A.G., EVANS, E.P., FORD, C.E., AND WEST, B.J. 1968. Studies on the induction of translocations in mouse spermatogonia. I. The effect of dose-rate. *Mutation Research* **6**:427–436.

SÉGUIN, E. 1846. *Le traitment moral, l'hygiene et l'education des idiots*. Paris: Bailliere.

————. 1866. *Idiocy: Its treatment by the physiological method* (translated from the French version, above). New York: Wood.

ŠEVC, J., KUNZ, E., AND PLAČEK, V. 1976. Lung cancer in uranium miners and long-term exposure to radon daughter products. *Health Physics* **30**:433–437.

ŠEVCOVĀ, M., ŠEVC, J., AND THOMAS, J. 1978. Alpha irradiation of the skin and the possibility of late effects. *Health Physics* **35**:803–806.

SHAPIRO, J. 1954. *An evaluation of the pulmonary radiation dosage from radon and its daughter products*. U.R. 298. Rochester, N.Y.: University of Rochester Atomic Energy Project.

SHORE, R.E., ALBERT, R.E., AND PASTERNACK, B.S. 1976. Follow-up study of patients treated by X-ray epilation for tinea capitis. Re-survey of post-treatment illness and mortality experience. *Archives of Environmental Health* **31**:21–28.

SHORE, R.E., HEMPELMANN, L.H., KOWALUK, E., MANSUR, P.S., PASTERNACK, B.S., ALBERT, R.E., AND HAUGHIE, G.E. 1977. Breast neoplasms in women treated with X-rays for acute postpartum mastitis. *Journal of the National Cancer Institute* **59**:813–822.

SIGLER, A.T., LILIENFELD, A.M., COHEN, B.H., AND WESTLAKE, J.E. 1965. Radiation exposure in parents of children with mongolism (Down's Syndrome). *Bulletin of the Johns Hopkins Hospital* **117**:374–399.

SILVERBERG, E. 1980. Cancer statistics, 1980. *Ca-A Cancer Journal for Clinicians* **30**:23–44.

SMITH, P.G., AND DOLL, R. 1976. Late effects of X-irradiation in patients treated for metropathia haemorrhagica. *British Journal of Radiology* **49**:224–232.

――――. 1978. Age- and time-dependent changes in the rates of radiation-induced cancers in patients with ankylosing spondylitis following a single course of X-ray treatment. In *Late Biological Effects of Ionizing Radiation*, proceedings of a symposium, March, 1978. **Vol. 1**:205–218. International Atomic Energy Agency, Vienna. (These authors provided unpublished data on this series to the BEIR-III Committee.)

SMITH, P.G., DOLL, R., AND RADFORD, E.P. 1977. Cancer mortality among patients with ankylosing spondylitis not given X-ray therapy. *British Journal of Radiology* **50**:728–734.

SPIERS, F.W. 1979. Background radiation and estimated risks from low-dose irradiation. *British Journal of Radiology* **52**:508–509.

SPIESS, H., AND MAYS, C.W. 1970. Bone cancers induced by ^{224}Ra (ThX) in children and adults. *Health Physics* **19**:713–729.

STALLARD, H.B. 1962. The conservative treatment of retinoblastoma. *Transactions of the Ophthalmological Society of the United Kingdom* **82**:473–534.

STERNGLASS, E.J. 1977. Radioactivity. Chap. 15 of *Environmental Chemistry:* 477–515. Edited by J. O'M Bockris. New York: Plenum Press.

STEVENSON, A.C., MASON, R., AND EDWARDS, K.D. 1970. Maternal diagnostic X-radiation before conception and the frequency of mongolism in children subsequently born. *Lancet* **2**:1335–1337.

STEWART, A.M. 1973. Cancer as a cause of abortions and stillbirths: The effect of these early deaths on the recognition of radiogenic leukemias. *British Journal of Cancer* **27**:465–472.

STEWART, A.M., AND KNEALE, G.W. 1968. Changes in the cancer risk associated with obstetric radiography. *Lancet* **1**:104–107.

――――. 1970a. Radiation dose effects in relation to obstetric X-rays and childhood cancers. *Lancet* **1**:1185–1188.

――――. 1970b. Letter in response to: Burch, P.R.J., Prenatal radiation exposure and childhood cancer, in *Lancet* **2**:1189. Reply is in *Lancet* **2**:1190.

STEWART, A., PENNYBACKER, W., AND BARBER, R. 1962. Adult leukemias and diagnostic X-rays. *British Medical Journal* **2**:882–890.

STEWART, A.M., WEBB, J.W., GILES, B.D., AND HEWITT, D. 1956. Preliminary communication: Malignant disease in childhood and diagnostic irradiation in utero. *Lancet* **2**:447.

STEWART, A.M., WEBB, J.W., AND HEWITT, D. 1958. A survey of childhood malignancies. *British Medical Journal* **1**:1495–1508.

SZTANYIK, L.B. 1978. Late radiobiological effects of A-bombing in Japan. In *Late Biological Effects of Ionizing Radiation*, proceedings of a symposium, March, 1978. **Vol. 1**:61–70. International Atomic Energy Agency, Vienna.

TAKAHASHI, S. 1964. A statistical study of human cancer induced by medical irradiation. *Nippon Acta Radiologica* **23**:1510–1530.

TAKEICHI, N., HIROSE, F., AND YAMAMOTO, H. 1976. Salivary gland tumors in atomic bomb survivors, Hiroshima, Japan. *Cancer* **38**:2462–2468.

TAMPLIN, A.R., GOFMAN, J.W. 1970a. Radiation-induced breast cancer. *Lancet* **1**:297.

_____. 1970b. The Colorado Plateau: Joachimsthal revisited? An analysis of the lung cancer problem in uranium and hard rock miners. Supplement to testimony of January 28, 1970. In *Underground Uses of Nuclear Energy*, Hearings before the Subcommittee on Air and Water Pollution of the Committee on Public Works, U.S. Senate, 91st Congress, First Session, on S.B. 3042, Part I, November 18–20, 1969:351–377.

_____. 1970c. Radiation-induction of human breast cancer. Ibid.:378–388.

_____. 1970d. ICRP publication-14 versus the Gofman-Tamplin report (ICRP = International Commission on Radiological Protection). Ibid.:419–425.

_____. 1970e. Osteogenic sarcoma induction in the beagle dog with alpha-emitting radionuclides: (a) Further validation of the linear hypothesis of radiation carcinogenesis, (b) Absence of any suggestion of safe radiation threshold for bone cancer induction. Supplementary testimony to the Joint Committee on Atomic Energy, February 18, 1970. In *Underground Uses of Nuclear Energy*, Hearings before the Subcommittee on Air and Water Pollution of the Committee on Public Works, U.S. Senate, 91st Congress, Second Session, on S.B. 3042, Part II, August 5, 1970: 1452–1464.

_____. 1970f. Allowable occupational exposures and employee's compensation. Ibid.:1476–1481.

TASK GROUP ON LUNG DYNAMICS (for Committee II of ICRP) 1966. Deposition and retention models for internal dosimetry of the human respiratory tract. *Health Physics* **12**:173–207.

TAYLOR, K.W., PATT, N.L., AND JOHNS, H.E. 1979. Variations in X-ray exposures to patients. *The Journal of the Canadian Association of Radiologists* **30**:6–11.

TERZAGHI, M., AND LITTLE, J.B. 1975. Repair of potentially lethal radiation damage in mammalian cells is associated with enhancement of malignant transformation. *Nature* **253**:548–549.

TJIO, J.H., AND LEVAN, H. 1956. The chromosome number in man. *Heriditas* **42**: 1–6.

TRIMBLE, B.K., AND DOUGHTY, J.H. 1974. The amount of hereditary disease in human populations. *Annals of Human Genetics (London)* **38**:199–223. (Also known as the *British Columbia Survey*.)

UCHIDA, I.A., AND CURTIS, E.J. 1961. A possible association between maternal radiation and mongolism. *Lancet* **2**:848–850.

UCHIDA, I.A., AND FREEMAN, C.P.V. 1977. Radiation-induced nondisjunction in oocytes of aged mice. *Nature* **265**:186–187.

UCHIDA, I.A., HOLUNGA, R., AND LAWLER, C. 1968. Maternal radiation and chromosome aberrations. *Lancet* **2**:1045–1049.

UCHIDA, I.A., LEE, C.P.V., AND BYRNES, E.M. 1975. Chromosome aberrations induced in vitro by low doses of radiation: Nondisjunction in lymphocytes of young adults. *American Journal of Human Genetics* **27**:419–429.

UNSCEAR (United Nations Scientific Committee on the Effects of Atomic Radiation)—All page references in the text are to the 1977 report unless another year is explicitly given.

_____. 1966. Report to the General Assembly, Official Records: Twenty-First Session, Supplement No. 14 (A/6314). United Nations, New York.

_____. 1969. Report to the General Assembly, Official Records: Twenty-Fourth Session, Supplement No. 13 (A/7613). United Nations, New York.

_____. 1977. *Sources and effects of ionizing radiation.* Report to the General Assembly, with annexes. United Nations, New York.

UPTON, A.C. 1977. Radiobiological effects of low doses: Implications for radiological protection. *Radiation Research* **71**:51–74.

VARMA, V.M., BEIERWALTES, W.H., NOFAL, M.M., NISHIYAMA, R.H., AND COPP, J.E. 1970. Treatment of thyroid cancer: Death rates after surgery and after surgery followed by sodium iodide I-131. *Journal of the American Medical Association* **214**: 1437–1442.

VITAL STATISTICS, DIVISION OF, National Center for Health Statistics 1976. Mortality from cancer, United States white population, 1973–1974. In *Statistical Bulletin* **57**:7. Metropolitan Life, One Madison Avenue, New York 10010.

VOELZ, G.L. 1975. What we have learned about plutonium from human data. *Health Physics* **29**:551–561.

VOELZ, G.L., HEMPELMANN, L.H., LAWRENCE, J.N.P., AND MOSS, W.D. 1979. A 32-year medical follow-up of Manhattan Project plutonium workers. *Health Physics* **37**:445–485.

VOELZ, G.L., STEBBINGS, J.H., HEMPELMANN, L.H., HAXTON, L.K., AND YORK, D.A. 1978. Studies on persons exposed to plutonium. In *Late Biological Effects of Ionizing Radiation*, proceedings of a symposium, March, 1978. **Vol. 1**:353–367. International Atomic Energy Agency, Vienna.

WAGONER, J.K. 1979. *Uranium: the United States experience, a lesson in history.* A Report of the Environmental Defense Fund, 1525 18th Street, N.W., Washington, D.C. 20036.

WAGONER, J.K., ARCHER, V.E., LUNDIN, F.E. JR., HOLADAY, D.A., AND LLOYD, J.W. 1965. Radiation as the cause of lung cancer among uranium miners. *New England Journal of Medicine* **273**:181–188.

WANEBO, C.K., JOHNSON, K.G., SATO, K., AND THORSLUND, T.W. 1968. Breast cancer after exposure to the atomic bombings of Hiroshima and Nagasaki. *New England Journal of Medicine* **279**:667–671.

WANG, Y.S. 1975. Measurement of ionizing radiation from color television receivers by thermo-luminescent dosimeters. *Health Physics* **28**:78–80.

WARKANY, J. 1971. *Congenital malformations:* p. 328. Chicago: Year Book Medical Publishers.

WATSON, J.D. 1970. *Molecular biology of the gene. 2nd ed.* Menlo Park, California: W. A. Benjamin, Inc.

WATSON, J.D., AND CRICK, F.H.C. 1953. Genetical implications of the structure of deoxyribonucleic acid. *Nature* **171**:964–967.

WEITL, F.L., RAYMOND, K.N., AND DURBIN, P.W. 1980. Synthetic enterobactin analogs. Carboxamide-2, 3-dihyroxyterephthalate conjugates of spermine and spermidine. A preprint from *Divisions of Materials and Molecular Research and Biology and Medicine,* Lawrence Berkeley Laboratory; and Department of Chemistry, University of California, Berkeley, California 94720. (Popularly known as the work on LICAM-C.)

WILKENING, M.H., CLEMENTS, W.E., AND STANLEY, D. 1972. Radon-222 flux measurements in widely separated regions. In *The Natural Radiation Environment:* 717–730. Edited by J.A.S. Adams, W.M. Lowder, and T.F. Gesell. U.S. Energy Research and Development Administration Report CONF-720805-P2. (Also cited p.114, UNSCEAR 1977.)

WOLF, U., PORSCH, R., BAITSCH, H., AND REINWEIN, H. 1965. Deletion on short arms of a B-chromosome without "cri-du-chat" syndrome. *Lancet* **1**:769.

WOLFF, S., ATWOOD, K.C., RANDOLPH, M.L., AND LUIPPOLD, H.E. 1958. Factors limiting the number of radiation-induced chromosome exchanges. I. Distance: evidence from non-interaction of X-ray and neutron-induced breaks. *Journal of Biophysical and Biochemical Cytology* **4**:365–372.

WOLFF, S., AND BODYCOTE, J. 1975. The induction of chromatid deletions in accord with the breakage-and-reunion hypothesis. *Mutation Research* **29**:85–91.

WOLFF, S., AND LUIPPOLD, H.E. 1956. The production of two chemically different types of chromosomal breaks by ionizing radiation. *Proceedings of the National Academy of Sciences* (U.S.) **42**:510–514.

WOOD, J.W., JOHNSON, K.G., AND OMORI, Y. 1967. *In utero* exposure to the Hiroshima atomic bomb: An evaluation of head size and mental retardation: twenty years later. *Pediatrics* **39**:385–392.

WORK GROUP ON RADIATION EXPOSURE REDUCTION, Interagency Task Force on Ionizing Radiation 1979. *Draft Report,* February 20, 1979. Department of Health, Education, and Welfare, Public Health Service, Center for Disease Control, Atlanta, Georgia 30333.

WRIXON, A.D., AND WEBB, G.A.M. 1974. Miscellaneous sources of ionizing radiations in the United Kingdom: The basis of safety assessments and the calculation of population dose. In *Population Dose and Standards for Man and His Environment,* proceedings of a seminar, Portoroz, May, 1974:557–593. International Atomic Energy Agency Publication STI/PUB/375, Vienna.

YAMAMOTO, T., RABINOWITZ, Z., AND SACHS, L. 1973. Identification of the chromosomes that control malignancy. *Nature New Biology* **243**:247–250.

YAMAZAKI, J.N. 1966. A review of the literature on the radiation dosage required to cause manifest central nervous system disturbances from *in utero* and post-natal exposure. *Pediatrics* **37**:877–903.

ZELLWEGER, H., IONASESCU, V., SIMPSON, J., AND BURMEISTER, L. 1976. The problem of trisomy 22. *Clinical Pediatrics* **15**:601–606.

ZELLWEGER, H., AND SIMPSON, J. 1977. *Chromosomes of man* (Clinics in Developmental Medicine Nos. 65/66). Spastic International Medical Publications. Philadelphia: J.B. Lippincott Co.

INDEX